Lecture Notes in Computer Science   8298

Commenced Publication in 1973
Founding and Former Series Editors:
Gerhard Goos, Juris Hartmanis, and Jan van Leeuwen

Bijaya Ketan Panigrahi
Ponnuthurai Nagaratnam Suganthan
Swagatam Das
Shubhransu Sekhar Dash (Eds.)

Swarm, Evolutionary, and Memetic Computing

4th International Conference, SEMCCO 2013
Chennai, India, December 19-21, 2013
Proceedings, Part II

 Springer

Volume Editors

Bijaya Ketan Panigrahi
IIT Delhi, New Delhi, India
E-mail: bijayaketan.panigrahi@gmail.com

Ponnuthurai Nagaratnam Suganthan
Nanyang Technological University, Singapore
E-mail: epnsugan@ntu.edu.sg

Swagatam Das
Indian Statistical Institute, Kolkata, India
E-mail: swagatamdas19@yahoo.co.in

Shubhransu Sekhar Dash
SRM University, Tamil Nadu, India
E-mail: munu_dash_2k@yahoo.com

ISSN 0302-9743   e-ISSN 1611-3349
ISBN 978-3-319-03755-4   e-ISBN 978-3-319-03756-1
DOI 10.1007/978-3-319-03756-1
Springer Cham Heidelberg New York Dordrecht London

Library of Congress Control Number: 2013954557

CR Subject Classification (1998): F.1, I.2, H.3, F.2, I.4-5, J.3, H.4

LNCS Sublibrary: SL 1 – Theoretical Computer Science and General Issues

Typesetting: Camera-ready by author, data conversion by Scientific Publishing Services, Chennai, India

Printed on acid-free paper

Springer is part of Springer Science+Business Media (www.springer.com)

Preface

This LNCS volume contains the papers presented at the 4th International Conference on Swarm, Evolutionary and Memetic Computing (SEMCCO 2013) held during December 19–21, 2013, at SRM University, Chennai, India. SEMCCO is regarded as one of the prestigious international conference series that aims at bringing together researchers from academia and industry to report and review the latest progresses in the cutting-edge research on swarm, evolutionary, memetic and other computing techniques such as neural and fuzzy computing, to explore new application areas, to design new nature-inspired algorithms for solving hard problems, and finally to create awareness about these domains to a wider audience of practitioners.

SEMCCO 2013 received 350 paper submissions from 20 countries across the globe. After a rigorous peer-review process involving 1,100 reviews, 126 full-length articles were accepted for oral presentation at the conference. This corresponds to an acceptance rate of 36% and is intended to maintain the high standards of the conference proceedings. The papers included in this LNCS volume cover a wide range of topics in swarm, evolutionary, memetic, fuzzy, and neural computing algorithms and their real-world applications in problems from diverse domains of science and engineering.

The conference featured distinguished keynote speakers: Prof. Marios M. Polycarpou, President, IEEE Computational Intelligence Society and Director, KIOS Research Center for Intelligent Systems and Networks Department of Electrical and Computer Engineering, University of Cyprus; Prof. Ferrante Neri, Professor of Computational Intelligence Optimization, De Montfort University, UK; Dr. M. Fatih Tasgetiren, Associate Professor of Industrial Engineering, Yasar University, Turkey; Dr. Dipti Srinivasan, Associate Professor, Department of Electrical and Computer Engineering, National University of Singapore. The other prominent speakers were Dr. P.N. Suganthan, NTU, Singapore; Dr. Adel Nasiri, Department of Electrical Engineering and Computer Science, University of Wisconsin-Milwaukee, USA; Dr. Ravipudi Venkata Rao, NIT, Surat, India; and Dr. Swagatam Das, ISI, Kolkata, India.

We take this opportunity to thank the authors of the submitted papers for their hard work, adherence to the deadlines, and patience with the review process. The quality of a referred volume depends mainly on the expertise and dedication of the reviewers. We are indebted to the Program Committee/Technical Committee members, who produced excellent reviews in short time frames.

We would also like to thank our sponsors for providing all the logistical support and financial assistance. First, we are indebted to SRM University Management and Administration for supporting our cause and encouraging us to organize the conference at SRM University, Chennai, India. In particular, we would like to express our heartfelt thanks for providing us with the necessary financial support and infrastructural assistance to hold the conference. Our sincere thanks to Thiru T.R. Pachamuthu, Chancellor, Shri P. Sathyanarayanan, President, Dr. M. Ponnavaikko, Vice-Chancellor, Dr. N. Sethuraman, Registrar, and Dr. C. Muthamizhchelvan, Director (E&T) of SRM University, for their encouragement and continuous support. We thank Prof. Carlos A. Coello Coello, Prof. Nikhil R. Pal, and Prof. Rajkumar Roy for providing valuable guidelines and inspiration to overcome various difficulties in the process of organizing this conference.

We would also like to thank the participants of this conference. Finally, we would like to thank all the volunteers who made great efforts in meeting the deadlines and arranging every detail to make sure that the conference could run smoothly. We hope the readers of these proceedings find the papers inspiring and enjoyable.

December 2013   Bijaya Ketan Panigrahi
                                                 Swagatam Das
                                                 P.N. Suganthan
                                                 S.S. Dash

Organization

Chief Patron

Thiru T.R. Pachamuthu

Patron

Shri P. Sathyanarayanan

Honorary Chairs

Nikhil R. Pal, India
Carlos A. Coello Coello, Mexico
Rajkumar Roy, UK
M. Ponnavaikko, India

General Chairs

B.K. Panigrahi, India
Swagatam Das, India
P.N. Suganthan, Singapore

Program Chairs

S.S. Dash, India
Zhihua Cui, China
J.C. Bansal, India

Program Co-chairs

K. Vijaya Kumar, India
A. Rathinam, India

Steering Committee Chair

P.N. Suganthan, Singapore

Publicity Chairs

S.S. Dash, India
S.C. Satpathy, India
N.C. Sahoo, Malaysia

Special Session Chairs

Sanjoy Das, USA
Wei-Chiang Hong, Taiwan

R. Rajendran, India
E. Poovammal, India

Tutorial Chair

S.K. Udgata, India

Technical Program Committee

Abbas Khosravi	Deakin University, Australia
Ahmed Y. Saber	Senior Power System Engineer - R&D Department, OTI/ETAP, CA, USA
Aimin Zhou	East China Normal University, China
Almoataz Youssef Abdelaziz	Ain Shams University, Cairo, Egypt
Athanasios V. Vasilakos	University of Western Macedonia, Greece
Ayman Abd El-Saleh	Multimedia University, Cyberjaya, Malaysia
Balasubramaniam Jayaram	Indian Institute of Technology Hyderabad, India
Carlos A. Coello Coello	CINVESTAV-IPN, México
Chilukuri K. Mohan	Syracuse University, USA
Chanan Singh	Texas A&M University, USA
Dipankar Dasgupta	University of Memphis, USA
Dinesh Kant Kumar	RMIT, Australia
Esperanza García-Gonzalo	Oviedo University, Spain
Ganapati Panda	IIT Bhubaneswar, India
G. Kumar Venayagamoorthy	Clemson University, USA
G.A. Vijayalakshmi Pai	PSG College of Technology, Coimbatore, India
Gerardo Beni	University of California, Riverside, USA
Halina Kwasnicka	Wroclaw University of Technology, Poland
Hisao Ishibuchi	Japan
Hong-Jie Xing	Hebei University, China
Janusz Kacprzyk	Systems Research Institute, Poland
John MacIntyre	University of Sunderland, UK
Jeng-Shyang Pan	National Kaohsiung University of Applied Sciences, Taiwan
Juan Luis Fernández Martínez	Universidad de Oviedo, Spain
Kalyanmoy Deb	IIT Kanpur, India
Konstantinos E. Parsopoulos	University of Ioannina, Greece
K. Vaisakh	Andhra University, India
Laxmidhar Behera	IIT Kanpur, India
Leandro Nunes de Castro	Universidade Presbiteriana Mackenzie, Brazil
Lingfeng Wang	The University of Toledo, USA

M.A. Abiso	King Fahd University of Petroleum & Minerals, Saudi Arabia
Maurice Clerc	France Telecom R&D, France
Manoj Kumar Tiwari	IIT Kharagpur, India
Martin Middendorf	University of Leipzig, Germany
Meng Hiot Lim	NTU, Singapore
N.C. Sahoo	IIT Bhubaneswar, India
Oscar Castillo	Tijuana Inst. Technology, Mexico
Peng Shi	University of Adelaide, Australia
Pei Chan Chang	Taiwan
P.K. Dash	SOA University, India
Quan Min Zhu	University of the West of England, Bristol, UK
Rafael Stubs Parpinelli	State University of Santa Catarina, Brazil
Saeid Nahavandi	Deakin University, Australia
Samrat Sabat	University of Hyderabad, Hyderabad, India
Satchidananda Dehuri	Ajou University, South Korea
Shu-Heng Chen	National Chengchi University, Taipei, Taiwan, ROC
S.G. Ponnambalam	Monash University, Malaysia
Siba K. Udgata	University of Hyderabad, Hyderabad, India
Saman K. Halgamuge	Australia
Sanjoy Das	Kansas State University, USA
S. Baskar	Thiagarajar College of Engineering, India
Somanath Majhi	IIT, Guwahati, India
Tan Kay Chen	National University of Singapore, Singapore
Vincenzo Piuri	Università degli Studi di Milano, Italy
V. Ravi	IDRBT, Hyderabad, India
Wei-Chiang Hong	Oriental Institute of Technology, Taiwan
Xin-She Yang	Middlesex University, London, UK
X.Z. Gao	Aalto University, Finland
Yew-Soon Ong	Nanyang Technological University, Singapore
Yuehui Chen	University of Jinan, China
Yuhui Shi	Xi'an Jiaotong-Liverpool University, China
Yucheng Dong	Sichuan University, China
Zhao Xu	Hong Kong Polytechnic University, Hong Kong
Zong Woo Geem	Gachon University, South Korea
S. Baskar	Thiagrajar College of Engineering, Madurai, India
P. Somsundaram	Anna University, Chennai, India
D. Devaraj	Kalasalingam University, India
C. Christopher Asir Rajan	Pondicherry University, India

Technical Review Board

Pratihar, Dilip
P.P., Rajeevan
Panda, Sidhartha
Panda, Ganapati
Pandit, Manjaree
Panigrahi, Siba
Parillo, Fernando
Pant, Millie
Pattnaik, Shyam
Pluhacek, Michal
Puhan, Niladri
Qian, Bin
Rao, Ravipudi
Rocky, Taif Hossain
Rout, Pravat Kumar
Rybnik, Mariusz
Rajagopal, V.
Rahman, Humyun Fuad
Rajasekhar, Anguluri
Ramasamy, Savitha
Ravi, V.
Ravishankar, Jayashri
Ren, Ye

S., Sudha
Saikia, Lalit
Salehinejad, Hojjat
Samiei Moghaddam, Mahmoud
Saxena, Anmol Ratna

Selvakumar, A. Immanuel
Senroy, Nilanjan
Shariatmadar, Seyed Mohammad
Sharma, Shailendra
Shukla, Anupam
Singh, Madhu
Singh, Mukhtiar
Singh, Pramod Kumar
Swarup, Shanti
Sabat, Samrat
Salkuti, Surender Reddy
Samantaray, Subhransu
Satapathy, Suresh Chandra
Schaefer, Gerald
Senkerik, Roman
Sethuraman, Kowsalya
Shieh, Chin-Shiuh
Shrivastava, Ashish
Shrivastava, Nitin Anand
Singh, Bhim
Singh, Manohar
Singh, Sanjeev
Sinha, Dr. Nidul

Sishaj P. Simon
Skanderová, Lenka
Sun, Jianyong

Swain, Akshaya
Thangaraj, Radha
Thomas, Mini
Tiwari, Manoj
Tang, Ke
Thelukuntla, Chandra Shekar
Torkaman, Hossein
Udgata, S.K.
V., Ravikumarpandi
Vaisakh, K.
Verma, Nishchal
Vijay, Ritu
Wang, Lingfeng
Wang, Shengyao
Willjuice Iruthayarajan, M.
Xie, Liping
Yang, Xin-She
Yusof, Norazah
Yussof, Salman
Zamuda, Ales
Zapotecas Martínez, Saúl
Xie, Feng
Xue, Bing
Zelinka, Ivan
Zhihua, Cui
Zhou, Aimin
Zhuhadar, Leyla

Organizing/Technical Program Committee

R. Jegatheesan, SRM University
R. Ramanujam, SRM University
N. Chellammal, SRM University
C.S. Boopathy, SRM University
D. Suchithra, SRM University
K. Mohanraj, SRM University
N. Kalaiarasi, SRM University
R. Sridhar, SRM University
D. Sattianandan, SRM University
C. Bharathiraja, SRM University
S. Vidyasagar, SRM University
C. Subramanian, SRM University

Table of Contents – Part II

Critical Issues in Model-Based Surrogate Functions in Estimation
of Distribution Algorithms 1
  Roberto Santana, Alexander Mendiburu, and Jose A. Lozano

Sandholm Algorithm with K-means Clustering Approach
for Multi-robot Task Allocation 14
  Murugappan Elango, Ganesan Kanagaraj, and S.G. Ponnambalam

Genetic Programming for Modeling Vibratory Finishing Process: Role
of Experimental Designs and Fitness Functions 23
  Akhil Garg and Kang Tai

Non-fragile Robust PI Controller Design Using Co-variance Matrix
Adaptation Evolutionary Strategy.................................. 32
  K. Mohaideen Abdul Kadhar and S. Baskar

Meta Heuristic Approaches for Circular Open Dimension Problem 44
  N. Madhu Sudana Rao, M. Aruna, and S. Bhuvaneswari

Protein Function Prediction Using Adaptive Swarm Based Algorithm ... 55
  Archana Chowdhury, Amit Konar, Pratyusha Rakshit, and
  Ramadoss Janarthanan

Reduction of Bullwhip Effect in Supply Chain through Improved
Forecasting Method: An Integrated DWT and SVM Approach 69
  Sanjita Jaipuria and S.S. Mahapatra

An Ant Colony Optimization Algorithm for the Min-Degree
Constrained Minimum Spanning Tree Problem...................... 85
  V. Venkata Ramana Murthy and Alok Singh

Multiobjective Differential Evolution Algorithm Using Binary Encoded
Data in Selecting Views for Materializing in Data Warehouse 95
  Rajib Goswami, Dhruba Kumar Bhattacharyya, and
  Malayananda Dutta

Robust Protective Relay Setting and Coordination Using Modified
Differential Evolution Considering Different Network Topologies 107
  Joymala Moirangthem, Bijaya Ketan Panigrahi,
  Krishnanand K.R., and Sanjib Kumar Panda

Real-Coded Genetic Algorithm and Fuzzy Logic Approach
for Real-Time Load-Tracking Performance of an Autonomous Power
System 119
    Abhik Banerjee, V. Mukherjee, and S.P. Ghoshal

Short Term Load Forecasting (STLF) Using Generalized Neural
Network (GNN) Trained with Adaptive GA 132
    D.K. Chaturvedi and Sinha Anand Premdayal

Gene Selection Using Multi-objective Genetic Algorithm Integrating
Cellular Automata and Rough Set Theory 144
    Soumen Kumar Pati, Asit Kumar Das, and Arka Ghosh

Fusion at Features Level in CBIR System Using Genetic Algorithm..... 156
    Chandrashekhar G. Patil, Mahesh T. Kolte, and
    Devendra S. Chaudhari

New Bio-inspired Meta-Heuristics - Green Herons Optimization
Algorithm - for Optimization of Travelling Salesman Problem
and Road Network 168
    Chiranjib Sur and Anupam Shukla

A Comparative Analysis of Results of Data Clustering with Variants
of Particle Swarm Optimization 180
    Anima Naik, Suresh Chandra Satapathy, and K. Parvathi

Hybrid Particle Swarm Optimization Technique for Protein Structure
Prediction Using 2D Off-Lattice Model 193
    Nanda Dulal Jana and Jaya Sil

Software Effort Estimation Using Functional Link Neural Networks
Optimized by Improved Particle Swarm Optimization 205
    Tirimula Rao Benala, Rajib Mall, and Satchidananda Dehuri

Improved Feature Selection Based on Particle Swarm Optimization
for Liver Disease Diagnosis 214
    Gunasundari Selvaraj and Janakiraman S.

Groundwater System Modeling for Pollution Source Identification
Using Artificial Neural Network 226
    Raj Mohan Singh and Divya Srivastava

Stochastic Analysis for Forecasting the MW Load of Plug-In Electric
Vehicles 237
    C.S. Indulkar and K. Ramalingam

Biometric Based Personal Authentication Using Eye Movement
Tracking   248
    Atul Dhingra, Amioy Kumar, Madasu Hanmandlu, and
    Bijaya Ketan Panigrahi

Accelerated Simulation of Membrane Computing to Solve the N-queens
Problem on Multi-core   257
    Ali Maroosi and Ravie Chandren Muniyandi

A Genetic Algorithm Optimized Artificial Neural Network
for the Segmentation of MR Images in Frontotemporal Dementia   268
    R. Sheela Kumari, Tinu Varghese, C. Kesavadas,
    N. Albert Singh, and P.S. Mathuranath

Intelligent Computation and Kinematics of 4-DOF SCARA Manipulator
Using ANN and ANFIS   277
    Panchanand Jha and Bibhuti Bhusan Biswal

Hybrid Neuro-Fuzzy Network Identification for Autonomous
Underwater Vehicles   287
    Osama Hassanein, G. Sreenatha, and Tapabrata Ray

Prediction of Protein Structural Class by Functional Link Artificial
Neural Network Using Hybrid Feature Extraction Method   298
    Bishnupriya Panda, Ambika Prasad Mishra, Babita Majhi, and
    Minakhi Rout

ANN Modeling of a Steelmaking Process   308
    Dipak Laha

Crop Yield Forecasting Using Neural Networks   319
    Mukesh Meena and Pramod Kumar Singh

Non-linear Dynamic System Identification Using FLLWNN with Novel
Learning Method   332
    Mihir Narayan Mohanty, Badrinarayan Sahu,
    Prasanta Kumar Nayak, and Laxmi Prasad Mishra

Analysis of Transient Stability Based STATCOM for Neural Network
Controller in Cascaded Multilevel Inverter   342
    P.K. Dhal and C. Christober Asir Ranjan

Emotion Recognition System by Gesture Analysis Using Fuzzy Sets   354
    Reshma Kar, Aruna Chakraborty, Amit Konar, and
    Ramadoss Janarthanan

Automatic Eye Detection in Face Images for Unconstrained Biometrics
Using Genetic Programming   364
    Chandrashekhar Padole and Joanne Athaide

Neural Network Based Gesture Recognition for Elderly Health Care
Using Kinect Sensor 376
    Sriparna Saha, Monalisa Pal, Amit Konar, and
    Ramadoss Janarthanan

City Block Distance for Identification of Co-expressed MicroRNAs 387
    Sushmita Paul and Pradipta Maji

Extreme Learning Machine Approach for On-Line Voltage Stability
Assessment.. 397
    P. Duraipandy and D. Devaraj

Quadratic Fuzzy Bilevel Chance Constrained Programming
with Parameters Following Weibull Distribution 406
    Animesh Biswas and Arnab Kumar De

Message Passing Methods for Estimation of Distribution Algorithms
Based on Markov Networks 419
    Roberto Santana, Alexander Mendiburu, and Jose A. Lozano

Application of Neural Networks to Automatic Load Frequency
Control 431
    Soumyadeep Nag and Namitha Philip

RNN Based Solar Radiation Forecasting Using Adaptive
Learning Rate 442
    Ajay Pratap Yadav, Avanish Kumar, and Laxmidhar Behera

Energy Efficient Aggregation in Wireless Sensor Networks for Multiple
Base Stations.. 453
    Nagarjuna Reddy Busireddy and Siba K. Udgata

An Intelligent Method for Handoff Decision in Next Generation
Wireless Network 465
    Laksha Pattnaik, Mihir Narayan Mohanty, and Bibhuprasad Mohanty

Path Planning for the Autonomous Underwater Vehicle 476
    Andrey Kirsanov, Sreenatha G. Anavatti, and Tapabrata Ray

A Game Theoretic Approach for Reliable Power Supply in Islanded DG
Grids.. 487
    Rohan Mukherjee, Rupam Kundu, Sanjoy Das,
    Bijaya Ketan Panigrahi, and Swagatam Das

Classification of Day-Ahead Deregulated Electricity Market Prices
Using DCT-CFNN 499
    S. Anbazhagan and Narayanan Kumarappan

Multi-Objective Approach for Protein Structure Prediction 511
    S. Sudha, S. Baskar, and S. Krishnaswamy

Clustering Based Analysis of Spirometric Data Using Principal
Component Analysis and Self Organizing Map   523
    Mythili Asaithambi, Sujatha C. Manoharan, and
    Srinivasan Subramanian

Feature Selection of Motor Imagery EEG Signals Using Firefly
Temporal Difference Q-Learning and Support Vector Machine   534
    Saugat Bhattacharyya, Pratyusha Rakshit, Amit Konar,
    D.N. Tibarewala, and Ramadoss Janarthanan

Optimal Build-or-Buy Decision for Component Selection of Application
Package Software   546
    P.C. Jha, Ramandeep Kaur, Shivani Bali, and Sushila Madan

Text and Data Mining to Detect Phishing Websites and Spam
Emails   559
    Mayank Pandey and Vadlamani Ravi

Intelligent Fault Tracking by an Adaptive Fuzzy Predictor
and a Fractional Controller of Electromechanical System – A Hybrid
Approach   574
    Tribeni Prasad Banerjee and Swagatam Das

Differential Evolution and Bacterial Foraging Optimization Based
Dynamic Economic Dispatch with Non-smooth Fuel Cost Functions   583
    Kanchapogu Vaisakh, Pillala Praveena, and Kothapalli Naga Sujatha

Permutation Flowshop Scheduling Problem Using Classical NEH,
ILS-ESP Operator   595
    Vanita G. Tonge and Pravin Kulkarni

Analysis of Human Retinal Vasculature for Content Based Image
Retrieval Applications   606
    Sivakamasundari J. and Natarajan V.

Activity Recognition Using Multiple Features, Subspaces
and Classifiers   617
    M.M. Sardeshmukh, M.T. Kolte, and D.S. Chaudahri

Advanced Optimization by Progressive Mapping Search Method
of PSO and Neural Network   625
    Dong Hwa Kim, Jin Ill Park, and X.Z. Gao

Optimal Placement of DG in Distribution System Using Genetic
Algorithm   639
    D. Sattianadan, M. Sudhakaran, S.S. Dash, K. Vijayakumar, and
    P. Ravindran

Intelligent Controllers in Path Tracking of a Manipulator with Bounded
Disturbance Torque 648
  Neha Kapoor and Jyoti Ohri

Multiscale and Multilevel Wavelet Analysis of Mammogram Using
Complex Neural Network 658
  E. Malar, A. Kandaswamy, and M. Gauthaam

Author Index 669

Table of Contents – Part I

A Populated Iterated Greedy Algorithm with Inver-Over Operator
for Traveling Salesman Problem.................................... 1
   M. Fatih Tasgetiren, Ozge Buyukdagli, Damla Kiziay, and
   Korhan Karabulut

Meta-modeling and Optimization for Varying Dimensional Search
Space... 13
   Kalyanmoy Deb, Soumil Srivastava, and Akshay Chawla

A General Variable Neighborhood Search Algorithm for the No-Idle
Permutation Flowshop Scheduling Problem......................... 24
   M. Fatih Tasgetiren, Ozge Buyukdagli, Quan-Ke Pan, and
   Ponnuthurai Nagaratnam Suganthan

Design of Non-uniformly Weighted and Spaced Circular Antenna
Arrays with Reduced Side Lobe Level and First Null Beamwidth Using
Seeker Optimization Algorithm 35
   Gopi Ram, Durbadal Mandal, Sakti Prasad Ghoshal, and Rajib Kar

Covariance Matrix Adaptation Evolutionary Strategy for the Solution
of Transformer Design Optimization Problem...................... 47
   Selvaraj Tamilselvi and Subramanian Baskar

Load Information Based Priority Dependant Heuristic for Manpower
Scheduling Problem in Remanufacturing 59
   Shantanab Debchoudhury, Debabrota Basu, Kai-Zhou Gao, and
   Ponnuthurai Nagaratnam Suganthan

A Tree Based Chemical Reaction Optimization Algorithm for QoS
Multicast Routing... 68
   Satya Prakash Sahoo, Sumaiya Ahmed, Manoj Kumar Patel, and
   Manas Ranjan Kabat

A New Improved Knowledge Based Cultural Algorithm for Reactive
Power Planning... 78
   Bidishna Bhattacharya, Kamal K. Mandal, and Niladri Chakraborty

BFO-RLDA: A New Classification Scheme for Face Images Using
Probabilistic Reasoning Model................................... 88
   Lingraj Dora, Sanjay Agrawal, and Rutuparna Panda

Optimal Stable IIR Low Pass Filter Design Using Modified Firefly
Algorithm..   98
    Suman K. Saha, Rajib Kar, Durbadal Mandal, and
    Sakti Prasad Ghoshal

Firefly Algorithm with Various Randomization Parameters:
An Analysis..   110
    Nadaradjane Sri Madhava Raja, K. Suresh Manic, and
    V. Rajinikanth

Reducing Power Losses in Power System by Using Self Adaptive Firefly
Algorithm..   122
    B. Suresh Babu and A. Shunmugalatha

A Soft-Computing Based Approach to Economic and Environmental
Analysis of an Autonomous Power Delivery System Utilizing Hybrid
Solar – Diesel – Electrochemical Generation   133
    Trina Som and Niladri Chakraborty

Parameter Adaptation in Differential Evolution Based on Diversity
Control   146
    S. Miruna Joe Amali and Subramanian Baskar

Data Clustering with Differential Evolution Incorporating
Macromutations   158
    Goran Martinović and Dražen Bajer

Improved Adaptive Differential Evolution Algorithm with External
Archive...   170
    Rammohan Mallipeddi and Ponnuthurai Nagaratnam Suganthan

Fuzzy Clustering of Image Pixels with a Fitness-Based Adaptive
Differential Evolution..   179
    Soham Sarkar, Gyana Ranjan Patra, Swagatam Das, and
    Sheli Sinha Chaudhuri

Performance Study of a New Modified Differential Evolution Technique
Applied for Optimal Placement and Sizing of Distributed Generation ...   189
    S. Kumar, D. Pal, Kamal K. Mandal, and Niladri Chakraborty

An Approach to Solve Multi-criteria Supplier Selection While
Considering Environmental Aspects Using Differential Evolution   199
    Sunil Kumar Jauhar, Millie Pant, and Aakash Deep

Comparison between Differential Evolution Algorithm and Particle
Swarm Optimization for Market Clearing with Voltage Dependent
Load Models   209
    Deep Kiran, Bijaya Ketan Panigrahi, and A.R. Abhyankar

Multipopulation-Based Differential Evolution with Speciation-Based
Response to Dynamic Environments   222
    Souvik Kundu, Debabrota Basu, Sheli Sinha Chaudhuri

A Modified Differential Evolution for Symbol Detection
in MIMO-OFDM System   236
    Aritra Sen, Subhrajit Roy, and Swagatam Das

Lévy Flight Based Local Search in Differential Evolution   248
    Harish Sharma, Shimpi Singh Jadon, Jagdish Chand Bansal, and
    K.V. Arya

An Adaptive Differential Evolution Based Fuzzy Approach for Edge
Detection in Color and Grayscale Images   260
    Satrajit Mukherjee, Bodhisattwa Prasad Majumder,
    Aritran Piplai, and Swagatam Das

A Differential Evolution Approach to Multi-level Image Thresholding
Using Type II Fuzzy Sets   274
    Ritambhar Burman, Sujoy Paul, and Swagatam Das

Differential Evolution with Controlled Annihilation and Regeneration
of Individuals and a Novel Mutation Scheme   286
    Sudipto Mukherjee, Sarthak Chatterjee, Debdipta Goswami, and
    Swagatam Das

Differential Evolution and Offspring Repair Method Based Dynamic
Constrained Optimization   298
    Kunal Pal, Chiranjib Saha, and Swagatam Das

Adaptive Differential Evolution with Difference Mean Based
Perturbation for Practical Engineering Optimization Problems   310
    Rupam Kundu, Rohan Mukherjee, and Swagatam Das

Transmission Line Management Using Multi-objective Evolutionary
Algorithm   321
    K. Pandiarajan and C.K. Babulal

Normalized Normal Constraint Algorithm Based Multi-Objective
Optimal Tuning of Decentralised PI Controller of Nonlinear
Multivariable Process – Coal Gasifier   333
    Rangasamy Kotteeswaran and Lingappan Sivakumar

Simulated Annealing Based Real Power Loss Minimization Aspect
for a Large Power Network   345
    Syamasree Biswas (Raha), Kamal Krishna Manadal, and
    Niladri Chakraborty

Hybrid Artificial Bee Colony Algorithm and Simulated Annealing
Algorithm for Combined Economic and Emission Dispatch Including
Valve Point Effect... 354
    Sundaram Arunachalam, R. Saranya, and N. Sangeetha

Spectrum Allocation in Cognitive Radio Networks Using Firefly
Algorithm... 366
    Kiran Kumar Anumandla, Shravan Kudikala,
    Bharadwaj Akella Venkata, and Samrat L. Sabat

Bi-objective Optimization in Identical Parallel Machine Scheduling
Problem 377
    Sankaranarayanan Bathrinath, S. Saravana Sankar,
    S.G. Ponnambalam, and B.K.V. Kannan

Teaching-Learning-Based Optimization Algorithm in Dynamic
Environments 389
    Feng Zou, Lei Wang, Xinhong Hei, Qiaoyong Jiang, and
    Dongdong Yang

A Novel Ant Colony Optimization Algorithm for the Vehicle Routing
Problem 401
    Srinjoy Ganguly and Swagatam Das

Implementation of Fractional Order PID Controller for Three
Interacting Tank Process Optimally Tuned Using Bee Colony
Optimization 413
    U. Sabura Banu

Artificial Bee Colony-Based Approach for Optimal Capacitor Placement
in Distribution Networks...................................... 424
    Attia El-Fergany, Almoataz Y. Abdelaziz, and
    Bijaya Ketan Panigrahi

Grammatical Bee Colony 436
    Tapas Si, Arunava De, and Anup Kumar Bhattacharjee

Artificial Bee Colony Algorithm for Probabilistic Target Q-coverage
in Wireless Sensor Networks................................... 446
    S. Mini, Siba K. Udgata, and Samrat L. Sabat

Chaos Synchronization in Commensurate Fractional Order Lü System
via Optimal $PI^\lambda D^\mu$ Controller with Artificial Bee Colony Algorithm 457
    Anguluri Rajasekhar, Shantanu Das, and Swagatam Das

Cooperative Micro Artificial Bee Colony Algorithm for Large Scale
Global Optimization Problems.................................. 469
    Anguluri Rajasekhar and Swagatam Das

Improvement in Genetic Algorithm with Genetic Operator Combination (GOC) and Immigrant Strategies for Multicast Routing in Ad Hoc Networks 481
    P. Karthikeyan and Subramanian Baskar

Ensemble of Dying Strategies Based Multi-objective Genetic Algorithm.. 492
    Rahila Patel, M.M. Raghuwanshi, and L.G. Malik

Effect of Photovoltaic and Wind Power Variations in Distribution System Reconfiguration for Loss Reduction Using Ant Colony Algorithm.. 504
    H.A. Abdelsalam, Almoataz Y. Abdelaziz, R.A. Osama, and Bijaya Ketan Panigrahi

Inter-species Cuckoo Search via Different Levy Flights 515
    Swagatam Das, Preetam Dasgupta, and Bijaya Ketan Panigrahi

Cuckoo Search Algorithm for the Mobile Robot Navigation 527
    Prases Kumar Mohanty and Dayal R. Parhi

Automatic Generation Control of Multi-area Power System Using Gravitational Search Algorithm 537
    Rabindra Kumar Sahu, Umesh Kumar Rout, and Sidhartha Panda

Design and Simulation of FIR High Pass Filter Using Gravitational Search Algorithm 547
    R. Islam, Rajib Kar, Durbadal Mandal, and Sakti Prasad Ghoshal

Solution of Optimal Reactive Power Dispatch by an Opposition-Based Gravitational Search Algorithm 558
    Binod Shaw, V. Mukherjee, and Sakti Prasad Ghoshal

A Novel Swarm Intelligence Based Gravitational Search Algorithm for Combined Economic and Emission Dispatch Problems 568
    Hari Mohan Dubey, Manjaree Pandit, Bijaya Ketan Panigrahi, and Mugdha Udgir

Particle Swarm Optimization Based Optimal Reliability Design of Composite Electric Power System Using Non-sequential Monte Carlo Sampling and Generalized Regression Neural Network 580
    R. Ashok Bakkiyaraj and Narayanan Kumarappan

A Bacteria Foraging-Particle Swarm Optimization Algorithm for QoS Multicast Routing.. 590
    Rohini Pradhan, Manas Ranjan Kabat, and Satya Prakash Sahoo

Performance Evaluation of Particle Swarm Optimization Algorithm for Optimal Design of Belt Pulley System 601
    Pandurengan Sabarinath, M.R. Thansekhar, and R. Saravanan

Optimal Sizing for Stand-Alone Hybrid PV-WIND Power Supply
System Using PSO 617
    D. Suchitra, R. Jegatheesan, M. Umamaheswara Reddy, and
    T.J. Deepika

A Peer-to-Peer Dynamic Single Objective Particle Swarm Optimizer 630
    Hrishikesh Dewan, Raksha B. Nayak, and V. Susheela Devi

Aligned PSO for Optimization of Image Processing Methods Applied
to the Face Recognition Problem 642
    Juan Luis Fernández-Martínez, Ana Cernea,
    Esperanza García-Gonzalo, Julian Velasco, and
    Bijaya Ketan Panigrahi

Optimal Operation Management of Transmission System with Fuel Cell
Power Plant Using PSO 652
    S. Vidyasagar, K. Vijayakumar, and D. Sattianadan

PID Tuning and Control for 2-DOF Helicopter Using Particle Swarm
Optimization 662
    A.P.S. Ramalakshmi, P.S. Manoharan, and P. Deepamangai

Optimal Location and Parameter Selection of Thyristor Controlled
Series Capacitor Using Particle Swarm Optimization 673
    S. Devi and M. Geethanjali

A New Particle Swarm Optimization with Population Restructuring
Based Multiple Population Strategy 688
    Qingjian Ni, Cen Cao, and Huimin Du

Small Signal Stability Constrained Optimal Power Flow Using Swarm
Based Algorithm 699
    Mani Devesh Raj and Periyasami Somasundaram

Online Voltage Stability Assessment of Power System by Comparing
Voltage Stability Indices and Extreme Learning Machine 710
    M.V. Suganyadevi and C.K. Babulal

A Peer-to-Peer Particle Swarm Optimizer for Multi-objective
Functions 725
    Hrishikesh Dewan, Raksha B. Nayak, and V. Susheela Devi

A Novel Improved Discrete ABC Algorithm for Manpower Scheduling
Problem in Remanufacturing 738
    Debabrota Basu, Shantanab Debchoudhury, Kai-Zhou Gao, and
    Ponnuthurai Nagaratnam Suganthan

Optimal Partial-Retuning of Decentralised PI Controller of Coal
Gasifier Using Bat Algorithm 750
   Rangasamy Kotteeswaran and Lingappan Sivakumar

Optimal Velocity Requirements for Earth to Venus Mission Using
Taboo Evolutionary Programming 762
   M. Mutyalarao, Amaranathan Sabarinath, and M. Xavier James Raj

Author Index 773

Critical Issues in Model-Based Surrogate Functions in Estimation of Distribution Algorithms

Roberto Santana, Alexander Mendiburu, and Jose A. Lozano

Intelligent Systems Group
Department of Computer Science and Artificial Intelligence
University of the Basque Country (UPV/EHU)
Paseo Manuel de Lardizabal 1, 20080, San Sebastian, Guipuzcoa, Spain
{roberto.santana,alexander.mendiburu,ja.lozano}@ehu.es

Abstract. In many optimization domains the solution of the problem can be made more efficient by the construction of a surrogate fitness model. Estimation of distribution algorithms (EDAs) are a class of evolutionary algorithms particularly suitable for the conception of model-based surrogate techniques. Since EDAs generate probabilistic models, it is natural to use these models as surrogates. However, there exist many types of models and methods to learn them. The issues involved in the conception of model-based surrogates for EDAs are various and some of them have received scarce attention in the literature. In this position paper, we propose a unified view for model-based surrogates in EDAs and identify a number of critical issues that should be dealt with in order to advance the research in this area.

Keywords: estimation of distribution algorithms, surrogate functions, function approximation, probabilistic modeling, most probable configuration, abductive inference.

1 Introduction

Surrogate functions are approximations of objective or fitness functions that usually allow a more efficient search for optimal solutions in evolutionary algorithms (EAs). There is a variety of techniques used to construct surrogate functions in EAs [17,44]. They include instance-based learning methods, machine learning methods, and statistical learning methods [44]. In this position paper we focus on methods that are based on the use of probabilistic models for estimation of distribution algorithms (EDAs) [22,24]. These methods combine machine learning techniques and statistical procedures to learn and exploit the models.

The characteristic feature of EDAs with respect to other EAs is the use of probabilistic modeling to capture the most relevant features of the selected solutions. EDAs have been praised for their capacity to capture and exploit the interactions between the problem variables, limiting to a large extent the disruption of partial solutions [21,43]. In many cases, the probabilistic model learned

B.K. Panigrahi et al. (Eds.): SEMCCO 2013, Part II, LNCS 8298, pp. 1–13, 2013.

by EDAs is able to explicitly represent the problem structure which amounts to produce in each generation a candidate model for problem decomposition.

Since probabilistic models are a by-product of EDAs, a natural question is to what extent can these models be used as surrogates and which are the tasks that can be accomplished with this type of surrogates. These questions have been seldom addressed in the literature from a general perspective. When considering probabilistic models as surrogates, the focus has been on a particular type of EDAs, those based on Markov networks [5,6]. Furthermore, while the main application of surrogates are in the replacement of the original fitness value by its approximation, there are several scenarios in which they can be used in an indirect way (e.g., comparing and ranking solutions, partial evaluation, etc.). One of our contributions in this paper is addressing all these issues from a common perspective, pointing to the links with other relevant aspects of probabilistic modeling in EDAs. We also expand our analysis to cover uses of model-based surrogates for multi-objective problems (MOP) [11].

The paper is organized as follows. In the next section, we introduce EDAs and discuss the role of probabilistic modeling in these algorithms. Section 3 proposes a classification for model-based fitness-surrogates. Section 4 analyzes alternatives for learning model-based surrogates, and different criteria to assess their quality are reviewed in Section 5. Model-based fitness surrogates of multi-objective functions are discussed in Section 6. The conclusions of our paper and some lines for future work are presented in Section 7.

2   Estimation of Distribution Algorithms

In this paper, the joint generalized probability distribution of $\mathbf{x}$ is represented as $p(\mathbf{X} = \mathbf{x})$ or $p(\mathbf{x})$. $p(\mathbf{x}_S)$ will denote the marginal generalized probability distribution for $\mathbf{X}_S$. We use $p(X_i = x_i \mid X_j = x_j)$ or, in a simplified form, $p(x_i \mid x_j)$, to denote the conditional generalized probability distribution of X_i given $X_j = x_j$.

In EDAs, the new population of solutions is sampled from a probability distribution, which is estimated from a database that contains the selected solutions from the current generation. Thus, the interactions between the different variables that represent the solutions are explicitly expressed through the joint probability distribution associated with the solutions selected at each generation. A pseudo-code of EDAs is described in Algorithm 1.

The termination criteria of an EDA can be a maximum number of generations, a homogeneous population or no improvement after a specified number of generations. The probabilistic model learned at step 5 has a significant influence on the behavior of the EDA from the point of view of complexity and performance.

Algorithm 1. Estimation of distribution algorithm

---

1 Set $t \Leftarrow 0$. Generate M solutions randomly.
2 **do** {
3   Evaluate the solutions using the fitness function.
4   Select a set D_t^S of $N \leq M$ solutions according to a selection method.
5   Calculate a probabilistic model of D_t^S.
6   Generate M new solutions sampling from the distribution represented in the model.
7 $t \Leftarrow t + 1$
8 } **until** Termination criteria are met.

2.1 Probabilistic Modeling in EDAs

The main role of probabilistic modeling in EDAs is to capture an accurate representation of the regularities of the selected solutions. Frequently, these regularities correspond to the most common configurations of subsets of variables and patterns of interactions between the variables. Probabilistic models learned by EDAs can be classified according to the type of learning they use into two groups: 1) Models that apply parametrical learning; 2) Models that apply structural *and* parametric learning. In the first case, the structure of the model is known a priori and only the parameters are learned from data. In the second case, the structure and the parameters are learned from data. The original, an still primary application of a probabilistic model in EDAs is to generate new solutions. However, probabilistic models of fitness functions can be applied in different situations:

– To create surrogate functions that help to diminish the number of evaluations for costly functions [30,41,42].
– To obtain models of black box optimization problems for which an analytical expression of the fitness function is not available.
– To unveil and extract problem information that is hidden in the original formulation of the function or optimization problem [6,37].
– To design improved (local) optimization procedures based on the model structure [7,32,34,41].

2.2 MOEDAs

In MOPs, two or more, often conflicting, objectives have to be simultaneously optimized. Different variants of MOEDAs have been applied to these problems [21,25,48]. Particularly relevant for our analysis is the recently introduced MOEDA based on the joint probabilistic modeling of variables and objectives [20]. In this approach, a variable $Y_i, i \in \{1 \ldots k\}$ is associated to the objective f_i in such a way that Y_i takes values in the image of f_i, i.e. $y_i = f_i$.

A probability distribution $\hat{p}(x_1, \ldots, x_n, y_1, \ldots, y_k)$ is defined as the joint probability distribution of variables and objectives. The selected solutions from which

$\hat{p}$ is learned should correspond to good candidate sets for Pareto set approximations [20]. The probabilistic model $\hat{p}(x_1, \ldots, x_n, y_1, \ldots, y_k)$ will eventually capture conditional probabilistic relationships between objectives and variables. This model will capture the variable-objective mapping.

The key issue here is that the dependencies represented in the model could serve as a characterization of the relationships in the Pareto set approximations, possibly revealing characteristic patterns in this set of solutions.

3   Types of Model-Based Fitness Surrogates

In this section we propose a general classification of model-based fitness surrogates according to their use and the type of models they are based on. We start by identifying two situations in which surrogate functions may be needed:

1. λ-error surrogate: Approximating the fitness function to a desired level of accuracy λ.
2. α-ranking surrogate: Using surrogate values to rank solutions with a level of accuracy α.

Let $\hat{f}(\mathbf{x})$ be a surrogate function of $f(\mathbf{x})$. $\hat{f}(\mathbf{x})$ is a λ-error surrogate if $|f(\mathbf{x}) - \hat{f}(\mathbf{x})| < \lambda$, $\forall \mathbf{x}$. The λ-error surrogate defines a family of parametric functions that depend on λ.

$\hat{f}(\mathbf{x})$ is an α-ranking surrogate if:

$$q\left(sign(f(\mathbf{x}) - f(\mathbf{y})) = sign(\hat{f}(\mathbf{x}) - \hat{f}(\mathbf{y}))\right) \geq \alpha \qquad (1)$$

$$sign(\mathbf{x}) = \begin{cases} -1 \text{ for } \mathbf{x} < 0 \\ 0 \text{ for } \mathbf{x} = 0 \\ 1 \text{ for } \mathbf{x} > 0 \end{cases} \qquad (2)$$

where q gives the proportion of pairs of solutions $\mathbf{x}, \mathbf{y}$, out of all possible pairs, that satisfy that the ordering relationship between $\mathbf{x}$ and $\mathbf{y}$, defined by f is respected by the surrogate function. If $\alpha = 1$, then the surrogate function produces the same ranking that the original fitness function for any set of solutions.

Examples of models that can be respectively analyzed as a λ-error surrogate and an α-ranking surrogate are the Markov fitness model (MFM) model [5] and the Boltzmann distribution used in the context of of EDAs [28].

The MFM is based on a Markov network formed by a set of maximal cliques $K = \{K_1, \ldots, K_m\}$. Then, for any solution $\mathbf{x}$, the model of the fitness function is given by:

$$-ln(f(\mathbf{x})) = \sum_i \alpha_i V_{K_i}(\mathbf{x}) \qquad (3)$$

where V_k are the characteristic functions of a Walsh decomposition of the fitness function, and α_i are the model coefficients [5]. Given a sufficiently-sized set of solutions and their fitness, the MFM can be found solving a system of equations in the parameters.

The Boltzmann probability distribution $\hat{p}(\mathbf{x})$ is defined as

$$\hat{p}(\mathbf{x}) = \frac{e^{\frac{f(\mathbf{x})}{T}}}{\sum_{\mathbf{x}'} e^{\frac{f(\mathbf{x}')}{T}}}, \tag{4}$$

where $\sum_{\mathbf{x}'} e^{\frac{f(\mathbf{x}')}{T}}$ is the so-called partition function, and T is the temperature of the system that can be used as a parameter to smooth the probabilities.

By definition, the MFM provides a λ-error surrogate model where λ can be estimated as the greatest difference, among all the solutions, between the original fitness value and its approximation. The Boltzmann distribution guarantees that $sign(\hat{p}(\mathbf{x}^i) - \hat{p}(\mathbf{x}^j)) = sign(f(\mathbf{x}^i) - f(\mathbf{x}^j))$. Therefore, the Boltzmann distribution is an 1-ranking surrogate model of $f(\mathbf{x})$.

4   Learning of Model-Based Surrogates of Single-Objective Problems

The question of how to learn a model-based surrogate is a fundamental one. Particularly, in optimization domains for which we intend to extract as much knowledge as possible from the fitness function with the minimal number of function evaluations. In this section we analyze probabilistic modeling in EDAs from the perspective of fitness surrogates.

When a sufficiently large set of evaluated solutions is available, and the structure of the problem is known, i.e., the cliques of the Markov network, a MFM can be learned in a straightforward way from the data. If the structure is not available, then it has to be recovered from the data and this is accomplished using statistical methods for learning probabilistic graphical models (PGMs) from data [40]. Computing the Boltzmann distribution requires the computation of the partition function which is infeasible when the dimension space of the solutions grows. Therefore, instead of computing the Boltzmann distribution, usually a PGM is learned from the data. We call this approximation PGM-based approach.

The MFM and PGM-based approaches coincide in that both need to learn a structural representation from data when it is not available a priori. However, they differ in the way parameters are computed, and the way they are applied in EDAs.

4.1   Fitness-Blind versus Fitness-Aware Model Computation

In most commonly used EDAs, the probabilistic model is learned from the set of selected solutions. Marginal probabilities are computed based on the frequencies of the solutions in the selected set. No information about the fitness of the solutions is directly encoded in the model. The rationale is that since solutions have been selected according to their fitness, and the goal of the algorithm is to "model the best solutions", all relevant information has been already considered at the time of selection.

However, disregarding the fitness information of the selected solutions, at the time of learning the model, or even not using the fitness information of the non selected solutions means that valuable information obtained from searching the space of solutions is wasted. This is particularly remarkable if we intend to use the PGM as fitness surrogate.

In [36], the idea of learning the marginal probabilities of the PGM from the fitness values of all the evaluated solutions was proposed and applied to different EDAs. Similar ideas have been shown to improve the efficiency of EDAs that learn multivariate models [29,46]. Other methods [27] follow an intermediate approach in which solutions are first classified according to their fitness into two or more groups, and then one or more models are learned using the class labels associated to the solutions. These methods are able to incorporate, to a greater extent, the information contained in the fitness values.

In this paper we introduce the terms of *fitness-blind* and *fitness-aware* model-based fitness surrogates to refer to methods that respectively use non or extensive information about the fitness during learning of the probabilistic model. We state that the design of fitness-aware model learning methods is a critical issue for model-based surrogates. Results confirming the benefits of fitness-aware learning for diminishing the number of function evaluations [29,36,46] are an example of the potential of these methods for learning more accurate surrogates.

5   Evaluation of the Models as Surrogates

Once a model has been learned, one important question is how to evaluate the quality of the model as a surrogate. In this section we review the methods used for evaluating model-based surrogates. Evaluation of the models is mostly approached comparing the original fitness values and the approximations produced by the model on a set of solutions. Two different elements of this process can be identified:

1. The method for generating the solutions that are later used to evaluate the models.
2. The measures for evaluating the models from the solutions and their associated objective evaluations.

The way the sample of solutions is selected is usually a question overlooked in the literature. However, we emphasize this is a very important question.

Let us suppose the number of solutions to be generated is k. We identify as relevant the following procedures to generate them:

- The k solutions are randomly generated [6].
- The k solutions correspond to the best known values (for a single objective) of the function or they are the selected solutions [6,15,35].

− Solutions correspond to the k most probable configurations (MPC) of the model [14,16].

The way solutions are sampled is very related to the criteria taken into consideration and the measures used to evaluate the model. Among the measures that can serve to evaluate different facets of the models are:

− Correlation between the probabilities assigned by the models to the solutions and their fitness values [6].
− Distance between the ranking of solutions induced by the fitness functions and their models.
− Expected fitness value of the model, i.e. $\sum_x \hat{p}(x) f(x)$.
− Entropy of the model.
− Sum of the probabilities assigned to the solutions [35].

Some methods used for generating solutions better fit with some particular approaches to measure the quality of the model. For random solutions, we can compare different models in terms of the correlations or the expected fitness values. In [6], the analysis of the correlation has been successfully employed to analyze the fitness modeling capabilities of EDAs based on Markov networks. The entropy of the model can also be used. A model that assigns the same or very similar probability to all the solutions is of scarce interest.

If the k best known solutions are used to evaluate the models, all the previous criteria can be used but, in addition, we can evaluate the capacity of the model to generate solutions different to those that have been previously evaluated (exploration, or generalization capability of the model). The exploration capability can be estimated by computing first the total probability assigned to the best solutions [35]. If the sum of the probabilities given by the model to the k best solutions is very high (e.g. $\sum_x p(\mathbf{x}) = 0.9$) then we can assume its capacity of exploration is very limited. The k most probable configurations can be computed using algorithms that employ abductive inference and dynamic programming as those used in [26] to generate better solutions at an earlier step of the evolution.

Few available implementations of EDAs incorporate methods for constructing and using model-based fitness surrogates and evaluate their quality. Some of the methods described above for generating the solutions and some measures to evaluate the quality of the models have been implemented as part of the MATEDA-2.0 software [38]. A critical issue for extending the application of model-based fitness surrogates is their implementation as part of available software.

The main aspect to be emphasized from the analysis presented in this section is that while models can serve as surrogate to approximate the fitness of solutions, carefully selected solutions can be also very important to obtain an accurate evaluation of the models as fitness surrogates.

6   Model-Based Fitness Surrogates of Multi-objective Problems

Extending model-based surrogates to MOPs is a critical issue for the applicability of these algorithm. The problem of fitness surrogates for MOPs is more complex than in the single-objective case because different classes of surrogates can be designed for different types of possible approximations. Among the approximation tasks that can be approached using model-based surrogates are:

1. Learning a single model of each objective function.
2. Learning a joint model of all the objectives.
3. Learning a model of the Pareto set.

The first task can be approached with the same methods analyzed for the single-objective case. However, notice that probabilistic models of a single objective could incorporate, as input variables, the information about the other objectives. This type of information should be particularly useful when there is some degree of redundancy or statistical dependency between the objectives.

Several objectives can be simultaneously estimated by using multi-dimensional classifiers [1,12]. Nevertheless, learning this type of classifiers is not, in general, an easy task.

Models of the Pareto set can output the probability that a given solution, its objective vector, or a combination of both, belongs to the Pareto set. This type of model could not be used as a surrogate of the individual objective functions but can serve to estimate the "global" fitness of a solution, understanding this fitness value as the capacity of the solution to belong to the Pareto set.

Understanding the differences between these three approximation tasks is an important question for the conception of model-based surrogates for MOPs. We briefly review some of the statistical methods used in multi-objective optimization to represent the relationships between variables and objectives. These methods can be instrumental in the conception of strategies for model-based fitness surrogates in MOEDAs.

1. Analysis of the objectives correlation matrix [13,23]: In [13], PCA is used for detecting conflicting objectives. A method based on a different, unsupervised, feature selection is proposed in [23].
2. Explicit modeling of variable dependencies [3,25,31,47]: This is the main goal of several variants of multi-objective EDAs.
3. Joint clustering of variables and objectives [45]. Similar solutions are grouped by finding so-called modules of the decision space [45]. Biclustering and dendrogram visualization are used with this purpose.
4. Objective-based mixture modeling of variables' dependencies [2]: Solutions are first clustered based on their objective similarity, and then a model of the variables relationships is learned in each cluster.
5. Gaussian joint modeling of objectives and variables [19,20]: In [19], a Gaussian Bayesian network is used to represent dependencies between objectives, between variables, and between objectives and variables. In [18,20],

multi-dimensional Bayesian networks, used for multi-label classification tasks [1,12], serve to model the dependencies between variables and objectives.

6. Gaussian process (GP) models to predict objective values [8,49]: The idea is to predict the Pareto-optimal set by evaluating as few designs as possible and using Gaussian processes.

Some of the methods included above are natural candidates to be applied as fitness surrogates in MOPs. They have been mainly used for generation of solutions during the sampling step and for understanding the types of relationships between the variables and objectives of the problem. Statistical methods from other areas such as quantitative genetics have also application to design model-based fitness surrogates in MOEDAs [39].

7 Conclusions

In this paper we have analyzed a number of critical issues related with the design and application of fitness surrogates constructed from probabilistic graphical models. A classification of model-based fitness surrogates according to the type of approximation problem they can be used for has been proposed. We have also emphasized the importance that fitness-aware learning of the probabilistic models has for taking advantage of the information available about the fitness function. We have analyzed the commonly applied methods for evaluating the quality of the model-based surrogates and discussed the usually overlooked problem of how to select a sample of solutions for evaluating the models. Finally, we have analyzed the different approaches to model-based surrogates for MOPs and identified the available methods for variable-objective mapping.

There are several areas where further work is required:

- We have focused our analysis on the use of model-based surrogates in the context of EDA applications. However, surrogate models constructed from probabilistic models can be used within other EAs like genetic algorithms [4]. The conception of methods that extend the use of probabilistic models to other EAs is a topic worth to research.
- The application of probabilistic modeling has been mainly constrained to problems with binary and continuous representation. Recent results in other domains like permutations [9,10] show that PGMs can be also applied in these domains with important gains in efficiency. Some authors have proposed the use of this type of models also as fitness surrogates [33] and more work is needed in this direction.
- Theoretical work is needed to obtain effective learning methods for model-based fitness surrogates for MOPs and for providing a taxonomy of the different approximation problems that arise in this domain.

Acknowledgements. This work has been partially supported by Saiotek and Research Groups 2007-2012 (IT-242-07) programs (Basque Government), TIN2010-14931, and COMBIOMED network in computational biomedicine (Carlos III Health Institute).

References

1. Bielza, C., Li, G., Larranaga, P.: Multi-dimensional classification with Bayesian networks. International Journal of Approximate Reasoning 52(6), 705–727 (2011)
2. Bosman, P.A.: Design and Application of Iterated Density-Estimation Evolutionary Algorithms. PhD thesis, Universiteit Utrecht, Utrecht, The Netherlands (2003)
3. Bosman, P.A., Thierens, D.: Multi-objective optimization with diversity preserving mixture-based iterated density estimation evolutionary algorithms. International Journal of Approximate Reasoning 31(3), 259–289 (2002)
4. Brownlee, A.E.I., Regnier-Coudert, O., McCall, J.A., Massie, S., Stulajter, S.: An application of a GA with Markov network surrogate to feature selection. International Journal of Systems Science 44(11), 2039–2056 (2013)
5. Brownlee, A.E.I., McCall, J., Shakya, S.K.: The Markov Network Fitness Model. In: Shakya, S., Santana, R. (eds.) Markov Networks in Evolutionary Computation, vol. 14, pp. 125–140. Springer (2012)
6. Brownlee, A.E.I., McCall, J., Zhang, Q., Brown, D.: Approaches to selection and their effect on fitness modelling in an estimation of distribution algorithm. In: Proceedings of the 2008 Congress on Evolutionary Computation, CEC 2008, Hong Kong, pp. 2621–2628. IEEE Press (2008)
7. Butz, M.V., Pelikan, M., Llorá, X., Goldberg, D.E.: Automated global structure extraction for effective local building block processing in XCS. Evolutionary Computation 14(3), 345–380 (2006)
8. Campigotto, P., Passerini, A., Battiti, R.: Active learning of Pareto fronts. Technical Report DISI-13-001, University of Trento (2013)
9. Ceberio, J., Irurozki, E., Mendiburu, A., Lozano, J.A.: A review on estimation of distribution algorithms in permutation-based combinatorial optimization problems. Progress in Artificial Intelligence 1(1), 103–117 (2012)
10. Ceberio, J., Mendiburu, A., Lozano, J.A.: The Plackett-Luce ranking model on permutation-based optimization problems. In: 2013 IEEE Congress on Evolutionary Computation (CEC), pp. 494–501. IEEE (2013)
11. Coello, C., Lamont, G., Van Veldhuizen, D.: Evolutionary Algorithms for Solving Multi-objective Problems. Springer-Verlag New York Inc. (2007)
12. de Waal, P.R., van der Gaag, L.C.: Inference and learning in multi-dimensional Bayesian network classifiers. In: Mellouli, K. (ed.) ECSQARU 2007. LNCS (LNAI), vol. 4724, pp. 501–511. Springer, Heidelberg (2007)
13. Deb, K., Saxena, D.K.: On finding Pareto-optimal solutions through dimensionality reduction for certain large-dimensional multi-objective optimization problems. KanGAL Report 2005011, Kanpur Genetic Algorithms Laboratory (KanGAL). Indian Institute of Technology Kanpur (2005)
14. Echegoyen, C., Mendiburu, A., Santana, R., Lozano, J.A.: Analyzing the k most probable solutions in EDAs based on Bayesian networks. In: Exploitation of Linkage Learning in Evolutionary Algorithms, Evolutionary, pp. 163–189. Springer (2010)
15. Echegoyen, C., Mendiburu, A., Santana, R., Lozano, J.A.: Toward understanding EDAs based on bayesian networks through a quantitative analysis. IEEE Transactions on Evolutionary Computation 16(2), 173–189 (2012)
16. Höns, R., Santana, R., Larrañaga, P., Lozano, J.A.: Optimization by max-propagation using Kikuchi approximations. Technical Report EHU-KZAA-IK-2/07, Department of Computer Science and Artificial Intelligence, University of the Basque Country (November 2007)

17. Jin, Y.: Surrogate-assisted evolutionary computation: Recent advances and future challenges. Swarm and Evolutionary Computation 1(2), 61–70 (2011)
18. Karshenas, H.: Regularized model learning in EDAs for continuous and multiobjective optimization. PhD thesis, Technical University of Madrid, Spain (2013)
19. Karshenas, H., Santana, R., Bielza, C., Larrañaga, P.: Continuous estimation of distribution algorithms based on factorized Gaussian Markov networks. In: Shakya, S., Santana, R. (eds.) Markov Networks in Evolutionary Computation, pp. 157–173. Springer (2012)
20. Karshenas, H., Santana, R., Bielza, C., Larrañaga, P.: Multi-objective optimization based on joint probabilistic modeling of objectives and variables. IEEE Transactions on Evolutionary Computation (accepted for publication, 2013)
21. Larrañaga, P., Karshenas, H., Bielza, C., Santana, R.: A review on probabilistic graphical models in evolutionary computation. Journal of Heuristics 18(5), 795–819 (2012)
22. Larrañaga, P., Lozano, J.A. (eds.): Estimation of Distribution Algorithms. A New Tool for Evolutionary Computation. Kluwer Academic Publishers, Boston (2002)
23. López, A., Coello, C.A., Chakraborty, D.: Objective reduction using a feature selection technique. In: Proceedings of the Genetic and Evolutionary Computation Conference, GECCO 2008, pp. 673–680. ACM, New York (2008)
24. Lozano, J.A., Larrañaga, P., Inza, I., Bengoetxea, E. (eds.): Towards a New Evolutionary Computation: Advances on Estimation of Distribution Algorithms. Springer (2006)
25. Marti, L., Garcia, J., Berlanga, A., Coello, C.A., Molina, J.M.: On current model-building methods for multi-objective estimation of distribution algorithms: Shortcommings and directions for improvement. Technical Report GIAA2010E001, Department of Informatics of the Universidad Carlos III de Madrid, Madrid, Spain (2010)
26. Mendiburu, A., Santana, R., Lozano, J.A.: Introducing belief propagation in estimation of distribution algorithms: A parallel framework. Technical Report EHU-KAT-IK-11/07, Department of Computer Science and Artificial Intelligence, University of the Basque Country (October 2007)
27. Miquélez, T., Bengoetxea, E., Larrañaga, P.: Evolutionary computation based on Bayesian classifiers. International Journal of Applied Mathematics and Computer Science 14(3), 101–115 (2004)
28. Mühlenbein, H., Mahnig, T.: Evolutionary algorithms: from recombination to search distributions. In: Theoretical Aspects of Evolutionary Computing, pp. 137–176. Springer, Berlin (2000)
29. Munetomo, M., Murao, N., Akama, K.: Introducing assignment functions to Bayesian optimization algorithms. Information Sciences 178(1), 152–163 (2008)
30. Oriols-Puis, Bernardó-Manilla, E., Pastry, K., Goldberg, D.E.: Substructures surrogates for learning decomposable classification problems: Implementation and first results, London, UK, pp. 2875–2882. ACE Press (2007)
31. Pelikan, M., Sastry, K., Goldberg, D.E.: Multiobjective estimation of distribution algorithms. In: Pelikan, M., Sastry, K., Cantú-Paz, E. (eds.) Scalable Optimization via Probabilistic Modeling: From Algorithms to Applications. SCI, pp. 223–248. Springer, Heidelberg (2006)

32. Pereira, F.B., Machado, P., Costa, E., Cardoso, A., Ochoa, A., Santana, R., Soto, M.R.: Too busy to learn. In: Proceedings of the 2000 Congress on Evolutionary Computation, CEC 2000, La Jolla Marriott Hotel La Jolla, California, USA, pp. 720–727. IEEE Press (July 2000)

33. Regnier-Coudert, O.: Bayesian network structure learning using characteristic properties of permutation representations with applications to prostate cancer treatment. PhD thesis, Robert Gordon University (2013)

34. Rivera, J.P., Santana, R.: Design of an algorithm based on the estimation of distributions to generate new rules in the XCS classifier system. Technical Report ICIMAF 2000-100, CEMAFIT 2000-78, Institute of Cybernetics, Mathematics and Physics, Havana, Cuba (June 2000)

35. Santana, R.: An analysis of the performance of the mixture of trees factorized distribution algorithm when priors and adaptive learning are used. Technical Report ICIMAF 2002-180, Institute of Cybernetics, Mathematics and Physics, Havana, Cuba (March 2002)

36. Santana, R.: Factorized distribution algorithms: Selection without selected population. In: Proceedings of the 17th European Simulation Multiconference, ESM-2003, Nottingham, England, pp. 91–97 (2003)

37. Santana, R., Armañanzas, R., Bielza, C., Larrañaga, P.: Network measures for information extraction in evolutionary algorithms. International Journal of Computational Intelligence Systems 6(6), 1163–1188 (2013)

38. Santana, R., Bielza, C., Larrañaga, P., Lozano, J.A., Echegoyen, C., Mendiburu, A., Armañanzas, R., Shakya, S.: Mateda-2.0: A MATLAB package for the implementation and analysis of estimation of distribution algorithms. Journal of Statistical Software 35(7), 1–30 (2010)

39. Santana, R., Karshenas, H., Bielza, C., Larrañaga, P.: Quantitative genetics in multi-objective optimization algorithms: From useful insights to effective methods. In: Proceedings of the 2011 Genetic and Evolutionary Computation Conference, GECCO 2011, Dublin, Ireland, pp. 91–92 (2011)

40. Santana, R., Shakya, S.: Probabilistic graphical models and Markov networks. In: Shakya, S., Santana, R. (eds.) Markov Networks in Evolutionary Computation, pp. 3–19. Springer (2012)

41. Sastry, K., Pelikan, M., Goldberg, D.: Efficiency enhancement of genetic algorithms via building-block-wise fitness estimation. In: Proceedings of the 2004 Congress on Evolutionary Computation, CEC 2004, Portland, Oregon, pp. 720–727. IEEE Press (2004)

42. Shakya, S., McCall, J., Brown, D.: Using a Markov network model in a univariate EDA: An empirical cost-benefit analysis. In: Beyer, H.-G., O'Reilly, U.-M. (eds.) Proceedings of Genetic and Evolutionary Computation Conference, GECCO 2005, Washington, D.C, USA, pp. 727–734. ACM Press (2005)

43. Shakya, S., Santana, R. (eds.): Markov Networks in Evolutionary Computation. Springer (2012)

44. Shi, L., Rasheed, K.: A survey of fitness approximation methods applied in evolutionary algorithm. In: Tenne, Y., Goh, C.-K. (eds.) Computational Intelligence in Expensive Optimization Problems, pp. 3–28. Springer (2010)

45. Ulrich, T., Brockhoff, D., Zitzler, E.: Pattern identification in Pareto-set approximations. In: Proceedings of the Genetic and Evolutionary Computation Conference, GECCO 2008, pp. 737–745. ACM, New York (2008)

46. Valdez-Peña, I.S., Hernández-Aguirre, A., Botello-Rionda, S.: Approximating the search distribution to the selection distribution in EDAs. In: Proceedings of the Genetic and Evolutionary Computation Conference, GECCO 2009, pp. 461–468. ACM, New York (2009)

47. Zhang, Q., Li, H.: MOEA/D: A multiobjective evolutionary algorithm based on decomposition. IEEE Transactions on Evolutionary Computation 11(6), 712–731 (2007)

48. Zhou, A., Zhang, Q., Jin, Y.: Approximating the set of Pareto-optimal solutions in both the decision and objective spaces by an estimation of distribution algorithm. IEEE Transactions on Evolutionary Computation 13(5), 1167–1189 (2009)

49. Zuluaga, M., Sergent, G., Krause, A., Püschel, M.: Active learning for multiobjective optimization. In: Proceedings of the 30th International Conference on Machine Learning (ICML 2013), pp. 462–470 (2013)

Sandholm Algorithm with K-means Clustering Approach for Multi-robot Task Allocation

Murugappan Elango[1], Ganesan Kanagaraj[1], and S.G. Ponnambalam[2]

[1] Thiagarajar College of Engineering, Maduai, Tamil Nadu, India
[2] School of Engineering, Monash University Malaysia, Bandar Sunway, Malaysia
{memech,gkmech}@tce.edu, sgponnambalam@monash.edu

Abstract. Multi-robot systems are becoming more and more significant in industrial, commercial and scientific applications. The current attempts made by the researchers concentrate only on minimizing the distance between the robots and the targets, and not much importance is given to the balancing of workloads among robots. Auction based mechanism are popularly used to allocate tasks to multiple robots. This paper attempts to develop mechanisms to address the above two issues with objective of minimizing the distance travel by 'm' robots and balancing the work load of 'N' targets between 'm' robots equally. The proposed approach has three stages, stage I bundles the 'N' targets into 'n' clusters of targets using commonly adopted K-means clustering technique with the objective of minimizing the distance between the 'n' targets and its cluster centroids, this gives the legal bundles and also reduces the search space. Stage II calculates the biding distance based of the shortest path from the current robot position to bundle or bundle combinations. In stage III bundles are allocated to the each robot using Sandholm algorithm. The performance of the proposed method is tested with small and large size bench mark problem instances.

1 Introduction

Robot teams are increasingly becoming a popular alternative to single robots for a variety of difficult robotic tasks, such as planetary exploration or flexible automation. Robot teams offer many advantages over single robots: robustness (due to redundancy), efficiency (due to parallelism), and flexibility (due to reconfigurability). However, an important factor for the success of a robot team is the ability to coordinate the team members in an effective way. Coordination involves the allocation and execution of individual tasks through an efficient (preferably decentralized) mechanism for sharing the workload in a cost effective manner. Current scenario does not concentrate on sharing the load. Chandran et al [1] pointed out that in multiple traveling salesman problems the less addressed criterion is the balancing of workloads amongst salespersons. Bektas [2] points out that multiple traveling salesman problems is a generalization of the well known traveling salesman problem and although there exists a wide body of the literature for the TSP and the

B.K. Panigrahi et al. (Eds.): SEMCCO 2013, Part II, LNCS 8298, pp. 14–22, 2013.

VRP, the MTSP has not received the same amount of attention. Simmons et al [3] reckons that individual robots construct "bids," which describe their estimates of the expected information gain and costs of traveling to various locations. Diaz and Stenz [4] points out that multi robot coordination, if made efficient and robust, promises high impact on automation. Vries and Vohra [5] conclude that because of substitution effects between the different assets, bidders have preferences not just for particular items but for sets of items. For this reason, economic efficiency is enhanced if bidders are allowed to bid on bundles or combinations of different assets. Elmaghraby and Keskinocak [6] accept that combinatorial auctions are a powerful tool for auctioning off multiple non-identical units with complementarities or synergies and they allow a bidder to submit a bid for a group of items, or package bids, and the bidder wins either all, or none of the items in a package. Mataric et al [7] believes that multiple cooperating robots hold the promise of improved performance and increased fault tolerance for large-scale problems such as planetary survey and habitat construction and also states that multi-robot coordination is a complex problem

Most of the researchers concentrate only on minimizing the distance between the robots and the targets, and some of the researches focus on balancing the work load among the robots but very few papers was addressed taking the distance minimization and work load balancing as an objective. When there is more than one robot it resembles a Multiple Traveling Salesman Problem wherein all the robots would be used to visit all the targets by making proper utilization of the resources (available robots).Thus the aim of this paper is to bring out a mechanism which works on both the objective. As the number of robots and targets increase the solution field also gets increased thus it becomes an NP (Non deterministic time polynomial) Hard Problem. Since Multi-Robot task allocation like mTSP is NP hard number of solution methods for minimizing the distance objective were reported in literature are for mTSP -Branch and bound algorithm, Crossbar hopefield neural network, Genetic algorithm, For $mTSP$MD - Integer linear programming, $mTSP$TW- Decomposition heuristic, Genetic algorithm, Graph theory – precedence graphs. Also with only the work load balancing objective the solution methods reported in the literature is Heuristic approach, clustering approach, From the above the cluster based solution for mTSP is addressed in Chandran et al. [1] most recently only for balancing of work load objective. Thus there exists a wide gap in finding the solution under clustering based approach for Multi-Robot task allocation with two objectives under consideration. Few heuristics proposed for mTSP routing and scheduling problems are heuristic approach, branch and bound algorithm, constraint relaxation approach, Tabu search, decomposition heuristic, genetic algorithm based approach, and Graph theory based methodology.

From literature survey it was found that during the allocation of robots to targets distance between the targets and the robots were given paramount importance. Not much attention was given to the sharing of work load between the robots which led to improper utilization of the resources and created an imbalance in the workload shared.

This paper attempts to develop mechanisms to address the above two issues with objective of minimize the travel distance and to balance the distance traveled by each robot for the better utilization of 'm' robots with 'N' targets. The proposed approach has three stages, stage I bundles the 'N' targets into 'n' clusters of targets using commonly adopted K-means clustering technique with the objective of minimizing the distance between the 'n' targets and its cluster centroids, this gives the legal bundles and also reduces the search space. Stage II calculates the biding distance based of the shortest path from the current robot position to bundle or bundle combinations. In stage III bundles are allocated to the each robot using Sandholm algorithm [8-9].

2   Problem Description

Multi-robot routing is a class problem where a team of mobile robots must visit a set of locations for some purpose (e.g., delivery or acquisition) with routes that optimize certain criteria (e.g., minimization of consumed energy, completion time, or average latency). Such routing problems, including Vehicle Routing Problems (VRP) and several variants of the Multiple Traveling Salesman Problem (mTSP), have been studied from a centralized point of view in operations research, and recently in robotics with a focus on decentralized approaches. The cost per unit distance of idleness is assumed to be unit cost. The different possible combinations for a given number of robots and targets is given by the formula m^N. Where 'm' is the total number of robots and N is the total number of targets. If the search is made for all combination it become a time consuming process, and NP hard so in the present work the targets are bundled into 'k' no clusters the robots are allow to bid on the bundle and bundle combination and the optimal allocation of bundle is determined by sandholm algorithm.

Initially k is equal to m, the clustering is done based on minimizing the sum of targets-to-cluster centroids distance (SD_k), summed over all 'k' clusters, Then, for each robot the biding cost on each bundle is calculated based on the shortest path possible using standard TSP procedure. Finally the robot are allocated to the bundle based on the generalized vickery auction to achieve balanced allocation between robots .

Indices h = centroid index, i = target index, k = bundle index, ki= bundle cluster target index, a,b= cluster distance matrix index

Sets $s^i = \{x_i, y_i\}_{i=1}^{N}$,

$ss_k = \{x_{ki}, y_{ki}\}_{ki=1}^{kn}$,

$\{d_{a,b}\}_k$ = distance matrix corresponds to data set SS_k,

se = subset of $\{d_{a,b}\}_k$,

Variables SD_k is the sum of distance for k th cluster from its robot to its cluster points, N = Total number of target, kn = Total Number of target in k th cluster, Y_i = decision variable 0-1 continuous variable that allot the target, PL_k is the minimum Path length connecting the city in the data set SS_k, , $x_{a,b}$ = decision variable, $x_{a,b}$ =1 if the $d_{a,b}$ is used in solution , otherwise $x_{a,b}$ =0,

2.1   Allocation of Target to Bundle 'k" with Minimum SD_k

For the given target coordinates as cluster centroid C^1; C^2..... ,C^k minimizing the sum of the distance between each point S^i and to its nearest cluster centroid C^h using

$$\min_{c^1\ldots c^k} SD_k = \sum_{i=1}^{N} \min_{h=1,\ldots,k} |s^i - c^h| \tag{1}$$

$$SS_k = s^i \times Y_i \tag{2}$$

2.2   Finding the Biding Distance for All Robot and Bundle Combination

$$\min \quad PL_k = \sum_{a=1}^{kn} \sum_{b>1}^{kn} d_{a,b}\, x_{a,b} \tag{3}$$

Subject to (i). symmetric TSP constraint

$$\sum_{b<a}^{kn} x_{b,a} + \sum_{b.>a}^{kn} x_{a,b} = 2 \quad \text{for all a.} \tag{4}$$

(ii) sub tour elimination constraint

$$\sum_{a\in se} \sum_{b\notin se,b>a}^{kn} x_{a,b} + \sum_{a\notin se} \sum_{b\in se,b>a}^{kn} x_{a,b} \geq 2 \tag{5}$$

For all proper point subsets se in ss_k, [se]>=3 for all a; b>a

2.3   Allocation of Robot to the Bundle of Targets in a Balanced Manner Using the Following Steps

Step 1: Generate Biding table based on all robot-bundle combination
Step 2: Construct the Sandholm allocation tree [8-9] based on the minimum bid distance. The higher bid distance is not considered for allocation tree since the objective is to minimization
Step 3: Identify the optimal path in the tree which gives minimum total distance. Then allocate the bundle in the optimal path to the respective robot.

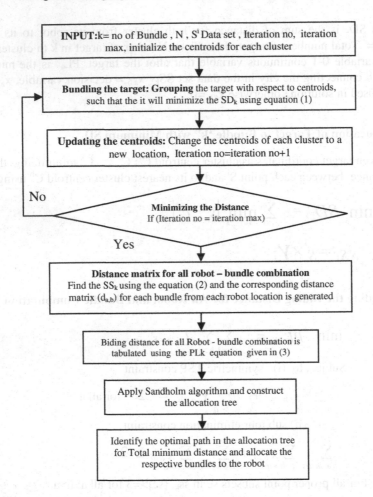

Fig. 1. The proposed Sandholm algorithm with K-means Clustering procedure for Multi-Robot Task Allocation

3   Numerical Illustrations

For the purpose of illustrating Sandhom algorithm with K-means clustering, we consider the following Data set. The program is coded in Matlab Version 7.0 and run on PC Pentium-D 2.80 GHz processor

Table 1. Data-set for S^i

Robot R1	Robot R2	Target	T_A	T_B	T_C
20	80	x	10	22	66
20	20	y	10	44	55

The target is bundled into B1 and B2 using K-mean clustering method. The bundle B1 has T_C target alone and the bundle B2 has T_A and T_B targets. Now the Distance matrix for all robot and bundle combination is generated ie the R1 B1, R1 B2, R2 B1, R2 B2. These entire symmetric distance matrix is solved for shortest path length PLk using equation (3). This path length calculated is tabulated as the biding   cost of the robot to the corresponding bundle

Table 2. Bids placed by robots

Bidder	Bundle bids	
	B1	B2
Robot R1	115.6	74.3
Robot R2	75.4	169.54

The bid place by the robot on the R1 B1B2 and R2 B1B2 combination is not considered since our objective is to allocate the target to each robot in a balanced manner ie each robot must be utilized properly. Since for the same bundle there exit two bids we select the lowest bid alone. Now the Sandholm algorithm is used to generate the allocation tree as given below.

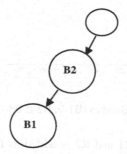

Fig. 2. Allocation tree for Table 2

From the above tree, we find the minimum distance traveled by each robot will occur if the following bids are selected (R1, B2, 74.3) (R2, B1, 75.4) the optimal allocation vector is X* = (0110), the total distance traveled by the R1 and R2 robot is 74.3+75.4 = 149.7. To find the contribution of each robot on the solution first remove the R1 from bidding scenario and now obtain the optimal allocation of the bids X*=(0011), The total distance traveled by the R2 is 244.94. The marginal contribution of R1 to the problem is – (149.7-244.94) = 95.24. Similarly remove R2 from the biding scenario then the optimal allocation vector is X*= (1100). The total distance traveled by the R1 is 189.9. The marginal contribution of R2 on the solution is – (149.7-189.9) = -40.2.

4   Results and Discussions

To evaluate the proposed procedure data set given in Chandran et al [3] is taken and
the corresponding bundle bids placed by two robots are given in Table.3.

Table 3. Bids placed by robots

Bidder	Bundle bids					
	B1	B2	B3	B1&B2	B2&B3	B1&B3
Robot R1	245.8	213.4	171.1	337.9	290.9	265.5
Robot R2	239.7	139.4	245.4	274	266	324.1

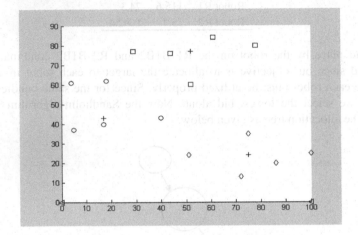

Fig. 3. Bundling of targets into 3 Bundles (B1-◊, B2-□ B3-○) Robot < I Centroides +

The present robot position and R1 and R2 is added as first node to the each bundle
combination and the distance matrix is generated and the shortest path length PL_k is
computed using equation (3) and the bidding cost for all combination is tabulated in the
Table 3.

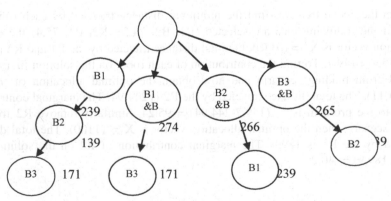

Fig. 4. Allocation Tree for the Table 3

The allocation tree shows that minimum travel distance is achieved when the following bids are selected (R1, B3&B1, 265.5) and (R2, B2, 139.4). The optimal allocation vector is X*=(000001010000). The total distance traveled by R1 and R2 is 404.9. If the R1 is removed from the biding scene then the optimal allocation vector is X*=(000000010001). Yielding a minimum total distance traveled by for R2 is 463.5. Therefore the marginal contribution of R1 to the solution is -(404.9 - 463.5)= 58.5. If R2 is removed from the biding scene the optimal allocation vector is X*=(010001000000) which yield a minimum total distance traveled by the R1 as 478.9. The marginal contribution of R2 to the solution is –(404.9 -478.9)= 73.9. The proposed method is further validated for its performance with a bench mark vrp data set Eil22.Vrp and compared with the results with angular method and saving matrix method and Z saving method quoted in [10-11]. The comparison results along with the optimal value obtained from linear programming method are presented in Table 4.

Table 4. Result Comparison with other methods

Bidder	Proposed method	Angular method	Saving matrix method	z-savings	Optimal
R1	159.52	158.706	288.99	136.28	**265.58**
R2	139.26	156.749	295.58	171.305	**22.31**
Total	**298.78**	**315.455**	**584.57**	**307.59**	**287.89**

Osman et al (2007) modeled the same problem as vehicle routing problem and uses the Z-saving method to obtain the solution. From Table 4, it is clear that the Sandholm Algorithm with K-means Clustering Approach for Multi-Robot Task Allocation provides the best solution among three existing methods and also the solution is very near to the optimal solution.

5   Conclusions

The proposed Sandholm algorithm with K-means Clustering approach for Multi-Robot Task Allocation mechanism is designed to meet both the minimizing the distance traveled by each robot and to share the distance between the robots such that the robot is utilized in a better way. This was achieved by bundling the targets into B1, B2, …etc., .the biding is placed in a balance manner with the all robot - bundle combination. The Sandholm Algorithm used for bundle allocation and the K-means Clustering for producing the legal bundle together can be used effectively for solving small and large size multi-robot task allocation problems.

In the present work all bundles will not be allotted to a single robot. This work is general outline of implementing the Sandholm algorithm and clustering method for mutirobot task allocation problem, the detail study will improve the solution quality in a better way.

References

1. Chandran, N., Narendran, T.T., Ganesh, K.: A clustering approach to solve the multiple travelling salesmen problem. International Journal of Industrial and Systems Engineering 1(3), 372–387 (2006)
2. Bektas, T.: The multiple traveling salesman problem: an overview of formulations and solution procedures. Omega 34(3), 209–219 (2006)
3. Simmons, R., Apfelbaum, D., Burgard, W., Fox, D., Moors, M., Thrun, S., Younes, H.: Coordination for multi-robot exploration and mapping. In: AAAI/IAAI, pp. 852–858 (2000)
4. Dias, H.B., Stentz, A.: Opportunistic optimization for market-based multirobot control. In: IEEE/RSJ International Conference on Intelligent Robots and Systems, vol. 3, pp. 2714–2720. IEEE (2002)
5. De Vries, S., Vohra, R.V.: Combinatorial auctions: A survey. INFORMS Journal on Computing 15(3), 284–309 (2003)
6. Elmaghraby, W., Keskinocak, P.: Combinatorial auctions in procurement. In: The Practice of Supply Chain Management: Where Theory and Application Converge, pp. 245–258. Springer, US (2004)
7. Matarić, M.J., Sukhatme, G.S., Østergaard, E.H.: Multi-robot task allocation in uncertain environments. Autonomous Robots 14(2-3), 255–263 (2003)
8. Sandholm, T., Suri, S., Gilpin, A., Levine, D.: CABOB: A fast optimal algorithm for combinatorial auctions. In: International Joint Conference on Artificial Intelligence, vol. 17(1), pp. 1102–1108. Lawrence Erlbaum Associates Ltd. (2001)
9. Sandholm, T.: Algorithm for optimal winner determination in combinatorial auctions. Artificial intelligence 135(1), 1–54 (2002)
10. Elango, M., Nachiappan, S.P., Prabakaran, S.: "Hybrid Methodologies for Balanced Multi-Robot Task Allocation and Path Minimization. Indian Journal of Industrial and Applied Mathematics 3(1), 1–18 (2011)
11. Parlaktuna, O., Sipahioflu, A., Yazici, A.: A VRP-Based Route Planning for a Mobile Robot. Group Turk J. Elec. Engin. 15(2), 187–197 (2007)

Genetic Programming for Modeling Vibratory Finishing Process: Role of Experimental Designs and Fitness Functions

Akhil Garg and Kang Tai

School of Mechanical and Aerospace Engineering, Nanyang Technological University,
50 Nanyang Avenue, Singapore 639798, Singapore
{akhil1,mktai}@ntu.edu.sg

Abstract. Manufacturers seek to improve efficiency of vibratory finishing process while meeting increasingly stringent cost and product requirements. To serve this purpose, mathematical models have been formulated using soft computing methods such as artificial neural network and genetic programming (GP). Among these methods, GP evolves model structure and its coefficients automatically. There is extensive literature on ways to improve the performance of GP but less attention has been paid to the selection of appropriate experimental designs and fitness functions. The evolution of fitter models depends on the experimental design used to sample the problem (system) domain, as well as on the appropriate fitness function used for improving the evolutionary search. This paper presents quantitative analysis of two experimental designs and four fitness functions used in GP for the modeling of vibratory finishing process. The results conclude that fitness function SRM and PRESS evolves GP models of higher generalization ability, which may then be deployed by experts for optimization of the finishing process.

Keywords: vibratory finishing; fitness function, vibratory modeling, GPTIPS, experimental designs, finishing modeling.

1 Introduction

Despite availability of empirical and industrial information on vibratory finishing process, its fundamentals are still mostly developed through trial-and-error approach [1]. Very few models exist that explain the mechanism of vibratory finishing process [2-5]. Hashimoto [6] formulated empirical relationship between the output process parameters (surface roughness, stock removal rate and optimum polishing time) and input parameters (time and initial surface roughness) based on the fundamentals on vibratory process. Sofronas and Taraman [7] used response surface methodology (RSM) to formulate the polynomial model that explicitly describe relationship between five input parameters (Brinell hardness, projection width, processing time, media size and frequency of bowl) and three output parameters (surface roughness reduction, projection height reduction, edge radiusing). In another application of RSM, relationship between four input parameters (burnishing speed, feed, ball force, frequency and amplitude of vibration) and two output parameters (surface roughness

B.K. Panigrahi et al. (Eds.): SEMCCO 2013, Part II, LNCS 8298, pp. 23–31, 2013.

and micro hardness) was established [8]. Recently, Garg and Tai [9] proposed hybrid genetic programming-neural network method (GP-ANN) to model the vibratory finishing process, and found that hybrid method outperforms the standardized GP method. From the literature, it is obvious that focus of researchers have shifted towards the practice of advanced soft computing methods such as GP, ANN, fuzzy logic (FL), etc., since these methods are void of statistical assumptions and possesses the ability to capture the dynamics of the process.

Among these methods, GP has the ability to automate and evolve the model structure and its coefficients [10-18, 34]. The mathematical model developed using GP relates the input process parameters to the output process parameters. In context of symbolic regression problems, extensive literature has been published, that point improvement in performance of functioning of GP, but less focus has been paid to choice of experimental design and fitness function.

In GP, the mathematical models are built from the symbolic regression of the data points obtained from the systems/processes. This implies that the nature of data set obtained i.e. sampling of data points plays a key role in efficient learning/training of GP model. Data points obtained from the system comprise of input process parameters and output process parameters. The output process parameter values could change drastically with change in input parameter values. In other words, dynamics of the system is stored in the values of input and output process parameters. Therefore, sampling of data points should be done carefully so that the model formed from it is able to respond to the system dynamics. The data collection process is itself computationally expensive, and therefore the sampling of data points should focus towards collecting as minimum number of samples that represents system characteristics. Methods used to sample data points are known as Design of Experiment (DOE) methods [13]. DOE methods such as full factorial (FF), latin hypercube sampling (LHS) and response surface (RS) design sample data points from the system by adopting different mechanism. The choice of appropriate design method is essential in efficient training of GP models [13, 19].

In addition to experimental design methods, fitness function is highly responsible for the evolution of generalised models. This is because in GP, solutions are searched globally throughout the model space with direction of search guided by fitness function. Model selection criteria such as Akaike's information criteria (AIC), predicted residual error sum of squares (PRESS), Bayesian information criteria (BIC), final prediction error (FPE) and structural risk minimization (SRM) [21-27], that takes into account the number of data samples (sample size) and size of the model can be deployed as fitness function in GP for efficiently guiding the evolutionary search towards an optimum solution. However, the choice of an appropriate fitness function is unclear, which means an improper deployment of fitness function could results in over-fitting of the GP model on testing samples. Given the set of fitness functions, it is therefore important to understand, how each of them have impact on the performance of the GP model.

In the present work, a quantitative analysis is conducted for studying the effect of fitness functions across two experimental designs, on the performance of GP in modeling of vibratory finishing process. Surface finish reduction model is obtained from the study conducted by Sofronas and Taraman [7]. Two set of twenty-seven data points are generated from the model [7] using two experimental designs such as FF and LHS respectively. Each data set is fed into GP for training of models. Five fitness functions used are PRESS, SRM, AIC, FPE and BIC. The performance of GP is evaluated for each fitness function across two experimental designs. The objective of the paper is to find out the best fitness function and experimental design that evolves GP models of higher generalization ability.

The remainder of the paper is organized as follows. In Section 2, problem of vibratory finishing process is discussed. Section 3 provides brief introduction on GP. Section 4 provides results and discussion. Finally, Section 5 concludes with recommendations for future work.

2   Experimental Database of Vibratory Finishing Process

Vibratory finishing process is widely used because of its versatility, consistency and efficiency. This process gained its popularity in 1960 in the metal working sector. In present work, the RSM model developed by Sofronas and Taraman [7] for prediction of surface finish reduction of vibratory machine processed work piece is used. The model initially contains five input process parameters but it was further reduced to three using statistical method of analysis of variance. Three process input parameters considered are processing time (x_1), media size (x_2) and vibratory frequencies (x_3), and the output parameter considered is surface finish reduction (y).

Two data sets, each of twenty-seven points are generated by using two experimental designs methods such as FF and LHS respectively. In FF design, the sample size of data points generated is of order n^m, where m is number of decision variables and n is the number of levels (low, medium, high, etc). In this study, value of m and n is three and default settings in MATLAB are used for implementing FF method. LHS is a hypercube design consisting of a matrix of j rows (number of level of decision variables) and l columns (number of decision variables). The columns are the random permutations of combinations of decision variables. More details about these two experimental designs methods can be found in [20, 28-29]. Nature of the data sets generated using two experimental design methods is shown in Table 1 and Table 2.

Table 1. Descriptive statistics of the data set generated using FF experimental design

Parameter	x_1	x_2	x_3	y
Mean	70	0.875	1743.3	22.88
Standard error	7.33	0.04	40.07	1.77
Median	60	0.875	1730	21.57
Standard deviation	38.12	0.20	208.23	9.23
Kurtosis	-1.56	-1.56	-1.50	-0.33
Skewness	0.404	0	0.103	0.66
Minimum	30	0.625	1500	9.94
Maximum	120	1.125	2000	44.20

Table 2. Descriptive statistics of the data set generated using LHS experimental design

Parameter	x_1	x_2	x_3	y
Mean	77.56	0.88	1759.10	22.91
Standard error	5.38	0.030	29.50	1.56
Median	77.80	0.88	1759.3	22.11
Standard deviation	27.99	0.15	153.29	8.124
Kurtosis	-1.227	-1.173	-1.190	-0.431
Skewness	-2.14E-5	-0.012	-0.017	0.370
Minimum	32.69	0.62	1509.71	9.946
Maximum	122.6	1.145	2009.7	40.57

Each of the data set generated using experimental design method is further fed into GP algorithm. Five fitness functions: PRESS, SRM, AIC, FPE and BIC are used. The mathematical formula of each fitness function is shown in Table 3, where b is the number of nodes of GP tree (size of model), SSE is the sum of square of error of GP model on the training data and N is the number of training samples.

Table 3. Fitness function and mathematical formulae

Fitness function	Mathematical formulae
PRESS	$SSE/N \; (1+2b/N)$
SRM	$SSE/N \; (1- ((b/N -(b/N \log (b/N)) + (\log (b/N)/2N))^{1/2})^{-1}$
AIC	$N \log(SSE/N)+ b$
FPE	$SSE/N \; (N+b/N-b)$
BIC	$SSE/N + \log (N) (b/N)(SSE/N-b)$

3   Genetic Programming

Widely used soft computing method, genetic programming, is based on Darwinian theory of "Survival of the fittest". GP algorithm has been extensively applied in solving symbolic regression problems of various processes. GP algorithm works on the principle of GA but there exists difference between them [30]. GP evolves models represented by tree structures of varying sizes, while GA gives solutions in crisp values of binary or real form. GP algorithm starts with initialization of population. The population represents the number of models. The model is formed by randomly combining the elements from the functional and terminal set.

The elements of the function set can be chosen from basic mathematical operators (+, - , ×, /) and also Boolean algebraic operators (eg. AND and OR) or any other user defined expressions. The elements of the terminal set comprises of input process parameters and constants. The performance of the models is evaluated using fitness function as specified by the user. Based on performance, models from the initial population are selected for genetic operation such as crossover, reproduction and mutation. The performance of new population formed is again evaluated. This phenomenon of generating new population/generation continues till the termination criterion is satisfied. The termination criterion is specified by the user. It is the threshold error of the model or maximum number of generations, whichever is achieved earlier.

The present work uses popular variant of GP, namely, multi-gene genetic programming (MGGP), developed by Hinchliffe et al., [31] and Hiden [32]. The main difference between the traditional GP and multigene GP is that in multigene GP, number of trees makes a model. All of the genes are combined by weights (different for each gene) and a constant term added to it gives the final formulae (mathematical model). MGGP is implemented using the software GPTIPS [33].

GPTIPS is implemented using the parameter settings as shown in Table 4 for each fitness function across two experimental designs. Trial-and-error method is used to select the parameter settings (see Table 2). The function set consists of broader set of elements so as to evolve variety of non-linear forms of mathematical models. The values of population size and number of generations fairly depend on the complexity of the data. Based on literature review by Garg and Tai (2012), the population size and number of generations should be fairly large for data of higher complexity, so as to find the models with minimum error. Maximum number of genes and maximum depth of the gene influences the size and the number of models to be searched in the global space. The maximum number of genes and maximum depth of gene is chosen at 4 and 4 respectively. For each data set, first thirteen data samples are used for training, while remaining for testing the generalization ability of the model. The best model is selected based on minimum error on training data.

In this way, we have 5 best models for each data set, corresponding to five fitness functions. The performance of the models is discussed and compared in Section 4.

Table 4. Parameter settings for GP

Parameters	Values assigned
Training data	13
Testing data	14
Runs	35
Population size	300
Generations	100
Tournament size	2
Termination criteria	0.25
Max depth of tree	4
Max genes	4
Functional set	(multiply, plus, minus, square, sin, divide, cos, power)
Terminal set	$(x_1, x_2, x_3, [-10\ 10])$

4   Results and Discussion

The performance of the best GP models formed from five fitness functions for two data sets is compared. The performance is evaluated using root mean square error (RMSE). Table 5 and Table 6 shows the RMSE on the testing data and size of the best GP model evolved, when the five fitness functions are used in GP for two designs data set.

Comparison of performance of fitness functions on GP for FF designed data set

From Table 5, it is obvious that SRM fitness function when used in GP, gives better generalization ability of GP model when compared to other fitness functions. SRM fitness function not only gives better generalisation ability but also evolved model of lower complexity. Among fitness functions, PRESS, AIC, FPE and BIC, PRESS fitness function gives better generalisation ability of the GP model. Among, AIC, FPE and BIC, all three have shown comparable performance of GP model. Fitness function, namely, AIC, FPE and BIC shows signs of over-fitting of GP model, since model has high values of RMSE on testing data.

Table 5. RMSE on testing data and size of the best GP model evolved when GP is applied on FF designed data set

Fitness function	PRESS	SRM	AIC	FPE	BIC
RMSE	4.62	1.30	31.94	33.92	35.30
Size (b)	20	19	11	10	10

Comparison of performance of fitness functions on GP for LHS designed data set

From Table 6, it is obvious that PRESS and SRM fitness function when used in GP, gives better generalization ability of model when compared to other fitness functions. Though, SRM and PRESS fitness function gives models of similar generalisation ability but SRM based GP model has lower complexity. Among, AIC, FPE and BIC, all three have shown comparable performance of GP model. The GP model evolved using fitness function, AIC, FPE and BIC shows signs of over-fitting, since it has high values of RMSE on testing data.

From Table 5 and 6, LHS designed data set gives lower values of RMSE of GP model on testing data for five fitness functions. This indicates that LHS designed data set is able to evolve the GP model that captures dynamics of the process quite well.

Table 6. RMSE on testing data and size of the best GP model evolved when GP is applied on LHS designed data set

Fitness function	PRESS	SRM	AIC	FPE	BIC
RMSE	0.11	0.20	21.85	21.34	23.99
Size (b)	65	16	12	11	11

5   Conclusion and Future Work

An application of GP in modeling of vibratory finishing process is introduced to study the effect of the fitness functions on the performance of GP for two designed data sets. The results conclude that for both the generated data sets, the fitness functions, namely, SRM and PRESS have shown better performance of GP models than those of the other fitness functions such as AIC, BIC and FPE. Between PRESS and SRM, both have shown comparable performance. In terms of complexity of the models, SRM fitness function evolved GP model of lower complexity when compared to PRESS. Thus, the model formed from the fitness function SRM, can be deployed in practice due to its higher generalization ability. Between FF and LHS designs, LHS designed data set results in better performance of GP models on all five fitness functions. Thus, we can conclude that LHS designed data set is able to train GP effectively to evolve model, which captures the dynamics of the process satisfactorily.

For highly dynamic and chaotic systems such as those of stock market data, the performance of GP models need to be studied across different fitness functions. Future work will include studying the effects of various fitness functions on the performance of GP in modeling of stock market data.

References

1. Domblesky, J., Evans, R., Cariapa, V.: Material removal model for vibratory finishing. International Journal of Production Research 42, 1029–1041 (2004)
2. Gillespie, L.: A quantitative approach to vibratory deburring effectiveness, Society of Manufacturing Engineers, Technical paper MR 75-11 (1975)
3. Brust, P.C.: Surface improvement by vibratory cascade finishing process. Society of Manufacturing Engineers, Dearborn (1997)
4. Davidson, D.A.: Mechanical Surface Preparation - Mass Finishing Processes. Metal Finishing 1, 75 (2006)
5. Wang, S., Timsit, R.S., Spelt, J.K.: Experimental investigation of vibratory finishing of aluminum. Wear 243, 147–156 (2000)
6. Hashimoto, F.: Modelling and optimization of vibratory finishing process. CIRP Annals Manufacturing Technology 45, 303–306 (1996)
7. Sofronas, A., Taraman, S.: Model Development and Optimization Of Vibratory Finishing Process. Int. J. Prod. Res. 17, 23–31 (1979)

8. Pande, S.S., Patel, S.M.: Investigations on vibratory burnishing process. International Journal of Machine Tool Design and Research 24, 195–206 (1984)
9. Garg, A., Tai, K.: A Hybrid Genetic Programming-Artificial Neural Network Approach for Modeling of Vibratory Finishing Process. In: International Proceedings of Computer Science and Information Technology, ICIIC 2011-International Conference on Information and Intelligent Computing, Hong Kong, November 25-26, vol. 18, pp. 14–19 (2011)
10. Garg, A., Tai, K.: Comparison of regression analysis, Artificial Neural Network and genetic programming in Handling the multicollinearity problem. In: Proceedings of 2012 International Conference on Modelling, Identification and Control (ICMIC 2012), Wuhan, China, June 24-26, pp. 353–358. IEEE (2012)
11. Garg, A., Tai, K.: Review of genetic programming in modeling of machining processes. In: Proceedings of 2012 International Conference on Modelling, Identification and Control (ICMIC 2012), Wuhan, China, June 24-26, pp. 653–658. IEEE (2012)
12. Garg, A., Tai, K.: Comparison of statistical and machine learning methods in modelling of data with multicollinearity. Int. J. Modelling, Identification and Control 18(4), 295–312 (2013)
13. Garg, A., Tai, K.: Selection of a Robust Experimental Design for the Effective Modeling of the Nonlinear Systems using Genetic Programming. In: Proceedings of 2013 IEEE Symposium Series on Computational Intelligence and Data mining (CIDM), Singapore, April 16-19, pp. 293–298 (2013)
14. Garg, A., Bhalerao, Y., Tai, K.: Review of Empirical Modeling Techniques for Modeling of Turning Process. International Journal of Modelling, Identification and Control 20(2), 121–129 (2013)
15. Garg, A., Rachmawati, L., Tai, K.: Classification-Driven Model Selection Approach of Genetic Programming in Modelling of Turning Process. International Journal of Advanced Manufacturing Technology (in press, 2013), doi:10.1007/s00170-013-5103-x
16. Garg, A., Savalani, M.M., Tai, K.: State-of-the-Art in Empirical Modelling of Rapid Prototyping Processes. Rapid Prototyping Journal (in press, 2013)
17. Garg, A., Sriram, S., Tai, K.: Empirical Analysis of Model Selection Criteria for Genetic Programming in Modeling of Time Series System. In: Proceedings of 2013 IEEE Conference on Computational Intelligence for Financial Engineering & Economics (CIFEr), Singapore, April 16-19, pp. 84–88 (2013)
18. Garg, A., Tai, K., Lee, C.H., Savalani, M.M.: A Hybrid M5-Genetic Programming Approach for Ensuring Greater Trustworthiness of Prediction Ability In Modelling of FDM Process. Journal Of Intelligent Manufacturing (in press, 2013), doi:10.1007/s10845-013-0734-1
19. Can, B., Heavey, C.: Comparison of experimental designs for simulation-based symbolic regression of manufacturing systems. Computers & Industrial Engineering 61, 447–462 (2011)
20. Akaike, H.: A new look at the statistical model identification. IEEE Transactions on Automatic Control 19, 716–723 (1974)
21. Barron, A.R.: Predicted squared error: a criterion for automatic model selection. Self-Organizing Methods in Modeling 54, 87–103 (1984)
22. Miller, A.J.: Subset selection in regression. CRC Press, Florida (2002)
23. Moody, J.: Prediction risk and architecture selection for neural networks. Nato Asi Series F Computer and Systems Sciences, vol. 136, p. 147 (1994)
24. Rust, R.T., et al.: Model selection criteria: An investigation of relative accuracy, posterior probabilities, and combinations of criteria. Management Science 41, 322–333 (1995)

25. Schwarz, G.: Estimating the dimension of a model. The Annals of Statistics 6(2), 461–464 (1978)
26. Vapnik, V.N.: Statistical learning theory. John Wiley and Sons, Inc., USA (1998)
27. Croarkin, C., Tobias, P.: NIST/SEMATECH e-handbook of statistical methods. NIST/SEMATECH (July 2006),
    http://www.itl.nist.gov/div898/handbook
28. Harris, C.M., Hoffman, K.L., Yarrow, L.A.: Using integer programming techniques for the solution of an experimental design problem. Annals of Operations Research 58, 243–260 (1995)
29. Yildiz, G., Eski, O.: An artificial neural network based simulation metamodeling approach for dual resource constrained assembly line. In: Kollias, S.D., Stafylopatis, A., Duch, W., Oja, E. (eds.) ICANN 2006. LNCS, vol. 4132, pp. 1002–1011. Springer, Heidelberg (2006)
30. Koza, J.R.: Genetic programming: on the programming of computers by means of natural selection. MIT Press, Cambridge (1992)
31. Hinchliffe, M., Hiden, H., Mckay, B., Willis, M., Tham, M., Barton, G.: Modelling chemical process systems using a multi-gene genetic programming algorithm. Late breaking paper, GP 1996, Stanford, USA, pp. 28–31 (1996)
32. Hiden, H.G.: Data-Based Modelling using Genetic Programming. PhD Thesis, Dept. Chemical and Process Engineering, University of Newcastle, UK (1998)
33. Searson, D.P., Leahy, D.E., Willis, M.J.: GPTIPS: an open source genetic programming toolbox for multigene symbolic regression. In: Proceedings of the International MultiConference of Engineers and Computer Scientists, pp. 77–80. Citeseer (2010)
34. Garg, A., Vijayaraghavan, V., Mahapatra, S.S., Tai, K., Wong, C.H.: Performance evaluation of microbial fuel cell by artificial intelligence methods. Expert Systems with Applications (2013), http://dx.doi.org/10.1016/j.eswa.2013.08.038

Non-fragile Robust PI Controller Design Using Co-variance Matrix Adaptation Evolutionary Strategy

K. Mohaideen Abdul Kadhar and S. Baskar

Electrical & Electronics Engineering department
Thiagarajar College of Engineering
{makeee, sbeee}@tce.edu

Abstract. This paper discusses the application of Co-variance Matrix Evolutionary Strategy (CMA-ES) in the design of non-fragile robust PI controller. The desired maximum sensitivity of the closed loop system is considered as an objective and success rate of stability under probabilistic controller uncertainty is taken as a constraint for non-fragile robust PI controller design problem. Success rate of stability is calculated using Monte Carlo simulation (MCS) under probabilistic controller perturbation. CMA-ES finds the optimal controller parameter based on robustness objective and non-fragileness constraint. The Single Input Single Output (SISO) first order sugar cane raw juice neutralization process and second order Irrigation canal systems are considered as a test systems. The performance of the CMA-ES designed non-fragile robust PI controller is compared with the flat phase concept based PI controller and Astrom suggested PI controller for both test systems. Simulation results demonstrated that CMA-ES based non-fragile robust PI controller has better performance in robustness as well as non-fragileness.

Keywords: CMA-ES, non-fragile robust PI controller, maximum sensitivity, probabilistic parametric perturbation.

1 Introduction

Robustness is the ability of the controller which makes the closed loop system to be stable even under the effect of uncertainties. Many of the robust controller design methods considered only the plant side uncertainty and doesn't consider controller side uncertainty. Because, it is assumed that there are no uncertain parameters occurred in the controller side [1]. But in reality, there are some unavoidable amount of uncertainty exists in the controller due to the dynamics of analogue controller and the effect of quantization error in digital controllers [2, 3].

L. H. Keel and Bhattacharya proposed the importance of considering controller uncertainty in robust controller design based on the results of various robust controllers' instability due to controller uncertainty. If the uncertainties in the controller parameters make the closed loop system unstable then the controller is said to be a fragile controller [1, 3]. Whidbhone et al [2] proposed a method for the reduction of controller's fragility by minimizing closed loop pole sensitivity without

B.K. Panigrahi et al. (Eds.): SEMCCO 2013, Part II, LNCS 8298, pp. 32–43, 2013.

considering the performance of the closed loop system. Zhisheng et al designed the non-fragile H_∞ robust controller considering both controller and plant perturbations [4]. L. H. Keel, Bhattacharya, Whidbhone and Zhisheng are analyzed the fragility characteristic in higher order robust controllers.

Most of the industries have implemented PI and PID type controllers because of its simplicity, easy implementation and good performance [5]. Thus, it is imperative to analyze the fragility of PID controllers. Datta et al., Ho , designed the less fragile PID controllers based on the maximum l_2 norm parametric stability margin without considering the performance characteristics of the closed loop system [6, 7]. Irinel-Constantin et al suggested a geometric approach to find the stability region of the PID controller, based on stability crossing boundaries for SISO systems and they found the maximum deviation of the controller parameters within the closed loop stability boundary [15].Alfaro suggested a Fragility Index (FI) for classifying the various PID controllers based on the Maximum sensitivity (Ms) of the closed loop system. Also, Alfaro classified the PID controllers in to three categories namely i) fragile controller ii) Non-fragile controller and iii) Resilient controller, based on Fragility Index (FI) [3].

Based on the literature survey, it is found that the design of Non-fragile robust PID controller that can tolerate plant uncertainty as well as controller uncertainty is of immediate necessity. Many researchers analyzed the fragility of the designed PID controller [6, 7, 15], but they are not including the controller's fragility criterion in the robust PID controller design. By considering the efficiency of evolutionary algorithms in controller design, non-fragile robust PI controller design is formulated as an optimization problem. Recently, CMA-ES algorithm is successfully applied as an efficient optimization tool for optimizing nonlinear, multi-modal real world optimization problems.

In this paper, Co-variance Matrix Adaptation Evolutionary Strategy is used for the design of non-fragile robust PI controller. The desired maximum sensitivity (Ms=1.4) is considered as an objective and the success rate of stability under probabilistic controller perturbation is taken as a constraint for non-fragile robust PI controller design problem. The Single Input Single Output first order sugar cane raw juice neutralization process and second order Irrigation canal system[8] are chosen as a test systems for the design of CMA-ES based non-fragile robust PI controller. Consideration of robustness as well as non-fragileness in a controller design which gives the better robust controller.

The rest of the paper is organized as follows, Section 2 discusses the problem formulation; Section 3 describes the implementation of CMA-ES in non-fragile robust PI controller design; Simulation results are given in Section 4; Conclusion is on Section 5.

2   Problem Formulation

In this paper, an ideal PI controller structure given in equation (1) is chosen for the design of non-fragile robust PI controller. The maximum sensitivity (M_S) of the closed loop system given in equation (1) is considered as a design parameter for the design of non-fragile robust PI controller [4, 7]. M_S has a good geometrical   interpretation with Nyquist diagram and the inverse of M_S (i.e $\frac{1}{M_S}$) is the shortest distance from the critical point -1+j0 to the Nyquist curve of the open loop transfer function(L=GK) as shown in figure 1.

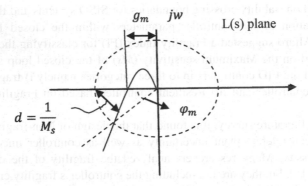

Fig. 1. Nyquist curve Loop transfer function

$$K(s) = k_c \left(1 + \frac{1}{T_i s}\right); \; M_s(x) = \max_\omega \left|\frac{1}{1+G(j\omega)K(j\omega)}\right| \qquad (1)$$

where, $G(s)$ is the plant to be controlled, x is controller parameter vector (i.e $x = [k_c, T_i]$). Maximum sensitivity (M_S) of the closed loop system gives the information about the closed loop system's sensitivity under the effect of parameter variations in closed loop system. The maximum sensitivity as $(M_S = 1.4)$ which gives the good phase and gain margin for maximum robustness [3, 5]. Hence, desired M_S value is chosen as 1.4 for robustness objective in non-fragile robust PI controller design.

2.1   Controller Uncertainty Modeling

The controller parameters (k_p and T_i) are perturbed as shown in equation (2).

$$k_{p\delta} = k_p(1 + \delta) \, ; T_{i\delta} = T_i(1 + \delta) \qquad (2)$$

where, $k_{p\delta}$ and $T_{i\delta}$ are the perturbed controller parameters and δ is the parametric perturbation. If the perturbed controller parameter vector arranged as $x_\delta = [k_{p\delta}, T_{i\delta}]$ then, the perturbed controller and the maximum sensitivity($M_s(x_\delta)$) are given in equation (3).

$$K_\delta(s) = k_{p\delta}(1 + \frac{1}{T_{i\delta}s}) \; ; \; M_s(x_\delta) = \max_\omega \left| \frac{1}{1+G(j\omega)K_\delta(j\omega)} \right| \tag{3}$$

Usually, perturbation as in the equation (3) is considered as a step change in the plant or controller parameters i.e δ is a single scalar [3]. But this type of uncertain behavior doesn't mean the actual real time perturbations. Hence, probabilistic perturbation is used in this paper to mimic the real time uncertain behaviors of controller parameters [11].

2.2   Probabilistic Approach

The maximum sensitivity bound in the range of 1.2 to 2 which gives the guaranteed robustness to the closed loop system [3, 5]. If the M_s value is in between the above specified range (i.e. M_S =1.2 to 2) then the closed loop system is stable. Lower $M_S \approx 1.2$ gives better robustness and Larger $M_S \approx 2$ gives aggressive and less acceptable robustness [7]. By using this maximum sensitivity bound, success rate of stability under probabilistic controller perturbation is evaluated using Monte Carlo Simulation (MCS).

2.3   Evaluation of Non-fragileness Constraint

MCS is a method for iteratively evaluating a deterministic model using sets of random numbers as inputs [9, 10]. In this paper, $q \times n$ number of random samples are generated by using normal distribution with zero mean and 0.1 standard deviation as N (0, 0.1) for uncertain parameters. where, 0.1 represent the 10% of uncertain parameters. The generated random samples are added to the controller parameters as per the equation (2). Under random variation of controller parameters, the stability of the closed loop system is represented using a discrete limit state function based on the maximum sensitivity bound and given in the equation 4 [9,10].

$$I_{M_s(x_\delta)} = \begin{cases} 1 & if \;\; 1.2 < M_s(x_\delta) \leq 2 \\ 0 & otherwise \end{cases} \tag{4}$$

By using MCS, the probability of success rate ($P_s(x_\delta)$) for stability is calculated using the q number of binary data from the limit state function as in the equation (5).

$$P_s(x_\delta) = \frac{1}{q}\sum_{i=1}^{q} I_{M_{si}(x_\delta)}(G(s),K(s,x_\delta)) \tag{5}$$

where, q is the total number of samples , $I_{M_{si}(x_\delta)}$ limit state function at the ith sample, n is the number of controller parameters . This probability of success rate for stability is used as a constraint in the design of non-fragile robust PI controller.

2.4   Objective Function

An error function $J(x)$ is used as an objective to achieve the desired maximum sensitivity in non-fragile robust PI controller design and it is given in equation (6).

$$J(x) = |M_s(x) - M_{sd}| \qquad (6)$$

where, $M_s(x)$ is the actual maximum sensitivity and M_{sd} is the desired maximum sensitivity value (M_{sd} =1.4). CMA-ES finds the optimal controller parameter vector $x= [k_c, T_i]$ by minimizing the error function $J(x)$ while satisfying the non-fragileness constraint as follows.

$$\text{Minimize } J(x)$$
$$\text{Subject to}$$
$$\frac{1}{q}\sum_{i=1}^{q} I_{M_{si}(x_\delta)}(G(s), K(s, x_\delta)) \geq 0.8 \qquad (7)$$

In equation (7), non-fragileness constraint is set as 0.8 for achieving at least 80% of success rate in closed loop stability under probabilistic controller perturbation.

2.5   Test Systems

The dynamic model of the sugar cane raw juice neutralization process [8] is given in equation (8).

$$G_1(s) = \frac{0.55}{1+62s}e^{-10s} \qquad (8)$$

The second order irrigation canal system [8] model $G_2(s)$ is shown in equation (9).

$$G_2(s) = \frac{1.25*e^{-600s}}{(1+300*s)(1+60*s)} \qquad (9)$$

3   CMA-ES in Non-fragile Robust PI Controller Design

CMA-ES was proposed by Hansen and Ostermeier in 2001. The basic idea in this stragety is moving the population in the form of multivariate normal distribution. The distribution takes the form of hyper ellipsoid and search history of the population is used for moving the population to optimum one [11, 12]. CMA-ES algorithm code is downloaded from [11] and the CMA-ES code is customized for handling constraints for the design of non-fragile robust PI controller.

3.1   Constraint Relaxation and Fitness Function

By using ε_c constraint relaxation method, the constraint violation was relaxed up to the generation control limit. The ε_c level is set to zero up to the generation control limit g_c, to obtain the solutions with no constraint violation.

$$\varepsilon_c(0) = v(x_i) \tag{10}$$

After the generation control limit g_c, constraint is violated as follows.

$$\varepsilon_c(g) = \begin{cases} \varepsilon_c(0)\left(1 - \dfrac{g}{g_c}\right)^{cp}, & 0 < g < g_c \\ 0, & g \geq g_c \end{cases} \tag{11}$$

Where x_i is the top i^{th} individual and i= $(0.05* \lambda)$. The recommended parameter ranges are [13] :$g_c \in [0.1g_{max}, 0.8g_{max}]$ and $cp \in [2,10]$. Due to this constraint relaxation, the individual with best objective are considered for next generation even it has high constraint violation. After constraint relaxation, penalty parameter less constraint handling scheme is employed to find the fitness function. The fitness function for any solution x is given as follows:

$$F(x) = \begin{cases} J(x) & if\ x\ is\ feasible \\ J_{max} + \varepsilon_c(g) & otherwise \end{cases} \tag{12}$$

where,
$F(x)$ - Fitness function,
$J(x)$ - Objective function
J_{max} - objective function value of the worst feasible solution in the population

3.2   Initialization

The initial CMA-ES parameters are set as population size(λ)=10; max_Feval=1000, m=0, σ=0, $P_\sigma^{(0)} = P_c^{(0)} = 0.25(x_u - x_l)$, $CM^{(0)} = I, \mu = \frac{\lambda}{2}$. where, x_l, x_u are upper and lower bounds of controller parameters respectively.

3.3   Controller Parameter Setting

The solution vector for SISO system is arranged as x= [k_c, T_i].

The lower and upper bounds of the solution vector are set as follows.

   Sugar cane raw juice neutralization process x_l= [0, 0]; x_u= [5, 10].

   Irrigation canal system x_l= [0, 0]; x_u= [1, 500];

The dimension for SISO non-fragile robust PI controller: n=2.

3.4   Co-variance Matrix Adaptation Evolutionary Strategy

Step 1: Generate $\lambda \times n$ random controller parameter matrix of x as follows.

$$x_k^{(g)} = m^{(g)} + \sigma^{(g)}N\left(0, CM^{(g)}\right) \text{ where } 1 < k < \lambda \tag{13}$$

Step 2: Stop if the termination criteria is met as in the section 3.5.

Step 3: Calculate the fitness value (F) based on objective and constraint violation as in equation (12).

Step 4: Sort the solutions based on fitness value and Select the best μ number of individuals (x_μ) from the λ population.

Step 6: Update the mean $m^{(g+1)}$ using $m^{(g+1)} = \sum_{i=1}^{\mu} w_i x_{i:\lambda}^{(g+1)}$ (14)

$$\text{where, } w_i = \frac{ln(\mu+1)-ln(i)}{\mu(ln(\mu+1))-\sum_{j=1}^{\mu} ln(j)} \quad for\ i = 1\ to\ \mu\ ; \tag{15}$$

This weighted average gives the new mean to move the population towards optimal solution. The variance of effective selection mass [12] is calculated from the equation
$$\mu_{eff} = \left(\sum_{i=1}^{\mu} w_i^2\right)^{-1}$$
Step7: Adaptation of global step size using evolution path

$$P_\sigma^{(g+1)} = (1 - c_\sigma).P_\sigma^{(g)} + \sqrt{c_\sigma(2 - c_\sigma)} \frac{\sqrt{\mu_{eff}}}{\sigma^g}(CM^{-1/2})^{(g)}\left((x)_\mu^{(g+1)} - (x)_\mu^g\right) \tag{16}$$

$$\sigma^{(g+1)} = \sigma^{(g)}\exp^*\left(\frac{c_\sigma}{d}\left(\frac{\|P_\sigma^{G+1}\|}{E(\|N(0,I)\|)}\right) - 1\right) \tag{17}$$

Step 8: Update Co-variance matrix using the evolution path $P_c^{(g+1)}$

$$p_c^{g+1} = (1 - C_c)P_c^{(g)} + \sqrt{C_c(2 - C_c)}.\frac{\sqrt{\mu}}{\sigma^{(g)}}(< x >_\mu^{(g+1)} - < x >_\mu^g) \tag{18}$$

Then the covariance matrix $CM^{(g)}$ is extended from the evolution path

$$CM^{(g+1)} = \left(1 - C_{cov}\right).CM^g + \frac{C_{cov}}{\mu_{eff}}P_c^{(g+1)}\left(P_c^{(g+1)}\right)^T + (1 - \frac{1}{\mu_{eff}})\frac{C_{cov}}{\sigma^{(g)^2}}\sum_{i=1}^{\mu}(x_i^{g+1} - <x>_\mu^g)(x_i^{g+1} - <x>_\mu^g)^T) \tag{19}$$

Step 9: The updated CMA-ES parameters $m^{(g+1)}$, $\sigma^{(g+1)}$, $CM^{(g+1)}$ are used to generate $\lambda \times n$ random controller parameter matrix of x using the equation (13) for the next generation (g+1), set g=g+1, return to step 3. This procedure is repeated until the stopping criteria met.

3.5   Stopping Criteria

The recommendations of stopping criteria in the design of non-fragile robust PI controller are given as below.

- max_Feval: stop if maximum function evaluation is reached.
- TolFun: Tolerance value for objectives is assumed to 10^{-5}. Stop if all the fitness function (F) values of the last 20 generation are below TolFun.
- TolX: Tolerance value for co-ordinates is assumed to 10^{-5}[12].

4   Simulation Results

All the simulations are done in MATLAB R2009b software on a 32 bit core2duo processor PC operating at 2.93 GHz with 3GB RAM. Initialization and controller parameter settings are done as in the section 3.

4.1   Controllers

The CMA-ES designed non-fragile robust PI controller for both sugar cane raw juice neutralization process and irrigation canal system arc given in Table 1. Table 1 shows the controller parameters and their corresponding maximum sensitivity, probability of success rate under 20% probabilistic perturbations.

Table 1. Controller parameters and maximum sensitivity for both systems

	Sugar cane raw juice neutralization process			Irrigation canal system		
	Controller parameters	Ms	$P_s(x)$	Controller parameters	Ms	$P_s(x)$
CMAES-PI	kp=4.3365, ki=46.3593	1.4	1	kp=0.1920, ki=410.09.	1.4	1
C.A.Monje-PI [8]	kp=1.2749, ki=24.51.	1.36	0.9	kp=0.5511, ki=0.0008, kd=80.13.	1.83	0.6
Astrom-PI [14]	kp=1.76, ki=29.32.	1.32	0.7	kp=0.00262, ki=5.86.	1.58	0.9

From Table 1, it is clear that CMA-ES based PI controller has more success rate of stability under probabilistic perturbation for both systems.

4.2   Time Domain Analysis

Figure 2 and Figure 3 shows the closed loop step response of three controllers' for sugar cane raw juice neutralization process and Irrigation canal system respectively. From the Figures 2 and 3, CMA-ES based non-fragile robust PI controller has less over shoot and quick response than other PI controllers for both systems.

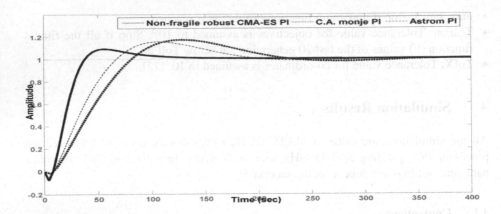

Fig. 2. Closed loop step response of three controllers for sugar cane neutralization process

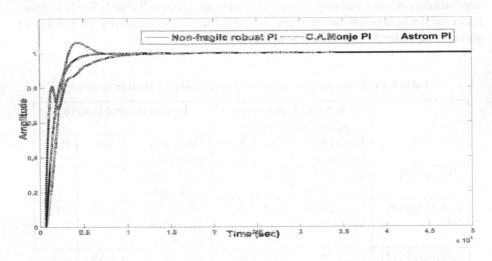

Fig. 3. Closed loop step response of three controllers for Irrigation canal system

4.3 Robustness Analysis

Figure 4 and 5 shows the response of the load disturbance rejection of the three controllers for sugar cane raw juice neutralization process and Irrigation canal system respectively. From figure 4 and 5, it is clear that CMA-ES designed Non-fragile robust PI controller reject the input load disturbance quickly than other controllers for both systems.

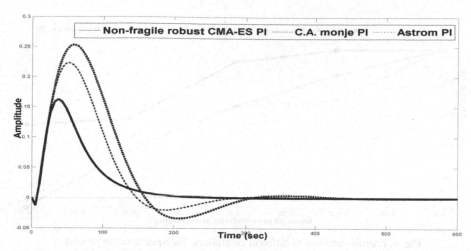

Fig. 4. Load disturbance rejections of the controllers for sugar cane neutralization process

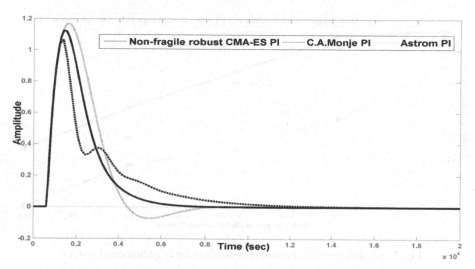

Fig. 5. Load disturbance rejections of the controllers for Irrigation canal system

4.4   Fragility Analysis

To check the fragile characteristic of the controller's, the mean of random number is increased from 0.1 to 0.5 and the corresponding probability of success rate for stability is plotted against the mean of the perturbation level. Figure 5 and 6 shows the comparison results of three controller's success rate against the increasing perturbation in controllers for sugar cane raw juice neutralization process and Irrigation canal system respectively. From figure 5 and 6 CMA-ES designed non-fragile robust PI controller has near 80% success rate of closed loop stability up to 0.5 mean of random perturbations. Astrom based PI controller and flat phase concept based PI controller are not able to withstand its closed loop stability whenever the perturbations increased.

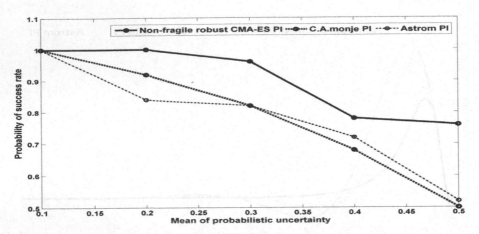

Fig. 6. Fragility analysis of different controllers for neutralization process

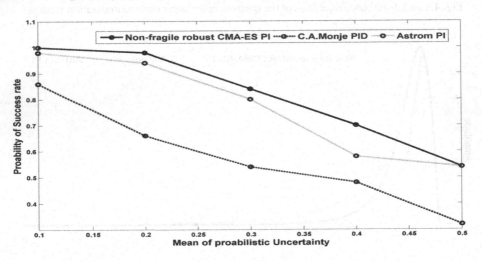

Fig. 7. Fragility analysis of different controllers for Irrigation canal system

5   Conclusion

In this paper, non-fragile robust PI controller is designed using Co-variance Matrix Adaptation Evolutionary Strategy (CMA-ES) for sugar cane raw juice neutralization process and Irrigation canal system. Parametric probabilistic controller perturbation is used to check the robustness and fragileness of the designed controller. CMA-ES based non-fragile robust PI controller has better command tracking and load disturbance rejection characteristic than Astrom based PI controller and flat phase concept based PI controller for both systems. In controller fragility, CMA-ES based PI controller has maximum success rate of stability under the probabilistic controller perturbation for both systems. CMA-ES based non-fragile robust PI controller is better in robustness as well as non-fragileness. Hence, CMA-ES based non-fragile robust PI controller is suitable for real time applications where there is a fragility problem.

Acknowledgment. This research was supported by Indian government via University Grants Commissions' Maulana Azad National Fellowship (MANF) scheme (MANF File no: MANF-MUS-TAM-3045). The authors would like to thank the principal and management of Thiagarajar College of Engineering for their continuous encouragement and providing the facilities for the research.

References

1. Keel, L.H., Bhattacharyya, S.P.: Robust, Fragile or Optimal. IEEE Transactions on Automatic Control 42(8) (August 1997)
2. Whidborne, J.F., Istepanian, R.S.H., Wu, J.: Reduction of Controller Fragility by Pole Sensitivity Minimization. IEEE Transactions on Automatic Control 46(2) (February 2001)
3. Alfaro: PID controller fragility. ISA Transactions 46(4), 555–559 (2007)
4. Duan, Z., Huang, L., Wang, L.: Robustness analysis and synthesis of SISO systems under both plant and controller perturbations. Systems & Control Letters 42, 201–216 (2001)
5. Astrom, K.J.: Control system Design (2002)
6. Datta, A., Ho, M.-T., Bhattacharyya, S.P.: Structure and Synthesis of PID Controllers. Springer, London (2000)
7. Ho, M.T.: Non-fragile PID controller design. In: 39th IEEE Conference on Decision and Control, Sydney, Australia (December 2000)
8. Monje, C.A., Calderon, A.J., Vinagre, B.M., Chen, Y., Feliu, V.: On Fractional PI^λ Controllers: Some Tuning Rules for Robustness to Plant Uncertainties. Nonlinear Dynamics 38, 369–381 (2004)
9. Wittwer, J.W.: "Monte Carlo Simulation Basics From" Vertex42.com (June 1, 2004), http://www.vertex42.com/ExcelArticles/mc/MonteCarloSimulation.html
10. Ray, L., Stengel, R.F.: A Monte Carlo approach to the analysis of control system robustness. Automatica 29(1), 229–236 (1993)
11. Hansen, https://www.lri.fr/~hansen/cmaesintro.html
12. Hansen, N.: The CMA Evolution Strategy: A Tutorial (June 28, 2011)
13. Takahama, T., Sakai, S., Iwane, N.: Solving Nonlinear Constrained Optimization Problems by the ε Constrained Differential Evolution. In: 2006 IEEE Conf. on Systems, Man, and Cybernetics, Taipei, October 8-11 (2006)
14. O'Dwyer, A.: Handbook of PI and PID Controller Tuning Rules. Imperial College Press (2009)
15. Mor˜arescu, I.-C.: Stability Crossing Boundaries and Fragility Characterization of PID Controllers for SISO Systems with I/O Delays. In: ACC 2011 (2011)

Meta Heuristic Approaches for Circular Open Dimension Problem

N. Madhu Sudana Rao, M. Aruna, and S. Bhuvaneswari

School of Computing, SASTRA University, Thanjavur, India
{madhu031083,bhuvana2392}@gmail.com, aruna92@outlook.com

Abstract. This paper discusses the circular open dimension problem (CODP), where set of circles of different radii has to be packed into a rectangular strip of predetermined width and variable length. The circle packing problem is one of the variant of cutting and packing problems. We propose four different nature inspired Meta heuristic algorithms for solving this problem. These algorithms are proved to be the best in finding local solutions. The algorithms are based on food foraging process and breeding behavior of some biological species such as bat, bee, firefly and cuckoo. Circle packing problem is one of the NP hard problems. It is very difficult to solve NP hard problems exactly, so the proposed approaches tries to give approximate solution within the stipulated time. The standard benchmark instances are used for comparison, and it is proved that firefly is giving the best solution.

Keywords: CODP, CPP, Meta heuristic, local search.

1 Introduction

Circle packing problem comes under optimization problems. As it is very difficult to solve exactly, we use different approximation algorithms. In real time the cutting and packing problems are encountered in paper cutting, wireless sensor node deployment and food industry. The application areas mentioned are mainly concerned about minimizing wasted portion, storage space. The approaches specified in this paper give approximate solutions within reasonable computation time.

Circle packing problem has two categories: uniform sized circle packing and arbitrary sized circle packing. In uniform sized circle packing, set of circles with same radius have to be packed into solution space. Many researchers have found efficient solutions for uniform sized circle packing problem. In arbitrary sized circle packing problem set of circles with different radii will be packed without any overlapping. Circular open dimension problem comes under ACP family. This paper provides different approaches for CODP problem.

More precisely, set of N circles (1, 2, ..., n) with different radii $r_i (i = 1, 2, ..., n)$ should be packed into a rectangular strip of predetermined width W and unrestricted length L without overlapping. By overlapping, it is meant that the circles should not exceed the boundary of the solution space and also that the circles should not collide with one another. The objective is to minimize L with less penalty (overlapping).

B.K. Panigrahi et al. (Eds.): SEMCCO 2013, Part II, LNCS 8298, pp. 44–54, 2013.

Initially the circles are placed randomly into the strip. The circle configuration $(x_1, y_1, x_2, y_2, \ldots, x_n, y_n)$ can be ensured right, if it satisfies the following constraints:

$$|x_i| + |r_i| \leq X + L \quad \forall \, 1 \leq i \leq n. \tag{1}$$

$$|x_i| - |r_i| \geq X \quad \forall \, 1 \leq i \leq n. \tag{2}$$

$$|y_i| + |r_i| \leq Y + W \quad \forall \, 1 \leq i \leq n. \tag{3}$$

$$|y_i| - |r_i| \geq Y \quad \forall \, 1 \leq i \leq n. \tag{4}$$

$$|r_i| + |r_j| \leq \sqrt{(x_i - x_j)^2 + (y_i - y_j)^2} \quad \forall \, 1 \leq i < j \leq n. \tag{5}$$

Where, (X, Y) represents the starting coordinate of the strip.

If the equations (1), (2), (3), (4), (5) are satisfied, the configuration is further subjected to length reduction.

Penalty function (P) is defined based on the constraints to calculate penalty of an arrangement. Overlapping in this kind of packing can occur in two ways as mentioned.

$$P_{ix_1} = (x_i + r_i) - (X + L) \quad \forall \, 1 \leq i \leq n. \tag{6}$$

$$P_{ix_2} = x_i - ((x_i - r_i) + (x_i - X)) \quad \forall \, 1 \leq i \leq n. \tag{7}$$

$$P_{iy_1} = (y_i + r_i) - (Y + W) \quad \forall \, 1 \leq i \leq n. \tag{8}$$

$$P_{iy_2} = y_i - ((y_i - r_i) + (y_i - Y)) \quad \forall \, 1 \leq i \leq n. \tag{9}$$

$$P_{ij} = (r_i + r_j) - \sqrt{(x_i - x_j)^2 + (y_i - y_j)^2} \quad \forall \, 1 \leq i < j \leq n. \tag{10}$$

$$P = (P_{ix_1})^2 + (P_{ix_2})^2 + (P_{iy_1})^2 + (P_{iy_2})^2 + (P_{ij})^2 \tag{11}$$

The value of P gives the overall penalty of the configuration. If each of the value of P_{ix}, P_{iy}, P_{iz} is less than or equal to 0, then it denotes that there is no penalty or overlapping in the present configuration. The equations (6) & (7), (8) & (9) give the penalty of the circles extending the vertical and horizontal boundaries respectively. The equation (10) gives the penalty of overlapping circles.

2   Literature Review

To solve circle packing problem several methods have been proposed. The two main classifications of circle packing problems are construction based approach and perturbation based approach. In construction based approach, circles are packed one by one until all the circles are successfully packed whereas perturbation based approach starts with initial configuration which may contain overlapping which is then iteratively improved.

Most of the algorithms used for solving ACP follows construction based approach. Hakim Akeb. Mhand Hifi (2008) proposed an approach which combines beam search and look ahead strategy for solving ACP. On subsequent research Hakim Akeb (2010) proposed an algorithm which solves the ACP using greedy procedures, beam strategies, and a look-ahead search. In his later release (2011) he proposed an augmented beam search algorithm which combines binary search, beam search and multi start strategy. A mathematical model has been proposed for CPP by Yu. G. Stoyan (2004). Yaohua He·Yong Wu (2012) has proposed an approach for arbitrary sized circle packing using genetic algorithm. Huang (2005) proposed two greedy algorithms. One is B1.0 which tries to pack the circles using maximum-hole degree rule. Another algorithm is B1.5 which improves B1.0 by adding self-look-ahead search technique.

Some of the existing approaches which come under perturbation are listed. An Iterated tabu search proposed by Zhanghua Fu, Wenqi Huang, Zhipeng L (2012) which starts with randomly generated initial solution and then tries to pack circles without overlapping using tabu search procedure. A simulated annealing approach proposed by Mhand Hifi , Vangelis Th. Paschos, Vassilis Zissimopoulos (2004) defines an energy function which concentrates on placing circles on the left corner of the rectangle. A mathematical model have been constructed by Stoyan, Y.G., Yaskov, G.N (1998) solves the problem by a method which uses branch and bound algorithm and the gradient method. An adaptive Tabu Search (ATS) by Zhipeng Lu (2010) is also one among them.

Meanwhile UCP have been solved by many efficient algorithms. Non linear programming approach proposed by Maranas (1995). Huang and Ye (2010) proposed a physically inspired model and new heuristic to solve this problem. In 2011 he introduced another method called the quasi-physical global optimization. We know that the CPP problems are NP hard problems. As it is very difficult to solve NP hard problems exactly, the proposed heuristic approaches give approximate solution.

3   Proposed Approach

In this paper four nature inspired Meta heuristic approaches are used to solve CODP. These algorithms follow breeding behavior and food foraging process of some biological species such as Bat, Bee, Cuckoo and Firefly. These algorithms come under perturbation based approaches. Additionally it uses optimization technique for smoothening the result. It starts with randomly generated coordinates which is then iteratively improved to best configuration. In each iteration, if all the circles are successfully configured then the length of the rectangle is monotonously decreased.

3.1   Bat Algorithm

Bat algorithm is based on echolocation behavior of bats [13]. With the help of echolocation bats can identify the distance and type of prey. It also detects the moving speed of small insects. Even in the complete darkness the bat could able to find its prey. Each bat has its own velocity (V) and the pulse emitted by bats lasts for few thousandths of a second. When the bat hunts for prey it increases the rate of pulse emission per second [12].When the bat is more close to the prey, it decreases its loudness (A). The loudness and rate are updated only if the bat moves towards optimal solution [12]. For simplicity, three rules are used:

1. Bats use echolocation to find distance and type of prey
2. Each bat flies randomly with a fixed frequency f_{min}, varying wavelength λ , loudness A_0 and varying velocity V_i at position X_i to search for prey. It automatically changes its rate of pulse emission and loudness when it is close to the prey.
3. The loudness varies in the range A_0 to A_{min} .

Steps:
1. Initialize the velocity V_i , loudness A_i , rate of pulse emission r_i and frequency f_i of the bat population X_i (i=1, 2,....,n).
2. For specified period of generation, new solution is generated by adjusting frequency.
3. If the new solution of particular bat is found to be best, then that particular solution is considered to be best in that generation. The best solution is carried over to next generation.

3.1.1   Bat Algorithm in CODP
Each bat is considered as one configuration in circular open dimension problem. The objective function is considered to be penalty function. Initially the bats are assigned with random coordinates (x, y), velocity (v), loudness (A) and rate of pulse emission (r).

ALGORITHM
Objective function f(x)
Set length L to maximum
While limited time has not been elapsed **do**
Initialize the bat population X_i (i = 1, 2, ..., n) and V_i
Initialize frequency f_i at X_i
Initialize rate of pulse r_i and the loudness A_i for each bat
While (t <Max Generation)
    Generate new solution randomly from equation (1)
$X_i \leftarrow$ Optimization (X_i)
Evaluate the penalty f(X_i)
If (random no >r_i) **then**
    Select the best solution
    Generate local solution for the best solution from equation (2)
End if
If (random no < A_i & f (X_i) < f (X_*)) **then**
    Accept the generated new solution
    Update r_i and A_i using equation (3) & (4)
End if
    Rank the bats and find current best configuration X_*
End while
If ($f(X_*) == 0$)
    L=L-(L/10000)
End if
End while

The new solution(x_i^t , y_i^t) is given by,

$$x_i^t = x_i^{t-1}+\text{rand}, y_i^t = y_i^{t-1}+\text{rand} \tag{1}$$

The local solution is generated as follows,

$$x_{new} = x_{old}+\varepsilon A^t, \ y_{new} = y_{old}+\varepsilon A^t \tag{2}$$

Where ε random number $\in$ [-1, 1], $A^t = <A_i^t>$ is average loudness of all bats in that generation.

Loudness and rate of pulse emission of bat is updated as,

$$A_i^{t+1} = \alpha A_i^t, \tag{3}$$

$$r_i^{t+1} = r_i^0[\text{1-exp} (\gamma t)] \tag{4}$$

Where α, γ are constant and is set to 0.1. The initial loudness is in the range [0, 1] and rate of pulse is in the range [0, 1].

3.2   Bee Colony Optimization Algorithm

This algorithm is based on food searching behavior of honey bees [14]. This technique generates neighborhood solutions, so it is used for optimization problems.

In nature, the colony of bees moves in multiple directions simultaneously in search of food. Usually scout bees are sent out for searching flowers which has more nectar. Those bees that found a patch which is rated above certain threshold quantity of honey goes to the dance floor to perform "waggle dance" [14]. Through this waggle dance honey bees communicates with each other. It conveys three pieces of information about a flower: the direction in which the flower with more nectar is found, distance between hive and flower, the quality (amount of honey). Based on the information given by scout bees more bees are sent to best site i.e. the site which has more nectar.

3.2.1   Bee Colony Optimization in CODP

Each bee is considered to be one configuration of circles with x and y coordinates. Initially the bees are assigned with random x and y coordinates. The neighborhood search is carried as mentioned in BCO algorithm, and then the solution is iteratively improved to give globally best solution.

ALGORITHM
Objective function f(x)
Set length L to maximum
While limited time has not been elapsed **do**
Initialize the bee population X_i (i = 1, 2, ..., n)   with random coordinates
Evaluate penalty for each bee$f(X_i)$
While (t< Maximum generation)
        Select best configurations (s) for neighborhood search
        More number of neighborhood search for best (b) site
        X_i ← Optimization (X_i)
        Evaluate the penalty f(X_i)

Generate neighborhood for (s-b) configurations
$X_i \leftarrow$ Optimization (X_i)
Evaluate the penalty $f(X_i)$
Rank and find best configuration X_*
End while
If $(f(X_*) == 0)$
L=L-(L/10000)
End if
End while

The neighborhood search for the best site is generated as follows,

$$x_i = x_i + \text{random}, \quad y_i = y_i + \text{random} \tag{1}$$

random number is in the range [0,1].

3.3   CUCKOO Search

This algorithm slightly differs from other algorithms in a way that it is based on the breeding nature of cuckoo [15]. Cuckoos generally don't build its own nest and lay their eggs on some other birds nest. If the host bird discovers that the eggs are not their own, then it will either throw the cuckoos egg or ditch its nest. This kind of cuckoo search follows some rules. They are

1. Each cuckoo will lay only one egg at a time and place it in a randomly chosen nest.
2. The number of host nests remains constant.
    The quality of the solution or the fitness of an egg in a particular nest is measured from the objective function.

CUCKOO Procedure in CODP

1. Fix the number of host nests.
2. Each nest represents a solution.
3. Generate initial coordinates for each nest and calculate its penalty.
4. For the first iteration generate new coordinates for a nest from (1).
5. Update the coordinates using the equation (1) for the rest of the iteration and calculate the penalty at last.
6. Select a nest randomly.
7. If the penalty calculated in step 5 is less than the penalty of the randomly chosen nest then update its coordinates with the coordinates as given in step 5.
8. Find the nest with the least penalty value.
9. If this value equals zero then reduce the length of the strip and move on to the next iteration until the time doesn't exceeds the specified one.

ALGORITHM
Objective function f(x)
Set length L to maximum
While limited time has not been elapsed **do**
     Initialize n host nests X_i (i = 1, 2, ..., n) with random coordinates
While (t <Max Generation)
     Generate a solution for cuckoo randomly using equation (1)
     $X_i \leftarrow$ Optimization (X_i)
     Evaluate the penalty f (X_i)

     Evaluate its penalty f (X_i)
     Choose a nest (j) from n host nests randomly
If ($f(X_i$)> $f(X_j$)),
     Replace j with new solution
End if
     Rank and find best configuration X_*
If ($f(X_*$) ==0)
     L=L-(L/10000)
End if
End while
     New solution $(x_1, y_1, x_2, y_2 ... ..., x_n, y_n)$ for a cuckoo X_i is generated using the
following equation

$$x_i^{t+1} = x_i^t + \alpha(1/t^\lambda), \qquad y_i^{t+1} = y_i^t + \alpha(1/t^\lambda) \qquad (1)$$

Where, t represents the current iteration number
α represents a value between 0 and 1.

3.4   Firefly Algorithm

This technique is based on food foraging behavior of fireflies [16]. Firefly produces a
flashing light. The brightness of this light is responsible for attracting the prey or
some other firefly towards the one considered. For simplicity following rules are
considered. They are

1. Attractiveness is proportional to the brightness of firefly; less bright firefly
    will be attracted towards the brighter firefly.
2. Brightness decreases as the distance between the firefly increases.
3. Brightness is calculated based on the objective function. The objective
    function here gives the penalty of the configuration.

Firefly Algorithm in CODP

1. Generate initial coordinates for the fireflies X_i and calculate its penalty
    $f(X_i$) using the penalty function.
2. Each firefly represents a solution.
3. Find the firefly which has the minimum penalty value and consider it as the
    best for that particular iteration.

4. Compare the penalty of each firefly with every other firefly and the distance between them is calculated using the equation (1).
5. The coordinates of the firefly which has the maximum penalty value will be changed in accordance with the coordinates of the best among the two, as represented by the equations (2) & (3).
6. This is followed by the optimization of the firefly.
7. The firefly which has the least penalty value will be considered the best firefly.
8. If this value equals to zero then the length of the strip will be reduced and the next iteration follows.
9. The algorithm goes on with the iteration until it reaches the specified amount of time.

ALGORITHM
Objective function f(x)
Set length L to maximum
While limited time has not been elapsed **do**
    Initialize the population of fireflies X_i (i = 1, 2, ..., n) with random coordinates
    Light intensity I_j at X_i is determined by f(X_i)
    Initialize absorption coefficient γ
While (t <Maximum Generation)
For i = 1: n all n fireflies
For j = 1: n all n fireflies
If $(f(X_j)$ $< f(X_i)$)
    Move firefly i towards j
        $X_i \leftarrow$ Optimization (X_i)
    Evaluate the penalty $f(X_j)$
End If
    Evaluate the new solution penalty and update light intensity
End for j
End for i
    Rank the fireflies and find the current best configuration X_*
End While
If $(f(X_*) ==0)$
    L=L-(L/10000)
End If
End while

The main feature of firefly is that each firefly tries to learn from the best firefly at that instance. That is it generates $O(n^2)$ number of local solution in each generation. The distance (r) between any two fireflies (i, j) is obtained by the formula

$$r_{ij} = \sqrt{(x_i - x_j)^2 + (y_i - y_j)^2}$$ (1)

Where (x_i, y_i) represents the coordinates of the ith firefly in a solution.
A firefly i, move towards a brighter firefly j with the movement given by

$$x_i = x_i + \beta_0 e^{-\gamma r_{ij}^2}(x_j - x_i) + \alpha\,(rand - 0.5) \qquad (2)$$

$$y_i = y_i + \beta_0 e^{-\gamma r_{ij}^2}(y_j - y_i) + \alpha\,(rand - 0.5) \qquad (3)$$

Where the second term defines attraction and the last term in the equation is for randomization where α is the randomization parameter and (x_i, y_i) represents the coordinates of the ith firefly, and $rand \in [0,1]$.

3.5   Optimization Technique

The optimization technique that has been used in this paper tries to pack all the circles without any overlapping.

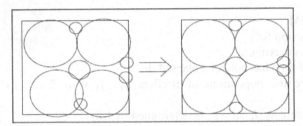

Fig. 1. Optimization

The procedure for optimization technique is given below,

1.   All the circles placed inside the rectangle/strip as initial step.
2.   Then each circle is checked with every other circle for overlapping
3.   If there is any overlapping then the coordinates for overlapping circle is randomly generated. goto step 2
4.   If randomly generated coordinate is not improved within 10 iteration, then the algorithm proceeds to next circle.

ALGORITHM
For all circles
If (x_i, y_i) overlaps with boundary of rectangle
          Place the circle (x_i, y_i) inside the boundary
End If
End For
For all circles   i=1 :n
If (x_i, y_i) overlaps with (x_k, y_k)
          Generate random coordinates for i^{th} circle
Else
                    Increment i
End if
If i^{th} circle is not improved within 10 iteration
                    Increment i
End if
End for

4   Comparison

The algorithms proposed in this paper are implemented in Java language.These algorithms has been run on the Linux cluster with 15 nodes. Specifications of the server is Operating System:RedHat enterprises Linux 4,Processor :Intel Pentium 4 XEON 4,Clock Speed :1.9Ghz,RAM:2GB,SCSI Hard disks:108 GB,Network car:Fiber Optics Gigabit Ethernet,Tape Drive :40 GB DLT tape drive.Node specification is Processor :Intel Pentium 4,Clock Speed :1.7 GHz,,RAM :256 MB,IDE Hard disks :40 GB,Network Card:10/100 Mbps.Standard benchmark instances [17] are taken and the result obtained from each algorithm is tabulated in Table 1. Some of the KBG instances are considered and the time limit is set to 24 hours for all such instances. Number of circles in each instance is 25 and the maximum limit is set to 75.Our experimentation results shown that FIREFLY algorithms showing better performance .ALL the four algorithms are executed for the same amount of time but still firefly shows improvement, because each Firefly is learning from all other Fireflies.

Table 1. Comparison table

INSTANCE	TIME-hours	BAT	BEE	CUCKOO	FIREFLY
KBG1	24	47.4615	57.2246	48.0153	**45.8519**
KBG2	24	29.5769	36.2814	29.1162	**28.6225**
KBG4	24	19.1647	23.1729	19.1226	**18.4778**
KBG5	24	11.6090	36.9330	9.0987	**8.9722**
KBG6	24	35.7591	49.2979	36.3068	**34.2985**
KBG7	24	8.7980	9.4068	11.0939	**6.9193**
KBG8	24	6.1209	6.2897	5.9829	**5.7165**
KBG21	24	6.9007	8.4632	6.7559	**6.7001**
KBG32	24	2.3756	2.3861	1.9732	**1.9614**

5   Conclusion

As mentioned earlier Cutting and packing problems are NP-hard problems, the proposed approaches give approximate solutions. Nature inspired algorithms such as (Bat, Bee, cuckoo, Firefly) are used for solving CODP because they are proved to give best local solution. As finding local solution is one of the major functions in CODP these algorithms are used.

Standard instances are taken and all the above specified algorithms are executed for 24 hours. For all the sample KBG instances, it is proved that firefly is giving best approximate solution when compared to other algorithms in specified time. Firefly gives best result because it generates $O(n^2)$ number of local solution in each generation. The proposed approach can be extended in these areas: different optimization function for different scenarios, use of different solution space for packing circles, nature inspired algorithms can be extended with some functions.

References

1. Akeb, H., Hifi, M., Negre, S.: An augmented beam search-based algorithm for the circular open dimension problem. Comput. Ind. Eng. 61(2), 373–381 (2011)
2. Stoyan, Y.G., Yas'kov, G.: A mathematical model and a solution method for the problem of placing various-sized circles into a strip. European Journal of Operational Research 156, 590–600 (2004)
3. He, Y., Wu, Y.: Packing non-identical circles within a rectangle with open length. J. Global Optim. (2012), doi:10.1007/s10898-012-9948-6
4. Huang: Greedy algorithms for packing unequal circles into a rectangular container. Journal of the Operational Research Society 56, 539–548 (2005)
5. Fu, Z., Huang, W., Zhipeng: Iterated tabu search for the circular open dimension problem. European Journal of Operational Research 225, 236–243 (2013)
6. Hifi, M., Paschos, V.T., Zissimopoulos, V.: A simulated annealing approach for the circular cutting problem. European Journal of Operational Research 159, 430–448 (2004)
7. Stoyan, Y.G., Yaskov, G.N.: Mathematical model and solution method of optimization problem of placement of rectangles and circles taking into account special constraints. International Transactions in Operational Research 5(1), 45–57 (1998)
8. Lü, Z.P., Hao, J.K.: Adaptive Tabu Search for course timetabling. European Journal of Operational Research 200(1), 235–244 (2010)
9. Maranas, C.D., Floudas, C.A., Pardalos, P.M.: New results in the packing of equal circles in a square. Discrete Mathematics 142(1), 287–293 (1995)
10. Huang, W.Q., Ye, T.: Greedy vacancy search algorithm for packing equal circles in a square. Operations Research Letters 38(5), 378–382 (2010)
11. Huang, W.Q., Ye, T.: Global optimization method for finding dense packings of equal circles in a circle. European Journal of Operational Research 210(3), 474–481 (2011)
12. Yang, X.-S.: A New Metaheuristic Bat-Inspired Algorithm. In: González, J.R., Pelta, D.A., Cruz, C., Terrazas, G., Krasnogor, N. (eds.) NICSO 2010. SCI, vol. 284, pp. 65–74. Springer, Heidelberg (2010)
13. Altringham, J.D.: Bats: Biology and Behaviour. Oxford Univesity Press (1996)
14. Pham, D.T., Ghanbarzadeh, A., Koc, E., Otri, S., Rahim, S., Zaidi, M.: The Bees Algorithm. Technical Note, Manufacturing Engineering Centre, Cardiff University, UK (2005)
15. Yang, X.-S., Deb, S.: Cuckoo search via Lévy flights. In: Proc. of World Congress on Nature & Biologically Inspired Computing (NaBIC 2009), India, pp. 210–214. IEEE Publications, USA (2009)
16. Yang, X.-S.: Firefly algorithm, Lévy flights and global optimization. In: Bramer, M., Ellis, R., Petridis, M. (eds.) Research and Development in Intelligent Systems XXVI, pp. 209–218. Springer, London (2010)
17. http://www.packomania.com

Protein Function Prediction Using Adaptive Swarm Based Algorithm

Archana Chowdhury[1], Amit Konar[1], Pratyusha Rakshit[1],
and Ramadoss Janarthanan[2]

[1] ETCE Department, Jadavpur University, Kolkata, India
[2] CSE Department, TJS College of Engineering, Chennai, India
{chowdhuryarchana,pratyushar1}@gmail.com,
konaramit@yahoo.co.in, srmjana_73@yahoo.com

Abstract. The center of attention of the research in bioinformatics has been towards understanding the biological mechanisms and protein functions. Recently high throughput experimental methods have provided many protein-protein interaction networks which need to be analyzed to provide an insight into the functional role of proteins in living organism. One of the important problems of post-genomic era is to predict the functions of unannotated proteins. In this paper we propose a novel approach for protein function prediction by utilizing the fact that most of the proteins which are connected in protein-protein interaction network, tend to have similar functions. The method randomly associates unannotated protein with functions from the possible set of functions. Our approach, Artificial Bee Colony with Temporal Difference Q-Learning (ABC-TDQL), then optimizes the score function which incorporates the extent of similarity between the set of functions of unannotated protein and annotated protein, to associate a function to an unannotated protein. The approach was utilized to predict protein function of Saccharomyces Cerevisiae and the experimental results reveal that our proposed method outperforms other algorithms in terms of precession, recall and F-value.

Keywords: Bioinformatics, protein function prediction, Protein – protein interaction network, annotated protein, Artificial Bee Colony algorithm, Temporal Difference Q- Learning.

1 Introduction

The presence of growing amount of data generated from the application of high throughput technologies in various genome projects has encouraged the need for computational techniques to provide understanding of such data. The recent initiation of proteomics technologies such as yeast two-hybrid or mass spectrometry [1] has allowed the construction of networks representing physical interactions among proteins which is known as protein-protein interaction networks (PPI). The introduction of high-throughput techniques have resulted in an amazing number of new proteins been identified. However, the function of a large number of these

B.K. Panigrahi et al. (Eds.): SEMCCO 2013, Part II, LNCS 8298, pp. 55–68, 2013.
© Springer International Publishing Switzerland 2013

proteins still remains unknown. For example, even the most-studied species, Saccharomyces Cerevisiae, is reported to have more than 26 percent of its proteome` with unknown molecular functions [2]. Discovering the functions of an uncharacterized protein can facilitate understanding the protein itself, which in turn can support the implementation of medical, diagnostic, or pharmacogenomic studies.

Several algorithms have been developed to predict protein functions, on the basic assumption that proteins with similar functions are more likely to interact. Among them, Deng proposed the Markov random field (MRF) model, which predicts protein functions based on the annotated proteins and the structure of the PPI network [3], [4]. Schwikowski proposed neighbor counting approach to predict the function of an unannotated protein based on the frequencies of the functions among its neighbors [5]. Hishigaki used a chi-square statistics [6] to calculate the significance of the functions of neighbors considering both directly and indirectly connected proteins. These two methods are based on the local graph and limit the annotations of an unknown protein by its interacting neighbors.

A number of computational approaches for protein function prediction have been developed over the years. These methods utilize different information to predict protein function. Earlier methodologies focus on estimating the function based on genomic sequence analysis, for example, analyzing sequence similarity between proteins listed in the databases [7] using programs[8], [9], using the gene fusion method or 'Rosetta stone' to infer yet unknown functions for protein[10], exploring the principle on similarity of phylogenetic trees for protein function prediction. With the development of high-throughput experimental techniques, various high-throughput biological data, such as microarray gene expression profiles and mutant phenotype, have also been used to assign functions to novel proteins [11], [12].

In recent years, more and more research turned to predicting protein functions semantically by combining the inter-relationships of function annotation terms in a scheme such as GO with the topological structure information in the PPI network.. The inter-relationships are usually represented as functional similarities between annotation terms in the annotation scheme. To predict protein functions semantically, various methods were proposed to calculate functional similarities between annotation terms [13]. For instance, Resink [14] used the concept of information content to calculate the semantic similarity between two GO terms. Jiang et al. [15] and Lin [16] improved Resink's method by scaling the similarity to a fixed range.

In this paper, we aim to predict the function of an unannotated protein by using the topographical information of PPI network and function of annotated protein. We have tried to analyze the effect of annotated proteins which are either directly or indirectly connected to unannotated protein. Though semantic similarity could have been used in the paper we have used GO based method for its simplicity to represent functional similarity. For this task we have employed the use of Artificial Bee Colony with Temporal Difference Q-Learning (ABC-TDQL) [22]. An adaptive memetic algorithm incorporates an adaptive selection of memes (units of cultural transmission) from a meme-pool to improve the cultural characteristics of the individual member of a population-based meta-heuristic search algorithm. ABC-TDQL provides a novel approach to design an adaptive memetic algorithm by utilizing the composite benefits of ABC for global search and TDQL for local refinement [17]. It is shown that ABC-TDQL with a modification of solution representation scheme can give very promising results if applied to the optimization problem.

The rest of this paper is organized as follows: Section 2 give a brief idea about the definition and formulation of the problem as well as the scheme for solution representation. Section 3 provides an overview of the Artificial Bee Colony with Temporal Difference Q-learning. Experiments and results are provided in Section 4. Section 5 concludes the paper.

2   Background of the Problem

2.1   Problem Definition

Let us consider a PPI network with N proteins. The PPI network is modeled as an undirected graph. The nodes in the graph characterize unique proteins and the interactions between them are represented by the edges. The PPI network can also be represented by a binary data matrix $Z_{N \times N}$ where $z_{ij}=z_{ji}=1$ indicates an interaction between proteins p_i and p_j while $z_{ij}=z_{ji}=0$ denotes absence of interaction among them. A diagrammatic representation of a PPI network is exemplified in Fig. 1(a) with 'p' as unannotated protein. The same network with six proteins is represented in the form of matrix Z of dimension 6×6 in Fig. 1(b).

However, there are evidences where functions of all proteins in the PPI network are not known and hence proteins remain functionally unannotated. Given the PPI data matrix $Z_{N \times N}$, a protein function prediction algorithm attempts to find a set of possible functions $F(p)$ of an unannotated protein p based on the functions $F(p')$ of all annotated proteins p' in the PPI network. In other words, both the topological structure of the PPI network and the functional information of the annotated proteins are used to predict the functions of unannotated ones. It is noteworthy that the protein function prediction should be in accordance to the principle that proteins interacting with each other are more likely to possess same functions.

In order to assign functions to unannotated protein p, first the function set $F(p')$ of each annotated protein p' is considered. The set of all possible functions in the network, excluding the unannotated protein p, is defined as $F= F(p_1)UF(p_2)U...UF(p_N)$ with $|F|=D$. A small illustration of the fact is given as follows. Let $F(p_1)=\{f_1, f_3\}$, $F(p_2)=\{f_1, f_5\}$, $F(p_3)=\{f_1, f_4\}$, $F(p_4)=\{f_1, f_2, f_5\}$ and $F(p_5)=\{f_1, f_3, f_4\}$. Hence $F=F(p_1)UF(p_2)UF(p_3)UF(p_4)UF(p_5)=\{f_1, f_2, f_3, f_4, f_5\}$. The objective is now to predict $F(p)$ from F given matrix Z in Fig. 1(b).

Since the functions can be assigned to the unannotated protein p in a number of ways satisfying the aforementioned condition, a fitness function (measuring the accuracy of the function prediction) must be defined. The problem now turns out to be an optimization problem of finding a set of functions $F(p)$ of optimal adequacy as compared to all other feasible sets of functions for unannotated protein p.

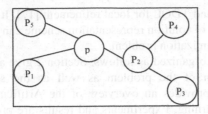

Fig. 1. (a). PPI network with ten proteins and 'p' as unannotated protein

Z=		p1	p2	p3	p4	p5	p
	p1	0	0	0	0	0	1
	p2	0	0	1	1	0	1
	p3	0	1	0	0	0	0
	p4	0	1	0	0	0	0
	p5	0	0	0	0	0	1
	p	1	1	0	0	1	0

Fig. 1. (b). Matrix representation of PPI network of Fig. 1(a)

2.2   Formulation of the Problem

The efficacy of protein function prediction can be improved by taking the composite benefit of the topological configuration of the PPI network and the functional categories of annotated proteins through Gene Ontology (GO). Here, the protein functions are annotated using GO terms. Any function f here is represented as a vector $\vec{f}$ of dimension K, with K as the number of GO terms in the network. The j-th element of the function vector $f_j \in \{0, 1\}$ indicates the occurrence of the GO notation term to annotate f. However, GO is basically represented as a directed acyclic hierarchical structure in which a GO term may have multiple parents/ancestor GO terms. Hence, if a function f is annotated by a GO term g, then f is also annotated with ancestor GO terms of g. Let us consider an example with five GO terms in the network and consider any function f being annotated by the fourth GO term with its ancestors being the second and third GO terms. There can be three possible arrangements of GO terms annotating function f (2, 3, 4) satisfying the stated condition. In Fig. 2 the three cases are shown. For each of the three circumstances, function f is represented by a vector $\vec{f}$ of dimension 5 as shown in Fig. 3.

With this representation scheme of protein functions, the similarity between a predicted function $f \in F(p)$ of unannotated protein p and a real function $f' \in F$ of the PPI network can be computed as follows.

$$sim(f,f') = \frac{\vec{f}.\vec{f'}}{\left\|\vec{f}\right\|\left\|\vec{f'}\right\|} \qquad (1)$$

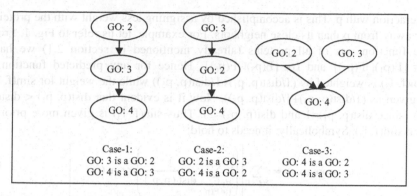

Case-1:   Case-2:   Case-3:
GO: 3 is a GO: 2   GO: 2 is a GO: 3   GO: 4 is a GO: 2
GO: 4 is a GO: 3   GO: 4 is a GO: 2   GO: 4 is a GO: 3

Fig. 2. Example of hierarchical arrangement of GO terms annotating a protein function

0	1	1	1	0

Fig. 3. Protein function encoding scheme in the proposed method

It is evident from (1) that $\text{sim}(f, f') = 1$ if $f = f'$. On the contrary, if there is no common GO term between f and f', $\text{sim}(f, f') = 0$. The adequacy of assigning a function f to unannotated protein p is evaluated by measuring a grade, denoted as $\text{score}(p, f)$. Three important facts are taken care for designing $\text{score}(p, f)$.

1. It assigns function f to protein p based on the similarity between f and all other protein functions available in the given network. This conforms to the fact that the proteins with similar functions interact more frequently to construct the PPI network. By way of explanation, let us consider (1) with predicted function $f \in F(p)$ and existing real function $f' \in F$. A high value of $\text{sim}(f, f')$ indicates a high functional correlation between the predicted and the real network function with most of the GO terms in common. It in turn signifies a high degree of certainty in assigning the function to unannotated protein p. Let us consider only one real function of the PPI network, represented by $f' = \{1, 0, 1, 1, 1\}$, for simple illustration and two alternatives of f, given as $f_1 = \{0, 1, 1, 1, 0\}$ and $f_2 = \{0, 1, 0, 1, 0\}$ respectively. From (1), we have $\text{sim}(f_1, f') = 2/(\sqrt{3} \times \sqrt{4}) = 0.577$ and $\text{sim}(f_2, f') = 1/(\sqrt{2} \times \sqrt{4}) = 0.3535$. If the same scenario follows for all other functions of the same PPI network, it implies a relatively higher confidence in inferring f_1 as a function of p than f_2. Consequently, considering the cumulative effects of all functions $f' \in F$

$$\text{score}(p, f) \propto \sum_{\forall f' \in F} \text{sim}(f, f') \tag{2}$$

2. The contribution of the function $f' \in F$ to annotate the protein p is not only dependent on the similarity measure with respect to the predicted function f. Instead, it will be more relevant to assign different weights for all $f' \in F$ depending upon the distance of protein p' from p, provided $f' \in F(p')$. Let this distance be symbolized by $\text{dist}(p, p')$. To improve the reliability on $\text{sim}(f, f')$, it is weighted by $1/\text{dist}(p, p')$, $\forall p'$ such that $f' \in F(p')$. The underlying premise is that proteins far away from p contribute less functional information than those having direct

interaction with p. This is accomplished by assigning less weight with the proteins far away from p than its close neighbors. For example, let us refer to Fig. 1. From the function sets of all proteins (already mentioned in section 2.1) we have $f_3 \in \{F(p_1) \cap F(p_5)\}$ and $f_4 \in \{F(p_3) \cap F(p_5)\}$. Hence for any predicted function f, $sim(f, f_3)$ is weighted by $(1/dist(p, p_1) + 1/dist(p, p_5))$ while the weight for $sim(f, f_4)$ is given as $(1/dist(p, p_3) + 1/dist(p, p_5))$. Now it is evident that $dist(p, p_1) < dist(p, p_3)$ (since $dist(p, p_1) = 1$ and $dist(p, p_3) = 2$). Thus $sim(f, f_3)$ is given more priority than $sim(f, f_4)$. Symbolically, it needs to hold:

$$score\,(p, f) \propto \sum_{\forall f' \in F} \left[\left(\sum_{\substack{\forall p', \\ f' \in F(p')}} \frac{1}{dist\,(p, p')} \right) \times sim\,(f, f') \right] \tag{3}$$

3. Intuitively, if a function f' is common to almost all proteins, i.e. almost all proteins in the dataset have the function f', we are more likely to believe that the unannotated protein also has the same function. Referring to section 2.1 and Fig. 1, we can infer that the possibility of assigning f_1 as a function of unannotated p is high. In order to accomplish this concept, the number of proteins having function f' is calculated and is denoted as $n_{f'}$. Then the function $f' \in F$ with high $n_{f'}$ is given more preference to annotate p. This is achieved by incorporating a term, $n_{f'}/N$, in the weight of $sim(f, f')$.

Considering the aforementioned points, the score of the unannotated protein being annotated by the predicted function f is evaluated by (4).

$$score\,(p, f) \propto \sum_{\forall f' \in F} \left[\left(\sum_{\substack{\forall p', \\ f' \in F(p')}} \frac{1}{dist\,(p, p')} \right) \times \frac{n_{f'}}{N} \times sim\,(f, f') \right] \tag{4}$$

2.3   Solution Representation and Cost Function Evaluation

In the proposed method for maximum D functions in the PPI network, consisting of N proteins, a solution $\vec{X}_i$ is a vector of dimension D. The entries of $\vec{X}_i$ belong to $\{0, 1\}$. The j-th parameter of $\vec{X}_i$ is interpreted as follows:

If $x_{i,j} = 1$, then the j-th function f_j is predicted as a function of protein p.   (5.a)
If $x_{i,j} = 0$, then f_j is not predicted as a function of protein p.   (5.b)

As an example, consider the solution encoding scheme in Fig. 4. Let there are D=8 functions available in the network among which, the second, third, fifth and seventh have been predicted as assigned functions of unannotated protein p.

0	1	1	0	1	0	1	0

Fig. 4. Solution encoding scheme in the proposed method

In order to judge the quality of the function prediction yielded by such a solution $\vec{X}_i$, the entire contribution by the set of predicted functions (denoted by set $F(p) = \{f_j| \ x_{i,j} = 1 \ \text{for} \ j = [1, D]\}$) to annotate protein p is used for fitness function evaluation. Symbolically,

$$\text{fit}(\vec{X}_i) = \sum_{\forall f \in F(p)} \text{score}(p, f) \tag{6}$$

3 An Overview of Artificial Bee Colony with Temporal Difference Q-Learning

The Artificial Bee Colony with Temporal Difference Q-Learning (ABC-TDQL) [22] includes an ABC (with NP employed and NP onlooker bees) for global exploration and a TDQL for adaptive selection of scale factors for the individual members of the ABC by accessing the Q-table. The row indices of the Q-table represent states S_1, S_2, ..., S_{NP} of the population (based on fitness measure) obtained from the last update of the Q-table. The column indices correspond to uniformly quantized values of the scale factors F_1, F_2, ..., F_{10} to be used in ABC. The steps of ABC-TDQL are given below.

1. Initialization: ABC-TDQL starts with a population of NP, D-dimensional food sources (solutions) $\vec{X}_i(G) = [x_{i,1}(G), x_{i,2}(G), ... x_{i,D}(G)]$ for i = [1, NP] at generation G=0 within the prescribed minimum and maximum bounds $\vec{X}_{min} = \{x_{min-1}, x_{min-2}, ... x_{min-D}\}$ and $\vec{X}_{max} = \{x_{max-1}, x_{max-2}, ... x_{max-D}\}$. Each food source $\vec{X}_i(G)$ is assigned a fitness value (nectar amount) $\text{fit}(\vec{X}_i(G))$. The entries for the Q-table are initialized as small values.

2. Adaptive Selection of Parameters of the ABC for Employed Bee Phase: The scale factor $F = F_j$ is randomly selected for individual food source from the meme pool $\{F_1, F_2, ..., F_{10}\}$ satisfying (6) with r as a random number between (0, 1).

$$\sum_{m=1}^{j-1} Q(S_i, 10F_m) \bigg/ \sum_{n=1}^{10} Q(S_i, 10F_n) < r \leq \sum_{m=1}^{j} Q(S_i, 10F_m) \bigg/ \sum_{n=1}^{10} Q(S_i, 10F_n) \tag{7}$$

3. Employed Bee Phase of Artificial Bee Colony: An employed bee produces a modification $\vec{X'}_i(G) = [x_{i,1}(G), x_{i,2}(G), ... x'_{i,j}(G), ... x_{i,D}(G)]$ on the position in her memory $\vec{X}_i(G) = [x_{i,1}(G), x_{i,2}(G), ..., x_{i,j}(G), ..., x_{i,D}(G)]$ and tests $\text{fit}(\vec{X'}_i(G))$. The value of $x'_{i,j}(G)$ parameter in $\vec{X'}_i(G)$ solution is computed using the following expression:

$$x'_{i,j}(G) = x_{i,j}(G) + 2 \times (F - 0.5) \times (x_{i,j}(G) - x_{k,j}(G)) \tag{8}$$

Here F is the scale factor in [0, 1] adaptively selected from the meme pool in step-2, j and k are randomly selected such that $j \in [1, D]$, $k \in [1, NP]$, $k \neq i$. The bee replaces $\vec{X}_i(G)$ by $\vec{X'}_i(G)$ if $\text{fit}(\vec{X'}_i(G)) > \text{fit}(\vec{X}_i(G))$.

4. Ranking of the Members and State Assignment: The food sources are sorted in descending order of probability of selection by onlooker bee as in (9).

$$\text{prob(i)} = \text{fit}(\vec{X}_i\,(G)) \Big/ \sum_{j=1}^{NP} \text{fit}(\vec{X}_j\,(G)), \forall i \qquad (9)$$

5. Reward/Penalty Based Q-table Updating: Let a member at state S_i on selection of F_j moves to a new state S_k. Then $Q(S_i, 10F_j)$ will be updated following (11) with

$$\text{reward}(S_i, 10F_j) = \begin{cases} \text{fit}(\vec{X}_i'(G)) - \text{fit}(\vec{X}_i(G)), & \text{if fit}(\vec{X}_i'(G)) > \text{fit}(\vec{X}_i(G)) \\ -K \text{ (however small)}, & \text{otherwise} \end{cases} \qquad (10)$$

$$Q(S_i, 10F_j) = (1-\alpha)Q(S_i, 10F_j) + \alpha(\text{reward}(S_i, 10F_j) + \gamma \max_{F'} Q(S_k, 10F')) \quad (11)$$

Here, the learning rate α determines to the extent the newly acquired information will override the old information and the discount factor γ determines the importance of future rewards.

6. Onlooker Bee Phase: Every onlooker bee probabilistically selects a food source from the population of the G-th iteration depending on the probability value associated with that food source, as calculated in (9). Next steps 2 to 5 are repeated.

7. Scout Bee Phase: The abandoned food source is reinitialized randomly by the scout.

8. Convergence: After each evolution, we repeat from step 2 until the termination condition is satisfied.

4   Experiments and Results

Protein-protein interaction data of Saccharomyces Cerevisiae were obtained from BIOGRID [19] database (http://thebiogrid.org/). To reduce the effect of noise, the duplicated interactions and self interactions were removed. The final dataset consists of 69,331 interaction protein pairs involving 5386 annotated proteins. The GO terms [20] and GO annotation dataset [21] used in the experiments were downloaded from Saccharomyces Genome Database (SGD). The GO consortium provides a structured standard vocabulary for describing the function of gene products. It is divided into three categories: biological process, molecular function and cellular component, represented by directed acyclic graphs in which nodes correspond to GO terms and edges to their relationships. For each protein, GO terms were extracted from SGD. We filtered out all regulatory relationships, and maintain only the is_a relationships resulting in 15 main functional categories for Saccharomyces Cerevisiae. The functional categories of Saccharomyces Cerevisiae are provided in Table 1.

Let $\{f_{r1}, f_{r2}, \ldots, f_m\}$ be the set of n real functions of protein p and $\{f_{p1}, f_{p2}, \ldots, f_{pm}\}$ denotes the set of m functions predicted by protein function assignment scheme. It is obvious that $1 \le m$, $n \le D$. To evaluate the effectiveness of our proposed method in inferring protein functions, as well as to compare the relative performance of our proposed technique with respect to other methods, three performance metrics are defined in (12) to (14).

$$Precision = \frac{\sum\limits_{j=1}^{m} \max\limits_{i=1}^{n}(sim(f_{r_i}, f_{p_j}))}{m} \qquad (12)$$

$$Recall = \frac{\sum\limits_{i=1}^{n} \max\limits_{j=1}^{m}(sim(f_{r_i}, f_{p_j}))}{n} \qquad (13)$$

$$F - value = \frac{2 \times Precision \times Recall}{Precision + Recall} \qquad (14)$$

Table 1. Gene Ontology classes used for annotating Saccharomyces Cerevisiae proteins

Serial Number	GO Term	Function Name
1	GO:0008150	Biological process
2	GO:0003674	Molecular function
3	GO:0005575	Cellular component
4	GO:0051169	Nuclear transport
5	GO:0003723	RNA binding
6	GO:0005198	Structural molecule activity
7	GO:0016020	Membrane
8	GO:0006974	Response to DNA damage stimulus
9	GO:0006520	Cellular amino acid metabolic process
10	GO:0005975	Carbohydrate metabolic process
11	GO:0006811	Ion transport
12	GO:0006325	Chromatin organization
13	GO:0007005	Mitochondrion organization
14	GO:0070925	Organelle assembly
15	GO:0006091	Generation of precursor metabolites and energy

A high value of each of these three metrics indicates superiority of an algorithm over others. The evaluation of theses metrics were conducted on test datasets with number of proteins in the network N= [20, 200] for a particular unannotated protein. Here, we have tested efficacy of our proposed method by predicting functions of some proteins with known functions and evaluating their results. The raw data set consists of 118,363 interactions involving 6593 Sacharomyces Cerevisea proteins, of which 75,748 interactions are unique. The dataset is pruned by removing unannotated protein, self-interactions and repeated interactions to obtain the final dataset which consists of 69,331 interaction pairs involving 5386 annotated proteins. So we have considered approximately 82% of proteins in Saccharomyces Cerevisiae. We have used only biological process for our experiment. Using the proposed method it was observed that 80% of functions were predicted accurately.

In our study, we have compared the relative performance of the proposed scheme with Differential Evolution with Temporal Difference Q-Learning (DE-TDQL) [17], ABC [18], and Differential Evolution (DE) [23]-based strategies with same fitness measure and also with the existing Neighbor Counting (NC) approach [24] in Table-3 and Fig. 6-8 for predicting functions of protein YKL181W. We employ the best parametric set-up for all these algorithms as prescribed in their respective sources and are represented in Table-2.

We report here results for only the above mentioned protein in order to save space. It is to be noted that the omitted results for different proteins follow a similar trend as those reported in Table-3 and Fig. 5-8. For all the evolutionary algorithm-based prediction schemes, the population size is kept at 50 and the maximum function evaluations (FEs) is set as 300000. We employ the best parametric set-up for NC as prescribed in [24]. The GO tree of the function for which result is being predicted is shown in Fig 5 where the leaf nodes represent the real function. It can be observed from Table 3 and Fig 5 that our proposed algorithm is able to predict comparatively more number of functions as well as more specific functions than other algorithms taken into consideration. It is evident from Table-3 and Fig. 5-8 that our algorithm outperforms others with respect to the aforementioned performance metrics irrespective of number of proteins in the network.

Table 2. Parameter tuning of different competitor algorithms

Parameters	Algorithms			
	DE	ABC	DE-TDQL	ABC-TDQL
Population Size	50	50	50	50
Crossover Ratio	0.9	×	0.9	×
Scale Factor	(0,2]	(0,1]	adaptive	adaptive
Limit Cycle	×	50	×	50
Learning Rate α	×	×	0.25	0.25
Discount Factor β	×	×	0.8	0.8

Table 3. Comparative analysis for predicting functions of YKL181W by various methods with N=80

Protein	Real Function	Real Functions Predicted by Different Algorithms				
		ABC-TDQL	DE-TDQL	ABC	DE	NC
YKL181W	GO:0006015	✓	✓	✓	×	×
	GO:0009156	✓	×	×	×	×
	GO:0009165	✓	×	✓	✓	✓
	GO:0016310	✓	✓	×	✓	×
	GO:0031505	✓	✓	✓	×	×
	GO:0044249	×	✓	×	✓	✓

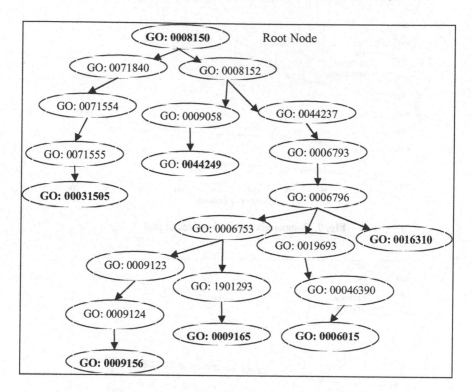

Fig. 5. GO tree of function used in result prediction

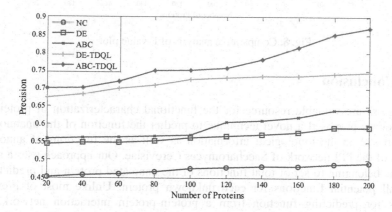

Fig. 6. Comparative analysis of precision plot

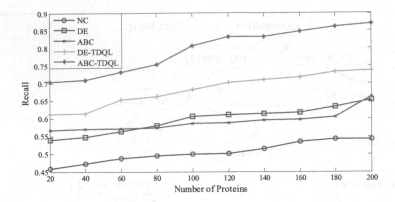

Fig. 7. Comparative analysis of recall plot

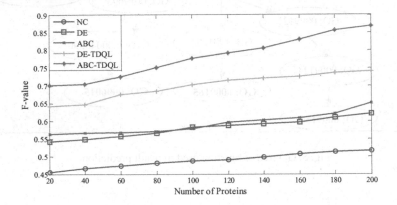

Fig. 8. Comparative analysis of F-value plot

5   Conclusion

PPI network are valuable resource for the functional characterization of protein. In this paper we proposed a novel technique to predict the function of the unannotated protein based on the topological information as well as the functions of annotated proteins of the PPI network of Saccharomyces Cerevisiae. Our approach uses a set of functions belonging to set of total functions of the annotated protein and predicts the set of all potential functions for each unknown protein. Unlike most of previous methods for predicting function from a protein-protein interaction network, our approach does not entirely depend on the assumption that two interacting proteins are likely to have the same function or share functions. Our algorithm achieves superior performances when compared with other state-of-the-art approaches. Recent advances in bioinformatics have generated an explosive amount of biological data, so one of the future directions of research may be to integrate the heterogeneous data sources to generate more reliable resources for function prediction.

References

[1] Shoemaker, B.A., Panchenko, A.R.: Deciphering protein-protein interactions. Part i. Experimental techniques and databases. PLoS Computational Biology 3(3), 337–344 (2007)

[2] Breitkreutz, B.J., et al.: The BioGRID Interaction Database: 2008 Update. Nucleic Acids Research 36(Database issue), D637–D640 (2008)

[3] Deng, M.H., Zhang, K., Mehta, S., Chen, T., Sun, F.Z.: Prediction of protein function using protein-protein interaction data. Journal of Computational Biology 10(6), 947–960 (2003)

[4] Deng, M.H., Chen, T., Sun, F.Z.: An integrated probabilistic model for functional prediction of proteins. Journal of Computational Biology 11(2-3), 463–475 (2004)

[5] Schwikowski, B., Uetz, P., Field, S.: A network of protein-protein interactions in yeast. Nature Biotechnology 18, 1257–1261 (2000)

[6] Hishigaki, H., Nakai, K., Ono, T., Tanigami, A., Takagi, T.: Assessment of predition accuracy of protein function from protein-protein interaction data. Yeast 18, 523–531 (2001)

[7] Hodgman, T.C.: A historical perspective on gene/protein functional assignment. Bioinformatics 16, 10–15 (2000)

[8] Pearson, W.R., Lipman, D.J.: Improved tools for biological sequence comparison. Proc. Natl. Acad. Sci. U. S. A. 85, 2444–2448 (1988)

[9] Wu, L.F., Hughes, T.R., Davierwala, A.P., Robinson, M.D., Stoughton, R., Altschuler, S.J.: Large-scale prediction of Saccharomyces cerevisiae gene function using overlapping transcriptional clusters. Nat. Genet. 31, 255–265 (2002)

[10] Marcotte, E.M., Pellegrini, M., Ng, H.L., Rice, D.W., Yeates, T.O., Eisenberg, D.: Detecting protein function and protein-protein interactions from genome sequences. Science 285, 751–753 (1999)

[11] Deane, C.M., Salwinski, L., Xenarios, I., Eisenberg, D.: Protein interactions: two methods for assessment of the reliability of high throughput observations. Mol. Cell Proteomics 1, 349–356 (2002)

[12] Brown, M.P., Grundy, W.N., Lin, D., Cristianini, N., Sugnet, C.W., Furey, T.S., Ares Jr., M., Haussler, D.: Knowledge-based analysis of microarray gene expression data by using support vector machines. Proc. Natl. Acad. Sci. U. S. A. 97, 262–267 (2000)

[13] Chen, G., Wang, J., Li, M.: GO semantic similarity based analysis for huaman protein interactions. In: Proceedings of 2009 International Joint Conference on Bioinformatics, Systems Biology and Intelligent Computing, pp. 207–210 (2009)

[14] Resnik, P.: Using information content to evaluate semantic similarity in a taxonomy. In: Proceedings of International Joint Conference for Artificial Intelligence, pp. 448–453 (1995)

[15] Jiang, J., Conrath, D.: Semantic similarity based on corpus statistics and lexical taxomy. In: Proceedings of International Conference Research on Computational Linguistics, pp. 19–33 (1997)

[16] Lin, D.: An information-theoretic definition of similarity. In: Proceedings of the Fifteenth International Conference on Machine Learning, pp. 296–304 (1998)

[17] Bhowmik, P., Rakshit, P., Konar, A., Nagar, A.K., Kim, E.: DE-TDQL: an adaptive memetic algorithm. In: Congress on Evolutionary Computation, pp. 1–8 (June 2012)

[18] Bhattacharjee, P., Rakshit, P., Goswami, I., Konar, A., Nagar, A.K.: Multi-robot path-planning using artificial bee colony optimization algorithm. In: NaBIC 2011, pp. 219–224 (2011)

[19] Stark, C., Breitkreutz, B.J., Reguly, T., Boucher, L., Breitkreutz, A., Tyers, M.: BioGRID: a general repository for interaction datasets. Nucleic Acids Res. 34, D535–D539 (2006)

[20] Ashburner, M., Ball, C., Blake, J., Botstein, D., Butler, H., Cherry, J., Davis, A., Dolinski, K., Dwight, S., Eppig, J.: Gene ontology: tool for the unification of biology. Nature Genetics 25, 25–29 (2000)

[21] Dwight, S., Harris, M., Dolinski, K., Ball, C., Binkley, G., Christie, K., Fisk, D., Issel Tarver, L., Schroeder, M., Sherlock, G.: Saccharomyces Genome Database (SGD) provides secondary gene annotation using the Gene Ontology (GO). Nucleic Acids Research 30, 69–72 (2002)

[22] Rakshit, P., Konar, A., Das, S., Nagar, A.K.: ABC-TDQL: AN Adaptive Memetic Algorithm. In: 2013 IEEE Symposium Series on Computational Intelligence, Singapore (accepted, to be published, 2013)

[23] Storn, R., Price, K.V.: Differential evolution–A simple and efficient adaptive scheme for global optimization over continuous spaces. Institute of Company Secretaries of India, Chennai, Tamil Nadu. Tech. Report TR-95-012 (1995)

[24] Schwikowski, B., Uetz, P., Fields, S.: A network of protein-protein interactions in yeast. Nature Biotechnology 18, 1257–1261 (2000)

Reduction of Bullwhip Effect in Supply Chain through Improved Forecasting Method: An Integrated DWT and SVM Approach

Sanjita Jaipuria and S.S. Mahapatra

Department of Mechanical Engineering
National Institute of Technology
Rourkela,769008, Odisha, India
{sanjita.jaipuria,mahapatrass2003}@gmail.com

Abstract. In a supply chain, forecasting method directly influences the bullwhip effect (BWE) and net-stock amplification (NSAmp) which adversely impact on performance of supply chain. However, such adverse effects can be moderated through use of realistic and accurate demand forecasting models. In the present study, an integrated approach of discrete wavelet transforms (DWT) analysis and least-square support vector machine (LSSVM) is proposed for demand forecasting. Initially, the proposed DWT-LSSVM model is tested and validated using a data set from open literature. A comparative study between Autoregressive Integrated Moving Average (ARIMA) and proposed model has been made. Further, the model is tested with demand data collected from two different manufacturing firms. It is observed that proposed model outperforms ARIMA model in respect to accurate estimation of demand and reduce BWE.

Keywords: Supply chain unscertainty, Bullwhip effect, ARIMA, Discrete wavelets, Least-square support vector machine.

1 Introduction

Identification of sources of uncertainties within a supply chain and finding remedial measures after a thorough analysis is considered as a crucial activity for the improvement of supply chain performance [1, 2]. One of the major adverse effects of uncertainty is the amplification of order in the upward stream of a supply chain termed as bullwhip effect (BWE) [3, 4, 5]. Five major causes can be assigned to bullwhip effect. They are demand forecasting, order batching, price fluctuations, supply shortages and non-zero lead-time and BWE can be reduced through controlling these causes [6, 7]. Among the five causes, accurate demand forecasting is one of the most challenging tasks for the researchers as well as the practitioners. Generally, demand follows a time series pattern and various time series models can be explored to mitigate the BWE. Wright et al. [8] have analysed the impact of ordering policy and forecasting method (Holt and Brown's models) on BWE through simulating a four stage supply chain. Luong [9] has examined the effect of autoregressive coefficient and lead time on BWE for a two stage supply chain

B.K. Panigrahi et al. (Eds.): SEMCCO 2013, Part II, LNCS 8298, pp. 69–84, 2013.
© Springer International Publishing Switzerland 2013

employing base-stock inventory control policy using first order autoregressive model AR(1). Further, the model is modified for higher order autoregressive model AR (p) [10]. Chen et al. [11] have employed the exponential smoothing forecasting method to quantify BWE for a two stage supply chain. Hong et al. [12] have compared the AR (1) stationary demand process with moving average (MA), exponentially weighted moving average (EWMA) and mean square error-optimal (MSE-optimal) for two stage supply chain employed with order-up-to-level policy to analyse the influence of three forecasting techniques on BWE. Zhang [13] have studied the effect of autoregressive moving average (ARMA) parameters on BWE. Bandyopadhyay et al. [14] have formulated generalized expression to evaluate BWE for five different replenishment policies like, $(R, \hat{D})$, $(R, \gamma O)$, (R, S), $(R, \beta IP)$ and $(R, \gamma O, \beta IP)$ using autoregressive moving average ARMA (p, d) with fixed lead time. Duc et al. [15] have further improved this model to autoregressive integrated moving average ARIMA (1, 1) process and investigated the influence of autoregressive coefficients, moving average parameters and lead time on BWE. It is concluded that BWE exists only when the autoregressive coefficient is higher than the moving average parameter. Gilbert [16] has proposed generalized expression for quantifying the BWE representing the demand with ARIMA time series process for a multistage supply chain. It is proved that BWE is high when lead time is long and demand is autocorrelated. It has also been reported that BWE depends only on the total of lead times not on number of stages in a multistage supply chains. Boute et al.[17] tested different demand forecasting methods like MA, exponential smoothing (ES), minimum mean square error MMSE for order-up-to-level policy in a two stage supply chain and reported that reduction in BWE (dampening the order variability) may lead to adverse effect on the inventory holding cost and customer service level. ARIMA time series model is mainly suitable for linear time series behaviour. In real time series, data is generally followed with a non-linear pattern. Support vector machine (SVM) is a self-learning technique which possesses the capability to recognise the pattern of a given data series and ability for non-linear prediction. The technique is proposed by Vapnik [18] and further adopted in various area of research for prediction [19, 20, 21, 22, 23, 24, 25, 26, 27]. SVM is based on the unique theory of the structural risk minimization principle to estimate a function by minimizing an upper bound of the generalization error. It is hardly affected from the over-fitting problem and finally produces a high generalized performance. Another major property of SVM is that training SVM is equivalent to solving a linearly constrained quadratic programming problem so that the solution of SVM is always unique and globally optimal. A proficient forecasting model should have the ability to recognise the pattern i.e. can capture the variation based on time domain. Wavelet transform theory is a mathematical tool which provides information about a given data series based on time domain and frequency domain. Hence, recently wavelet theory is adopted as a special tool along with the forecasting model to capture the variation in data series in a better manner [28, 29, 30, 31, 32].

This research proposes an integrated approach of discrete wavelet theory (DWT) and least square-support vector machine (LSSVM) to enhance the accuracy of the forecasting model so that performance of supply chain can be improved by reducing the BWE. The proposed integrated approach denoted as DWT-LSSVM model can be used for demand forecasting when data series is non-stationary and non-linear. In order to validate the proposed model, a comparative study has been performed between ARIMA and proposed model considering an example data set from open literature. Three case studies from manufacturing firms dealing with different products and operating under different environmental conditions are considered. The forecasting performance of the DWT-LSSVM model is compared with ARIMA model through estimating the mean square error (MSE) value. It is observed that MSE value is comparatively less in case of DWT-LSSVM model. A better forecasting model leads to reduction in BWE and net stock amplification (NSAmp). To prove this further, order quantities are determined by implementing the base-stock policy for the considered cases and BWE and NSAmp values are estimated.

2   The Time Series Model

In a time series model, times varying past values are taken into account to develop the model for prediction. The time series model can be mathematically represented by Eq. (1).

$$X_{t+1} = f_\theta \left(x_t + x_{t-1} + ... + x_{t-N+1} \right) \tag{1}$$

where, x_{t+1} is the unknown value to be predicted from the current and past value of the variable x.

There are many time series forecasting models are available for predicting demand. The autoregressive process (AR) of order p denoted as AR (p) is presented in Eq. (2) where Y_t is the forecasted demand for period t and $Y_{t-1}, Y_{t-2}, ..., Y_{t-p}$ are the time lagged values of the demand variable (Y). The moving average (MA) model of order q can be represented by the Eq. (3). The combination of AR and MA process is known as ARMA (p, q). A typical ARMA (p, q) model can be mathematically represented by Eq.(4). However, ARMA model has the limitation that it can be applied to predict stationary data series. In order to make prediction from non-stationary data series, the ARMA model is extended by allowing differencing to convert the data series into stationary form and called ARIMA model [33]. A data series may contain seasonal effect. Thus the non-seasonal ARIMA process can be denoted as ARIMA (p, d, q) whereas seasonal one is represented as ARIMA (p, d, q) (P, D, Q)$_s$. The ARIMA(1,1,1) process can be represented through Eq.(5) and ARIMA(1,1,1)(1,1,1) can be given by Eq.(6) [34].

$$Y_t = c + \phi_1 Y_{t-1} + \phi_2 Y_{t-2} + ... + \phi_p Y_{t-p} + e_t \tag{2}$$

$$Y_t = c - \theta_1 e_{t-1} - \theta_2 e_{t-2} - ... - \theta_p e_{t-q} + e_t \tag{3}$$

$$Y_t = c + \phi_1 Y_{t-1} + \phi_2 Y_{t-2} + ... + \phi_p Y_{t-p} - \theta_1 e_{t-1} - \theta_2 e_{t-2} - ... - \theta_q e_{t-q} + e_t \tag{4}$$

$$Y_t = c + (1 + \phi_1) Y_{t-1} - \phi_1 Y_{t-2} + e_t - \theta_1 e_{t-1} \tag{5}$$

$$Y_t = c + (1+\phi_1)Y_{t-1} - \phi_1 Y_{t-2} + (1+\Phi_1)Y_{t-12} - (1+\phi_1+\Phi_1+\phi_1\Phi_1)Y_{t-13} + (\phi_1+\phi_1\Phi_1)$$
$$Y_{t-14} - \Phi_1 Y_{t-24} + (\Phi_1+\phi_1\Phi_1)Y_{t-25} - \phi_1\Phi_1 Y_{t-26} + e_t - \theta_1 e_{t-1} - \Theta_1 e_{t-12} + \theta_1\Theta_1 e_{t-13}$$

$$(6)$$

where,

p = non-seasonal order of the autoregressive part
d = non-seasonal degree of differencing involved
q = non-seasonal order of moving average part
P = seasonal order of the autoregressive part
D = seasonal degree of differencing involved
Q = seasonal order of moving average part
s = number of period per season
c = constant term
ϕ_j = non-seasonal j^{th} autoregressive parameter
θ_j = non-seasonal j^{th} moving average parameter
e_{t-q} = error term at t-q
e_t = error term at time t
Φ_j = seasonal j^{th} autoregressive parameter
Θ_j = seasonal j^{th} moving average parameter

3   Proposed Model

Generally, forecasting models are based on the past data pattern. For improving the forecasting accuracy, the model should have the ability to capture the past data pattern. Wavelet transform (WT) analysis is a powerful mathematical tool has the capability to provide the data information based on time and frequency domain. Wavelets are the small waves located in different time domain and frequency. The mathematical representation of wavelet is shown in Eq. (7).

$$\int_{\infty}^{\infty} \psi(t)\,dt = 0 \qquad (7)$$

While WT analysis deals with continuous sample of data, it is known as continuous wavelet transforms (CWT). The wavelet analysis is efficient and capable of retaining accuracy when the scaling factor a and shifting factor τ of the basic wavelet function (also called mother wavelet designated as $\psi_{a,\tau}$) is limited to only discrete values. This process is known as discrete wavelet transformation (DWT). In case of DWT, wavelets are discretely sampled. Recently, WT has been widely used as an efficient computational technique for extracting information about non-stationary signals [35, 36].

If $a = a_0^j, \tau = ka_0^j\tau_0, a_0 > 0, \tau_0 \in R, \forall j,k = 0,1,2,3,\dots,m \in Z$ then

$\left(\psi_{a,\tau}(t)\right)$ can be rewritten as follows:

$$\psi_{j,k}(t) = a_0^{-j/2}\psi\left[a_0^{-j}\left(t - ka_0^j\tau_0\right)\right] = a_0^{-j/2}\psi\left(a_0^{-j}t - k\tau_0\right) \qquad (8)$$

Therefore, DWT can be expressed through Eq. (9)

$$W_f(j,k) = a_0^{-j/2} \int_{-\infty}^{+\infty} f(t)\psi \times \left(a_0^{-j}t - k\tau_0\right)dt \qquad (9)$$

The most efficient and simple way of choosing position and scale value is power of two form logarithm called dyadic scale and position i.e. $a_0=2$, $\tau_0=1$. Then DWT becomes change to binary form and it can be defined by Eq. (10).

$$W_f(j,k) = 2^{-j/2} \int_{-\infty}^{+\infty} f(t)\psi \times \left(2^{-j}t - k\right)dt \qquad (10)$$

where, $W_f(a,\tau)$ and $W_f(j,k)$ reflects the characteristics of original time series in frequency (a or j) and time domain (τ or k). While a or j is small, the frequency resolution is very low but the time domain is very high. When a or j become large, the frequency resolution is high but time domain is low. In a discrete time series f (t) in which f (t) occurs at the discrete integer time steps t, the dyadic discrete wavelet transformation can be written as Eq. (11).

$$W_f(j,k) = \sum_{j,k \in z} f(t) 2^{-j/2} \psi \left(2^{-j}t - k\right) \qquad (11)$$

The original input signal can be reconstructed using Eq. (12).

$$f(t) = \sum_{j,k \notin z} W_f(j,k)\psi_{j,k}(t) \qquad (12)$$

The wavelet coefficients $W_f(j,k)$ are decomposed into two parts-an approximation (or low frequency) coefficient (cA_n) at level-n through a low pass-filter $l(\psi_{i\,k}(t))$, and detail (or high frequency) coefficients ($cD_1,cD_2,cD_3,...,cD_n$) at different levels of $1,2,...,n$ through the high-pass filter $h(\psi_{i,k}(t))$ as given in Eq.(13). (cA_n) at level-n provides background information on the original data through low pass filter and detail coefficients ($cD_1,cD_2,cD_3,...,cD_n$) at different levels of $1,2,...,n$ contains the detail information such as period, break and jump using high pass filter. The original signal can be expressed through Eq. (13).

$$f(t) = cA_n l\left(\psi_{i,k}(t)\right) + \sum_{n=1} cD_n h\left(\psi_{i,k}(t)\right) \qquad (13)$$

The Eq. (13) can be represented in simplified way through Eq. (14).

$$f(t) = cA_n(t) + \sum cD_n(t) \qquad (14)$$

Daubechies wavelet family is usually written as 'dbN' where, db is the 'surname', and N is the order of wavelet [26]. For example db5 represents decomposition of original data into five levels using Daubechies wavelet family, it provide approximation coefficient as cA_5 and detail coefficient of $cD_1,cD_2,...,cD_5$. For DWT analysis Daubechies wavelet family has been used here. The subseries of approximations and details so obtained are used as inputs to LSSVM model for prediction. The support vector machine (SVM) is a learning machine based on statistical theory. It has the ability to predict both linear and non-linear data series by mapping. The formulation of LS-SVM for prediction can be presented as follows [37]:

Consider a given training data set {x_i, y_i}, i=1, 2... N, where, $x_i \in R$ is the input data series and $y_i \in R$ is the output data set. The following regression model can be constructed by using non-linear mapping function $\phi(x)$ Eq. (15).

$$y = w^T \phi(x) + b \tag{15}$$

The quadratic loss function is used for LSSVM goal optimization, while inequality constraints into equality constraints. Therefore, the optimization problem becomes as follows:

$$\min \ C(w,e) = \frac{1}{2} w^T w + \frac{1}{2} \gamma \sum_{i=1}^{N} e_i^2 \tag{16}$$

where, w-weight vector and b-the bias term, γ - penalty factor and e_i-loss function(regression error).

subject to equality constraints

$$y = w^T \phi(x_i) + b + e_i \quad i=1, 2... N \tag{17}$$

SVM minimizes the cost function C containing a penalized regression error. The first part of the cost function (Eq. 16) is a weight decay which is used to regularize weight sizes and penalize large weights. Due to regularization, the weights converge to fixed values. Large weights fail the generalization ability of the LSSVM because they can have excessive variance. The second part of Eq. (16) is the regression error for all training data and the regularization parameter γ, which has to be optimized by the user, gives the relative weight of this part as compared to the first part. The constraint shown by Eq. (17) gives the definition of regression error. To solve this optimization problem, Lagrange function is constructed as (Eq. (18)):

$$L(w,b,e,\alpha) = \frac{1}{2} \|w\|^2 + \gamma \sum_{i=1}^{N} e_i^2 - \sum_{i=1}^{N} \alpha_i \left\{ w^T \phi(x_i) + b + e_i - y_i \right\} \tag{18}$$

where, α_i are the Lagrange multipliers, $\gamma > 0$, α_i,b can be calculated based on Karush-Kuhn-Tucker(KKT) conditions. So LSSVM model for nonlinear system becomes:

$$y_i = w.\phi(x) + b = \sum_{i=1}^{k} \alpha_i k(x_i, x) + b \tag{19}$$

where, $k(x, x_i) = \phi(x)^T \phi(x_i)$ is the kernel function

There are different types of kernel functions like linear kernel, polynomial kernel, radial basis function kernel (RBF_kernel) and multilayer perceptron kernel in LSSVM analysis to map train data into kernel space. In this research work the RBF_kernel has been used, this can be mathematically represented as Eq. (20):

$$K(x_i, x_j) = \exp\left(-\frac{\|x_i - x_j\|^2}{\sigma_{sv}^2}\right) \tag{20}$$

where, σ_{sv}^2 is the squared variance of the Gaussian function. To obtained support vector it should be optimized by user. In order to achieve good generalized model it is very important to make a careful selection for the tuning parameters like α and γ.

Throughout the LSSVM analysis radial basis kernel function has been used as kernel function, to find the minimum cost value in space the optimization function 'grid-search' has been used and for estimating the model parameters 'crossvalidate function' has been used.

4   Model Validation

To validate and assess the performance of proposed DWT-LSSVM model, an example data set (monthly sales data for printing and writing paper between the year 1963 and 1972) is considered [34]. A time series plot is shown in Figure 1. From Figure 1, it can be observed that data series is non-stationary in nature as the data points are not horizontally scattered around a constant mean. Then ACF and PACF plot are analysed. It is found that data series is non-stationary and possesses seasonal effect. To convert the data series into stationary form, first it is seasonally differentiated by lag-12. To test the existence of non-stationary/stationary time series plot is plotted for the resultant data series and found resultant data series is still non-stationary. Therefore, to make stationary the resultant data series is non-seasonally differenced with lag-1, the resultant time series plot is shown in Figure 2. From the Figure 2, it is identified that resultant data series is stationary. Next, ACF and PACF plots are plotted to identify the order of autoregressive (AR) and moving average (MA) terms from Figure 3 and Figure 4 respectively. From the plots, it can be concluded that large number of spikes seems to be significant. Hence, the model identified is ARIMA $(p, 1, q) (P, 1, Q)_{12,}$ and the parameters p, q, P and Q are yet to be determined. Therefore, randomly fourteen different model settings are selected for analysis purpose. In Table.1, fourteen models are listed by varying the value of p, q, P and Q with forecasted mean square error (MSE) for twenty-four months ahead.

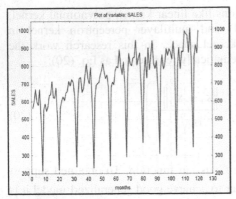

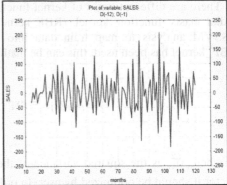

Fig. 1. Time series plot of sales data for example dataset

Fig. 2. ACF plot of differenced sales data for example dataset

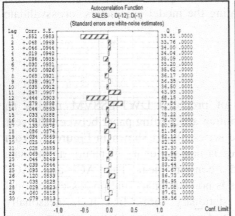

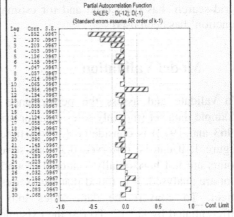

Fig. 3. ACF plot of differenced sales data for example dataset

Fig. 4. PACF plot of differenced sales data for example dataset

Further, the original dataset is applied to DWT and decomposed into five levels using the wavelet family db4. The resulting approximation data subseries (cA5) and five detail data subseries (cD1, cD2... cD5) are shown pictorially in Figure 5. The whole data contained in these subseries are divided into training and testing part. Training part contained 96-month of data i.e. 80% of whole data set and testing part is contained with 24-months (20%). Initially, the training data is used to train the LSSVM model and obtained the optimal model parameters setting as described in the Table 1. Then, the testing data is applied to LSSVM model to predict the 24-months of data with model parameter setting as described in Table.1and MSE value is estimated. From Table 1, it can be observed that the MSE value estimated for the predicted data set using DWT-LSSVM model is much less than all the selected fourteen ARIMA models. This signifies DWT-LSSVM is a better forecasting model than the ARIMA. To test the performance of DWT-LSSVM model suitable for any type of data series, two demand patterns from two different firms has been considered as case studies.

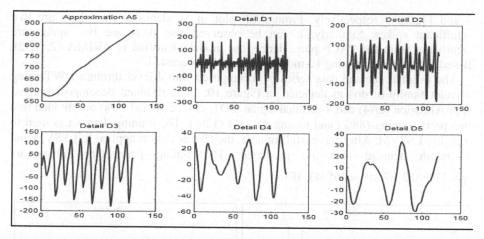

Fig. 5. Decomposed data series of sales data for example dataset

Table 1. ARIMA models and DWT-LSSVM model for example dataset

MODELS	MSE	MODELS	MSE
ARIMA(0,1,1)(0,1,1)$_{12}$	5248.200	ARIMA(0,1,1)(1,1,0)$_{12}$	9587.796
ARIMA(1,1,1)(0,1,1)$_{12}$	5477.935	ARIMA(1,0,1)(0,1,2)$_{12}$	5792.225
ARIMA(0,1,2)(0,1,1)$_{12}$	5490.433	ARIMA(1,1,1)(1,1,0)$_{12}$	9979.237
ARIMA(0,1,1)(0,1,2)$_{12}$	5262.050	ARIMA(1,1,0)(0,1,1)$_{12}$	7963.264
ARIMA(0,1,1)(1,1,1)$_{12}$	5272.198	ARIMA(0,1,1)(0,1,0)$_{12}$	13884.479
ARIMA(0,1,3)(0,1,1)$_{12}$	5416.394	ARIMA(1,1,0)(1,1,0)$_{12}$	15529.235
ARIMA(1,1,1)(1,1,1)$_{12}$	5505.864	ARIMA(1,1,0)(0,1,1)$_{12}$	25091.383

DWT-LSSVM   7.267

Training data set = 80% (96 months), Testing data set = 20% (24 months),
DWT (Db4, 5 layer decomposition), γ =576676.98, σ^2 = 6373154.086

5   Case Studies

Case I: ABC Pvt. Ltd.
ABC Pvt. Ltd. is situated in the Eastern part of India dealing with automotive parts and accessories and supplies to majors automobile companies in India. Its annual turnover is 871000 USD. One of its major products is fan shroud and its demand is difficult to predict. The demand data of fan shroud for 96-months (April 2005-March 2013, 8 years) is collected and to plotted in Figure 6 to identify the demand pattern. Next, to examine the existence of seasonality and non-stationary in data series ACF and PACF graphs are plotted. From the plot, it is identified that data series is non-stationary and possesses no seasonal effect. To make the data series stationary, it is differenced with lag-1 as shown in Figure 7. From Figure 7, it can be observed that it is stationary in nature. Further, ACF and PACF plots are plotted as shown in Figure

8 and Figure 9 respectively. From ACF plot, it is identified that there are two significant spikes. Similarly, it can be observed that there are two spikes are significant from the PACF plot. Hence, the model identified is ARIMA (2, 1, 2). Based on this model setting 12-months demand is forecasted.

The original demand data series is decomposed into 4-level through DWT using wavelet family of db4 as depicted in Figure 10. The resultant decomposed signal approximation (cA4) and 4-detailed signal (cD1, cD2, cD3 and cD4) are divided into two parts training (88%) and testing data set (12%). The training data set is used to train the LSSVM. After successful training, the testing data is applied to LSSVM and 12-month demand data are predicted. The tuning parameters values are $\gamma = 3778865.67$ $\sigma^2 = 265043.383$.

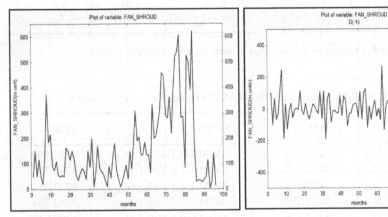

Fig. 6. Time series plot for ABC Pvt. Ltd   **Fig. 7.** Differenced time series plot for ABC Pvt. Ltd

Case II: MNO Pvt. Ltd.

MNO Pvt. Ltd. is a well-known steel processing industry of India and its plants are located in different parts of the country. The annual turnover of the company is 335 million dollars. The demand data from January 2009 to February 2013 collected from a plant located in southern part of India in metric ton per month. A similar procedure discussed in above case studies is followed to identify the model from this data series. The time series plot is shown in Figure 11 this signifies non-stationary nature of data. Next, ACF and PACF plots are plotted for the original data series and found that there is no seasonal effect and it is non-stationary in nature. From the time series plot, it can be observed that the resultant differenced series is non-stationary so again it is differenced with lag-1. The time series plot for the double differenced data series is shown in Figure-12. Further, ACF and PACF plots are plotted for the resultant data series as shown in Figures 13 and Figure14 respectively. From the ACF plot, it can be observed that there is significant lag at lag-1. From PACF, most significant lag is observed at lag-1 and lag-2. Therefore, the ARIMA model identified is ARIMA (2, 2, 1). Using this parameters setting, 12-months demand is forecasted.

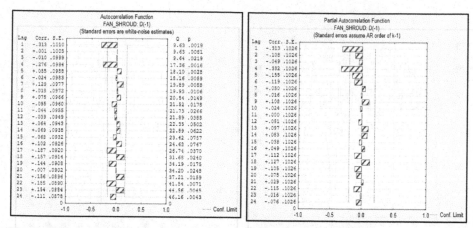

Fig. 8. ACF plot of data series differenced by lag-1 for ABC Pvt. Ltd

Fig. 9. PACF plot of data series differenced by lag-1 for ABC Pvt. Ltd

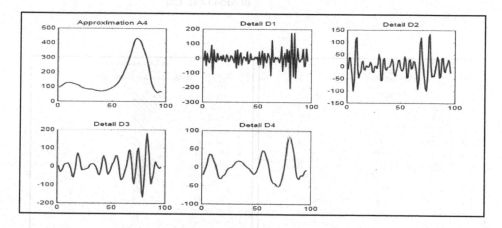

Fig. 10. Decomposed data series for ABC Pvt. Ltd

The original demand data series is decomposed into 3-level through DWT using wavelet family of db4 as depicted in Figure 15. Similar to case-I the resultant decomposed signal approximation (cA3) and 3-detailed signal (cD1, cD2, and cD3) are divided into two parts training (76%) and testing data set (24%). The training data set is used to train the LSSVM. After successful training, the testing data is applied to LSSVM and 12-month demand data are predicted. The tuning parameters values are $\gamma = 128689932$ $\sigma^2 = 7145220115$.

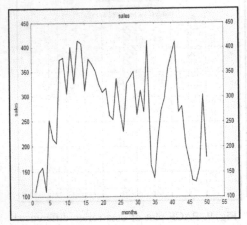

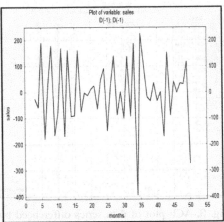

Fig. 11. Time series plot for MNO Pvt. Ltd.   **Fig. 12.** Double differenced time series data of MNO Pvt. Ltd

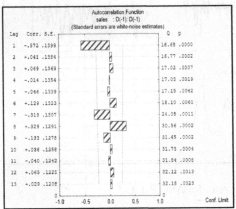

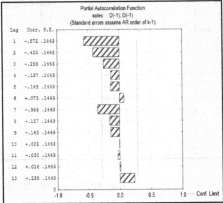

Fig. 13. PACF plot of double differenced time series data of MNO Pvt. Ltd   **Fig. 14.** PACF plot of double differenced time series data of MNO Pvt. Ltd

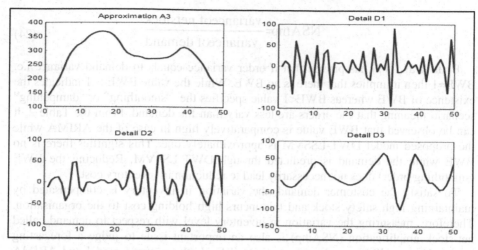

Fig. 15. Decomposed series of data of MNO Pvt. Ltd

6   Results and Discussions

Using Eq. (21), the forecast errors are estimated from the forecasted demand value estimated from both ARIMA and DWT-LSSVM as described in Table 2. From the Table 2, it can be observed that the MSE values for DWT-LSSVM model are comparatively very less than that of ARIMA model. Hence, it can be agreed that the proposed model DWT-LSSVM has high forecasting accuracy. From previous literature, it has been proved that a better forecasting model always moderate the BWE [6]. To validate this further, the order quantities (or production quantities) are estimated using the Eq. (22) applying base-stock-policy [9, 10, 13] in which lead time (L) and review period (R) is taken as one period. $\hat{D}_t^L$ is the forecasted demand during the lead time L at time period t, $\hat{D}_{t-1}^L$ is the demand during the lead time L at t-1 and $\hat{D}_{t-1}^L$ represents the actual demand at time period t-1. Using the estimated order quantity q_t, the BWE is estimated for all the considered cases using Eq. (23). The estimated BWE are given in Table 2 for the two cases.

$$MSE = \frac{(\text{actual demand - forecasted demand})^2}{\text{number of forecasted period}}$$ (21)

$$q_t = \left(\hat{D}_t^L - \hat{D}_{t-1}^L \right) + D_{t-1}$$ (22)

$$BWE = \frac{\text{variance of order}}{\text{variance of demand}}$$ (23)

$$NSAmp = \frac{variance\,of\,netstock}{variance\,of\,demand} \qquad (24)$$

Bout et al., [17] has proved that if order variance equals to demand variance i.e. BWE=1 then it implies that there is no BWE. While the value BWE > 1 indicates the existence of BWE whereas BWE<1 value specifies the "smoothing" or "dampening" scenario meaning that the orders are less vary than the demand. From the Table 2, it can be observed that BWE value is comparatively high in case of the ARIMA while the proposed model DWT-LSSVM is approximately one. This signifies there is no BWE while the demand is predicted through DWT-LSSVM. Reducing the BWE (smoothing order) does not necessarily lead to reduction in inventory cost.

To satisfy the customer demand, the variation in inventory is compensated by maintaining high safety stock and this incurs high holding cost to the organisation. Therefore, measuring the variation in inventory level with respect to demand called net-stock amplification (NSAmp) is also an important issue to judge a forecasting model. Hence, NSAmp values are estimated for both proposed model and ARIMA model using Eq. (24) as described in Table 2. From the Table 2, it can be identified that NSAmp value is comparatively less in case of DWT-LSSVM than ARIMA. From the above analysis, it can be confirmed that forecasting accuracy of the DWT-LSSVM is high as compared to the ARIMA.

Table 2. Estimated performance parameters

Cases	ARIMA			DWT-LSSVM		
	MSE	BWE	NSAmp	MSE	BWE	NSAmp
Case I: ABC Pvt. Ltd.	178544.011	1.27	1.02	0.0007	0.9998	0.0004
Case II: MNO Pvt. Ltd.	12046.7679	1.18240	0.87025	0.0031	0.9998	0.0066

7   Conclusions

In this research, an integrated approach of discrete wavelet theory and least square support vector machine (DWT-LSSVM model) is proposed to make improvement is forecasting accuracy and to improve the inventory performance so as supply chain performance can be improved. Hence, to validate the model, an example data set is tested from the open source. The proposed model is applied to demand data from two different industries representing different production process and operating environment. A comparative study between the time series ARIMA model and the proposed model is made on two datasets based on forecasting error in terms of mean square error (MSE). The analysis shows that DWT-LSSVM model invariably gives less forecasting error in comparison to ARIMA model. Using a base-stock policy, bullwhip effect for both two cases is quantified as ratio of order variance to demand variance (BWE). It is observed that reduced forecasting error leads to diminish the bullwhip effect. If the demands are estimated by DWT-LSSVM model, BWE approaches approximately equal to unity indicating no bullwhip effect. Also, the NSAmp value in case of DWT-LSSVM model is less as compared to ARIMA model. From the analysis it can be conclude that the proposed model is a better forecasting model as compared to the ARIMA time series model as it not only help in controlling the order variation but also help in controlling the inventory variation so that operations can be smoothened and total supply chain cost can be reduced.

References

1. Davis, T.: Effective supply chain management. Sloan Management Review, 35–46 (Summer 1993)
2. van der Vorst, J.G.A.J., Beulens, A.J.M.: Identifying sources of uncertainty to generate supply chain redesign strategies. International Journal of Physical Distribution and Logistics Management 32, 409–430 (2002)
3. Forrester, J.W.: Industrial dynamics–A major breakthrough for decision making. Harvard Business Review 36, 37–66 (1958)
4. Forrester, J.W.: Industrial Dynamics. MIT Press, Cambridge (1961)
5. Sterman, J.: Modelling managerial behaviour: Misperceptions of feedback in a dynamic decision making experiment. Management Science 35, 321–339 (1989)
6. Lee, H.L., Padmanabhan, V., Whang, S.: The Bullwhip effect in supply chains. Sloan Management Review 38, 93–102 (1997a)
7. Lee, H.L., Padmanabhan, V., Whang, S.: Information Distortion in a Supply Chain: The Bullwhip Effect. Management Science 43, 546–558 (1997b)
8. Wright, D., Yuan, X.: Mitigating bullwhip effect by ordering policies and forecasting methods. International Journal of Production Economics 113, 587–597 (2008)
9. Luong, H.T.: Measure of bullwhip effect in supply chains with autoregressive demand process. European Journal of Operational Research 180, 1086–1097 (2007)
10. Luong, H.T., Phien, N.H.: Measure of bullwhip effect in supply chains: The case of high order autoregressive demand process. European Journal of Operation Research 183, 197–209 (2007)
11. Chen, F., Drezner, Z., Ryan, J.K., Simchi-Levi, D.: The impact of exponential smoothing forecasts on the bullwhip effect. Naval Research Logistics 47, 269–286 (2000)
12. Hong, L., Ping, W.: Bullwhip effect analysis in supply chain for demand forecasting technology. System Engineering-Theory and Practice 27, 26–33 (2007)
13. Zhang, X.: Evolution of ARMA Demand in supply chain. Manufacturing and Service Operations Management 6, 195–198 (2004)
14. Bandyopadhyay, S., Bhattacharya, R.: A generalized measure of bullwhip effect in supply chain with ARMA demand process under various replenishment policies. International Journal of Advance Manufacturing Technology (2013), doi:10.1007/s00170-013-4888-y
15. Duc, T.T.H., Luong, H.T., Kim, Y.-D.: A measure of bullwhip effect in supply chains with a mixed autoregressive-moving average demand process. European Journal of Operational Research 187, 243–256 (2008)
16. Gilbert, K.: An ARIMA supply chain model. Management Science 51, 305–310 (2005)
17. Boute, R.N., Lambrecht, M.R.: Exploring the bullwhip effect by mean of spreadsheet simulation. Informs Transaction on Education 10, 1–9 (2009)
18. Vapnik, V.: The Nature of Statistical Learning Theory. Springer, New York (1995)

19. Chauchard, F., Cogdill, R., Roussel, S., Roger, J.M., Bellon-Maurel, V.: Application of LS-SVM to non-linear phenomena in NIR spectroscopy: Development of a robust and portable sensor for acidity prediction in grapes. Chemometrics and Intelligent Laboratory Systems 71(2), 141–150 (2004)
20. Lu, C.-J., Lee, T.-S., Chiu, C.-C.: Financial time series forecasting using independent component analysis and support vector regression. Decision Support System 47, 115–125 (2009)
21. Kim, K.-J.: Financial time series forecasting using support vector machines. Neurocomputing 55, 307–319 (2003)
22. Zhiqiang, G., Huaiqing, W., Quan, L.: Financial time series forecasting using LPP and SVM optimization by PSO. Soft Computing 17, 805–818 (2013)
23. Sudheer, C., Shrivastava, N.A., Panigrahi, B.K., Mathur, S.: Streamflow forecasting by SVM with quantum behaved particle swarm optimization. Neurocomputing 101, 18–23 (2013)
24. Hong, W.-C., Dong, Y., Zhang, W.Y., Chen, L.-Y., Panigrahi, B.K.: Cyclic electric load forecasting by seasonal SVR with chaotic genetic algorithm. International Journal of Electrical Power & Energy Systems 44, 604–614 (2013)
25. Sudheer, C., Shrivastava, N.A., Panigrahi, B.K., Mathur, S.: Groundwater Level Forecasting Using SVM-QPSO. In: Panigrahi, B.K., Suganthan, P.N., Das, S., Satapathy, S.C. (eds.) SEMCCO 2011, Part I. LNCS, vol. 7076, pp. 731–741. Springer, Heidelberg (2011)
26. Sudheer, C., Maheswaran, R., Panigrahi, B.K., Mathur, S.: A hybrid SVM-PSO model for forecasting monthly streamflow. Neural Computing and Application, 1–9 (2013)
27. Partal, T., Cigizoglu, H.K.: Prediction of daily precipitation using wavelet-neural networks. Hydrological Sciences Journal 54, 234–246 (2009)
28. Peixian, L., Zhixiang, T., Lili, Y., Kazhong, D.: Time series prediction of mining subsidence based on a SVM. Mining Science and Technology 21, 557–562 (2011)
29. Khan, A.A., Shahidehpour, M.: One day ahead wind speed forecasting using wavelets. In: IEEE/PES Power Systems Conference and Exposition, PSCE 2009, Seattle, WA, pp. 1–5 (2009)
30. Wei, S., Song, J., Khan, N.I.: Simulating and predicting river discharge time series using a wavelet-neural network hybrid modelling approach. Hydrological Process. 26, 281–296 (2012)
31. Zhang, J., Tan, Z.: Day ahead electricity price forecasting using WT, CLSSVM and EGARCH model. Electrical Power and Energy Systems 45, 362–368 (2013)
32. Aggarwal, S.K., Saini, L.M., Kumar, A.: Electricity price forecasting using wavelet domain and time domain features in a regression based technique. International Journal of Recent Trends in Engineering 2, 33–37 (2009)
33. Box, G.E.P., Jenkins, G.M., Reinsel, G.C., Jenkins, G.: Time Series Analysis: Forecasting and Control, 3rd edn. Prentice-Hall, Englewood Cliffs (1994)
34. Makridakis, S., Wheelwright, S.C., Hyndman, R.J.: Forecasting methods and applications, 3rd edn. John Wiley & Sons Inc., Singapore (1998)
35. Daubechies, I.: The wavelet transforms time–frequency localization and signal analysis. IEEE Transactions on Information Theory 36, 961–1005 (1990)
36. Kim, C.-K., Kwak, I.-S., Cha, E.-Y., Chon, T.-S.: Implementation of wavelets and artificial neural networks to detection of toxic response behaviour of chironomids (Chironomidae: Diptera) for water quality monitoring. Ecological Modelling 195, 61–71 (2006)
37. Shengxian, C., Yanhui, Z., Jing, Z., Dayu, Y.: Experimental Study on Dynamic Simulation for Biofouling Resistance Prediction by Least Squares Support Vector Machine. In: 2012 International Conference on Future Electrical Power and Energy Systems, Energy Procedia, vol. 17, pp. 74–78 (2012)

An Ant Colony Optimization Algorithm
for the Min-Degree Constrained Minimum Spanning
Tree Problem

V. Venkata Ramana Murthy and Alok Singh

School of Computer and Information Sciences
University of Hyderabad, Hyderabad 500046, India
murthy.582@gmail.com, alokcs@uohyd.ernet.in

Abstract. Given a connected edge-weighted undirected graph, the min-degree constrained minimum spanning tree (MDCMST) problem seeks on this graph a spanning tree of least cost in which every non-leaf node have a degree of at least d in the spanning tree. This problem is $\mathcal{NP}$-Hard for $3 \leq d \leq \lfloor \frac{n}{2} \rfloor$ where n is the number of nodes in the graph. In this paper, we have proposed an ant colony optimization based approach to this problem. The proposed approach has been tested on Euclidean and random instances both. Computational results show the effectiveness of the proposed approach.

Keywords: Ant Colony Optimization Algorithm, Combinatorial Optimization, Min-Degree Constrained Minimum Spanning Tree Problem, Swarm Intelligence.

1 Introduction

Given a connected edge-weighted undirected graph $G = (V, E)$, where V denotes the set of nodes and E denotes the set of edges, the Min-Degree Constrained Minimum Spanning Tree (MDCMST) Problem consists in finding a spanning tree of G with minimum cost such that every internal node, i.e., non-leaf node must have a degree of at least d in the spanning tree. Almeida et al.[1] introduced MDCMST problem and proved its $\mathcal{NP}$-Hardness for $4 \leq d \leq \lfloor \frac{n}{2} \rfloor$, where n is the number of nodes in the graph. The case $d = 3$ was shown $\mathcal{NP}$-Hard later in [2]. It is pertinent to mention here that MDCMST problem reduces to well known minimum spanning tree problem in case of $d = 2$.

MDCMST problem finds practical application in the domain of telecommunication network while designing the access points that route traffic between a main network and a large number of end-users. Only in case a certain minimum number of end-users are connected to each of these access points, the cost of installing expensive routing equipments at these access points can be justified [3]. It also finds application in facility location where in order to justify the existence of a facility, it has to service a certain minimum number of clients [3].

While introducing MDCMST, Almeida et al. [1] also provided integer programming formulations based on single and multi-commodity flows and solved these formulations using branch-and-bound algorithms. A new formulation for MDCMST problem using Miller-Tucker-Zemlin constraints [4] was proposed by Akgün and Tansel [3]. This new

B.K. Panigrahi et al. (Eds.): SEMCCO 2013, Part II, LNCS 8298, pp. 85–94, 2013.
© Springer International Publishing Switzerland 2013

formulation was also solved using a branch-and-bound algorithm. This new branch-and-bound algorithm was faster in comparison to branch-and-bound algorithms of [1].

A problem specific heuristic based on modified Prim's algorithm and an artificial bee colony (ABC) algorithm for the MDCMST problem have been proposed in [5]. For both employed and onlooker bee phase, this ABC algorithm generates neighboring solutions by deleting an edge from the solution under consideration and inserting in its place another edge that can connect the two resulting components. This edge is selected from another solution that is chosen randomly. If there are more than one edge that can connect the two components in the randomly chosen solution, then one such edge is chosen randomly. If min-degree constraint gets violated in this process for some internal nodes then ABC algorithm tries to satisfy the min-degree constraint of these nodes by moving enough leaf nodes from internal nodes having excess leaf nodes to these nodes. However, it is not always possible to satisfy the min-degree constraints and further processing in case of failure depends on the phase. If failure happens in employed bee phase then employed bee solution is replaced with a randomly generated solution. In case failure happens in onlooker bee phase, simply the worst possible fitness is assigned to the corresponding infeasible onlooker bee solution. The best solution obtained through ABC algorithm is improved further through a local search. The ABC algorithm and heuristic were tested on Euclidean as well as random graph instances. On both types of graph instances, the heuristic and ABC approach performed quite similar for small values of d. However, for larger values of d, ABC algorithm outperformed the heuristic by a large margin.

In this paper, we have proposed an ant-colony optimization (ACO) approach to the MDCMST problem. The performance of the proposed ACO approach has been compared with ABC approach of [5] on same instances as used in [5]. Our ACO approach clearly outperformed the ABC approach on random instances, whereas the performances of the two approaches are comparable on Euclidean instances.

The remainder of this paper is structured as follows: Section 2 provides a brief introduction to ACO algorithm. Section 3 describes our proposed ACO approach to MDCMST problem. Computational results are presented in Section 4, whereas Section 5 presents some concluding remarks and directions for future research.

2   Ant Colony Optimization Algorithm

Ant colony optimization algorithms belong to the class of *swarm intelligence based algorithms*, i.e., class of algorithms inspired by the collective intelligent behavior of *swarm or group of organisms*. Ant colony optimization algorithms are inspired by the cooperative foraging behavior of natural ant colonies. While walking, ants deposit on the ground a substance called *pheromone*, forming in this way a pheromone trails. Ants can smell pheromone, and its presence influences the choice of their paths, i.e., ants choose probabilistically the paths marked by high pheromone concentrations. The pheromone trail allows the ants to find their way back to the food source (or to the nest). While searching for a path from nest to food source and back, ants tracing the shortest path will return sooner, and, therefore, immediately after their return, concentration of pheromone will be more on this path. This influences other ants to follow this path thereby facilitating even higher pheromone concentration on this path. As a result, after some time, almost whole colony of ants starts following this path. Thus pheromone trail allows a colony of ants to find the shortest paths between their nest and food source. This feature of real ant colonies is exploited in artificial ant colony optimization algorithms to solve optimization problems.

Since Dorigo et al. [6,7] developed first ACO algorithm called Ant System, several variants have been reported in the literature. The basic idea behind ACO is to model the problem as some kind of search on a graph. The ACO algorithm iteratively distributes a set of artificial ants (ants for short) on this graph to perform randomized walks on the graph in search of good solutions. Individual ants do not, in general, find good solutions on their own. Good solutions emerge from cooperative interaction among ants. This cooperative interaction is achieved through the use of two rules. The first is the probabilistic *state-transition rule* that is used when an ant chooses the next node to visit. The other is *pheromone-update rule* that changes the preference degree of a node/edge based on the quality of solutions containing that node/edge. Variations in these two rules lead to different ACO algorithms. Interested readers may refer to [8] for an excellent introduction to ant colony optimization and a detailed survey of different variants of ACO algorithms and their applications. Some recent applications of ACO can be found in [9,10,11].

3   ACO Approach for MDCMST Problem

In our ACO approach, each solution is constructed by following a three stage procedure. In first stage, $\lfloor \frac{n}{\psi \times d} \rfloor$ nodes are selected to become internal nodes using state-transition rule where $\psi > 1.0$ is a parameter to be determined empirically. In the second stage, Prim's algorithm is applied to construct a minimum spanning tree over the graph induced by the set of selected internal nodes. In the third stage, remaining nodes are connected to these internal nodes in such a manner that min-degree constraint is satisfied for each internal node. To achieve this, each internal node is considered one-by-one in some random order and nodes not in the tree are attached one-by-one to this internal node in increasing order of the cost of their edge to this internal node till the degree constraint of this internal node is satisfied. This process is repeated for each internal node. If still some unconnected nodes remain then each of them is connected to the tree via the least cost edge connecting that node to some internal node. The solution thus obtained is improved further through a local search which is described at the end of this section. This improved solution is considered to be the final solution generated by an ant. Other salient features of our ACO algorithm is described in subsequent subsections. It is to be noted here that the idea of first selecting internal nodes and constructing a minimum spanning tree on them has been used in [12,13,14] in the context of leaf-constrained minimum spanning tree problem.

3.1   Definition of Pheromonal Components

Pheromone is associated with the nodes of the underlying graph and denotes the learned desirability of a node to be an interior node. The pheromone associated with a node v_i is denoted by τ_i.

3.2   State-Transition Rule

While determining the set of interior nodes, at each step our ACO algorithm selects a node v_i from the set of nodes not yet included in the set of interior nodes with probability $p(v_i)$. This probability is proportional to pheromone concentration on the node v_i, i.e.,

$$p(v_i) = \frac{\tau_i}{\sum\limits_{v_j \in V-I} \tau_j}$$

where I is the set of nodes already selected to act as one of interior node. Clearly, the probability of selection of a node depends only on the concentration of pheromone on it. This deviates from most standard ACO algorithms, where this probability is also influenced by a heuristic term measuring the static desirability of a vertex. Another difference with most other ACO algorithms is the absence of exponent α in determining this probability. A similar approach was used in [13,15].

Probability values associated with different nodes can be computed efficiently in the following manner. Initially, $I = \emptyset$ and the denominator is the sum of pheromone concentration on all the nodes of the graph. After each step, we add the node selected to I and denominator is updated simply by subtracting from it the pheromone value of the node selected.

3.3   Pheromone Update Rule

After the end of each iteration, i.e., when every ant has build its solution, pheromones on the nodes are updated according to the best solution found during that iteration. First, to simulate the effect of pheromone evaporation, pheromone concentration on each node is reduced by multiplying it with a persistence factor $\rho(0 \leq \rho \leq 1)$. Then the pheromone concentration on the interior nodes of the best solution of that iteration is augmented by $\frac{1}{10+C(S_{itbest})-C(S_{best})}$, where S_{itbest} is the best solution of that iteration and S_{best} is the best solution found since the beginning, and $C(S_{itbest})$ and $C(S_{best})$ are their costs. Clearly, maximum pheromone augmentation of 0.1 takes place when $C(S_{itbest})$ $= C(S_{best})$. In all other cases, pheromone is augmented by an amount which is less than 0.1.

3.4   Local Search

The solution constructed using three step procedure is improved further through the application of a local search. This local search consists of repeatedly swapping the leaf nodes between two internal node if such a swap can reduce the cost of the spanning tree.

Algorithm 1 provides the pseudo-code for our ACO approach for MDCMST problem where N_a is the number of ants, $f(MT)$ is the cost of the min degree constrained spanning tree MT and $Local\_Search(MT)$ is a function that applies the local search described in section 3.4 on MT.

Algorithm 1. Pseudo-code of our ACO Approach for MDCMST Problem

---

Input: Set of parameters for our ACO Approach and an instance for MDCMST Problem
Output: Best solution found

Initialize pheromone values on each node;
$cost\_best \leftarrow \infty$;
$best \leftarrow \emptyset$;
while *termination condition is not satisfied* **do**
    $cost\_iter\_best \leftarrow \infty$;
    $iter\_best \leftarrow \emptyset$;
    for $i \leftarrow 1$ **to** N_a **do**
        Select the set S of $\lfloor \frac{n}{\psi \times d} \rfloor$ internal nodes using state transition rule;
        Compute the minimum spanning tree T on subgraph induced by S;
        $MT \leftarrow T$;
        forall the $v_j \in S$ *in some random order* **do**
            while *min-degree constraint of* v_j *is not satisfied* **do**
                add the least-cost edge connecting v_j to an unconnected node to MT;
            end
        end
        while *an unconnected node u remain* **do**
            add the least-cost edge connecting u to one of the internal node to MT;
        end
        $MT \leftarrow Local\_Search(MT)$;
        if $f(MT) < cost\_iter\_best$ **then**
            $cost\_iter\_best \leftarrow f(MT)$;
            $iter\_best \leftarrow MT$;
        end
    end
    if $cost\_iter\_best < cost\_best$ **then**
        $cost\_best \leftarrow cost\_iter\_best$;
        $best \leftarrow iter\_best$;
    end
    Update pheromones using *iter_best* through pheromone update rule;
end
return *best*;

4　Computational Results

We have implemented our ACO approach in C and executed it on a Linux based 3.0 GHz Core 2 Duo system with 2GB of RAM. We have taken 15 ants ($N_a = 15$) in each iteration and allowed our approach to execute for 1000 iteration. We have used $\rho = 0.985$ and $\psi = 1.3$ in our ACO approach. All the pheromone values have been initialized to 10. All these parameter values are chosen empirically. Clearly, the maximum pheromone concentration that can be sustained with the chosen value of persistence factor $\rho = 0.985$ and maximum pheromone augmentation of 0.1 is about 6.667. Such a pheromone initialization aids in wider exploration of the search space at the beginning of ACO algorithm.

Table 1. Comparison of ABC and ACO approaches for Euclidean instances of size 50 with different min degree constraints

Name	d	ABC				ACO			
		Best	Average	SD	Time(s)	Best	Average	SD	Time(s)
E50.1	3	6.61	6.71	0.08	4.97	6.54	6.58	0.03	3.72
E50.2	3	6.41	6.66	0.12	5.04	6.58	6.61	0.03	3.77
E50.3	3	6.28	6.48	0.12	4.65	6.40	6.46	0.04	4.09
E50.4	3	5.90	6.12	0.09	4.83	6.12	6.15	0.03	4.11
E50.5	3	6.52	6.60	0.04	5.05	6.46	6.52	0.03	3.83
E50.1	5	7.68	7.91	0.12	5.07	7.91	8.00	0.06	2.82
E50.2	5	7.57	8.01	0.17	5.39	8.00	8.04	0.04	2.74
E50.3	5	7.55	7.73	0.12	5.62	7.71	7.72	0.02	3.00
E50.4	5	6.94	7.06	0.12	5.15	7.12	7.16	0.03	3.26
E50.5	5	7.66	7.81	0.11	4.95	7.78	7.79	0.01	3.00
E50.1	10	10.33	10.70	0.26	5.47	11.45	11.46	0.02	2.18
E50.2	10	10.08	10.24	0.12	4.55	10.81	10.81	0.00	2.17
E50.3	10	9.41	9.65	0.15	5.71	10.32	10.32	0.00	2.18
E50.4	10	8.81	9.03	0.16	5.70	9.57	9.57	0.00	2.17
E50.5	10	9.59	9.81	0.15	5.25	9.96	9.96	0.00	1.99

Table 2. Comparison of ABC and ACO approaches for Euclidean instances of size 100 with different min degree constraints

Name	d	ABC				ACO			
		Best	Average	SD	Time(s)	Best	Average	SD	Time(s)
E100.1	3	9.06	9.29	0.14	15.59	9.02	9.10	0.05	21.57
E100.2	3	9.08	9.42	0.15	13.56	8.99	9.06	0.05	21.05
E100.3	3	9.54	9.62	0.06	16.30	9.21	9.32	0.07	21.96
E100.4	3	9.53	9.67	0.09	16.23	9.36	9.53	0.08	23.36
E100.5	3	9.61	9.80	0.12	16.62	9.55	9.63	0.06	20.81
E100.1	5	10.99	11.22	0.13	18.20	10.73	10.91	0.12	15.99
E100.2	5	10.69	11.10	0.26	16.81	10.76	10.90	0.07	15.78
E100.3	5	10.98	11.29	0.17	16.71	10.99	11.17	0.13	15.23
E100.4	5	11.23	11.44	0.14	17.40	11.34	11.40	0.06	16.07
E100.5	5	11.25	11.61	0.22	16.74	11.40	11.55	0.10	15.62
E100.1	10	14.54	14.88	0.23	19.28	14.54	14.67	0.12	9.98
E100.2	10	14.00	14.24	0.22	18.57	14.11	14.24	0.09	11.56
E100.3	10	14.80	15.02	0.11	18.47	14.80	14.97	0.13	10.75
E100.4	10	14.26	14.58	0.22	17.70	14.59	14.69	0.07	10.32
E100.5	10	14.66	15.23	0.29	18.68	15.29	15.38	0.07	10.49

To test the performance of our approach, we have used the same 25 test instances as used in [5]. These instances comprise 15 Euclidean and 10 random instances. The Euclidean instances are originally the instances of Euclidean Steiner tree problem and

Table 3. Comparison of ABC and ACO approaches for Euclidean instances of size 250 with different min degree constraints

Name	d	ABC				ACO			
		Best	Average	SD	Time(s)	Best	Average	SD	Time(s)
E250.1	3	15.92	16.08	0.10	96.81	15.59	15.70	0.12	273.51
E250.2	3	15.65	15.85	0.12	89.05	15.35	15.57	0.13	296.32
E250.3	3	15.56	15.72	0.10	89.52	15.39	15.48	0.07	284.62
E250.4	3	15.95	16.09	0.11	96.59	15.72	15.91	0.11	286.20
E250.5	3	15.82	15.95	0.08	103.74	15.49	15.64	0.08	272.22
E250.1	5	19.22	19.59	0.15	98.34	18.54	19.05	0.20	195.69
E250.2	5	19.05	19.29	0.22	106.52	18.69	19.03	0.21	203.36
E250.3	5	18.29	19.10	0.33	95.35	18.54	18.74	0.17	191.98
E250.4	5	19.20	19.73	0.21	99.53	19.10	19.37	0.18	172.76
E250.5	5	18.77	19.23	0.26	89.88	18.81	19.03	0.17	170.54
E250.1	10	24.05	25.23	0.49	96.16	24.11	24.66	0.28	108.78
E250.2	10	24.81	25.49	0.33	105.29	24.91	25.16	0.17	107.14
E250.3	10	24.13	24.88	0.30	108.72	23.87	24.20	0.20	106.63
E250.4	10	25.08	25.69	0.30	104.29	24.36	25.11	0.43	102.73
E250.5	10	24.14	25.06	0.54	104.99	24.57	25.02	0.22	101.73

consist of randomly distributed points in a unit square. These points can be considered as the nodes of a complete graph, whose edge weights are the Euclidean distances among them. These instances are available from http://people.brunel.ac.uk/~mastjjb/jeb/info.html There are 15 Euclidean instances for each of 50, 100 and 250 nodes and the first 5 instances of each size are used for MDCMST problem. Random instances are due to Julstrom [16] who created and used them for minimum routing cost spanning tree problem. There are 7 random instances for each of 100 and 300 nodes and the first 5 instance of each size are used here. For these random instances, edge-weights are uniformly distributed in [0.01, 0.99]. Each Euclidean instance has the name of the form $En.i$, where n is the number of nodes in the instance and i is its number. Similarly, each random instance has the name of the form $Rn.i$. Each of these 25 instances is subjected to three different min degree constraints, i.e., $d \in \{3, 5, 10\}$. This created a total of 75 test cases. Like ABC approach of [5], for each of these 75 test cases, we have executed our ACO approach 10 independent times.

Tables 1–5 report the results of our ACO approach and compare it with ABC approach of [5]. For each test case, these tables report the best and average solution quality obtained by ABC & ACO approaches along with the standard deviation of solution values and average execution time in seconds. Tables 1–3 are devoted to Euclidean instances whereas last two tables are for random instances. On 30 test cases involving random instances, our proposed ACO approach completely dominates the ABC approach as its best as well as average solution quality are better than those of ABC approach in all the cases. On 45 test cases involving Euclidean instances, the best solution obtained by ACO approach is better than ABC approach on 18 test cases, same as ABC on 2 test cases and worse than ABC on 25 test cases whereas the average solution quality of

Table 4. Comparison of ABC and ACO approaches for random instances of size 100 with different min degree constraints

Name	d	ABC				ACO			
		Best	Average	SD	Time(s)	Best	Average	SD	Time(s)
R100.1	3	3.49	3.60	0.07	16.82	3.05	3.11	0.05	21.48
R100.2	3	3.51	3.62	0.06	16.99	2.80	2.87	0.04	22.88
R100.3	3	3.81	3.98	0.08	15.04	3.21	3.29	0.04	22.62
R100.4	3	3.38	3.54	0.07	16.95	2.88	2.91	0.02	21.83
R100.5	3	3.78	3.86	0.06	17.03	3.22	3.25	0.02	24.34
R100.1	5	4.52	4.93	0.18	17.49	4.09	4.12	0.02	15.39
R100.2	5	4.80	5.00	0.10	16.79	4.04	4.07	0.02	16.28
R100.3	5	5.00	5.24	0.12	18.18	4.25	4.32	0.04	15.81
R100.4	5	4.66	4.85	0.12	17.39	3.89	3.93	0.04	15.90
R100.5	5	4.93	5.17	0.13	17.40	4.31	4.40	0.05	16.89
R100.1	10	7.75	7.96	0.17	18.25	7.45	7.54	0.08	10.57
R100.2	10	7.73	8.12	0.27	17.67	6.96	7.14	0.11	10.03
R100.3	10	7.72	8.10	0.28	19.78	7.37	7.39	0.03	11.04
R100.4	10	7.60	7.85	0.15	18.99	6.89	7.18	0.13	11.00
R100.5	10	7.94	8.53	0.32	19.07	7.34	7.35	0.02	10.58

Table 5. Comparison of ABC and ACO approaches for random instances of size 300 with different min degree constraints

Name	d	ABC				ACO			
		Best	Average	SD	Time(s)	Best	Average	SD	Time(s)
R300.1	3	6.29	6.33	0.02	137.93	5.56	5.61	0.04	489.50
R300.2	3	6.25	6.39	0.06	136.20	5.77	5.83	0.03	456.29
R300.3	3	6.21	6.26	0.03	143.01	5.61	5.66	0.03	431.84
R300.4	3	6.49	6.58	0.05	136.56	5.93	5.96	0.03	462.16
R300.5	3	6.17	6.24	0.04	137.00	5.49	5.61	0.07	443.40
R300.1	5	8.05	8.17	0.08	140.84	6.87	6.98	0.06	286.43
R300.2	5	8.14	8.23	0.06	123.97	7.21	7.27	0.04	300.52
R300.3	5	7.91	8.07	0.08	140.88	7.14	7.19	0.04	301.25
R300.4	5	8.26	8.41	0.10	141.34	7.25	7.46	0.11	327.46
R300.5	5	7.97	8.12	0.10	130.14	7.00	7.11	0.06	299.93
R300.1	10	11.97	12.39	0.21	141.28	10.42	10.63	0.15	172.55
R300.2	10	12.07	12.41	0.24	132.44	10.85	11.03	0.12	180.45
R300.3	10	12.17	12.35	0.14	137.34	10.81	11.00	0.13	167.23
R300.4	10	12.67	12.80	0.09	148.80	10.99	11.20	0.18	194.25
R300.5	10	12.16	12.36	0.18	155.13	10.93	11.06	0.09	183.56

ACO is better than ABC on 33 test cases, same as ABC on 1 test case and worse than ABC on 11 test cases. On Euclidean instances, in comparison to ABC approach, the solution quality of ACO improves with increase in number of nodes as can be seen in table 3.

Considering all the instances together, on a total of 75 test cases, best solution obtained by ACO approach is better than, equal to and worse than ABC on 48, 2 and 25 cases respectively. As far as average solution quality is concerned, ACO approach is better than, equal to and worse than ABC on 63, 1 and 11 test cases respectively. It can also be seen from tables 1–5 that on smaller instances ACO takes less time in comparison to ABC, whereas the situation is reversed on larger instances. This is due to the usual computational overhead associated with ACO as it builds each solution from scratch. Another interesting observation that can be drawn from these tables is that ACO takes more time for smaller values of d on test cases involving same number of nodes. This is due to the fact that for smaller values of d, there are more interior nodes to select through ACO.

5   Conclusions

In this paper, we have proposed an ant colony optimization (ACO) approach to the min-degree constrained minimum spanning tree problem and compared its performance with a previously proposed artificial bee colony (ABC) algorithm on Euclidean as well as random graph instances. Our ACO approach completely outperformed the ABC approach on random instances as its best as well as average solution quality is better than ABC approach in all the cases. However, in case of Euclidean instances though our ACO approach is better than ABC approach in terms of average solution quality in most cases, its performance is inferior in terms of best solution quality on slightly more than half of the cases.

As a future work, we intend to extend our ACO approach to a version of the problem where different nodes have different min-degree constraints.

References

1. Almeida, A.M., Martins, P., Souza, M.C.: Min-Degree Constrained Minimum Spanning Tree Problem: Complexity, Proprieties, and Formulations. Technical Report 6/2006, Centre for Operational Research, University of Lisboa (2006)
2. Almeida, A.M., Martins, P., Souza, M.C.: md-MST is $\mathcal{NP}$-Hard for $d \geq 3$. Electronic Notes in Discrete Mathematics 36, 9–15 (2010)
3. Akgün, I., Tansel, B.C.: Min-Degree Constrained Minimum Spanning Tree Problem: New Formulation via Miller-Tucker-Zemlin Constraints. Computers & Operations Research 37, 72–82 (2010)
4. Miller, C., Tucker, A., Zemlin, R.: Integer Programming Formulation of Travelling Salesman Problems. Journal of ACM 7, 326–329 (1960)
5. Murthy, V., V.R., Singh, A.: Solving the Min-Degree Constrained Minimum Spanning Tree Problem Using Heuristic and Metaheuristic Approaches. In: Proceedings of the Second IEEE International Conference on Parallel, Distributed and Grid Computing (PDGC 2012), pp. 716–720. IEEE Press (2012)
6. Dorigo, M., Maniezzo, V., Colorni, A.: Positive Feedback as a Search Strategy. Technical Report 91-016, Dipartimento di Elettronica, Politecnico di Milano, Milan, Italy (1991)
7. Dorigo, M., Maniezzo, V., Colorni, A.: The Ant System: Optimization by a Colony of Cooperating Agents. IEEE Transactions on Systems, Man and Cybernetics – Part B 26, 29–42 (1996)

8. Dorigo, M., Stützle, T.: Ant Colony Optimization. MIT Press, Cambridge (2004)
9. Sundar, S., Singh, A., Rossi, A.: New Heuristics for Two Bounded-Degree Spanning Tree Problems. Information Sciences 195, 226–240 (2012)
10. Potluri, A., Singh, A.: Hybrid Metaheuristic Algorithms for Minimum Weight Dominating Set. Applied Soft Computing 13, 76–88 (2013)
11. Sundar, S., Singh, A.: New Heuristic Approaches for the Dominating Tree Problem. Applied Soft Computing (in press, 2013), doi:10.1016/j.asoc.2013.07.014
12. Julstrom, B.A.: Codings and Operators in Two Genetic Algorithms for the Leaf-Constrained Minimum Spanning Tree Problem. International Journal of Applied Mathematics and Computer Science 14, 385–396 (2004)
13. Singh, A., Baghel, A.S.: New Metaheuristic Approaches for the Leaf-Constrained Minimum Spanning Tree Problem. Asia-Pacific Journal of Operational Research 25, 575–589 (2008)
14. Singh, A.: An Artificial Bee Colony Algorithm for the Leaf-Constrained Minimum Spanning Tree Problem. Applied Soft Computing 9, 625–631 (2009)
15. Solnon, C., Fenet, S.: A Study of ACO Capabilities for Solving the Maximum Clique Problem. Journal of Heuristics 12, 155–180 (2006)
16. Julstrom, B.A.: The Blob code is Competitive with Edge-Sets in Genetic Algorithms for the Minimum Routing Cost Spanning Tree Problem. In: Proceedings of the Genetic and Evolutionary Computation Conference 2005 (GECCO 2005), vol. 1, pp. 585–590. ACM Press, New York (2005)

Multiobjective Differential Evolution Algorithm Using Binary Encoded Data in Selecting Views for Materializing in Data Warehouse

Rajib Goswami, Dhruba Kumar Bhattacharyya, and Malayananda Dutta

Department of Computer Science and Engineering,
Tezpur University, Tezpur, PIN: 784028, India
{rgos,dkb,malay}@tezu.ernet.in

Abstract. In this paper, we define the view selection process for materializing in data warehouse as a multiobjective optimization problem. We have implemented multiobjective Differential Evolution (DE) algorithm for binary encoded data to solve this problem. In our approach, to control population in intermediate generations of the differential evolution process by maintaining diversity in solution space with necessary elitism, the solutions of intermediate generations are first ranked according to their pareto dominance levels and then the diversity among solution vectors in solution space is measured. The algorithm is found to be suitable in selecting significant representitive solutions from a large number of nondominating solutions of the view selection problem.

Keywords: Data warehouse, View materialization, Differential evolution algorithm, Multiobjective optimization.

1 Introduction

View materialization for reducing query processing costs in data warehouse applications requires a large amount of space. Materialized views are updated or maintained in response to changes in the base data. Therefore, it is necessary to select an appropriate set of views to materialize in order to increase performance, with optimized query processing and view maintenance costs. This is known as the *materialized view selection problem* [1–3]. Thus, the materialized view selection problem entails the following: *Given a set of data warehouse queries, select a set of views to materialize so that the total query processing cost and view maintenance cost is minimized.* Research on this problem started in the early 90s when several heuristic greedy algorithms were proposed [1–5].

It has been observed that when the dimension of the data warehouse grows, the solution space grows exponentially and therefore it becomes very difficult to find an optimal solution to this problem. In fact, the problem is NP-hard [6, 1–3, 7]. Therefore various stochastic or evolutionary algorithms, data mining and clustering based approaches etc. have been proposed using different data structures and notations [8–12]. Looking at the similarity of complex computational

B.K. Panigrahi et al. (Eds.): SEMCCO 2013, Part II, LNCS 8298, pp. 95–106, 2013.

and optimization problems with biological evolution, different evolutionary algorithms have been developed to tackle such problems [13, 14]. In this paper we define the view selection process for materializing in data warehouse as a multi-objective optimization problem. In recent literature on application of evolutionary computing techniques, we find that diversed types of complex multiobjective problems have been addressed by multiobjective evolutionary algorithms [15, 16]. We have implemented multiobjective Differential Evolution (DE) algorithm for binary encoded data to solve the problem of view selection for materializing in data warehouse.

2 The Problem of Selecting Views for Materializing in Data Warehouse

In data warehouses, a view consists of the result of an aggregation function on some other views or base tables of the warehouse produced while generating responses to queries. Thus, views are dependent on the contents of other views and base tables. To make query response faster, optimization is critical in selecting some or all of these views for materializing in the data warehouse. The view selection for materializing problem is to select some or all of the views those are generated frequently while processing queries on a data warehouse, such that, the space requirement to materialize the selected views is less than or equal to the space reserved for that, and if the selected views are materialized, the total query processing cost and materialized view maintenance cost becomes minimum.

The view selection process for materializing in data warehouse may be defined by a Query Processing Plan represented by a Directed Acyclic Graph (DAG) [17]. This DAG representation considers a set of frequent OLAP queries on a data warehouse on a specific period. It is assumed that the overall query processing efficiency will be maintained if the intermediate views generated in the middle of processing these queries are considered for materializing. The Query Processing Plan DAG framework to represent the view selection problem was originally defined by Yang et al. in [17] as Multiple View Processing Plan (MVPP) framework. The DAG in this framework represents a query processing strategy on a data warehouse. The leaf nodes of the DAG correspond to the base relations and the root nodes represent the responses of queries.

Definition 1. *Query processing tree for a query q is a DAG, $T_q = (V, A)$, where,*

- *V is the set of vertices representing intermediate select, join and project sub-expressions of the query q,*
- *A is the set of arcs $\{a_1, a_2, \cdots, a_n\}$, such that each arc $a_i \in A$, either*
  - *connects a vertex $u_i \in V$ to $v_i \in V$, directing u_i to v_i, if v_i returns a number of rows of a database relation by processing rows of database relation at u_i,*
  - *or connects a leaf node or base relation $b_j \in B_q$ to $v_i \in V$, directing b_j to v_i, where B_q are the base tables used by q such that the processing at v_i needs the data in b_j,*

- *or it is connecting a vertex $v_i \in V$ to the root node representing the final response of the query q.*

Definition 2. *An MVPP Directed Acyclic Graph (DAG) G is a graph generated by merging query processing trees $T_{q_i}, i = 1, \cdots, n$, for a set of queries $Q = \{q_1, q_2, \cdots, q_n\}$ on a data warehouse considered, whenever sub-graphs of the query processing trees are shared.*

To generate the MVPP DAG framework, all the considered frequent queries are analyzed and all the independent selection, projection, join and base relations are identified to represent as vertices of the DAG as defined in Definition 1 and 2. An MVPP DAG may be constructed as depicted in Fig. 1. The view selection problem using MVPP DAG framework is to select a set of nodes from the MVPP DAG excluding the leaf and root nodes to materialize, considering the space constraint, such that the total query processing cost and materialized view updating cost is minimum.

2.1   The Cost Model

The query processing cost $Q_G(M)$ for a set of materialized views M, of an MVPP DAG G is expressed as Equation 1, where, V is the set of vertices of G and $M \subseteq V$, R is the set of root nodes of G, f_q is the access frequency of query $q \in R$, and $C_a^q(v)$ is the query processing cost of query q by accessing vertices $v \in V$ when M is materialized.

$$Q_G(M) = \sum_{q \in R} f_q(C_a^q(v)). \tag{1}$$

The materialized view maintenance cost of an MVPP DAG G may be expressed as:

$$U_G(M) = \sum_{m \in M} f_m(C_u^m(r)) \tag{2}$$

where, V is the set of vertices of G representing views, $M \subseteq V$ is the set of views materialized, f_m is the maintenance frequency of materialized view $m \in M$, $C_u^m(r)$ is the cost of updating materialized view $m \in M$ by accessing the vertices r, $r \subset V$.

2.2   The View Selection Problem as Multiobjective Optimization Problem Representation

By using Equation 1 and 2, if V is the set of vertices of MVPP DAG G, and M is the set of views that are materialized, i.e. $M \subseteq V$, then under the constraint $\sum_{v \in M} A_v \leq A$, where A_v denotes the space required for materializing the view v and A is the total space available for materializing the views; the view selection problem is to find M to minimize:

$$\mathbf{y} = \mathbf{f}(M) \equiv (Q_G(M), U_G(M)). \tag{3}$$

If S_0 and S_1 are two solutions of the Equation 3 under the constraint $\sum_{v \in M} A_v \leq A$, then S_0 dominates S_1, expressed as $S_0 \prec S_1$, iff both the following logical conditions 4 and 5 are satisfied.

$$(Q_G(S_0) \leq Q_G(S_1)) and (U_G(S_0) \leq U_G(S_1)) \tag{4}$$

$$(Q_G(S_0) < Q_G(S_1)) or (U_G(S_0) < U_G(S_1)). \tag{5}$$

If $S_0 \nprec S_1$ and $S_1 \nprec S_0$, then S_0 and S_1 are said to be non-dominating solutions. The view selection for materializing in data warehouse is the problem of finding out a set of non-dominating solutions, which is an approximation to the *true Pareto front* of the problem defined by Equation 3.

2.3   Solution Representation

To represent solutions of MVPP DAG framework as suggested by Yang et al. in [17], all views represented as vertices in an MVPP DAG are labelled and indexed. The solutions are represented as a string of 1s and 0s such that if a particular view is selected for materialization, then the corresponding bit in the solution string is represented as 1 and else 0. For m number of views of an MVPP DAG considered for selection, the views are indexed from 0 to $m - 1$. The solution strings of length m are represented such that if i^{th} view v_i is selected for materialization then the ith bit of the solution string is set to 1 and else it is set to 0.

3   Multiobjective Differential Evolution Algorithm in Selecting Views to Materialize in Data Warehouse

The Differential Evolution (DE) algorithm is a stochastic parallel direct search method for global optimization problems over continuous space using NP D-dimensional parameter vectors $x_{i,g}$, $i = 1, 2, \cdots$, NP, representing NP as the population size for generation g of an evolutionary system [18]. For mutation, in one variant of DE, known as *DE/rand/1/bin*, new population vectors are generated by finding the weighted difference between two random population and then by adding it to a third random population vectors of the NP population. The DE introduced by Storn and Price in [18] was originally designed for global optimization problem over continuous spaces using solution population of real vectors. Gong et al. in [19] used *forma analysis* [20, 21] to derive discrete DE operators for discrete otimization problem where *formae basis* [21] based *DE mutation operator template* M_{de} is defined as Equation 6 below.

$$M_{de}(x_1, x_2, x_3, F, \Psi_i) = \{m \in S | D_{\Psi_i}(x_1, m) = k \wedge k = F \times D_{\Psi_i}(x_2, x_3)\}. \tag{6}$$

Here, x_1 represents the base vector selected from the population, x_2 and x_3 are the vectors of the population to produce the difference, m representing the mutant vector and Ψ_i represents the basis constructed for the ith dimension.

3.1 Adapting Multiobjective DE with Binary Encoded Data in View Selection

For using binary encoded data in multiobjective DE, to generate the mutant vector, the *forma basis* may be used as discussed in sub-section 3. In our solution representation of the problem of data warehouse view selection for materializing, we have defined each solution as a string of bits. To adapt our solution representation with multiobjective DE, each population vector of the evolutionary system is considered as the solution string of bits where each bit represents a decision variable of a population vector. Thus a set of NP initial solutions $x_1, x_2, \cdots, x_{NP}$ that satisfy the space constraint are generated for a given MVPP DAG G. Using this population of size NP, in each generation of a evolutionary process g, against each solution vector $x_i, i = 1, 2, \cdots, NP$, a mutant vector $v_{i,g+1}$ is to be generated. In our solution representation, each bit is in single dimension that may take either 1 or 0 as value representing whether a particular view is selected or not. Therefore, *restricted-change mutation operation* [19] may be applied for this solution representation. Thus the mutant vector $v_{i,g+1}$ is generated as stated in line number 7 of Algorithm 1. The trial vector $u_{i,g+1}$ is formed by crossover as stated in line 11 of Algorithm 1.

To adapt the problem of view selection to materialize in Data Warehouse, the query processing cost and materialized view maintenance cost of the given MVPP DAG G, $Q_G(x_{i,g})$, $Q_G(u_{i,g+1})$ and $U_G(x_{i,g})$, $U_G(u_{i,g+1})$ are computed using Equation 1 and Equation 2. If $u_{i,g+1} \prec x_{i,g}$ then $x_{i,g+1}$ is set as $u_{i,g+1}$, else if $x_{i,g} \prec u_{i,g+1}$, then $u_{i,g+1}$ is discarded. Otherwise, in case $u_{i,g+1} \not\prec x_{i,g}$ and $x_{i,g} \not\prec u_{i,g+1}$, $u_{i,g+1}$ is appended to the population for next generation $g+1$. Thus the population may go on increasing. To control the population growth in each generation of DE, when the population size touches a limit, a technique is used to filter out NP elite solution population that maintains diversity in the solution population (see Algorithm 2). This evolutionary process is continued till it reaches a maximum number of generation specified, say g_{max}. The dominated solutions in the final population are then deleted to return the non-dominated solutions of the problem.

Promoting Diversity in Solution Population. In our approach, to promote diversity in solution space with necessary elitism in the population of intermediate generations of the DE process, the solutions of intermediate generations are ranked according to their pareto dominance levels as it is done in Nondominated Sorting Genetic Algorithm II (NSGA-II) by Deb et al. [13]. For each solution of the population, the maximum distance to other solution vectors in the population is measured by *Simple Matching Co-efficient (SMC) distance* measure [22]. The solution population is then first sorted in ascending order of their pareto fronts and then on descending order of their maximum distances to other solutions in the population. From the doubly sorted solution population, the top NP solutions are selected as next generation population.

The runtime complexity of our algorithm is found to be $O(g_{max}.N^2)$. In the problem discussed here, the solution space of the problem increases exponentially

---

Algorithm 1. Multiobjective Differential Evolution using Binary Encoded Data for selecting view to materialize in data warehouse

---

Require: NP, g_{max}, F, CR, D, MVPP DAG G, constraints;

Ensure: A set of nondominated solutions;

1. Generate NP random vectors $x_1, x_2, \cdots, x_{NP}$ of dimension D that satisfy the specified constraints;
2. $N \leftarrow NP$; $g \leftarrow 1$;
3. **repeat**
4.   **for** $i = 1$ to N **do**
5.   select x_i and $x_{r_1}, x_{r_2}, x_{r_3}$, such that $x_i \neq x_{r_1} \neq x_{r_2} \neq x_{r_3}$;
6.   **for** $j = 1$ to D **do**
7. $v_{j,i} \leftarrow D_{\Psi_j}(x_{r_1}, round(F.D_{\Psi_j}(x_{r_2}, x_{r_3})))$

$$\text{where } round(F.D_{\Psi_j}(x_{r_2,g}, x_{r_3,g})) = \begin{cases} 1, & \text{if } random[0,1] < F \wedge (D_{\Psi_j}(x_{r_2,g}, x_{r_3,g}) = 1) \\ 0, & \text{otherwise} \end{cases}$$

$$D_{\Psi_j}(x_{r_2}, x_{r_3}) = \begin{cases} 0, & \text{if } x_{j,r_2} = x_{j,r_3} \\ 1, & \text{otherwise} \end{cases}$$

8.   **end for**
9. $rand_i = random[1, D]$;
10.   **for** $j = 1$ to D **do**
11. $u_{j,i} \leftarrow \begin{cases} v_{j,i}, & \text{if}(random[0,1] \leq CR) \text{or} j = rand_i \\ x_{j,i}, & \text{otherwise} \end{cases}$
12.   **end for**
13.   **if** u_i satisfies the constraints **then**
14.   Evaluate query processing cost and materialized view maintenance cost of G for u_i, x_i ;
15.   **if** $u_i \prec x_i$ **then**
16. $x_i \leftarrow u_i$
17.   **else**
18.   **if** $x_i \nprec u_i$ **then**
19. $NP \leftarrow NP + 1$; Append u_i to the population;
20.   **end if**
21.   **end if**
22.   **end if**
23.   **end for**
24.   **if** $NP > N$ **then**
25.   Keep elite N members from NP population in the list and discard rest;
26. $NP \leftarrow N$; $g \leftarrow g + 1$;
27.   **end if**
28. **until** $g < g_{max}$
29. **return** Nondominated solutions from the final population list ;

Algorithm 2. Selecting elite N solutions by NSGA-II based nondominated sorting and SMC based diversity in solution space

---

Require: NP, Solution population $x_1, x_2, \cdots x_{NP}$, N ($N < NP$) ;

Ensure: Elite N solution population ;

1. Do nondominated sorting of the population $x_1, x_2, \cdots x_{NP}$ and assign each solution population vector with corresponding pareto-front;
2. For each $x_i, i = 1, 2, \cdots, NP$ compute maximum SMC distance to other solutions in the solution population Max_i and assign it to x_i;
3. Sort the NP solution population in ascending order of their pareto-front and descending order of Max_i;
4. **return** The top N solution population from the sorted list.

with the dimension of the problem. Threfore the space complexity increases with the size of the problem. However, the space complexity of DE is relatively low compared to some other similar optimization techniques.

3.2   Filtering Representative Solutions from Nondominated Solutions Obtained

From large number of nondominated solutions yielded by multiobjective optimization, finding significant representation set is useful for decision makers [23]. Therefore, for filtering significant solutions from the obtained solutions, we select solutions that are relatively distant from others. For doing this, first the SMC based maximum distance with other solution vectors in the solution set, say $Max_i, i = 1, 2, \cdots, n$, of every solution vector S_i of n number of non dominated solutions is computed. Then the mean μMax and standard deviation σMax of $Max_i, i = 1, 2, \cdots, n$, are computed. A solution S_i is discarded if it's $Max_i < (\mu Max + C.\sigma Max)$, where C is a real constant that may be specified as positive, negative or zero, depending on number of solutions we want to filter out from the population.

4   Experimentation and Discussion

The effectiveness of multiobjective DE using binary encoded data in handling the problem of view selection for materializing in data warehouses, is studied using TPC-H [24] benchmark data warehouse. The TPC-H schema is built and loaded in Oracle10g RDBMS for experimentation. The TPC-H benchmark queries are generated using *qgen* utility of TPC-H framework and three queries are selected and reconstructed with minor changes for constructing a test MVPP DAG which goes well with our application. The test MVPP DAG is constructed as depicted in Fig. 1. The candidate views for selection are labelled as $v_1, v_2, \cdots, v_{16}$ in Fig. 1. The sizes of candidate views for selecting are computed using *EXPLAIN PLAN* utility of Oracle10g. Though there are differences in space requirement for different rows of different relations, yet the diferences are comparatively very small considering the space availability for materializing the views in a data warehouse. In our experimentation, to make the cost computation process simpler, it is assumed that the space requirement of each row of the candidate views are equal. In our experimentation it is observed that when NP is chosen to be in between 100 to 250 the results are found better for analysis. The results presented in this paper are based on 242 initial solution population. In [18], Storn and Price suggest effective range of F between 0.4 and 1. The crossover control parameter CR controls how many parameters are expected to change in a solution vector. In our experimentation, significant results are found when CR is chosen as 0.6 and F is chosen to be 0.5. The number of iterations g_{max} in DE is fixed depending upon the complexity of the objective functions. In an instance of experimentation, result of which is discussed here, the g_{max} value is set as 40.

In one of our experimentation using the MVPP DAG presented in Fig. 1, we put a space constraint for materializing as maximum 80000 rows. Initially

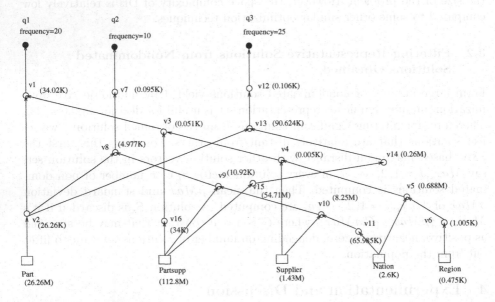

Fig. 1. An example MVPP graph using TPC-H benchmark data warehouse

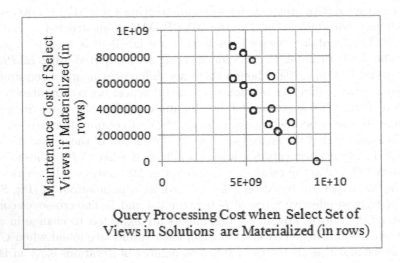

Fig. 2. Distribution of randomly generated 242 solutions in objective function space

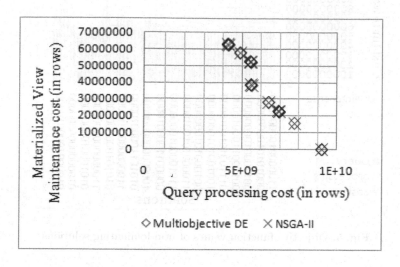

Fig. 3. Distribution of nondominated solutions after 40 iterations

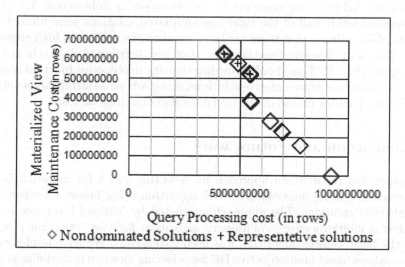

Fig. 4. Distribution of significant representetive solutions in objective space

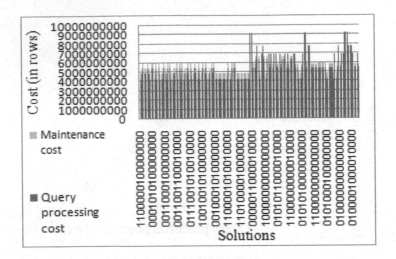

Fig. 5. Objective function values of nondominating solutions

242 non-duplicate solutions were generated which satisfy the space constraint. It has been observed in Fig. 3 that the solutions yielded by both NSGA-II [13] and multiobjective DE algorithms are distributed in same curve in the objective function space, i.e., in same *pareto front*. Also, it has been observed that the solutions yielded by multiobjective DE are equally well distributed over the objective function space like NSGA-II.

When the value of the constant C, as discussed in Sub-section 3.2, is set as 0, approximately half of the total nondominated solutions were filtered out. Another observation is that there are large number of solutions in high crowding density region of objective function space but are distributed distantly in their vector space (Fig. 5). Thus if only crowding density in objective function space is used for filtering out representetive solutions, some otherwise significant solutions in selecting views for materializing in data warehouse may be lost.

5   Conclusion and Future work

This paper has reported an approach for selecting views for materializing in data warehouse using multioblective DE algorithm using binary encodede representation of solutions. The approach suggested by Michael Lawrence in [25] presented a multiobjective evolutionary algorithm for view selection problem where the basic Genetic algorithm was used extensively. We have implemented *forma analysis* based multiobjective DE for selecting views to materialize in data warehouse for efficient OLAP query processing. Though the approach presented here is a scalable one, yet analysis of solutions with very high dimensional vectors often becomes too complex and at present the input multiple query processing plan used in our experimentation are generated offline by a seperate procedure, and therefore a very simple MVPP DAG based experimentation is presented in this paper. Moreover, it is expected that Transaction Processing council (TPC) will come-up with voluminous benchmark test dataset for this kind of experimentation on data warehouse that may be used for our future research.

References

1. Harinarayan, V., Rajaraman, A., Ullman, J.: Implementing data cubes efficiently. In: Proceedings of ACM SIGMOD International Conference on Management of Data, ACM SIGMOD, Montreal, Canada, pp. 205–216 (1996)
2. Gupta, H., Harinarayan, V., Rajaraman, A., Ullman, J.: Index selection for olap. In: Proceedings of the Thirteenth International Conference on Data Engineering, ICDE 1997, pp. 208–219. IEEE Computer Society, Washington, DC (1997)
3. Gupta, H., Mumick, I.S.: Selection of views to materialize under a maintenance cost constraint. In: Beeri, C., Bruneman, P. (eds.) ICDT 1999. LNCS, vol. 1540, pp. 453–470. Springer, Heidelberg (1998)
4. Nadeua, T., Teorey, T.: Achieving scalability in olap materialized view selection. In: Proceedings of ACM Fifth International Workshop on Data Warehousing and OLAP, DOLAP 2002, Virginia, USA, pp. 28–34. ACM (2002)
5. Serna-Encinas, M.T., Hoya-Montano, J.A.: Algorithm for selection of materialized views: based on a costs model. In: Proceedings of Eighth International Conference on Current Trends in Computer Science, Morella, Mexico, pp. 18–24 (September 2007)
6. Gupta, A., Mumick, I.: Maintenance of materialized views: Problems, techniques, and applications. IEEE Data Engineering Bulletin 18(2), 3–18 (1995)
7. Gupta, H.: Selection and maintenance of views in a data warehouse. Ph.d. thesis (1999)
8. Derakhshan, R., Stantic, B., Korn, O., Dehne, F.: Parallel simulated annealing for materialized view selection in data warehousing environments. In: Bourgeois, A.G., Zheng, S.Q. (eds.) ICA3PP 2008. LNCS, vol. 5022, pp. 121–132. Springer, Heidelberg (2008)
9. Loureiro, J., Belo, O.: An evolutionary approach to the selection and allocation of distributed cubes. In: Proceedings of Database Engineering and Applications Symposium, IDEAS 2006, Delhi, India, pp. 243–248. IEEE (2006)
10. Sun, X., Wang, Z.: An efficient materialized views selection algorithm based on PSO. In: Proceedings of International Workshop on Intelligent Systems and Applications 2009, Wuhan, China, pp. 1–4 (2009)
11. Qingzhou, Z., Xia, S., Ziqiang, W.: An efficient ma-based materialized views selection algorithm. In: Proceedings of the 2009 IITA International Conference on Control, Automation and Systems Engineering, Zhangjiajie, China, pp. 315–318 (2009)
12. Goswami, R., Bhattacharyya, D.K., Dutta, M.: Selection of views for materializing in data warehouse using MOSA and AMOSA. In: Wyld, D.C., Zizka, J., Nagamalai, D. (eds.) Advances in Computer Science, Engineering & Applications. AISC, vol. 166, pp. 619–628. Springer, Heidelberg (2012)
13. Deb, K., Pratap, A., Agarwal, S., Meyarivan, T.: A fast and elitist multiobjective genetic algorithm: NSGA-II. IEEE Transactions on Evolutionary Computation 6(2), 182–197 (2002)

14. Das, S., Suganthan, P.N.: Differential evolution: A survey of the state-of-the-art. IEEE Transactions on Evolutionary Computation 15(1), 4–31 (2011)
15. Zhou, A., Qu, B.Y., Li, H., Zhao, S.Z., Suganthan, P.N., Zhang, Q.: Multiobjective evolutionary algorithms: A survey of the state of the art. Swarm and Evolutionary Computation 1(1), 32–49 (2011)
16. Sengupta, S., Das, S., Nasir, M., Suganthan, P.N.: Risk minimization in biometric sensor networks an evolutionary multi-objective optimization approach. Soft Computing 17(1), 133–144 (2013)
17. Yang, J., Karlapalem, K., Li, Q.: Algorithm for materialized view design in data warehousing environment. In: Proceedings of VLDB 1997, Athens, Greece, pp. 136–145 (1997)
18. Storn, R., Price, K.: Differential evolution-a simple and efficient heuristic for global optimization over continuous spaces. Journal of Global Optimization 11, 341–359 (1997)
19. Gong, T., Tuson, A.: Differential evolution for binary encoding. In: 11th Online World Conference on Soft Computing in Industrial Applications, WSC11 (2006)
20. Radcliffe, N.J.: Equivalenc class analysis of genetic algorithms. Complex Systems, 183–205 (1991)
21. Radcliffe, N.J.: Forma analysis and random respectful recombination. In: Proceedings of the International Conference on Genetic Algorithms - ICGA 1991, pp. 222–229. Morgan Kaufmann, San Francisco (1991)
22. Sokal, R., Michener, C.: A statistical method for evaluating systematic relationships. University of Kansas Science Bulletin 38, 1409–1438 (1958)
23. Benson, H.P., Sayin, S.: Towards finding global representations of the efficient set in multiple objective mathematical programming. Naval Research Logistics (NRL) 44(1), 47–67 (1997)
24. Transaction Processing Council: TPC-H benchmark specification (2008), Published at http://www.tpc.org/hspec.html
25. Lawrence, M.: Multiobjective genetic algorithms for materialized view selection in olap data warehouses. In: Proceedings of the 8th Annual Conference on Genetic and Evolutionary Computation, pp. 699–706. ACM (2006)

Robust Protective Relay Setting and Coordination Using Modified Differential Evolution Considering Different Network Topologies

Joymala Moirangthem[1], Bijaya Ketan Panigrahi[2], K.R. Krishnanand[3], and Sanjib Kumar Panda[3]

[1] Electrical Instrumentation and Control Engineering, SOA University, Bhubaneswar, India
[2] Electrical Engineering, Indian Institute of Technology, Delhi, India
[3] Electrical and Computer Engineering, National University of Singapore, Singapore
{joy.mala,krishkr09}@gmail.com, bkpanigrahi@ee.iitd.ac.in,
eleskp@nus.edu.sg

Abstract. In real power system, the system may be subjected to operate in different network topologies due to single line outage contingencies, network reconfiguration and maintenance. These changes in the network would lead to operational inconsistency of directional overcurrent relays. To overcome this problem, a set of new coordination constraints corresponding to each network topology needs to be formulated. Directional Overcurrent Relays (ODCRs) problem can be formulated as a nonlinear optimization problem and also in addition to nonlinearity, the optimization problem encounter a large number of coordination constraints. This paper presents a modified Differential Evolution (DE) algorithm to handle such type of Optimal Directional Overcurrent Relays problem. Modified DE computes the optimal time dial setting and pickup current setting in terms of discrete values which collectively minimize the total operating time of the relays. To verify the performance of the proposed method, similar evolutionary computation methods such as the Genetic Algorithm (GA) approaches are also implemented using the same database. The proposed method has been verified on 8-bus test system. The results indicate that the proposed method can obtain better results than the method compared in terms of total operating time and convergence performance for both fixed and changed network topologies.

Keywords: Differential Evolution Algorithm, Directional overcurrent relays, Relay coordination, Pickup current settings, Time dial settings, Time multiplier settings.

1   Introduction

One of the fundamental tasks in a power system protection is to disconnect the faulty section from the network at a minimum time when any type of fault occurs. Directional Overcurrent Relays is commonly used for the protection of interconnected networks and looped distribution network [1]-[3]. Selecting suitable settings (TDS & Ip) ensures the effective coordination between primary relays and backup relays even in case of different fault conditions [1].

B.K. Panigrahi et al. (Eds.): SEMCCO 2013, Part II, LNCS 8298, pp. 107–118, 2013.
© Springer International Publishing Switzerland 2013

Several optimization algorithms have been proposed and applied for the coordination of DOCRs. The coordination problem can be formulated as Linear Programming Problem (LPP), in which pickup current settings are assumed to be known and operating time of relay is a linear function of TDS. After the problem formulation as LPP, it can be solved by linear programming techniques such simplex [1], [4], [5] two-phase simplex [6] and dual simplex methods [7]. The use of conventional techniques leads to the introduction of slack or surplus variables for each inequality constraint which would result in undesirable increase in the number of variables handled. Hence, only fewer constraints can be considered in conventional techniques. In [8]-[10], Genetic Algorithm (GA), Particle Swarm Optimization (PSO) and Modified PSO are proposed to determine the optimal settings of the relay.

A network topology may change due to system contingencies, maintenance activities and network reconfiguration. The change in the network topology could cause the variation in the fault current which lead to incoordination of directional overcurrent because the parameters set for each relay was for fixed network. A new coordination constraint is formed by considering the coordination constraints for each topology to the main coordination problem of the fixed network [11]. In [11], a hybrid GA is proposed to solve the coordination problem considering the effects of the different network topologies and also at the same it improves the convergence of the conventional GA. In this method, the pickup current settings are coded into genetic strings as discrete variables and to determine the optimal TDS as continuous variables for each genetic string, LP is used. In [12], the DOCR problem is formulated as an interval linear programming (ILP) problem. The obtained ILP problem, which has no equality constraints corresponding to each relay pair, is converted to standard linear programming (IP) thereby, reducing the number constraints in new formulation.

In this paper, a modified Differential Evolution is developed to determine the optimal discrete value of TDS and Ip, satisfying the set of inequality coordination constraints which are related to different network topologies. Modified DE also improves the convergence performance. In conventional DE the scaling factor may get stuck to local optimum as the parameters are tuned constant value and not tailored for handling discrete variables. The proposed method is applied to 8 bus test system and the results show robust coordination against topological uncertainty.

The paper is organized as follows. In Section 2, the coordination problem in fixed network topology and different network topologies is presented. In Section 3, describes about the modified differential evolutionary algorithm which has been applied to solve the problem. In Section 4, the proposed method is tested on 8 bus model test systems and the results are discussed by comparing with the existing techniques. Finally, conclusions are summarized in Section 5.

2   Overcurrent Relay Coordination Problem

In the coordination problem of directional overcurrent relays (DOCRs), the target is determine the optimal TDS and Ip for each relay so that the overall operating times of primary relays are minimized without violating any coordination constraints. The relay coordination problem for both fixed and different network topologies are presented in this section. The transient network during partial fault clearance can be ignored in this study since the relays operate based on the local current measurements available to them and the transient currents decay very soon for large networks considered in such studies.

2.1   Problem Formulation for Main Network Topology

Mathematically, for a fixed network topology the DOCRs problem can be formulated as non-linear optimization problem as follows:

$$Minimize \ J = \sum_{i=1}^{n} T_{pri\_Near}^{i} \tag{1}$$

where n is the number of relays and $T_{pri\_Near}^{i}$ is the operating time of the ith relay for near end fault.

2.1.1   Relay Characteristics

The operating time of ith overcurrent relay is a function of Time Dial Setting (TDS_i), Pickup Current Setting (I_{p_i}) and the fault current passing through the relay (I_{f_i}). The relay characteristics are given by constants a and b.

$$T_i = F_i\left(TDS_i, I_{p_i}, I_{f_i}\right) = \frac{(a \times TDS_i)}{\left(I_{f_i} / I_{p_i}\right)^b - 1} \tag{2}$$

2.1.2   Limits on the Relay Settings

The bounds on the relay settings can be represented as

$$I_{p_i}^{\min} < I_{p_i} < I_{p_i}^{\max} \tag{3}$$

$$TDS_i^{\min} < TDS_i < TDS_i^{\max} \tag{4}$$

Overcurrent relay coordination involves the appropriate settings of TDS_i (discrete) and I_{p_i} (discrete). The lower limit of I_{p_i} is the minimum tap available. The upper limit of I_{p_i} is the maximum tap available. Similarly TDS_i has also lower and upper limit values based on the relay current-time characteristic.

2.1.3   Coordination Criteria

Coordination constraint between the primary and backup relays is illustrated as,

$$T_{backup} - T_{primary} \geq CTI \tag{5}$$

where, T_{backup} is the operating time of backup relay and $T_{primary}$ is the operating time of the primary relay. The Coordination Time Interval (*CTI*) ensures that the operating time of the backup relay must be greater than the corresponding primary relay for all the faults considered (all fault types, normal and single-contingency conditions). The value of *CTI* is normally selected between 0.2 to 0.5 s.

2.2   Problem Formulation of Changed Network Topologies

The fault current passing through the relays changes when the network topology is changed. Owing to the changed fault current, the operating time of primary and backup relays will also change and this change in the operating time leads to the incoordination. To overcome this problem, a new set of coordination constraints is added to the coordination constraints of main topology. Considering the different network topologies due to single line outage contingencies, the coordination constraint is reformulated as follows:

$$T^s_{backup} - T^s_{primary} \geq CTI, s \in S \qquad (6)$$

where T^s_{backup} and $T^s_{primary}$ are the operating time of backup and primary relays for the sth network topology. S is the set of all topologies which have been obtained under single line outages contingencies of the main topology.

3   Modified Differential Evolution (DE)

The differential evolution (DE) algorithm inspired evolutionary computing, proposed by Storn and Price [13], is a stochastic, population based optimization method. DE has been successfully applied in many engineering fields such as power systems [14], mechanical engineering [14], pattern recognition [14] etc. due to its simplicity in implementation, robustness and fast convergence. The modified algorithm customized for the problem at hand is as follows.

3.1   Initialization

It begins with randomly initiated population of N D–dimensional parameter vectors, which represents the potential solutions of the global optimum. The total number of iterations or generations is represented by G. Each ith vector at g^{th} iteration is produced using corresponding minimum and maximum limits, using a uniformly distributed random variable. This causes the initial solutions to be spread over the search space without any bias. For all equations of the algorithm, integers $i \in [1, N]$, $j \in [1, D]$ and $g \in [1, G]$.

$$X_i^g = \left[x_{(i,1)}^g, x_{(i,2)}^g, \dots, x_{(i,j)}^g, \dots, x_{(i,D-1)}^g, x_{(i,D)}^g \right] \qquad (7)$$

Each element in the candidate vector has lower and upper numerical bounds, which are characteristic of the system being optimized.

$$X_i^{lower} = \left[x_1^{lower}, x_2^{lower}, \ldots, x_j^{lower}, \ldots, x_{(D-1)}^{lower}, x_D^{lower}\right] \tag{8}$$

$$X_i^{upper} = \left[x_1^{upper}, x_2^{upper}, \ldots, x_j^{upper}, \ldots, x_{(D-1)}^{upper}, x_D^{upper}\right] \tag{9}$$

$$x_{(i,j)}^1 = x_j^{lower} \times \left(1 - rand_{(i,j)}\right) + x_j^{upper} \times rand_{(i,j)} \tag{10}$$

It is notable that the optimization here contains physically dissimilar variables; the candidate vector is represented as a concatenation of those variables.

$$X_i^g = \left[TDS_{(i,1)}^g, TDS_{(i,2)}^g, \ldots, TDS_{(i,n)}^g, Ip_{(i,1)}^g, Ip_{(i,2)}^g, \ldots, Ip_{(i,n)}^g\right] \tag{11}$$

3.2   Mutation

This step modifies the potential vectors to be tested against the rest of the current vectors, going through a sorting process to ensure that only the best is transferred to the next iteration. It can be done through one of the many ways shown using mutually exclusive random indices a, b, c, d, e and index of the best vector.

1) "DE/rand/1":

$$M_i^g = X_a^g + \lambda\left(X_b^g - X_c^g\right) \tag{12}$$

2) "DE/best/1":

$$M_i^g = X_{best}^g + \lambda\left(X_a^g - X_b^g\right) \tag{13}$$

3) "DE/rand-to-best/1":

$$M_i^g = X_i^g + \lambda\left(X_{best}^g - X_i^g\right) + \gamma\left(X_a^g - X_b^g\right) \tag{14}$$

4) "DE/best/2":

$$M_i^g = X_{best}^g + \lambda\left(X_a^g - X_b^g\right) + \gamma\left(X_c^g - X_d^g\right) \tag{15}$$

5) "DE/rand/2":

$$M_i^g = X_a^g + \lambda\left(X_b^g - X_c^g\right) + \gamma\left(X_d^g - X_e^g\right) \tag{16}$$

Obtaining the modified vector M_i^g is dependent on the control parameters λ and γ, which can be intelligently modified to handle discrete variables. Instead of using them as just multipliers, in this algorithm they are treated as operators on the differential vectors which can multiply adaptive weights and also discretize the differential vectors operated upon.

$$\lambda(\theta) = \left\{ \overline{\overline{(\theta \times \Lambda)}} \middle| \Lambda = \Lambda_0 + \delta \right\} \tag{17}$$

$$\gamma(\theta) = \left\{ \overline{\overline{(\theta \times \Omega)}} \middle| \Omega = \Omega_0 + \delta \right\} \tag{18}$$

The double-bar operator represents discretization of the variable to the nearest possible state as allowed for TDS or Ip values. θ represents a generic multi-dimensional matrix of real numbers. Λ and Ω are multipliers which start with Λ_0 and Ω_0 values respectively, but are modified by a Gaussian random variable δ, which has standard deviation of unity over a mean value (μ^g) given by the normalized mean of the current population's objective values. If the mean of objective values are relatively small, larger is the perturbation, leading to higher explorative capabilities. As the iteration progresses, the mean value becomes relatively higher and the probability of smaller perturbations becomes high, leading to more exploitative capabilities of the population.

$$F^g = \left[f(X_1^g), f(X_2^g), \ldots, f(X_i^g), \ldots, f(X_{(N-1)}^g), f(X_N^g) \right]^T \tag{19}$$

$$\mu^g = \left(\frac{\min(F^g) - N^{-1} \sum_{i=1}^{N} f(X_i^g)}{\max(F^g)} \right) \tag{20}$$

where F^g is the column vector containing the objective values of the current population. The values of μ^g are reasonable for mutation operation only if all values in F^g are non-negative. Since the objective of the problem studied is total operating time, this criterion is satisfied automatically.

3.3   Crossover

It determines the intermixing of the mutant population with the original population. Depending on Cr, either mutant element or the original population is selected to a crossed population as shown below.

$$c_{(i,j)}^g = \begin{cases} m_{(i,j)}^g & if\ (rand_{(i,j)} \leq Cr)\ \ or\ \ j = j_{rand} \\ x_{(i,j)}^g & otherwise \end{cases} \tag{21}$$

where $c_{(i,j)}^g$ is the jth element of the vector C_i^g, $m_{(i,j)}^g$ is the jth element of the vector M_i^g and $x_{(i,j)}^g$ is the jth element of the vector X_i^g. The value j_{rand} is a random integer generated such that $j_{rand} \in [1,D]$. The value of $Cr \in (0,1)$ is generally taken high such that the crossed population would have higher probability of having larger percentage of mutated portions.

3.4   Selection

From the crossed population and the current population, candidate vectors are selected for the next generation, purely based on merit (or objective function value). N vectors giving the best objective values when both populations combined are selected.

$$X_i^{g+1} = \begin{cases} C_i^g & if \quad f(C_i^g) \le f(X_i^g) \\ X_i^g & otherwise \end{cases} \tag{22}$$

The procedure is repeated till specific criteria for termination is reached.

4   Case Study

In order to assess the proposed method, the developed modified DE is applied to 8-bus test-system shown in Fig.1. The system data is given in [9]. : The overcurrent relays having IEC standard inverse-type characteristics is considered for research work. The network consists of 14 relays shown in Fig 1. The TDS can vary from 0.05 to 1.1 with a step of 0.01 and the Ip can vary from 0.5 to 2.5 with a step of 0.25. The ratios of the CTs are shown in Table 1. CTI is assumed to be 0.3, a=0.14 and b=0.02. The primary/backup relay pairs and the corresponding fault current are shown in Table 2.

The proposed modified DE is capable of solving discrete non-linear optimization problems. The DOCRs coordination is solved for fixed network topology using the GA and modified DE and was coded in MATLAB with total number of variables 28 and population size of 20 individuals. The maximum number of generation count used is 1000. The modified DE performs best with the last strategy in DE. The scaling factor Λ_0 and Ω_0 are taken to be as 0.5 and 0.3 respectively after many trials. The crossover rate used is 0.8. In GA, its own individual best performance for this problem is found empirically when the probability of selection, crossover and mutation are taken as 0.6, 0.5 and 0.02 respectively. The optimal time dial setting and pick up current setting of each overcurrent relay are computed for two cases.

Case 1) Coordination problem considering fixed network topology
Case 2) Coordination problem considering changed network topology

Table 1. CT ratio for 8 bus system

Relay no	CT ratio	Relay no	CT ratio
1	1200/5	8	1200/5
2	1200/5	9	800/5
3	800/5	10	1200/5
4	1200/5	11	1200/5
5	1200/5	12	1200/5
6	1200/5	13	1200/5
7	800/5	14	800/5

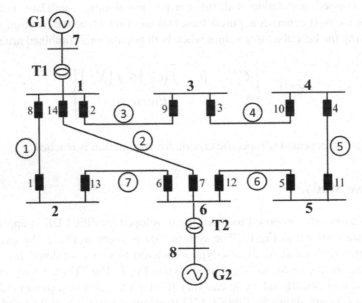

Fig. 1. 8-bus test-system, 14 relay pairs (Nodes, branches and relays are labelled. Node labels are in bold and branch labels are circled. Line outage numbers and branch labels are the same.)

The optimal values are shown in Table 3. From the results obtained by developing GA and modified DE, it shows the latter gave better optimal solution than GA for both the cases. Table 4 shows the coordination constraints number, number of incoordination and percentage of incoordination for fixed network and changed in the network topology due to single line outages contingencies. The parameters already set for fixed network topology would no longer make the system operate without any incoordination when there is a changed in the network topology because of the fault current variations. Table 5 shows the obtained optimal settings for fixed network and after consideration of different network topologies.

Table 2. Primary/Backup Relay Pairs and Fault Currents in Fixed Network Topology

Primary/Backup pairs		Near-End Fault Current	
Primary Relay No	Backup Relay No	Primary Relay (KA)	Backup Relay (KA)
1	6	2.6671	2.6671
2	1	5.2841	1.5791
2	7	5.698	2.0258
3	2	3.6274	3.6274
4	3	2.4216	2.4216
5	4	1.3651	1.3651
6	5	4.5068	0.7049
6	14	5.2354	1.4855
7	5	4.0438	0.2404
7	13	4.188	0.3959
8	7	5.1201	1.402
8	9	4.4388	0.6668
9	10	1.43	1.43
10	11	2.5382	2.5382
11	12	3.789	3.789
12	13	5.3675	1.6259
12	14	5.7953	2.086
13	8	2.4943	2.4943
14	1	4.188	0.3959
14	9	3.8957	2.0271

To verify the robustness of the modified DE, the results of the cases 1 and 2 are compared for an arbitrary relay pair. The operating time of primary and backup pairs are shown in Table 6 for every single line outage contingency.

Table 3. Optimal Settings of Relays for 8-Bus Test-System for Fixed Network Topology

Relay Number	Genetic Algorithm, GA		Proposed DE Algorithm	
	TDS	Ip	TDS	Ip
1	0.23	1.25	0.36	0.5
2	0.58	1	0.26	2.5
3	0.52	0.5	0.2	2
4	0.35	0.5	0.14	1.75
5	0.18	0.5	0.18	0.5
6	0.49	0.5	0.35	1.25
7	0.59	0.75	0.23	2.25
8	0.51	0.75	0.26	2
9	0.13	1	0.25	0.5
10	0.13	1.7	0.21	1.25
11	0.41	0.5	0.46	0.5
12	0.59	0.5	0.42	1.5
13	0.41	0.5	0.29	0.75
14	0.55	0.75	0.37	1.5
Objective Function Value (s)	11.9424		10.2864	

Table 4. Number of incoordination Constraints due to Single line Outage

Line Outage No	Coordination Constraints No.	Incoordination Constraints No.	Percentage of Incoordination
1	12	3	25
2	12	4	33
3	10	1	10
4	11	4	36.4
5	11	2	18.2
6	10	2	20
7	12	3	25

Table 5. Optimal Settings of Relays for 8-Bus Test-System

Relay Number	DE, Case 1		DE, Case 2	
	TDS	Ip	TDS	Ip
1	0.36	0.5	0.55	0.75
2	0.26	2.5	0.6	1.25
3	0.2	2	0.4	1.75
4	0.14	1.75	0.3	1.75
5	0.18	0.5	0.45	0.5
6	0.35	1.25	0.5	1.5
7	0.23	2.25	0.5	1.75
8	0.26	2	0.5	2
9	0.25	0.5	0.7	0.75
10	0.21	1.25	0.45	1.75
11	0.46	0.5	0.45	2.5
12	0.42	1.5	0.55	2.5
13	0.29	0.75	0.65	0.75
14	0.37	1.5	0.5	2.25
Objective Function Value (s)	10.2864		20.4	

Column 1 of Table 6 shows the line outage number and zero indicates the fixed network topology i.e. without any line outage. Columns 2 and 3 represents the operating time for backup and primary relays for case 1 and the incoordination constraint value is shown in column 4 for case 1. Columns 5, 6 and 7 show the operating time for backup relays, primary relays and incoordination constraint value for case 2. Near-end fault is created in line no. 3 (Relay 2 will act as primary and relay 7 as back for relay 2).

By employing the setting obtained from the case 1, the violation of four coordination constraints is caused by single line outage. It is seen from the Table 6, that setting obtained from case 2 removed all the violation constraints, thereby making solution robust against the single line outage even though the values of TDS and Ip are increased in multiple network topology. The objective function value shown in the Table 7 shows the advantage of proposed method over the GA.

Table 6. Operating Time of Primary/Backup Relay (2, 7) due to Single Line Outage Contingencies (for near-end faults)

Line Outage No.	Case 1			Case 2		
	Primary Operating Time	Backup Operating Time	Incoordination (CTI= 0.3)	Primary Operating Time	Backup Operating Time	Incoordination (CTI=0.3)
0	0.7766	0.3416	0.34	1.3662	0.6939	0.69
1	0.7908	0.9167	**0.1259**	1.3854	0.3497	0.3
2	-	-	-	-	-	-
3	-	-	-	-	-	-
4	0.7362	0.9133	**0.1771**	1.3106	0.419	0.42
5	0.7362	1.1182	0.38	1.3106	0.7495	0.75
6	0.7362	0.9133	**0.1771**	1.3106	0.419	0.4
7	0.7905	0.9159	**0.1254**	1.385	1.7339	0.3

Table 7. Optimal Settings of Relays for 8-Bus Test-System after Considering the Different Network Topologies

Relay Number	Genetic Algorithm, GA		Proposed DE Algorithm	
	TDS	Ip	TDS	Ip
1	0.490	1	0.55	0.75
2	0.62	1.5	0.6	1.25
3	0.62	0.75	0.4	1.75
4	0.39	1	0.3	1.75
5	0.44	0.5	0.45	0.5
6	0.48	1.5	0.5	1.5
7	0.74	1	0.5	1.75
8	0.69	1.25	0.5	2
9	0.96	0.5	0.7	0.75
10	0.52	1.75	0.45	1.75
11	0.91	0.75	0.45	2.5
12	0.67	2.5	0.55	2.5
13	0.67	1	0.65	0.75
14	0.65	1.75	0.5	2.25
Objective Function Value (s)	22.71		20.08	
No. of Function Evaluation	12000		9000	

5   Conclusion

This paper presents the reformulation of DOCRs coordination problem considering different network topologies. DOCRs can be formulated as a complex non-linear optimization problem .The proposed modified DE is applied to find the optimal settings of the DOCR without violating any of the coordination constraints. The algorithm is tailored for handling discrete variables and exhibit adaptive mutation as the state of the population changes. The proposed method provides the system robustness against network uncertainties caused through line outages.

References

1. Urdaneta, A.J., Nadira, R., Perez, L.G.: Optimal coordination of directional overcurrent relays in interconnected power systems. IEEE Trans. Power Del. 3(3), 903–911 (1988)
2. Abdelaziz, A.Y., Talaat, H.E.A., Nosseir, A.I., Hajjar, A.A.: An adaptive protection scheme for optimal coordination of overcurrent relays. Elect. Power Syst. Res. 61(1), 1–9 (2002)
3. Urdaneta, A.J., Perez, L.G., Restrepo, H.: Optimal coordination of directional overcurrent relays considering dynamic changes in the network topology. IEEE Trans. Power Del. 12(4), 1458–1464 (1997)
4. Urdaneta, A.J., Restrepo, H., Marquez, S., Sanchez, J.: Coordination of directional overcurrent relay timing using linear programming. IEEE Trans. Power Del. 11(1), 122–129 (1996)
5. Braga, A.S., Saraiva, J.T.: Co-ordination of directional overcurrent relays in meshed networks using simplex method. In: Proc. 1996 IEEE MELECON Conf., vol. 3, pp. 1535–1538 (1996)
6. Chattopadhyay, B., Sachdev, M.S., Sidhu, T.S.: An on-line relay coordination algorithm for adaptive protection using linear programming technique. IEEE Trans. Power Delivery 11, 165–173 (1996)
7. Abyaneh, H.A., Keyhani, R.: Optimal co-ordination of overcurrent relays in power system by dual simplex method. In: Proc. 1995 AUPEC Conf., Perth, Australia, vol. 3, pp. 440–445 (1995)
8. So, C.W., Li, K.K., Lai, K.T., Fung, K.Y.: Application of genetic algorithm for overcurrent relay coordination. In: Proc. Inst. Elect. Eng. Developments in Power System Protection Conf., pp. 66–69 (1997)
9. Zeineldin, H.H., El-Saadany, E.F., Salama, M.M.A.: Optimal coordination of overcurrent relays using a modified particle swarm optimization. Elect. Power Syst. Res. 76, 988–995 (2006)
10. Mansour, M.M., Mekhamer, S.F., El-Sherif El-Kharbawe, N.: A modified particle swarm optimizer for the coordination of directional overcurrent relays. IEEE Trans. Power Del. 22(3), 1400–1410 (2007)
11. Saberi Noghabi, A., Sadeh, J., Rajabi Mashhadi, H.: Considering different network topologies in optimal overcurrent relay coordination using a hybrid GA. IEEE Trans. Power Del. 24(4), 1857–1863 (2009)
12. Saberi Noghabi, A., Rajabi Mashhadi, H., Sadeh, J.: Optimal Coordination of Directional Overcurrent Relays Considering Different Network Topologies Using Interval Linear Programming. IEEE Trans. Power Del. 25(3), 1348–1354 (2010)
13. Storn, R.: Differential evolution: A simple and efficient adaptive scheme for global optimization over continuous spaces. Int. Comput. Sci. Inst., Berkely, CA, Tech. Rept. (1995)
14. Das, S., Suganthan, P.N.: Differential Evolution: A Survey of the State-of-the-Art. IEEE Trans. Evol. Comput. 15, 4–31 (2010)

Real-Coded Genetic Algorithm and Fuzzy Logic Approach for Real-Time Load-Tracking Performance of an Autonomous Power System

Abhik Banerjee[1], V. Mukherjee[2], and S.P. Ghoshal[3]

[1] Department of Electrical Engineering, Asansol Engineering College,
Asansol, West Bengal, India
[2] Department of Electrical Engineering, Indian School of Mines, Dhanbad, Jharkhand, India
[3] Department of Electrical Engineering, National Institute of Technology,
Durgapur, West Bengal, India
abhik_banerjee@rediffmail.com, vivek_agamani@yahoo.com,
spghoshalnitdgp@gmail.com

Abstract. This paper focuses on the application of real-coded genetic algorithm (RGA) to determine the optimal controller parameters of an autonomous power system model for its load tracking performance analysis. To determine the real-time parameters of the studied model, Sugeno fuzzy logic (SFL) is used. RGA is applied to obtain the controller parameters for transient response analysis under various operating conditions and fuzzy logic is applied to develop the rule base of the SFL model. The developed fuzzy system gives the on-line controller parameters for different operating conditions. Time-domain simulation of the investigated power system model reveals that the proposed RGA-SFL yields on-line, off-nominal controller parameters, resulting in on-line terminal voltage response. To show the efficiency and effectiveness of RGA, binary coded genetic algorithm is taken for the sake of comparison.

Keywords: Automatic voltage regulator, load-tracking performance, optimization, real-coded genetic algorithm, Sugeno fuzzy logic.

1   Introduction

Independent power producers (IPPs) are participating in the power market to supply reliable power to the consumers [1]. The main requirement of the distributed generation (DG) is focused due to the restructuring of the electric power industry and the increase of electric power demand. So, in modern power system, the use of the DG becomes more important because of the stringent present-day energy crisis. Generally, a DG system consists of small-scale power generators that are located close to the load centre. The main advantages of the employment of the DG systems are that consumers can generate electric power with or without grid backup and the surplus power generation can be sold back to the grid under low load-demand conditions. For example, a hybrid fuel cell-diesel engine generator (DEG)

B.K. Panigrahi et al. (Eds.): SEMCCO 2013, Part II, LNCS 8298, pp. 119–131, 2013.

system promises a lot of opportunities in remote areas which are far from the utility grid and DEGs may be employed to generate power for the connected loads [2].

The main function of the automatic voltage regulator (AVR) is to control the terminal voltage by adjusting the generator excitation under any load condition. Despite significant studies in the development of advanced control strategies, the classical proportional-integral-derivative (PID) controllers [3] remain the controllers of choice to control the AVR because of its simple structure and robustness to variations of the system parameters. Proper selection of the PID controller parameters is necessary for the satisfactory operation of the AVR.

Recently, evolutionary computation techniques such as genetic algorithm (GA) [4] and particle swarm optimization [5] have been applied to obtain the optimal PID controller parameters. Traditional, binary coded GA suffers from few drawbacks when applied to multi-dimensional and high-precision numerical problems [6]. The situation may be improved if GA is used with real number data, called as real-coded genetic algorithm (RGA) [7]. Sugeno fuzzy model for on-line tuning of the PID controller has been adopted in [5, 8].

Off-line conditions are sets of nominal system operating conditions, which is given in the SFL table and in real-time environment these input operating conditions vary dynamically and become off-nominal. This necessitates the use of very fast acting SFL to determine the off-nominal controller parameters for off-nominal input operating conditions occurring in real-time.

The objectives of this paper are (a) to determine the off-line, nominal controller parameters by employing either RGA or GA, (b) to explore the suitability of the SFL-based controller for on-line real-time environment, (c) to critically examine the performance of the proposed controller of the autonomous power system for practical implementation under any sort of input disturbances and (d) to establish the suitability of the RGA-SFL over the GA-SFL for the present application.

The rest of the paper is documented in the following headings. The next section describes the proposed autonomous power system model. In Section 3, the mathematical modeling of the present problem is formulated. A brief description of the RGA is given in Section 4. In Section 5, a short review of the SFL is done. Section 6 highlights on the input parameters of the studied autonomous power system model and those of the adopted algorithms. Simulation-based results of the present work are presented and discussed in Section 7. Finally, concluding remarks are focused in Section 8.

2   Autonomous Power System Model

An autonomous power system model of a typical DEG consisting of a speed governor and an AVR with a PID controller [5] is considered in the present work and is presented in Fig. 1. The upper half blocks of Fig. 1 represent the standard mechanical model of a DEG with a speed governor and the lower half blocks represent the electrical model of a DEG with an AVR [5]. Parameters of the speed governor are the droop R and a tunable integral controller gain K_{ii}. The objective of this integral controller is to eliminate the steady-state frequency error of the studied model.

The parameters H and D shown in Fig. 1 are p.u. inertia constant and the p.u. damping constant of the DEG, respectively.

Table 1 depicts the transfer function [9] and the parameter limits of the different components of the studied model.

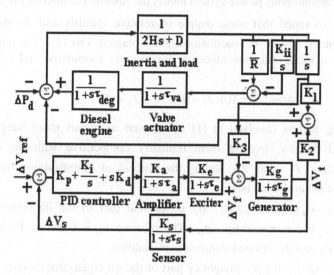

Fig. 1. Block diagram of the studied autonomous power system model

Table 1. Transfer functions and parameter limits of different components of the studied autonomous power system model

Component	Transfer function	Parameter limits
PID controller	$G_{PID}(s) = K_p + \dfrac{K_i}{s} + sK_d$	$0.0001 \leq K_p,\ K_i,\ K_d \leq 1.0$
I controller	$G_I(s) = \dfrac{K_{ii}}{s}$	$0.0001 \leq K_{ii} \leq 1.0$
Amplifier	$G_{amplifier}(s) = \dfrac{K_a}{1 + s\tau_a}$	$10 \leq K_a \leq 40\ ;\ 0.02\ s \leq \tau_a \leq 1.0\ s$
Exciter	$G_{exciter}(s) = \dfrac{K_e}{1 + s\tau_e}$	$1 \leq K_e \leq 10\ ;\ 0.4\ s \leq \tau_e \leq 1.0\ s$
Generator	$G_{generator}(s) = \dfrac{K_g}{1 + s\tau_g}$	K_g depends on load (0.7-1.0); $1.0\ s \leq \tau_g \leq 2.0\ s$
Sensor	$G_{sensor}(s) = \dfrac{K_s}{1 + s\tau_s}$	$0.001\ s \leq \tau_s \leq 0.06\ s$
DEG	$G_{deg}(s) = \dfrac{1}{1 + s\tau_{deg}}$	$\tau_{deg} = 2.31\ s$
Valve actuator (VA)	$G_{VA}(s) = \dfrac{1}{1 + s\tau_{va}}$	$\tau_{va} = 0.82\ s$

3   Mathematical Problem Formulation

3.1   Eigenvalue Analysis

In the studied autonomous power system model the tunable parameters (K_p, K_i, K_d, and K_{ii}) are so tuned that some degree of relative stability and the damping of electromechanical modes of oscillations are obtained [10,11]. To satisfy these requirements, a multi-objective objective function is formulated and is presented in (1).

$$Min \quad J = 10 \times J_1 + 10 \times J_2 + J_3 + J_4 \tag{1}$$

The weighting factors involved in (1) are chosen to impart more weights to J_1 and J_2 , and thereby, making them mutually competitive with the other two components (like J_3 and J_4) during the process of optimization. The different components of (1) are stated below.

$J_1 = \Sigma_i(\sigma_0 - \sigma_i)^2$ if $\sigma_0 > \sigma_i$, σ_i is the real part of the ith eigenvalue. The relative stability is determined by $-\sigma_0$. The value of σ_0 is taken as -1.0 for the best relative stability and the optimal transient performance.

$J_2 = \Sigma_i(\xi_0 - \xi_i)^2$, if (β_i , imaginary part of the ith eigenvalue) > 0.0, ξ_i is   the damping ratio of the ith eigenvalue and $\xi_i < \xi_0$. Minimization of this objective function will minimize the maximum overshoot.

$J_3 = \Sigma_i(\beta_i)^2$, if $\sigma_i \geq -\sigma_0$. High value of β_i to the right of the vertical line at $-\sigma_0$ is to be prevented. Zeroing of J_3 will increase the damping further.

$J_4 =$ an arbitrarily chosen very high fixed value (say, 10^6), which will indicate some σ_i values $\geq$ 0.0. This means unstable oscillation occurs for that particular set of parameters. This set of particular parameters will be rejected during the process of optimization.

It is to be noted here that by minimizing J , closed loop system poles are, consistently, pushed further left of $j\omega$ axis with reduction in imaginary part also.

Thus, enhancing the relative stability and increasing the damping ratio above ξ_0 .

3.2   Design of Misfitness Function

The prime requirements of the minimization of (1) are to obtain higher relative stability and to achieve better damping of the electromechanical modes of oscillations. These ensure minimal incremental change in terminal voltage (ΔV_t (p.u.)) response. This may be achieved when minimized overshoot (o_{sh}), minimized undershoot (u_{sh}), lesser settling time (t_{st}), and lesser time derivative of incremental change in terminal voltage ($\frac{d}{dt}(\Delta V_t)$) of the small-signal/ transient response are achieved. To assess the performance of the eigenvalue analysis based minimization approach, modal analysis [10] is adopted. Based on the results of these, a misfitness function (MF) is designed in (2) [11].

$$MF = (o_{sh} \times 10^6)^2 + (u_{sh} \times 10^6)^2 + (t_{st})^2 + (\frac{d}{dt}(\Delta V_t) \times 10^6)^2 \qquad (2)$$

These are determined by modal analysis subsequent to $\Delta\delta = 5° = 0.0857$ rad, state perturbation [10].

3.3   Constraints of the Problem

The constrained optimization problem for the tuning of parameters of the studied autonomous power system is subject to the minimum and maximum limits of the tunable parameters (K_p, K_i, K_d, K_{ii}) as given in (3).

$$\left.\begin{array}{cc} K_p^{\min} \le K_p \le K_p^{\max}, & K_i^{\min} \le K_i \le K_i^{\max} \\ K_d^{\min} \le K_d \le K_d^{\max}, & K_{ii}^{\min} \le K_{ii} \le K_{ii}^{\max} \end{array}\right\} \qquad (3)$$

From the above discussions, the optimal values of the tunable parameters of the studied model are obtained by minimizing the J value (i.e. eigenvalue analysis) with the help of any of the optimizing techniques (RGA/GA). And, by adopting the modal analysis [10], the value of the MF is obtained.

4   Review of RGA and Its Application to Load-Tracking Problem

For effective genetic operation, the crossover and mutation operators which can deal directly with the floating point numbers are used in RGA. The different steps of RGA are [7] real coded initialization of each chromosome, selection operation based on computation of the fitness function and merit ordering, crossover and mutation operation, sorting of the fitness values in increasing order among the parents and the off-springs, selection of the better chromosomes as parents for the next generation, and updating of genetic cycle and fulfilling the stopping criterion.

5   Review of SFL for On-Line Tuning of Controller Parameters

The whole process of SFL can be categorized into three steps viz. fuzzification, Sugeno fuzzy inference, and Sugeno defuzzification. The details of the steps may be found in [5, 8].

6   Input Parameters

A comprehensive list of the parameter limits of the studied power system model are given in Table 1. For the simulation work, the other chosen values of the model are $K_a = 10$, $\tau_a = 0.1$ s, $K_e = 1.0$, $\tau_e = 0.4$ s, $K_r = 1.0$ $\tau_r = 0.05$ s, $\tau_{deg} = 2.31$ s, $\tau_{va} = 0.82$ s, $K_1 = 1.5$, $K_2 = 0.2$, $K_3 = 1.5$, $H = 1.9$, $D = 0.8$, $R = 0.074$. The value of K_g is load dependent [9]. Number of parameters to be optimized is four.

The minimum and the maximum limits of the tunable parameters are presented in Table I. For GA [5, 8], number of bits = (number of parameters) × 8 (for binary coded GA, as considered in the present work), population size = 60, number of iterations = 100, runtime = 30, crossover rate = 80%. and mutation probability = 0.001 are chosen. For RGA [7, 12], population size = 60, number of iterations = 100, runtime = 30, crossover rate = 80%., mutation probability = 0.001, crossover = single point crossover, mutation = Gaussian mutation, selection = Roulette wheel and selection probability = 1/3.

The software has been written in MATLAB-7.3 language and executed on a 3.0-GHz Pentium IV personal computer with 512-MB RAM.

7   Simulation Results and Discussions

For the present work, K_g is varied from 0.7 to 1.0 in steps of 0.1 and τ_g is varied from 1.0 to 2.0 in steps of 0.2. Thus, total 24 different sets of nominal input conditions are obtained. The algorithms employed for the present work are RGA, and GA. The results of interest including modal analysis based small-signal response characteristics are bold faced in the respective tables. For time-domain plots of the ΔV_t (p.u.), input step perturbation of 1% is applied either in reference voltage (ΔV_{ref}) or in load demand (ΔP_d). The major observations are documented below.

7.1   Eigenvalue-Based System Performance and Misfitness Function Analysis

Table 2 includes 8 different selected sets of input conditions and establishes optimization performance of RGA-based approach is better than GA-based approach. The modal analysis-based small-signal response profiles of the incremental changes of terminal voltages of studied model are also presented in Table II. It shows, RGA-based technique yields optimal controller gains and offers lesser value of the *MF*.

Table 2. Sugeno fuzzy rule base table, optimized controller gains, optimum J values and modal analysis based transient response profile of incremental change in terminal voltage with varying K_g and τ_g

K_g, τ_g	Algorithm	Optimal controller gains				J	Modal analysis-based transient response profile			
		K_p	K_i	K_d	K_{ii}		u_{sh} ($\times 10^4$)	o_{sh} ($\times 10^4$)	t_{st} (s)	MF ($\times 10^9$)
0.7,	GA	0.0946	0.0834	0.0109	0.1000	35.7153	-3.3255	8.7213	20.000	9.1119
1.0	RGA	0.1000	0.0845	0.0145	0.1000	**26.2980**	-0.0695	8.7227	18.811	**7.9629**
0.7,	GA	0.0644	0.0525	0.0050	0.1000	29.1682	-0.0101	8.7227	17.949	7.9308
1.2	RGA	0.1000	0.1000	0.0050	0.1000	**28.7676**	-0.1870	8.7227	8.438	**7.7833**
0.8,	GA	0.0849	0.0765	0.0082	0.1000	38.5021	-3.4694	8.7213	20.000	9.2097
1.0	RGA	0.1000	0.0726	0.0315	0.1000	**27.1475**	-0.0112	8.7213	14.275	**7.8099**
0.8,	GA	0.0889	0.0644	0.0138	0.1000	34.5489	-2.1180	8.7227	20.000	8.4572
1.2	RGA	0.1000	0.0797	0.0078	0.1000	**27.0290**	-0.0104	8.7227	12.539	**8.1658**
0.9,	GA	0.0895	0.0813	0.0080	0.1000	35.5397	-3.5925	8.7213	20.000	9.2967
1.0	RGA	0.1000	0.1000	0.0063	0.1000	**26.8785**	-0.0144	8.7213	7.152	**7.8572**
0.9,	GA	0.0998	0.0801	0.0080	0.1000	39.1675	-3.6027	8.7227	20.000	9.3066
1.2	RGA	0.1000	0.0620	0.0311	0.1000	**29.8006**	-0.0109	8.7227	12.450	**7.8636**
0.9,	GA	0.1000	0.0487	0.0050	0.0995	38.6098	-3.6532	8.7256	20.000	9.3483
2.0	RGA	0.1000	0.0905	0.0050	0.1000	**35.7949**	-0.8358	8.7256	17.120	**7.9766**
1.0,	GA	0.0737	0.0684	0.0050	0.1000	28.8732	-0.0093	8.7213	7.254	7.6587
1.0	RGA	0.1000	0.1000	0.0050	0.1000	**25.8896**	-0.0044	8.7213	5.572	**7.6571**

7.2 Analysis of the Transient Response of Change in Terminal Voltage

Fig. 2 is pertaining to the comparative GA- and RGA-based time-domain transient response profiles of ΔV_t (p.u.) with 1% simultaneous step change in reference voltage and load demand for nominal set of input parameters. This figure portrays that RGA-based approach yields optimal ΔV_t (p.u.) response profile. The proposed RGA-based optimal controller gains settle the ΔV_t (p.u.) response quickly. Thus, the RGA-based controller gains perform better than the GA-based controller gains.

For on-line, off-nominal input sets of parameters, the SFL model is utilized to get the on-line, optimal controller gains and these controller gains also yield the optimal incremental change in terminal voltage response profile (Fig. 3). From Fig. 3 it is observed that RGA-SFL model yields optimal incremental change in terminal voltage response.

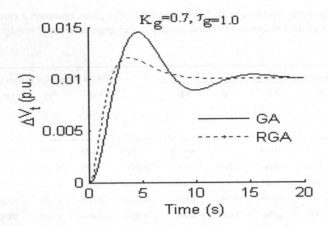

Fig. 2. Comparative GA-, and RGA-based time-domain transient responses of the incremental change in terminal voltage (p.u.) with 1% step change in reference voltage and load demand for nominal set of input parameters

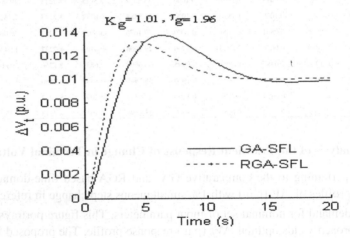

Fig. 3. Comparative GA-SFL-, and RGA-SFL-based time domain transient responses of the incremental change in terminal voltage (p.u.) with 1% step change in reference voltage and load demand for off-nominal set of input parameters

7.3   Convergence Profile

Fig. 4 portrays the comparative convergence profiles J value for the algorithms like GA and RGA and it indicates that RGA-based meta-heuristic offers faster convergence profile and lesser value of J than GA counterpart.

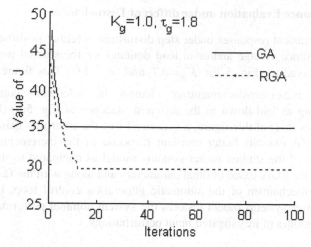

Fig. 4. Comparative GA-and RGA-based convergence profiles of J

7.4 SFL-Based Response

Table 3 illustrates the SFL-based off-nominal, on-line optimal gains, J values and the corresponding modal analysis based small-signal response profile of the incremental change in terminal voltage for on-line, off-nominal input set of parameters.

Table 3. Sugeno fuzzy based off-nominal, on-line optimal gains, J values and transient response profile of incremental change in terminal voltage

K_g, τ_g	Algori-thm-SFL	Optimal controller gains				J	Modal analysis-based transient response profile			
		K_p	K_i	K_d	K_{ii}		u_{sh} ($\times 10^4$)	o_{sh} ($\times 10^4$)	t_{st} (s)	MF ($\times 10^9$)
0.72, 1.42	GA-SFL	0.0798	0.0525	0.0050	0.1000	36.3182	-3.3692	8.7239	20.000	9.1457
	RGA-SFL	0.1000	0.0647	0.0117	0.1000	**29.9933**	-0.0165	8.7239	20.000	**8.0106**
0.87, 1.89	GA-SFL	0.0881	0.0516	0.0050	0.1000	40.3497	-3.2957	8.7254	20.000	9.0994
	RGA-SFL	0.1000	0.0475	0.0050	0.1000	**35.2068**	-0.0098	8.7254	13.654	**8.7997**
0.95, 1.67	GA-SFL	0.0948	0.0555	0.0050	0.1000	37.6234	-3.6710	8.7248	20.000	9.3598
	RGA-SFL	0.0525	0.0525	0.0207	0.1000	**34.9699**	-0.0110	8.7248	16.743	**7.8925**
1.01, 1.96	GA-SFL	0.0762	0.0315	0.0050	0.1000	38.4689	-3.7318	8.7255	20.000	9.4062
	RGA-SFL	0.1000	0.0525	0.0050	0.0240	**31.0984**	-0.0142	8.7255	18.917	**7.9714**

7.5   Performance Evaluation under different Disturbances

Time-domain transient responses under step disturbances (either positive or negative or zero) in reference voltage and/or in load demand for the studied power systems model are displayed in Fig. 5 for $K_g = 0.7$ and $\tau_g = 1.0$. This figure is achieved under certain increment/decrement/no change in reference voltage and/or loading/unloading as laid down in the different sketches of Fig. 5(a)-(f). From the different sketches (a–f) of this figure, it is noticed that the controller gains yielded by adopting the RGA exhibits better transient response of the incremental change in terminal voltage of the studied power systems model as compared to the GA-based approach. With the RGA-based optimal parameters and along with the faster action of the controlling mechanism of the automatic generation control loop, the proposed autonomous power systems model restores the system nominal performance quickly under different modes of investigated input perturbations.

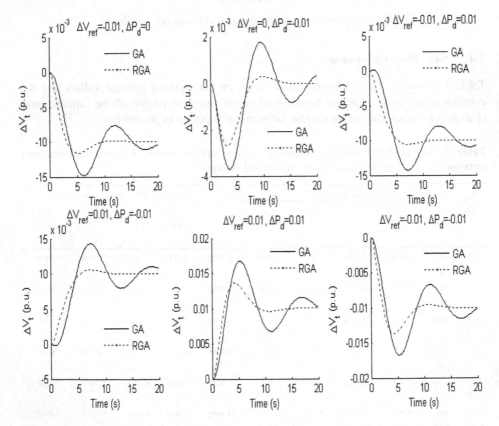

Fig. 5. Comparative GA- and RGA-based transient performance study for the studied model under different perturbations for nominal set of input parameters

7.6   Analysis of the Transient Response of Change in Frequency

Fig. 6 is pertaining to the comparative GA-, evolutionary programming (EP) [13] and RGA-based time-domain transient response profiles of Δf (p.u.) with 1% simultaneous step change in reference voltage and load demand for nominal set of input parameters. This figure portrays that RGA-based approach yields optimal Δf (p.u.) response profile. The proposed RGA-based optimal controller gains settle the Δf (p.u.) response quickly. Thus, the RGA-based controller gains perform better than either GA-based or EP-based controller gains.

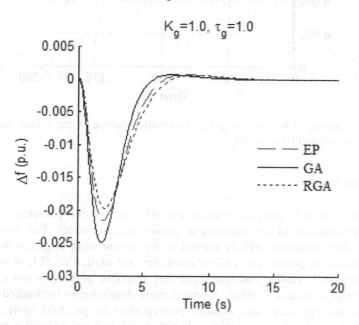

Fig. 6. Comparative GA-, and RGA-based time-domain transient responses of the incremental change in frequency (p.u.) with 1% step change in reference voltage and load demand for nominal set of input parameters

7.7   AVR without PID-controller

Fig. 7 presents the step response of the incremental change in terminal voltage of the studied power systems model without inclusion of the PID-controller. It is observed from this figure that the studied system is not capable to settle the terminal voltage to the desired value within a specified time. This necessitates the requirement of proper tuning of the controller gains.

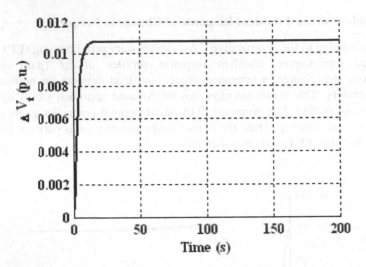

Fig. 7. Step response of incremental change in terminal voltage of the studied autonomous power systems without PID controller

8   Conclusion

In this paper, RGA is used to optimize the different tunable parameters of load-tracking performance of an autonomous power system model. For on-line, off-nominal system parameters SFL is applied in the present work to get on-line output terminal voltage response. The on-line computational burden of SFL is noticeably low. Consequently, on-line optimized transient response of incremental change in output terminal voltage is obtained. A time-domain simulation of the studied model is carried out under different sorts of input perturbations for practical application and exhibits a dynamic performance with truly optimized different controller gains. It is also presented that the DEG plays a significant role on maintaining the terminal voltage variations along with the optimized controller gains of the studied model. The potential benefit yielded by the RGA is compared to that yielded by GA for this specific application arena of power systems.

References

[1] Cheng, J.W.M., Galiana, F.D., McGillis, D.T.: Studies of bilateral contracts with respect to steady-state security in a deregulated environment. IEEE Transaction on Power Systems 13(3), 1020–1025 (1998)

[2] Wang, L., Lee, D.-J.: Load-tracking performance of an autonomous SOFC-based hybrid power generation/energy storage system. IEEE Transaction on Energy Conversions 25(1), 128–139 (2010)

[3] Astrom, K.J., Hang, C.C., Persson, P., et al.: Towards intelligent PID control. Automatica 28(1), 1–9 (1992)

[4] Krohling, R.A., Rey, J.P.: Design of optimal disturbance rejection PID controllers using genetic algorithm. IEEE Transaction on Evolutionary Computation 5(1), 78–82 (2001)

[5] Mukherjee, V., Ghoshal, S.P.: Intelligent particle swarm optimized fuzzy PID controller for AVR system. Electric Power Systems Research 72(12), 1689–1698 (2007)

[6] Devaraja, D., Selvabala, B.: Real coded genetic algorithm and fuzzy logic approach for real time tuning of proportional-integral-derivative controller in automatic voltage regulator system. Proc. IET Generation Transmission Distribution 3(1), 641–649 (2009)

[7] Sushil, K., Naresh, R.: Efficient real coded genetic algorithm to solve the non-convex hydrothermal scheduling problem. International Journal of Electrical Power and Energy Systems 29(10), 738–747 (2007)

[8] Ghoshal, S.P.: Multi-area frequency and tie-line power flow control with fuzzy logic based integral gain scheduling. Journal of The Institution of Engineers India Pt. EL 81, 135–141 (2003)

[9] Sadat, H.: Power System Analysis. Tata-McGraw-Hill, India (2003)

[10] Kundur, P.: Power System Stability and Control. Tata-McGraw-Hill, India (2006)

[11] Chatterjee, A., Ghoshal, S.P., Mukherjee, V.: Chaotic ant swarm optimization for fuzzy-based tuning of power system stabilizer. International Journal of Electrical Power and Energy Systems 33(3), 657–672 (2011)

[12] Amjady, N., Nasiri-Rad, H.: Solution of nonconvex and non-smooth economic dispatch by a new adaptive real coded genetic algorithm. Expert Systems with Applications 37(7), 5239–5245 (2010)

[13] Chatterjee, A., Ghoshal, S.P., Mukherjee, V.: A comparative study of single input and dual input power system stabilizer by hybrid evolutionary programming. In: Proc. World Cong. Nature & Biologically Inspired Computing 2009, NaBIC 2009, pp. 1047–1052 (December 2009)

Short Term Load Forecasting (STLF) Using Generalized Neural Network (GNN) Trained with Adaptive GA

D.K. Chaturvedi[*] and Sinha Anand Premdayal

Dept. of Electrical Engineering, Faculty of Engineering,
D.E.I. Dayalbagh, Agra, U.P. India 282005
dkc.foe@gmail.com

Abstract. The paper is mainly focus to develop an integration of GNN and wavelet based models for STLF. The model is trained by using error back-propagation algorithm, but there are certain inherent drawbacks of back-propagation algorithm. To overcome the drawbacks of back propagation algorithm such as slow learning, stuck in local minima, needs error gradient etc. genetic algorithm (GA) is proposed. The performance of GA is further improved by making an adaptive GA with the help of fuzzy system. The adaptive GA changes the GA parameters such as cross over probability and mutation rate during execution by using fuzzy system. The GNN-W-AGA is used to forecast electrical load and compared with GNN-W trained with backprop and actual data.

Keywords: Load Forecasting, GNN, Wavelet, Adaptive GA, Fuzzy System.

1 Introduction

The approaches of short-term load forecasting can be mainly divided into two categories: statistical methods and artificial intelligence methods. In statistical methods, equations can be obtained showing the relationship between load and its relative factors after training the historical data, while artificial intelligence methods try to imitate human beings' way of thinking and reasoning to get knowledge from the past experience and forecast the future loads.

The statistical category includes multiple linear regression [PAP 90], stochastic time series [1], general exponential smoothing [2], state space model [3], etc. Recently support vector regression (SVR) [4], which is a very promising statistical learning method, has also been applied to short-term load forecasting and has shown good results. Usually statistical methods can predict the load curve of ordinary days very well, but they lack the ability to analyze the load property of holidays and other anomalous days, due to the inflexibility of their structure. Expert system [5, 6], artificial neural network (ANN) [7] and fuzzy inference [8] belong to the artificial intelligence category. Expert systems try to get the knowledge of experienced operators and express it in an "if...then" rule, but the difficulty in this technique is

---

[*] SM IEEE.

B.K. Panigrahi et al. (Eds.): SEMCCO 2013, Part II, LNCS 8298, pp. 132–143, 2013.

sometimes the experts knowledge is intuitive and could not easily be expressed. Artificial neural network doesn't need the expression of the human experience and aims to establish a relational mapping between the input data set and the observed outputs. It is good at dealing with the nonlinear relationship between the load and its relative factors, but the shortcoming lies in over-fitting and long training time. Fuzzy inference is an extension of expert systems. It constructs an optimal structure of the simplified fuzzy inference that minimizes model errors and the number of the membership functions to grasp nonlinear behaviour of short-term loads, yet it still needs the experts experience to generate the fuzzy rules. Generally artificial intelligence methods are flexible in finding the relationship between load and its relative factors, especially for the anomalous load forecasting. [9-12] used the generalized neural network (GNN) approach for electrical STLF problem to overcome the problem of ANN. It is found that combinations of summation (Σ) neurons and product (Π) neurons at different layers are giving quite good results as compared to only summation neuron or product neuron in the whole network; which motivated to explore the possibilities of different combinations. Thus, a generalized neuron model has been developed that uses the fuzzy compensatory operators that are partly union and partly intersection given by Mizumoto [13] in his paper on pictorial representation of fuzzy connectives II in 1989.

Use of the sigmoid threshold function and ordinary summation or product as aggregation functions in the existing models fails to cope with the non-linearities involved in real life problems. To deal with these, the proposed model has both sigmoid and Gaussian functions with weight sharing. The generalized neuron model has flexibility at both the aggregation and threshold function level to cope with the non-linearity involved in the type of applications dealt with. The neuron has both Σ and π aggregation functions. The Σ aggregation function has been used with the sigmoid characteristic function while the π aggregation function has been used with the Gaussian function as a characteristic function [14-15].

Wavelet is a powerful tool that can be effectively utilized for the prediction of short-term loads. This can be integrated with the neural network for the forecasting. Wavelet decomposition techniques have been integrated successfully with neural networks [16-21] showing more accurate and acceptable results as compared to conventional methods.

In this paper, GNN-W based load forecasting technique has been developed which is trained using adaptive GA to overcome the problems of back-propagation gradient search algorithm.

2   Development of GNN-W for STLF

The proposed approach to forecasting is based on the wavelet transform (WT) and generalized neural network referred as GNN-W. The Db8 WT is used to decompose the given pattern as shown in Fig.2.

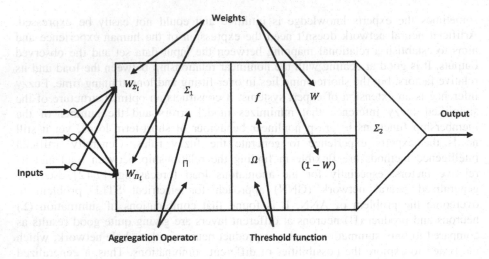

Fig. 1. Generalized Neural Network (GNN)

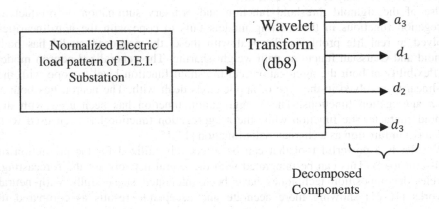

Fig. 2. A three resolution with Daubechies wavelet (db8)

These wavelet components are then used to train GNN to forecast each component one step ahead. The training vector used for first wavelet decomposed component as:

Input of training vector = $[a_3(t), a_3(t-1), a_3(t-2)]$

The output of training vector = $a_3(t+1)$

Then forecasted wavelet components are used to reconstruct the future behaviour of given pattern. The pseudo code of GNN-W is given below.

Pseudo code for GNN-W

Begin
Preparation of data
        Decompose the data using wavelet transform

> **for I = *1: no. of wavelet components***
>> Initialize the network parameters
>>> **While *(mean square error < error tolerance)***
>>>> Calculate GNN output
>>>> Calculate error
>>>> Modify weights and bias
>>> end
>>> Forecast wavelet components
>> end
>> Reconstruct forecasted pattern
>> Plot the forecasted data
> end

The training parameters for Generalized Neural Network Model and existing neural networks are given in Table 1.

Table 1. Parameters used for ANN-W and GNN-W models

Learning rate	-	0.0001
Momentum	-	0.9
Gain scale factor	-	1.0
Tolerance	-	0.002
All initial weights	-	0.95

3   Training of GNN-W Using Adaptive GA with Fuzzy System

The program is developed for feed-forward generalized neural network with adaptive Genetic Algorithm as the learning mechanism in the feedback loop to overcome some of the disadvantages of back propagation learning mechanism to minimize the error of GNN. The Genetic Algorithm is made adaptive by changing its parameters during execution using Fuzzy System.

Drawbacks of Back-propagation Learning Algorithm

The back-propagation learning algorithm has various drawbacks as follows [22]:

i.   The slowness of the learning process, especially when large training sets or large networks have to be used.

ii.   Network may get stuck in local minima.

iii. The learning rate and momentum have great effect of the training time. With constant step size of learning rate and momentum the convergence of back-propagation tends to be very slow and often yields sub-optimal solutions.

iv.   Initial weights also affect the training time.

v.   The neural network may not Converge at all if the initial weights are not selected properly [HIN 96].

vi.   The threshold function should be differentiable and non decreasing [FAU 94].

vii. The training time is a function of the error function [ESP 07].

viii.   The normalization range of training data and input output mapping also affect the training time and accuracy [CHA 96].

3.1   Advantages of GA

The central theme of research on genetic algorithms has been robustness, the balance between efficiency and efficacy necessary for survival in many different environments. The following are the advantages of GA [23]:

i.   The genetic algorithms are a set of sophisticated search and improve procedures based on the mechanics of natural genetics; the search is absolutely blind, but guided by pre-designated precise operators.
ii.   The potentials of genetic algorithms as a problem solving especially in finding near optimal solution.
iii. Genetic algorithms search from a population of points, not a single point.
iv.   Genetic algorithms use pay off information's (objective function), not derivatives or auxiliary knowledge.
v.   GA uses probabilistic transition rules, not deterministic rules.
vi.   Genetic algorithms work with a coding of the parameter themselves.
vii. GA uses probabilistic procedure to select input to produce outputs for the next generations that include only fittest among the input and output.

GAF Parameters

- Population size: 50
- Initial crossover probability: 0.9
- Initial mutation probability: 0.1
- Selection operator: tournament selection
- Number of generations: 100

In the adaptive Genetic Algorithm important GA parameters are:

i.   Crossover Probability (Pc), and
ii.   Mutation probability (Pm)

are proposed to be varied dynamically during execution of the program according to the fuzzy knowledge base which has been developed from the experience to maximize the efficiency of GA.

The philosophy behind varying these parameters is that the response of the optimization method depends on the stage of optimization, i.e. a high fitness value may require, a low cross over probability and high mutation probability for further improvement; alternatively, at low fitness values the response would be better with a relatively, a high cross over probability and a low mutation probability. The reason behind it is that at the time of starting high cross over probability (Pc) and low mutation probability (Pm) yield good results, because large number of crossover operation will produce better chromosome vectors whose fitness value are relatively high. This process will continue for some finite number of generations after that the fitness value of each chromosome vector becomes almost same (around 0.9). Beyond that the effect of crossover is not significant due to little variation in the chromosome vectors in that particular population. Hence, at this stage, the population can be diversified by the following means:

i.   By increasing the mutation rate of the chromosome vector to inculcate the new characteristics in the existing population.

ii.   By introducing new characteristics in chromosome vector in the existing population whose characteristics are different from the existing chromosome vectors and whose fitness value is relatively high (i.e. Keeping the population size (popsize) constant.

In the present work, a fuzzy system is used to control the values of Pc and Pm. For this purpose the proposed ranges of these parameters have been divided into low, medium and high membership function, and each is given some membership value.

4   Results

The figures 3 to 6 show the actual and predicted training of winter season for a_3, d_1, d_2, d_3 components. The error of training and testing performance are shown in figure 7 and 8. The GNN-W model forecasted output for combined load pattern is shown in figure 9 when trained using back-propagation. The GNN-W-GAF model forecasted output for testing results of recombined load signal is shown in figure 10. The testing performance of both these models also tabulated in Table – 2. The improvement in Maximum fitness using GNN-W-AGA is shown in figure 11. Variation in crossover and mutation probability during execution of GNN-GA Fuzzy for winter season is shown in figure 12.

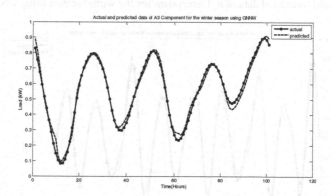

Fig. 3. Actual and forecasted data of a_3 Component for the winter season using GNN-W

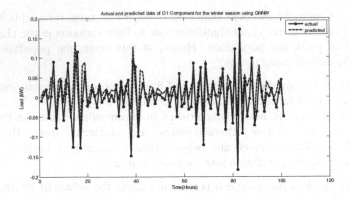

Fig. 4. Actual and forecasted data of d_1 Component for the winter season using GNN-W

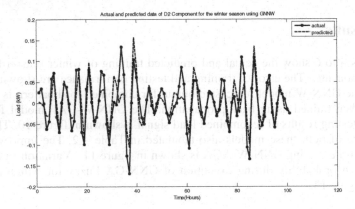

Fig. 5. Actual and forecasted data of d_2 Component for the winter season using GNN-W model

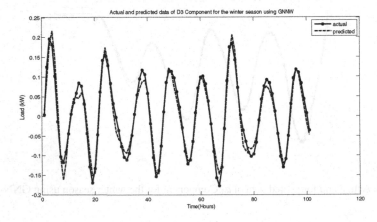

Fig. 6. Actual and forecasted data of d_3 Component for the winter season using GNN-W model

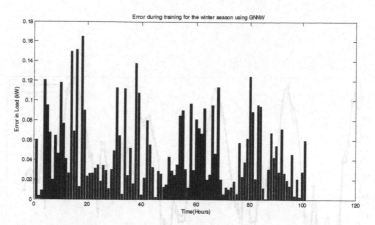

Fig. 7. Error during training for the winter season using GNN-W model

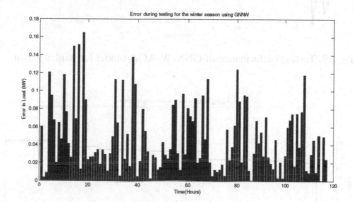

Fig. 8. Error during testing for the winter season using GNN-W model

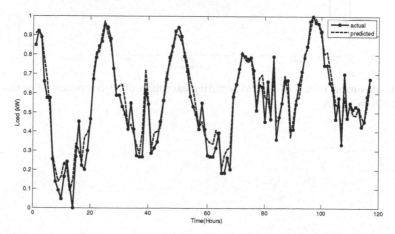

Fig. 9. Testing performance of GNN-W with backprop model for the winter season

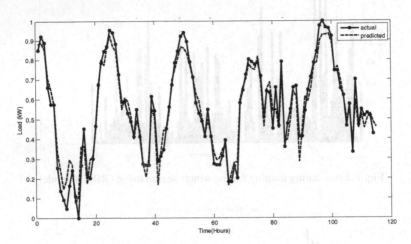

Fig. 10. Testing performance of GNN-W-AGA model for winter season

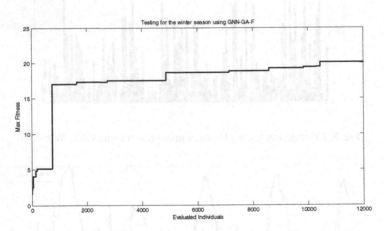

Fig. 11. Maximum Fitness of GA fuzzy during execution of a3 component of winter season using GNN-W- AGA

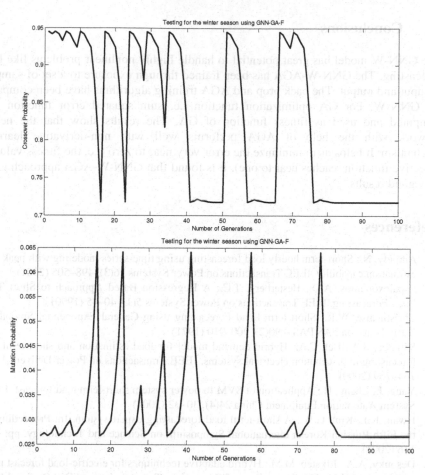

Fig. 12. Variation in Crossover and Mutation probability during execution of a3 component of winter season using GNN-W- AGA

Table 2. Training and testing performance of GNN-W models

Model	Testing RMSE	Training RMSE
GNN-W with backprop	0.06094	0.06202
GNN-W with AGA	0.0486	0.049

5   Conclusions

The GNN-W model has great potential to handle highly nonlinear problems like load forecasting. The GNN-W-AGA has been trained through exposure to a set of samples of input and output. The back prop and AGA training algorithms have been compared for GNN-W. For GA optimization function i.e. sum squared error function was computed and used as fitness function of GA. The results show that the neural network with the help of AGA performs well with non-derivative learning mechanism. It helps us to minimize the error very near to zero (i.e. the fitness value of objective function reaches near to one). It is found that GNN-W-AGA approach gives very good results.

References

1. Amjady, N.: Short-term hourly load forecasting using time-series modeling with peak load estimation capability. IEEE Transactions on Power Systems 16(3), 498–505 (2001)
2. Papalexopoulos, A.D., Hesterberg, T.C.: A Regression Based Approach to Short Term Load Forecasting. IEEE Transactions on Power Systems 5(1), 40–45 (1990)
3. Christiaanse, W.R.: Short term Load Forecasting using General Exponential Smoothing. IEEE Trans. on PAS PAS – 90(2), 900–910 (1971)
4. Villalba, S.A., Bel, C.A.: Hybrid demand model for load estimation and short-term load forecasting in distribution electrical systems. IEEE Transactions on Power Delivery 15(2), 764–769 (2000)
5. Yang, J., Cheng, H.: Application of SVM to power system short-term load forecast. Power System Automation Equipment China 24(4), 30–32 (2004)
6. Hwan, K.J., Kim, G.W.: A short-term load forecasting expert system. In: Proceedings of the Fifth Russian-Korean International Symposium on Science and Technology, pp. 112–116 (2001)
7. Desouky, A.A., Elkateb, M.M.: Hybrid adaptive techniques for electric-load forecast using ANN and ARIMA. IEE Proceedings of Generation, Transmission and Distribution 147(4), 213–217 (2000)
8. Kim, K.H., Youn, H.S., Kang, Y.C.: Short-term load forecasting for special days in anomalous load conditions using neural networks and fuzzy inference method. IEEE Transactions on Power Systems 15(2), 559–565 (2000)
9. Bunn, D.W.: Forecasting loads and prices in competitive power markets. Proceedings of the IEEE 88, 163–169 (2000)
10. Chaturvedi, D.K., Satsangi, P.S., Kalra, P.K.: Fuzzified Neural Network Approach for Load Forecasting Problems. Int. J. on Engineering Intelligent Systems 9(1), 3–9 (2001)
11. Chaturvedi, D.K., Kumar, R., Mohan, M., Kalra, P.K.: Artificial Neural Network learning using improved Genetic algorithm. J. IE(I), EL 82 (2001)
12. Chaturvedi, D.K., Satsangi, P.S., Kalra, P.K.: Load Frequency Control: A Generalized Neural Network Approach. Electric Power and Energy Systems 21, 405–415 (1999)
13. Mizumoto, M.: Pictorial representations of fuzzy connectives, Part II: cases of compensatory operators and self-dual operators. Fuzzy Sets and Systems 32, 45–79 (1989)
14. Chaturvedi, D.K., Mohan, M., Singh, R.K., Kalra, P.K.: Improved Generalized Neuron Model for Short Term Load Forecasting. Int. J. on Soft Computing - A Fusion of Foundations, Methodologies and Applications 8(1), 10–18 (2004)

15. Chaturvedi, D.K.: Soft Computing Techniques and its applications in Electrical Engineering. SCI, vol. 103. Springer, Heidelberg (2008)
16. Huang, C.-M., Yang, H.T.: Evolving wavelet-based networks for short term load forecasting. Proc. Inst. Elect. Eng., Gen., Transm., Distrib. 148(3), 222–228 (2001)
17. Oonsivilai, A., El-Hawary, M.E.: Wavelet neural network based short-term load forecasting of electric power system commercial load. In: Proc. IEEE Can. Conf. Electrical and Computer Engineering, pp. 1223–1228 (1999)
18. Chang, C.S., Fu, W., Yi, M.: Short term load forecasting using wavelet networks. Eng. Intell. Syst. Elect. Eng. Commun. 6, 217–223 (1998)
19. Chenthur Pandian, S., Duraiswamy, K., Christober Asir Rajan, C., Kanagaraj, N.: Fuzzy approach for short term load forecasting. Electric Power Systems Research 76, 541–548 (2006)
20. Banakar, A., Azeem, A.: Artificial Wavelet Neural Network and its application in Neurofuzzy models. Elsevier Applied Soft Computing (2008)
21. Ho, D.W.C., Zhang, P.A., Xu, J.: Fuzzy wavelet networks for function learning. IEEE Transactions on Fuzzy Systems 9, 200–211 (2001)
22. Chaturvedi, D.K., Das, V.S.: Optimization of Genetic Algorithm Parameters. In: National Conference on Applied Systems Engineering and Soft Computing (SASESC 2000), pp. 194–198. Organized by Dayalbagh Educational Institute, Dayalbagh (2000)
23. Fogarty, T.C.: Varying the Probability of Mutation in the Genetic Algorithm. In: Proceedings of 3rd International Conference in Genetic Algorithms and Applications, Arlington, VA, pp. 104–109 (1981)

Gene Selection Using Multi-objective Genetic Algorithm Integrating Cellular Automata and Rough Set Theory

Soumen Kumar Pati[1], Asit Kumar Das[2], and Arka Ghosh[3]

[1] Department of Computer Science/Information Technology,
St. Thomas' College of Engineering and Technology, 4, D.H. Road, Kolkata – 700023
[2] Department of Computer Science and Technology, Bengal Engineering
and Science University, Shibpur, Howrah – 711103
[3] Purabi Das School of Information Technology, Bengal Engineering
and Science University, Shibpur, Howrah-03
soumen_pati@rediffmail.com, akdas@cs.becs.ac.in,
arka.besu@gmx.com

Abstract. Feature selection is one of the most key problems in the field of machine learning and data mining. It can be done in mainly two different ways, namely, filter approach and wrapper approach. Filter approach is independent of underlying classifier logic and relatively less costly than the wrapper approach which is classifier dependent. Many researchers have applied Genetic algorithm (GA) as wrapper approach for feature selection. In the paper, a novel feature selection method is proposed based on the multi-objective genetic algorithm which is applied on population generated by non-linear uniform hybrid cellular automata. The fitness functions are defined one using set lower bound approximation of rough set theory and the other using Kullbak-Leibler divergence method. A comparative study between proposed method and some leading feature selection methods are given using some popular microarray cancer dataset to demonstrate the effectiveness of the method.

Keywords: Feature selection, Genetic algorithm, Multi-objective Evolutionary algorithm, Set lower bound approximation, Kullback-Leibler divergence.

1   Introduction

Data mining is the search of meaningful patterns or interesting information among huge set of redundant, noisy and inconsistent real life data. Features are characterization of data by which one can deduce some meaningful logic or rule from the data. There are many features in real life datasets, like gene microarray data, satellite GIS data, bio-medical data and so on, which are garbage and redundant in the sense that they do not have any active participation in mining task rather can degrade classification accuracy. As a result, only the significant features are selected as feature subset from the original feature set using various feature selection methods like CON [1], CFS [2], Single Objective Genetic Algorithm [3], NSGA-II [4] etc.

B.K. Panigrahi et al. (Eds.): SEMCCO 2013, Part II, LNCS 8298, pp. 144–155, 2013.

Evolutionary algorithms (EA) [5] [6] are imitation of natural evolution process for selecting the most feasible solution among many competing solutions. Genetic algorithm (GA) [3] is one of the most mature evolutionary strategies used for population based stochastic parallel search in which selection, crossover and mutation are three basic steps. Standard GA deals with only one fitness function or cost function but most of our daily real life problems are inherently multi-objective where simultaneous maximization or minimization of more than one competing fitness function value is required. The knowledge gathers about multi-objective GA and an extensive survey of stare of art research and development in multi objective Evolutionary algorithms can be found in [7]. The multi-objective evolutionary algorithm based on decomposition [8] is presented. Here neighborhood size parameter is tuned and show the better experimental results over fixed neighborhood size. There are many well-known methods present in the literature to handle more than one fitness function, like PAES [9], VEGA [10], MOGA [11], SEAMO [12], NSGA [13] and its descendent NSGA-II [4]. NSGA-II [4] gives very much promising result in finding the non-dominated pareto set as it is a pareto dominance based evolutionary algorithm. The major drawback of the method is its higher computational complexity $O(MN^2)$ (M= number of objectives and N= population size), which is very costly when population size increases.

In the proposed work, a novel feature selection method is introduced based on the multi-objective genetic algorithm which is applied on population generated by non-linear uniform hybrid cellular automata. The fitness functions are defined, one using set lower bound approximation of rough set theory and the other using Kullback-Leibler divergence method [14]. The method shows very promising result with less time complexity as there is no need of global calculation typical of other pareto based multi-objective optimization algorithm. It uses a steady state selection mechanism, no need for fitness sharing parameter used in NSGA or crowding distance used in NSGA-II [4]. It uses a unique jumping gene or Transposon [15] mechanism for mutation to preserve the diversity in the population. Cellular Automata (CA) [16] is well appreciated for its capability as an excellent random pattern generator. In the proposed method one dimensional non-linear uniform hybrid cellular automata is used for generating the population of binary strings where each feature is presented as a single bit in the entire string ('1' means presence of that feature and '0' means absence of feature).

The paper is organized into four sections. Section 2 describes the proposed feature selection method based on multi-objective genetic algorithm. The relate concepts of non-linear uniform hybrid cellular automata, rough set theory [17] and Kullback-Leibler divergence method [14] is described in this section which are used for setting the necessary environment for the application of genetic algorithm. The experimental results and performance of the proposed method for various benchmark gene expression datasets is evaluated in Section 3. Finally, conclusion and future work are drawn in Section 4.

2   Methodology

The Population generation is one of basic step in multi-objective evolutionary algorithm applied here for dimension reduction. A nonlinear hybrid uniform cellular automata is used for this purpose. Two fitness functions are defined separately using Set lower bound approximation and Kullback-Leibler divergence method [14]. Finally, the genetic algorithm based optimization method is introduced for selecting the most important genes from the gene expression dataset.The method uses simple selection step, single point crossover [9] step and a unique jumping gene or transposon mechanism [15] for mutation to preserve the diversity in the population.

2.1   Population Generation Using Nonlinear Hybrid Uniform Cellular Automata

Cellular Automata (CA) was firstly proposed by John Von Neumann [16]. The model is suggested with 2-dimension grid of cells. This model has the capability of self-reproduction and it is as powerful as universal Turing machine [18]. The proposed method uses a very simple version of CA which is widely known as one dimensional CA [16]. The method uses one dimensional grid of cells and generates four next state rules R_1, R_2, R_3 and R_4. Each cell of the grid has two states (0 or 1) and 3-neighborhood dependency.

i) R_1: $Next_{state(i)} = (L(i) \wedge C(i)) \vee (\sim L(i) \wedge R(i))$

ii) R_2: $Next_{state(i)} = (L(i) \wedge R(i)) \vee (C(i) \wedge \sim R(i))$

iii) R_3: $Next_{state(i)} = L(i) \oplus C(i) \oplus R(i)$

iv) R_4: $Next_{state(i)} = C(i) \oplus (L(i) \vee \sim R(i))$

Where, L(i) is the left cell value of current i-th cell, C(i) is the current i-th cell value and R(i) is the right cell value of C(i). For every cell, any one of the above four rules are used to get its next state but which rule will be applicable for which cell is fixed dynamically (thus known as hybrid CA). Among the above mentioned four rules, R_1, R_2 and R_4 are non-linear and R_3 is linear. So, it is non-linear hybrid CA which is used for population generation as described below with an example.

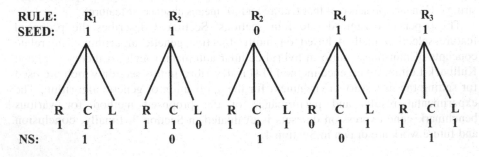

Fig. 1. Generation of next-state population using Cellular Automata

Firstly, a random seed of binary string with size equal to number of features in the dataset is considered. Say, there are five features in the dataset and the randomly generated seed is 11011. Now, to each cell of the seed any one rule of R_1 to R_4 is randomly assigned. Then, for each i-th cell of the seed L(i), C(i) and R(i) is set as shown in Fig. 1. Finally, associated rule to the cells are applied and next state value for each cell of the seed is obtained, which is together considered as new input seed and the same process is repeated for a certain number of times (i.e. population size). Now all seeds together will form a population.

2.2   Fitness Function

As Fitness function determines the quality of a chromosome in the population. So, a strong fitness function is imperative for giving good result. Our method uses two different fitness functions based on (a) Set lower bound approximation [17] and (b) Kullback-Leibler Divergence method [14].

2.2.1 Set Lower Bound Approximation

For calculating lower approximation [17] of a set of objects on an attribute subset P, universe of discourse U is partitioned into equivalence classes $[x]_P$ using indiscernible relation IND(P), defined in (1).

$$IND(P) = \{(x,y) \in (|U| \times |U|) | \forall a \in P, f_a(x) = f_a(y)\} \qquad (1)$$

Similarly, Equivalence classes $[x]_D$ are formed using (1) for the decision attribute. Thus, two different partitions U/P and U/D of equivalence classes $[x]_P$ and $[x]_D$ respectively, are formed. Now each class $[x]_D$ in U/D is considered to be the target sets X, i.e., $X \in U/D$. The lower approximation $\underline{P}X$ of X under P is computed using (2), for all $X \in U/D$. The positive region $POS_P(D)$ is obtained by taking the union of the lower approximations $\underline{P}X$ under P for all X in U/D, using (3). Then, dependency value of decision attribute D on P (i.e., $\gamma_P(D)$) is obtained using (4), which is dependent only on the set lower approximation value.

$$\underline{P}X = \{x | [x]_P \subseteq X\} \qquad (1)$$

$$POS_P(D) = \cup_{X \in U/D} \underline{P}X \qquad (3)$$

$$\gamma_P(D) = \frac{|POS_P(D)|}{|U|} \qquad (4)$$

2.2.2 Kullback-Leibler Divergence

The Kullback-Leibler (KL) [14] divergence is a primary equation of information theory that quantifies the proximity of two probability distributions. It is a measure in statistics [19] that quantifies in bits how close a probability distribution $p = \{p_i\}$ is to a model (or, candidate) distribution $q = \{q_i\}$. The KL divergence [12] is measured using (5).

$$D_{KL}(p||q) = \sum_{i=1}^{no.\,of\,feature} p_i log_2 \left(\frac{p_i}{q_i}\right) \qquad (5)$$

D_{KL} is non-negative (≥ 0) and not symmetric in p and q. Its value is zero if the distributions match exactly and can potentially equal perpetuity. According to the binary string population, candidate feature subset is created and associated probability distribution (q_i) is computed. Then the probability distribution (p_i) based on decision attribute over all samples is calculated. Thus, the $D_{KL}(p\|q)$ is computed using (5).Now, this model evaluates pair to pair D_{KL} value and mean of these D_{KL} value is used as another Fitness function.

2.3   Jumping Gene Mutation

Single bit mutation is very much popular in the GA literature [3] but it lacks diversity in population in some extent as the first bit of binary string generally does not change. To overcome the demerit, jumping gene or Transposon mutation methodology [15] is proposed. Jumping genes are a set of genes which can dynamically jump into the chromosome. These genes have a great potential for preserving the diversity among the members throughout the entire population which is very much crucial for search purpose.

Let, the original chromosome in the population is $(a_1a_2.....a_n)$. Randomly a jumping gene of length q ($q<<n$) say, ($b_1, b_2, ..., b_q$) is selected. Then randomly the starting position from where the original gene of the chromosome will be replaced by the jumping gene is chosen. Let the starting position be k, so after mutation the muted chromosome is $(a_1a_2...a_{k-1}b_1b_2...b_qa_{q+1}...a_n)$. This mutation method gives much promising result than the single bit mutation scheme. The proposed method is established as it only replaces a parent with offspring iff the offspring offers better solution (by measuring dominance or better global best).

Proposed feature selection method based on multi-objective genetic algorithm is pictorially depicted in Fig. 2.

3   Experimental Results and Performance Evaluation

Experimental studies presented here demonstrate the effectiveness of proposed feature selection technique. Experiments carried out on gene dataset publicly available at http://www-genome.wi.mit.edu/mpr   and   http://carrier.gnf.org/welsh/prostate   as training and test dataset are summarized in Table 1. The training dataset is used for forming optimal gene subset and test dataset is used for measuring the effectiveness of the method by computing classification accuracy.

Table 1. Summary of Gene expression (training/testing) dataset

Dataset	No. of Genes	Class Name	No. of Samples (class1/class2)
Leukemia	7129	ALL/AML	38(27/11)
Lung cancer	12533	MPM/ADCA	32(16/16)
Prostate cancer	12600	Tumor/Normal	102(52/50)

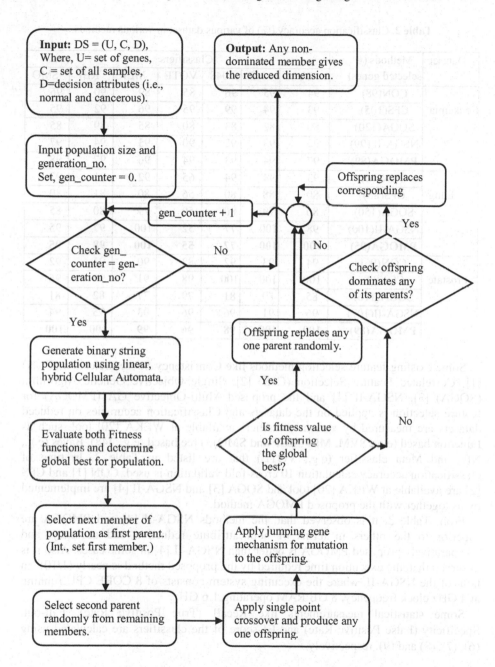

Fig. 2. Illustrate overall feature selection method

Table 2. Classification accuracy (%) of various dataset in various methods

Dataset	Methods (# selected genes)	Classifiers						
		SVM	NB	J48	VOTE	MLP	RBF	SMO
Leukemia	CON(98)	94	95	96	85	89	90	95
	CFS(105)	93	94	99	95	96	92	95
	SOGA(120)	80	82	83	80	85	89	85
	NSGA-II (99)	97	93	92	90	93	94	97
	PMOGA(89)	97	94	93	94	96	97	98
Lung	CON(90)	93	94	94	65	92	91	93
	CFS(85)	80	88	80	56	80	81	80
	SOGA(150)	80	79	80	50	79	80	85
	NSGA-II(100)	98	100	77	52	100	97	95
	PMOGA(95)	**100**	**100**	**77**	**55**	**100**	**98**	**95**
Prostate	CON(96)	94	93	92	82	90	91	92
	CFS(99)	100	100	100	98	91	99	96
	SOGA(116)	85	89	81	79	77	82	81
	NSGA-II(107)	96	91	96	96	93	95	94
	PMOGA(89)	**100**	**100**	**98**	**96**	**99**	**100**	**100**

Some existing feature selection methods like Consistency Subset Selection (CON) [1], Correlated Feature Selection (CFS) [2], Single Objective Genetic Algorithm (SOGA) [3], NSGA-II [4] and the proposed Multi-Objective GA (PMOGA) for feature selection is applied on the datasets and Classification accuracies on reduced datasets are measured by various classifiers available at WEKA [20] tool, such as Function based (e.g., SVM, MLP, RBF and SMO), Tree based (e.g., J48), Bayes (e.g., NB) and Meta classifier (e.g., VOTE) that are listed in Table 2. In time of classification accuracy calculation 10 cross-fold validation is used. CON [1] and CFS [2] are available at WEKA [20] tool and SOGA [3] and NSGA-II [4] are implemented by us together with the proposed PMOGA method.

From Table 2, it is observed that, the methods NSGA-II [4] and PMOGA are superior to the others in terms of both attribute reduction and accuracy, and comparatively proposed PMOGA is better than NSGA-II [4] in some cases. Also it is observed that, the execution time required by the proposed method is nearly $(1/10)^{th}$ in hour of the NSGA-II, where the executing system consists of 8 CORE CPU running at 4 GHz clock frequency, 8 GB RAM operating 1.6 GHz.

Some statistical measurements like Recall (True Positive Rate), Fall-out, Specificity (False Positive Rate) and F1-score of the classifiers are calculated using (6), (7), (8) and (9), respectively.

$$Recall = \frac{TP}{P} = \frac{TP}{TP + FN} \qquad (6)$$

$$Fall\_out = \frac{FP}{N} = \frac{FP}{FP + TN} \qquad (7)$$

$$Specificity = \frac{TN}{N} = \frac{TN}{FP + TN} = 1 - Fall\_out \qquad (8)$$

$$F1\_score = \frac{2 \times TP}{2 \times TP + FP + FN} \qquad (9)$$

Where, TP is the positive object classified as positive, FP is the positive object classified as negative, TN is the negative object classified as negative and FN is the negative object classified as positive. The calculated various statistical measurements are graphically shown in Fig. 3, Fig. 4 and Fig. 5 for three mentioned dataset for the classifiers SVM, NB and J48. It is observed that proposed method PMOGA gives better and more consistent measures compare to other methods.

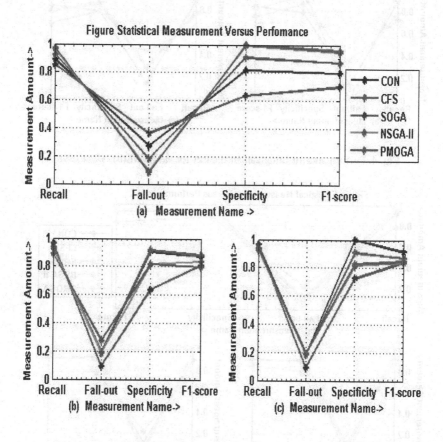

Fig. 3. Performance of Leukemia dataset for (a) SVM (b) NB (c) J48

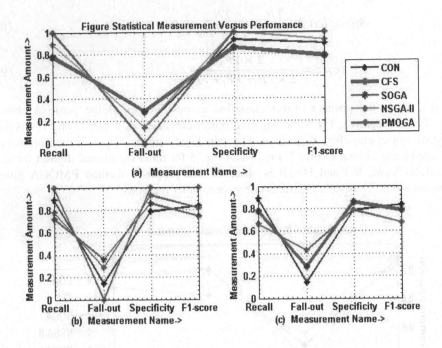

Fig. 4. Performance of Lung cancer dataset for (a) SVM (b) NB (c) J48

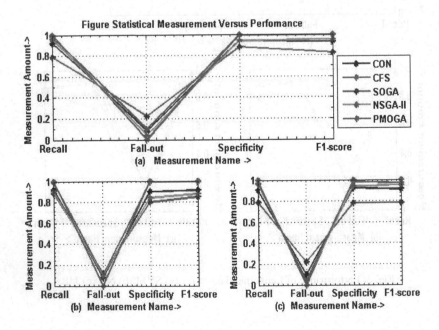

Fig. 5. Performance of Prostate cancer dataset for (a) SVM (b) NB (c) J48

The ROC curves (drawn by Matlab) of experimental dataset reduced by CON, CFS, SOGA, NSGA-II and PMOGA for SVM classifier are shown in Fig. 6, Fig. 7 and Fig. 8. It is observed that, the ROC graph corresponding to the proposed method PMOGA based on SVM classifier rises almost vertically from (0, 0) to (0, 1) and then horizontally to (1, 1) whereas the graph for other methods are not so vertical and horizontal. This indicates perfect and truly significant classification performance on the data set.

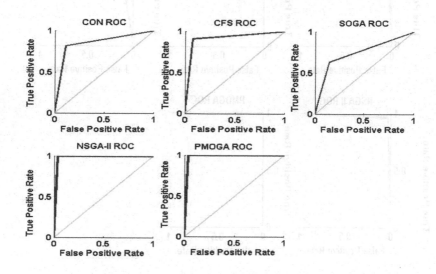

Fig. 6. ROC curve of Leukemia dataset for SVM classifier

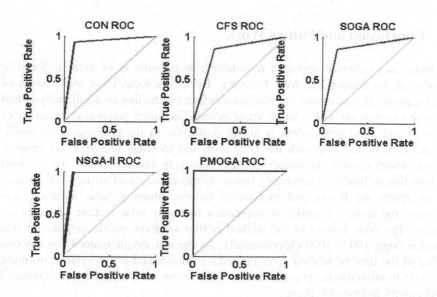

Fig. 7. ROC curve of Lung cancer dataset for SVM classifier

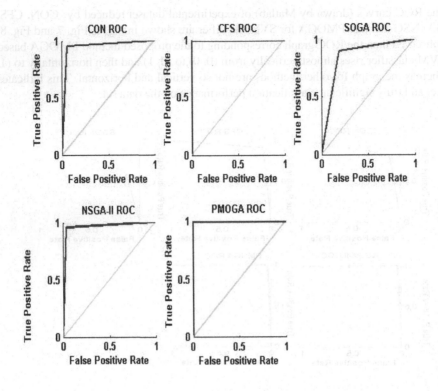

Fig. 8. ROC curve of Prostate cancer dataset for SVM classifier

4   Conclusion and Future Work

Systematic and unbiased approach to cancer classification is of great importance treatment of the disease and drug discovery. Biologists focus on a small subset of genes (features) that dominate the outcomes before conducting in depth analysis and expensive experiments with a larger set of genes. Therefore, automated discovery of this small and good gene subset is highly desirable. In the paper, a novel multi-objective evolutionary approach has been proposed to select important informative gene set, which classify the cancer dataset effectively and efficiently. The method uses two fitness functions separately based on the concepts of strong mathematics such as rough set theory and probability theory. Jumping gene mutation also overcomes the lack of diversity of population that may arise in case of single bit mutation. The only demerit of the method is that we have set the population size within the range 100 to 1000 experimentally. As the method guaranteed that any one member of the final population gives the reduced dimension of the system, in future we will try to minimize the population size and construct a classifier for each reduced dataset and try to ensemble them.

References

1. Yu, L., Liu, H.: Efficient feature selection via analysis of relevance and redundancy. The Journal of Machine Learning Research 5, 1205–1224 (2004)
2. Hall, M.A.: Correlation-based feature selection for machine learning. Diss., The University of Waikato (1999)
3. Goldberg, D.E., Holland, J.H.: Genetic algorithms and machine learning. Machine Learning 3(2), 95–99 (1988)
4. Deb, K., et al.: A fast and elitist multiobjective genetic algorithm: NSGA-II. IEEE Transactions on Evolutionary Computation 6(2), 182–197 (2002)
5. Schwefel, P.H.: Evolution and optimum seeking: the sixth generation. John Wiley & Sons, Inc. (1993)
6. Coello Coello, A.C., Lamont, B.G., Van Veldhuisen, D.A.: Evolutionary algorithms for solving multi-objective problems. Springer (2007)
7. Multi-objective Evolutionary Algorithms: A Survey of the State-of-the-art. Swarm and Evolutionary Computation 1(1), 32–49 (2011)
8. Zhou, A., Suganthan, P.N., Zhang, Q.: Decomposition Based Multiobjective Evolutionary Algorithm with an Ensemble of Neighborhood Sizes. IEEE Trans. on Evolutionary Computation 16(3), 442–446 (2012)
9. Knowles, J.D., Corne, D.W.: M-PAES: A memetic algorithm for multi-objective optimization. In: Proceedings of the 2000 Congress on Evolutionary Computation, vol. 1. IEEE (2000)
10. Zitzler, E., Lothar, T.: Multiobjective evolutionary algorithms: A comparative case study and the strength pareto approach. IEEE Transactions on Evolutionary Computation 3(4), 257–271 (1999)
11. Van Veldhuisen, D.A., Lamont, G.B.: Multi-objective evolutionary algorithm research: A history and analysis. Technical Report TR-98-03, Department of Electrical and Computer Engineering, Graduate School of Engineering, Air Force Institute of Technology, Wright-Patterson AFB, Ohio (1998)
12. Mumford, C.L.: Simple population replacement strategies for a steady-state multi-objective evolutionary algorithm. In: Deb, K., Tari, Z. (eds.) GECCO 2004. LNCS, vol. 3102, pp. 1389–1400. Springer, Heidelberg (2004)
13. Deb, K.: Multi-objective optimization. In: Multi-objective Optimization Using Evolutionary Algorithms, pp. 13–46 (2001)
14. Kullback, S., Leibler, R.A.: On Information and Sufficiency. Annals of Mathematical Statistics 22(1), 79–86 (1951), doi:10.1214/aoms/1177729694
15. Chaconas, G., Lavoie, B.D., Watson, M.A.: DNA transposition: jumping gene machine, some assembly required. Current Biology: CB 6(7), 817 (1996)
16. Von Neumann, J.: Theory of self-reproducing automata (1966)
17. Pawlak, Z.: Rough set approach to knowledge-based decision support. European Journal of Operational Research 99(1), 48–57 (1997)
18. Turing, A.: Universal Turing machine
19. Cover, T., et al.: Elements of information theory. Telecommunications, Wiley series (1991)
20. Hall, M., Frank, E., Holmes, G., Pfahringer, B., Reutemann, P., Witten, I.H.: The WEKA Data Mining Software: An Update. SIGKDD Explorations 11(1) (2009)

Fusion at Features Level in CBIR System
Using Genetic Algorithm

Chandrashekhar G. Patil[1,*], Mahesh T. Kolte[2], and Devendra S. Chaudhari[3]

[1,3] Department of Electronics and Telecommunication Engineering,
Government College of Engineering Amravati India
patilcg23@rediffmail.com, ddss@yahoo.com
[2] Maharashtra Institute of Technology College of Engineering, Pune, India
mtkolta@rediffmail.com

Abstract. The research in content based Image retrieval (CBIR) systems is becoming matured as more and more applications are building up over it. In order to imitate the way human being treat the image management, the conventional way of text based retrieval systems are being replaced by the visual content based systems. The image content has several dominant characteristics like color, texture and it is interesting to see the classification of images on content-basis can be achieved with these features. The color has different features like average, variance and texture can be represented by co-occurrence matrix. This different descriptor for the images can form a combined feature vector. However, in order to have optimum performance and to reduce the feature dimensionality for making system real-time, genetic algorithm (GA) based feature selection is used in this paper. The genetic algorithm can be used at the level of the feature elements selection; where important features are preserved while ignoring remaining We used the database of 10 classes and 100 images in each class for validation of CBIR system. We performed the experiments with and without GA and observed the usefulness of feature optimization. The result shows the effectiveness of these features for content based classification or image retrieval applications.

Keywords: Content based image retrieval (CBIR), Genetic Algorithm, Co-occurrence matrix, Feature vector, Edge Histogram Descriptor.

1   Introduction

With many ongoing multimedia applications, content- based image retrieval (CBIR) has recently gained more attention from the researcher around the world for image management and search of image of user's interest. Growing number of digital images are being created in various applications like academia, photography, hospitals, research, governance etc. In past or by conventional methods, the way used for image retrieval was metadata like tags, keyword indexing or just browsing. However, use of such metadata for searching for images can yield a lot of garbage content and

---

* Corresponding author.

B.K. Panigrahi et al. (Eds.): SEMCCO 2013, Part II, LNCS 8298, pp. 156–167, 2013.

additionally it needs all images to be tagged manually. With more and more multimedia information appear on the Internet and other digital multimedia as well as human beings' thirst for exact and fast retrieval, it is interesting to see how CBIR algorithms and data processing enables the image retrieval application and satisfies the users. The typical block diagram CBIR system is shown in fig 1, where query image is selected by user and CBIR system gives the group of similar images in response to the query.

The first Content-based image retrieval of its kind had been introduced by T. Kato in 1992. The enormous growth in images due to easy and cheaper availability of cameras, wide inclusion of images in governance and corporate processes, has already given some successful and popular CBIR systems such as QBIC, Virage, RetrievalWare, Photobook, Chabot, VisualSeek, WebSeek, MARS system, SurfImage, Netra, and CANDID etc. These are some CBIR systems where some of them are general and others are for specialized are like medical images retrieval system. Most Retrieval systems are based on similarity defined in terms of Visual features.

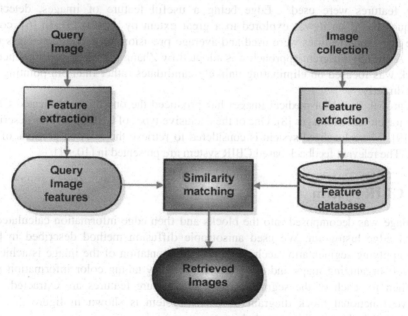

Fig. 1. Generic block diagram of CBIR system

In general, a database of images has to be stored in advance and appropriate features need to be extracted from these images. The set of features may include color, shape, texture, region or spatial features which are combined form the feature vectors. The user inputs a query image or query features. If the former, the features are first extracted from the image and are compared with the stored features of the database images. The images from database whose features are with the least distance from the query feature are chosen as a "retrieved images". The work in this paper presents the evolutionary computation based system for selecting the appropriate feature elements in order to maximize the system performance. We have used genetic algorithm tool to select optimum feature elements.

The remaining part of this paper is as follows. The next section 2 presents the relevant work done in the area of CBIR. Section 3 presents the methodology adopted in this work. The experimental results and discussion are reported in the section 4. Finally, paper is concluded in section 5 by highlighting the contribution of this work.

2   Relevant Work

It is normal to color, texture and shape information in various combinations have been the dominant traits used for image retrieval. Among these, color has been the most effective. Swain and Ballard were among the first to show the usefulness of color in object identification in [1]. It later transformed into its variants like a color histogram [2], color moments [3], and color correlogram [4]. This kind of work was extended in [8] for the CBIR system where efficient combination of multi-resolution color and texture features were used. Edge being a useful feature of images, detection techniques based on it was explored to a great extent by Amato [5]. In [6], color, texture and shape features were used and average precision for each image class was found. A slightly different approach was adopted by Zhang [7] where artificial neural network was focused on eliminating unlikely candidates rather than pin-pointing the targets directly.

The growth in digital medical images has produced the one of the dedicated CBIR system for blood cell images [8]. One of the exclusive types of CBIR system is described in the [9], where localized system is considered to retrieve the relevant portions of the image. The relevant feedback based CBIR system are presented in [10, 11].

3   CBIR System

The image was decomposed into the blocks and then edge information calculated in form of edge histogram. We used anisotropic diffusion method described in [12] before applying segmentation technique. The segmentation of the image is achieved using self-organizing maps and spectral clustering by taking color information as a cue. Then for each of the segments color and texture features are extracted. The cohesive functional block diagram of CBIR system is shown in figure 2. The methodology is described in steps below.

1) Querying: The user provides a sample image as the query for the system.

2) Extraction of the Low Level Features of the Image viz. i) Color, ii)Edge and iii)Texture.

3) Similarity computation: The system computes the similarity between the query images and the database images according to the aforementioned low-level visual features using a simple kNN classifier.

4) Retrieval: The system retrieves and presents a sequence of images ranked in decreasing order of similarity. As a result, the user is able to find relevant images by getting the top ranked images first.

In following subsections, each of the main steps of CBIR system is briefly described.

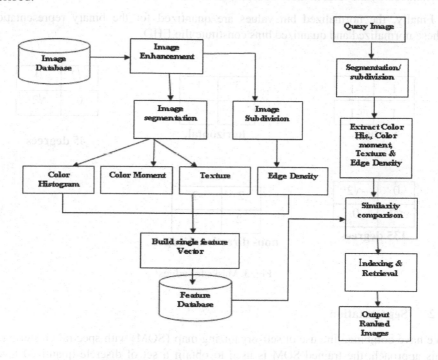

Fig. 2. Flowchart of proposed methodology

3.1   Edge Histogram Descriptor

Edges in images constitute an important feature to represent their content. Human eyes are sensitive to edge features for image perception. One way of representing such an important edge feature is to use a histogram. An edge histogram in the image space represents the frequency and the directionality of the brightness changes in the image. We will adopt the edge histogram descriptor (EHD) to describe edge distribution with a histogram based on local edge distribution in an image. The extraction process of EHD consists of the following stages.

1) An image is divided into 4 × 4 sub images.

2) Each sub image is further partitioned into non overlapping image blocks with a small size.

3) The edges in each image block are categorized into five types: vertical, horizontal, 45° diagonal, 135° diagonal, and non directional edges and they are filtered using masks (filters) shown in figure 3.

4) Thus, the histogram for each sub image represents the relative frequency of occurrence of the five types of edges in the corresponding sub image.

5) After examining all image blocks in the sub image, the five-bin values are normalized by the total number of blocks in the sub image.

Finally, the normalized bin values are quantized for the binary representation. These normalized and quantized bins constitute the EHD.

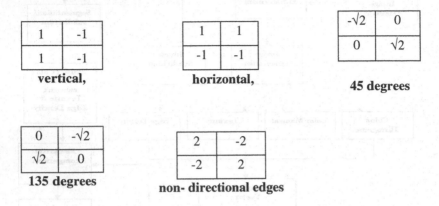

1	-1
1	-1

vertical,

1	1
-1	-1

horizontal,

-√2	0
0	√2

45 degrees

0	-√2
√2	0

135 degrees

2	-2
-2	2

non- directional edges

Fig. 3. Masks for edges

3.2   Segmentation

We have combined the use of self-organizing map (SOM) with spectral clustering. In this approach, the trained SOM is used to obtain a set of discrete quantized levels. These levels are reduced further to a set of optimum clusters obtained using the similarity-matrix to eliminate levels having similar values to those already present.

4   Color Feature Extraction

Color histogram is a powerful tool which has long been used for the purpose of segmentation. In Image Processing, a histogram of a grayscale image can be described as a representation of the frequencies of occurrence of discrete gray level. Each discrete level is called as a 'bin'. Naturally, a color histogram contains occurrences of each color obtained counting all pixels of a color image having that color. In the conventional color histogram, the pixels of the color image are represented in their respective bins based on their own color and not based on their relationship to other colors. However, a number of drawbacks arise from this approach. These are *(a)* the discrepancies such as changes in illumination and quantization errors are recorded as well, and *(b)* considering all values of color will lead to large number of indexing and data storage and processing. Hence, the logical and better way of drawing up the color histogram would be to build up the bins such that they use fewer quantization levels which represent the similarities between the colors. Hence, we use the segments extracted from the above algorithm. The histogram of the cluster is found. From the histogram, three color features are extracted i.e. mean, standard deviation and median. Thus with three features and three planes per cluster, we have 3x3 features per segment or cluster, per image.

4.1   Texture Feature Extraction

Texture is an important attribute that refers to innate surface properties of an object and their relationship to the surrounding environment. If we could choose appropriate texture descriptors, the performance of the CBIR should be improved. We will use a gray level co-occurrence matrix (GLCM), which is a simple and effective method for representing texture.

The co-occurrence matrix is statistical way to describe texture by statistically sampling the way certain grey-levels occur in relation to other grey-levels. It is calculated for each segment. For a position operator p, we can define a matrix $P(i, j)$ that counts the number of times a pixel with grey-level i occurs at position p from a pixel with grey-level j. i & j are not to be confused with image co-ordinates. For e.g. consider image I of dimensions MxN with x=1,2,...M & y=1,2,...N. Then suppose position p stands for one element to the right, if $i = I(x, y)$ and $j = I(x+1, y)$, then the co-occurrence matrix, $P(i, j) = P(i, j) + 1$. Texture is usually characterized by the values of energy, entropy, contrast and homogeneity. These values are readily obtained from the co-occurrence matrix by the following formulas.

$$Energy = \sum_i \sum_j P^2(i, j) \tag{1}$$

$$Entropy = \sum_i \sum_j P(i, j) \log P(i, j) \tag{2}$$

$$Contrast = \sum_i \sum_j (i-j)^2 P(i, j) \tag{3}$$

$$Homogenity = \sum_i \sum_j \frac{P(i, j)}{1+|i-j|} \tag{4}$$

For our purpose, we have used four positions for calculation the above values. These are one step right, one step left, one step up, and one step down. Thus for each images, we have 4x4 = 16 values per cluster which contribute to the texture feature.

4.2   Composite Feature Vector

Finally we have formed single feature vector by combining edge histogram and segment wise color and texture features. This feature vector will be used to find out the similarity between the query image and database images.

4.3   Genetic Algorithm

There are numerous attempts made by researchers for evolutionary model in the CBIR system. The genetic algorithm can be used at the level of the feature elements selection, where important features are preserved while ignoring remaining can employ the genetic algorithm. The composite feature vector to be used in image retrieval, feature elements may be very sensitive to additive noise due to intra class variations; therefore the recognition accuracy deteriorates drastically in such type of applications. Thus it is important to remove or suppress the effect of the feature elements which are sensitive to the noise and echo to optimize the recognition performance in high intra-class variation environment. This optimization problem can be handled using genetic algorithm.

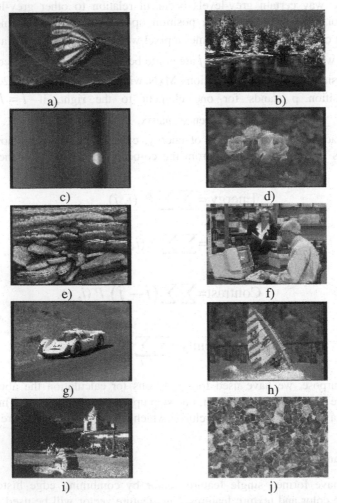

Fig. 4. Database sample images from each of the 10 classes which are (a) butterfly, (b) scenery, (c) sunset, (d) flowers, (e) rocks, (f) people, (g) cars, (h) yatch, (i) religious, (j) textures

The genetic algorithm is applied to the recognition problem of image class with the objective to find important feature elements that contributes more to classifier for distinguishing one word from others. Additionally, the number of feature elements are also reduced, which results into the reduction in the length of feature vector for further step of classification. The chromosome of GA was of length as same as that of feature vector. This chromosome has real value between 0 and 1, randomly generated at each position, in its first form and then it is modified by making 0 to the positions that has lesser value than some randomly generated value between 0 and 1. This modification helped in bringing the wide range variations in usable percentage of total feature elements. This enabled to evaluate the chromosome's performance of recognition with having even small percentage of elements. This chromosome was multiplied (element wise) with feature vector to be optimized, before using it for recognition.

5   Experimental Results and Discussion

We have used the Corel database. We selected 10 classes with 100 images for each class. We have performed image retrieval experiment by giving a query image to CBIR system. We focus on finding the cumulative match score(CMS) in each of the image classes . A typical graph that shows the CMS for Class a) is displayed in Figure 5.

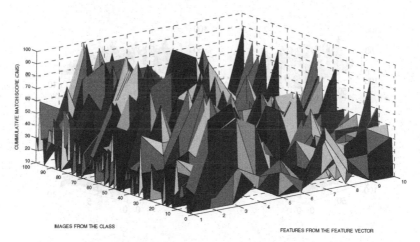

Fig. 5. The CMS evaluation for Class a) Images

The recall values for each of the classes were found by the ratio on the number of relevant images retrieved to the total number of relevant images in the database. From figure 6, (a) to (h) which correspond to the cumulative match score in each of the 10 classes mentioned, it can be seen that the score for classes a, b and d are comparatively higher as compared with other classes. The reason for this the uniform nature of images in database as compared with the other classes.

The CMS results are shown in figure 6 and 7 are for the 10 classes. It shows that recognition performance obtained with genetic algorithm is improved. The figure shows the GA based optimization performance for selection of feature elements and it can be sees that the performance increases as per the number of iterations. The figure 8 shows that the best optimized solutions of feature selection problem reduces the computational complexity in classifier as number of feature elements used for similarity calculation are reduced. Even after feature number reduction, it maintains or improves the image retrieval performance.

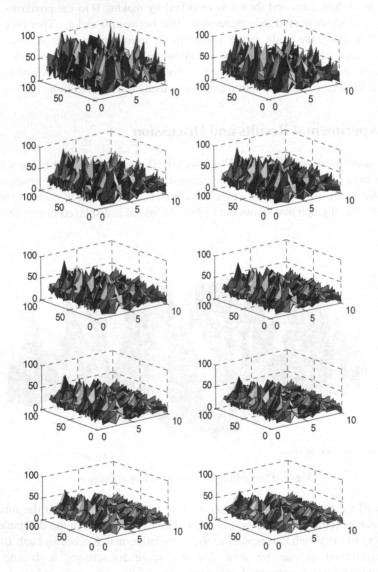

Fig. 6. Graphs of Query image v/s CMS without GA for each of the 10 classes enlisted in figure 4

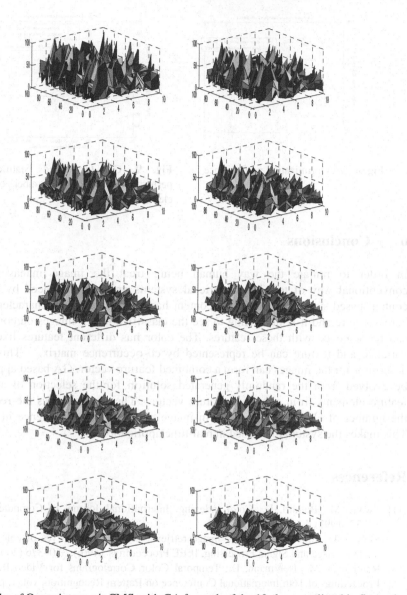

Fig. 7. Graphs of Query image v/s CMS with GA for each of the 10 classes enlisted in figure 4

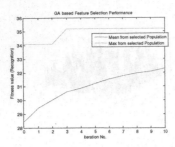

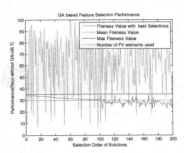

Fig. 8. GA Optimization performance

Fig. 9. GA Optimized Feature Vector performance & % number of feature elements used

6   Conclusions

In order to imitate the way human being treat the image management, the conventional way of text based retrieval systems are being replaced by the visual content based systems. The image content has several dominant characteristics like color, texture and it is interesting to see the classification of images on content-basis can be achieved with these features. The color has different features like average, variance and texture can be represented by co-occurrence matrix. This different descriptor for the images can form a combined feature vector. GA based approach can be evolved from the randomly generated solution for the selection of appropriate feature elements from combined feature vector. The results shows the reduction in the number of elements to be used in image representation and hence in classifier. This makes the system to be used in real-time applications.

References

[1] Swain, M., Ballard, D.: Color indexing. International Journal of Computer Vision 7, 11–32 (1991)
[2] Shih, J.-L., Chen, L.-H.: Color image retrieval based on primitives of color moments. Vision, Image and Signal Processing, IEEE Proceedings 149(6), 370–376 (2002)
[3] Rautiainen, M., Doermann, D.: Temporal Color Correlograms for Video Retrieval. In: Proceedings of 16th International Conference on Pattern Recognition, vol. 1, pp. 267–270 (August 2002)
[4] Eom, M., Choe, Y.: Fast Extraction of Edge Histogram in DCT Domain based on MPEG7. Proceedings of World Academy of Science, Engineering and Technology 9, 1307–6884 (2005) ISSN 1307-6884
[5] Amato, A., Di Lecce, V.: Edge Detection Techniques in Image Retrieval: The Semantic Meaning of Edge. In: 4th EURASIP Conference on Video/Image Processing and Multimedia Communications, Zagreb, Croatia, pp. 143–148.
[6] Hiremath, P.S., Pujari, J.: Content Based Image Retrieval using Color, Texture and Shape features. In: 15th International Conference on Advanced Computing and Communications, pp. 780–784. IEEE Computer Society (2007)

[7] Zhang, H.J., Shong, D.: A scheme for visual feature-based image indexing. In: Proceedings of SPIE Conference on Storage and Retrieval for Image and Video Databases III, San Jose, CA, vol. 2185, pp. 36–46 (February 1995)

[8] Seng, W.C., Mirisaee, S.H.: A Content-Based Retrieval System for Blood Cells Images. In: International Conference on Future Computer and Communication (2009)

[9] Rahmani, R., Goldman, S.A., Zhang, H., Cholleti, S.R., Fritts, J.E.: Localized Content-Based Image Retrieval. IEEE Transactions on Pattern Analysis and Machine Intelligence 30(11) (November 2008)

[10] Marakakis, A., Galatsanos, N., Likas, A., Stafylopatis, A.: Probabilistic relevance feedback approach for content-based image retrieval based on gaussian mixture models. IET Image Process. 3(1), 10–25 (2009)

[11] Bian, W., Tao, D.: Biased Discriminant Euclidean Embedding for Content-Based Image Retrieval. IEEE Transactions on Image Processing 19(2) (February 2010)

[12] Ilea, D.E., Whelan, P.F.: CTex—An Adaptive Unsupervised Segmentation Algorithm Based on Color-Texture Coherence. IEEE Transactions on Image Processing 17(10), pp.1926–1939 (2008)

[13] Shafimirza, Apparao, J.: Retrieval of Digital Images Using Texture Feature With Advanced Genetic Algorithm. Journal of Computer Trends and Technology 3(4) (2012)

New Bio-inspired Meta-Heuristics - Green Herons Optimization Algorithm - for Optimization of Travelling Salesman Problem and Road Network

Chiranjib Sur and Anupam Shukla

ABV-Indian Institute of Information Technology & Management, Gwalior
{chiranjibsur,dranupamshukla}@gmail.com

Abstract. Following the nature and its processes has been proved to be very fruitful when it comes to tackling the difficult hardships and making life easy. Yet again the nature and its processes has been proven to be worthy of following, but this time the discrete family is being facilitated and another member is added to the bio-inspired computing family. A new biological phenomenon following meta-heuristics called Green Heron Optimization Algorithm (GHOA) is being introduced for the first time which acquired its potential and habit from an intelligent bird called Green Heron whose diligence, skills, perception analysis capability and procedure for food acquisition has overwhelmed many zoologists. This natural skillset of the bird has been transferred into operations which readily favor the graph based and discrete combinatorial optimization problems, both unconstrained and constraint though the latter requires safe guard and validation check so that the generated solutions are acceptable. With proper modifications and modeling it can also be utilized for other wide variety of real world problems and can even optimize benchmark equations. In this work we have mainly concentrated on the algorithm introduction with establishment, illustration with minute details of the steps and performance validation of the algorithm for a wide range of dimensions of the Travelling Salesman Problem combinatorial optimization problem datasets to clearly validate its scalability performance and also on a road network for optimized graph based path planning. The result of the simulation clearly stated its capability for combination generation through randomization and converging global optimization and thus has contributed another important member of the bio-inspired computation family.

Keywords: Green Herons Optimization Algorithm, combinatorial optimization, graph based problems, bio-inspired meta-heuristics.

1 Introduction

The biologically inspired algorithms has been the new trend to capitalize on the intelligent behavior and approach of the various animals and organisms for food acquire, survival and sustaining the hardship of the nature that can be formulated as mathematical and algorithmic operations and models and can be utilized as optimization algorithm of the various discrete and continuous domain problems of the real world

B.K. Panigrahi et al. (Eds.): SEMCCO 2013, Part II, LNCS 8298, pp. 168–179, 2013.

problems. It is a common thing for the human when they are not good at something, they try to observe what other organisms do, what the nature does and depending on their study they come to a conclusion. This nature inspired meta-heuristics family is just an extension of such imitation of the natural phenomenon.

In this paper we have introduced another such type of nature inspired meta-heuristics called Green Heron Optimization algorithm inspired by the natural skill sets and perception of the green heron bird for catching aquatic prey through the process of baiting as any amateur fisher man would do for catching fishes. Quite astonishingly the bird has utilized its resources beautifully like its long extensible neck, speed, observation and analysis capability, long beak and most importantly patience, which is perhaps the only key for any success. The primary algorithm readily suits the problems having discrete representation of solution set ad graph based problems. The operation(s) of the algorithm produces better combinations of the solution set and also can produce a local search based operation which derives the better solution more quickly and convergence will be enhanced. The algorithm is applied on the Travelling Salesman Problem for certain dimensions depending upon the numbers of iteration.

There are many other nature inspired meta-heuristics which provided very optimistic results for many real world and benchmark problems but most of them are for the continuous variable problem where they persists on a certain range or all the real number line range. These are mainly Genetic Algorithm [6], Particle Swarm Optimization [7], Honey bee swarm [8], League Championship Algorithm [9], Cuckoo search [10], Simulated Annealing [12], Differential evolution [13], artificial immune system [14], harmony search [15], Glowworm swarm optimization [16] (specifically for multimodal optimization), Honey-bees mating optimization [17], differential search algorithm [19], Charged System Search [20], Krill Herd Algorithm [21], Virus Optimization Algorithm [22], Bacterial Foraging Optimization Algorithm [32], artificial weed colonies [36] etc. These algorithms are search algorithms for continuous search spaces and fail to deliver efficiently for the discrete combinatorial problems and graph based problem except a few of them are forged for discrete problems like discrete Genetic Algorithm [31], discrete Particle Swarm Optimization [30,34-35] which have limited opportunity to handle discrete problems. They mainly constitute an adaptive or multi-parameter dependent mathematical variation to hover in the acceptable range of the variables. However there are some members who are exclusively for the discrete problems like Intelligent Water Drops Algorithm (IWD) [18], Ant Colony Optimization (ACO) [33,37], Egyptian Vulture Optimization Algorithm [38,39] etc. So there is requirement of better discrete optimization algorithms which are more efficient. On the solution derivation of the travelling salesman problem there are a few techniques provided by many researchers like for deterministic approaches like [26-29] and nondeterministic approaches like [24-25] and genetic algorithm approaches [31]. The main problems the continuous domain algorithms face is the combination variation generation and link formation which is not required in continuous domain and this perhaps has led to the formation of exclusive discrete algorithms.

The remaining paper is arranged as Section 2 with Life Style of the Green Heron bird, Section 3 with the details of the operations of the algorithm, Section 4 with the steps of the implementation of the algorithm for Travelling Salesman Problem, Section 5 with results and Section 6 with conclusion and future works.

2   Life Style of Green Herons

The Green Heron bird [1-4] (Butorides virescens) resides on the freshwater or brackish water swampy marshes or wetlands with clumps of trees mainly in low lying areas where there are abundant scope of availability of fishes as their prey. They are nocturnal in habit and preference to stay back in sheltered areas during the daytime. But when hungry they generally feed during the daytime. Their main food consists of small fish, spider, frogs, grasshoppers, snakes, rodents, reptiles, aquatic arthropods, mollusks, crustaceans, insects, amphibians, vertebrate or invertebrate animals like leeches and mice, provided they can catch. Usually the Green Heron bird forages from a perch and there it stands with its body stretched out horizontally and lowered further, to insert its bill inside water for any unsuspecting prey. Green Heron is one among the few birds who can use tools for doing their daily jobs, the Green Heron will attract prey, mainly swarm of fishes, with bait (feathers, earthworms, bread crusts, tiny stick piece, insects, or even berries) when it drops on the water surface. The bait is dropped onto the water surface in order to attract fishes and all other water organisms that hover over the bait to sense its kind and food value. When any fish takes or tries to take the bait, the green heron bird grab hold the fish and eat the prey. This prey catching feature is being exploited as a meta-heuristic for complex problem solving and most importantly achieving optimization. The next section will describe in details the steps of the algorithm and its resemblance with the natural phenomenon of the Green Heron bird.

Fig. 1. Preying Habit with Bait of Green Heron Bird

Fig. 2. Green Heron Optimization Algorithm

3   Green Herons Optimization Algorithm

The Green Heron Optimization algorithm can be divided into the following basic operations which will perform different searches for heuristic sequence or path creation and will thus establish a solution for the algorithm. However the individual constraints unique to each kind of problems are required to be established into the computation through implementation and the operations are just guidelines of what should be happening with the solution set individually or as a whole.

3.1   Baiting – (Miss Catch, Catch, False Catch)

The baiting process is analogous to holding bait in the beak by the Green Heron bird and will drop at the appropriate place where there is chance of a catch. Similarly in the computation the bait is a solution that is arbitrarily generated and is held by the bird before it finds a good position through local search throughout the whole solution set. The bait and the prey is assumed as two individual solutions which takes part in the operation and there are three alternatives which the bait-prey pair will bring about altering the solution set and thus heuristically creating a new solution set or improving it. Now the three alternatives (the occurrences of which depends on the problem, its constraints, and the implementation and partly on probability and local search) are:

MISS CATCH – In this case the bait gets settled at one of its preferred place where it finds continuity and the bird fails to catch any prey and hence the number of solutions in the solution set tends to increase. Depending on the problem, the situation must be tackled. Like in TSP, scheduling problems, etc the missing node must be restored (may be from last, or at random) to sustain the validity of the solutions.

CATCH – In this case the bait helps the Green Heron bird to catch a prey and thus the solution set elements remains constant and one appropriate element is added and one inappropriate element is eliminated.

FALSE CATCH – Here the bird gets hold of a prey without using bait as sometimes fishes comes near the surface of the water. In this step an inappropriate element of the solution set is eliminated from the set. The depletion of a node in the form of a catch from the solution set, must be restored for establishment of validity for certain constraints of the problems or limitation on the part of the variables.

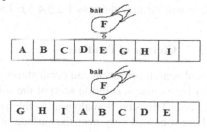

Fig. 3. Baiting Operation   **Fig. 4.** Attracting Prey Swarms

For the TSP problem, as the numbers of nodes are fixed and none should be repeated in the string, hence the replacement of the replaced and deletion of the excess due to miss catch phenomenon.

3.2   Attracting Prey Swarms

This Attracting Prey Swarms is also an equivalence of the local search operations that makes the algorithm quick convergent for constrained discrete problems solving the precedence criteria. But the step is little bit different from the Change of Position operation described previously. In this step the position of the bird sitting with the bait remains same but the swarm of fishes actually moves towards the fish or rather the bait is released and the fishes are attracted towards it. So for the solution set the point of release of the bait will remain same but the whole set will shift to create position for the best agent to receive the bait and this will help in a evolution like step where a shift can change the solution specially when the positions of the solution holds immense meaning and the correct sequence is of utmost importance. The example shown in Figure 4 will make the operation more clear. However this operation should be rare and occurs selectively for the iterations, only when there is no attachment in the initial positions of the solution set. This operation can be useful for problems like TSP, VRP, scheduling problems etc where the numbers of constraints are not present, but in problems like sequence ordering problems, routing, path planning, etc it can be useful selectively. However this operation can be operated on a selective portion of the solution set which is yet to be arranged or have not yet been lucky to engage in any kind of attachments. These local search processes are followed by the Baiting operation. It is to be mentioned that through the operations are described separately for convenience of understanding of the implementation with respect to any problem, in reality the operational steps are interweaved and cannot be operated separately unless some problems may be suited for and the key lies in proper studding the problem into the algorithm. In Figure 4 the operation occurs for the whole string of solution and is helpful for the solutions having fixed length, but in case of variable length solution like in routing, the operation must occur on the undecided portions of the solution. Like if the arranged sequence is 1,2,3,4,6,7,8,5 and the numerical precedence is respected, then movement of the portion from 6 to 5 occurs and the first four solution is kept intact. The secondary fitness will be helpful in deciding which portion to involve in movement. Now if the portion 6 to 5 moves right, then only one movement will arrange them as 1,2,3,4,5,6,7,8 which is the required arrangement.

3.3   Change of Position

Local search operation can occur through checking all (for small solution sets) or part (for long enough solution sets) of the solution sets for positions before it finds a suitable one. This step is analogous to the nature of the bird where it finds a suitable place where it can sit very near the surface of the water such that it can at any point f time can insert its beak inside water and take hold of a fish or aquatic animal whenever it comes near the surface naturally or due to the influence or temptation of the bait(s). This local search operation should count and made sure that too much time is not spend on a solution set if there are a number of solution sets to be taken care of in the iteration. In case of huge number elements, intensive local search strategy can be implemented for a selected zone to be checked or the low secondary fitness valued elements can be checked or any constraint of the problem can be utilized for such search and decision makings. In intensive local search the selected node is placed just by the side of the node where continuity can be established.

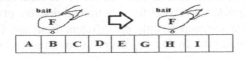

Fig. 5. Change of Position Operation

3.4   Fitness Function

There are two kind of fitness, one is primary fitness for the evaluation of complete path, but till the path is not complete there is another fitness involved called secondary fitness or incomplete fitness. Here each of the nodes is given a fitness value of 0-2 which implies how many neighbor nods are linked with it. Zero implies none, on implies on one, and two implies from both sides. This secondary fitness is helpful to decide which of the nodes need arrangement and which part is complete and thus helps in deciding the selecting the portion.

4   Steps of Green Heron Optimization Algorithm

The following steps are the details of the Green Heron Optimization Algorithm which are used for the simulation of the Travelling Salesman Problem datasets [23] ranging from the 16 to 280 dimensions.

Step 1: Initialize N solution strings (a set comprises of all the constituent nodes of the TSP as any discrepancy beyond this will land up the set as invalid solution) with random generation of all the nodes present for a dataset without repetition.

Step 2: Initialize the fitness matrix, however secondary fitness is unnecessary as all the nodes are connected.

Step 3: (For each string) Perform "Baiting" (with Miss Catch, Catch, False Catch) where position is selected with some intensive local search strategy where the nodes with least secondary fitness is searched (probability, random partial string, etc strategies can also be used). (need to take care of the duplicates)

Step 4: Perform "Change of Position" depending upon the requirement and initial search results. (Random positioning is done to see which combination yield best result)

Step 5: Perform "Attracting Prey Swarms".

Step 6: Complete "Baiting" operation. (End of For each string)

Step 7: Evaluate the fitness of each string.

Step 8: If New (derived out of combination of operation(s)) is better, then replace the old else don't.

Step 9: Select the best result and compare with global best. If better then set it as global best.

Step 10: After each iteration replace X% worst solutions with random initialization. (X depends on N and according to the exploration requirement)

Step 11: If number of iteration is complete then stop else continue from Step 3.

4.1   Road Network Description

The road network shown in Figure 6 consists of 25 nodes and 45 edges and is used for simulation of the GHOA and the results are shown in the next section. However there are several assumptions there are considered to make the simulation simple and objective oriented. There are a few considerations and approximations that are opted to ensure implementation simplicity of the road network and the application of the nature inspired heuristic possible. The vehicles considered here are of same size irrespective of its type and the velocity is considered constant. The road network parameters are modeled and changed randomly considering that the other vehicles from other regions are also making their normal transportation. The individual contribution is not considered, instead an average of all is considered. The four points Q, P, O and N are the point of investigation which can roughly decide whether the vehicle volume is scattered all over the network or not.

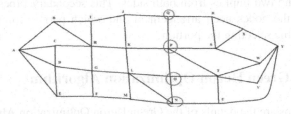

Fig. 6. Road Network

The GHOA algorithm and the details of the implementation for the road network is described below:

Step 1: Initialize the Road Graph matrix G = (V, E) and Road parameter matrix for each edge

Step 2: Initialize N Solution sets/Strings/Vectors with x<<n nodes where n is the maximum possible nodes that a string can hold and x is the number of initial randomly generated nodes. Also initialize the unit bit string marker with 0 (for not complete path) and can be 1 (when path is complete)

Step 3: Initialize the primary fitness and secondary fitness matrix.

Step 4: Prevent Duplicate nodes and Evaluate the secondary fitness of the initial strings (if any).

Step 5: Perform "Baiting" (with Miss Catch, Catch, False Catch) where position is selected with some intensive local search strategy where the nodes with least secondary fitness is searched (probability, random partial string, etc strategies can also be used).

Step 6: Perform "Change of Position" depending upon the requirement and initial search results.

Step 7: Perform "Attracting Prey Swarms".

Step 8: Complete "Baiting" operation.

Step 9: If the path is found complete then mark the string marker as 1 and no more operation is performed on it.

Step 10: Evaluate Primary Fitness of each complete string set of solution or with string marker as 1.

Step 11: When the numbers of solutions are greater than a certain percentage of the total number of strings then Update the Global Best result with the best complete path depending upon the Primary Fitness.

Step 12: Check Condition for stopping or Start from Step 2. [As the system is dynamic the next iteration must start from the initialization]

Step 13: If number of iteration is completed, provide the Best path for the vehicles for guidance.

5   Performance of GHOA Algorithm for TSP

In the table 1 the simulation result of the application of the green heron optimization algorithm for 50000 iterations on the various datasets [23], ranging from 16 to 280 dimensions, of the traveling salesman problem are provided in the form of best mean, standard deviation (SD), best and worst. There are graphical representations of the results to provide a pictorial view of the comparative study where the dataset number is the serial number (SN) in table 1.

Table 1. Results Of TSP Datasets Applied With Green Heron Optimization Algorithm

Dataset				GHOA			
SN	Name	Dim	Optimum	Mean	SD	Best	Worst
1	Ulysses16.tsp	16	74.11	75.18	0.047	74.11	78.27
2	att48.tsp	48	3.3524e+004	3.5436e+004	12.1	3.3613e+004	4.2996e+004
3	st70.tsp	70	678.5975	711.676	115.9	694	746
4	pr76.tsp	76	1.0816e+005	1.3319e+005	125.7	1.0816e+005	1.3757e+005
5	gr96.tsp	96	512.3094	643.97	69.4	573.16	806.4
6	gr120.tsp	120	1.6665e+003	1.7963e+003	46.8	1.7112e+003	1.8753e+003
7	gr202.tsp	202	549.9981	839.19	178.2	610.8	1005.9
8	tsp225.tsp	225	3919	4151.8	213.7	4058.9	5034.8
9	a280.tsp	280	2.5868e+003	2.77913e+003	986.1	2.6772e+003	3.1463e+003

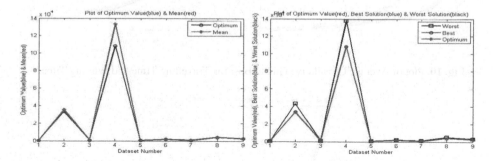

Fig. 7. Plot of Optimum & Mean for TSP, Plot of Optimum, Best & Worst Solution for TSP

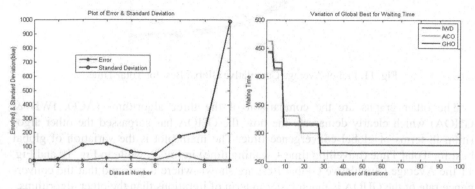

Fig. 8. Plot of Error & Standard Deviation for TSP, Plot for Global Best for Waiting Time

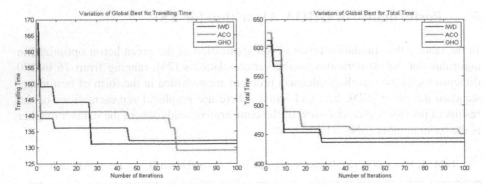

Fig. 9. Plot of Global Best for Travelling Time and Total Time

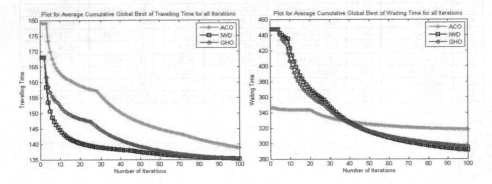

Fig. 10. Plot of Average Cumulative Global Best for Travelling Time and Waiting Time

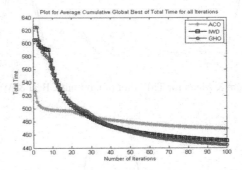

Fig. 11. Plot of Average Cumulative Global Best for Total Time

The other graphs are the comparison of the three algorithms (ACO, IWD & GHOA) which clearly demarcate the how the GHOA has surpassed the other algorithm in terms of global convergence time. The main plot is the variation of global best for Total Time (travelling time + waiting time) in Fig. 9, while in Fig. 10 and Fig. 11 the Average Cumulative Global Best are shown where it is found that the convergence rate of the GHOA is much faster in term of iterations than the other algorithms.

It must be mentioned that the three algorithms are run under only ten solution agents which is quite low and it is under this conditions the performance is evaluated. The main reasons for the enhanced performance of the GHOA algorithm are the success of the majority of the agents which are storing the solutions. In ACO and IWD, the algorithms work under the influence of the previous iterations and other agents due to the presence of pseudo communication (pheromone level in ACO & in silt in IWD where the graph is considered as river channels) among the agents. Hence the influence is partly explorative and the convergence rate is weak. Also it is found in the ACO and IWD that if the path forms a loop, then the path is either not optimized or wasted as the path is unacceptable. But in GHOA algorithm with the inclusion and exclusion of the nodes, the agents can revive. In GHOA if the repetition of nodes (that is a loop) occurs then the agent goes through a chain of node exclusion operation (false catch) to get revive its acceptability. The number of exclusion is random but is within range. The other plots in Figure 9-11are the variations of the other parameters individually for optimization of the algorithm. Another important feature of the GHOA is that it always starts form the initialization as it mostly exploration based algorithm, but for the ACO and IWD they depend on the previous iterations and solution. If ACO and IWD are made to start from initialization then its unique features (coordination and cooperation) are wasted and performance is hampered whereas if the parameters of the system change then the previous coordination and cooperation feature will misguide the present agents, but GHOA is fully randomized and hundred percent explorative algorithm with enhanced convergence rate and hence can be utilized in this kind of dynamic situations.

6   Conclusion

From the results of the simulation of the new meta-heuristics, it has clearly revealed the performance, potential of GHOA. The algorithm has been proven to produce promising solutions for all throughout the range or dimension of the traditional combinatorial problems and has shown quite good sign towards its robustness, scalability and convergence criteria.

From the plots of the simulation study for optimization of the datasets and the road network using the GHOA algorithm, we have tried to establish the effectiveness of the algorithm through the comparison with ACO and IWD algorithm which also has high success in the field of optimization and path finding and are among the few algorithms which are meant for the graph based problems and combinatorial optimization discrete problems. So overall in this paper a new multi-agent algorithm that GHOA has been described along with its opportunities and special task force for discrete and combinatorial optimization problems and its performance is compared with the traditional members of the bio-inspired computation family. The road network problem which has been optimized can be analyzed with this algorithm and is very vital for other dynamic systems where the system parameters changes with time and continuous monitoring of the system and optimization with quick convergence rate is considered.

References

1. http://en.wikipedia.org/wiki/Green_Heron
2. http://www.allaboutbirds.org/guide/Green_Heron/lifehistory
3. http://www.birdweb.org/birdweb/bird/green_heron
4. http://www.nhptv.org/natureworks/greenheron.htm
5. http://bermudaconservation.squarespace.com/
   storage/native-species-pags/green%20heron%20feeding%
   20DP.jpg?__SQUARESPACE_CACHEVERSION=1319462329360
6. Blum, C., Roli, A.: Metaheuristics in combinatorial optimization: Overview and conceptual comparison. ACM Comput. Surv. 35(3), 268–308 (2003)
7. Kennedy, J., Eberhart, R.: Particle swarm optimization. In: Proceedings of the IEEE International Conference on Neural Networks, vol. 4, pp. 1942–1948 (November/December 1995)
8. Karaboga, D.: An idea based on honey bee swarm for numerical optimization. Technical Report TR06, Erciyes University (October 2005)
9. Kashan, A.H.: League Championship Algorithm: A New Algorithm for Numerical Function Optimization. In: Proceedings of the 2009 International Conference of Soft Computing and Pattern Recognition (SOCPAR 2009), pp. 43–48. IEEE Computer Society, Washington, DC (2009)
10. Yang, X.-S., Deb, S.: Cuckoo search via Levy flights. In: World Congress on Nature & Biologically Inspired Computing (NaBIC 2009), pp. 210–214. IEEE Publication, USA (2009)
11. Yang, X.-S.: A New Metaheuristic Bat-Inspired Algorithm. In: González, J.R., Pelta, D.A., Cruz, C., Terrazas, G., Krasnogor, N. (eds.) NICSO 2010. SCI, vol. 284, pp. 65–74. Springer, Heidelberg (2010)
12. Kirkpatrick, S., Gelatt Jr., C.D., Vecchi, M.P.: Optimization by Simulated Annealing. Science 220(4598), 671–680 (1983)
13. Storn, R., Price, K.: Differential evolution - a simple and efficient heuristic for global optimization over continuous spaces. Journal of Global Optimization 11(4), 341–359 (1997)
14. Farmer, J.D., Packard, N., Perelson, A.: The immune system, adaptation and machine learning. Physica D 22(1-3), 187–204 (1986)
15. Geem, Z.W., Kim, J.H., Loganathan, G.V.: A new heuristic optimization algorithm: harmony search. Simulation 76(2), 60–68 (2001)
16. Krishnanand, K., Ghose, D.: Glowworm swarm optimization for simultaneous capture of multiple local optima of multimodal functions. Swarm Intelligence 3(2), 87–124 (2009)
17. Haddad, O.B., Afshar, A., Mariño, M.A.: Honey-bees mating optimization (HBMO) algorithm: a new heuristic approach for water resources optimization. Water Resources Management 20(5), 661–680 (2006)
18. Sur, C., Sharma, S., Shukla, A.: Multi-objective adaptive intelligent water drops algorithm for optimization & vehicle guidance in road graph network. In: 2013 International Conference on Informatics, Electronics & Vision (ICIEV), May 17-18, pp. 1–6 (2013)
19. Civicioglu, P.: Transforming geocentric cartesian coordinates to geodetic coordinates by using differential search algorithm. Computers & Geosciences 46, 229–247 (2012)
20. Kaveh, A., Talatahari, S.: A Novel Heuristic Optimization Method: Charged System Search. Acta Mechanica 213(3-4), 267–289 (2010)
21. Gandomi, A.H., Alavi, A.H.: Krill Herd Algorithm: A New Bio-Inspired Optimization Algorithm. Communications in Nonlinear Science and Numerical Simulation (2012)

22. Liang, Y.-C., Cuevas, J.R.: Virus Optimization Algorithm for Curve Fitting Problems. In: IIE Asian Conference 2011
23. TSP Datasets: http://elib.zib.de/pub/mp-testdata/tsp/tsplib/tsplib.html
24. Lin, S., Kernighan, B.W.: An effective heuristic algorithm for the traveling salesman problem. Operations Research 21, 498–516 (1973)
25. Helsgaun, K.: An effective implementation of the linkernighan traveling salesman heuristic. European Journal of Operational Research 126(1), 106–130 (2000)
26. Applegate, D., Bixby, R.E., Chvátal, V., Cook, W.: TSP Cuts Which Do Not Conform to the Template Paradigm. In: Jünger, M., Naddef, D. (eds.) Computational Combinatorial Optimization. LNCS, vol. 2241, pp. 261–304. Springer, Heidelberg (2001)
27. Hahsler, M., Hornik, K.: TSP Infrastructure for the Traveling Salesperson Problem (2007)
28. Dantzig, G.B., Fulkerson, D.R., Johnson, S.M.: Solution of a Large-scale Traveling Salesman Problem. Operations Research 2, 393–410 (1954)
29. Miller, Pekny, J.: Exact Solution of Large Asymmetric Traveling Salesman Problems. Science 251, 754–761 (1991)
30. Kennedy, J., Eberhart, R.C.: A Discrete Version of The Particle Swarm Algorithm. In: Proceedings of Conference on Systems, Man, and Cybernetics, pp. 4104–4108. IEEE Services Center, NJ (1997)
31. Guo, P., Wang, X., Han, Y.: A Hybrid Genetic Algorithm for Structural Optimization with Discrete Variables. In: 2011 International Conference on Internet Computing & Information Services (ICICIS), September 17-18, pp. 223–226 (2011)
32. Sur, C., Shukla, A.: Discrete bacteria foraging optimization algorithm for vehicle distribution optimization in graph based road network management. In: Thampi, S.M., Abraham, A., Pal, S.K., Rodriguez, J.M.C. (eds.) Recent Advances in Intelligent Informatics. AISC, vol. 235, pp. 351–358. Springer, Heidelberg (2014)
33. Dorigo, M., Gambardella, L.M.: Ant Colony System: A Cooperative Learning Approach to the Traveling Salesman Problem. IEEE Transactions on Evolutionary Computation 1(1), 53–66 (1997)
34. Chen, W.-N., Zhang, J.: A novel set-based particle swarm optimization method for discrete optimization problem. IEEE Transactions on Evolutionary Computation 14(2), 278–300 (2010)
35. Clerc, M.: Discrete Particle Swarm Optimization, illustrated by the Traveling Salesman Problem. In: New Optimization Techniques in Engineering. STUDFUZZ, vol. 141, pp. 219–239. Springer, Heidelberg (2004)
36. Kundu, D., Suresh, K., Ghosh, S., Das, S., Panigrahi, B.K., Das, S.: Multi-objective optimization with artificial weed colonies. Information Sciences 181(12), 2441–2454 (2011)
37. Sur, C., Sharma, S., Shukla, A.: Analysis & modeling multi-breeded Mean-Minded ant colony optimization of agent based Road Vehicle Routing Management. In: 2012 International Conference For Internet Technology and Secured Transactions, pp. 634–641 (2012)
38. Sur, C., Sharma, S., Shukla, A.: Egyptian Vulture Optimization Algorithm – A New Nature Inspired Meta-heuristics for Knapsack Problem. In: Meesad, P., Unger, H., Boonkrong, S. (eds.) IC2IT2013. AISC, vol. 209, pp. 227–237. Springer, Heidelberg (2013)
39. Sur, C., Sharma, S., Shukla, A.: Solving Travelling Salesman Problem Using Egyptian Vulture Optimization Algorithm - A New Approach. In: Kłopotek, M.A., Koronacki, J., Marciniak, M., Mykowiecka, A., Wierzchoń, S.T. (eds.) IIS 2013. LNCS, vol. 7912, pp. 254–267. Springer, Heidelberg (2013)

A Comparative Analysis of Results of Data Clustering with Variants of Particle Swarm Optimization

Anima Naik[1], Suresh Chandra Satapathy[2], and K. Parvathi[3]

[1] MITS, Rayagada, India
animanaik@gmail.com
[2] ANITS, Vishakapatnam
sureshsatapathy@ieee.org
[3] CUTM, Paralakhemundi
Kparvati16@gmail.com

Abstract. Particle Swarm Optimization (PSO) has been extensively studied, in recent past, for solving various engineering optimization problems. There have been many variants of PSO available in literatures. This paper presents a comparative analysis of few popular variants of PSO on the problem of data clustering. The investigated algorithms are evaluated on many real world datasets and few artificial datasets and clustering results are presented. Further, the results of statistical test on effectiveness of each investigated variants of PSO also demonstrated. The convergence characteristics of each variant are shown for different datasets. This study may be helpful to many researchers in choosing suitable PSO variants for their application.

Keywords: Data Clustering, PSO, Intra Cluster Distance.

1 Introduction

Data Clustering is a method of creating groups of objects, or clusters, in such a way that objects in one cluster are very similar and objects in different clusters are distinct. It is a kind of descriptive task in data mining field. There have been wide spread applications of data clustering in various fields ranging from engineering (e.g., machine learning, artificial intelligence, pattern recognition, mechanical engineering, and electrical engineering), computer sciences (e.g., web mining, spatial database analysis, textual document collection, and image segmentation), and life and medical sciences (e.g., genetics, biology, microbiology, paleontology, psychiatry, and pathology) to earth sciences (e.g., geography, geology, and remote sensing), social sciences (e.g., sociology, psychology, archeology, and education), and economics (e.g., marketing and business).

There are many clustering algorithms in literature. The traditional clustering algorithms are broadly classified to two catagories: hierarchical and partitional algorithms [1-3]. In this paper we have investigated partitional algorithm only. In this algorithm the clustering objective is to minimize the intra_cluster distance and maximize the inter_cluster distance so as to find compact and separable clusters.

B.K. Panigrahi et al. (Eds.): SEMCCO 2013, Part II, LNCS 8298, pp. 180–192, 2013.

Hence, clustering problem here can be well formulated as an optimization problem. Nature-inspired metahuristic algorithms are becoming popular in solving optimization problems [4-7]. The particle swarm optimization, a class of metaheuristic approach, was developed based on the swarm behavior, such as fish and bird schooling in nature [8-9]. The particle swarm optimizer (PSO) is an evolutionary computation technique.

Many researchers have worked on improving PSO performance in various ways, thereby deriving many interesting variants such as PSO with inertia weight (PSO-w) [10], PSO with constriction factor (PSO-cf) [11], Local version of PSO with inertia weight (PSO-w-local), Local version of PSO with constriction factor (PSO-cf-local) [12], UPSO [13], Fully informed particle swarm (FIPS) [14], FDR-PSO [15], CLPSO[16]. All these algorithms have been shown in good way in their respective papers with best performance in solving problems of different research areas. In this paper we have used all those algorithms for clustering data and compared their performance.

The rest of the paper is organized as follows: Section 2 presents an overview of the PSO algorithm, Section 3 presents PSO clustering. Experimental results are summarized in section 4. Section 5 gives the conclusion.

2   Particle Swarm Optimization

PSO can be considered as a swarm-based learning scheme. In PSO learning process, each single solution is referred to as a particle. The individual particles fly gradually towards the positions of their own and their neighbors' best previous experiences in a huge searching space. It shows that the PSO gives more opportunity to fly into desired areas to get better solutions. Therefore, PSO can discover reasonable solutions much faster. PSO define a proper fitness function that evaluates the quality of every particle's position. The position, called the global best (gbest), is the one which has the highest value among the entire swarm. The location, called it as personal best (pbest), is the one which has each particle's best experience. Based on every particle's momentum and the influence of both personal best (pbest) and global best (gbest) solutions, every particle adjusts its velocity vector at each iteration. The PSO learning formula is described as follows,

$$V_{i,m}(t + 1) = \tau . V_{i,m}(t) + c_1 * rand * \left(pbest_{i,m}(t) - X_{i,m}(t)\right) + c_2 * rand *$$
$$\left(gbest_m(t) - X_{i,m}(t)\right) \tag{1}$$

$$X_{i,m}(t + 1) = X_{i,m}(t) + V_{i,m}(t + 1) \tag{2}$$

Where m is the dimensional number, i denote the ith particle in the population, V is the velocity vector, X is the position vector and τ is the inertia factor, c_1 and c_2 are the cognitive and social lerning rates respectively. These two rates control the relative influence of the memory of particle and neighborhood.

3   PSO Clustering

In the context of clustering, a single particle represents the N_c cluster centriod vectors. That is, each particle X_i, is constructed as follows:

$$x_i = (m_{i,1}, m_{i,2}, \dots \dots m_{i,j} \dots \dots \dots m_{i,N_C}) \tag{3}$$

where $m_{i,j}$ refers to the j-th cluster centroid vector of the i-th particle in cluster C_{ij}. Therefore, a swarm represents a number of candidate clustering for the current data vectors. The fitness of particles are easily measured as the quantization error

$$J_e = \frac{\sum_j^{N_c} [\sum_{\forall z_p \in C_{ij}} d(z_p, m_j)/|C_{ij}|]}{N_c} \tag{4}$$

where d is Euclidean distance and $|C_{ij}|$ is the number of data vectors belonging to cluster C_{ij} i.e. the frequency of that cluster.

3.1   PSO Clustering Algorithm

Using PSO data vectors can be clustered as follows:

1. Initialize each learner to contain N, randomly selected cluster centroids.
2. For t = 1 to t_{max} do
   (a) For each learner i do
   (b) For each data vector z_p
      i.   Calculate the Euclidean distance $d(z_p, m_{ij})$ to all cluster centroids C_{ij}.
      ii.   Assign z_p to cluster C_{ij}. such that $(z_p, m_{ij}) = \min_{\forall c = 1,2, \dots \dots, N_c} d(z_p, m_{ic})$.
      iii. Calculate the fitness using equation (4)
   (c) Update the cluster centroids using equations (1) and (2).
      where t_{max}, is the maximum number of iteration

4   Simulation and Result

This section compares the results of all eight PSO Variants referred in the introduction part of this paper for solving data clustering problems for real and artificial datasets. The main purpose is to compare the quality of the respective clustering's, where quality is measured according to the following three criteria:

- the quantization error (as fitness value in our presented tables in the paper) as defined in equation (4).
- the intra-cluster distances, i.e. mean of maximum distance between two data vectors within a cluster of clusters i.e $\frac{1}{N_c}\sum_{i=1}^{N_c}[_{z_p, z_q \in C_i}^{\quad max} d(z_p, z_q)]$, where the objective is to minimize the intra-cluster distances.

- the inter-cluster distances, i.e. minimum distance between the centroids of the clusters, where the objective is to maximize the distance between clusters.

The latter two objectives respectively correspond to crisp, compact clusters that are well separated.

For all the results reported, averages over 40 simulations are given. All algorithms are run for 1200 function evaluations, and all PSO algorithms used 20 particles on K number of clusters.

A. Datasets Used

The following real-life and synthetic data sets are used in this paper. The real-life dataset are taken from UCI machine repository [17] and synthetic datasets are prepared manually. Here, n is the number of data points, d is the number of features, and K is the number of clusters.

1) Iris plants database (n = 150, d = 4, K = 3)
2) Glass (n = 214, d = 9, K = 6)
3) Wine (n = 178, d = 13, K = 3):
4) Wisconsin breast cancer data set (n = 683, d=9, K=2)
5) Pima Indian diabetes (n=768,d=8,K=2)
6) Haberman's Survival Data Set (n=306,d=3,K=2)
7) Hayes roth Dataset(n=160,d=4, K=3)
8) Ecoli Dataset(n=336,d=7,K=8)
9) Zoo Dataset(n=101,d=16,K=7)
10) Vowel Dataset(n=462,d=10,K=11)
11) Artificial data set1 (n=385,d=2,K=4): We generate a mixture of spherical, cube, rectangle and diamond clusters, as shown in Fig. 1. The total number of data points is 462 with 4 clusters.
12) Artificial data set2 (n=403, d=2,K=4): We generate a combination of same type of curve clusters , as shown in Fig. 2. The total number of data points is 403 with 4 curve clusters.

B. Population Initialization

For all PSO Variants , we randomly initialize cluster centroids. The cluster centroids are also randomly fixed between X_{max} and X_{min}, which denote the maximum and minimum numerical values of any feature of the data set under test, respectively.

C. Simulation Strategy

In this paper, while comparing the performance of algorithms, we focus on computational time required to find the solution. For comparing the speed of the algorithms, the first thing we require is a fair time measurement. The number of iterations or generations cannot be accepted as a time measure since the algorithms perform different amount of works in their inner loops, and they have different population sizes. Hence, we choose the number of *fitness function evaluations (FEs)* as a measure of computation time instead of generations or iterations. Since the algorithms are stochastic in nature, the results of two successive runs usually do not match. Hence, we have taken 40 independent runs (with different seeds of the random number generator) of each algorithm. The results have been stated in terms of the mean values and standard deviations over the 40 runs in each case.

Finally, we would like to point out that all the experiment codes are implemented in MATLAB. The experiments are conducted on a Pentium 4, 1GB memory desktop in Windows 7 environment.

D. Experimental Results

To judge the accuracy of the PSO Clustering, we let each of them run for a very long time over every benchmark data set, until the number of FEs exceeded 1200. Then, we note the result in terms of mean and standard deviation.

Table 1 to 6 summarizes the results obtained from the eight PSO Variants on 10 real life dataset and 2 synthetic datasets respectively. The values reported are averages over 40 simulations, with standard deviations to indicate the range of values to which the algorithms converge.

We used unpaired t-tests to compare the means of the results produced by the best and the second best algorithms. The unpaired t-test assumes that the data have been sampled from a normally distributed population. From the concepts of the central limit theorem, one may note that as sample sizes increase, the sampling distribution of the mean approaches a normal distribution regardless of the shape of the original population A sample size around 40 allows the normality assumptions conducive for performing the unpaired t-tests[18]. The result of t-test is given in Table 7. Form the t-test table it is clear that all the problems, except for Breast cancer dataset and Hayes roth Dataset the comparison of performance result have statistically significant.

Table 1. (Mean and Standard deviation over 40 independent runs) after each algorithm was terminated after running for 1200 FEs with the quantization error-based fitness function for real dataset

Agorithms		Iris Dataset			Glass Dataset		
		Fitness value	Intra cluster distance	Inter cluster distance	Fitness value	Intra cluster distance	Inter cluster distance
PSO-w	mean	**0.2832**	2.2006	2.1321	0.0438	5.2138	6.5425
	std	**0.0029**	0.0502	0.0963	0.0021	0.6548	7.3432
PSO-cf	mean	0.2954	2.4436	1.8481	**0.0395**	4.5193	10.0715
	std	0.0056	0.3734	0.3299	**0.0040**	0.8281	9.0813
PSO-w-local	mean	0.2924	2.4408	1.8412	0.0457	4.8108	6.9727
	std	0.0041	0.3532	0.3230	0.0024	0.8024	9.1866
PSO-cf-local	mean	0.2915	2.3666	2.0200	0.0445	4.8145	8.5215
	std	0.0044	0.3274	0.5094	0.0017	1.0436	8.2037
UPSO	mean	0.2916	2.3510	1.8771	0.0456	4.8447	7.5769
	std	0.0048	0.3734	0.5549	0.0021	0.9437	8.7510
FDR	mean	0.3246	2.2258	1.9359	0.0591	5.1942	4.7522
	std	0.0167	0.2635	0.2922	0.0062	0.8612	9.3653
FIPS	mean	0.2921	2.4703	1.8394	0.0458	4.8922	5.2455
	std	0.0050	0.3814	0.2756	0.0022	0.9647	6.4442
CLPSO	mean	0.2966	2.4094	1.9427	0.0490	5.0209	6.0050
	std	0.0049	0.3537	0.2923	0.0031	0.7282	7.2946

Due to space limitations we have considered results of IRIS dataset only in Fig 3 which shows the effect of varying number of clusters versus quantization error for Iris dataset is presented. As expected the quantization error goes down with increase in the number of clusters.

Figure 4.(a)-4(i) illustrate the convergence behavior of the different variants of PSO algorithms for different datasets. It is clear that in 7 cases PSO-cf, in 4 cases PSO-w and in 1 case FIPS show their superiority than other algorithm but from t-test table it is clear that the FIPS algorithm in comparison with other algorithm for Haysroth dataset is not statistically significant. Similarly PSO-cf algorithm in comparison with other algorithm for Breast cancer dataset is not statistically significant. From all Figure it is illustrated that convergence behavior of most of the algorithms exhibited a faster, but premature convergence to a large quantization error, while the PSO-cf algorithms had slower convergence, but to lower quantization errors in most cases.

Table 2. (Mean and Standard deviation over 40 independent runs) after each algorithm was terminated after running for 1200 FEs with the quantization error-based fitness function for real dataset

Agorithms		Wine Dataset			Breast cancer Data set		
		Fitness value	Intra cluster distance	Inter cluster distance	Fitness value	Intra cluster distance	Inter cluster distance
PSO-w	mean	338.5478	337.4092	328.1644	0.0597	16.9870	13.4433
	std	0.8299	0.9402	3.4486	0.0100	7.19e-15	0
PSO-cf	mean	**300.4487**	330.0486	422.5652	**0.0553**	16.9870	13.4433
	std	**1.4274**	14.1489	135.0956	**0.0283**	7.19e-15	0
PSO-w-local	mean	341.1881	341.7321	363.7254	0.0594	16.9870	13.4433
	std	1.5507	12.8166	61.7317	0.0256	7.19e-15	0
PSO-cf-local	mean	341.32	339.5085	370.8436	0.0690	16.9870	13.4433
	std	381.8323	13.2246	59.4894	0.0265	7.19e-15	0
UPSO	mean	340.5369	340.2944	378.7988	0.0740	16.9870	13.4433
	std	1.4231	10.9135	56.8953	0.0176	7.19e-15	0
FDR	mean	361.0162	340.3798	361.8864	0.0630	16.9870	13.4433
	std	10.9324	10.0163	51.8562	0.0312	7.19e-15	0
FIPS	mean	340.7071	341.7500	363.7845	0.0615	16.9870	13.4433
	std	1.8035	8.5898	46.7197	0.0145	7.19e-15	0
CLPSO	mean	343.8381	345.3000	329.2460	0.0629	16.9870	13.4433
	std	3.5914	7.6914	71.9199	0.0281	7.19e-15	0

Table 3. (Mean and Standard deviation over 40 independent runs) after each algorithm was terminated after running for 1200 FEs with the quantization error-based fitness function for real dataset

Agorithms		Pima Indian Diabates Data			Haberman's Survival Dataset		
		Fitness value	Intra cluster distance	Inter cluster distance	Fitness value	Intra cluster distance	Inter cluster distance
PSO-w	Mean	14.4579	729.4224	29.1512	5.1432	41.0284	5.0533
	Std	0.0058	0.1701	0.4060	0.1491	0.0656	0.6774
PSO-cf	Mean	**12.9109**	527.0603	58.6165	**3.6861**	28.8234	41.8921
	Std	**0.1545**	147.2876	20.0362	**0.4232**	3.6000	6.7169
PSO-w-local	Mean	14.5233	666.4104	40.7440	5.7066	32.1726	41.8921
	Std	0.0340	120.2595	17.6157	0.3094	3.9766	6.7169
PSO-cf-local	Mean	14.5244	648.0719	50.5252	5.7741	31.7580	34.3099
	Std	0.0384	129.3064	22.3962	0.2745	4.1801	10.3750
UPSO	Mean	14.5241	657.4033	44.4081	5.6702	32.0770	33.3491
	Std	0.0306	129.3883	18.1313	0.2502	3.6824	9.8801
FDR	Mean	14.9631	712.9630	33.9101	6.6930	34.9142	25.7607
	Std	0.3972	70.5667	8.7741	0.4539	4.4644	12.6104
FIPS	Mean	15.1726	706.3953	36.2068	5.6635	31.3672	35.7066
	Std	0.4347	74.6966	13.2739	0.2773	3.4865	9.8732
CLPSO	Mean	14.5665	707.0326	37.1064	5.9888	33.6676	28.8493
	Std	0.0559	74.5763	14.7293	0.3199	3.7428	10.1007

Table 4. (Mean and Standard deviation over 40 independent runs) after each algorithm was terminated after running for 1200 FEs with the quantization error-based fitness function for real dataset

Agorithms		Hayes roth Dataset			Ecoli Dataset		
		Fitness value	Intra cluster distance	Inter cluster distance	Fitness value	Intra cluster distance	Inter cluster distance
PSO-w	Mean	0.2856	3.7943	1.2422	0.0639	0.6885	0.2022
	Std	0.0182	0.0056	0.0785	0.0022	0.0571	0.0759
PSO-cf	Mean	0.3490	3.4242	1.6715	**0.0548**	0.6734	0.2245
	Std	0.0349	0.5361	0.5852	**0.0033**	0.0644	0.0926
PSO-w-local	Mean	0.2861	3.4789	1.5777	0.0642	0.6886	0.2130
	Std	0.0257	0.5074	0.5017	0.0017	0.0965	0.1079
PSO-cf-local	Mean	0.2820	3.3433	1.7454	0.0642	0.6733	0.2205
	Std	0.0189	0.5720	0.6023	0.0018	0.0715	0.1026
UPSO	Mean	0.2799	3.3605	1.7299	0.0640	0.6824	0.1922
	Std	0.0223	0.5336	0.6071	0.0022	0.0748	0.0943
FDR	Mean	0.2895	3.4024	1.6861	0.0713	0.6662	0.2008
	Std	0.0205	0.5524	0.6285	0.0035	0.0805	0.0856
FIPS	Mean	**0.2787**	3.2509	1.8398	0.0636	0.6921	0.1924
	Std	**0.0218**	0.5829	0.6214	0.0022	0.0585	0.0629
CLPSO	Mean	0.2927	3.5413	1.5242	0.0653	0.6756	0.1874
	Std	0.0325	0.4716	0.4532	0.0026	0.0584	0.0952

Table 5. (Mean and Standard deviation over 40 independent runs) after each algorithm was terminated after running for 1200 FEs with the quantization error-based fitness function for real dataset

Agorith ms		Zoo Dataset			Vowel Dataset		
		Fitness value	Intra cluster distance	Inter cluster distance	Fitness value	Intra cluster distance	Inter cluster distance
PSO-w	Mean	**0.0014**	1.6121	2.6875	**40.3612**	788.370	464.52
	Std	**9.54e-04**	1.1244e-15	2.22e-15	**2.5840**	170.28	201.855
PSO-cf	Mean	0.0033	1.6121	2.6875	42.3465	800.858	336.22
	Std	0.0015	1.1244e-15	2.22e-15	2.4465	121.565	153.92
PSO-w-local	Mean	0.0028	1.6121	2.6875	41.8766	815.5375	346.86
	Std	0.0021	1.1244e-15	2.22e-15	2.1676	127.43	177.9745
PSO-cf-local	Mean	0.0028	1.6121	2.6875	41.4532	799.6705	319.2503
	Std	0.0010	1.1244e-15	2.22e-15	1.8405	126.87	167.01
UPSO	Mean	0.0029	1.6121	2.6875	42.1284	820.5103	333.4838
	Std	0.0012	1.1244e-15	2.21e-15	1.9023	98.4752	144.9409
FDR	Mean	0.0031	1.6121	2.6875	49.3824	813.706	363.0656
	Std	0.0023	1.1244e-15	2.22e-15	4.9469	133.6519	188.4832
FIPS	Mean	0.0027	1.6121	2.6875	41.5465	801.186	328.2093
	Std	0.0011	1.1244e-15	2.22e-15	1.8433	126.9612	194.9740
CLPSO	Mean	0.0029	1.6121	2.6875	46.6196	810.179	350.2216
	Std	0.0018	1.1244e-15	2.22e-15	2.7013	102.2216	172.1102

Table 6. (Mean and Standard deviation over 40 independent runs) after each algorithm was terminated after running for 1200 FEs with the quantization error-based fitness function for artificial datasets

Agorith ms		Artificial dataset 1			Artificial dataset 2		
		Fitness value	Intra cluster distance	Inter cluster distance	Fitness value	Intra cluster distance	Inter cluster distance
PSO-w	Mean	1.9217	16.8278	7.0140	**0.1647**	1.5339	1.6915
	Std	0.0542	1.0433	4.1598	**0.0036**	0.0078	0.3068
PSO-cf	Mean	**1.6192**	16.2481	9.3947	0.1958	1.6692	1.4644
	Std	**0.1373**	2.4110	2.7588	0.0254	0.1494	0.3479
PSO-w-local	Mean	1.9609	16.4120	8.3280	0.1696	1.6762	1.5062
	Std	0.0500	2.3674	2.8088	0.0054	0.1075	0.3281
PSO-cf-local	Mean	1.9719	16.4936	8.8243	0.1718	1.6643	1.4636
	Std	0.0438	2.1851	2.3147	0.0062	0.1304	0.3215
UPSO	Mean	1.9850	16.2977	8.3507	0.1696	1.6511	1.4608
	Std	0.0560	2.3904	2.1578	0.0058	0.1661	0.4054
FDR	Mean	2.3063	16.4919	9.0748	0.2324	1.6596	1.5517
	Std	0.1531	2.2727	3.2635	0.0355	0.1199	0.2952
FIPS	Mean	1.9696	16.3439	8.5465	0.1705	1.6783	1.4239
	Std	0.0538	2.2250	2.2814	0.0066	0.1604	0.3367
CLPSO	Mean	2.0007	16.5929	8.4323	0.1722	1.6382	1.5745
	Std	0.0762	2.2270	2.8935	0.0079	0.1129	0.3200

Table 7. Results of the unpaired *t*-test between the best and the second best performing algorithms (for each data set) of Table 1 to Table 2

Dataset	Standard error	t	95% Confidence Interval	Two-tailed P	Significance
Iris	0.001	9.9614	-0.009959 to -0.006641	<0.0001	extremely statistically significant.
Glass	0.001	6.019	-0.005722 to -0.002878	<0.0001	extremely statistically significant
Wine	0.261	145.937 0	-38.618841 to - 37.579359	<0.0001	extremely statistically significant
Breast cancer Data	0.006	0.6795	-0.016112 to 0.007912	=0.4988	not statistically significant
Pima Indian Diabates	0.024	63.2828	-1.595668 to -1.498332	<0.0001	extremely statistically significant
Haberman's Survival Data	0.071	20.5384	-1.598341 to -1.315859	<0.0001	extremely statistically significant
Hayes roth Dataset	0.005	0.2434	-0.011017 to 0.008617	= -0.0012	not statistically significant
Ecoli	0.001	14.0329	-0.010048 to -0.007552	<0.0001	extremely statistically significant
Zoo	0.000	5.7849	-0.001747 to -0.000853	<0.0001	extremely statistically significant
Vowel Data	0.502	2.1770	-2.090629 to -0.093371	=0.0325	statistically significant.
Artificial Data 1	0.023	12.9610	-0.348965 to -0.256035	<0.0001	extremely statistically significant
Artificial Data 2	0.001	4.7751	-0.006943 to -0.002857	<0.0001	extremely statistically significant

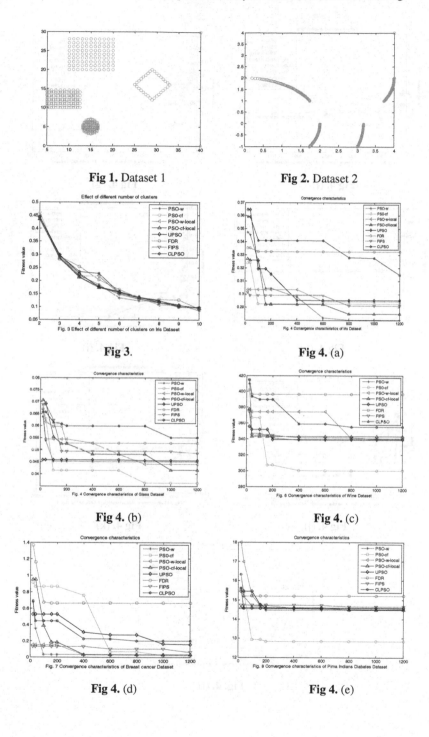

Fig 1. Dataset 1   **Fig 2.** Dataset 2

Fig 3.   **Fig 4.** (a)

Fig 4. (b)   **Fig 4.** (c)

Fig 4. (d)   **Fig 4.** (e)

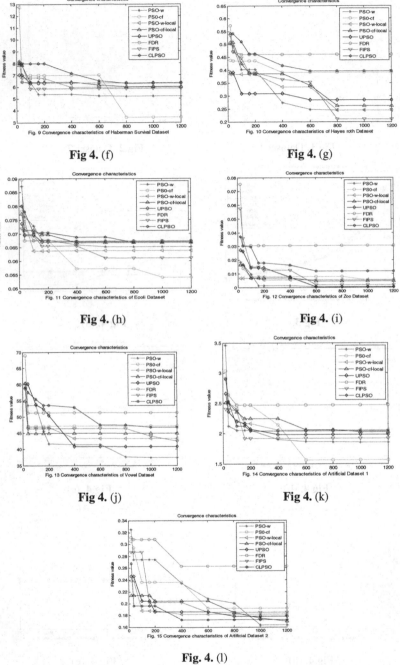

Fig 4. (f)   **Fig 4.** (g)

Fig 4. (h)   **Fig 4.** (i)

Fig 4. (j)   **Fig 4.** (k)

Fig. 4. (l)

5 Conclusion

This paper investigated the application of eight PSO variants to cluster data vectors. Their performance have been compared by clustering 10 real life data set and 2 artificial data set. It is clear that in 7 cases PSO-cf , in 4 cases PSO-w and in 1 case FIPS show their superiority than other algorithm. From simulations it is observed that convergence behavior of most of the algorithms exhibited a faster, but premature convergence to a large quantization error, while the PSO-cf algorithms had slower convergence, but to lower quantization errors with stable convergence in most cases. As further study some parameter tuning of PSO-cf can be done to improve the convergence characteristics. Our studies can be helpful to many researchers in choosing suitable PSO variants for their application.

References

[1] Han, J., Kamber, M.: Data Mining: Concepts and Techniques. Academic Press (2006)
[2] Jain, A.K., Murthy, M.N., Flynn, P.J.: Data Clustering: a review. Computing Survey, 264–323 (1999)
[3] Jain, A.K.: Data Clustering: 50 years beyond K-means. Pattern Recognition Letters 31, 651–666 (2010)
[4] Castillo, O., Martinez-Marroquin, E., Melin, P., Valdez, F., Soria, J.: Comparative study of bio-inspired algorithms applied to the optimization of type-1 and type-2 fuzzy controllers for an autonomous mobile robot. Information Sciences 192, 19–38 (2012)
[5] Kang, F., Li, J., Ma, Z.: Rosenbrock artificial bee colony algorithm for accurate global optimization of numerical functions. Information Sciences 181, 3508–3531 (2011)
[6] Kundu, D., Suresh, K., et al.: Multi-objective optimization with artificial weed colonies. Information Sciences 181, 2441–2454 (2011)
[7] Yang, X.S.: Nature-Inspired Metaheuristic Algorithms. Luniver Press (2008)
[8] Eberhart, R.C., Kennedy, J.: A new optimizer using particle swarm theory. In: Proc. 6th Int. Symp. Micromachine Human Sci., Nagoya, Japan, pp. 39–43 (1995)
[9] Kennedy, J., Eberhart, R.C.: Particle swarm optimization. In: Proc. IEEE Int. Conf. Neural Networks, pp. 1942–1948 (1995)
[10] Shi, Y., Eberhart, R.C.: A modified particle swarm optimizer. In: Proc. IEEE Congr. Evol. Comput. pp. 69–73 (1998)
[11] Clerc, M., Kennedy, J.: The particle swarm-explosion, stability, and convergence in a multidimensional complex space. IEEE Trans. Evol. Comput. 6(1), 58–73 (2002)
[12] Kennedy, J., Mendes, R.: Population structure and particle swarm performance. In: Proc. IEEE Congr. Evol. Comput., Honolulu, HI, pp. 1671–1676 (2002)
[13] Parsopoulos, K.E., Vrahatis, M.N.: UPSO—A unified particle swarm optimization scheme. Lecture Series on Computational Sciences, pp. 868–873 (2004)
[14] Mendes, R., Kennedy, J., Neves, J.: The fully informed particle swarm: Simpler, maybe better. IEEE Trans. Evol. Comput. 8, 204–210 (2004)
[15] Peram, T., Veeramachaneni, K., Mohan, C.K.: Fitness-distance-ratio based particle swarm optimization. In: Proc. Swarm Intelligence Symp., pp. 174–181 (2003)

[16] Liang, J.J., Qin, A.K., Suganthan, P.N., Baskar, S.: Comprehensive Learning Particle Swarm optimizer for Global Optimization of Multimodal Functions. IEEE Transactions on Evolutionary Computation 10(3) (2006)

[17] Mertz, C.J., Blake, C.L.: UCI Repository of Machine Learning Databases,

[18] http://www.ics.uci.edu/~mlearn/MLRepository.html

[19] Flury, B.: A First Course in Multivariate Statistics, vol. 28. Springer, Berlin (1997)

Hybrid Particle Swarm Optimization Technique for Protein Structure Prediction Using 2D Off-Lattice Model

Nanda Dulal Jana[1] and Jaya Sil[2]

[1]Department of Information Technology, National Institute of Technology,
Durgapur, West Bengal, India
nanda.jana@gmail.com
[2]Department of Computer Science and Technology,
Bengal Engineering & Science University, Shibpur, West Bengal, India
js@cs.becs.ac.in

Abstract. Protein Structure Prediction with lowest energy from its primary sequence of amino acids is a complex and challenging problem in computational biology, addressed by researchers using heuristic optimization techniques. Particle Swarm Optimization (PSO), a heuristic optimization technique having strong global search capability but often stuck at local optima while solving complex optimization problem. To prevent local optima problem, PSO with local search (HPSOLS) capability has been proposed in the paper to predict structure of protein using 2D off-lattice model. HPSOLS is applied on artificial and real protein sequences to conform the performance and robustness for solving protein structure prediction having lowest energy. Results are compared with other algorithms demonstrating efficiency of the proposed model.

Keywords: Protein Structure Prediction, Particle Swarm Optimization, Local Search, Off-lattice model.

1 Introduction

In computational biology, one of the most complex and challenging problem is the prediction of protein structure from the primary sequence of amino acids. A protein is represented by a sequence of 20 different amino acids. Biological functions are known from the structure of protein which plays an important role in drug design, disease prediction and many more. The structure with lowest energy of protein is associated with the structure of global minimum of the free energy consisting of the intermolecular interaction among protein atoms and surrounding solvent molecules [1]. Experimental methods like X-ray crystallography and Nuclear Magnetic Resonance (NMR) are time consuming and expensive to predict the structure of proteins. Therefore, computational method is an effective and necessary tool to predict the protein structure. Computational methods perform either considering the physical model or by applying a suitable global optimization method to predict the structure of a protein. Instead of considering all 20 different amino acids, the models are grouped into two classes of residues: hydrophobic (non-polar) and hydrophilic (polar) where 'H' represents hydrophobic and 'P' represents hydrophilic residues. These models include a family of HP lattice models [2] and HP off-lattice models [3].

B.K. Panigrahi et al. (Eds.): SEMCCO 2013, Part II, LNCS 8298, pp. 193–204, 2013.

In the paper, AB model proposed by Stillinger et al. [4] has been used where the hydrophobic monomers are labeled by 'A' and the hydrophilic or polar ones by 'B'. Based on the lowest free energy [1], many heuristic optimization methods such as Tabu Search algorithm [5], Differential Evolutionary algorithm [6] and particle swarm optimization algorithm [7, 8] have been developed to search for lowest free energy structure of a protein using 2D - AB off-lattice model.

Particle Swarm Optimization (PSO) is a population based search algorithm developed by Eberhart and Kennedy [9]. It has been successfully applied to many engineering optimization problems due to its simplicity, fast convergence and fewer parameters [10, 11]. However, PSO can easily trap into local optimum due to lack of diversity in the population. In order to improve performance of PSO, we have proposed hybrid PSO with local search (HPSOLS) algorithm. Proposed algorithm prevents the particles to fall into local optimum and improve the convergence rate and efficiency. In the paper, artificial and real protein sequences are used to show the ability of the HPSOLS algorithm and the results are compared with other algorithms.

The rest of the paper is organized as follows: an overview of AB off-lattice model, brief introduction of particle swarm optimization and Hill Climbing local search algorithm are presented in section 2. In section 3, the HPSOLS algorithm is described while in section 4, the results are compared with basic PSO and constriction PSO (CPSO). Section 5 concludes the paper with a possible direction in future works.

2   Background

2.1   AB Off-Lattice Model

AB off-lattice model, known as toy model was proposed by Stillinger et. al. in 1993 [4] where 20 amino acids are classified into hydrophobic and hydrophilic residues, labeled using letters 'A' and 'B' respectively. Two residues are linked by rigid unit-length bonds and the angle between two bonds can change freely. An n length protein sequence is represented by $(n-2)$ bend angles $\theta_2, \theta_3 \ldots \ldots, \theta_{n-1}$ at each of the non-terminal residues. We adhere the conventions that $-\pi < \theta_i < \pi$ and $\theta_i = 0$ reveals two continuous bond are on the same line while $\theta_i < 0$ and $\theta_i > 0$ represent rotation of amino acids in clockwise and counter clockwise direction respectively, as shown in Fig. 1.

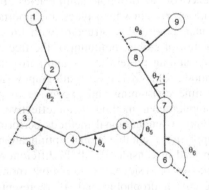

Fig. 1. 2D AB Off-Lattice model of a protein sequence with length 9

Where V_1 is the bending potentials, independent of protein sequence as defined by equation (2).

$$V_1(\theta_i) = \frac{1}{4}(1 - cos\theta_i) \qquad (2)$$

The nonbonded interactions V_2 have a species-dependent Lennard-Jones 12, 6 form are described in equation (3) and (4) respectively.

$$V_2(r_{ij}, \xi_i, \xi_j) = 4[r_{ij}^{-12} - C(\xi_i, \xi_j)r_{ij}^{-6}] \qquad (3)$$

$$C(\xi_i, \xi_j) = \frac{1}{8}(1 + \xi_i + \xi_j + 5\xi_i\xi_j) \qquad (4)$$

where r_{ij} denotes the distance between residue i and j of the chain and ξ_i, ξ_j are the variables encoded according to the residue species along the chain. For an AA pair, $C(\xi_i, \xi_j) = 1$ regarded as strongly attracting, for an AB pair, $C(\xi_i, \xi_j) = 0.5$, regarded as weakly attracting and for a BB pair, $C(\xi_i, \xi_j) = -0.5$, regarded as weakly repelling. Our objective is to find the minimum value of the equation (1). This minimum value is the lowest free energy of the structure of a protein.

2.2   Particle Swarm Optimization

The PSO algorithm uses a population of individual called particles where each particle represents a candidate solution to the optimization problem. Each particle has its own position and velocity to move around the search space. Particles have memory and each particle keep track of previous best position and corresponding fitness value called *pbest*, related only to a particular particle in the swarm. Another value called *gbest* is defined as the best value among all *pbest* in the swarm. The basic concept of PSO technique lies in accelerating each particle towards its *pbest* and *gbest* which ultimately leads to global optima.

In general, a swarm contains N particles and each particle moves in a D-dimensional search space. The position vector and velocity vector of ith particle is represented by $X_i = (x_{i1}, x_{i2}, ..., x_{iD})$ and $V_i = (v_{i1}, v_{i2}, ..., v_{iD})$ respectively. Each particle maintains a memory of its previous best position which is represented by $X_{pbest} = (x_{pbest1}, x_{pbest2}, x_{pbestD})$ and best of all the particles in the swarm by $X_{gbest} = (x_{gbest1}, x_{gbest2}, ..., x_{gbestD})$. At each generation, say t, particles update their velocities and positions in the search space using equations (5) and (6) respectively, which govern the working principle of PSO.

$$V_i(t + 1) = V_i(t) + c_1r_1\left(X_{pbesti}(t) - X_i(t)\right) + c_2r_2(X_{gbesti}(t) - X_i(t)) \qquad (5)$$

$$X_i(t + 1) = X_i(t) + V_i(t + 1) \qquad (6)$$

Here c_1 and c_2 are two positive constants referred to as cognitive and social parameters, which accelerate the particles towards the personal best and global best positions, respectively. Adjustment of these coefficients is very important in PSO, which allow particles to move far from the target region for small values whereas high values provide abrupt movement toward or past the target region in the search space [12]. The constants r_1 and r_2 are uniformly distributed random numbers in $[0, 1]$.

A constant, maximum velocity (V_{max}) is used to limit the velocities of the particles and improve the resolution of the search space. Large values of V_{max} facilitate global exploration, whereas smaller values encourage local exploitation. If V_{max} is too small, the swarm may not explore sufficiently in the search space while too large values of V_{max} risk the possibility of missing a good region. In the present investigation, the version of PSO proposed by Shi and Eberhart [13] has been considered, which incorporates a new parameter ω, known as the inertia weight factor into the velocity updating equation (5), modified as equation (7).

$$V_i(t + 1) = \omega * V_i(t) + c_1 r_1 \left(X_{pbesti}(t) - X_i(t) \right) + c_2 r_2 \left(X_{gbesti}(t) - X_i(t) \right) \quad (7)$$

The main role of the inertia weight factor ω is to control the magnitude of the velocities and alleviate the swarm explosion effect. In this paper, the inertia weight version of PSO as describe by equations (6) and (7) are used and called as basic PSO.

2.3   Hill Climbing - Local Search Algorithm

Hill Climbing (HC) is an optimization technique which belongs to the family of local search. It is an iterative algorithm that starts with an arbitrary solution to a problem, then attempts to find a better solution by incrementally changing a single element of the solution with a neighborhood function (F). If the change produces a better solution, an incremental change is made to the new solution, repeating until no further improvements can be found or stop with a specific condition. HC algorithm is used to local exploration for obtaining the local optimum (a solution that cannot be improved by considering a neighboring configuration) but it is not guaranteed to find the best possible solution (the global optimum) out of all possible solutions. The HC local search algorithm is hybridized with particle swarm optimization providing more flexibility in the motion of particles. In the proposed algorithm, the neighborhood function (F) has been designed to generate a new candidate solution, describe by equation (8).

$$New\ Solution\ (X_{new}) = Current\ Solution\ (X_c) + r * (1 - 2 * rand()) \quad (8)$$

Where r represents the changing range of original particles and $rand()$ is a random number between 0 to 1.

$$r = a - (a - b) * \frac{t}{G} \quad (9)$$

Where a is the initial value of r and b is the value decreased by each iteration t. G is the maximum number of generation.

Hill climbing algorithm is presented below.

Algorithm HC
Start
Initialization: Assume the current solution (base point) is X_c, the neighborhood function is F and N is the desired number of neighborhood points.

Set $k=1$.
Step1: Generate new solution (X_{new}) using equation (8)
Step2: Calculate $f(X_{new})$ and $f(X_c)$ \\ f is fitness function
Step3: If $f(X_{new}) < f(X_c)$, Then X_{new} is the best solution, set $X_c = X_{new}$
       Else return X_c as the best solution
Step4: If $k \neq N$, set $k=k+1$ and go to Step1

     Else Stop.

3   Particle Swarm Optimization and Local Search

PSO was originally designed as a numerical optimization technique based on swarm intelligence and proved its robustness and efficiency to solving non-linear, real-valued function optimization problem. However, when dealing with complex problems, quality of solution is affected as the number of iterations increases and it suffers from premature convergences. The former situation occurs when all particles converge to a single point as the speed of the particles decrease with time. Thereafter, forcing them to converge to the global best point found so far which is not to become global optima. PSO sometimes suffers from premature convergence due to many local minima in the search space. In general, convergence is a desirable property that swarms are allowed to search near the global minimum as time progresses. Unfortunately, in the context of many local minima, the convergence property may cause a swarm to become trapped in one of them and fail to explore more promising neighboring minima. To enhance the exploration capability and to avoid being trapped into local optima, a hybrid strategy is necessary to increase the diversity of the swarms in the search space. With this observation, a hybrid particle swarm optimization with local search algorithm has been proposed in the paper. In the proposed approach, hill-climbing (HC) algorithm is used to execute local search to find better solutions in the neighborhood search space as produced by PSO at each iteration.

3.1   HPSOLS Algorithm

In HPSOLS, each particle has a chance of self-improvement by applying local search algorithm before communicating with the population in which it belongs. Local search has been applied to all *pbest* (the best position found by each particle) of the swarm. In HPSOLS algorithm, r is used in equation (9) linearly decreased as the iteration increased.

HPSOLS Algorithm
Start
Initialize the parameters of PSO i.e. maximum iteration, Population size (P),
Inertia weight, Accelerating   Coefficients.
Step1: Randomly generate initial positions (X) and velocities (V) of the particles.
Step2: Calculate the fitness for each particle in X. Set *pbest*(P_i) and *gbest*(P_g). Set
    $G = 1$.

Step3: Perform Local Search i.e. HC algorithm on every $pbest(P_i)$ of the
       population found so far.
Step4: Update $pbest(P_i)$ and $gbest(P_g)$.
Step5: Update velocity using equation (7)
       Update position using equation (6)
Step6: Evaluate the fitness function for each particle of the population
Step7: Update $pbest(P_i)$ and $gbest(P_g)$.
Step8: If $G = maximum\ iteration$ then $gbest(P_g)$ is the solution.
       Stop;
       Else set $G = G +1$ and go to Step3.

After searching local optimum, the particle is regarded to be matured. PSO methods excite from a local optimum point so that there will be a greater chance to reach to a global optimum.

4　Experimental Studies

In the experiment, both artificial and real protein sequence are considered to conform robustness and performance of the proposed HPSOLS algorithm applied in protein structure prediction in 2D off-lattice model.

4.1　Artificial Protein Sequence

For experiments, two kinds of artificial sequences are considered. Firstly, 20 artificial protein sequences of length 5 as in Stillinger [4] are used, shown in Table1.

Table 1. Artificial Protein Sequence of length 5

Sequence			
AAAAA	AABAB	ABABB	BAABB
AAAAB	AABBA	ABBAB	BABAB
AAABA	AABBB	ABBBA	BABBB
AAABB	ABAAB	ABBBB	BBABB
AABAA	ABABA	BAAAB	BBBBB

Secondly, Fibonacci sequence is considered for obtaining an artificial protein sequence to predict protein structure in off-lattice model as studied in [14]. The Fibonacci sequence is defined below recursively as-

$$S_0 = A, \qquad S_1 = B, \qquad S_{i+1} = S_{i-1} * S_i$$

where * is the concatenation operator. The first few sequences are $S_2 = AB$, $S_3 = BAB$, $S_4 = ABBAB$ and so on. Hydrophobic residue A occurs isolated along the chain, while hydrophilic residue B occurs either isolated or in pairs and the molecules have a hierarchical string structure. We considered the Fibonacci sequences with length 13, 21,34 and 55 for experiments as artificial protein sequences are shown in Table 2.

Table 2. Fibonacci Sequences

A.S.	Sequence
S_{13}	ABBABBABABBAB
S_{21}	BABABBABABBABBABABBAB
S_{34}	ABBABBABABBABBABABBABABBABBABABBAB
S_{55}	BABABBABABBABBABABBABABBABBABABBABBA BABBABABBABBABABBAB

4.2 Real Protein Sequences

Real protein sequence given in Table 3 is considered to evaluate the performance of the proposed HPSOLS algorithm. In the experiment, K-D method [15] is applied to distinguish hydrophobic and hydrophilic residues of 20 amino acids in real protein sequences. The amino acids I, V, L, P, C, M, A, G are hydrophobic (A) and D, E, F, H, K, N, Q, R, S, T, W, Y are hydrophilic (P).

Table 3. Real Protein Sequences

R.S.	Sequence
1BXP	MRYYESSLKSYPD
1BXL	GQVGRQLAIIGDDINR
1EDP	CSCSSLMDKECVYFCHL
1EDN	CSCSSLMDKECVYFCHLDIIW
1AGT	GVPINVSCTGSPQCIKPCKDQGMRFGKCMNRKCHCTPK

4.3 Parameter Setting and Initialization

The proposed HPSOLS algorithm is compared with basic PSO [11] and PSO with a constriction factor (CPSO) [8], using artificial and real protein sequences with different lengths. The algorithms are implemented using MATLAB 7.6.0 (R2008a) applied on Intel (R) Core (TM) i7-2670QM CPU @ 2.20 GHz with 8 GB RAM on windows 7 Home Premium platform with same initial population but different number of generation based on the respective length of protein sequences. For the experiments, 5000, 12000, 14000, 16000 and 20000 number of generations of the protein sequences of length 5, 13, 21, 34 and 55 are considered respectively. Each algorithm runs 30 times and their mean and standard deviation are calculated. The population size for all approaches is set as 50. The inertia weight (ω) and acceleration coefficients (c_1 and c_2) for the basic PSO are set as $\omega = 0.732$ and $c_1=c_2 = 1.49$ while for CPSO, $c_1=c_2 = 2$. The parameters of the proposed HPSOLS algorithm are set to $c_1 = c_2 = 2.05$ and inertia weight (ω) decreases linearly from 0.9 to 0.4 with increasing generations. In order to obtain less computational time spent by local search in

HPSOLS algorithm, a small number of neighbors of the current solution is taken considering $N = 5$ and r is initially set to 0.2 and its value decreases by 0.05 in every iteration.

Table 4. Results on Artificial Protein Sequence of length 5

Sequence	HPSOLS		PSO		CPSO	
	Mean	Std. Dev.	Mean	Std. Dev.	Mean	Std. Dev.
AAAAA	-3.083	0.000	-3.017	0.089	-2.996	0.039
AAAAB	-1.931	0.000	-1.923	0.048	-1.903	0.012
AAABA	-2.675	0.000	-2.632	0.068	-2.583	0.069
AAABB	-0.888	0.000	-0.888	0.000	-0.880	0.004
AABAA	-2.655	0.000	-2.623	0.054	-2.576	0.037
AABAB	-1.474	0.000	-1.472	0.003	-1.452	0.010
AABBA	-0.962	0.000	-0.786	0.400	-0.901	0.035
AABBB	0.040	0.000	0.040	0.000	0.041	0.001
ABAAB	-1.721	0.000	-1.721	0.000	-1.692	0.016
ABABA	-2.562	0.000	-2.562	0.000	-2.476	0.036
ABABB	-0.958	0.000	-0.958	0.000	-0.951	0.004
ABBAB	-0.235	0.049	-0.118	0.137	-0.228	0.008
ABBBA	-0.475	0.000	-0.321	0.239	-0.448	0.016
ABBBB	-0.072	0.012	-0.044	0.023	-0.067	0.005
BAAAB	-0.526	0.000	-0.526	0.000	-0.520	0.003
BAABB	0.096	0.000	0.096	0.000	0.098	0.001
BABAB	-0.866	0.000	-0.866	0.000	-0.852	0.006
BABBB	-0.490	0.000	-0.490	0.000	-0.471	0.012
BBABB	-0.362	0.000	-0.362	0.000	-0.343	0.010
BBBBB	-0.680	0.000	-0.680	0.000	-0.657	0.010

4.4   Results with Artificial Protein Sequence

Table 4 presents mean and standard deviation of 30 runs of the algorithms on the 20 different artificial protein sequence (A. S.) of length 5. From the results it has been observed that the proposed method performs better than basic PSO and CPSO. Moreover, the proposed algorithm is more robust than basic PSO and CPSO on some artificial sequences.

From Table 5, it is clear that mean of minimum energy obtained by HPSOLS dominates the mean of the basic PSO and CPSO for all 13, 21, 34 and 55 length of artificial protein sequences in 30 runs. It has shown the better performance of the HPSOLS over the basic PSO and CPSO. In case of robust solution, the HPSOLS is placed in second position, compared with basic PSO and CPSO by considering standard deviation of first three artificial protein sequences in Table 5. But, in higher length of artificial sequence, the minimum energy obtained by the HPSOLS is robust than the other algorithms.

The convergence characteristics of each algorithm on artificial protein sequences of lengths 13, 21, 34 and 55 are shown in Fig. 2. The HPSOLS exhibits better convergence than the basic PSO and CPSO.

4.5   Results with Real Protein Sequence

The results of the experiments are listed in Table 6 representing the mean and standard deviation of 30 runs applied on 1BXP, 1BXL, 1EDP, 1EDN and 1AGT of real protein sequences. It has been observed that lowest energy obtained by HPSOLS algorithm is obviously better than that of other algorithms like basic PSO and CPSO. Therefore, the proposed method provides better performance in solving real protein sequences. The lowest energy obtained by the HPSOLS approach is highly robust than the basic PSO as revealed from the standard deviation of all real protein sequences. But robustness is slightly better than HPSOLS in CPSO except for 1BXP real protein sequence.

The convergence characteristics of HPSOLS, basic PSO and CPSO on real protein sequences are plotted in Fig. 3 showing earlier convergence of HPSOLS algorithm compare to other two algorithms.

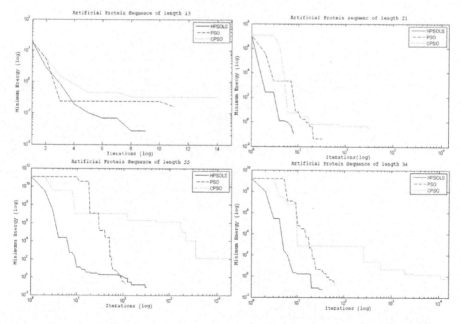

Fig. 2. Convergence characteristics of Artificial Protein Sequence with different lengths

Table 5. Results of Artificial Protein Sequence

A.S.	HPSOLS		PSO		CPSO	
	Mean	Std. Dev.	Mean	Std. Dev.	Mean	Std. Dev.
S_{13}	-2.738	0.416	-1.805	0.581	-0.919	0.274
S_{21}	-4.968	0.589	-3.851	1.022	-0.660	0.220
S_{34}	-6.051	1.080	-5.670	1.450	1.188	0.285
S_{55}	-8.328	1.207	-8.299	1.865	5474	1630

Table 6. Results of Real Protein Sequence

R.S.	HPSOLS		PSO		CPSO	
	Mean	Std. Dev.	Mean	Std. Dev.	Mean	Std. Dev.
1BXP	-2.423	0.0804	-1.835	0.430	-0.883	0.220
1BXL	-8.398	0.422	-6.468	1.300	-3.027	0.468
1EDP	-6.389	0.5923	-3.563	1.448	-1.313	0.481
1EDN	-7.095	0.917	-5.017	1.821	-0.805	0.348
1AGT	-16.965	2.069	-14.400	3.103	-0.049	0.590

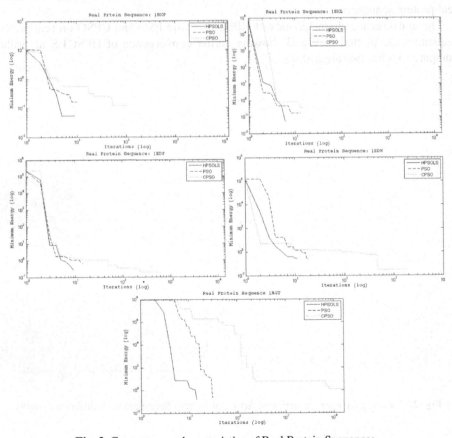

Fig. 3. Convergence characteristics of Real Protein Sequences

5   Conclusions

The paper presents a hybrid particle swarm optimization with local search for solving protein structure prediction problem. PSO has strong global search capability to solve many optimization problems. But, due to lack of diversity in their individuals particles can easily trapped into local minima when solving complex problem. In the paper local search algorithm is applied on *pbest* of all particles in each iteration to preventing particles fall into local optima and made exploration on their search space. The hybrid HPSOLS is used to solve protein structure prediction problem on 2D off-lattice model. Experimental results show that the proposed HPSOLS has better performance than basic PSO and CPSO. In future, we will implementing the 3D off lattice protein structure prediction using this proposed algorithm and controlling the parameters which are associated with HPSOLS.

References

1. Anfinsen, C.B.: Principles that Govern the Folding of Protein Chains. Science, pp. 223–230 (1973)
2. Dill, A.K., Bromberg, S., Yue, K., Fiebig, K.M., Yee, D.P., Thomas, P.D., Chan, H.S.: Principle of protein folding: a perspective from simple exact models. Protein Science 4(4), 561–602 (1995)
3. Honeycutt, J.D., Thirumalai, D.: The nature of folded states of globular proteins. Biopolymers 32(6), 695–709 (1992)
4. Stillinger, F.H., Head-Gordon, T., Hirshfel, C.L.: Toy Model for Protein Folding. Phys. Rev., 1469–1477 (1993)
5. Yue, X.II., Tang, H.W., Guo, C.H.: A Tabu search and its application in 2D HP off-lattice model. Comput. Appl. Chem. 22(12), 1101 1105 (2005)
6. Kalegari, D.H., Lopes, H.S.: A differential evolution approach for protein structure optimization using a 2D off-lattice model. International Journal of Bio-Inspired Computation 2(3), 242–250 (2010)
7. Liu, J., Wang, L.H., He, L.L., Shi, F.: Analysis of Toy Model for Protein Folding Based on Particle Swarm Optimization Algorithm. In: ICNC, pp. 636–645 (2005)
8. Zhang, X., Li, T.: Improved Particle Swarm Optimization Algorithm for 2D Protein Folding Prediction. In: 1st International Conference on Bioinformatics and Biomedical engineering (ICBBE 2007), pp. 53–56 (2007)
9. Kennedy, J., Eberhart, R.C.: Particle Swarm Optimization. In: Proceedings of IEEE International Conference on Neural Networks (ICNN 1995), pp. 1942–1948. IEEE Press, Perth (1995)
10. Ghosh, S., Das, S., Kundu, D., Panigrahi, B.K., Cui, Z.: An inertia-adaptive particle swarm system with particle mobility factor for improved global optimization. Neural Computing and Applocations 21(2), 237–250 (2012)
11. Panigrahi, B.K., Pandi Ravikumar, V., Das, S.: An Adaptive Particle swarm Optimization Approach for Static and Dynamic Economic Load Dispatch. International Journaul on Energey Conversion and Management 49, 1407–1415 (2008)

12. Eberhart, R.C., Shi, Y.: Particle swarm optimization: developments, applications and resources. In: Proceedings of the IEEE Congress of Evolutionary Computation, vol. 1, pp. 27–30 (2001)
13. Shi, Y., Eberhart, R.C.: A modified particle swarm optimizer. In: Proceedings of the IEEE Congress of Evolutionary Computation, pp. 69–73 (1998)
14. Stillinger, F.H.: Collective Aspects of Protein Folding Illustrated by a Toy Mode. Physical Review E, 2872–877 (1995)
15. Thorton, J., Taylor, W.R.: Structure Prediction. In: Findlay, J.B.C., Geisow, M.J. (eds.) Protein Sequencing, pp. 147–190. IRL Press, Oxford (1989)

Software Effort Estimation Using Functional Link Neural Networks Optimized by Improved Particle Swarm Optimization

Tirimula Rao Benala[1], Rajib Mall[2], and Satchidananda Dehuri[3]

[1] Department of Information Technology
Jawaharlal Nehru Technological University Kakinada, University College Of Engineering
Vizianagaram-535003, India
b.tirimula@gmail.com
[2] Department of Computer Science and Engineering
Indian Institute of Technology, Kharagpur
rajib@cse.iitkgp.ernet.in
[3] Department of System Engineering,
Ajou University, San 5, Woncheon-dong,
Yeongtong-gu, Suwon 443-749, South Korea
satchi@ajou.ac.kr

Abstract. This paper puts forward a new learning model based on improved particle swarm optimization (ISO) for functional link artificial neural networks (FLANN) to estimate software effort. The improved PSO uses the adaptive inertia to balance the tradeoff between exploration and exploitation of the search space while training FLANN. The Chebyshev polynomial has been used for mapping the original feature space from lower to higher dimensional functional space. The method has been evaluated exhaustively on different test suits of PROMISE repository to study the performance. The simulation results show that the ISO learning algorithm greatly improves the performance of FLANN and its variants for software development effort estimation.

Keywords: Software effort estimation, ISO, Back propagation, and FLANN.

1 Introduction

Software effort estimation is the process of prediction of effort, cost, schedule, and staffing levels for successful project management. Accurate software cost estimation is critical for the effective software project management. It significantly affects management activities such as resource allocation and creating reasonable schedule. The major contributing factor for accurate estimation is effort. This has led researchers to conduct extensive research on software effort estimation methods. In this paper, we investigate the use of Improved Particle Swarm Optimization algorithm (ISO) for tuning the control parameters of FLANN for software effort estimation. The improved PSO employs parameter automation strategy, velocity resetting, and

B.K. Panigrahi et al. (Eds.): SEMCCO 2013, Part II, LNCS 8298, pp. 205–213, 2013.
© Springer International Publishing Switzerland 2013

adapting the inertia in global search and thereby fine tuning the quality of the solution [3]. This work is an improvement of our earlier work PSO-FLANN[12].

FLANN proposed by Pao, is a flat network consisting of one input layer and an output layer for forming arbitrarily complex decision regions to guide real world applications. FLANN generates output (effort) by expanding the inputs (cost drivers) by nonlinear orthogonal functions like Chebyshev polynomial and then processing the final output layer. Each input neuron corresponds to a component of an input vector. The output layer consists of one output neuron that computes the software development effort as a linear weighted sum of the outputs of the input layer [10, 11]. The non-normal characteristics of the datasets always lead FLANN to low prediction accuracy and high computational complexity. To alleviate these drawbacks our proposed technique has been formulated to exploit the best features of ISO and FLANN a.k.a ISO-FLANN.

Functional link neural networks and cost estimation fundamentals are briefly reviewed in Section 2. The proposed approach is described in Section 3 and Section 4. In Section 5, numerical examples from Cocomo81 (Coc81), Nasa93, Maxwell dataset is used to evaluate the performance. Section 6 concludes this paper.

2   Background

In this section the background of this work is discussed. Software cost estimation and FLANN architecture are described in Subsection 2.1 and 2.2, respectively.

2.1   Software Effort Estimation

Software effort estimation (SEE) is one of the important steps in software project management. It can be defined as the task of estimating the total effort required to develop a software system [5]. SEE is incorporated by set of attributes (a. k. a, cost drivers) representing a software project to predict (or estimate) the cost, in terms of person-months, in turn to predict the required time to develop the software system [1, 8]. SEE assist the project managers to take strategic decisions such as bidding of a new project, managing development, maintenance or customization of software, planning and allocation of resources. According to Oliveira [8], the major bottlenecks for software projects are the schedule and effort (cost) to finish it; the ever changing dynamics of project scope make the process of cost estimation complex. Due to typical characteristics of each project, the accurate measurement of the cost and development time of software can be determined only after the project is completed [2, 8]. However, it is necessary to perform estimations before the project begins. There are various techniques and methods which can be employed to estimate software development effort, cost, and time. This paper introduces an innovative technique aimed to predict (estimate) the software development effort based on ISO and FLANN.

2.2   Architecture of FLANN

A typical FLANN structure is illustrated in Figure 1. FLANN is a single layer flat net with implicit hidden layer. The original input space is mapped into n-dimensional feature space (n is a user defined parameter, varies across the domains) by functional expansion such that the feature space becomes linearly separable. The Chebyshev polynomial functional expansion is widely considered as basis function in software cost estimation [12]. The output of the basis function is multiplied by random weights chosen in the range [-0.5, 0.5] and the summation of all such multiplications is feed to sigmoid function to predict the development effort in Person-Months [10, 11]. The learning process involves updating the weights of FLANN in order to minimize a given cost function. The weight vector is evolved by Improved Particle Swarm optimization (ISO), which has unique charactcristics like rapid convergence to global solutions and less number of parameters to be optimized.

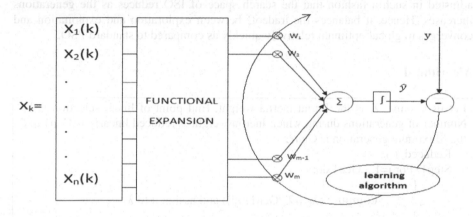

Fig. 1. FLANN Architecture

3   Improved Particle Swarm Optimization

The essence of ISO-FLANN architecture for software cost estimation is to predict the effort accurately by fine tuning the control parameters of FLANN by employing a new learning method based on ISO.

The Improved PSO relies on standard global version of PSO [3]. In order to circumvent the slow convergence rate to the global optimum and inefficiencies of PSO to fine tune the control parameters of the solution space, the ISO has been used in this work. The mathematical model for ISO is as follows.

$$\overrightarrow{v_k}(t+1) = \lambda \otimes \overrightarrow{v_k}(t) + \overrightarrow{c_1} \otimes \overrightarrow{r_1}(t) \otimes \left(\overrightarrow{p_k}(t) - \overrightarrow{x_k}(t)\right) + \overrightarrow{c_2} \otimes \overrightarrow{r_2}(t) \otimes \left(\overrightarrow{p_g}(t) - \overrightarrow{x_k}(t)\right) \tag{1}$$

$$\overrightarrow{x_k}(t+1) = \overrightarrow{x_k}(t) + \overrightarrow{v_k}(t+1) \tag{2}$$

The symbol $\otimes$ in equation (1) denotes point by point vector multiplication. λ is an adaptive inertia weight (detailed is described in algorithm-I); cognitive component c_1 and social component c_2 are non-negative real constants. Randomness (useful for good state space exploitation) is introduced via the vector of random numbers $\vec{r_1}$ and $\vec{r_2}$. These are usually selected as a uniform random number in the range [0, 1]. The steps of velocity update, position update, and fitness computations are repeated until a desired convergence criterion is met. The stopping criterion is usually that the maximum change in the best fitness should be smaller than the specified tolerance for a specified number of iterations, I, as shown in Eq. (3). Alternatively, the algorithm can be terminated when the velocity updates are close to zero over a number of iterations.

$$\left| f\left(\vec{p_g}(t)\right) - f\left(\vec{p_g}(t-1)\right) \right| \leq \epsilon, \quad t = 2,3,\ldots,I \quad (3)$$

The unique flavor of ISO is its adaptive inertia weight λ. The adaptive weight λ is adjusted in such a fashion that the search space of ISO reduces as the generations increases. Hence, it balances the tradeoff between exploration and exploitation and converges to global optimum relatively quickly as compared to standard PSO.

Algorithm-I

Let us assume, λ_0 is the Initial inertia weight, End point of linear selection is λ_1, Number of generations during which inertia weight is reduced linearly is Gen1 and the Maximum generation is Gen2.

  Reduced_( )
  Step1: For i=1.., Gen1 do:
     {
                 Compute $(\lambda_0 - ((\lambda_1/Gen1) \times i))$ and assign it to λ_1
     }

  Step 2: For i=Gen1+1..,Gen2 do:
     {
                 Compute $((\lambda_0 - \lambda_1) \times exp\left((((Gen1+1)-i)/i)\right))$ and assign it to λ_1
     }

4   ISO-FLANN Algorithm

In this section, we first propose the methodology for software cost estimation, next algorithm and finally performance evaluation metrics.

4.1   Methodology

ISO-FLANN is a typical two layer feed forward neural network consisting of an input layer and output layer with an implicit hidden layer. The nodes between input and hidden layer are connected without weight vector and the nodes between hidden layer and output layer are assigned with weight vector. Unlike FLANN, the weight vector is evolved by ISO Learning algorithm. There are n input nodes (n depends on the cost drivers of a particular dataset). The input nodes are expanded by a basis function to m number of nodes, where m is the functionally expanded nodes. In software cost estimation domain Chebyshev polynomial basis function is most effective function for functional expansion [10, 11]. The basis function maps the input space to higher dimension.

4.2 Algorithm-II

Let us assume, D is the dataset, tr and te are the training and testing parts respectively, p is the data point, l and h are the lower and higher dimensions respectively, and tc is the termination criteria, O is the output layer, w is the weighted sum, E is the error, current best fitness value is cf, Fitness value is F, gb represents global best, pv is the particle velocity, CG represents Cauchy and Gaussian Mutation .

Step1: Divide D $2/3^{rd}$ parts into tr and $1/3^{rd}$ part into te.
Step 2: For each p
    Step 2.1: Map from l to h.
Step3: For each particle initialize with small values from [-1, -1].
Step 4: While (!tc)
    {
        For each swarm
        {
            For each particle in the swarm
            {
                For each sample in the training sample
                {
                    Calculate w, and send it as input to O.
                    Calculate E.
                }
                Assign E to F.
                If(F is better than cf)
                {
                    Assign F to cf.
                }
            Assign cf to gb.
            }
            For each particle
            {
                Call Reduced_() and find pv.
                Update particle position.
            }
        }
        Apply CG if the position of the global best position is not improved
    }

4.3   Performance Evaluation Metrics

Three evaluation criteria were used to assess degree of accuracy to which the estimated effort matches actual effort. These evaluation criteria have been chosen as they are widely accepted bench mark metrics for performance evaluation in the software cost estimation literature. They are as follows: Mean Magnitude of Relative Error (MMRE), Median Magnitude of relative error (MdMRE), and PRED (0.25) [4, 9].

5   Datasets, Experiments, and Results

In this section, studies were carried out on three PROMISE repository datasets, namely, Cocomo81 (Coc81), Nasa93, Maxwell [8] to investigate performance of our methods. These datasets are available at http://code.google.com/p/promisedata/.

5.1   Dataset Preparation

Before the experiments, all input variables (a. k. a features) are normalized using min-max normalization in order to eliminate the possibility of unequal influences. The three real datasets shown in Table 1 are subjected to Leave-one-out cross-validation; in each iteration all the data points except for the single observation are used for training and the model is tested on that single observation. Table 1 provides an overview of the data sets, including number of features, size.   The skewness, minimum, mean and maximum of effort and size in Klocs.

Table 1. Descriptive statistics for public datasets

Dataset	Coc81	Nasa93	Maxwell
Features	17	17	27
Size	63	93	62
Units	Months	Months	Hours
Minimum Effort	6	8	583
Median	98	252	5189.5
Mean	683	624	8223.2
Maximu m Effort	11400	8211	63694
Skew	4.4	4.2	3.26

5.2   Cost Estimation Models

This study explored the feasibility of using different models based on FLANN. Out of the three functional expansions, namely, C-FLANN, P-FLANN and L-FLANN, C-FLANN based model is included in our experiments. Hereafter, C-FLANN will be annotated as FLANN. The proposed models using Improved Particle Swarm Optimization and Particle swarm optimization will be hereafter known as ISO-FLANN and PSO-FLANN. For a comprehensive evaluation of the proposed models, for comparison, other popular estimation models including, Functional Link Artificial Neural Networks (FLANN) [10, 11], and artificial neural networks (ANN), are also included in the experiments.

5.3   Experimental Procedure

For the purpose of validation, we adopt Leave-one out cross-validation to evaluate the generalization error of the methods. In this scheme for each dataset of n data points and given m candidate models, each model is trained with n-1 data points and then is tested on the sample that was left out. This process is repeated n times until every data point in dataset have been used as cross-validation instance. Then the average training error and testing error across all three trials are computed. The advantage of this scheme is that it does not matter how the data is split since each data point is assigned into a test set, a training set and a validation set respectively once. First, the performances of ISO-FLANN, BP-FLANN and PSO-FLANN are investigated. The best variants on training set are selected as the candidate for comparisons. Next, the optimizations of machines learning methods are conducted on the training dataset by searching through their parameter spaces. Thirdly, the training and testing results of the best variants of all estimation methods are summarized and compared. The experimental results and the analysis are presented in the next section.

5.4   Experimental Results

Tables 2 to 4 present a summary of all the methods applied on three PROMISE repository datasets given in Table 1. The second annotated column in each table shows performance of various methods with respect to performance metrics MMRE. Similarly, the third column and fourth column of each table summarizes the results with respect to performance metrics MdMRE and PRED(0.25) respectively. With these values it can be interpreted that the testing results in the proposed methods outperform the testing results in traditional methods.

Our experiments suggest that hybrid combination of ISO-FLANN improves the accuracy very efficiently when compared to BP-FLANN, PSO-FLANN and ANN.

Table 2. Results on Coc81 Dataset

Methods	MMRE		MdMRE		PRED(0.25)	
	Training	Testing	Training	Testing	Training	Testing
ISO-FLANN	0.008145	0.025319	0.006868	0.001597	1	1
BP-FLANN	0.0047	0.0119	0.0005913	0.00058568	1	1
PSO-FLANN	0.000072218	0.000026565	0.00092968	0.000086921	1	1
ANN	0.0053	0.0064	0.0045	0.0111	1	1

Table 3. Results on Nasa93 Dataset

Methods	MMRE		MdMRE		PRED(0.25)	
	Training	Testing	Training	Testing	Training	Testing
ISO-FLANN	0.0032	0.00016343	0.0034	0.0011	1	1
BP-FLANN	0.00094315	0.00035029	0.00076716	0.0009355	1	1
PSO-FLANN	0.00084454	0.000090888	0.00046056	0.00010601	1	1
ANN	0.0020	0.0053	0.0019	0.0042	1	1

Table 4. Results on Maxwell Dataset

Methods	MMRE		MdMRE		PRED(0.25)	
	Training	Testing	Training	Testing	Training	Testing
ISO-FLANN	0.01137	0.001349	0.00792	0.002363	1	1
BP-FLANN	0.005687	0.011517	0.000613	0.000679	1	1
PSO-FLANN	0.0000722	0.0000266	0.00093	0.0000869	1	1
ANN	0.005351	0.007901	0.004413	0.011444	1	1

6   Conclusion and Future Work

Software cost estimation by hybrid system using ISO and FLANN-an improvement of PSO-FLANN, has been presented in this work. We have evaluated the performance of ISO-FLANN. The experimental results show that our method gives improved performance as compared to conventional FLANN and outperforms the competitive techniques such as PSO-FLANN, and ANN. As a future work, our best effort may continue towards designing of new hybrid learning mechanisms for software effort estimation based on meta-heuristic techniques like Bat algorithm, artificial bee colony (ABC) algorithm, differential evolution (DE), and simulated annealing.

References

1. de Araújo, R.A., Oliveira, A.L.I., Soares, S.: A Shift-Invariant Morphological System for Software Development Cost Estimation. Expert Systems with Applications 38, 4162–4168 (2011)
2. Braga, P.L., Oliveira, A.L.I., Ribeiro, G.H.T., Meira, S.R.L.: Software Effort Estimation Using Machine Learning Techniques with Robust Confidence Intervals. In: Proceedings of IEEE International Conference on Tools with Artificial Intelligence (ICTAI), pp. 181–185 (2007)
3. Dehuri, S., Roy, R., Cho, S.-B., Ghosh, A.: An improved particle swarm optimized functional link artificial neural network (ISO-FLANN) for classification. The Journal of System and Software 85, 1333–1345 (2012)
4. Foss, T., Stensrud, E., Kitchenham, B., Myrtveit, I.: A Simulation Study of the Model Evaluation Criterion MMRE. IEEE Transactions on Software Engineering 29(11), 985–995 (2003)

5. Keung, J.W.: Theoretical Maximum Prediction Accuracy for Analogy-Based Software Cost Estimation. In: Proceedings of 15th Asia-Pacific Software Engineering Conference, pp. 495–502 (2008)
6. Mendes, E., Watson, I., Triggs, C., Mosley, N., Counsell, S.: A Comparative Study of Cost Estimation Models for Web Hypermedia Applications. Empirical Software Engineering 8, 163–196 (2003)
7. McQueen, J.B.: Some methods of classification and analysis of multivariate observations. In: Proceedings of the Fifth Berkeley Symposium on Mathematical Statistics and Probability, pp. 281–297 (1967)
8. Oliveira, A.L.I.: Estimation of software project effort with support vector regression. Neurocomputing 69(13-15), 1749–1753 (2006)
9. Stensrud, E., Foss, T., Kitchenham, B.A., Myrtveit, I.: An Empirical Validation of the Relationship Between the Magnitude of Relative Error and Project Size. In: Proceedings of the IEEE 8th Metrics Symposium, pp. 3–12 (2002)
10. Tirimula Rao, B., Sameet, B., Kiran Swathi, G., Vikram Gupta, K., Raviteja, C., Sumana, S.: A Novel Neural Network approach for Software Cost Estimation Using Functional Link Artificial Neural Networks. International Journal of Computer Science and Network Security (IJCSNS) 9(6), 126–131 (2009)
11. Tirimula Rao, B., Dehuri, S., Mall, R.: Functional Link Artificial Neural Networks for Software Cost Estimation. International Journal of Applied Evolutionary Computation (IJAEC) 3(2), 62–82 (2012)
12. Tirimula Rao, B., Chinnababu, K., Mall, R., Dehuri, S.: A Particle Swarm Optimized Functional Link Artificial Neural Network (PSO-FLANN) in Software Cost Estimation. In: Satapathy, S.C., Udgata, S.K., Biswal, B.N. (eds.) Proceedings of Int. Conf. on Front. of Intell. Comput. AISC, vol. 199, pp. 59–66. Springer, Heidelberg (2013)

Improved Feature Selection Based on Particle Swarm Optimization for Liver Disease Diagnosis

Gunasundari Selvaraj [1] and Janakiraman S. [2]

[1] Research Scholar, Pondicherry University
[2] Asst Prof, Pondicherry University
gunapondyuniv@gmail.com, jana3376@yahoo.co.in

Abstract. Dimensionality reduction of a feature set is a usual pre-processing step used for image classification to improve their accuracy. In this paper an automatic Computer Aided Diagnostic system (CAD) is proposed for detection of liver diseases like hepatoma and hemangioma from abdominal Computed Tomography (CT) images using an evolutionary approach for feature selection. The liver is segmented using adaptive thresholding. Histogram analyzer is used to fix the threshold and morphological operation is used for post processing. Rules are applied to remove the obstacles. Fuzzy c-Mean (FCM) clustering is used to extract the lesion from the segmented liver. Auto covariance features are extracted from the segmented lesion. The Binary Particle Swarm Optimization (BPSO) is applied to get the best reduced feature set. The textual information obtained after feature reduction was used to train Probabilistic Neural Network (PNN). The results obtained from different transfer functions are analyzed and compared.

Keywords: BPSO, Feature Selection, FCM, Morphological Operation, Covariance Matrix, PNN, Liver CAD System.

1   Introduction

Liver cancer is one of the leading causes of death in many countries. CT is often the favored method for identifying many different liver diseases, including liver cancer, since the image allows a physician to verify the presence of a tumor and to measure its size. CAD systems have been developed to help doctors to diagnose precisely. The goal of the development of these systems is to assist radiologists in interpreting radiographic images. Tumors can be benign or malignant. Benign tumors are not cancer cells and do not extend to tissues around them. Malignant tumors are cancer cells and can invade and damage nearby tissues and organs. In many fields such as data mining, pattern recognition and image processing, many numbers of features are often involved. In the same way in CAD system also many features are concerned. Feature reduction has to be done to improve their performance with a small feature subset. In feature subset selection problem, the prediction accuracy of the selected subset depends on the size of the subset as well as the features selected. Evolutionary computing can be applied to problems where traditional methods are hard to apply.

B.K. Panigrahi et al. (Eds.): SEMCCO 2013, Part II, LNCS 8298, pp. 214–225, 2013.

A well-known evolutionary computing algorithm is the Particle Swarm Optimization (PSO) Algorithms which are very capable to search large solution spaces. PSO is one of the most widely used evolutionary algorithms inspired from social behavior of animals. It is popular because it is very simple and inexpensive. There exists Binary Particle Swarm Optimization (BPSO) which is a binary version of PSO. In our work, the BPSO algorithm as a feature selector, and PNN as a classifier are integrated effectively. The selected best features from BPSO are fed to PNN classifier to classify the liver diseases. The computer aided liver disease diagnostic system can be divided into four parts. The first part is the segmentation of the liver and extraction of the lesion. The second and third part is the identification of features and best features and the last one is the recognition of the lesion. The rest of the paper is organized as follows. Section 2 reviews the past work. Section 3 briefly presents the BPSO. Section 4 describes the system structure. Section 5 discusses the implementation and results. Section 6 concludes the work.

2   Past Work

A lot of liver texture analysis techniques have been proposed and surveyed in the past [1] for CT imaging modalities to extract useful features for reliable liver tissue classification. Support Vector Machine (SVM) was designed by some authors to characterize liver diseases. Kernel-based Classifier is implemented [2] for classification of cyst, hepatoma and cavernous hemangioma. The features derived from the co-occurrence matrix, shape descriptors etc. are used to train the SVM for classification. CT liver images are characterized into normal, visible and invisible malignancy [3]. A CT liver image diagnostic classification system is developed which consists of a detect-before-extract (DBE) [4] system which automatically finds the liver boundary and a neural network liver classifier for classification. An automatic liver segmentation and classification system is developed in [5]. The orthogonal wavelet transform is used to compute horizontal, vertical and diagonal details. Statistical texture features are extracted and PNN is used for classification. The study and development of PNN, Linear Vector Quantization and Back Propagation Network for classification of fatty and cirrhosis liver diseases is reported in [6]. Kumar et al (2010, 2011, and 2012) reveals that curvelet transforms [7], [8], and [9] achieve better than wavelet transform for categorization. Mala et al (2010) and Gunasundari et al (2012) concluded that the performance of PNN is good when it is compared with other neural networks [10]. A classifier [11] consisting of three sequentially placed neural networks for four classes of hepatic tissues was developed. Eight co-occurrence texture features are calculated for six different values of the pixel spacing. A CAD system architecture [12] which is able to accurately classify hepatic as normal liver, hepatic cyst, hemangioma, and Hepatoma was presented. Genetic Algorithm based feature selection method was applied for feature selection. First Classifier consists of five multilayer perceptron neural networks and second Classifier consists of five different primary classifiers, namely one multilayer perceptron Neural Network, one PNN, and three k-nearest neighbor classifiers (K-NN), each fed with the combination of the five texture feature sets or with their reduced versions. Orthogonal moments [13] are used to classify the liver diseases from abdominal CT. Neural networks have been extensively used in pattern classification applications. [3-12]

A complementary particle swarm optimization algorithm [14] is used to find the best feature combinations. They used the complementary function to generate the new particles, and replace the 50% of the particles in the swarm. Chr-PmRF approach is designed [15] where PSO based sampling, Minimum Redundancy and Maximum Relevance mRMR based FS and Random Forest (RF) classifier successfully handle the troubles of customer churn prediction in telecommunication. Two wrapper based feature selection approaches [16], which are single feature ranking and BPSO based feature subset ranking is designed. Logistic maps and tent maps [17] are embedded in BPSO to find out the inertia weight of the BPSO. Chaotic binary particle swarm optimization is proposed to implement the Feature Selection (FS). Catfish binary particle swarm optimization [18] is proposed in which the catfish effect is applied. This effect is the introduction of catfish particles into the search space, which replaces particles with the worst fitness. Swarm intelligence FS algorithm is designed based on the initialization and update of only a subset of particles in the swarm [19]. An original two-phase FS method [20] that uses PSO is presented, which forms an initial core set of discriminatory features of the original feature space. This core set is then consecutively extended by searching for extra discriminatory features. Improved binary particle swarm optimization [21] is proposed to implement FS and K-NN method serves as an evaluator of the IBPSO for gene expression data categorization problems. A system that classifies lymph nodes from the ultrasound images is presented [22]. A FS algorithm that integrates the particle swarm optimization neural network with the Boltzmann function is implemented to select significant features. A novel FS method for the categorization of high dimensional cancer microarray data is designed which used filtering technique such as signal-to noise ratio (SNR) score and PSO [23]. A novel method for hepatitis disease diagnosis is designed [24], which is based on Rough Set, PSO and SVM. The proposed method is tested on the multi-core platform. Different spectral features are analyzed from transrectal ultrasound images for prostate cancer recognition [25]. A novel FS and classification method for hyperspectral images by combining the global optimization ability of PSO algorithm and SVM is reported [26]. Global optimal search performance of PSO is improved by using a chaotic optimization search technique. Granularity based grid search strategy is used to optimize the SVM model parameters. A combination of Integer-Coded Genetic Algorithm and PSO is coupled with the neural-network-based Extreme Learning Machine, is used for gene selection and cancer classification [27]. Semi supervised Ellipsoid ARTMAP algorithm combined with the PSO to distinguish tumor tissues with more than two categories through analyzing gene expression profiling is implemented [28].

3   Binary Particle Swarm Optimization

PSO is an evolutionary computation technique that was proposed by Kennedy and Eberhart [29]. It is initialized with a population of random solutions, called particles which fly around in the search space to find the best solution. Each particle in PSO should consider the current position, the current velocity, the personal best solution, pbest, and the gbest, to modify its position. The particles are manipulated according to the following equation:

$$v_i^{t+1} = w v_i^t + c1 \times rand \times (pbest_i - x_i^t) + c2 \times rand \times (gbest - x_i^t) \qquad (1)$$

$$x_i^{t+1} = x_i^t + v_i^{t+1} \qquad (2)$$

where v_i^t is the velocity of particle i at iteration t, w is a inertia weight, c1 and c2 are acceleration constant, rand is random number between 0 and 1, x_i^t is the current position of particle i at iteration t, pbest$_i$ is the best solution that the i-th particle has obtained so far, and gbest indicates the best solution the particle has obtained so far. The PSO starts with randomly placing the particles in a problem space. At each pass, the velocities of particles are computed using Eq. (1). After defining the velocities, the position of particles can be computed using Eq. (2). The process of changing particles' positions will continue until satisfying an objective function. In designing the binary version of PSO, some basic concepts of the velocity and position updating process must be modified. In binary space the position updating process cannot be performed using Eq. (2). A transfer function is necessary to map velocity values to probability values for updating the positions. The original BPSO was proposed by Kennedy and Eberhart [30] to allow PSO to operate in binary problem spaces. The roles of velocities are to present the probability of a bit taking the value 0 or 1. A sigmoid function as in Eq. (3) was employed to transform all real values of velocities to probability values in the interval [0, 1].

$$T(v_i^k(t)) = \frac{1}{1 + e^{-v_i^k(t)}} \qquad (3)$$

Where $v_i^k(t)$ indicates the velocity of particle i at iteration t in k-th dimension. After changing velocities to probability values, position vectors could be updated with the probability of their velocities as in Eq. (4):

$$x_i^k(t+1) = \begin{cases} 0 & if \quad rand \quad < T(v_i^k(t+1)) \\ 1 & if \quad rand \quad > T(v_i^k(t+1)) \end{cases} \qquad (4)$$

A transfer function defines the probability of changing a position vector's elements from 0 to 1and vice versa. The range of a transfer function should be bounded in the interval [0, 1], as they represent the probability that a particle should change its position. Some of the S and V type transfer functions are given in Eq. (5-8) [31]. V type of transfer functions is quite unlike from the s-shaped family, they need a new position updating rules. Eq. (9) should be used to update position vectors based on velocities.

$$S1: \quad T(x) = \frac{1}{1 + e^{-2x}} \tag{5}$$

$$S2: \quad T(x) = \frac{1}{1 + e^{(-x/2)}} \tag{6}$$

$$V1: \quad T(x) = \left| erf\left(\frac{\sqrt{\pi}}{2} x\right)\right| \tag{7}$$

$$V2: \quad T(x) = \tanh(x) \tag{8}$$

$$x_i^k(t+1) = \begin{cases} (x_i^k(t))^{-1} & if \quad rand \quad < T(v_i^k(t+1)) \\ x_i^k(t) & if \quad rand \quad > T(v_i^k(t+1)) \end{cases} \tag{9}$$

Where $x_i^k(t)$ indicates the velocity of particle i at iteration t in k-th dimension, $(x_i^k(t))^{-1}$ is the complement of $x_i^k(t)$

4   System Structure

The liver is segmented from abdominal CT images using adaptive thresholding and morphological opening and closing (Gunasundari et al 2012). Based on medical knowledge obstacles are removed automatically. The lesion is extracted using FCM. The textural features extracted from the lesion are given as input to BPSO to get the best features to identify the disease using PNN. System structure is shown in Fig. 1.

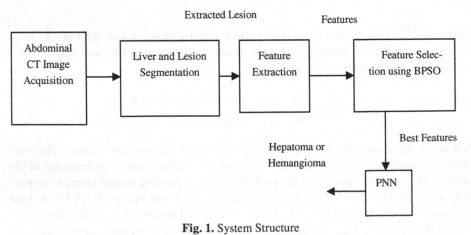

Fig. 1. System Structure

4.1   Image Acquisition

From the website "ctisus.org" the abdominal CT image is downloaded which is in JPEG format and it is created and maintained by The Advanced Medical Imaging Laboratory (AMIL).

4.2   Segmentation of Liver and Lesion

In Liver Segmentation, anatomical knowledge is used to identify the liver region. Normally the liver is located on the upper side of the image and takes up the major area in a CT image. Although the liver retains the constant intensity throughout, a fixed threshold is not possible since the intensity differs according to the patient slice and CT machine. The window size is fixed from a CT image. The histogram is drawn and analyzed for an area inside the window. The highest pitch in the histogram represents the middle intensity of the liver region and certain intensities which are having high density are considered to fix the threshold. The pixels in the determined range of intensity are extracted. Morphological opening followed by closing is applied with the flat structuring element to smooth contours. Opening breaks narrow isthmuses and eliminates sharp peaks whereas closing fuses narrow breaks and eliminates small holes. Based on certain conditions other regions located nearby in the liver can be detached. The first condition is the location of the object. The liver is located in a constant area in the upper left side of the image. The second condition is the area. The area of the liver is large when it is compared with the obstacles. The morphological operations are again applied after removing the obstacles. The image obtained after applying disk structuring element is converted to binary image, complemented and multiplied with the original image to get the segmented liver.

There are many kinds of liver diseases like hepatoma, hemangioma, cysts, cholangiocarcinoma etc. It is not easy to discriminate between these diseases. To distinguish it, the lesion must be extracted. The extraction of lesion is also not simple. The threshold can't be predetermined since the intensity of the lesion varies and it depends on CT machine. A technique independent of a varying intensity must be applied. This paper utilizes the version of the k-Means clustering and fuzzy logic. Fuzzy c-Means clustering is used to segment the lesion. The pixels of the input image are divided into 3 clusters. The first cluster includes pixels in the background. The second cluster includes pixels in the liver other than lesion and the third cluster includes pixels in the lesion. The post processing is done to remove some obstacles. Morphological closing followed by opening is applied again to the flat structuring element.

4.3   Auto Covariance Features

Auto-correlation coefficients reflect the inter-pixel correlation within an image. It is a mean removed version also called modified Auto Covariance features. Let the given image has size M*N. The modified auto-covariance coefficients are given by Eq. (10) and Eq. (11) [32]

$$\gamma\ (\Delta\ m,\quad \Delta\ n)\ =\ 1\ -\ A(\ \Delta\ m,\quad \Delta\ n)/A(0,0) \tag{10}$$

$$A(\Delta m,\Delta n)=\frac{1}{(M\ -\ \Delta m)(N\ -\ \Delta n)}\times\left|\sum_{x=0}^{M-1-\Delta m}\sum_{y=0}^{N-1-\Delta n}(f(x,y)-Mean\ )(f(x+\Delta m,y+\Delta n)-Mean\ )\right| \tag{11}$$

Mean = mean value of f (x, y)

4.4   Feature Selection Using Particle Swarm Optimization

The goal of the feature subset selection task is to obtain k dimensions from the whole feature space K where k < K, which optimize a criterion function. The features extracted are given to identify the optimal subset of features. The feature subset selection problem is defined as finding a subset L from F and which minimizes the misclassification rate of the PNN classifier Eq. (12). The BPSO algorithm is applied using S and V transfer functions. The cross-validation approach is used to train and validate the accuracy of a PNN network. The final accuracy of the model is calculated as the average of all accuracies among all test subsets.

$$J\ (L\ )\ =\ \min_{Y\ \subseteq\ F\ ,|Y|=\ k}\ J\ (Y\ ) \tag{12}$$

4.5   Probabilistic Neural Network (PNN)

PNNs are a special form of Radial Basis Function (RBF) network, which is widely used for pattern classification. The network learns from a training set T which is a collection of examples called instances. Each instance has an input vector and an output class. In a PNN, the operations are organized into a multilayered feed forward network with four layers such as Input layer, Pattern layer, Summation layer and Output layer [33]. Each hidden node hi in the network is joined to a single class node. If the output class of instance i is j, then hi is connected to class node Cj. Each class node Cj calculates the summation of the activations of the hidden nodes that are linked to it and passes this sum to a decision node. The decision node yields the class with the highest summed activation.

5   Implementation and Results

The abdominal CT images were downloaded and total number of different image slice considered for evaluation is 48. It includes 36 hepatoma and 12 hemangioma images. Since the liver is located in the left side of the CT image, the window slice is selected. Then the histogram is drawn to this window and analyzed. The intensity points with the maximum count are identified to fix the threshold. The pixels in the determined range of intensity are extracted. Morphological operations are applied and obstacles are removed from the rules. The lesion is extracted using FCM. The segmentation output of an image is shown in Table 1. The auto covariance features are extracted from the lesion. While calculating auto covariance features the positional difference varies from 1 to 12. The number of features extracted varies based on positional difference values. The possible feature set extracted is 2, 5, 9, 14, 27, 44, 65 and 90, as

Table 1. Segmentation Output

Input Image	Segmented Liver	Segmented Lesion

Table 2. Auto Covariance Features for different $(\Delta m, \Delta n)$

Max value of $(\Delta m + \Delta n)$, Possible values of $(\Delta m, \Delta n)$	No of Features	Accuracy with PNN (%)	Time in (Seconds) Feature Extraction of all images
$\Delta m + \Delta n = 6$ (0,1),(1,0),(1,1),(2,0),(0,2),(1,2),(2,1),(3,0),(0,3),(0,4),(4,0),(1,3),(3,1),(2,2),(0,5), (5,0),(1,4),(4,1), (2,3),(3,2), (0,6),(6,0),(1,5)(5,1),(2,4),(4,2),(3,3)	27	90	3.9
$\Delta m + \Delta n = 8$ (0,1),(1,0),(1,1),(2,0),(0,2),(1,2),(2,1),(3,0),(0,3),(0,4),(4,0),(1,3),(3,1),(2,2),(0,5),(5,0),(1,4),(4,1),(2,3),(3,2), (0,6),(6,0),(1,5)(5,1),(2,4), (4,2)(3,3), (0,7), (7,0),(6,1),(1,6),(2,5),(5,2),(3,4),(4,3),(0,8),(8,0),(1,7),(7,1),(2,6),(6,2),(3,5),(5,3),(4,4)	44	94	5.5
$\Delta m + \Delta n = 12$ (0,1),(1,0),(1,1),(2,0),(0,2),(1,2),(2,1),(3,0),(0,3),(0,4),(4,0),(1,3),(3,1),(2,2), (0,5), (5,0),(1,4),(4,1) , (2,3),(3,2),(0,6),(6,0),(1,5)(5,1),(2,4),(4,2),(3,3), (0,7), (7,0), (6,1), (1,6), (2,5), (5,2), (3,4), (4,3), (0,8),(8,0), (1,7),(7,1),(2,6),(6,2),(3,5), (5,3), (4,4), (0,9), (9,0), (8,1), (1,8),(2,7), (7,2),(3,6),(6,3),(5,4),(4,5),(0,10),(10,0) ,(1,9), (9,1), (2,8), (8,2)(3,7), (7,3), (4,6), (6,4), (5,5), (0,11), (11,0) ,(10,1) (1,10), (2,9), (9,2),(3,8), (8,3),(4,7),(7,4),(5,6),(6,5),(0,12),(12,0),(11,1),(1,11), (2,10), (10,2), (3,9), (9,3), (4,8), (8,4), (5,7),(7,5),(6,6)	90	98	8.1

shown in Table 2. The 90 features are given to the feature selection module to fetch the best feature set. In BPSO the Number of particles (Np) is varied to 20 or 30 and c1, c2=2. The Number of dimensions (Nd) is equal to 90. The number of maximum iteration is varied from 20 to 50. The Fitness function considered is the misclassification rate of PNN classifier. Four different transfer functions are employed to analyze the performance [Table 3-6]. The reduced feature set of size 46 is given as input to PNN for classification of disease and for analyzing the performance. The 33 images are considered for training and 15 images are considered for testing. The training sets produced the accuracy of 100% whereas testing set produces 97.9%. The time complexity of the system is analyzed by giving the features directly to the classifier without feature reduction. The training time for the classifier is more if the features are not reduced.

Table 3. Performance of S1 transfer function

Np	Nd	Nt	Gbest-Value	Features Selected	No of Features	Time Taken (in seconds)
10	90	30	0.0625	1 3 4 5 6 8 9 12 13 14 15 17 18 20 22 26 28 29 30 31 32 33 36 38 40 45 47 49 50 51 55 56 57 58 60 61 63 64 66 68 70 73 75 83 84 86 87 89	48	22.17
10	90	50	0.0833	2 3 4 6 7 8 9 11 12 14 15 16 19 21 22 23 25 26 28 31 33 34 36 39 40 41 42 45 46 47 49 51 52 53 54 56 57 58 60 61 62 66 69 70 71 72 73 74 75 76 78 79 80 82 84 85 87 90	40	34.7
20	90	30	0.0833	1 2 5 6 7 9 10 11 12 17 18 19 21 25 27 28 29 30 31 32 34 35 36 37 38 39 41 42 44 46 48 50 52 55 56 57 58 59 60 61 63 65 66 68 71 72 73 75 76 78 79 80 81 84 85 86 87 88 89 90	60	44.01

Table 4. Performance of S2 transfer function

Np	Nd	Nt	Gbest-Value	Features Selected	No of Features	Time Taken (in seconds)
10	90	30	0.0625	3 4 5 6 7 8 10 12 17 18 19 20 21 24 26 28 33 34 36 37 40 41 42 43 47 48 49 52 55 56 57 60 61 66 67 68 69 70 72 73 74 75 78 80 85 87	46	21.78
10	90	50	0.0833	1 2 3 6 7 9 11 12 14 16 17 18 20 21 22 26 28 35 37 38 39 41 45 46 49 50 51 52 54 56 57 58 59 60 62 64 66 67 68 69 70 71 73 74 75 76 79 80 81 82 84 86 87 90	54	35.8
20	90	30	0.0625	2 4 5 6 9 10 12 16 17 19 20 21 24 26 27 28 30 31 32 34 36 37 38 40 41 43 44 45 46 47 49 50 51 53 55 57 58 60 62 63 64 66 67 68 69 71 73 75 76 77 80 81 83 84 88 89	56	40.4

Table 5. Performance of V1 transfer function

Np	Nd	Nt	Gbest-Value	Features Selected	No of Features	Time Taken (in seconds)
10	90	30	0.0833	1 2 3 5 6 7 9 10 11 12 13 14 16 17 1 23 26 28 29 30 31 32 33 34 35 36 38 42 43 45 46 47 49 50 51 54 55 56 57 58 60 61 6 63 66 67 68 71 72 73 74 76 77 80 82 83 85 87 88 89 90	63	20.18
10	90	50	0.0833	1 2 3 5 6 8 9 10 12 13 14 15 17 18 19 20 23 24 26 27 28 29 31 32 33 34 37 38 39 40 42 43 45 46 47 48 50 51 53 55 60 62 63 64 65 67 68 69 70 72 73 74 75 76 78 79 80 82 83 84 85 86 87 89 90	65	39.28
20	90	30	0.0833	2 4 6 7 8 10 11 12 14 15 16 17 18 20 21 22 26 27 28 30 31 32 33 35 36 37 38 39 40 41 42 43 44 46 47 49 51 52 53 54 55 57 58 60 62 63 64 65 66 68 69 70 74 75 76 77 78 79 80 81 83 84 85 86 87 88 89 90	68	46.2

Table 6. Performance of V2 transfer function

Np	Nd	Nt	Gbest-Value	Features Selected	No of Features	Time Taken (in seconds)
10	90	30	0.0833	1 2 4 6 7 8 10 11 12 14 17 19 21 22 23 24 25 26 29 30 31 33 34 35 37 38 39 42 43 44 45 46 49 54 55 56 57 58 59 61 62 64 65 66 67 68 69 70 71 72 74 75 76 77 78 79 80 81 82 83 85 86 87 90	64	22.4
10	90	50	0.0625	1 2 4 5 6 7 8 9 10 11 12 13 17 18 19 20 21 23 24 27 28 29 32 34 35 36 37 40 41 44 45 49 50 51 53 56 57 58 60 61 62 64 66 68 69 70 71 72 76 78 79 81 82 83 84 85 86 87 88 89	60	36.4
20	90	30	0.0625	1 2 4 5 7 8 11 12 15 16 17 18 19 20 21 22 23 24 25 27 28 29 30 31 33 34 35 36 37 38 40 42 43 44 45 46 48 49 50 52 57 58 60 61 62 63 64 66 67 68 70 71 72 74 76 78 81 82 83 84 85 86 89	63	43.48

6   Conclusion and Future Work

The proposed CAD system is used to segment the liver using adaptive threshold followed by morphological operations. The lesion is extracted using FCM. The auto covariance features are extracted from the segmented lesion. The best features are selected using BPSO. The time complexity to train the neural network is minimized after reducing the feature set using BPSO. By varying the number of particles, iterations and transfer function the system is analyzed. The performance of S2 transfer function is better when it is compared with others. The best features are given as input to a classifier like PNN to classify hepatoma and hemangioma. In comparisons, auto covariance features yields better result in PNN with the high accuracy of 98%. In future, it will be tested on a large number of images and different type of diseases

References

1. Gunasundari, S., Janakiraman, S.: A Study of Textural Analysis Methods for the Diagnosis of Liver Diseases from Abdominal Computed Tomography. International Journal of Computer Applications 74(11), 7–12 (2013)
2. Lee, C.C., Chiang, Y.C., Tsai, C.L., Chen, S.H.: Distinction of Liver Disease from CT images using Kernel-based Classifiers. ICMED 1(2), 113–120 (2007)
3. Mir, A.H., Hanmandlu, M., Tandon, S.N.: Texture analysis of CT images. IEEE Engineering in Medicine and Biology 14(6), 781–786 (1995)
4. Chen, E.L., Chung, P.C., Chen, C.L., Tsai, H.M., Chang, C.I.: An Automatic Diagnostic System for CT Liver Image Classification. IEEE Transactions on Biomedical Engineering 45(6), 783–794 (1998)
5. Mala, K., Sadasivam, V.: Automatic segmentation and classification of diffused liver diseases using wavelet based texture analysis and Neural Network. In: Proc. of International Conference of IEEE on INDICON, pp. 216–219 (2005)
6. Mala, K., Sadasivam, S.: Classification of Fatty and Cirrhosis Liver Using Wavelet-Based Statistical Texture Features and Neural Network Classifier. International Journal of Software Informatics 4(2), 151–163 (2010)
7. Kumar, S.S., Moni, R.S.: Diagnosis of Liver Tumor from CT Images using Curvelet Transform. International Journal of Computer Application Special Issue on CASCT 1, 1–6 (2010)
8. Kumar, S.S., Moni, R.S., Rajeesh, J.: Contourlet Transform Based Computer-Aided Diagnosis System for Liver Tumors on Computed Tomography Images. In: Proc. of International Conference of IEEE on Signal Processing, Communication, Computing and Networking Technologies, pp. 217–222 (2011)
9. Kumar, S.S., Moni, R.S., Rajeesh, J.: Liver tumor diagnosis by gray level and contourlet coefficients texture analysis. In: International Conference on Computing, Electronics and Electrical Technologies, pp. 557–562 (2012)
10. Gunasundari, S., Suganya Ananthi, M.: Comparison and Evaluation of Methods for Liver Tumor Classification from CT Datasets. International Journal of Computer Applications 39(18), 46–51 (2012)
11. Glestos, M., Mougiakakou, S.G., Matsopoulos, G.K., Nikita, K.S., Nikita, A.S., Kelekis, D.: Classification of hepatic lesions from CT images using texture features and neural networks. In: Proc. of 23rd Annual EMBS International Conference of IEEE on Engineering in Medicine and Biology Society, vol. 3, pp. 2748–2752 (2001)
12. Mougiakakou, S.G., Valavanis, I., Nikita, A., Nikita, K.S.: Differential diagnosis of CT focal liver lesions using texture features, feature selection and ensemble driven classifiers. Artificial Intelligence in Medicine 41, 25–37 (2007)
13. Bharathi, V.S., Ganesan, L.: Orthogonal moments based texture analysis of CT liver images. Pattern Recognition Letters 29, 1868–1872 (2008)
14. Chuang, L.Y., Jhang, H.F., Yang, C.H.: Feature Selection using Complementary Particle Swarm Optimization for DNA Microarray Data. In: Proc. of International Conference of Engineers and Computer Scientists, Hong Kong (2013)
15. Idris, A., Rizwan, M., Khan, A.: Churn prediction in telecom using Random Forest and PSO based data balancing in combination with various feature selection strategies. Computers and Electrical Engineering 38, 1808–1819 (2012)
16. Xue, B., Zhang, M., Browne, W.N.: Single Feature Ranking and Binary Particle Swarm Optimization Based Feature Subset Ranking for Feature Selection. In: Proc. of International conference of ACSC Melbourne, Australia, pp. 27–36 (2012)

17. Chuang, L.Y., Yang, C.H., Li, J.C.: Chaotic maps based on binary particle swarm optimization for feature selection. Applied Soft Computing 11, 239–248 (2011)
18. Chuang, L.Y., Tsai, S.W., Yang, C.H.: Improved binary particle swarm optimization using catfish effect for feature selection. Expert Systems with Applications 38, 12699–12707 (2011)
19. Martinez, E., Alvarez, M.M., Trevino, V.: Compact cancer biomarkers discovery using a swarm intelligence feature selection algorithm. Computational Biology and Chemistry 34, 244–250 (2010)
20. Pedrycz, W., Park, B.J., Pizzi, N.J.: Identifying core sets of discriminatory features using particle swarm optimization. Expert Systems with Applications 36, 4610–4616 (2009)
21. Chuang, L.Y., Chang, H.W., Tu, C.J., Yang, C.H.: Improved binary PSO for feature selection using gene expression data. Computational Biology and Chemistry 32, 29–38 (2008)
22. Chang, C.Y., Lai, C.C., Lai, C.T., Chen, S.J.: Integrating PSONN and Boltzmann function for feature selection and classification of lymph nodes in ultrasound images. J. Vis. Commun. Image R. 24, 23–30 (2013)
23. Sahu, B., Mishra, D.: A Novel Feature Selection Algorithm using Particle Swarm Optimization for Cancer Microarray Data. Procedia Engineering 38, 27–31 (2012)
24. He, F., Yang, H.M., Wang, G., Cui, G.D.: A Novel Method for Hepatitis Disease Diagnosis based on RS and PSO. In: Proc. of International Conference of 4th Electronic System Integration Technology Conference, pp. 1289–1292 (2012)
25. Mohamed, S.S., Salama, M.A.: Prostate Cancer Spectral Multi feature Analysis Using TRUS Images. IEEE Transactions on Medical Imaging 27(4), 549–556 (2008)
26. Yang, H.C., Zhang, S.B., Deng, K.Z., Du, P.J.: Research into a Feature Selection Method for Hyperspectral Imagery Using PSO and SVM. Journal of China University of Mining & Technology 17(4), 0473–0478 (2007)
27. Saraswathi, S., Sundaram, S., Sundararajan, N., Zimmermann, M., Hamilton, M.N.: ICGA-PSO-ELM Approach for Accurate Multiclass Cancer Classification Resulting in Reduced Gene Sets in Which Genes Encoding Secreted Proteins Are Highly Represented. IEEE/ACM Transactions on Computational Biology and Bioinformatics 8(2), 452–463 (2011)
28. Xu, R., Anagnostopoulos, G.C., Wunsch II, D.C.: Multiclass Cancer Classification Using Semisupervised Ellipsoid ARTMAP and Particle Swarm Optimization with Gene Expression Data. IEEE/ACM Transactions on Computational Biology and Bioinformatics 4(1), 65–77 (2007)
29. Kennedy, J., Eberhart, R.C.: Particle swarm optimization. In: Proc. of the IEEE International Conference on Neural Networks, USA, vol. 4, pp. 1942–1948 (1995)
30. Kennedy, J., Eberhart, R.C.: A discrete binary version of the particle swarm algorithm. In: Proceedings of the IEEE International Conference on Computational Cybernetics and Simulation (1997)
31. Mirjalili, S., Lewis, A.: S-shaped versus V-shaped transfer functions for binary Particle Swarm Optimization. Swarm and Evolutionary Computation 9, 1–14 (2013)
32. Huang, Y.L., Chen, J.H., Shen, W.C.: Diagnosis of Hepatic Tumors with Texture Analysis in Non enhanced Computed Tomography Images. Acad. Radiol. 13, 713–720 (2006)
33. El Emary, I.M.M., Ramakrishnan, S.: On the Application of Various Probabilistic Neural Networks in Solving Different Pattern Classification Problems. World Applied Sciences Journal 4(6), 772–780 (2008)

Groundwater System Modeling for Pollution Source Identification Using Artificial Neural Network

Raj Mohan Singh and Divya Srivastava

Department of Civil Engineering, Motilal Nehru National Institute of Technology,
Allahabad-211004, India
rajm@mnnit.ac.in, rajm.mnnit@gmail.com

Abstract. Groundwater contamination is serious threat to health of human being and environment. It is difficult and expensive to remediate the polluted aquifers. Identification of unknown pollution sources is first step towards adopting any remediation strategy. The proposed methodology characterizes concentration breakthrough curves in terms of statistical parameter such as average value, maximum value, standard deviation, skewness and kurtosis. The characterized parameters are utilized in a feed forward multilayer artificial neural network (ANN) to identify the sources in terms of its location, magnitudes and duration of activity. The characterized breakthrough curves parameters serve as inputs to ANN model. Unknown pollution source characteristics are outputs for ANN model. Experimentations are performed with different number of training and testing patterns.

Keywords: Breakthrough curve, groundwater flow and transport, characterization of inputs, pollution source identification, ANN.

1   Introduction

Contamination of groundwater poses serious threat to the environment. The contamination of aquifer not only threatens public health and the environment, it also involves large amounts of money in fines, lawsuits, and cleanup costs. Once groundwater is contaminated, it may be difficult and expensive to clean up. Sometimes it is impossible to clean it up to drinking water standards. Polluted groundwater may prevent the use of groundwater for drinking and other domestic and agricultural purposes. Presence of certain chemical pollutants may also prevent its use for various specific purposes.

A problem commonly encountered in remediation of contaminated sites and health risk assessment studies, is the identification of contamination source location in space and time using a set of historical observation data at monitoring sites. Once source location and release histories at a site are identified, reconstruction of the spread of contaminant plumes can be evaluated and the remediation system design and risk assessment studies may be completed. The first step towards remediation is to identify the source of pollution, which is responsible for the observed pollution scenario. Only then, the transport of the pollutant can be predicted, and a suitable remedial measure can be taken.

B.K. Panigrahi et al. (Eds.): SEMCCO 2013, Part II, LNCS 8298, pp. 226–236, 2013.

The identification of unknown pollution sources in groundwater is a complex multidimensional inverse problem. A source is characterized by its location, magnitude and duration of activity. Contamination observed at certain observation well may be caused from more than one location. At each potential location, magnitude of source fluxes may be varying and operating with different disposal periods. Thus, there is huge combination of source characteristics in terms of its location, magnitude and disposal periods. Also, present observed concentration at an observation well is employed to identify the source characteristic that caused the contamination, so the problem is inverse in nature. Various aspects of groundwater management for potential pollution source identification are available in literature [1,2,3,4,5,6,7,8].

An improved genetic algorithm (IGA) is proposed to determine the contaminant source location, leak rate, and release period. The results obtained from IGA agreed with those obtained from linear and nonlinear programming approaches [9]. Progressive genetic algorithm (PGA), in which the GA is combined with the groundwater simulation model, is also employed for the source identification problem [10]. Results indicated that the initial guess does not influence the identified solution. Singh et al. (2004) identified unknown pollution source using an artificial neural network [11]. They considered simple as well as complex scenarios. Geostatistical based approach is used for contaminant source identification in a two-dimensional aquifer where the model uncertainty is caused by variability in hydraulic conductivity [12]. Some recent work are available elsewhere [13,14,15]. Present work does systematic characterization of pollution breakthrough curves and its subsequent utilization in source identification by ANN. This aspect is not adequately addressed in literature.

2   Artificial Neural Network

The ANN is a broad term covering a large variety of network architecture, the most common of which is a multilayer perceptron feedforwrd network with back propagation algorithm [16]. There is no definite formula that can be used to calculate the number of hidden layer(s) and number of nodes in the hidden layer(s) before the training starts, and usually determined by trial-and-error experimentation. The back propagation algorithm is used for training of the feed forward multi-layer perceptron using gradient descent [17, 18]. Present paper utilized Levenberg- Marquardt (LM) backpropagation algorithm to optimize the weights and biases in the network. LM algorithm is more powerful and faster than the conventional gradient descent technique [19]. Basics and details of ANN are available in literature [20].

3   Simulation of Groundwater Flow and Contaminant Transport

The partial differential equations describing groundwater flow and contaminant transport are called the governing equations. To solve these governing equations additional information in the form of initial conditions and boundary conditions are necessary. Governing equations, with specified initial conditions and boundary conditions constitute the mathematical model for the aquifer system. Mathematical model is solved to simulate the physical processes in the aquifer system.

Governing Equation for Groundwater Flow and Transport

The governing equations representing physics of groundwater flow and contaminant transport are derived using Eulerian approach, and applying the principle of conservation of mass to an infinitesimal fixed control volume [21,22,23].

Groundwater flow equation

The proposed methodology is utilized in this study for groundwater systems under steady state flow conditions. The governing equation describing for the steady state two-dimensional areal flow of groundwater through a non-homogenous anisotropic and saturated aquifer can be written in Cartesian tensor notation [24] as:

$$\frac{\partial}{\partial x_i}\left(T_{ij}\frac{\partial h}{\partial x_j}\right) = W; \qquad\qquad i,j = 1,2 \qquad\qquad (1)$$

where, T_{ij}= transmissivity tensor (L^2T^{-1})= $K_{ij}b$; K_{ij}=hydraulic conductivity tensor (LT^{-1}); b= saturated thickness of aquifer (L); h= hydraulic head (L); W =volume flux per unit area (positive sign for outflow and negative sign for inflow) (LT^{-1}); x_i, x_j=Cartesian coordinates(L).

Contaminant transport equation

The governing equation describing transient two-dimensional areal transport of a nonreactive, nonradioactive solute through a saturated aquifer, in Cartesian notation, can be written [25] as:

$$\frac{\partial(cb)}{\partial t} = \frac{\partial}{\partial x_i}(bD_{ij}\frac{\partial c}{\partial x_j}) - \frac{\partial}{\partial x_j}(bcv_i) - \frac{c'W}{\varepsilon}; \qquad\qquad i,j=1,2 \qquad\qquad (2)$$

where, t = time (T); c= concentration of the dissolved chemical species (ML^{-3}); D_{ij}= coefficient of hydrodynamic dispersion (second-order tensor) (L^2T^{-1}); c'= concentration of the dissolved chemical in a source or sink fluid (ML^{-3}); v_i= seepage velocity in the direction $x_i(LT^{-1})$; ε = effective porosity of the aquifer (dimensionless).

The first term on the right side of equation (2) represents dispersive and diffusive (hydrodynamic dispersion) transport. The second term on the right side of the equation represents advective transport due to migration of the contaminant along with flowing groundwater under hydraulic gradient. The third term on the right side of the equation represents a fluid source or sink.

Development of ANN identification models requires simulation of flow and transport process in the groundwater system. Specifications of the equations that represent the flow and transport processes; boundary conditions of the aquifer; and initial conditions in the aquifer are integral part of groundwater simulation process. The well-known groundwater flow and transport simulator MOC (Method of Characteristics) developed by U.S.G.S.[26] is utilized for simulating the flow and transport processes in the aquifer.

In this study, the product of the liquid volume disposal rate and the solute concentration of the source are treated as a single variable called source flux or disposal flux. A groundwater pollution source is assumed to be constant at each potential source location during a single disposal period. A groundwater pollution source is completely identified or characterized if its location, magnitude, and the time period during which it is active are specified. The number of source locations and disposal time horizons, sparsity of observation data available, location of observation wells relative to the actual source locations, heterogeneity of the aquifer, parameter estimation uncertainties in the specified boundary conditions etc. add to the ill-posedness [27] and hence, complexity of this identification problem. The identification of unknown pollution sources is an ill-posed inverse problem, since contaminant fate and transport processes are irreversible[10].

In the problem discussed here, contaminants are considered to be conservative and all geologic and geochemical parameters of the aquifer and the contaminant are assumed to be known initially. The contaminant transport in a 2D unconfined aquifer with steady state conditions is considered. In this study, all the unknown sources are considered to be point sources.

4   Breakthrough Curves Characterization and Methodology Development for Unknown Source Identification

Universal function approximation capability of a feed forward multiplayer perception with back-propagation algorithm is utilized to solve this tedious source identification problem. A groundwater flow and transport simulation model[23] is used to simulate observation data for a large number of randomly selected specified pollution source fluxes and source fluxes generated by random generation and Latin hypercube sampling. Latin Hypercube Sampling (LHS) is used for uniform sampling of source fluxes. In LHS technique, data used for each simulation comes uniformly from different sub intervals in the specified ranges. LHS is a method for stratifying a univariate margin. These simulated data are used for ANN models development for unknown source identification. Observed concentration values characteristics corresponding to different time steps at an observation site constitute models input. Source fluxes responsible for these concentration values are treated as the output for training of the models. In this way, inverse nature of the source identification problem is formulated in ANN framework. Schematic representation of proposed ANN methodology involving the procedure as outline is in Figure 1.

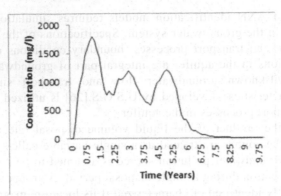

Break through curve Characterization

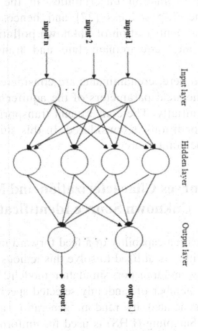

Fig. 1. Schematic of groundwater pollution source identification

Breakthrough Curves Characterization

The ANN model, discussed above, work on input-output relationship. The contaminant source identification in groundwater is formulated as an inverse problem by characterizing breakthrough curve (BTC) of simulated concentration as input and source fluxes as output of the model. Different ANN models were developed that differed in the manner of presenting the breakthrough curve to the input layer of ANN model.

Statistical characterization of BTC

The breakthrough curve is characterized by statistical analysis of simulated concentrations. There are five statistical parameters, which are used to characterize the breakthrough curve for generation of inputs of ANN models. These five statistical parameters are average value, maximum value, standard deviation, skewness and kurtosis. In some of the ANN models four statistical parameters are used. These four statistical parameters are mass (summation of concentrations in the breakthrough curve), average value, standard deviation and skewness.

Determination of Network Architecture

ANN architecture determines the number of connection weights (free parameters) and the way information flows through the network. Determination of appropriate network architecture (or topology) is the most important and also, the most difficult tasks in the ANN model building process. An artificial neural network learns the approximation of the desired mapping (input vector to desired output vector) by repeatedly modifying network weights. It is done using an algorithm or learning rule. The entire process is called training. In training phase known patterns are presented to the network and its weights are adjusted to produce required outputs. Then, in the testing or recognition phase, the patterns are again presented to the network and it produces the outputs based on the weights fixed during the training phase. The time spend on calculating weights in training mode is much longer than the time required running the finalized neural network in the recognition or testing mode.

Choosing a successful network geometry is highly problem dependent. Network inputs and outputs are the inputs and outputs of the problem considered. The number of hidden layers and the number of nodes in hidden layer are to be selected on the basis of experimentation in the training phase. For a specified performance with specified number of hidden layer and hidden node training algorithm iterates in different number of epochs.

Performance Criteria

The performance of the developed methodology is evaluated by estimation of normalized error (NE) necessary to define the criteria by which performance is evaluated. To judge the predictive accuracy, the following statistical parameter is used for quantifying the errors. The NE, which is a measure of the methodology performance, is defined as:

$$NE = \frac{\sum |X_0 - X_i|}{\sum X_0} \tag{3}$$

where X_0=actual value and X_i = model predicted value. NE value indicates the performance of the developed methodology for source identification.

5   Illustrative Application of the Developed Methodology

The performance of the methodology is evaluated for a study area with varying numbers of locations of observation wells, and pollution sources (Fig.2). A ten-year time domain divided into forty equal time steps is considered. The sources are assumed to release the pollutant in the aquifers during the first five years of the ten-year time domain. It is further assumed that the source releases the pollutants into the aquifer at a constant rate during one year.

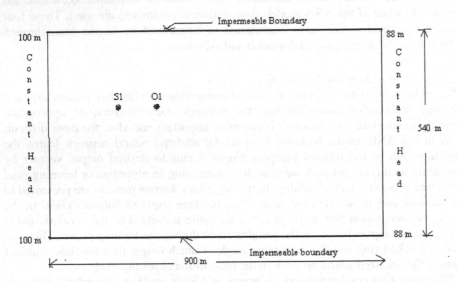

Fig. 2. Study area showing for performance evaluation of methodology

Table 1. Flow and transport parameter values used for simulating observed data for Scenario 1 and Scenario 2

Parameter	Value
Kxx (m/s)	0.0001
Kyy (m/s)	0.0001
ε	0.20
αL(m)	30.5
αT(m)	12.2
b (m)	30.5
Δx(m)	91.5
Δy(m)	91.5
Δt(month)	3

Table 2. Source flux values used for simulating observed data for Scenario 1

Source fluxes1 at S1	
Year 1	48.8
Year 2	0.0
Year 3	10.0
Year 4	42.0
Year 5	36.0

1Unit of source flux is in grams per second (g/s)

The illustrative application of the methodology assumes that the solute is conservative, and that gradients of fluid density, viscosity, and temperature do not affect the velocity distribution. The groundwater system is assumed to be with steady state flow and transient transport condition. ANN models are developed utilizing 100 patterns. More or less than 100 patterns, may be utilized in this scenario. The finite difference grid size and aquifer parameter values are given in Table 1 and Table 2 respectively.

6   ANN Model and Results

A simple scenario of single potential sources (1-potential sources) and one observation well is considered. For development of ANN based model, the source fluxes magnitudes (500 in numbers) are generated randomly between specified ranges for the potential location. These source fluxes are utilized to perform 100 simulations. Taking each time 5 source fluxes that represent five years of individual active period respectively, the flow and transport simulation model, MOC, is utilized for these simulations. Each simulated breakthrough curve is characterized by five statistical parameters i.e. maximum value, average value, standard deviation, skewness and kurtosis. These five statistical parameters are used as input for development of ANN model to predict source fluxes. The developed ANN methodology is applied to identify contaminant source location in two scenarios. Total data sets are partitioned into training set and testing set. The 70% of total data sets is used for training and 30% for testing. All the data sets are scaled into range (0; 1).

To determine an efficient architecture for the ANN model, a number of experiments were performed with different network architectures with varying numbers of hidden layers and nodes. In the course of experimentation, it was observed that single hidden layer architectures lacked generalization ability when applied to identification problem. In earlier work [11] also, it was observed that a network with two hidden layers performed better than the network with single hidden layer. Better performance with two hidden layers may be due to the complexity and nonlinearity involved in mapping of the input to the output of the problem.

The network with 5 input values, 5 target values per pattern and 5 neurons in each of the first and second hidden layers represented as 5-5-5-5 performed better for ANN

Model. This choice is based on the evaluation results for different architectures of the ANN models as shown in Table 3. It is evident that both for the training and testing mode, this architecture performs better. NE is 18% in training and 23 % in testing. Plot for error versus number of iteration obtained by ANN Model 5-5-5-5 is shown in Fig.3.

Table 3. Performance evaluations during the Training and Testing for ANN Model

ANN Models	Normalized Error (%)	
	Training	Testing
5-5-4-5	19	25
5-5-5-5	18	23
5-5-6-5	19	39
5-5-7-5	19	23

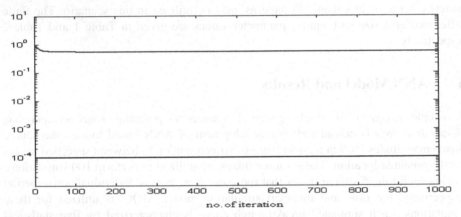

Fig. 3. Plot Error versus Number of Iteration for the ANN Model 5-5-5-5

Embedded optimization technique used seven observation well compared to only four in this study [28]. Singh et al. (2004) used 160 inputs (40 concentration measurement values at each observation wells) in ANN based methodology [11]. This work employed characterization of breakthrough curve instead of using the complete breakthrough curve to reduce the inputs. Total number of inputs reduced to 16 by the characterization. Though NE value in this study is slightly higher compared to earlier methods, but it considerably reduces the dimensionality of the problem.

7   Conclusions

Methodology based on ANN techniques are employed for unknown source identification in groundwater system. Identification results establish potential applicability of complex problem of source identification in groundwater sources. The evaluations carried out in this study are certainly not extensive. One limitation of our study is that the effects of parameter uncertainty are not addressed. The methodologies developed are applied to homogenous confined aquifer only. Also, steady state flow and transient contaminant transport conditions are assumed. A typical conservative pollutant from point sources is assumed to be responsible for the observed contamination. The proposed methodology may be extended to real life situations for complex groundwater systems considering heterogeneity of the medium and parameter uncertainties in the flow and transport parameters.

References

1. Atmadja, J., Bagtzoglou, A.C.: Pollution source identification in heterogeneous porous media. Water Resour. Resear. 37, 2113 (2001)
2. Liu, C., Ball, W.P.: Application of inverse methods to contaminant source identification from aquitard diffusion profiles at Dover AFB, Delaware. Water Resour. Res. 35, 1975–1985 (1999)
3. Gorelick, S.M., Evans, B., Remson, I.: Identifying sources of groundwater pollution: An optimization approach. Water Resour. Res. 19, 779–790 (1983)
4. Wagner, B.J.: Simultaneous parameter estimation and contaminant source characterization for coupled groundwater flow and contaminant transport modeling. J. of Hydrol. 135, 275–303 (1992)
5. Skaggs, T.H., Kabala, Z.H.: Recovering the release history of a groundwater contaminant plume: Method of quasi-reversibility. Water Resour. Res. 31, 2669–2673 (1995)
6. Skaggs, T.H., Kabala, Z.H.: Limitations in recovering the history of a groundwater contaminant plume. J. Contam. Hydrol. 33, 347–359 (1998)
7. Woodbury, A.D., Ulrych, T.J.: Minimum relative entropy inversion: the release history of a groundwater contaminant. Water Resour. Res. 32, 2671–2681 (1996)
8. Woodbury, A.D., Sudicky, E., Ulrych, T.J., Ludwig, R.: Three dimensional plume source reconstruction using minimum relative entropy inversion. J. Contam. Hydrol. 32, 131–158 (1998)
9. Aral, M.M., Guan, G.: Genetic algorithms in search of groundwater pollution sources. In: Advances in Groundwater Pollution Control and Remediation, pp. 347–369. Spinger (1996)
10. Aral, M.M., Guan, J., Maslia, M.L.: Identification of contaminant source location and release history in aquifers. J. of Hydrologic Engrg. 6, 225–234 (2001)
11. Singh, R.M., Datta, B., Jain, A.: Identification of unknown groundwater pollution sources using artificial neural networks. Journal of Water Resources Planning and Management, ASCE 130(6), 506–514 (2004)
12. Sun, A.Y.: A robust geostatistical approach to contaminant source identification. Water Resour. Res. 43, 1–12 (2007)
13. Singh, R.M., Datta, B.: Artificial Neural Network Modeling for Identification of Unknown Pollution Sources in Groundwater with Partially Missing Concentration Observation Data. Water Resources Management 21(3), 557–572 (2007)
14. Chadalavada, S., Datta, B., Naidu, R.: Optimal identification of groundwater pollution sources using feedback monitoring information: a case study. Environmental Forensics 13(2), 140–153 (2012)
15. Jha, M., Datta, B.: Three-Dimensional Groundwater Contamination Source Identification Using Adaptive Simulated Annealing. J. Hydrol. Eng. 18(3), 307–317 (2013)

16. Rumelhart, D.E., Hinton, G.E., Williams, R.J.: Learning internal representation by error propagation. In: Parallel Distributed Processing, vol. 1, pp. 318–362. MIT Press, Cambridge (1986)
17. Bishop, C.M.: Neural Networks for Pattern Recognition. Oxford University Press, India (1995)
18. Hagan, M.T., Menhaj, M.B.: Training feed forward networks with the Marquaradt algorithm. IEEE Trans. Neural Netw. 6, 861–867 (1994)
19. Kisi, O.: Streamflow forecasting using different artificial neural network algorithms. J. Hydrol. Eng. 12(5), 532–539 (2007)
20. Haykin, S.: Neural networks: A comprehensive foundation, 696 p. Mac-Millan, New York (1994)
21. Bear, J.: Dynamics of Fluids in Porous Media. Dover Publication Inc., New York (1972)
22. Bear, J.: Hydraulics of Groundwater. Elsevier, New York (1979)
23. Freeze, R.A., Cherry, J.A.: Groundwater. Prentice-Hall, Inc., N.J. (1979)
24. Pinder, G.F., Bredehoeft, J.D.: Application of the digital computer for aquifer evaluations. Water Resour. Res. 4, 1069–1093 (1968)
25. Bredehoeft, J.D., Pinder, G.F.: Mass transport in flowing water. Water Resour. Res. 9, 194–210 (1973)
26. Konikow, L.F., Bredehoeft, J.D.: Computer model of two-dimensional solute transport and dispersion in groundwater. U. S. Geol. Surv. Tech. Water Resources Invest. Book 7 (1978)
27. Datta, B.: Discussion of "Identification of contaminant source location and release history in aquifers" by Mustafa M. Aral, Jiabao Guan, and Morris L. Masia. J. of Hydrologic Engineering 7, 399–401 (2002)
28. Mahar, P.S.: Optimal identification of groundwater pollution sources using embedding technique. PhD. Thesis, I.I.T., Kanpur (1995)

Stochastic Analysis for Forecasting the MW Load
of Plug-In Electric Vehicles

C.S. Indulkar[1,*] and K. Ramalingam[2,**]

[1] Indian Institute of Technology, Delhi
indulkar@ieee.org
[2] Airports Authority of India, Delhi
drramalingamk@gmail.com

Abstract. This paper proposes a Monte Carlo analysis for forecasting the MW load of plug-in electric vehicles. The method considers the number of vehicles in a city, Wh/km, km per vehicle, vehicles on chargers, and power factor of chargers. Using the Monte Carlo method, the range of the MW load is forecasted, considering the associated ranges of the various parameters and variables.

Keywords: Plug-in Electric vehicle, load forecasting, Monte Carlo method, stochastic analysis, battery chargers.

1 Introduction

Current transportation systems are heavily based on the century-old technology of internal combustion engines (ICE). Transport electrification is a necessary trend to improve efficiency, performance, and sustainability of transportation systems. A long-term transportation electrification goal is to integrate the transportation industry with the electric power industry, generate more and more electricity from carbon-free and renewable energy sources, and use such electricity in transportation.

In India, the pollution due to vehicular emissions continues to pose problems, with air quality deteriorating in major Indian cities. Both the industry and consumers are looking for viable alternatives for personal mobility and the industry seems to be laying a bet on electric vehicles (EV). EVs on Indian roads are expected to be a common sight as early as 2015. According to Ernst and Young, a mass market for the EV in India is still eight to 10 years away. The market for such cars is at a nascent stage even globally. Infrastructural issues have forever been cited as the primary reason for EVs not hitting the roads. But besides the dearth of recharge points, the ambiguity in electrical sockets, and the shortage of electricity, one of the biggest issues for the EVs, not having taken off, is their batteries. In the near future, cars altering from IC engines to plug-in hybrid vehicles (PEV) and EVs will be a major shift in personal mobility. The whole infrastructure for charging EVs will have to be

---

* Professor and Head of Electrical Engineering Department.
** Regional Executive Director (Southern Region) of the Airports Authority of India.

B.K. Panigrahi et al. (Eds.): SEMCCO 2013, Part II, LNCS 8298, pp. 237–247, 2013.
© Springer International Publishing Switzerland 2013

set-up from scratch, from public charging points to personal charging stations for individual EV owners.

Opportunities lie in manufacturing of batteries, electric motors and controllers, electric drives, and a range of electrical parts, including the wiring harness, charger and integrated circuits. Maintenance and servicing demand for these components will create several completely new lines of big business. Prices of EVs are expected to come down drastically as companies manufacturing such cars achieve economies of scale. The government has shown interest by setting up a National Mission for Hybrid and Electric cars. The government approved a Rs.230, 000 million plan to the production of electric (EV) and hybrid vehicles over the next eight years, targeting 6 million units by 2020.While some sops have already been announced, the government may, in the next couple of years, reduce taxes and duties on such non-polluting vehicles and may even provide some rebates for car owners that makes EVs very attractive to middle- class car buyers.

In [1], Alec Brooks et al describe an internet-based system for aggregating electric vehicle charging load and manage it in real time for system services. In [2], E. Ungar and K. Fell investigate the additional load impact of plug-in hybrid vehicle (PEV) electric vehicle (EV) that are expected to penetrate the market and stress the need for managed charging. Authors of [2]   forecast the impact of PEV smart charging and stress the importance of daytime charging via public chargers which is important for the commercial success of PEVs. They have also calculated   the MW load and charging projections for the "top ten" metropolitan areas in the US. In [3], a Monte Carlo simulation approach has been adopted for the derivation of the system load due to EVs based on a model representing real commuting patterns. Since the model variables are characterized by a stochastic behavior and are correlated, a multivariate distribution function has been built by means of copula function and the respective marginal empirical distributions

Plug-in Electric vehicles (PEVs) have been identified in [4]-[5] as a vital technology to reduce carbon emissions and dependence on petroleum. PEVs, either plug-in hybrid electric vehicles (PHEVs) or pure electric vehicles (EVs), adopt similar drive–train configurations as hybrid electric vehicles (HEVs), but are characterized by larger battery capacity and the capability of being recharged from the electric grid. Therefore, a portion of the energy obtained from fuel can be replaced by electricity from the power system.

The emerging fleet of PEVs in several countries will introduce a considerable amount of additional load on the power systems in future. Power consumption by electric vehicles is usually estimated based on the results of the energy calculations. There is still uncertainty [4] regarding the size and configuration of future PEVs. Some PEVs may be pure EVs, without an internal combustion engine. Others may be designed to operate initially in EV mode and then switch to a charge-sustaining mode.

In [5], a comparative study is carried out by simulating four EV charging scenarios, i.e. uncontrolled domestic charging, uncontrolled off-peak domestic charging, "smart" domestic charging and uncontrolled public charging, where the commuters are capable of recharging at the workplace. The proposed four EV charging scenarios take into account the expected future changes in the electricity tariff in the electricity market place and appropriate regulation of EV's battery charging loads. Results have shown that a 10% market penetration of EVs in the studied system [5] would increase the daily peak demand by up to 17.9%, while a 20% of EV penetration would lead to a 35.85% increase in peak load, for the scenario of uncontrolled domestic charging. The worst-case scenario is that all EVs start charging when drivers arrive home at the peak load time. Uncontrolled public charging reflects the effect of price incentives on the charging of EVs. It is a more realistic charging scenario, where smart metering and advanced communication techniques are widely used in the charging systems. Uncontrolled public charging is a more realistic charging scenario, where EV owners are able to charge both at the workplace and home.

In studies pertaining to the MW load estimation of EVs, several simplifications can be made:

- Battery chargers are assumed to charge at the same time, and the batteries are charged from the fully discharged state,
- The power demand of the battery charging loads depend on
  - ✓ the number of EVs,
  - ✓ the time of switching on/off of the EVs battery charging, and
  - ✓ the initial state-of–charge at the beginning of the charging process.

The start times and initial state-of-charge of the battery have an element of randomness, but the general driving pattern is influenced by traffic habits and by the electricity rate structure. Since all EVs do not start charging simultaneously, the time of switching on an individual charger is a random variable. It is determined by the tariff structure and the pattern of the vehicle usage. The initial state of charge of the EV battery is the residual capacity. It is assumed to be a random function of the distance travelled after its last charge.

In this paper, the Monte Carlo analysis is used to determine the MW load and the charging projections for a large metropolitan area, such as Mumbai. A penetration of EVs by 10 % of the present total vehicles is assumed to replace diesel vehicles in Mumbai. That is, about 100,000 EVs is expected in Mumbai in the next 5-8 years.

The accuracy of a load forecast due to EV penetration is crucial to any electric utility, since it dictates the timing and characteristics of major system additions. As forecast that is too low can easily result in lost revenue from sales to neighboring utilities or even in load curtailment. On the other hand, forecasts that are too high can result in severe financial problems due to an excessive investment in plant that is not fully utilized, or is operated at low capacity factors.

Demand forecasts are used to determine the capacity of generation, transmission, and distribution system additions, and energy forecasts determine the type of facilities. For example, if a demand forecast stated that 100 MW capacities is needed and a corresponding annual energy forecast stated the need for only 200,000 MWh, installation of a peaking generating unit would be sufficient, instead of a base load unit. The difference in cost between these two is often substantial.

2   Monte Carlo Analysis

In predicting the EV load by the stochastic Monte Carlo simulation, the variation of several parameters and the interaction among them can be considered straightforwardly. The Monte Carlo simulation thus provides more information on the overall calculation of the MW load due to PEV charging with simultaneous parameter variations. If the MW load, P is a function of the random variables X_1, X_2, X_3, etc; and if the sample value of each random variable were known (say $X_1=x_{11}$, $X_2=x_{12}$, $X_3=x_{13}$, etc.), then a sample value of P (say P_1) could be computed. Then if another set of sample values were chosen for the random variables, then another sample value of P could be computed. One could compute many such sample values of P. In this paper, the calculation of the PEV load is simulated on the computer for 100 trials, where for each trial, new parameter and operating variable values are chosen randomly from within a given tolerance range. Uniform probability distribution is assumed for variations in parameter and operating variables. For uniform distribution, all values have an equal chance of occurring, within the assumed tolerance range. In general, deterministic analysis makes it difficult to see which variables impact the MW load the most. However, in Monte Carlo simulation, it's easy to see the inputs that have the biggest effect on the MW load. Therefore, the normalized sensitivity analysis has also been carried out using the seed parameter values for the parameters/variables. The normalized sensitivities of the parameters are determined by increasing the seed values one at a time by 1%, and the effect of the parameter on the changed values of the MW load are calculated.

3   PEV Electrical Vehicles

The MW load depends on the number of PEVs available locally, the charging voltage, and the likelihood that the vehicle is charging. The total energy required to charge the batteries depends on the kilometers driven and the energy consumption per km by the vehicle. Two cases, as in [2], are examined: one in which the vehicles are all charged during a 12-hour-period and another in which the vehicles are all charged during an 8-hour period. It is assumed that the PEVs will be capable of charging either at Level 1, or at Level 2. Level 1 charger has specifications to operate at 120V/15-A, 0.8 power factor. Level 2 Charger has specifications to operate at 240-V/30-A, 0.9 power factor.

In this paper, the number of average kilometers driven per vehicle daily in the metropolitan area is taken as 45 km approximately. PEVs typically require 90-250 Wh/km. Energy in kWh does not provide the capability to meet the peak demand. Therefore, back-up power also needs to be considered for those times that the facility would be unavailable. Hence, energy and MW load are both considered in this paper, using Monte Carlo analysis. The data used to carry out the statistical Monte Carlo analysis is given in Table 1.

The ranges given in Table 1 are used for each parameter/variable to calculate the total PEV loads in MW in a single trial, where the sample values of each range are selected randomly using the uniform distribution, and represented by a single row of the Excel sheet. One hundred such rows are similarly calculated on the Excel sheet. The 100 rows are then sorted out and arranged so that the first row represents the lowest PEV load in MW and the hundredth row represents the highest PEV load.   The Monte Carlo analysis thus gives the expected result of the forecasted range of load power in MW, when the various parameters and variables are allowed to vary statistically.

Table 1. Data Range and Seeds for Monte Carlo Analysis

Total number of vehicles = 100000		
	Range	Seed number
Wh/km per vehicle	90-250	170
Km per vehicle	30-60	45
The hours per vehicle are calculated from kW capacity of Level 1 (or Level 2) charger		
PEVs on Level 1 chargers	20-30%	20%
Remaining PEVs, out of a total of 100,000 are on Level 2 chargers		
Input power factors of Level 1 chargers	0.8-0.9	0.85
Input power factors of Level 2 chargers	0.85-0.95	0.9

The random numbers are generated using the Data Analysis, Random Number Generation function on the Excel sheet. A "random seed" number, as shown in Table 1, is selected for each parameter (variable) within the specified range and the MW load calculated for the first row. The random seeds to develop the first row are used so that the remaining 99 rows, using uniform distribution,   can be reproduced on the Excel sheet, if necessary.

The normalized sensitivity values of MW load with respect to the vehicle parameters of Wh/km and km/vehicle respectively, as expected, are both equal to zero. The load sensitivities with respect to   power factors (PF_1 and PF_2) of Level 1 and Level 2 chargers, and with respect to the percentage of PEVs on Level 1 chargers are shown in Table 2.

Table 2. Normalised Sensitivities of MW Load with respect to Parameters / Variables

Parameters/variables	Sensitivity of parameters/variables
PF$_1$	0.055
PF$_2$	0.944
Percentage of PEV1%	-0.180

Table 3. MW Load Charging Projections for the Mumbai Area

Output Row No. of Monte Carlo analysis	Wh/km Range 90-250	km/vehicle Range 30-60	Power factor of Level 1 Chargers Range 0. 8- 0..9	Power factor of Level 2 Chargers Range 0.85-0..95	PEVs on Level 1 Chargers Range 10-30 %	Balance PEVs on Level 2 Chargers	MW load on Level 1 Charger	MW load on Level 2 Charger	Total MW Load if everyone charges	MW Load if charging is staged over 8 hours	MW Load if charging is staged over 12 hours
Seed values	170	45	0.85	0.9	20000	80000	30.6	518.4	549	68.265	45.75
1	169	53	0.85	0.85	27677	72323	42	446	488	61	41
2	212	54	0.88	0.86	28020	71980	44	446	490	61	41
3	208	55	0.86	0.87	27771	72229	40	454	495	62	41
4	213	44	0.81	0.86	25799	74201	39	458	496	62	41
5	199	32	0.89	0.86	25160	74840	38	461	499	62	42
6	206	56	0.85	0.85	23914	76086	38	515	553	69	46
7	209	59	0.84	0.93	14585	85415	23	583	606	76	50
8	148	35	0.81	0.94	14402	85598	23	583	606	76	51
9	101	43	0.85	0.95	12749	87251	18	588	607	76	51
10	224	37	0.88	0.95	11536	88464	17	590	607	76	51
11	101	58	0.90	0.95	10099	89901	16	596	612	76	51

As expected, the normalized sensitivities of the MW load with respect to the parameters- km/vehicle, and the energy consumed per km by the vehicle- are zero. The power factor of Level 2 chargers has considerable influence on the increase of MW load compared to the power factor of Level 1 chargers. If the percentage of PEVs on Level 1chargers is increased, the MW load will in fact decrease.

Table 3 gives the results of the eleven (top 5, middle 1and bottom 5) rows of the one-hundred Monte Carlo trials for the Mumbai area and for the corresponding assumed tolerance ranges for the parameters. The first five rows correspond to the lower MW loads and the last five rows correspond to the higher MW loads. The middle row corresponds to an intermediate load. The total PEVs assumed in the Mumbai area are 100,000. The table shows that the total MW load increases from the lowest value of 61 MW to the highest value of 76 MW, if charging is staged over 8 hours. If, the charging is staged over 12 hours the MW load requirement is much less and varies between 41 MW to 51 MW.

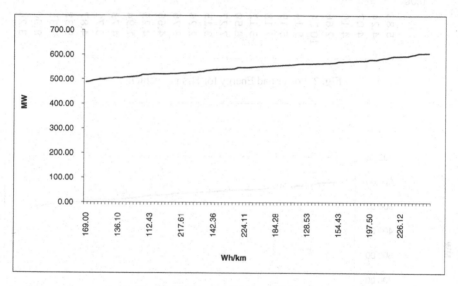

Fig. 1. MW versus Wh/km of Vehicles

Fig.1 shows the variation of MW with Wh/km. It is observed that the MW load, as expected, increases proportionally with the energy consumption per km for the vehicles. Fig.2 shows that when the total loads for 100.000 vehicles changes from minimum 488MW to maximum 607 MW, the total energy consumption changes from a minimum of 280 MWh to a maximum of 1495 MWh. This is interpreted to mean that installation of peaking generating unit would be sufficient to provide power to the EVs in Mumbai.

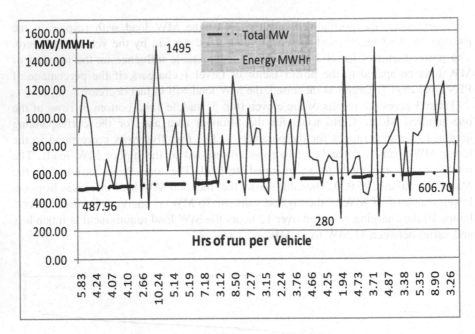

Fig. 2. Power and Energy for Hrs per vehicle

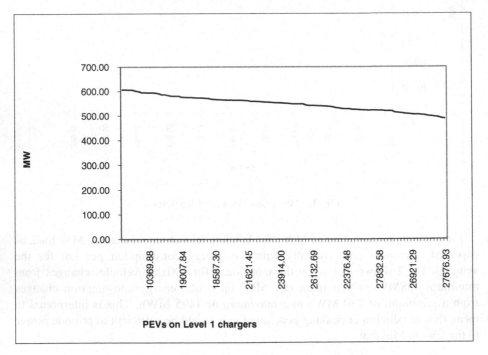

Fig. 3. MW load versus PEVs on Level 1 chargers

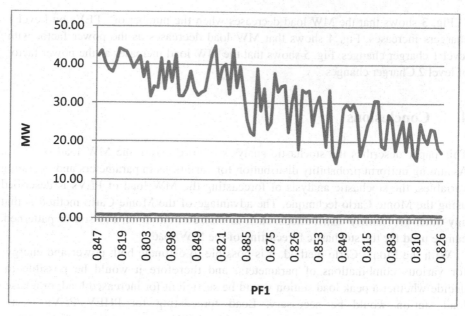

Fig. 4. MW load versus power factor of Level 1 chargers

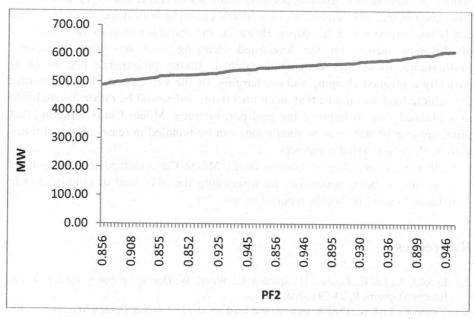

Fig. 5. MW load versus power factor of Level 2 chargers

Fig. 3 shows that the MW load decreases when the number of PEVs on Level 1 chargers increases. Fig. 4 shows that MW load decreases as the power factor with level 1 charger changes. Fig. 5 shows that the MW load increases as the power factor of level 2 Charger changes

4   Conclusions

This paper describes the stochastic analysis of forecasting the MW load of PEVs. Assuming uniform probability distribution for variations in parameters and operating variables, the stochastic analysis of forecasting the MW load of PEVs is described using the Monte Carlo technique. The advantage of the Monte Carlo method is that any other probability distributions, such as discrete, binomial, Poisson or patterned, can be used for the stochastic forecasting of the MW load.

With the Monte Carlo method, it is possible to estimate both power and energy for various combinations of parameters, and therefore it would be possible to decide whether a peak load station would be sufficient for increased load, or a base load station would be necessary. Load forecasting for PHEVs/PEVs is an interdisciplinary research of power systems and transportation sector. Forecasting mainly depends on previous statistical data [1]. Thus, one needs exact travel/tour history of each vehicle, such as accurate statistics of travel kms, type of car, day type, season, etc. The forecasting of vehicles' charging with respect to time of the day is not carried out in this paper. However, the influence of stochastic variation of different factors on the forecasted charging load has been presented. Furthermore, these days 'demand dispatch' is taking prominence [1], which is basically a planned charging and discharging, of the vehicles. In that framework, the vehicle load will not be that much uncertain, and would be rather dispatchable in a planned way to improve the grid performance. Monte Carlo solutions that often involve 10,000 or more simulations can be handled in reasonable real times with modern fast digital computers.

Further work regarding comparison of the Monte Carlo method with fuzzy logic programming is being undertaken for forecasting the MW load of plug-in electric vehicles and the results will be reported soon.

References

1. Brooks, A., Lu, E., Reicher, D., Spirakis, C., Weihl, B.: Demand dispatch. IEEE Power & Energy Magazine 8, 20–29 (2010)
2. Ungar, E., Fell, K.: Plug in, turn on, and load up. IEEE Power & Energy Magazine 8, 30–35 (2010)

3. Lojowska, A., Kurowicka, D., Papaefthymiou, G., van der Sluis, L.: Stochastic Modeling of Power Demand Due to EVs Using Copula. IEEE Trans. Power Systems 27(4), 1960–1968 (2012)
4. Wu, D., Aliprantis, D.C., Gkritza, K.: Electric Energy and Power Consumption by Light-Duty Plug-In Electric vehicles. IEEE Trans. Power Systems 26(2), 738–746 (2011)
5. Qian, K., Zhao, C., Allan, M., Yuan, Y.: Modeling of Load Demand due to EV battery charging in distribution systems. IEEE Trans. Power Systems 26(2), 802–810 (2011)

Biometric Based Personal Authentication
Using Eye Movement Tracking

Atul Dhingra[1], Amioy Kumar[2], Madasu Hanmandlu[2], and Bijaya Ketan Panigrahi[2]

[1] Netaji Subhas Institute of Technology, New Delhi, India
dhingra.atul@nsitonline.in
[2] Indian Institute of Technology, New Delhi, India
{amioy.iitd,mhmandlu,bijayaketan.panigrahi}@gmail.com

Abstract. The paper provides an insight into the newly emerging field of Eye Movement Tracking (EMT), spanning across various facets of EMT, from acquisition to authentication. The second most cardinal problem of machine learning after overfitting, i.e. Curse of Dimensionality is dealt with using a novel method of error analysis on EMT based personal authentication through a dimensionality reduction algorithm. We apply both static and dynamic methods for the dimensionality reduction in EMT to achieve promising results of personal authentication and compare these results based on speed and accuracy of both the methods. A decision tree classifier is used in two cases (static and dynamic) of EMT for the classification. The novel method presented in this paper is not limited to EMT and it can be emulated for other biometric modalities as well.

Keywords: EMT, Dimensionality Reduction, Biometrics, Authentication.

1 Introduction

Biometrics is a branch that deals in identification and authentication using traits that are unique to an individual such as fingerprint, palm print, gait etc. Biometrics in its inchoate stage was used mostly by law enforcement agencies to keep the mischief-makers of the society under surveillance by culling various biometrics trait imprints left by the criminals on the scene of crime, such as fingerprints, the gait size etc and comparing it with the annals available with the security departments. Today biometrics has transcended these boundaries and apart from handling security issues, biometric traits especially eye movement tracking are being used in a wide variety of applications which are discussed in detail in section 2.1.

Biometrics can be broadly classified into two distinct types, viz., static biometrics and behavioral biometrics. Static biometrics has been out there for long time and has been used widely for authentication in the form of iris, fingerprint, face etc. The behavioral biometrics on the other hand is a relatively newer concept, especially Eye Movement Tracking (EMT) which makes use of physiological and behavioral aspects [1], making the authentication process more secure and difficult to replicate. In this paper we will investigate Eye Movement as a means for the development of an authentication system and provide a brief overview of the myriad types of applications associated with EMT.

B.K. Panigrahi et al. (Eds.): SEMCCO 2013, Part II, LNCS 8298, pp. 248–256, 2013.

1.1   Prior Works and Motivations

One of the many scientists who started to work towards the field of EMT and emphasized the grandness of eye movements in vision and perception was Descartes (1596-1650). The first known substantial work on this field was by French ophthalmologist Emile Javal in [3] who found out that eye follows a unique pattern of fixation and saccades. Kasprowski and Ober [4] in 2004 used a 9 point jumping simulation for extracting the data from user. The features extracted such as fixation count, average fixation duration, average saccade amplitudes; average saccade velocities etc. were converted to cepstrum features during the processing stage. The substantial results from classification provided an impetus for further exploration of human eye movements. A few recent developments that have taken place in this realm are from the contribution of Holland and Komogortsev [9], who have adopted a very different philosophy of using the eye movements in conjunction with the oculomotor plant.

The recent developments in the field of EMT rallied our disposition towards taking up research work in the field. It is also due to the fact that EMT has shown multidimensional applications discussed in section 2.1, motivated us towards working in the field of EMT.

In this paper, we will be exploring both static and dynamic dimensionality reduction methods for error analysis in authentication using EMT that is explained in detail in section 5. The rest of the paper is arranged as follows: section 2 gives an overview of EMT, section 3 talks about the feature extraction and analysis, section 4 talks about dimensionality reduction and preprocessing and finally section 5 presents the experiment and results performed on various datasets used in this experiment.

2   Eye Movement Tracking

When a user looks at any object, its eye follows a definite path through the entire object to register the complete image of the object. If we replace the random object with some systemized simulation, the eye follows a unique pattern, and this pattern is repeated each time when a user is presented with a similar simulation. This pattern forms the basic principle authentication using EMT works on. This pattern constitutes of fixations and saccades constitute the EMT signal. As this pattern is obtained in a form of a signal, basic signal processing and heuristic knowledge about eye movements can be cashed in to extract meaningful features.

2.1   Personal Authentication Using EMT

For a typical authentication process, the cardinal and foremost step is data acquisition. The accuracy to which a dataset is acquired decides the consequent performance indices at the time of classification. The dataset collation process for Eye Movement is done using tracking the eye movement in response to the simulation process which can be broadly classified into two different categories, Static and Dynamic simulation, which are presented to the user depending upon the user end application. The most commonly used simulation techniques are Jumping Point Simulation (dynamic) which constitutes a grid generally of 3x3, i.e. a 9- point simulation where each point defines the position the jumping point can take. The user has to follow the jumping point for the duration of simulation which varies according to the device used for the acquisition. The disadvantage of this method is that the user has no free will and he/she moves his/her eyes in response to the stimulus of the jumping point. This leads to losing all the information from brain and thereby nullifying the feature that makes EMT stand out from rest of the prevalent biometric modalities. The method that nullifies this disadvantage of jumping point simulation is text simulation (static). In this technique a text is presented to the user, which is read with a free will, there is no restriction on the eye to follow any particular simulation pattern, and hence this is a much better technique for simulation as compared to the jumping point simulation from the point of involvement of the brain activity into the simulation process. But it has its own drawback that it can introduce Learning Effect [1]. This problem can be solved by presenting different text to the user every time a simulation is taking place, but care should be taken such that the different text presented should be of the same difficulty level so that the number of saccade and fixations the eye follows doesn't change drastically, and the authentication can follow. Choice of the simulation depends upon the type of application, jumping point simulation being the preferred choice in the case of authentication using EMT.

After extracting features from the signal, classification processes follows to classify the new sample to its respective class. There are many classifiers like k-nearest neighbor, SVM, Bayes, neural networks etc. which can be used to perform the classification. We have made use of decision tree classifier for this experiment. It is a non-metric method and gives a set of rules on the basis of heuristics that can be understood better. Finally the efficiency of the authentication process is calculated in terms of performance metrics like FAR, FRR and HTER.

2.2   EMT versus Iris Authentication

Iris as a biometric trait is one of the mostly accepted and used biometric traits. Iris acquisition is done manually most of the times as one of the major challenges of automated iris recognition is to capture a high-quality image of the iris while remaining harmless to the individuals. Iris images must be acquired with sufficient resolution and sharpness in order to support recognition. These images should have good contrast in the interior iris pattern without glaring the eye of the individual. In the manual procedure, the user needs to adjust the camera to get the iris in focus and needs to be within six to twelve inches of the camera. Moreover, iris is a fallacious trait which can be replicated with ease using either 3D representation of iris or coercing an unconscious or for the matter of fact, a dead person.

On the contrary Eye Movement Acquisition is a robust method, where authentication cannot be done unless a person is fully conscious. Even effects of alcohol have been proved to affect eye movements. Therefore coercion or drugging a person to gain access is also unachievable. For authentication using EMT we just need sensors to sense the eye movements in response to the simulation presented to the user. The output is obtained in the form of signal representing the path followed by the eye. EMT stands out as a better authentication technique and a lot of work is still to be done before it replaces the current technologies in authentication.

2.3   Why EMT?

EMT is a highly robust method for authentication as it not only depends on the physiological aspects but the behavioral aspects as well. The latter are more difficult to forge as to replicate the brain to produce the same effect in accordance to the eye movements is highly inaccurate with the present knowledge of neural networks available. EMT apart from authentication also has myriad applications, some of which include: (i) Eye-Password [2] based security applications, (ii) providing an alternative communication means to patients; one such system uses Touch Free Computing [5], (iii) lie detection, as the eye movement is directly linked to the brain's response because any fluctuation in the brain activity would reflect the eye movements, (iv) WWW pages [6], where a thermal plot is created depicting the area that has a high density of fixations during the test run by users and help them to strategically place the links at the position of high fixations to draw attention to the users and (v) liveliness detection. Note that better lie detectors could be formed using the fact that there is a change in brain activity and hence the eye movements when a person is telling a lie and it would be very difficult for a person to sham both physical (eye movements) and brain activities associated with it simultaneously.

3   Feature Extraction and Tools Used

In this section, we will present different types of features and talk about the classification process that is required for any authentication process.

3.1   EMT Features

Unlike common metrics like Iris, where we can extract the features using Gabor filter, in the case of EMT features we have no such privilege of specific predefined methods. For extracting the EMT features, we have to either apply heuristic knowledge with basic signal processing techniques or go in for the methods published earlier [1] - [10]. There are a total of 15 features that can be extracted and these includes: eye positions (Lx, Ly, Rx, Ry), eye velocity (V_L, V_R), angles (θ_L, θ_R), signals (S_L, S_R), eye distance (ED), and Fourier transform of both the left and the right eye for both horizontal and vertical axes. These features are now described briefly.

Eye Position: When the eye is presented with a stimulus, the eye follows a specific pattern unique to an individual. Due to this property of the eye movement, we can use the eye positions as features.

Eye Velocity: The underlining principle used in eye-position can be extended to the time-domain by taking the change of eye position with respect to the time leading to the eye velocity. This implies that eye-velocity patterns will also be unique for each user, it is given by:

$$v = \sqrt{(x_{i+1} - x_i)^2 - (y_{i+1} - y_i)^2} \tag{1}$$

where x_i and y_i are the horizontal and vertical positions of the eye at the ith instance. This is calculated both for the left (V_L) and the right (V_R) eye.

Eye Movement Direction: The direction in which the eye moves is unique, given by

$$\theta = \frac{x_{i+1} - x_i}{\sqrt{v_x^2 + v_y^2}} \times \text{sgn}(y_{i+1} - y_i) \tag{2}$$

where v_x and v_y are velocities in the horizontal and the vertical directions respectively.

Signal: The eye velocity coupled with the eye movement gives us a high potential feature. This is the ratio of the velocity to the eye movement direction at the ith instance, given by,

$$signal(\phi) = \frac{\sum_{i \in (\theta = \phi)} v_i}{\sum_{i \in (\theta = \phi)} \theta_i} \tag{3}$$

Eye Distance: This can be calculated simply as a function of the position of eye in the horizontal and the vertical directions as,

$$\text{Eye Distance} = \sqrt{(RX_i - LX_i)^2 + (RY_i - LY_i)^2} \tag{4}$$

Frequency Domain Analysis: The frequency domain analysis like Fast Fourier Transform of eye movements also provides some vital characteristics of the eye.

3.2   Classification

Classification in the field of Machine Learning is the approach that is followed to find out the class to which a new observation belongs based on the classification that is done using the test data. There are different types of algorithms which can be used to perform this task efficiently. In this paper we have focused our attention on decision tree algorithm.

4   Preprocessing

The basic aim of preprocessing is to reduce the complexity of the data by modifying the data such that the essential features of the data are retained. These features accurately represent the learning examples and predict the classes for the new examples using supervised learning algorithms. Methods used for preprocessing try to deal with problems of "Over fitting" and "Curse of Dimensionality" in machine learning applications. In the paper we focus our attention on the latter.

Dimensionality Reduction: "Curse of dimensionality" is a situation in machine learning problems which arises when the dimension of the feature vector increases enormously. In this situation, learning of a new test example by the learner becomes highly difficult computationally and intuitively. To counter this problem of machine learning, we make use of dimensionality reduction where the higher order dimensions are abridged into lower dimensions without losing any vital information. This doesn't include outlier removal which is a very different concept where in a samples is completely removed. In dimensionality reduction we represent all the information from higher dimensions into lower dimension space. For example, a million-dimension dataset can be represented accurately, say, by a few hundred- dimension dataset, but containing all the aspects of the million-dimension. In this paper we have used t-SNE algorithm [8] for the dimensionality reduction.

5   Experiments and Results

5.1   Databases

In this paper, we have focused our attention on 3 datasets for experimentation. The details of datasets are given in Table 1. The data is partitioned using data partitioning method or holdout method, where the data is divided in three-fold ratio, i.e. the training data size is three times that of the testing data. For each of the dataset, the training data set contains 15 samples as compared to the 5 samples in testing data set. The static and dynamic methods are applied after a removing the outliers based on the velocity threshold value from the dataset.

Table 1. Various database used for the experiment

Database	Total number of users	Number of samples per user
Database 1[7]	11	20
Database 2[1]	11	20
Database 3[1]	41	20

5.2   Experiments

The dataset obtained from three-fold holdout is used for the experiment where a two class classification is done on the dataset. We work with 15 different features as explained in section 3.1. Here we have used an algorithm called, t-SNE [8] to perform dimensionality reduction on the dataset in the following two ways as explained in detail below.

5.2.1   Static Dimensionality Reduction

This method is simplest form of dimensionality reduction in which features are progressively added till all the 15 features have been added to form a feature matrix with each sample containing 15 features. The classifier used in each case was decision tree. By this method, computation is reduced drastically as we focus primarily on finding the best features out of a set of features we have. The concept of dimensionality reduction that is used here is to stop adding more features whenever overall best score is obtained.

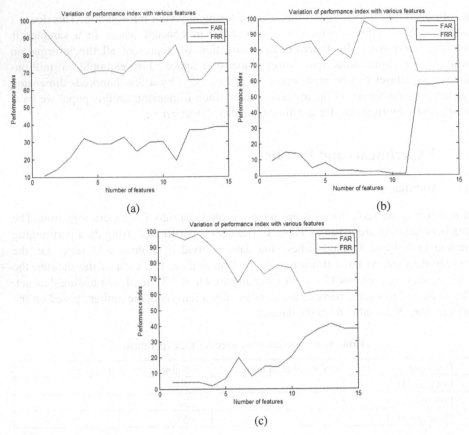

Fig. 1. Dynamic multi-class scores on (a) Database 1 (b) Database 2 and (c) Database 3

Figure 1 shows the performance index versus the number of features for the dynamic multi-class calculation performed on the three databases. A total of 15 features as discussed in Section 3.1 are used for this method. Figure 1 show how the values of these indices change as the number of features are successively added. We see that for Database 1, the optimal value of the pair (FAR, FRR) occurs at the feature number (n) = 12 and n=13 with FAR=36.72% and FRR=65.45%. For database 2, the optimal value is obtained for at n=12 and n=13 with FAR=57.27% and FRR=65.45%. For database 3, the minimum pair (FAR, FRR) is found at n=11, with FAR=32.36% and FRR=60%. The third database being the biggest of the all the databases used in this experiment shows better and more comprehensible results than the other two database with HTER=45%.

5.2.2   Dynamic Dimensionality Reduction
This method employs the dimensionality reduction using t-SNE [8] algorithm where the basic intuition behind performing the reduction is to reduce all 15 dimensions (total features) progressively that all the vital information of 15 features is well coalesced into lower dimensions. The intuition behind this method is explained in great detail in Section 4. The t-SNE algorithm is applied dynamically working on 15

dimensions and the dimensionality reduction algorithm is run iteratively, converting the given dimension into lower dimensions ranging from 14 to 2. Please note that the dimensionality reduction on the x index in Figure 2 shows the iteration number. This means index 2 on x-axis implies that dimensionality reduction is carried out from 15 to 14; whereas index 3 means that the reduction is from 15 to 13 so on and so forth.

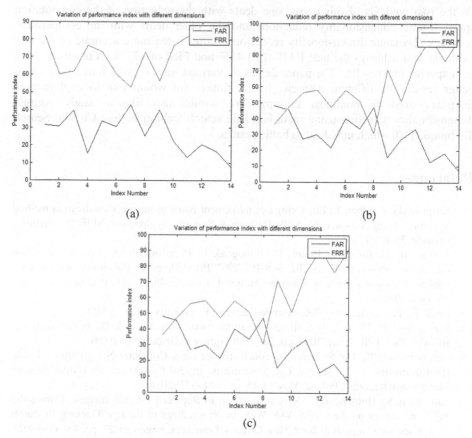

Fig. 2. Dynamic dimensionality reduction on (a) Database 1 (b) Database 2 and (c) Database 3

In Figure 2, for database 1, index (n) =2, where n=6 gives the optimal value for the pair (FAR, FRR) where FAR=30.3%, FRR=60%. This means that when the dimensionality reduction is carried out to 13 or 9 from 15, when this value is observed. Similarly, for database 2, we observe the optimal performance index (FAR, FRR) occurs at n=5, i.e., when the dimension is reduced to 10 from 15 with FAR=21.45%, FRR=47.2%. For database 3 the lowest error in terms of FAR, FRR value is observed at n=3, that when the dimensionality reduction is employed over 15 features to reduce it to 12 features that are representative of all the 15 features, such that the value of FAR=44.72%, FRR=60%.

The most promising results are obtained for the Dynamic dimensionality reduction algorithm, with dimension equal to 10 with optimal performance index, FAR=21.45%, and FRR=47.2% for database 2. This is a novel approach for the error analysis in the case of EMT, but this method is not limited to EMT and can be easily employed on other biometric modalities as well.

6   Conclusions and Future Work

Of the two methods of this paper, one deals with the reduction of the computation speed (Static dimensionality reduction) and the other deals with the computation accuracy (Dynamic dimensionality reduction). Latter is the more accurate of the two methods as it achieves the best FAR of 21.45% and FRR of 47.2% as observed from the experimental results. The paper delves on various ways by which to obtain much better results on different datasets. In the future, we would like to explore new features based on nonlinear entropy. We would also like to study optimal dimensionality reduction using meta heuristic search techniques like Cuckoo Search Technique [10] which may lead to better results.

References

1. Kasprowski, P., Ober, J.: Enhancing eye movement based biometric identification method by using voting classifier. In: SPIE Defence & Security Symposium, SPIE Proceedings, Orlando, Florida (2005)
2. Kumar, M., Garfinkel, T., Boneh, D., Winograd, T.: Reducing Shoulder-surfing by Using Gaze-based Password Entry. In: SOUPS 2007 Proceedings of the 3rd Symposium on Usable Privacy and Security, Carnegie Mellon University, Pittsburgh, PA, July 18-20, pp. 13–19 (2007)
3. Javal, É.: Physiologie de la lecture et de l'écriture Paris, Félix Alcan (1905)
4. Kasprowski, P., Ober, J.: Eye Movements in Biometrics. In: Maltoni, D., Jain, A.K. (eds.) BioAW 2004. LNCS, vol. 3087, pp. 248–258. Springer, Heidelberg (2004)
5. Lewandowski, T.: The System of a Touch free Personal Computer Navigation by Using the Information on the Human Eye Movements. In: 3rd Conference on Human System Interactions, Rzeszów, Poland, May 13-15, pp. 674–677 (2010)
6. Josephson, S., Holmes, M.E.: Visual Attention to Repeated Internet Images: Testing the Scanpath Theory on the World Wide Web. In: Proceedings of the Eye Tracking Research & Application Symposium 2002, New Orleans, Louisiana, March 25-27, pp. 43–49 (2002)
7. Kasprowski, P., Ober, J.: Eye Movement in Biometrics. In: Proceedings of Biometric Authentication Workshop, European Conference on Computer Vision in Prague, The IEEE/IARP International Conference on Biometrics (ICB) (2004)
8. van der Maaten, L.J.P., Hinton, G.E.: Visualizing High-Dimensional Data Using t-SNE. Journal of Machine Learning Research 9, 2579–2605 (2008)
9. Holland, C., Komogortsev, O.V.: Biometric Identification via Eye Movement Scan paths in Reading. In: International Joint Conference on Biometrics (IJCB), October 11-13, Washington, DC, pp. 1–8 (2011)
10. Panda, R., Agrawal, S., Bhuyan, S.: Edge Magnitude based Multilevel Thresholding using Cuckoo Search Technique. Expert Systems with Applications 40(18), 7617–7628 (2013)

Accelerated Simulation of Membrane Computing to Solve the N-queens Problem on Multi-core

Ali Maroosi and Ravie Chandren Muniyandi

Research Center for Software Technology and Management,
Faculty of Information Science and Technology, University Kebangsaan Malaysia, Malaysia
ali.maroosi@gmail.com, ravie@ftsm.ukm.my

Abstract. Membrane computing or P Systems are distributed and parallel computing device that inspired their computation from cell biology. In this study, a new model of membrane computing with active membranes is defined for solving the N-queens problem. The model contains two membranes, but the inclusion of several objects and rules within each membrane. This model increases the parallelism of previous Membrane computing with active membranes because several rules can evolve concurrently and more than one queen can be exchanged during each step. Number of communication rules are also decreased. Communication rules decrease speed on multi-core processing because communications and synchronizations between threads and cores that are necessary for communication rules are very time consuming process. Multi-core processing is used to exploit the parallelism of membrane computing for solving N-queens problem.

Keywords: active membrane systems, membrane computing, multi-core processing, N-queens.

1   Introduction

The N-queens problem is applied in different fields of study, such as parallel memory storage approaches, image processing, physical and chemical studies as well as networks [1]. The N-queens problem is classified as a non-deterministic polynomial (NP) class problem, which is intractable for large N values. The goal when solving the N-queens problem is placing N-queens on an N × N board so no queen threatens other queens using standard chess queen moves, while no more than one queen should be in the same column, row, ascending diagonal, or descending diagonal.

Membrane computing [2] is a theoretical method inspired by the way livings cells work, which facilitates the production of computational models of real-life problems. Membrane computing is an extension of molecular computing, which zooms out from the molecular level and focuses on other parts of the cell, as found in distributed systems. Several membrane computing variants have been reported in the literature, which vary in the way cells are created and dissolved, how rules are applied, the distribution of cells, etc.

B.K. Panigrahi et al. (Eds.): SEMCCO 2013, Part II, LNCS 8298, pp. 257–267, 2013.

An important application of membrane computing models is solving computationally intensive problems in polynomial or even linear time [3,4]. Membrane computing often trades the execution time for a large amount of space when solving these complicated problems. The main components of membrane computing are as follows: (i) the membrane structure, which delimits the compartments where (ii) multi-sets of objects evolve according to (iii) biochemically inspired rules. The rules process the objects and membranes [5]. There are cell-like, tissue-like, and spiking-like membrane systems [6–8], which process the multi-sets in compartments defined by membranes. Several simulators have also been proposed for implementing membrane computing [9–11]. Cell-like Membrane computing are divided into active, probabilistic, and stochastic membrane systems. In this study, a membrane computing with active membranes was used to develop the proposed model.

The N-queens problem has been modeled in the membrane computing framework with active membranes. The first study of the N-queens problem using membrane computing was introduced by Gutierrez-Naranjo et al. who applied it to a 4-queens problem that included 65536 elementary membranes [12]. Depth-first search was later introduced into membrane computing by Gutierrez-Naranjo et al. [13] who used it to solve the N-queens problem. Gutierrez-Naranjo et al. [14] improved the speed of solving the N-queens problem by using membrane computing as a local search strategy.

In this study, a new membrane computing with active membranes is defined to solve the N-queens problem. The proposed active membranes system is an improvement on previous approaches because it decreases the number of unnecessary communication rules and membranes. The number of rules that can be evolved simultaneously during each step is also increased in the proposed model, which makes this active membranes model suitable for parallel implementation.

2   Active Membrane Systems

Active membrane systems have different elements (Fig. 1), including skin membranes and delimiting regions where multiple sets of objects (chemical substances) and sets of evolution rules (reactions) are placed.

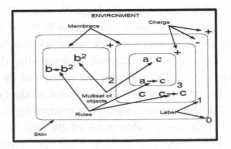

Fig. 1. Membrane structure

Active membrane systems are defined formally as a tuple $\pi = (O, H, \mu, w_1, ..., w_m, R)$, where:

(1) $m \geq 1$ (the initial degree of the system, which is equal to the number of membranes present in the system initially);

(2) O is the alphabet of objects;

(3) H is a finite set of membrane labels;

(4) μ is a membrane structure that comprises m membranes with initially neutral polarizations, with labels from H;

(5) $w_1, . . . , w_m$ are the strings over O, which describe the multi-sets of objects placed in the m regions of μ;

(6) R is a finite set of rules, which are defined as follows:

> (a) Object evolution rules: $[a \rightarrow u]_h^\alpha$ for $h \in H$, $\alpha \in \{+,-, 0\}$ (electrical charges), $a \in O$ and u is a string over O that describes a multi-set of objects associated with membranes, which depends on the label and the charge in the membranes;

> (b) "In" communication rules: $a[]_h^\alpha \rightarrow [b]_h^\beta$ for $h \in H$, $\alpha, \beta \in \{+,-, 0\}$, $a, b \in O$. An object is introduced into the membrane and possibly modified, where the initial charge α is changed to β;

> (c) "Out" communication rules: $[a]_h^\alpha \rightarrow []_h^\beta b$ for $h \in H$, $\alpha, \beta \in \{+,-, 0\}$, $a, b \in O$. An object is released from the membrane and possibly modified, where the initial charge α is changed to β;

> (d) Dissolving rules: $[a]_h^\alpha \rightarrow b$ for $h \in H$, $\alpha \in \{+,-, 0\}$, $a, b \in O$. The object a dissolves the membrane h and moves to the surrounding region as object b. All of the remaining objects in h also move to the surrounding region.

> (e) Division rules: $[a]_h^\alpha \rightarrow [b]_h^\beta [c]_h^\gamma$ for $h \in H$, $\alpha, \beta, \gamma \in \{+,-, 0\}$, $a, b, c \in O$. A membrane is divided into two membranes. The objects inside the membrane are replicated, except for a, which may be modified in each membrane.

These rules are applied according to the following principles.

All rules are applied in a maximally parallel manner (during each step, all objects that can evolve should evolve) or, more specifically, one membrane object is used by one rule (chosen in a non-deterministic way) at most during each step. However, any object that evolves under any one rule must evolve during one step. Rules (b) to (e) cannot be applied simultaneously in a membrane during one computation step. The rules associated with the membranes labeled with h are applied to the membranes with that label. Further information about active membranes systems has been described by Paun [9].

3   Proposed Active Membrane System for the N-queens Problem

Based on the definition of active membrane systems given in Section II, our model for $\pi = (O, H, \mu, w_1, ..., w_m, R)$ is as follows.

-The degree of our system is $m = 2$.

-The alphabet of objects for the N-queens puzzle is as follows: $O = \{R_1,..., R_N, C_1,....., C_N, u_{-N+1},..., u_{N-1}, d_2,..., d_{2N-1}\}$, where $R_i; i = 1,..., N$ represent the rows on the $N \times N$ board, $C_j; j = 1,..., N$ represent the columns on the board, $d_q; q = 2,...,2N$, and $u_p; p = -N+1,..., N-1$ are the ascending and descending diagonals of the $N \times N$ puzzle board.

-The label of the model is $H = \{1,2\}$ and the initial membrane structure is a membrane with two compartments $\mu = [[]_2^0]_1^0$ and zero polarizations.

-The initial multi-sets are $w_1 = \{D_{cnt(q)} \ U_{cnt(p)} \mid q = 2,...,2N, p = -N+1,..., N+1\}$, where $D_{cnt(q)}$ s($U_{cnt(p)}$)s are the counters used to count the number of descending (or ascending) diagonals that are present in the skin, which are equal to zero in the initial state. In the initial state, the objects that represent the rows and columns occur in the membrane with label 2. Thus, $w_2 = \{R_1,..., R_N, C_1,....., C_N\}$.

The set of rules are as follows.

(a) $[R_i \ C_j \rightarrow R_i.C_j]_2^0$;$i = 1,....,N, j = 1,...,N$

where R_i is the object for the ith row on the board, C_j is the object for the jth column on the board, and $R_i.C_j$ are multi-sets of objects, which show that a queen is located in the ith row and the jth column or square (i,j) on the board. First, R_i s (rows on the board) reacts with C_j s (columns on the board) and produces $R_i.C_j$ s (the squares (i, j) where the queens are located). Rule (a) is executed in a maximally parallel manner. In one step, one object of a membrane is used by at most one rule (chosen in a non-deterministic manner), but any object that evolves via any one rule must evolve. Therefore, each of the two objects produced (for example, $R_i.C_j$ and $R_k.C_s$) by rule (a) cannot be the same, i.e., $i \neq k$ and $j \neq s$. This result indicates that the queens do not intersect in the rows ($i \neq k$) and columns ($j \neq s$), and that this property prevails during the simulation period.

(b) $[R_i.C_j]_2^0 \rightarrow []_2^0 R_i.C_j \ u_{i-j} \ d_{i+j} + D_{cnt(i+j)} \ +U_{cnt(i-j)};$
     $i = 1,....,N, j = 1,...,N$

Rule (b) sends out objects $R_i.C_j$ from membrane two to the skin membrane and generates objects u_{i-j} and d_{i+j}, which represent the ascending and descending diagonals related to square (i, j), and increases counters $D_{cnt(q)}$ and $U_{cnt(p)}$. The counters $D_{cnt(q)}$ where $q = i + j$ and $U_{cnt(p)}$ where $p = i - j$ in the skin membrane count the number of queens present in the qth descending diagonal and the pth ascending diagonal, respectively. These counters are used to calculate the decrease in the number of collisions when a queen is removed from square (i, j) and the increase in the number of collisions when a queen is placed on square (i, j). The total number of collisions on the board is the number of queens present in the ascending diagonal, with more than one queen, plus the number of queens that exist in the descending diagonal, with more than one queen. Therefore, the reduction in the number of collisions when a queen is removed from (i, j) is as follows:

$$colli_{Re\,moved}(R_i.C_j) = \begin{cases} 2 & (D_{cnt(i+j)} > 1) \text{ and } (U_{cnt(i-j)} > 1) \\ 1 & (D_{cnt(i+j)} > 1) \text{ or } (U_{cnt(i-j)} > 1) \\ 0 & (D_{cnt(i+j)} \leq 1) \text{ and } (U_{cnt(i-j)} \leq 1) \end{cases}.$$

When a queen is placed in the new square (i, j), the following intersection is added on the board:

$$colli_{Placed}(R_i.C_j) = \begin{cases} 2 & (D_{cnt(i+j)} > 0) \text{ and } (U_{cnt(i-j)} > 0) \\ 1 & (D_{cnt(i+j)} = 0) \text{ or } (U_{cnt(i-j)} = 0) \\ 0 & (D_{cnt(i+j)} = 0) \text{ and } (U_{cnt(i-j)} = 0) \end{cases}.$$

Thus, no intersection is added on the board when a queen is placed in a square with no queen in the diagonals.

(c) $[R_i.C_j \ u_{i-j} \ d_{i+j} \ R_k.C_s \ u_{k-s} \ d_{k+s} \ D_{cnt(i+j)} \ U_{cnt(i-j)}$
$D_{cnt(k+s)} \ U_{cnt(k-s)} \ D_{cnt(i+s)} \ U_{cnt(i-s)} \ D_{cnt(k+j)} \ U_{cnt(k-j)} \rightarrow$
$R_i.C_s \ u_{i-s} \ d_{i+s} \ R_k.C_j \ u_{k-j} \ d_{k+j} \ -D_{cnt(i+j)} \ -U_{cnt(i-j)}$
$-D_{cnt(k+s)} \ -U_{cnt(k-s)} \ +D_{cnt(i+s)} \ +U_{cnt(i-s)} \ +D_{cnt(k+j)}$
$+U_{cnt(k-j)}]_1^+$;

for $i, j, k, s \in \{1,....,N\}, i \neq k$ and $Colli_{Removed}(R_i.C_j) + Colli_{Removed}(R_k.C_s) \geq Colli_{Placed}(R_i.C_s) + Colli_{Placed}(R_k.C_j)$.

Rule (c) allows any possible exchanges (i, j) and (k, s) during each execution time step. According to the principles of membrane computing, one object on a membrane is used by a maximum of one rule, i.e., each object u_q (ascending diagonal) and d_q (descending diagonal) is used by only one rule (exchange). Thus, one exchange does not affect other exchanges. The definition of this new active membrane structure and the use of membrane computing principles means that more than one exchange can be performed during each step, so one exchange does not affect other exchanges. This rule consumes $R_i.C_j$, u_{i-j}, d_{i+j}, $R_k.C_s$, u_{k-s}, and d_{k+s} objects, and produces $R_i.C_s$, u_{i-s}, d_{i+s}, $R_k.C_j$, u_{k-j}, and d_{k+j}. The value of $D_{cnt(q)}$ changes with this rule and reduced $(-D_{cnt(q)})$ when a queen is removed from the square (i,s) where $q = i + j$ and increases $(+D_{cnt(q)})$ when a queen is added to square (i,s) where $q = i + s$.

Similar changes are also observed for U-counters. Rule (c) is executed when the number of reduced collisions exceeds the added collisions when exchanging (i,j) and (k,s).

(d) $[D_{cnt(2)},.....,D_{cnt(2N)},U_{cnt(-N+1)},.....,U_{cnt(N+1)}]_1^+ \rightarrow []_1^-$ $yes;$

  If all $D_{cnt(q)} \leq 1$ and $U_{cnt(p)} \leq 1; q = 2,...,2N,$

  $p = -N + 1,...,N + 1.$

Rule (d) sends "yes" (solved queen) to the environment and changes the polarization of the membrane to $(-)$, which stops the execution of all other rules. This rule executes when all of the ascending and descending diagonal queen counters are equal or less than one ($D_{cnt(q)} \leq 1, U_{cnt(p)} \leq 1$), which means that there are no collisions in the ascending and descending diagonals. According to rule (a), the queens have no collisions in the rows and columns. Thus, we solve the N-queens problem when rule (d) is executed.

(e) $[Cnt_{restart}]_1^+ \rightarrow [+Cnt_{restart}]_1^+;$ if for all $i, j, k, s \in \{1,.....,N\},$

  $i \neq k$ and $Colli_{Removed}(R_i.C_j) + Colli_{Removed}(R_k.C_s) \leq$

  $Colli_{Placed}(R_i.C_s) + Colli_{Placed}(R_k.C_j).$

Rule (e) counts the number of steps when there are no improvements on the board. During these steps, the number of collisions added to the board is greater than or equal to the number of collisions removed from the board by all possible exchanges. In this situation, counter $Cnt_{restart}$ increases. This counter is used to restart the membrane computing model in rule (f).

(f) $[Cnt_{restart}]_1^+ \rightarrow []_1^-$ $restart;$if $Cnt_{restart} = User\_Const$

When the counter $Cnt_{restart}$ reaches $User\_Const$, rule (f) restarts the model, where $User\_Const$ is a constant number, which is determined by the user and the optimum number obtained experimentally (we obtained $User\_Const = 5$ in our experiment). This indicates that the membrane system should be restarted after a certain number of unsuccessful steps to resolve and reduce conflicts on the board. According to rule (f), if there are collisions on the board (the model cannot solve the problem until this point) but there is no exchange to improve the collisions on the N × N board using rule (*c*), we restart our membrane model by re-initialization. Rule (*a*) is executed in the initial state and assigns queens non-deterministically to squares in the initial state. Thus, each time that the membrane model is restarted, it is initialized with a new assignment by rule (a).

4   Simulations and Results

4.1   Simulation of the New Active Membrane System

In this section, we report the results of the simulations using the proposed membrane computing model of the N-queens membrane. The previous approach described in [14] used several different membranes and each membrane contained only one object. Thus, each membrane lacked sufficient parallelism and several communication rules were executed between the membranes.

First, the communications between two membranes occurs in the skin, followed by those from the skin to the destination membrane. This process reduced the execution speed in previous approaches. Our new active membrane system has fewer membranes and there are several objects within each membrane. This process reduces the number of communication rules between membranes and increases the execution speed. The speed of finding a solution to the N-queens problem with different numbers of queens on one processor unit in a sequential manner is compared in the following sections, where the time required for restarting was also recorded. These simulations were conducted on a computer using a one-processor Intel core i5 (with two cores at 2.45 GHz) with 4 GB of RAM running a Visual C++ program. The previous simulations were conducted on different machines. The simulations in [13] and [14] were conducted on a computer with an Intel Pentium dual CPU E2200 at 2.20 GHz with 3 GB of RAM. The approximate times in previous studies were compared with the times on our computer (Intel core i5, 2.45 GHz).

We ran the programming code for the approach described in [14] on our computer to make a comparison.

The initial state of our simulations was random and the natural state of membrane systems (when applying the rules) was non-deterministic. Thus, 100 runs were conducted for each N during our simulations and the average simulation time was recorded. Table 1 shows that the proposed active membranes system was faster than [14]. The method in [13] with N = 20 took 5796 s whereas our method had a simulation time of 0.0045 s with N = 20. In some cases, such as N = 200, our model was almost 1000 times faster than the previous approaches Table 1 shows comparisons between our approach and previous approach.

Table 1. Comparison of the evaluation times using proposed active membrane systems and previous studies

Number of queens	Previous approach [14]		Proposed active membrane system	
	Average number of steps	Average time (s) afte programming [14] on our computer	Average number of steps	Average time (s)
10	141.35	0.0074	13.62	0.0042
20	166.25	0.061	11.79	0.0077
30	270.9	0.282	10.16	0.0123
40	272.7	0.642	9.14	0.0200
50	382.4	1.793	9.00	0.0291
60	453.8	3.623	9.05	0.0405
70	495.45	6.27	8.78	0.0525
80	637.6	12.11	8.29	0.0656
90	625	17.87	8.2	0.0804
100	757.6	30.21	8.15	0.1005
110	745.75	42.25	7.92	0.1213
120	841.75	58.63	7.90	0.1390
130	891.25	80.16	7.90	0.1614
140	983.7	115.5	7.60	0.1875
150	979.75	142.3	7.58	0.2130
160	1093	200.6	7.53	0.2389
170	1145.5	251.3	7.50	0.2780
180	1206.25	323.5	7.48	0.3034
190	1272.25	404.5	7.45	0.3403
200	1365.25	530.1	7.40	0.3778
300	—	1851	7.01	0.8499
400	—	4623	7.00	1.5325
500	—	9524	7.01	2.5019

4.2   Multi-core Processing Simulation

This research increased parallelism of active membrane systems. In another words this research increased the number of rules that can be executed simultaneously in one step. This study defined new active membrane system model in which it has two membranes with a lot of objects and rules inside them that can be evolve simultaneously. Previous models had a lot of membranes with just one object inside them that these membranes should communicate each step that decreases speed of model. We used multi-core to exploit parallelism advantages of proposed active membrane system. Simulation time for one active membrane that processed on two or four cores has been shown in Table 2 and Table 3. Simulation results show that speed of proposed model respect to previous model increases when number of cores is increased. For example for N=200 speed up for new membrane system on two cores is 1.68 while for previous one that has lower parallelism is 1.12 and speed up on four cores respect to one core for new model is 3.11 while for previous approach is 1.8 times. Since proposed model also decreases unnecessary membranes and communication rules speed up of proposed model on one core 697 times faster than previous approach for N=200.

Table 2. Comparison between proposed membrane model and previous membrane model [14] on one, two cores

| | on Intel core i5, 2.45GHz with two cores | | | | | | | |
| Number of queens (N) | Previous model | | | Proposed membrane model | | | Speed up of proposed model to previous model | |
	One core (s)	Two cores (s)	Speed up on Two/one cores	One core (s)	Two cores (s)	Speed up on Two /one cores	Speed up on one core proposed/ previous	Speed up on two cores proposed/p revious
100	30.3	27	1.12	0.117	0.07	1.63	258	385
200	530	441	1.2	0.760	0.452	1.68	697	975
300	1850	1412	1.31	2.416	1.38	1.75	765	1023
400	4623	3502	1.32	5.740	3.26	1.76	805	1074
500	9524	7054	1.35	10.70	5.9	1.81	890	1195

Table 3. Comparison between proposed membrane model and previous membrane model [14] on one, four cores

Number of queens (N)	Previous membrane model			Proposed membrane model			Speed up of proposed model to previous model for four cores
	One core (s)	four cores (s)	Speed up on four/one cores	One core (s)	four cores (s)	Speed up on four/one cores	
100	21	11.4	1.8	0.082	0.026	3.11	423
200	358	170	2.1	0.514	0.153	3.36	1111
300	1300	610	2.13	1.70	0.483	3.52	1262
400	3300	1466	2.25	4.10	1.13	3.61	1297
500	5910	2558	2.31	6.65	1.83	3.63	1397

(on Intel cori7, 3.6GHz with four cores)

5   Conclusions

Besides the above mentioned styles there are more useable format specifications: This study improved parallelism of membrane computing for solving N-queens problem. In proposed model number of communication rules is decreased. Communication rules decrease speed on multi-core processing. For communication rules it is necessary to communicate between threads and cores that is very time consuming process. Several rules can also be evolved in defined model in parallel way. In some cases, our models were almost 1000 times faster than those in previous studies. Parallelism of proposed model lets us to efficiently use multi core processing for speed up the solving the problems (see Table. 2).

Acknowledgment. This work has been supported by the Fundamental Research Grant Scheme (FRGS) of the Ministry of Higher Education (Malaysia; Grant code: FRGS/1/2012/ SG05/UKM /02/3).

References

1. Bell, J., Stevens, B.: A survey of known results and research areas for n-queens. Journal of Discrete Mathematics 309, 1–31 (2009)
2. Paun, G.: A quick introduction to membrane computing. Journal of Logic and Algebraic Programming 79, 291–294 (2010)
3. Maroosi, A., Muniyandi, R.C.: Membrane Computing Inspired Genetic Algorithm on Multi-Core Processors. Journal of Computer Science 9, 264–270 (2013)
4. Gutierrez-Naranjo, M.A., Perez-Jimenez, M.J., Riscos-Nunez, A.: A linear–time Tissue P system based Solution for the 3–coloring problem. Electronic Notes in Theoretical Computer Science 171, 81–93 (2007)

5. Paun, G.: Tracing some open problems in membrane computing. Romanian Journal of Information Science and Technology 10, 303–314 (2007)
6. Ishdorj, T., Leporati, A., Pan, L., Zeng, X., Zhang, X.: Deterministic solutions to QSAT and Q3SAT by spiking neural P systems with pre-computed resources. Theoretical Computer Science 411, 2345–2358 (2010)
7. Linqiang, P., Alhazov, A.: Solving HPP and SAT by P systems with active membranes and separation rules. Acta Informatica 43, 131–145 (2006)
8. Linqiang, P., Zeng, X., Zhang, X., Jiang, Y.: Spiking neural P systems with weighted synapses. Neural Processing Letters 35, 13–27 (2012)
9. Paun, G., Rozenberg, G., Salomaa, A.: The Oxford Handbook of Membrane Computing. Oxford University Press (2010)
10. García-Quismondo, M., Gutiérrez-Escudero, R., Pérez-Hurtado, I., Pérez-Jiménez, M.J., Riscos-Núñez, A.: An overview of P-lingua 2.0. In: Păun, G., Pérez-Jiménez, M.J., Riscos-Núñez, A., Rozenberg, G., Salomaa, A. (eds.) WMC 2009. LNCS, vol. 5957, pp. 264–288. Springer, Heidelberg (2010)
11. Gutierrez-Naranjo, M.A., Perez-Jimenez, M.J., Riscos-Nunez, A.: Available membrane computing software. Applications of Membrane Computing in Natural Computing Series, pp. 411–436 (2006)
12. Gutierrez-Naranjo, M.A., Martnez-del-Amor, M.A., Perez-Hurtado, I., Perez-Jimenez, M.J.: Solving the N-queens puzzle with P systems. In: Seventh Brainstorming Week on Membrane Computing, Spain, vol. 1, pp. 199–210 (2009)
13. Gutiérrez-Naranjo, M.A., Pérez-Jiménez, M.J.: Depth-first search with P systems. In: Gheorghe, M., Hinze, T., Păun, G., Rozenberg, G., Salomaa, A. (eds.) CMC 2010. LNCS, vol. 6501, pp. 257–264. Springer, Heidelberg (2010)
14. Gutierrez-Naranjo, M.A., Perez-Jimenez, M.J.: Local search with P systems: A case study. International Journal of Natural Computing Research 2, 47–55 (2011)

A Genetic Algorithm Optimized Artificial Neural Network for the Segmentation of MR Images in Frontotemporal Dementia

R. Sheela Kumari[1], Tinu Varghese[2], C. Kesavadas[3],
N. Albert Singh[4], and P.S. Mathuranath[5]

[1] Sree Chitra Tirunal Institute for Medical Science and Technology Trivandrum, Kerala
sheela82nair@gmail.com
[2] Noorul Islam University, Kumara coil, Thuckalay, Tamilnadu
tinuannevarghese@gmail.com
[3] Department of Radiology, Sree Chitra Tirunal Institute for Medical Science and Technology,
Trivandrum, Kerala
chandkesav@yahoo.com
[4] Noorul Islam University, Kumara coil, Thuckalay, Tamilnadu
albertsingh@rediffmail.com
[5] Department of Neurology, National Institute of Mental Health and Neurosciences, Banglore
psmathu@yahoo.com

Abstract. Frontotemporal Dementia (FTD) is an early onset dementia with atrophy in frontal and temporal regions. The differential diagnosis of FTD remains challenging because of the overlapping behavioral symptoms in patients, which have considerable overlap with Alzheimer's disease (AD). Neuroimaging analysis especially Magnetic Resonance Image Imaging (MRI) has opened up a new window to identify, and track disease process and progression. In this paper, we introduce a genetic algorithm (GA) tuned Artificial Neural Network (ANN) to measure the structural changes over a period of 1year. GA is a heuristic optimization method based on the Darwin's principle of natural evolution. The longitudinal atrophy patterns obtained from the proposed approach could serve as a predictor of impending behavioral changes in FTD subjects. The performance of our computerized scheme is evaluated and compared with the ground truth information. Using the proposed approach, we have achieved an average classification accuracy of 95.5 %, 96.5% and 98% for GM, WM and CSF respectively.

Keywords: Frontotemporal Dementia (FTD), Alzheimer's disease (AD), Magnetic Resonance Imaging (MRI), Genetic algorithm (GA), Artificial Neural Network (ANN).

1 Introduction

Frontotemporal Dementia (FTD) is the second most common cause of presenile dementia [1] and has an age of onset between 35-75yrs. This disease is characterized by atrophy in the frontal and temporal regions [2]. However, behavioral disturbances are more prominent and constitute the main feature distinguishing FTD from other

B.K. Panigrahi et al. (Eds.): SEMCCO 2013, Part II, LNCS 8298, pp. 268–276, 2013.

forms of dementia. Three main syndromic variants of FTD are behavioural variant FTD (fvFTD), progressive nonfluent aphasia (PNFA), and semantic dementia (SD)[3]. Among these, behavioral variant is the commonest. Each of these clinical variants are associated with characterestic patterns of brain atrophy.

Neuroimaging analysis has broadened and extended our understanding of where and how extensively brain regions have atrophied in neurodegeneration. Although it has its own limitation including that of subjectivity, conventional visual interpretation of Magnetic Resonance Imaging (MRI) is a useful tool in supporting clinical decision making during diagnostic processes. Segmentation is the fundamental preprocessing step in which MR images are partitioned into some non-overlapping and meaningful homogenous regions[4]. The goal of MR image processing is to partition the image into grey matter (GM), white matter (WM) and Cerebrospinal fluid (CSF). The segmented images are then used to calculate separate tissue volumes and total brain volume.The GM and WM volume obtained from the segnmentation procedure can act as the predictor of neuronal loss in FTD patients. Moreover, the quantification of brain tissue volume may be of great interest in the differential diagnosis of FTD from other types of dementia.

Fuzzy C means (FCM) is the most widely used technique for the segmentation of MR images[5]. But the main drawback of FCM is that the intensity values of background and CSF are almost same. Hence, the efficiency of the algorithm is considerably reduced in the case of noisy MR images and leads to some misclassification[6,7]. In such case, segmentation methods based on artificial intelligence that, utilizes artificial neural network approaches is perhaps more accurate in tissue classification. An accurate and effective segmentation of MR images facilitates the better understanding of the disease progression.

Texture analysis is an important and active research area in machine learning. Researchers have proposed various approaches (co-occurrence matrices, wavelet based methods, Fourier transform methods, and intensity histogram methods etc) for texture feature extraction [8]. Among these, Laws Texture Energy Measures (LTEM) in texture classification has showed better performance in terms of accuracy and processing time [9]. In this paper we used LTEM for brain tissue classification.

The back propagation algorithm (BP) in ANN uses gradient descent for finding the correct node's weight combination, which results in minimization of errors in a known training data set. Hence, the efficiency depends on the initial parameter setting like varying the hidden neurons, momentum and learning rate. Also, the local minima problems in ANN can be overcome by optimized Genetic Algorithms (GAs) by locating the global maximum in a search space [10]. Some studies have employed GA [11] in combination with FCM [12] for the segmentation of MR images. But studies on the longitudinal atrophic patterns using GA guided approach are even sparse. Hence, in this study we have designed a novel revolutionary automated GA for the longitudinal assessment of atrophy rate in FTD in the clinical environment.

2   Materials and Methods

2.1   Participants

A total of 15 FTD subjects participated in this study. The Patients were selected from the Dementia Clinic of the Department Of Neurology, SCTIMST, Thiruvananthapuram,

Kerala. Written informed consent for the study, which was approved by the Ethical Committee, SCTIMST, Thiruvananthapuram, Kerala, was obtained from the caregiver. All subjects, after informed consent, were subjected to a baseline evaluation which included a clinical examination by a neurologist in the dementia clinic, a detailed neuropsychological evaluation and an MRI. The MRI and neuropsychometric assessment were repeated during the annual follow up.

2.2   MRI Imaging

The MRI imaging procedure was done in the Department of Radiology at SCTIMST. MRI scanning was performed on a 1.5 Tesla Seimens Magnetom – Avanto, SQ MRI scanner. In all subjects, structural MR images of the entire brain were obtained using a three dimensional , Flash Spoiled Gradient echo Sequence with the standard parameters TR = 11ms; TE = 4.94 ms; flip angle = 150 ; slice thickness = 1 mm; matrix size = 256x 256. The images were post processed in the well equipped Brain Mapping Unit of SCTIMST, Trivandrum.

2.3   MRI Data Preprocessing

MR image contains both cerebral and non cerebral tissues. The goal of preprocessing is to remove the noncerebral tissues such as scalp, meninges etc. Among the various preprocessing methods, skull stripping is used for removing the nonbrain tissues. Most common techniques adopted for skull stripping are region growing [13] and morphological operation [14]. Mathematical morphology has showed a supposed rate of 95.5% than region growing. Therefore, in this analysis mathematical morphology is used for skull stripping. The block diagram of the proposed methodology is shown in Fig.1.

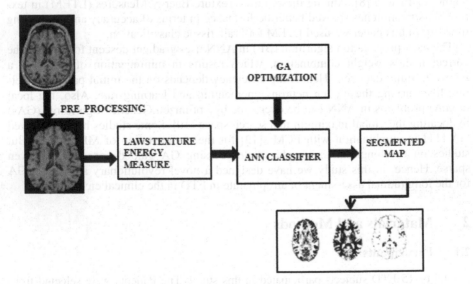

Fig. 1. Block diagram of proposed method

2.4   Texture feature Extraction

Texture feature extraction is the process in which texture features were extracted from the skull stripped MR image. The basis of texture classification is the prior knowledge of texture category in an observed image. Image texture is an important visual indicator of both spatial discrepancy and display of the central image elements. The spatial discrepancy most often visualized as gray level values and texture features have to be derived from these gray tones of the image [15]. In this analysis textural properties are derived from a 2D convolution kernel (masks). To generate the Texture Energy Measures (TEM) at each pixel, these masks are convolved with the image pixel. The texture descriptions used are level (L), edge (E), spot(S), wave (W) and ripple (R). L5 = (1, 4, 6, 4, 1), E5 = (-1, -2, 0, 2, 1), S5 = (-1, 0, 2, 0, -1), W5 = (-1, 2, 0, -2, -1), R5 = (1, -4, 6, -4, 1).

2.5   Genetic Algorithm

Genetic Algorithms (GA) are most powerful optimization technique due to its excellent global optimization ability[16]. John Holland first introduced GA in 1960s, which is based on the principles of natural selection by Charles Darwin. It is a heuristic method for finding most adaptive solution in search domain. In GA, the optimization is inculcated through the natural exchange of genetic material between parents. The evolution starts from the random selection of initial population. Then the fitness value of each individual is evaluated from the fitness function Φ (x). Based on the fitness value, multiple individuals are selected from the current population. The stochastically selected population is then modified by the genetic operation crossover and mutation.

Selection: In the selection phase, an integer Np (population size) that defines the search domain is selected on the basis of the previous knowledge. Then a decision variable xi is selected with in the limit (x_{imin}, x_{imax}) [17]. After each generation two sets of chromosomes are probabilistically chosen based on their fitness (defined in equation 4). The fitness evaluation is the key component in GA, which measures the better performance of an individual relative to others

Crossover: The two selected individuals are used for crossover. This operation produces superior offsprings by fusing parts of parent chromosomes. In crossover, new strings are formed by random selection of crossover points between the preferred individuals.

Mutation: The basic operation behind the mutation is migration. The mutation operation follows the migration operation [18] to generate a newly diverse population, which increases the search space. This can be applied by randomly flipping bits within an individual after the crossover operation. For this sake a new mutation operator is employed and created a new value x_i^G

$$x_i^{G+1} = \begin{cases} x_i^{G+1} + \rho(x_i^{min} - x_i^G), \text{if } \tau < \dfrac{x_i^{G+1} - x_i^{min}}{x_i^{max} - x_i^{min}} \\ x_i^{G+1} + \rho(x_i^{max} - x_i^G), \text{otherwise} \end{cases} \tag{1}$$

Where I = 1,2 ….n and n the total number of individuals in a population Np, τ, are ρ random numbers in the range [0, 1]. The flow chart of the working algorithm is given in Fig.2.

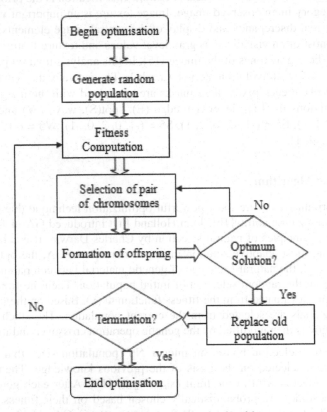

Fig. 2. Flow diagram of Genetic algorithm

3   Classification Using GA Tuned ANN

The obtained images were post – processed in the fully equipped Brain Mapping lab. Our classification approach has been to create a Genetic Algorithm tuned Artificial Neural Network (GAANN). A fully connected feed forward Neural Network has implemented the proposed algorithm. The implementation followed an optimization procedure by optimizing the factors such as the number of neurons in the hidden layer, the learning rate and the momentum factor. In this specific application a fixed and equal number of neurons are selected in the input and output layer. Let NI and NO represents the size of the neurons in the input and output layer respectively. The number of hidden layers in this problem is restricted and made as one. The range of the optimization is represented as two sets of arrays $R_{min} = \{Nh_{min}, Lr_{min}, Mc_{min}\}$ and $Rmax = \{Nh_{max}, Lr_{max}, Mc_{max}\}$ where, Nh is the number of neurons in the hidden layer, Lr is the learning rate and Mc is the momentum factor.

Let us define an activation function f, as the sum of weighted input and bias ie,

$$y_k^p = f(s_k^p), s_k^p = \sum_j w_{j_{.k}} y_j^p + \theta_k \tag{2}$$

y_k^p is the output of the kth neuron when a pattern P is fed, $w_{j,k}$ is the weight from the jth neuron and θ_k is the bias value of the kth neuron in the hidden layer and it is defined by hyperbolic tangent activation function,

$$\tanh(x) = \frac{e^x - e^{-x}}{e^x + e^{-x}} \tag{3}$$

As a result of optimal training, the Mean Square Error (MSE) is formulated as,

$$MSE = \sum_{p \in T} \sum_{k=1}^{N_o} (t_k^p - y_k^{p,o})^2 \tag{4}$$

Where t_k^p is the target output and $y_k^{p,0}$ is the actual output of the kth neuron in the output layer O, for the pattern P in the training set. GAANN algorithm utilizes the framed fitness function to evolve a better solution. All of the analysis was performed in MATLAB 7.10 framework on windows XP, which aims at developing a CAD system for the analysis of MR images in FTD in a longitudinal basis. The optimally designed ANN has a three-layer architecture: an input layer, hidden layer and an output layer. In this analysis the number of neurons in the input layer is equal to the number of feature vector extracted (25 TEM).

Our optimization analysis using GAANN classifier is performed with the learning rate and the momentum constant varied from 0 to 1. The crossover and mutation probability of the GA is selected as 0.5 and 0.01 respectively. For this training a maximum of 100 generations is performed with a population size of 50. During each GAANN generation, the best fitness score (minimum MSE) achieved by the population at the optimum dimension is stored. Hence the proposed algorithm was used to generate an optimized ANN with the parameters Nh = 143, Lr = 0.5882 and Mc = 0.9989.

4 Results and Discussions

The proposed method evolved a GAANN classifier for the segmentation of MR images in FTD subjects. A feed forward network was set up with a backpropogation algorithm. An optimized artificial neural network was set up with the proper parametric setting. Hence, the analysis results a condensed network configuration in the search space rather than the complex one. Finally, the analysis extended to all images in the data set and optimum results were obtained. Segmentation results of an FTD subjects in the baseline and visit are shown in Fig 3 and Fig 4.

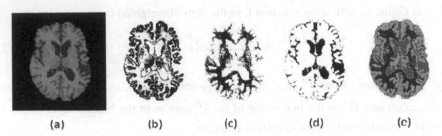

Fig. 3. Segmentation of a baseline MR brain image (FTD): (a) Original image (b) GM (c) WM (d) CSF (e) Segmentation map using GAANN algorithm

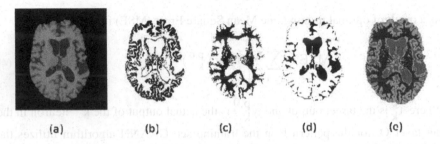

Fig. 4. Segmentation of a follow up MR brain image (FTD): (a) Original image (b) GM (c) WM (d) CSF (e) Segmentation map using GAANN algorithm

The results of both skull stripping and segmentation were validated quantitatively by two expert neuroradiologists . The Performance evaluations of GAANN have been done on the basis of Accuracy, Sensitivity, Specificity and Youden index parameter measures. Average segmented volume of 15 FTD subjects in the baseline and visit after 1 year is shown in Table 1 and it illustrates the GM cortex loss annually in FTD subjects.

In this proposed approach, we have obtained a high classification accuracy by comparing baseline images with 1 year follow up images. The average classification accuracy of GM, WM and CSF in the baseline and visit is 95.5 %, 96.5% and 98% respectively. Table 2 presents a comparison of performance evaluation factors of baseline and visit.

Table 1. Volume of Segmented tissues

Class	GAANN Volume		
	GM(mm^3)	WM(mm^3)	CSF(mm^3)
Base	371612	669986	285136
Visit	354828	654872	295038

Table 2. Quantitative Validation of Segmented Results

Class	Accuracy (%)			TPR	FPR	Sensitivity(%)	Specificity(%)	Youden index (%)
	GM	WM	CSF					
Base	96.57	97.21	98.31	94.25	0.01	94.09	99.06	93.16
Visit	95.83	96.02	98.56	90.12	0.01	90.12	98.28	89.41

5   Conclusion

In this paper we have proposed a novel approach to image segmentation using genetic algorithm. The strength of the study is the use of a fully automated CAD system for producing objective results without any external expertise. This technique can be used to enhance the clinicians' confidence by offering quantitative evaluation of brain degeneration, especially in the context of dreaded demending diseases like FTD. In FTD, both qualitative and quantitative analysis is important to understand the disease process in its early stage. Hence the application of GA plays vital role in the disease diagnosis. The comparative experimental results had shown that the proposed methodology is effective in the longitudinal evaluation of structural changes in MR images. Using the proposed approach, we have achieved an average classification accuracy of GM, WM and CSF in baseline and follow-up visit are 95.5 %, 96.5% and 98% respectively Moreover, the proposed approach incorporates considerable flexibility into the segmentation procedure. The main advantages of GAANN over the existing techniques are easy to implement; robustness of algorithms and application to large scale system dealing with images.

References

1. Ratnavalli, E., Brayne, C., Dawson, K., Hodges, J.R.: The prevalence of Frontotemporal dementia. Neurology 58(11), 1615–1621 (2002)
2. Go, C., Mioshi, E., Yew, B., Hodges, J.R., Hornberger, M.: Neural correlates of behavioural symptoms in behavioural variant Frontotemporal dementia and Alzheimer's disease: Employment of a visual MRI rating scale, Dement Neuropsychol. Dement Neuropsychol. 6(1), 12–17 (2012)
3. Huey, E.D., Goveia, E.N., Paviol, S., Pardini, M., Krueger, F., Zamboni, G., Tierney, M.C., Wassermann, E.M., Grafman, J.: Executive dysfunction in Frontotemporal dementia and Corticobasal syndrome. Neurology 72(5), 453–459 (2009)
4. Gonzalez, R.C., Woods, R.E.: Digital Image Processing. Addison-Wesley, Massachusetts (1992)
5. Kannan, S.R., Sathya, A., Ramathilagam, S., Devi, R.: Novel segmentation algorithm in segmenting medical images. Journal of Systems and Software 83(12), 2487–2495 (2010)
6. Kannan, S.R., Ramathilagam, S., Devi, R., Hines, E.: Strong fuzzy c-means in medical image data analysis. Journal of Systems and Software 85(11), 2425–2438 (2012)

7. He, Y., Hussaini, M.Y., Ma, J., Shafei, B., Steidl, G.: A new fuzzy c-means method with total variation regularization for segmentation of images with noisy and incomplete data. Pattern Recognition 45(9), 3463–3471 (2012)

8. Reed, R.T., du Buf, J.M.H.: A review of recent texture segmentation and feature extraction techniques. Comput. Vis. Graphics Image Processing 57(3), 359–372 (1993)

9. Christodoulou, Michaelides, S.C., Pattichis, C.S.: Multifeature Texture Analysis for the Classification of Clouds in Satellite Imagery. IEEE Transactions on Geoscience and Remote Sensing 41(11), 2662–2668 (2003)

10. Yeh, J.Y., Fu, J.C.: A hierarchical genetic algorithm for segmentation of multi-spectral human–brain MRI. Expert Systems with Applications 34(2), 1285–1295 (2008)

11. Ma, H., Zhang, Y., Jia, G.: Medical images segmentation using modified genetic fuzzy clustering algorithm. Computer Engineering and Design 23(13), 2357–2359 (2006)

12. Jamshidi, O., Pilevar, A.H.: Automatic Segmentation of Medical Images Using Fuzzy c-Means and the Genetic Algorithm. Journal of Computational Medicine, 1–7 (2013)

13. Adams, R., Bischof, L.: Seeded region growing. IEEE Transactions on Pattern Analysis and Machine Intelligence 16(6), 641–646 (1994)

14. Roslan, R., Jamil, N., Mahmud, R.: Skull Stripping Magnetic Resonance Images Brain Images: Region Growing versus Mathematical Morphology. International Journal of Computer Information Systems and Industrial Management Applications (3), 150–158 (2011) ISSN 2150-7988

15. Jafari-Khouzani, K., Siadat, M.R., Soltanian-Zadeh, H., Elisevich, K.: Texture Analysis of Hippocampus for Epilepsy. Proceedings of SPIE (5) (2003)

16. Chiang, C.-L.: Improved Genetic Algorithm for Power Economic Dispatch of Units with Valve-Point Effects and Multiple Fuels. IEEE Transactions on Power Systems 20, 1690–1699 (2005)

17. Dheeba, J., Tamil Selvi, S.: A CAD System for Breast Cancer Diagnosis Using Modified Genetic Algorithm Optimized Artificial Neural Network. In: Panigrahi, B.K., Suganthan, P.N., Das, S., Satapathy, S.C. (eds.) SEMCCO 2011, Part I. LNCS, vol. 7076, pp. 349–357. Springer, Heidelberg (2011)

18. Goldberg, D.E.: Genetic Algorithm in Search, Optimization and Machine Learning. Addison-Wesley Publishing Company (1989)

Intelligent Computation and Kinematics of 4-DOF SCARA Manipulator Using ANN and ANFIS

Panchanand Jha and Bibhuti Bhusan Biswal

Department of Industrial Design, National Institute of Technology, Rourkela, 769008, India
Jha_ip007@hotmail.com, bbbiswal@nitrkl.ac.in

Abstract. The inverse kinematics of manipulator comprises the computation required to find the joint angles for a given Cartesian position and orientation of the end effector. There is no unique solution for the inverse kinematics thus necessitating application of appropriate predictive models from the soft computing domain. Artificial neural network and adaptive neural fuzzy inference system techniques can be gainfully used to yield the desired results. This paper proposes structured artificial neural network (ANN) model and adaptive neural fuzzy inference system (ANFIS) to find the inverse kinematics solution of robot manipulator. The ANN model used is a multi-layered perceptron Neural Network (MLPNN). Wherein, gradient descent type of learning rules is applied. An attempt has been made to find the best ANFIS configuration for the problem. It is found that ANFIS gives better result and minimum error as compared to ANN.

Keywords: Inverse Kinematics, D-H Notations, ANN, ANFIS.

1   Introduction

The Robot manipulator is composed of a serial chain of rigid links connected to each other by revolute or prismatic joints. Each robot joint location is usually defined relative to the neighboring joint. The relation between successive joints is containing a 4x4 homogeneous transformation matrix that has orientation and position data of robots. Conversion of the position and orientation of robot manipulator end-effectors from Cartesian space to joint space is called as inverse kinematics problem. The corresponding joint values must be computed at high speed by the inverse kinematics transformation [1]. For a manipulator with n degree of freedom, at any instant of time the joint variable is denoted by $i = \theta(t)$, $i = 1, 2, 3 \ldots\ldots\ldots$n and position variables by $x_j = x(t)$, $j = 1, 2, 3 \ldots\ldots$m. The relations between the end-effectors position $x(t)$ and joint angle $\theta(t)$can be represented by forward kinematic equation

$$x(t) = f(\theta(t)) \tag{1}$$

Where, f is a nonlinear continuous and differentiable function.

On the other hand, with the desired end effectors position, the problem of finding the values of the joint variables is inverse kinematics, which can be solved by,

$$\theta(t) = f'(x(t)) \tag{2}$$

B.K. Panigrahi et al. (Eds.): SEMCCO 2013, Part II, LNCS 8298, pp. 277–286, 2013.
© Springer International Publishing Switzerland 2013

Inverse kinematics solution is not unique due to nonlinear, uncertain and time varying nature of the governing equations [2].

The simulation and computation of inverse kinematics using soft computing technique is particularly useful where less computation times are needed, such as in real-time adaptive robot control [3], [4], [5]. If the number of degrees of freedom increases, traditional methods will become more complex and quite difficult to solve inverse kinematics [6].Many research contributions have been made related to the neural network-based inverse kinematics solution of robot manipulators [7].

Use of soft computing technique is not new in the field of multi-objective and NP-hard problem to arrive at a very reasonable optimized solution. Soft computing technique is used to find inverse kinematics solution which yields multiple and precise solutions with an acceptable error and are suitable for real-time adaptive control of robotic manipulators [8]. The study of previous work shows that the most of the researchers [9] and [11] have adopted methods like ANN, ANFIS etc. for simple problem. The features of adopted techniques are found quite matching and hence suitable for the present problem having complexity and involving multiple parameters. Therefore, the main aim of this work is focused on minimizing the mean square error of the neural network-based as well as ANFIS based solution of inverse kinematics problem. The result of each technique is evaluated by using inverse kinematics equations to obtain information about their error. In other words, the angles obtained for each joint are used to compute the Cartesian coordinate for end effector.

2   Kinematic Modeling of SCARA Manipulator

The Denavit-Hartenberg (D-H) notation and methodology are used in this section to derive the kinematics of robot manipulator. The coordinate frame assignment and the DH parameters are depicted in Fig. 1, and listed in Table 1 respectively.

Table 1. The D-H Parameters

SN	θ_i (degree)	d_i (mm)	a_i (mm)	α_i (degree)
1	$\theta_1=\pm120$	0	$a_1=250$	0
2	$\theta_2=\pm130$	0	$a_2=150$	180
3	0	$d_3=150$	0	0
4	θ_4	$d_4=150$	0	0

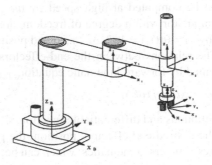

Fig. 1. D-H frames of the SCARA robot

Where (p_x, p_y, p_z) represents the position and $\{(n_x, n_y, n_z), (o_x, o_y, o_z),$ $and\,(a_x, a_y, a_z)\}$ represents the orientation of the end-effector.

$$\theta_2 = \tan^{-1}\left(\frac{s_2}{c_2}\right) = \tan^{-1}\left[\frac{\pm 2a_1 a_2 \sqrt{1 - c_2^2}}{p_x^2 + p_y^2 - a_1^2 - a_2^2}\right] \tag{3}$$

$$\theta_1 = \tan^{-1}\left(\frac{s_1}{c_1}\right) = \tan^{-1}\left[\frac{(a_1 + a_2 c_2)p_y - a_2 s_2 p_x}{(a_1 + a_2 c_2)p_x + a_2 s_2 p_y}\right] \tag{4}$$

$$d_3 = -p_z - d_4 \tag{5}$$

$$\theta_4 = \tan^{-1}\left[\frac{-n_x s_{12} + n_y c_{12}}{n_x c_{12} + n_y s_{12}}\right] \tag{6}$$

It is obvious from the representation given in equations (3) through (6) that there exist multiple solutions to the inverse kinematics problem. So to know which solution holds good to study the inverse kinematics, all joints variables are obtained and compared using forward kinematics solution. This process is been applied for θ_1, θ_2, d_3 and θ_4, to choose the correct solution.

3   Architectures of ANN and ANFIS

3.1   Architecture of MLFF Neural Network

It is well known that neural networks have the better ability than other techniques to solve various complex problems. Inverse kinematics is a transformation of a world coordinate frame (X, Y, and Z) to a link coordinate frame (θ_1, θ_2, d_3, and θ_4). This transformation can be performed on input/output work that uses an unknown transfer function. MLP neural network's neuron is a simple work element, and has a local memory. A neuron takes a multi-dimensional input, and then delivers it to the other neurons according to their weights. This gives a scalar result at the output of a neuron. The transfer function of an MLP, acting on the local memory, uses a learning rule to produce a relationship between the input and output. For the activation input, a time function is needed [11].

A block diagram of the structure is shown in Fig. 2. Each of the signals from the input neurons is multiplied by the value of the weights of the connection, w_j, between the respective input neurons and the hidden neuron.

The aim of the training phase is to minimize this average sum squared error over all training patterns. The speed of convergence of the network depends on the training rate, η and the momentum factor, α. In this work, a two hidden layer neural network with three inputs, P_x, P_y and P_z, and four outputs, θ_1, θ_2, d_3, and θ_4 was trained using the back-propagation algorithm described earlier, along a trajectory of the end-effector in the x-y plane.

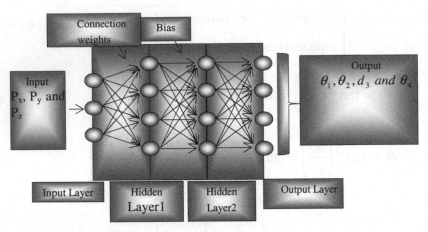

Fig. 2. Multi-layered perceptron neural network structure

3.2   Architecture of ANFIS

The ANFIS can perform the mapping relation between the input and output data through a learning algorithm to optimize the parameters of a given FIS. The ANFIS architecture consists of fuzzy layer, product layer, normalized layer, de-fuzzy layer, and summation layer. A typical architecture of ANFIS is shown in Fig. 3, in which a circle indicates a fixed node, whereas a square indicates an adjustable node. For example, we consider two inputs x, y and one output z in the FIS. The ANFIS used in this paper implements a first-order Sugeno FIS. Among many fuzzy systems, the Sugeno fuzzy model is the most widely applied, because of its high interpretability and computational efficiency, and built-in optimal and adaptive techniques [3].

For a first-order Sugeno fuzzy system, the typical rule set can be expressed as:

Rule 1: If x is $A1$ and y is $B1$, then $z1 = p1x + q1y + r1$
Rule 2: If x is $A2$ and y is $B2$, then $z2 = p2x + q2y + r2$

where Ai and Bi are the fuzzy sets in the antecedent, and pi, qi, and ri are the parameters that are assigned during the training procedure. As in Fig. 3, the ANFIS consists of five layers. Every ith node in the first layer is an adaptive node with a node output defined by:

$$O_i^1 = \mu_{A_i}(x), \qquad i = 1,2$$

$$O_i^1 = \mu_{B_{i-2}}(y), \qquad i = 3,4$$

where $\mu_{A_i}(x)$ and $\mu_{B_{i-2}}(y)$ can adopt any fuzzy membership function (MF).

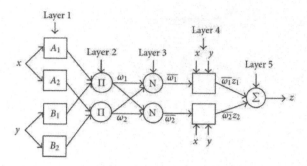

Fig. 3. Architecture of ANFIS

The hybrid learning algorithm [3], combining the LSM and the back propagation algorithm can be used to solve this problem. This algorithm converges much faster because it reduces the dimension of the search space of the back propagation algorithm. During the learning procedure, the premise and consequent parameters are tuned until the desired response of the FIS is achieved. The hybrid learning algorithm is divided into two steps: forward pass and a backward pass. In the forward pass, while the premise parameters are held fixed, the network inputs propagated forward until layer 4, where the consequent parameters are identified by the LSM. In the backward pass, the consequent parameters are held fixed while the error signals are propagated from the output end to the input end, and the standard back propagation algorithm updates the premise parameters. Fig. 3 shows the procedure of ANFIS training. This paper considers three ANFIS structure with first-order Sugeno fuzzy system for joint variables. Gaussian MFs with product inference rule are used at the fuzzification layer.

4   Simulation Results and Performance Analysis

4.1   MLFF Simulation and Results

The proposed work is performed on the Matlab Neural Networks Toolbox. The training functions employed are 'trainoss' and 'trainlm', to validate the performance of MLFF neural network for inverse kinematics problem. Then, the weights and biases are calculated for the network.. In this work the training data sets were generated by using equation (3) through (6). A set of 1000 data sets were first generated as per the formula for the input parameter px, py and pz coordinates in inches.

The following parameters were taken: Learning rate 0.08; Momentum parameter 0.081; Number of epochs 10000; Number of hidden layers 2; Number of inputs 3 and Number of output 4.

The mean square curve shown in Fig. 4 through Fig. 7 shows the building knowledge procedure for the new path which gives an indication for the success of the proposed algorithm. As shown in result, the used solution method gives the chance of selecting the output, which has the least error in the system. So, the solution can be obtained with less error as shown in Fig. (4) through (7) for the best validation performance of the obtained data with the desired data.

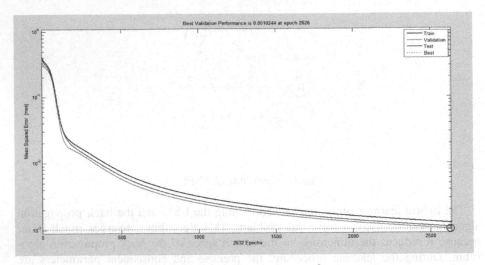

Fig. 4. Mean square error for θ_1

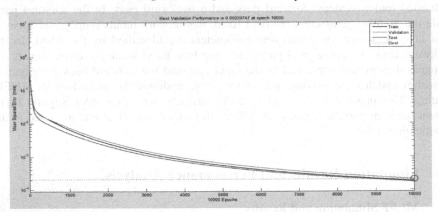

Fig. 5. Mean square error for θ_2

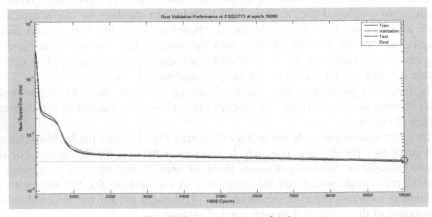

Fig. 6. Mean square error for d$_3$

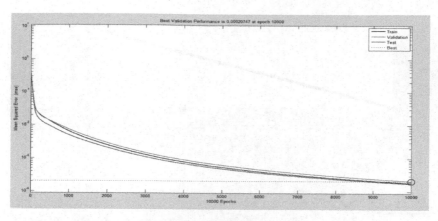

Fig. 7. Mean square error for θ_4

4.2   ANFIS Simulation and Results

Data set were generated by using inverse kinematic equations. The coordinates (px, py and pz) and the angles ($\theta 1$, $\theta 2$, d_3 and $\theta 4$) are used as training data to train ANFIS network with Gaussian membership function with hybrid learning algorithm. Table 2 shows configuration of ANFIS. Fig. 8 through Fig. 11 shows the validation curve for the problem of learning the inverse kinematics of the 4-DOF SCARA manipulator. Table 3 gives the average errors of joint variables using ANFIS and MLFF. These errors are small and the ANFIS algorithm is, therefore, acceptable for obtaining the inverse kinematics solution of the robotic manipulator.

Table 2. Configuration of ANFIS

Number of nodes	734
Number of linear parameters	343
Number of nonlinear parameters	63
Total number of parameters	406
Number of training data pairs	700
Number of fuzzy rules	343

Table 3. Comparison of results

Sl.	MSE of MLPNN	MSE of ANFIS
1	0.0076	0.00030124
2	0.00471	0.00002849
3	0.00031	0.00026932
4	0.00584	0.00039377

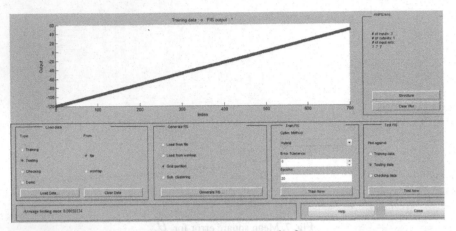

Fig. 8. Mean square error for θ_1

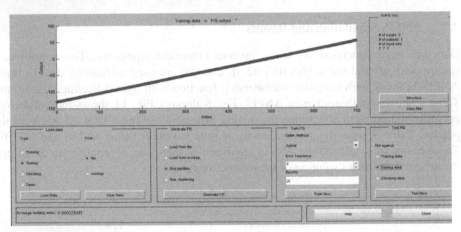

Fig. 9. Mean square error for θ_2

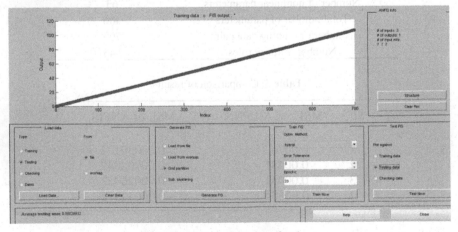

Fig. 10. Mean square error for d_3

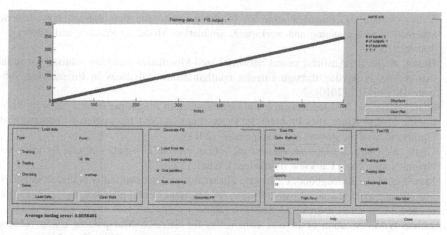

Fig. 11. Mean square error for θ_4

5   Conclusions

In this paper, we have selected two methods which are ANN and ANFIS to obtain the solution of inverse kinematics of 4 DOF SCARA manipulator. In this approach forward and inverse kinematic model of 4 DOF SCARA manipulator is used to generate the data set for training the ANN and ANFIS model. The difference in desired and predicted data with ANN, gives poor results as compared to ANFIS. Also, the ANFIS accumulate small number of epoch with hybrid learning algorithm.

Therefore, ANFIS can be used for accurate and fast solution of inverse kinematics. Future research will revise the rules, inputs, number and type of membership functions, the epoch numbers used, and training sample to further refine the ANFIS model.

References

1. Shital, S., Chiddarwar, N., Ramesh, B.: Comparison of RBF and MLP neural networks to solve inverse kinematic problem for 6R serial robot by a fusion approach. Engineering Applications of Artificial Intelligence 23, 1083–1092 (2010)
2. Koker, R.: Reliability-based approach to the inverse kinematics solution of robots using Elman's networks. Engineering Applications of Artificial Intelligence 18, 685–693 (2005)
3. Alavandar, S., Nigam, M.J.: Neuro-Fuzzy based Approach for Inverse Kinematics Solution of Industrial Robot Manipulators. Int. J. of Computers, Communications & Control 3, 224–234 (2008)
4. Hasan, A., et al.: An adaptive-learning algorithm to solve the inverse kinematics problem of a 6 D.O.F serial robot manipulator. Advances in Engineering Software 37, 432–438 (2006)
5. Husty, M.L., Pfurner, M., Schrocker, H.P.: A new and efficient algorithm for the inverse kinematics of a general serial 6R manipulator. Mechanism and Machine Theory 42, 66–81 (2007)

6. Yahya, S., et al.: Geometrical approach of planar hyper-redundant manipulators: Inverse kinematics, path planning and workspace. Simulation Modeling Practice and Theory 19, 406–422 (2011)
7. Hasan, A., et al.: Artificial neural network-based kinematics Jacobian solution for serial manipulator is passing through singular configurations. Advances in Engineering Software 41, 359–367 (2010)
8. Olaru, A., et al.: Assisted Research and Optimization of the proper Neural Network Solving the Inverse Kinematics Problem. In: Proceedings of 2011 International Conference on Optimization of the Robots and Manipulators (2011)
9. Olaru, A., Olaru, S.: Optimization of the robots inverse kinematics results by using the Neural Network and LabView simulation. IPCSIT 13 (2011)
10. Mayorga, R.V., Sanongboon, P.: Inverse kinematics and geometrically bounded singularities prevention of redundant manipulators: An Artificial Neural Network approach. Robotics and Autonomous Systems 53, 164–176 (2005)
11. Jasim, W.M.: Solution of Inverse Kinematics for SCARA Manipulator Using Adative Neuro-Fuzzy Network. International Journal on Soft Computing (IJSC) 2, 4 (2011)
12. Haykin, S.: Neural networks a comprehensive foundation (1994)

Hybrid Neuro-Fuzzy Network Identification
for Autonomous Underwater Vehicles

Osama Hassanein, G. Sreenatha, and Tapabrata Ray

School of Engineering and Information Technology,
UNSW@ADFA, Canberra, ACT, Australia
{o.hassan,s.anavatti,t.ray}@adfa.edu.au

Abstract. Autonomous Underwater Vehicles (AUVs) are ideal platforms
for aquatic search and rescue operations and exploration. The AUV poses
serious challenges due to its complex, inherently nonlinear and time-varying
dynamics. In addition, its hydrodynamic coefficients are difficult to model accurately because of their variations under different navigational conditions and
manoeuvring in uncertain environments. This paper introduces an identifier
scheme for identification of non-linear systems with disturbances based on Hybrid Neuro-Fuzzy Network (HNFN) technique. The method comprises of an automatic structure-generating phase using entropy based technique. The accuracy
of the model is suitably controlled using the entropy measure. To improve the
accuracy and also for generalization of the model to handle different data sets,
Differential Evolution technique (DE) is employed. Finally, Hardware In-Loop
(HIL) simulation and real-time experiments using the proposed algorithm to
identify the 6-DOF UNSW Canberra AUV's dynamics are implemented. The
modelling performance and generalisation capability are seen to be superior
with our method.

1   Introduction

AUVs are widely used for scientific, commercial and military underwater applications, some of which necessitate accurate positioning and path control. The modelling, system identification and control of these vehicles are still major active areas of
research and development. System identification, mathematical or artificial intelligent
model of the system, is a crucial part in the design, analysis and control of the system
and generally, the system models are classified as white-box, gray-box and black-box
[1]. White-box modelling requires the complete dynamics of a system to be known
prior to its use and, then the system identification problem becomes a parameter identification problem [2]. Parameter estimation techniques involve methods such as Maximum Likelihood Estimators [3], State Space methods [4] and other robust estimation
methods [5,6]. The white-box modelling may not be appropriate for modelling the
dynamics of AUV system due to the uncertainties and nonlinearities involved. A
black-box model requires no physical insight into the dynamics of a plant but relies
completely on the input-output data and has two phases, model structure determination and model parameter calculations. The black-box identification technique is used
in this research.

B.K. Panigrahi et al. (Eds.): SEMCCO 2013, Part II, LNCS 8298, pp. 287–297, 2013.
© Springer International Publishing Switzerland 2013

Two identifiers of nonlinear systems were developed based on fuzzy system models, with initially known model structures and parameters in [7]. They simulated the chaotic glycolytic oscillator and the results showed that, by incorporating some linguistic descriptions, they were greatly improved. A chaotic optimisation method called Chaotic Ant Swarm (CAS) was introduced to solve the problem of designing a fuzzy system based on the fitness theory in [8].

The Auto Regression (AR) model was used to predict disturbances in an AUV's dynamics [9]. Several techniques have been used to estimate and adapt already known underwater vehicle model parameters off-line [10-12]. Various kinds of neural network structures for identification of AUV systems were investigated in [13-14]. They developed an independent model for each single degree of freedom of Twin Burger 2 AUV, which can be called as Single Degree of Freedom Neural Network Identification (SDFNNI).

The Hybrid Neural Fuzzy Network (HNFN) systems possess the advantages of both NNs and Fuzzy systems, where NNs provide an essentially low-level learning and computational power to process large amounts of data while fuzzy logic provides a structural framework that utilises and exploits these low-level capabilities [15-16]. Hence, a Fuzzy Neural Network (FNN) has great potential for application to model the AUVs [17]. The Neuro-Fuzzy modelling techniques presented in [18] was a powerful approach and has been demonstrated to the identification of an Ocean Voyager AUV.

The Differential Evolution (DE) appeared in a written article as a technical report by R. Storn in 1995 [19]. Since then, the DE has drawn the attention of many researchers. DE operates through similar computational steps as employed by a standard Evolutionary Algorithm (EA). Unlike traditional EAs, the DE-variants perturb the current generation population members with the scaled differences of randomly selected and distinct population members [20].

In this paper, an auto-generating mechanism with entropy based differential evolution neuro-fuzzy system modelling is proposed to generate an adaptive Hybrid Neuro-Fuzzy Netwotk (HNFN) model for UNSW Canberra AUV without any prior knowledge of the physical relationship inside the system. This method builds on the method proposed by the authors [21] where a Fuzzy Neural Model is proposed for Under Water Vehicles. Here, a Hybrid Neuro-Fuzzy Network is proposed. In addition, in this paper, a method based on Entropy measure is introduced to add fuzzy rules and thus control the accuracy of the model, practically starting with no fuzzy rules. The information required to model the system is only the input-output data available from the real-time tests. The process of identification is carried out in two steps. The first step is the off-line procedure and the second step is online procedure. The results are validated using the HIL data and experimental input-output data from the model shown in Fig. 1.

This paper is organized as follows. Section 2 describes the structure of the HNFN model. Section 3 presents HNFN modelling mechanism. Next, the results of HIL simulations and real-time experiments of the AUV are described in section 4. Finally, Section 5 concludes the paper.

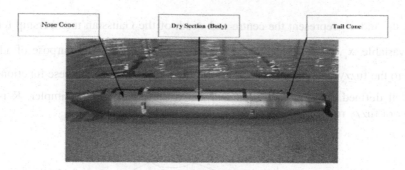

Fig. 1. AUV at UNSW Canberra

2   Structure of Hybrid Neuro-Fuzzy Network (HNFN) Model

Hybrid Neural Fuzzy Network (HNFN) uses the Functional Link Neural Network (FLNN) to the consequent part of the fuzzy rules. The consequent part of the HNFN model is a nonlinear combination of input variables [22]. The FLNN is a single-layer neural structure capable of forming arbitrarily complex decision regions by generating nonlinear decision boundaries with nonlinear Function Expansion (FE). Fig.2 presents the structure of the proposed HNFN system identifier. The HNFN model realises a fuzzy if–then rule in the following form

$$R^{(l)}: \quad \text{IF}(x_1 \text{ is } F_1^l \text{ and} .... \text{ and } x_n \text{ is } F_N^l) \text{ THEN}$$

$$\hat{y}_j = \sum_{i=1}^{M} w_{ij} \phi_i(x) \quad = \quad w_{1j}\phi_1 + w_{2j}\phi_2 + ... + w_{jM}\phi_M \tag{1}$$

where x_i and $\hat{y}_i$ are the input and local output variables, respectively, F_N^l is the linguistic term of the precondition part with the Gaussian membership function, N is the number of input variables, w_{ij} is the link weight of the local output, ϕ_M is the basis trigonometric function of the input variables, M is the number of basis functions and j, the jth fuzzy rule. As shown in Fig.2 no computation is performed in layer 1 as each node in it transmits only directly input values to the next layer. Each fuzzy set is described by a Gaussian membership function and the fuzzy system part chosen to be designed in this study has a product inference engine, singleton fuzzifier and Gaussian membership function in the form of;

$$\hat{y}(k+1) = \frac{\sum_{j=1}^{R}\left(\sum_{i=1}^{M} w_{ij}\phi_i\right)\prod_{i=1}^{N}\left(\exp\left(-0.5\frac{\left(x_i - c_{ji}\right)^2}{\left(\sigma_{ji}\right)^2 + \varepsilon}\right)\right)}{\sum_{j=1}^{R}\left(\prod_{i=1}^{N}\left(\exp\left(-0.5\frac{\left(x_i - c_{ji}\right)^2}{\left(\sigma_{ji}\right)^2 + \varepsilon}\right)\right)\right)}. \tag{2}$$

where c_{ji} and σ_{ji} represent the centre and width of the Gaussian membership for the input variable x_i, respectively, and $\varepsilon > 0$ is a small constant, the purpose of adding which to the fuzzy membership functions is that, even if σ_{ji}'s $= 0$, these functions are still well defined. This modification will make the adaptive law simpler. R is the number of fuzzy rules and y the output from the HNFN identifier.

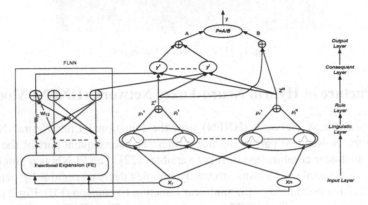

Fig. 2. Structure of proposed HNFN identifier

2.1   Functional Link Neural Network (FLNN) Structure

Fig.3 describes the FLNN structure in which, as the input data usually incorporate high-order effects, the dimensions of the input space artificially increase using a FE. Accordingly, the input representation is enhanced and linear separability is achieved in the extended space. The HNFN model adopts the FLNN structure to generate complex nonlinear combinations of input variables in the consequent part of the fuzzy rules. The theory behind the FLNN for multi-dimensional function approximation is discussed in [22, 23].

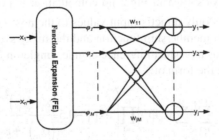

Fig. 3. FLNN structure

The FLNN is a single-layer network while the input variables generated by the linear links of neural networks are linearly weighted and the functional link acts on an element of the input variables by generating a set of linearly independent functions and orthogonal polynomials for a FE, and then evaluates these functions of the variables as the arguments. In the FLNN, a set of basis functions, ϕ, and a fixed number of weight parameters, W, represent the function f. The linear sum of the jth node is given by;

$$\hat{y}_j = \sum_{i=1}^{M} w_{ij}\phi_i(x) = w_{1j}\phi_1 + w_{2j}\phi_2 + \dots\dots + w_{jM}\phi_M. \quad (3)$$

where $w_{ij} = [w_{j1}, \dots\dots, w_{jM}]$ is the weight vector associated with the jth output from the FLNN and $\hat{y}_j$ is the local output from the FLNN structure.

3 HNFN Modelling Mechanism

In this study, a tool is offered for modelling automatically the AUV system without any prior knowledge of the physical relationship. Sets of input-output data with different operating conditions and disturbances are the only information required for generating the model of the system. The proposed mechanism is a combination of two stages. The first stage is the off-line procedure and the second one is the on-line procedure.

3.1 Off-Line Procedure

The off-line stage as a first step in generating the mode comprises of a structure-generating phase and parameter-learning phase.

Structure-Generating Phase. The membership functions and rules of the HNFN model are generated automatically based upon the reception of incoming input-output data. The first step in the structure-generating is to determine the criteria that should be used to extract and generate new fuzzy rules of the system. For each incoming pattern, the rule firing strength is used to calculate the entropy values between data points and current membership functions to determine whether a new rule should be added or not. The entropy measure calculation is given by [24];

$$ENT_j = \sum_{i=1}^{N} L_{ij}^{(2)}(1 - L_{ij}^{(2)}). \quad (4)$$

where $L_{ji}^{(2)} = \exp\left(-0.5\frac{\left(x_i - c_{ji}\right)^2}{\left(\sigma_{ji}\right)^2 + \varepsilon}\right)$ is the firing strength for each rule and the maximum entropy measure is determined as $ENT_{MAX} = \max_{1 \leq X \leq R(t)} ENT_j \cdot$, where $R(t)$ is the number of existing rules at time t. If $ENT_{Max} \leq \overline{ENT}$, then a new rule is generated and added to the model. $\overline{ENT}$ is a pre-specified threshold. A low threshold leads to fewer rules, whereas a high threshold leads to more rules. Therefore, the selection of the threshold value $\overline{ENT}$ will critically affect modelling accuracy. Once a new rule has been generated, the next step is to assign the initial mean and variance to the new membership function and the corresponding output and variance for the consequent part. After the model is generated, the error between the data used in generating phase and the output of generated model are calculated. If the error and its RMSE value meet the design demand in terms of model accuracy and computational time, then the generated model will enter to the next step, otherwise, the $\overline{\text{ENT}}$ threshold should be changed as previously described.

Parameter-Learning Phase Using BP: During the generating process of the model structure according to the current input-output data set, the parameter-learning procedure is involved to adjust the parameters of the model based on the same data. The BP algorithm is used to adapt the HNFN model parameters c_{ji}, σ_{ji} and w_{ji} based on the following objective function;

$$E(k) = \frac{1}{2}(y_m(k+1) - y_f(k+1))^2.$$ (5)

where $E(k)$ is error between the HNFN model and the actual plant outputs. If $Z(k)$ represents the parameter to be adapted at iteration k in the fuzzy model, the training algorithm seeks to minimize the value of the objective function [25] by

$$z(k+1) = z(k) - \alpha \frac{\partial E}{\partial Z}.$$ (6)

In this technique, the HNFN is adapted in two ways: the BP algorithm is applied to tune the membership function parameters in the antecedent part and the parameters of the FLNN; and the consequent part of the fuzzy rules is adapted through the FLNN. The learning rate, α, in Eq. 6 has a significant effect on the stability and convergence of the system [26]. A higher learning rate may enhance the convergence rate but can reduce the stability of the system.

Parameter-Learning Phase Using DE: In DE, an initial population is generated and, for each parent vector from the current population (target vector), a mutant vector (donor vector) is obtained. Finally, an offspring is formed by combining the donor with the target vector. A tournament is then held between each parent and its offspring with the better being copied to the next generation [27]. The DE learning algorithm consists of four major steps as follows:

Initialization step: The first step is the coding of the HNFN model parameters into an individual as shown in Equation (7) where i and j represent the ith input variable and the jth rule, respectively. The number of individuals is determined according to the generation and population size.

$$Individual = c_{j1}, c_{j2}, ..., c_{jM}, \sigma_{j2}, \sigma_{j2}, ..., \sigma_{jM}, b_1, b_2, ..., b_M, \sigma_1, \sigma_2, ..., \sigma_M.$$ (7)

Evaluation step: The objective function is used to provide a measure of how individuals have performed in the problem domain. In the minimization problem, the fit individuals will have the lowest numerical value of the associated problem objective function. The cost function that attempts to optimize the whole parameters is ITSE (Integral Time of Square Error) over the total simulation time.

$$ITSE = \int_{t_1}^{t_2} e^2 dt, \quad J_{E1} = Max(ITSE), \quad F_{E1} = 1/J_{E1}.$$
(8)

where J_{E1} and F_{E1} are the objective function and fitness function of each degree of freedom separately for all population in the range, respectively.

Mutation and crossover step: This operation enables DE to explore the search space and maintain diversity. The simplest form of this operation is that a mutant vector is generated by multiplying an amplification factor.

$$\vec{V}_{z,t} = \vec{x}_{r_1,t} + H \times (\vec{x}_{r_2,t} - \vec{x}_{r_3,t})$$
(9)

where r_1, r_2 and r_3 are random numbers (1, 2,..., PS), $r_1 \neq r_2 \neq r_3 \neq z$, x is a decision vector, PS is the population size, H is a positive control parameter for scaling the DE and t the current generation. For more details, readers are referred to [28].

Reproduction and selection step: To keep the population size constant over subsequent generations, the next step of the algorithm calls for selection to determine whether the target or the trial vector survives to the next generation, i.e., at $G = G + 1$. The selection operation is described as

$$\vec{X}_{i,G+1} = \vec{U}_{i,G} \quad if \; f(\vec{U}_{i,G}) \leq f(\vec{X}_{i,G})$$
$$= \vec{X}_{i,G} \quad if \; f(\vec{U}_{i,G}) > f(\vec{X}_{i,G})$$
(10)

where $f(x)$ is the objective function to be minimized.

3.2   ON-LINE Procedure

Generally, the basic objective of the proposed model is identifying the behaviour of the original plant online with consistent performance and high accuracy in the presence of uncertainties. Therefore, the generated HNFN model is equipped with online adaptation algorithm to enhance the generality and accuracy of the model during the online operations conditions. The BP algorithm minimizes a given cost function, (5), by adjusting the parameters of model as mentioned in equation 6.

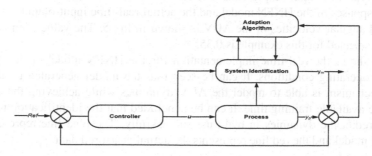

Fig. 4. Tracking of error function between process and HNFN model

4   AUV Modelling Results

This study evaluated the performance of the proposed HNFN mechanism to model nonlinear dynamics for AUV. In this section, the identification algorithm is needed to be tested for autonomous manoeuvring of the AUV. To achieve this, a real-time Hardwar-In-Loop (HIL) simulation technique is developed and used in order to validate the proposed mechanism. Next, real-time experiment is conducted to validate the identification technique for the AUV.

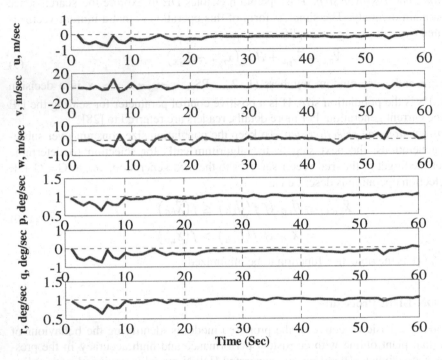

Fig. 5. AUV HNFN identification HIL results: Coupled dynamics

The identification of coupled 6-DOF of the AUV is further investigated by HNFN based on real-time input-output data. The HIL simulation for identification and prediction responses of the HNFN model and the actual real-time input-output data of the linear and angular velocities of the AUV is shown in Fig 5. The value of the entropy threshold selected for this example is 0.35.

Fig. 6 shows the real-time implementation for the HNFN model of the AUV at real-time operating conditions. It can be seen that the model generated by the proposed mechanism is able to model the AUV dynamics while achieving the training within the available training time. It can be concluded that the identification model is able to predict the dynamics in real-time successfully. The blue line represents the identified model and the red line represents the actual measured data.

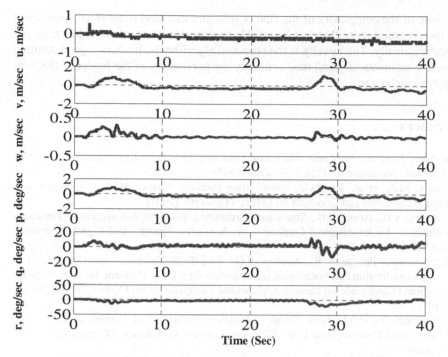

Fig. 6. AUV HNFN identification experimental results: Coupled dynamics

Table 1. AUV HNFN model HIL RMSE values: Coupled dynamics

DOF	Linear Velocities			Angular Velocities		
	u	v	w	φ	θ	ψ
RMSE (HIL)	1.32e-05	2.18e-05	2.09e-09	0.0025	1.33e-04	1.36e-6
RMSE (Exper.)	0.0017	0.0029	0.0110	0.0157	0.0157	0.0053
Rules No.	4	3	4	3	4	4

Table 1 shows the RMSE values of the modelling errors of the predicted response of the proposed modelling mechanism and the corresponding number of the generated rules for each DOF with HIL and real-time experiment. Results indicate that the model adapts itself with changes in the test regime very well.

5   Conclusion

Real time validation using HIL simulation shows a good correlation for HNFN identification. The experimental validation for the system identification of AUV dynamics enhances this. The results showed good match between the identified model and the actual measured data. The modelling performance and generalisation capability are seen to be superior with the proposed method.

In spite of the complexity of the HNFN structure that lead to more computational time, the proposed algorithm was being able to generate its structure and tune its parameters optimally. The novelty in the proposed algorithm is, it offers a good solution to generate automatically and tune optimally the parameters of the model of the nonlinear dynamic systems.

References

1. Sjöberg, J., et al.: Nonlinear Black-Box Modeling In System Identification: A Unified Overview. Automatica 31(12), 1691–1724 (1995)
2. Khalik, M.A., et al.: Parameter Identification Problem: Real-Coded GA Approach. Applied Mathematics and Computation 187(2), 1495–1501 (2007)
3. Morgera, S.D., Armour, B.: Structured Maximum Likelihood Autoregressive Parameter Estimation. In: International Conference on Acoustics, Speech, And Signal Processing, ICASSP 1989 (1989)
4. Salman, S.A., Puttige, V.R., Anavatti, S.G.: Real-Time Validation and Comparison of Fuzzy Identification and State-Space Identification for a UAV Platform. In: 2006 IEEE International Conference on Control Applications, Computer Aided Control System Design. IEEE (2006)
5. Soderstrom, T., et al.: Least Squares Parameter Estimation of Continuous-Time ARX Models from Discrete-Time Data. IEEE Transactions on Automatic Control 42(5), 659–673 (1997)
6. Kim, J., et al.: Estimation of Hydrodynamic Coefficients for an AUV Using Nonlinear Observers. IEEE Journal of Oceanic Engineering 27(4), 830–840 (2002)
7. Wang, L.X.: Design and Analysis of Fuzzy Identifiers of Nonlinear Dynamic Systems. IEEE Transactions on Automatic Control 40(1), 11–23 (1995)
8. Li, L., Yang, Y., Peng, H.: Fuzzy System Identification via Chaotic Ant Swarm. Chaos, Solitons & Fractals 41(1), 401–409 (2009)
9. Healey, A.J.: Model Based Predictive Control of Auvs for Station Keeping in a Shallow Water Wave Environment, Dtic Document (2005)
10. Petrich, J., Neu, W.L., Stilwell, D.J.: Identification of a Simplified Auv Pitch Axis Model for Control Design: Theory and Experiments. In: Oceans (2007)
11. Conte, G., et al.: Evaluation of Hydrodynamics Parameters of a Uuv. A Preliminary Study. In: First International Symposium on Control, Communications and Signal Processing (2004)
12. Faruq, A., et al.: Optimization of Depth Control for Unmanned Underwater Vehicle Using Surrogate Modeling Technique. In: 2011 4th International Conference on Modeling, Simulation and Applied Optimization, ICMSAO (2011)
13. Ishii, K., Ura, T., Fujii, T.: A Feedforward Neural Network for Identification and Adaptive Control of Autonomous Underwater Vehicles. In: 1994 IEEE International Conference on Neural Networks, IEEE World Congress on Computational Intelligence (1994)
14. Ishii, K., Fujii, T., Ura, T.: A Quick Adaptation Method in a Neural Network Based Control System for Auvs. In: Proceedings of the 1994 Symposium on Autonomous Underwater Vehicle Technology, Auv 1994 (1994)
15. Nauck, D., Klawonn, F., Kruse, R.: Foundations of Neuro-Fuzzy Systems. John Wiley & Sons, Inc. (1997)
16. Sun, F., et al.: Neuro-Fuzzy Adaptive Control Based on Dynamic Inversion for Robotic Manipulators. Fuzzy Sets And Systems 134(1), 117–133 (2003)

17. Lei, Z., et al.: Fuzzy Neural Network Control of Auv Based on Ipso. In: IEEE International Conference on Robotics And Biomimetics, Robio 2008 (2008, 2009)
18. Bossley, K.M., Brown, M., Harris, C.J.: Neurofuzzy Identification of an Autonomous Underwater Vehicle. International Journal of Systems Science 30(9), 901–913 (1999)
19. Storn, R., Price, K.V.: Differential evolution: A simple and efficient adaptive scheme for global optimization over continuous spaces (ICSI, USA, Tech. Rep. TR-95-012 (1995), http://icsi.berkeley.edu/storn/litera.html
20. Das, S., Suganthan, P.N.: Differential Evolution: A Survey of the State-of-the-Art. IEEE Trans. on Evolutionary Computation 15, 4–31 (2011)
21. Hassanein, O., Sreenatha, G., Ray, T.: Improved Fuzzy Neural Modeling for Underwater Vehicles. Int. J. World Academy of Science, Engineering and Technology 71, 1208–1215 (2012)
22. Cheng-Hung, C., Cheng-Jian, L., Chin-Teng, L.: A Functional-Link-Based Neurofuzzy Network for Nonlinear System Control. IEEE Transactions on Fuzzy Systems 16(5), 1362–1378 (2008)
23. Patra, J.C., et al.: Identification of Nonlinear Dynamic Systems Using Functional Link Artificial Neural Networks. IEEE Transactions on Systems, Man, and Cybernetics, Part B: Cybernetics 29(2), 254–262 (1999)
24. Beyhan, S., Alci, M.: Fuzzy Function Based ARX Model and New Fuzzy Basis Function Models for Nonlinear System Identification. Applied Soft Computing J. 10, 439–444 (2010)
25. Wang, L.X.: A course in fuzzy systems and control. Prentic Hall Inc., USA (1997)
26. Salman, A., Sreenatha, G., Jin, Y.C.: Indirect Adaptive Fuzzy Control of Unmanned Aerial Vehicle. In: Proc. 17th Congr. Int. Federation of Automatic Control, Seoul, Korea, pp. 13229–13243 (2008)
27. Elsayed, S.M., Sarker, R.A., Essam, D.L.: Differential evolution with multiple strategies for solving CEC2011 real-world numerical optimization problems. In: Proc. IEEE Congr. on Evolutionary Computation, New Orleans, US, vol. I, pp. 1041–1048 (2011)
28. Chang, C.S., Xu, D.Y.: Differential evolution based tuning of fuzzy automatic train operation for mass rapid transit system. IEEE Proc. Electric Power Applications 147(3), 206–212 (2000)

Prediction of Protein Structural Class by Functional Link Artificial Neural Network Using Hybrid Feature Extraction Method

Bishnupriya Panda, Ambika Prasad Mishra, Babita Majhi, and Minakhi Rout

{panda.bishnupriya,ambikaprasad.mishra,babita.majhi,
minakhi.rout}@gmail.com

Abstract. During last few decades' accurate prediction of protein structural class has been a challenging problem. Efficient and meaningful representation of protein molecule plays a significant role. In this paper Chou's pseudo amino acid composition along with amphiphillic correlation factor and the spectral characteristics of the protein has been used to represent protein data. Thus a protein sample is represented by a set of discrete components which incorporate both the sequence order and the sequence length effects. On the basis of such a statistical framework a simple functionally linked artificial neural network has been used for structural class prediction.

Keywords: AAC, AmPseAAC, DCTAmPseAAC, Functional link artificial neural network (FLANN), Protein Domain, Structural Class.

1 Introduction

In molecular biology, sequence to structure prediction plays a significant role. Specifically in protein molecular biology, function of protein molecule is highly dependent on the structure of protein molecule. Protein structural class plays a significant role in determining protein folding. Protein database is growing every day. So a computationally efficient method is highly required for protein structural class prediction. Levitt and Chothia (1976) reported 10 structural classes, 4 principal and 6 small classes in a dataset of 31 globular proteins. However biological community recognizes 4 principal classes depending on percentage of alpha helices and beta strand.

1. α class : Contains more than 45% alpha strands and less than 5% beta strands.

2. β class : Contains more than 45% beta strands and less than 5% alpha strands.

3. α+β class : Contains more than 30% alpha helices and more than 20 % beta strands and beta strands are anti- parallel.

4. α/β class : Contains more than 30% alpha helices and more than 20 % beta strands and beta strands are parallel.

B.K. Panigrahi et al. (Eds.): SEMCCO 2013, Part II, LNCS 8298, pp. 298–307, 2013.

Though Amino acid composition of protein is highly related to cell activity it is difficult to predict a protein molecule of different arranging orders from amino acid composition. Accurate determination of protein structural class is a two step process: Effective representation of protein sequence and then developing a prediction model. Many in-silico structural class prediction algorithm and methods have been proposed earlier.

Amino Acid Composition (AAC) is highly related to protein structural class [1]. Several classification methods such as distance classifier, principal component analysis [2], Bayesian classifier, fuzzy clustering [3], support vector machine [4] and multilayer artificial neural network [5] have been proposed in the literature. Though many promising results have been achieved, AAC of protein lacks sequence order and sequence length information. Sequence order and sequence length information also play a significant role in predicting protein structural class because amino acid composition do not differentiate between protein molecules of different sequence order and sequence length. In this paper along with pseudo amino acid composition, amphiphillic correlation factors of protein molecule [6] and the spectral characteristics of the protein [7] has been used to capture the sequence order information. Many authors have proposed neural network as a good candidate for classification of protein structural class. But how to choose the number of layers and number of neurons in each layer to enhance the classification accuracy is highly complex problem. To alleviate this problem in this paper we propose a low complexity single layer single neuron neural network known as functional link artificial neural network (FLANN) [8] for classification of protein structural class.

This paper is organized as follows: Section 2 describes the Amino Acid Composition of data and design of Amphiphillic Pseudo Amino Acid Composition of data using Hydrophilicity and Hydrophobicity of amino acids and Spectral characteristic of protein. Working principle and discussion of functional expansion of all the three types are carried out in Section 3. Section 4 deals with the results obtained from the simulation study followed by discussions. Finally Section 5 presents the conclusion of the investigation.

2   Preliminaries

A. Protein as Amino Acid Composition(AAC)

Amino acid composition representation of protein molecule is a 20-dimensional feature vector in Euclidian space. The protein x in the composition space is defined as

$$P(x) = [p_1(x), p_2(x).....p_{20}(x)] \tag{1}$$

Where

$$P_k(x) = \frac{f_k(x)}{\sum_{i=1}^{20} f_i(x)} i, k = 1,2.....20 \tag{2}$$

Where $f_k(x)$: Occurrence frequency of 20 constituent amino acid for protein x
      $P(x)$: Protein x in composition space

B. Protein as Amphiphillic Amino Acid Composition(AmPseAAC)

Sequence order and Sequence length information of a protein must be retained. However protein sequence length varies widely which poses an additional problem. Chou [9] has proposed an effective way of representing protein character sequence by some of its physiochemical properties. Hydrophobicity and Hydrophilicity of protein molecule play important role in folding of protein molecule. Suppose a protein molecule is represented by $P_1P_2P_3$.......P_l where P_1 represents the residue at location 1 along with the sequence and so on. The sequence order effect along with a protein chain is approximated by a set of sequence order correlation factor which is defined as

$$\theta_\tau = \frac{1}{L-1}\sum_1^{L-\tau}\theta\left(P_i,P_\tau\right),\left(i=1,2,3....\lambda\right) \tag{3}$$

In (3) L and θ_τ denote length θ_τ order correlation factor. The correlation function $\theta\left(P_i,P_\tau\right)$ is calculated as

$$\theta\left(P_i,P_\tau\right)=H\left(P_i\right)*H\left(P_j\right) \tag{4}$$

Where $H(P_i)$ and $H(P_j)$ refers to Hydrophobicity values of the amino acids P_i and P_j respectively.

In (3) θ_1 is first tier correlation factor and θ_2 is second tier correlation factor.

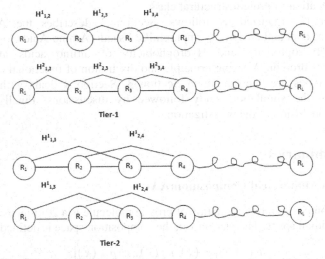

Fig. 1. A schematic representation to show sequence order correlation factor using Hydrophobicity and Hydrophilicity values

Before substituting the Hydrophobicity and Hydrophilicity values in (3) they are subjected to some standard conversion. The objective of the conversion is to make the coded sequence zero mean over the 20 amino acids. The standard conversion is described by the following expression:

$$h^1(R_i) = \frac{h_0^1(R_i) - \sum_{k=1}^{20} h_0^1(R_k)/20}{\sqrt{\sum_{u=1}^{20} [h_0^1(R_u) - \sum_{k=1}^{20} h_0^1(R_k)/20]^2 / 20}}$$

(5)

$$h^2(R_i) = \frac{h_0^2(R_i) - \sum_{k=1}^{20} h_0^2(R_k)/20}{\sqrt{\sum_{u=1}^{20} [h_0^2(R_u) - \sum_{k=1}^{20} h_0^2(R_k)/20]^2 / 20}}$$

3 Spectral Characteristics of Protein

3.1 Fourier Transform Based Feature Representation of Protein

Preserving the periodicity of patterns plays a significant role in class prediction. Hydrophobicity of amino acids can be used to establish a pattern in protein molecules. Sequence pattern of the protein molecule can be transformed to a discrete frequency domain. This can be achieved with the help of discrete Fourier transform. The DFT of a protein sequence (p) can be given as

$$X(k) = \sum_{n=1}^{L} H(P_n) e^{(-j2\Pi nk/L)}, k = 1,2...L \qquad (6)$$

Where X(k) represents periodicity features and the compositional patterns by sinusoidal waves with different frequencies. The low frequency components have more biological significance than high frequency noisy components. These components are chosen for forming the feature vector. Discrete Cosine transformation is a form of DFT which involves low computational complexity and assumes even symmetry. This does not introduce any discontinuity in time domain unlike DFT. Therefore DCT has been chosen as a better substitute of DFT in feature representation.

3.2 Discrete Cosine Transformation

The Discrete Cosine Transformation (DCT) of the coded protein sequence (P) is defined as

$$G(K) = \alpha(k) \sum_{n=0}^{L-1} H(p_n) \cos\left[\frac{(2n+1)k\pi}{2L}\right], k = 0,1,2,...,L-1$$

$$where$$

$$\alpha(k) = \begin{cases} \sqrt{\dfrac{2}{L}}, & k \neq 0 \\ \sqrt{\dfrac{1}{L}}, & k = 0 \end{cases}$$

L : length of protein molecule

G(0) is DC component and remaining are called harmonic of the sequence. Here the low frequency DCT components represent the global information of the coded sequence. The type of protein is represented by the curve of the hydrophobic values whose global shape is determined by low frequency DCT components. Here the DCT components represent the spectral characteristic of the protein molecules.We have used 10 low frequency DCT component of each protein molecule to represent the

So a protein sample is represented as:

$$P = \begin{bmatrix} P_1 \\ P_2 \\ . \\ . \\ . \\ P_{20} \\ P_{20+1} \\ . \\ . \\ P_{20+2\lambda} \\ P_{20+2\lambda+1} \\ . \\ . \\ . \\ P_{20+2\lambda+\delta} \end{bmatrix}$$

Where

$$P_u = \begin{cases} \dfrac{f_u}{\displaystyle\sum_{i=1}^{20} f_i + w\sum_{j=1}^{2\lambda}\theta_j + w\sum_{k=1}^{\delta}\gamma_k} & (1 \le u \le 20) \\[4ex] \dfrac{w\theta_{u-20}}{\displaystyle\sum_{i=1}^{20} f_i + w\sum_{j=1}^{2\lambda}\theta_j + w\sum_{k=1}^{\delta}\gamma_k} & (21 \le u \le 20+2\lambda) \\[4ex] \dfrac{w\gamma_{u-(20+2\lambda)}}{\displaystyle\sum_{i=1}^{20} f_i + w\sum_{j=1}^{2\lambda}\theta_j + w\sum_{k=1}^{\delta}\gamma_k} & (20+2\lambda+1) \le u \le (20+2\lambda+\delta) \end{cases} \tag{8}$$

and   w=0.01

f_i : frequency of amino acid

θ_j : jth rank of coupling factor that harbors jth sequence order correlation factor

γ_k : low frequency DCT components

We have chosen 10 low frequency DCT components for each protein molecule i.e $\delta=10$.

4   Data Set

In order to predict the structural class we have used 3 different standard dataset. The dataset constructed by Chou [10] contains 204 proteins. The average sequence similarity scores in the protein classes are 21% for α ,30% for β,15% for α/β and 14% for α+β. Therefore there is no significant sequence similarity between protein molecules in the dataset. Another two datasets constructed by Zhou [11] contains 277 and 498 proteins. The number of protein domains in each class is listed in Table -1.

Table 1. Details of protein datasets

Dataset	All α	All β	α+β	α/β
204 domain	52	61	46	45
277 domain	70	61	81	65
498 domain	107	126	136	129

The Functional Link Artificial Neural Network (FLANN) has been developed as an alternative architecture to the well known Multilayer Perceptron (MLP) network with application to both function approximation and pattern recognition. The FLANN proposed by Pao [12] is a single layer artificial neural network structure, a nonlinear network with simple operations and provides comparable performance as that of multilayer artificial neural network. The weights of the network are updated using simple LMS algorithm using (9).

$$w(k+1) = w(k) + 2 * \mu * e(k) * \phi \qquad (9)$$

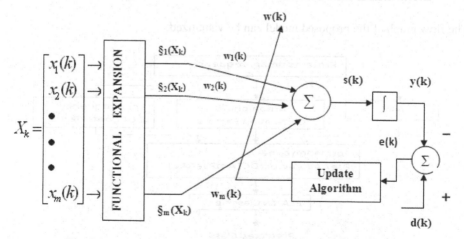

Fig. 2. A simple functional link artificial neural network architecture

Fig. 2 shows an adaptive FLANN architecture with one neuron and nonlinear inputs. The nonlinearity in the input is introduced by trigonometric expansions of input values. After nonlinear mapping of the input features simple linear combiner is used to obtain the output which is then passed through a nonlinear function. According to Covers theorem, a complex pattern classification problem cast in a high-dimensional space is more likely to be linearly separable than in a low dimensional space. The functional expansion block makes use of a functional model comprising of a subset of orthogonal sine and cosine basic functions and the original pattern along with its outer products. For an input pattern consisting of (x_1, x_2) can be expanded using trigonometric functions as

$$\varphi(x) = \left[x_1, \sin\pi(x_1), \cos\pi(x_1), x_2, \sin\pi(x_2), \cos\pi(x_2), \ldots \right] \tag{10}$$

The intermediate output $s(k)$ is calculated as

$$s(k) = \phi(k).W(k) \tag{11}$$

Where $\phi(k)$: input vector after trigonometric expansion
The final output, $y(k)$ is given as

$$y(k) = tanh(s(k)) \tag{12}$$

The output of the FLANN is compared with the target value to give the error value

$$e(k) = d(k) - y(k) \tag{13}$$

Weights of the network are update using simple LMS rule.

5   Simulation and Result

The flow graph of the proposed model can be visualized

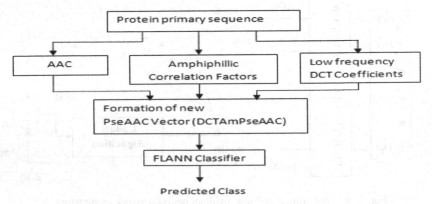

Fig. 3. The flow graph of the proposed FLANN based classification scheme

Initially for each of the standard protein dataset the Amino acid composition (AAC), Amphiphillic Pseudo amino acid (AmPseAAC) composition and the spectral characteristics features are extracted using the formulae as described in Section 2. Then each of the feature patterns is expanded to five terms using the trigonometric expansion. The nonlinearly mapped input pattern is weighted, added together and passed through the activation function, tanh ( ) to give the final value, y(k). The output of FLANN is compared with the target value to produce the error. Then the simple LMS based algorithm is used to update the weights of the classifier and process continues until the error square is minimum. The value of the error square corresponding to each iteration is stored and plotted in Figs. 4-6 to show the convergence characteristics for 204, 277 and 498 domain protein dataset respectively.

The prediction accuracy is more in case of 498 domains due to more number of duplicates. It is more difficult to predict the α+β class due to more number of helices and strands. Here 20 AAC features, 20 Amphiphillic correlation factor and 10 low frequency DCT components have been embedded to form the DCTAmPseAAC feature representation of protein. As this representation of protein captures more features prediction accuracy is higher for this.

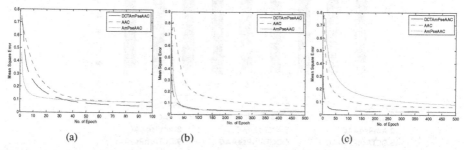

(a)   (b)   (c)

Fig. 4. Comparison of convergence characteristics of FLANN based classifier using AAC, AmPseAAC and DCTAmPseAAC features (a) for the 204 protein domain (b) for the 277 protein domain and (c) for the 498 protein domain respectively

Table 2. Comparison of classification accuracy of three different protein domain datasets with AAC, AmPseAAC and DCTAmPseAAC features

Data Set	Features	Classification Accuracy				
		All α	All β	All α+β	All α/β	Overall Accuracy
	AAC	53.8	45	46.6	100	56.81
204	AmPseAAC	90	17.6	30	68	63.63
	DCTAmPseAAC	94.2	94.2	70.2	86.79	87.25
	AAC	22.7	71.5	74.1	76.9	57.97
277	AmPseAAC	100	52.1	66.7	72.3	71.05
	DCTAmPseAAC	92.6	86.7	91.1	95.31	89.59
	AAC	75	60	50	62.9	58.89
498	AmPseAAC	63	92	52.9	88.5	74.72
	DCTAmPseAAC	93.8	95	94.8	95.68	94.12

The value of λ is chosen as 10 for finding the correlation factor up to 10th tier to preserve sequence order information. It is observed that the α+β class is more difficult to predict as it contains more variability of helices. The classification accuracy of the model is compared using both AAC and AmPseAAC in all the three data sets. Table-2 shows the comparison result of prediction accuracy for 204, 277 and 498 protein domain datasets with AAC and AmPseAAC features. The same is also represented in histogram in Fig. 7. It is evident from Table 2 that DCTAmPseAAC feature representation of the protein data gives better accurate classification result than AmPseAAC and AAC.

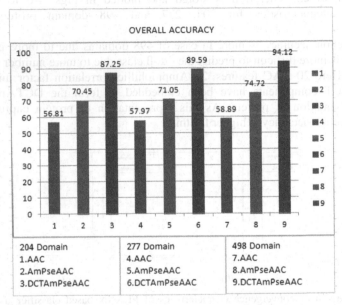

Fig. 5. Comparison of overall classification accuracy of three protein datasets using AAC, AmPseAAC and DCTAmPseAAC features

Table 3. Comparision of Classification accuracy with different feature representation using MLP and FLANN

Dataset	Feature	Overall Accuracy	
		MLP	FLANN
204 Domain	AAC	85.21	56.81
	AmPseAAC	85.62	70.45
	DCTAmPseAAC	86.76	87.25
277 Domain	AAC	81.56	57.97
	AmPseAAC	83.93	71.05
	DCTAmPseAAC	86.64	89.59
498 Domain	AAC	88.51	58.89
	AmPseAAC	89.65	74.72
	DCTAmPseAAC	91.96	94.12

6   Conclusion

In this paper the low complexity neural network FLANN has been used as classifier. The accuracy of the model is enhanced as DCTAmPseAAC representation of the proteins is supplied to the model. The comparison study of the proposed model with MLP shows higher prediction accuracy .In representation of protein molecule we have considered only Hydrophobicity and Hydrophilicity. However other physiochemical properties can also be incorporated. Therefore it is suggested that if more number of features are added then the classification accuracy can further be enhanced.

References

1. Chou, K.C.: A novel approach to predicting protein structural classes in a (20-1)-D amino acid composition space. Proteins 21(4), 319–344 (1995)
2. Du, Q.S., Jiang, Z.Q., He, W.Z., Li, D.P., Chou, K.C.: Amino acid principal component analysis (AAPCA) and its applications in protein structural class prediction. J. Bimol. Struct. Dynam. 23, 635–640 (2006)
3. Ding, Y.S., Zhang, T.L., Chou, K.C.: Prediction of protein structure classes with pseudo amino acid composition and fuzzy support vector machines network. Protein Peptide Lett. 14, 811–815 (2007)
4. Cai, Y.D., Liu, X.J., Xu, X., Zhou, G.P.: Support vector machines for predicting protein structural class. BMC Bioinformatics 2, 3 (2001)
5. Cai, Y., Zhou, G.: Prediction of protein structural classes by neural network. Biochimie 82(8), 783–785 (2000)
6. Panda, B., Mishra, A.P., Majhi, B., Rout, M.: Development and performance evaluation of FLANN based model for protein structural class prediction (in press)
7. Sahu, S.S., Panda, G.: A novel feature representation method based on Chou's pseudo amino acid composition for protein structural class prediction. Computational Biology and Chemistry 34, 320–327 (2010)
8. Majhi, R., Panda, G., Sahoo, G.: Development and performance evaluation of FLANN based model for forecasting of stock markets. Expert Systems with Applications 36, 6800–6808 (2009)
9. Chou, K.C.: Prediction of protein cellular attributes using pseudo amino acid composition. Proteins 43, 246–255 (2001)
10. Chou, K.C.: A key driving force in determination of protein structural classes. Biochem. Biophys, Res. Commun. 264, 216–224 (1999)
11. Zhou, G.P.: An intriguing controversy over protein structural class prediction. J. Protein Chem. 17(8), 729–738 (1998)
12. Pao, Y.H.: Adaptive pattern recognition & neural networks. Addison-Wesley, Reading (1989)

ANN Modeling of a Steelmaking Process

Dipak Laha

Department of Mechanical Engineering
Jadavpur University, Kolkata, India
dipaklaha_jume@yahoo.com

Abstract. In a steelmaking shop, the output 'yield' is considered as an important performance measure while producing a specific amount of steel. It represents the operational efficiency of the steelmaking shop. It is the objective of management to maintain a high percentage of the yield. The present study was performed considering the open-hearth process of a steelmaking shop. The best subset regression analysis is applied to determine the most influencing variables influencing the output of the steelmaking process. Then, the multi-layer feed forward neural network with Levenberg-Marquardt (L-M) backpropagation algorithm is presented to predict the output yield of steel. In the present investigation, 0.0001 of MSE is set as a goal of the network training. The overtraining is given cognizance during the model building. The overall average of absolute percentage error (APE) of the model is found to be 0.5145% and the predicted yield based on the neural network is found to be in good agreement with the testing data set.

Keywords: Yield of steel, open-hearth process, backpropagation neural networks, best subset analysis, Levenberg-Marquardt algorithm.

Nomenclature

$\bar{W}$:   vector of weight connected between neuron j to previous neurons

$\bar{X}$:   vector of inputs

λ: scalar factor

d_{jp}:   desired output of the j-th neuron for pattern p

o_{jp}:   actual output of the j-th neuron for pattern p

NP: number of training patterns

n: learning step for updating weights

$w_{ji(n)}$:   weight of the link between neurons i and j for n-th learning step

$\Delta w_{ji(n)}$:   change in the weight factor for the weight $w_{ji(n)}$

δ_{pj}:   error term

J: number of neurons in the hidden layer

B.K. Panigrahi et al. (Eds.): SEMCCO 2013, Part II, LNCS 8298, pp. 308–318, 2013.

η: learning rate

α: momentum coefficient

p: number of patterns

d_p: desired output for the p-th pattern

o_p: actual output for the p-th pattern

F_n: weight update function for the nth iterations

JM: Jacobean matrix containing the first order derivatives of the network errors

μ: Marquardt parameter

e: vector of network errors

I: identity matrix

β: a scalar quantity

Y_{act} : actual value of yield factor

Y_{pred} : predicted value of yield factor

1   Introduction

Since the steelmaking process (Couderier et al., 1978) is very complex and stochastic in nature, modeling and predicting the operational efficiency of the steelmaking shop is reasonably difficult. For the purpose of modeling a complex process, different me-thodologies such as neural network (NN), multiple regression model, and response surface methodology have been successfully utilized in a wide variety of complex processes. Among these techniques, it has been shown that the predictive quality of the NN is better compared to other methodologies due to its good learning ability. The NN being inspired by the biological nerve system is a tool of artificial intelli-gence used for data classification, pattern recognition, and simulation of various com-plex systems (Jalali-Heravi et al., 2008). Also, this tool has been considered for the prediction of mechanical behavior of materials, and response parameters of various machining processes.

Karnik et al. (2008) used a multilayer feed forward backpropagation NN to model for analyzing the effects of drilling process parameters on delamination factor.

Pal et al. (2008) developed a multilayer NN model to predict the ultimate tensile stress of welded plates and compared with the multiple regression analysis. It was found that the welding strength using the model is better than that using multiple re-gression analysis.

Bezerra et al. (2007) used multilayer NN perceptron architecture to predict the shear stress – strain behavior from carbon fiber / epoxy and glass fiber / epoxy compos-ites. They showed the predictive quality of the network improves with increasing the neurons in the hidden layers and the number of training instances.

The most commonly used ANN model is based on backpropagation with gradient descent algorithm in a training process. Recently, literature review reveals that there are some research work (Mukherjee and Routroy, 2012; Tsai et al., 2008; Jalali-Heravi et al. 2008) on successfully implementation of the Levenberg-Marquardt Backpropagation algorithm on modeling of nonlinear multiple response process behavior in manufacturing and other industries.

Mukherjee and Routroy (2012) used L-M algorithm and Quasi-Newton algorithm for modeling multiple-response grinding process. They have shown that these algorithms converge faster and can predict the nonlinear behavior of multiple-response grinding process well.

Tsai et al. (2008) implemented multiple regression analysis and backpropagation NN with L-M algorithm to build a predicting model for cutting Quad Flat Non-lead packages by using a Diode Pumped Solid State Laser System.

Jalali-Heravi et al. (2008) presented L-M NN for modeling and predicting heparanase inhibitors' activity. The L-M algorithm shows a better performance compared with backpropagation and conjugate gradient algorithms.

The application of a multilayer feed forward backpropagation NN for modeling the parameters, especially on prediction of output 'yield' of the steelmaking process was not reported in the literature. However, there are some literature on ANN modeling of a steelmaking process to predict output parameters, like temperature of the liquid metal and the volume of necessary oxygen blow (Falkus et al., 2003), metallurgical length, shell thickness at the end of the mould and billet surface temperature (Gresouvnik et al., 2012), percentage of phosphorus in the final composition of steel (Monteiro and Sant'Anna, 2012; Shukla and Deo, 2007). A comprehensive description of modern steelmaking processes along with physical and mathematical modeling and solution methodologies based on AI-based techniques, especially ANN, GA, CFD, and FLUENT software is provided by Mazumdar and Evans (2009).

This paper presents the application of a multi-layer feed forward NN with Levenberg-Marquardt (L-M) backpropagation algorithm to model and predict the steelmaking process parameters. The present study is carried out based on the data on monthly basis for the input and output parameters of an open hearth process. The process data was collected from a steelmaking shop, located in Eastern India.

2   Important Input Process Parameters

The 'yield' of steel determines the operational efficiency of the steelmaking shops, i.e., it determines how much percentage of hot metal, scrap, and the iron ore are being converted into steel ingots having desirable compositions. It is the management objective to maintain a high percentage of the yield. The term 'yield' can be defined in different ways. One way to define yield in Equation (1) is on the basis of iron content in the output and input of the furnace, i.e.,

$$yield = \frac{Fe-content\ in\ steel\ ingot}{Fe-content\ in\ hotmetal, scrap\ and\ iron\ ore} \tag{1}$$

The 'yield' is defined here as the ratio of tonnage of the steel ingot and the tonnage of the hot metal, the scrap, and the iron ore, taking into consideration of data on the weekly or monthly basis.

The a-priori reasoning that formed the basis for considering the following ten variables are described below.

- Fuel rate (FLRT) – If FLRT is increased, the temperature of the molten mass in the furnace will be high. In general, the oxidation of iron will be high that leads to losses in the form of vapor and slag. So, there will be an adverse effect of the FLRT on the yield. The unit of fuel rate in SI unit is KJ/kg mole. However, the unit of fuel rate is commonly used in steel industry as Mkcal/ton.

- Hot metal rate (HMRT) – If charging of HMRT is increased, carbon and other impurities will go to the slag and also some iron in the slag reducing the magnitude of the yield. It is expressed in kg/ton of steel.

- Heat time (HTTM) – If HTTM is increased then during the time all reactions will be continued and even after oxidation of all impurities in the pig iron, iron will be started oxidizing with excess oxygen. Also due to vaporization there will be some losses in iron. So, the yield will decrease. It is expressed in hours.

- Scrap charged (SCH) – For melting, the scrap takes long time. There is a possibility for iron to get oxidized and will go to the slag. Part of it straightway reacts with hot metal resulting excessive boiling, which will lead to fume formation. Hence, there will be losses in iron. It is expressed in kg/ton of steel.

- Oxygen rate (XGNRT) – When amount of oxygen lancing is increased, there is a heavy formation of fume and as a result, iron gets vaporized and gets lost in the atmosphere. Due to high temperature there is extensive carbon oxidation reaction during melting and also during refining time resulting the fume formation and thus decreases the yield. It is expressed in Nm/ton of steel.

- Production (PRDN) – Apart from supplying raw materials production generally increases due to the increase in the heat input and the oxygen input. It is expressed in ton/month.

- Mould sticker (MST) – Some metals get stuck in the mould. If there is increase in loss in mould sticker the yield will be decreased. It is expressed in ton/month.

- Metal lost (MLT) – Increase in metal loss leads to decrease in the yield. Depending on the FLRT, the temperature of the molten mass in the furnace will be high. As a result, the oxidation of iron will be high that leads to losses in the form of vapor and slag. It is expressed in ton/month.

- Ore rate (ORRT) – Reduction of iron is a high exothermic reaction. So, all the concerned reactions are slowed down and more time is needed, resulting in a huge loss in iron either in the form of slag or fumes. It is expressed in kg/ton of steel.

- Heat size (HSZ) – It depends upon the amount of hot metal and scrap. So, depending upon the hot metal scrap ratio heat size will be affected. Here, "heat size" means that each heat is of 3.5 to 4 hours duration in the open-hearth process and the capacity of the hot metal in the vessel is about 200 tons and 100 tons respectively. Heat is measured in KJ/kg of steel. It is expressed in ton/heat.

3   Best Subset Regression Analysis

The best subset regression procedure (Rencher and Pun, 1980) is used to select subset of variables from group of variables as it is not possible to select all variables at a time. The general method is to select the smallest subset that fulfills certain statistical criteria. The best subset regression procedure is a method to determine the most likely group of variables for further analysis. The reason for using a subset of variables rather than a full set is because the subset model may actually estimate the regression coefficients and predict future responses with smaller variance than the full model using all predictors.

The statistics R^2, R_{adj}^2, C_p, and MSE are calculated by the best subset procedure using MINITAB 16 English. In this study, after establishing a-priori metallurgical cause-effect relationship among all these variables, the best subset regression analysis has been applied to obtain the most significant variables influencing the output yield of steel. Based on these statistical results, the significant variables are finally selected for further processing.

4   The L-M Backpropagation Algorithm

The slow convergence of the gradient descent back-propagation algorithm which is frequently used in the common NN model results in a local minimum during training. To overcome this disadvantage, some improved algorithms have been found effective in the literature, such as quasi-Newton algorithm, scaled conjugate gradient algorithm, and L-M algorithm.   A quasi-Newton method attains faster convergence near a local or global optimum, but, is not as sensitive to accuracy as the conjugate-gradient method. The L-M method bridges the gap between these two techniques, resulting in improved performance, convergence and predicting values in many experimental studies (Tsai et al., 2008; Jalali-Heravi et al., 2008).

4.1   Mathematical Background

Like the quasi-Newton method and the conjugate-gradient methods, the Levenberg-Marquardt algorithm avoids the need to use the Hessian matrix (Hagan and Menhaj, 1994).

When the neural network has a multilayer perceptron with a single output neuron, it is trained by minimizing the cost function, $C_{av}(w)$, in the form of sum of squares error given as

$$C_{av}(w) = \frac{1}{2N} \sum_{i=1}^{N} [d(i) - F(x(i), w)]^2 \qquad (2)$$

Using the Levenberg-Marquardt algorithm, the adjustment of the weight error (Δw) is computed as

$$\Delta w = [H + \mu I]^{-1} g \qquad (3)$$

The Hessian matrix and the gradient vector of the cost function, $C_{av}(w)$, are defined as

$$g(w) = \frac{\partial C_{av}(w)}{\partial w} \qquad (4)$$

$$H(w) = \frac{\partial C_{av}(w)}{\partial w^2} \qquad (5)$$

However, due to the complexity difficulty of Equation (5), especially when the dimension of the weight vector (w) is high, the Hessian matrix can be approximated as

$$Hw \approx JTJ \tag{6}$$

The use of this approximation in equation (6) is justified when the Levenberg-Marquardt algorithm is applied in close proximity of a local optimum. Hence, the Levenberg-Marquardt algorithm due to the approximation of the Hessian matrix is a first-order optimization problem and is suitable for nonlinear least-squares.

The regularizing or loading parameter μ, in Equation (3) is a critical factor in operating the Levenberg-Marquardt method. If we set μ equal to zero, this method becomes Newton' method. On the other hand, if we consider large value of μ so that the value μI is much higher than the H in Equation (3), then it functions as a gradient des cent method. From these two special cases, it follows that at each iteration of this method, value of μ should be such that the matrix $((H + \mu)$ will be a positive definite.

4.2   The Neural Network Procedure

The steps involved in the training of a multilayer feed forward NN are given below:

Inputs. Consider a set of inputs and desired outputs, known as training patterns. All the inputs and desired outputs are normalized in the range [-1, 1] using the expression, given by

$$X_{norm} = \frac{2(X - X_{min})}{(X_{max} - X_{min})} - 1 \tag{7}$$

Step 1. Initialize all of the synaptic weights of the links of the neurons between the layers by assigning small random values to all the links. Let us assume unipolar sigmoid transfer function and the input and output of j-th neuron in the hidden and the output layer is given as

$$O_j = \frac{1}{1 + e^{-\lambda inp_j}} \tag{8}$$

$$inp_j = \overline{W}^T X \tag{9}$$

Step 2: Set $kp = 1$. Set $epochs = 1$.

Step 3. Determine the synaptic weights that are required to produce the desired output for the kp-th pattern based on the weight update function, F_n, using L-M algorithm in order to minimize the sum of the squared error (SSE) for N-number of output neurons, as given as:

$$(n+1) = Fn + \alpha \Delta wji(n) \tag{10}$$

$$SSE = \frac{1}{2} \sum_{i=1}^{N} (d_{ip} - o_{ip})^2 \tag{11}$$

$$F_o = -g_o \tag{12}$$

$$F_n = -[JM^T \times JM + \mu I]^{-1} \times JM^T \times e \tag{13}$$

In the L-M algorithm, the update function, F_n, can be computed using Equations 12-13. The parameter μ should be multiplied by some factor, say, a scalar β when a tentative step would increase of the performance function E_n. On the other hand, when the step decreases of the function E_n, μ is divided by β.

Step 4. If $kp<NP$, $kp = kp+1$ and return to Step 3; Otherwise, go to Step 5.

Step 5. Compute MSE considering all the training patterns as given by:

$$MSE = \frac{1}{NP} \sum_{p=1}^{NP}(d_{ip} - o_{ip})^2 \tag{14}$$

Step 6: If ($MSE < MSE_{target}$), then stop; Otherwise, go to Step 7.

Step 7: epochs=epochs+1. If (epochs> epochs_{max}), then stop; Otherwise, return to Step 2.

Outputs. Obtain MSE at the end of the training process.

5   Computational Results

In the present study, we selected a number of input variables on the basis of the technological relationship existing between the variables under consideration and the output yield. For the open-hearth process, we considered ten variables and fifty-four input-output data patterns on monthly basis. After establishing a-priori metallurgical cause-effect relationship among all these variables, the best subset regression analysis (described in Section 3) is employed to obtain the most significant variables, HMRT, HTSZ, ORRT, and SCH influencing the output yield of steel as shown in Table 1. The ANN was developed with the HMRT, HTSZ, ORRT, and SCH as the input process parameters to predict the output yield of steel. The ANN program was coded in MATLAB 8 for Windows 8 operating system. A three-layer feed forward network with log-sigmoid transfer function was selected. The proper number of neurons in the hidden layer is problem specific for successful training of the network and was obtained by varying different number of neurons in the hidden layer using trial and error method. If there are too few neurons, it can result in under-fitting whereas too many neurons lead to over-fitting (Karnik et al., 2008). Also, prolonged training exceeding certain epochs has the tendency of memorizing the input-output data patterns resulting

Table 1. Results obtained from the best subset regression analysis

Variables	R^2	R^2_{adj}	Cp	MSE
HMRT, ORRT, SCH, XGNRT	95.4	95.1	18.4	0.0048401
HMRT, HSZ, ORRT, SCH	**96.2**	**95.9**	**8.1**	**0.0044227**
HMRT, MST, ORRT, SCH	95.3	94.9	20.5	0.0049209
HMRT, ORRT, PRDN, SCH	94.7	94.2	29.0	0.0052336
FLRT, HMRT, ORRT, SCH	94.6	94.2	29.5	0.0052534

Table 2. Data set for steel making process parameters for the training purpose

Sl. No	HMRT	HSZ	ORRT	SCH	Y_{act}	Y_{pred}	APE
1	776	209.65	123	69.48	0.86	0.8654	0.628
2	819	210.89	135	59.08	0.86	0.8624	0.279
3	788	211.60	115	80.66	0.82	0.8182	0.220
4	830	202.79	121	70.50	0.82	0.8190	0.122
5	851	206.00	148	63.80	0.82	0.8186	0.171
6	824	211.20	122	72.80	0.82	0.8222	0.268
7	796	210.45	143	69.60	0.84	0.8421	0.250
8	855	213.68	191	55.60	0.83	0.8291	0.108
9	822	215.10	167	62.00	0.84	0.8415	0.178
10	808	215.60	174	62.80	0.85	0.8482	0.212
11	803	214.87	144	76.20	0.83	0.8231	0.831
12	838	204.30	164	74.10	0.79	0.7902	0.025
13	887	209.60	170	51.80	0.82	0.8229	0.354
14	822	213.15	160	77.30	0.80	0.8002	0.025
15	832	212.60	140	74.15	0.81	0.8097	0.037
16	734	214.80	148	85.20	0.84	0.8409	0.107
17	763	216.20	180	76.80	0.84	0.8386	0.167
18	844	211.80	184	57.00	0.83	0.8319	0.229
19	826	211.70	187	65.00	0.82	0.8241	0.500
20	828	214.68	165	73.92	0.80	0.8066	0.825
21	838	213.59	168	64.30	0.82	0.8256	0.683
22	872	208.52	186	59.77	0.81	0.8037	0.778
23	794	214.79	166	75.55	0.83	0.8253	0.566
24	836	210.65	195	72.30	0.79	0.7919	0.241
25	804	212.42	146	73.40	0.83	0.8277	0.277
26	757	215.33	138	82.10	0.84	0.8349	0.607
27	817	214.71	147	69.90	0.83	0.8308	0.096
28	800	209.67	154	71.06	0.83	0.8314	0.169
29	801	209.58	163	56.50	0.88	0.8715	**0.966**
30	784	212.52	147	65.51	0.87	0.8687	0.149
31	869	206.66	137	60.25	0.82	0.8205	0.060
32	845	209.75	162	56.53	0.84	0.8361	0.464
33	755	213.94	157	71.66	0.87	0.8682	0.207
34	776	211.90	149	69.00	0.86	0.8618	0.209
35	757	212.90	132	74.12	0.86	0.8636	0.419
36	775	209.79	123	63.60	0.89	0.8831	0.775
38	744	208.70	179	79.60	0.83	0.8330	0.361
38	819	201.92	114	75.50	0.81	0.8096	0.049

Table 3. Data set for steel making process parameters for the testing purpose

Sl. No.	HMRT	HSZ	ORRT	SCH	Y_{act}	Y_{pred}	APE
1	786	209.25	123	63.86	0.87	0.8780	0.920
2	841	211.90	164	61.10	0.83	0.8305	0.060
3	810	215.00	176	65.60	0.84	0.8370	0.357
4	772	216.80	165	83.80	0.81	0.8134	0.420
5	813	211.50	145	68.20	0.84	0.8349	0.607
6	762	214.67	146	75.91	0.86	0.8498	1.186
7	737	210.73	174	74.70	0.85	0.8625	**1.471**
8	804	207.25	121	74.98	0.83	0.8218	0.988

Table 4. Data set for steel making process parameters for the validation purpose

Sl. No.	HMRT	HTSZ	ORRT	SCH	Y_{act}	Y_{pred}	APE
1	824	215.69	149	65.58	0.84	0.8376	0.286
2	844	213.25	165	57.00	0.85	0.8381	**1.400**
3	846	215.23	162	64.60	0.82	0.8233	0.402
4	850	209.26	160	57.90	0.83	0.8313	0.157
5	832	211.50	149	58.92	0.85	0.8453	0.553
6	768	211.66	131	72.89	0.86	0.8586	0.163
7	797	208.21	120	69.17	0.85	0.8483	0.200
8	818	211.21	106	71.34	0.83	0.8308	0.096

Table 5. Configuration and parameters for training of the proposed L-M NN

Network configuration	4-10-1
Transfer function used in the hidden layer	log- sigmoid transfer function
Number of patterns used for training	38
Number of patterns used for testing	8
Number of patterns used for validation	8
Maximum number of epochs	100
MSE (target)	0.00001
Marquardt parameter μ	0.01
Factor β	10

in poor generalization ability. Therefore, in this study, 100 epochs to be completed or a MSE of 0.00001 was set as stopping criterion. For ANN modeling, all 54 data set was separated into three groups: training, testing and validation sets. These data samples were randomly placed in these sets. The training set consisted of 38 input-output patterns and was used for model generation. However, the test set comprised 8 input patterns and was used to take care of the generalized ability and overtraining of the

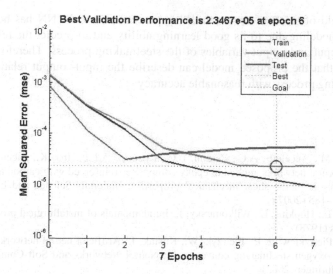

Fig. 1. Performance curves with the variation of MSE and epochs

ANN model. The rest data set, i.e., 8 out of 54 was used to evaluate the generated model. In the present investigation, 0.00001 of MSE was set as an error goal of network training. The network is trained in batch training mode. The details of the parameters employed for training of the network using L-M algorithm are shown in Table 5. The training process was stopped either by the MSE goal or the maximum number of training epochs, depending on which is reached earlier. It is observed at the end of the training process that the network architecture with [4-10-1] yields the least MSE of 0.000020374 (using Equation 9) after 100 epochs and therefore is selected for modeling. The trained ANN was initially selected considering 38 input data patterns which were employed for the training purpose. For each input pattern, the predicted or desired output by the network is compared with the actual output value. It was found from the results of Table 2 that the predicted value closely matches the corresponding actual output and the maximum APE was seen to be 0.965909%. The trained network was then tested using test set of 8 input patterns and from the results in Table 3, the maximum APE for testing patterns was found to be 1.47059%. As expected, the predicted errors from the testing patterns are slightly higher than those from the training input patterns. The performance of the trained network is also checked with the validation set. From the results of validation sets in Table 4, the maximum APE was seen to be 1.4% and is in good agreement with the testing data set. Figure 1 shows for the proposed NN model that the performance curves during training, testing and validation converge to a satisfactory MSE of 0.000023467 after 6 epochs approximately.

6   Conclusions

In the present work, the Levenberg-Marquardt backpropagation algorithm has been used as a weight updating method in the multilayer feed forward back propagation neural network to predict the relationship between the input parameters and the output parameter (yield of steel) of the steelmaking process. The L-M NN has been found effective for modeling due to its good learning ability and to predict the relationship between the input and output variables of the steelmaking process. Therefore, it may be concluded that the proposed model can describe the input- output relationship of the steel- making process with reasonable accuracy.

References

1. Bezerra, E.M., Ancelotti, A.C., Pardini, L.C., Rocco, J.A.F.F., Iha, K., Ribeiro, C.H.C.: Artificial neural networks applied to epoxy composites reinforced with carbon and E-glass fibers: Analysis of the shear mechanical properties. Materials Science and Engineering A 464, 177–185 (2007)
2. Couderier, L., Hopkins, L., Wilkomirsky, I.: Fundamentals of metallurgical processes. Paragon Press (1978)
3. Falkus, J., Pietrzkiewicz, P., Pietrzyk, W., Kusiak, J.: Artificial neural network predictive system for oxygen steelmaking converter. In: Neural Networks and Soft Computing, pp. 825–830. Springer (2003)
4. Gresovnik, I., Kodelja, T., Vertnik, R., Sarler, B.: Application of artificial neural networks to improve steel production process. In: Proceedings of the IASTED International Conference on Artificial Intelligence and Soft Computing, pp. 249–255 (2012)
5. Hagan, M.T., Menhaj, M.B.: Training feedforward networks with the Marquardt algorithm. IEEE Transactions on Neural Networks 5, 989–993 (1994)
6. Jalali-Heravi, M., Asadollahi-Baboli, M., Shahbazikhah, P.: QSAR study of heparanase inhibitors activity using artificial neural networks and Levenberg-Marquardt algorithm. European Journal of Medicinal Chemistry 43, 548–556 (2008)
7. Karnik, S.R., Gaitonde, V.N., Campos Rubio, J., Esteves Correia, A., Abrão, A.M., Paulo Davim, J.: Delamination analysis in high speed drilling of carbon fiber reinforced plastics (CFRP) using artificial neural network model. Materials and Design 29, 1768–1776 (2008)
8. Mazumdar, D., Evans, J.W.: Modeling of steelmaking processes. CRC Press (2009)
9. Monteiro, L.V., Sant'Anna, A.M.O.: Application of Neural network for modeling steelmaking process. Congrso Latino-lberoameroamericano de investigacion Oprative, 1618–1627 (2012)
10. Mukherjee, I., Routroy, S.: Comparing the performance of neural networks developed by using Levenberg-Marquardt and Quasi-Newton with the gradient descent algorithm for modelling a multiple response grinding process. Expert Systems with Applications 39, 2397–2407 (2012)
11. Pal, M., Pal, S.K., Samantaray, A.K.: Artificial neural network modeling of weld joint strength prediction of a pulsed metal inert gas welding process using arc signals. Journal of Materials Processing Technology 202, 464–474 (2008)
12. Rencher, A.C., Pun, F.C.: Inflation of R2 in best subset regression. Technimetrics 22, 49–53 (1980)
13. Shukla, A.K., Deo, B.: Mathematical modeling of phosphorus prediction in BOF steelmaking process: A fundamental approach to produce low phosphorus steels and ensure direct tap practices. In: International Conference on Metal and Alloys, METALL 2007 (2007)
14. Tsai, M.J., Li, C.H., Chen, C.C.: Optimal laser-cutting parameters for QFN packages by utilizing artificial neural networks and genetic algorithm. Journal of Materials Processing Technology 208, 270–283 (2008)

Crop Yield Forecasting Using Neural Networks

Mukesh Meena and Pramod Kumar Singh

Computational Intelligence and Data Mining Research Lab
ABV- Indian Institute of Information Technology and Management Gwalior
mukesh.iiitm@gmail.com, pksingh@iiitm.ac.in

Abstract. The crop production forecasting has become an important issue, now, as it is a key factor for our economy and sustainable development on account of increased demand of the food grains with growing population. It helps farmers and government to develop a better post-harvest management at local / regional / national level, e.g., transportation, storage, distribution. Additionally, it helps farmers to plan next year's crop and government to plan import/export strategies. This work is based on the yield forecasting of the pearl millet (bajra) in the Jaipur region of Rajasthan, India. The proposed method uses a back propagation artificial neural network to forecast current yield of the crop with respect to the environmental factors using time series data. The obtained results are encouraging and much better in comparison to a recent fuzzy time series based methods for forecasting.

Keywords: Crop yield forecasting, Pearl millet, Time series, Correlation analysis, Neural network.

1 Introduction

Forecasting is the use of historic data to determine the direction of future trends. It is an age old phenomenon and finds its application in almost every walk of life, e.g., weather forecasting [1], economic forecasting [2], energy forecasting [3], transport forecasting [4], sales forecasting [5], technology forecasting [6], crop yield forecasting [7]. As risk and uncertainty are central to forecasting, it is not possible to forecast with 100% accuracy. Therefore, the forecasting methods aim to reduce the forecasting error and obtain the best possible forecast.

The crop production forecasting is determining future value of a crop yield for any given region/country for a particular year or season. It has gained significance due to the rapidly growing population, industrialization and globalization. A successful forecast of a crop yield bears significant profits. An accurate crop yield forecast helps farmers in storage management and planning for the next year's crop and helps governments for better post-harvest management in terms of storage, transportation and distribution at local / regional / national level, and plan import/export strategies accordingly. It is particularly useful for us as our economy primarily depends on agriculture and agriculture based products. Moreover, almost two-third of the employed class in our country lives on the business of agriculture. In spite of this, there is a high degree of uncertainty as the agriculture is heavily dependent on rains.

B.K. Panigrahi et al. (Eds.): SEMCCO 2013, Part II, LNCS 8298, pp. 319–331, 2013.

The crop yield is affected by the physical factors, the economic factors, and the technological factors [8]. The prime *physical factors* are temperature, humidity, rainfall, soil, and topography. For example, the moisture requirements vary from plant to plant and region to region; regions having low maximum temperature are not suitable for plant growth whereas agriculture is successful in the tropical regions, where temperature is high throughout the year. The prime *economic factors* are market, transport facilities, capital, labour, and government policies. For example, the supply of labour determines the character and type of agriculture; the government policies may restrict / promote a crop and influence agricultural land use. The Government may restrict or force the cultivation of a crop. The prime *technological factors* are fertilizers, pesticides, machinery and high yielding variety seeds. The scientific and technological development has a great impact on the crop production. The use of primitive methods of farming results in poor farm yield whereas the use of modern farm technologies increases the farm yield substantially. For example, per hectare yield of rice in India is only 2000 kg in comparison to about 5600 kg in Japan due to scientific and technological differences in farming.

In this study, we present our back propagation artificial neural network based approach to forecast yield of the pearl millet (bajra) in the Jaipur region of Rajasthan, India. However, in absence of vast and varied data required for forecasting, we use data related to physical factors only, which we collected through official websites and by other official means from the government of Rajasthan and the government of India. Here, we use the monthly data for every season as our primary concern is to obtain a high degree of accuracy in the forecasting. In other words, this study aims to provide a simple computational method which uses available data to the best possible extent to obtain a high degree of accuracy in the forecasting. However, this is not a maiden attempt to a novel problem (agricultural production forecasting). Kumar et al. [9] present a fuzzy time series model and two variations of it to forecast wheat production. The results clearly indicate that the models are not appropriate as the forecasting error is high; it is probably because they use only previous years' yield to forecast. Kumar and Kumar [7] too present a fuzzy time series model for wheat forecasting. Here, too the authors use only previous years' yield to forecast and obtain poor results.

Rest of the paper is organized as follows. Section 2 includes the data analysis part. The proposed forecasting method is presented in Section 3. Section 4 presents simulation results and is followed by the conclusion in Section 5.

2   Factors Affecting the Crop Production

An analysis of the available historical data indicates following relationship between the crop yield and the physical factors.

2.1   Variation of Crop Yield with Rainfall

The rainfall is one of the important factors that affect the crop production. Figure 1 represents a scatter plot of the total seasonal yield given in kg per hectare and the total seasonal rainfall (July – September). It is observed that for extremely low rainfall and the extremely high rainfall the yield is low and for average rainfall (300 mm – 600 mm) the yield is average or high. It indicates that the crop requires moderate rainfall; extremely high or low rainfall may be devastating for the crop.

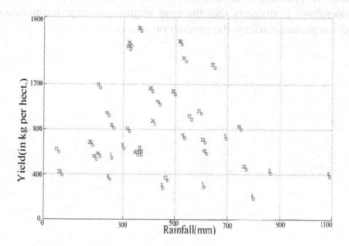

Fig. 1. Plot between yield Vs total rainfall

2.2   Variation of Crop Yield with Humidity

Humidity is another important meteorological factor that plays a vital role for growth of the crop. A scatter plot of the given yield and the average humidity is presented in Figure 2. It shows that pearl millet production is high for high humid conditions and low for low humid conditions. Therefore, we conclude that the crop requires high humidity.

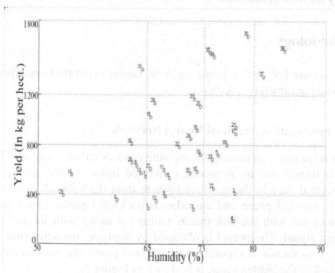

Fig. 2. Plot between yield and average humidity

2.3   Variation of Crop Yield with Temperature

Figure 3 represents a scatter plot of the yield and the average temperature. It is observed that the production is low for low and high temperature, and high for average temperature. It suggests that the crop requires average temperature whereas low and high temperature affects the production adversely.

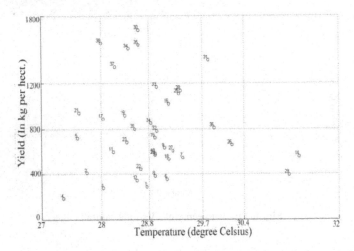

Fig. 3. Plot between yield and average temperature

The above analysis of the three most prominent factors for the crop yield indicates that though the pearl millet has a wide adaptability to grow under varying stress of rainfall, temperature and moisture, it requires average rainfall and temperature, and high humidity for high production.

3   Methodology

In this work, we use back propagation artificial neural network; hence, present it and its computational parameters briefly.

3.1   Back Propagation Artificial Neural Network

It is build by connecting elementary processing devices called neurons. The signal or information is transmitted by means of connected links. As the name suggests the error is propagated back to the previous layer to train the network. It consists of two phases: one is forward phase and the other is backward phase. In forward phase, a weight is associated with the link that is multiplied along with the net input or the incoming input signal. The output is obtained by applying the activation function on the net input. It is shown in Figure 4. In backward phase the error is calculated and propagated back to the hidden layer. It is shown in Figure 5.

Here, i, j and k are the index for i_{th} input neuron, j_{th} hidden neuron and k_{th} output neuron respectively. The w_{ji} is a weight between the link connecting a hidden neuron and a input neuron and w_{kj} is a weight between the link connecting a output neuron and a hidden neuron. $Nout_j$ is the output of the hidden neuron j, which is computed as shown in equation 1.

$$Nout_j = \sum_{i=1}^{n} w_{ji} * input_i \qquad (1)$$

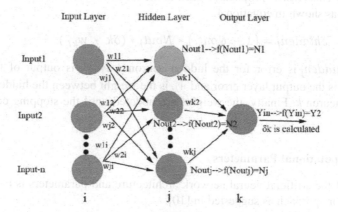

Fig. 4. Forward phase of back propagation

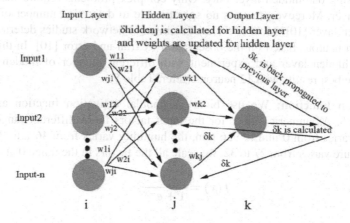

Fig. 5. Backward phase of back propagation

The f($Nout_j$) is activation of the j_{th} hidden neuron represented by N_j. Y_{in} is output of a neuron in the output layer. The output of k_{th} neuron in the output layer is computed as shown in equation 2.

$$Y_{ink} = \sum_{i=1}^{n} w_{kj} * N_j \tag{2}$$

The $f(Y_{in})$ is activation of the output neuron and is represented as $Y2$ in Figure 4. The δk is the output layer error. This error term is computed as shown in equation 3.

$$\delta k = (Y1 - Y2) * (1 - Y2) * Y2 \tag{3}$$

Here, δk is output layer error, $Y1$ is target output and $Y2$ is computed output of the output layer. This error is propagated back to the hidden layer. The hidden layer error is computed as shown in equation 4.

$$\delta hidden_j = (1 - Nout_j) * Nout_j * (\delta k * w_{kj}) \tag{4}$$

Here, $\delta hidden_j$ is error for the hidden neuron j, $Nout_j$ is output of the hidden neuron j, δk is the output layer error and w_{kj} is the weight between the hidden neuron j and output neuron k. Finally, the weights are updated until the stopping condition is reached.

3.2 Computational Parameters

Our study of the artificial neural network architecture and parameters is based on the trail-and-error approach as suggested in [10].

Number of Neurons in the Hidden Layer: There is no evidence that suggests using more than two hidden layers in artificial neural network. Most of the problems are solved using one hidden layer only. Only complex problems require more than one hidden layer. Moreover, there is no specific rule to determine number of neurons in the hidden layer [10]. Most of the artificial neural network studies determine number of hidden neurons based on the observation by trial-and-error [10]. In this work, we use one hidden layer and experiment with different number of hidden neurons to obtain the best results with 12 neurons (refer, Table 5).

Activation Function: We use binary sigmoidal activation function as shown in equation 5. As numeric values for the input factors lie in different ranges, e.g., the rainfall varies from 0 mm to 956 mm, the humidity varies from 46% to 90% and the temperature varies from 27 to 32, we scale all the factors in the range 0 and 1.

$$f(x) = \frac{1}{1 + e^{-x}} \tag{5}$$

Weight: The weights connecting input neuron to the hidden neuron and the weights connecting hidden neuron to the output neuron may be initialized to zero or any random value. In this work, we initialize the weights randomly between 0 to1, which are further updated using the gradient descent rule as shown in equation 6.

$$weight(new) = weight(old) - \alpha * \delta E/\delta w \tag{6}$$

Here, α is learning rate and $\delta E / \delta w$ is first derivative of the cost function $E(n)$ as shown in equation 7.

$$E(n) = 1/2(\Sigma(Y1(n) - Y2(n))^2) \tag{7}$$

Learning Rate: It determines speed of convergence of the system. Its value ranges between 0 and 1 [11]. A low learning rate slows and a high learning rate hasten converge of the system to the global optima. However, a fast learning rate may trap the system into a local optima. In view of the results obtained in [12] we start with a learning rate of 0.1 and increase it as long as the error is not increasing in order to avoid trapping in local optima. Afterwards, we reduce the learning rate to achieve best results.

Momentum Factor: It is added to the weight update formula for faster convergence. It helps to avoid being trapped into the local optima and its value too ranges between 0 and 1. The weight update formula for the back propagation artificial neural network with momentum factor is shown in equation 8[11].

$$\begin{aligned} weight(t + 1) = weight(t) + \alpha * \delta k * x + mf[weight(t) \\ - weight(t - 1)] \end{aligned} \tag{8}$$

Here, *mf* is momentum factor, α is learning rate and *x* is an input from the previous neuron. As its value is determined heuristically, we use a trail-and-error approach to determine its appropriate value for our problem and observe that the best result is obtained for its value of 0.9.

Stopping Condition: Usually a threshold value of the error or a fixed number of epochs is considered as the stooping criteria [11]. In this work, the stopping condition is minimum of 1000 epochs (fixed number of epochs) or error 1e-10 (threshold value of the error) whichever condition occurs earlier.

4   Results and Discussion

4.1   Data Set

In this work, we use the pearl millet (bajra) crop in the Jaipur region of Rajasthan, India. The pearl millet is a rain fed crop and sown during monsoon season, i.e., in kharif season. Though many factors affect the yield of pearl millet, we consider only the physical factors (climatic conditions) because of an easy availability of the data. As the climatic condition requirements for any crop are different throughout the life cycle of the crop, we consider environmental factors of each month as individual factor in our study. In in this manner there are 24 factors for three months as in Rajasthan pearl millet is sown in the month of July and harvested at the end of the month of September.

The 24 factors are average monthly rainfall, maximum temperature in a month, minimum temperature in a month, average monthly humidity, mean sea level pressure, mean wind speed (km/h), maximum sustained speed (km/h) and number of days of rain occurred in the three months of crop life cycle, i.e., July, August and September. These factors are shown in Table 1.

Table 1. 24 factors affecting the pearl millet (bajra) production

Factors		
July rainfall	Aug rainfall	Sep rainfall
July maximum temperature	Aug maximum temperature	Sep maximum temperature
July minimum temperature	Aug minimum temperature	Sep minimum temperature
July humidity	Aug humidity	Sep humidity
July mean sea level pressure	Aug mean sea level pressure	Sep mean sea level pressure
July mean wind speed	Aug mean wind speed	Sep mean wind speed
July maximum sustained speed	Aug maximum sustained speed	Sep maximum sustained speed
July number of days of rain	July number of days of rain	July number of days of rain

The relevant data are obtained from different sources. The crop production related data are collected from the Ministry of Agriculture, Government of Rajasthan and other online sources of Government of Rajasthan [13, 14]. The meteorological data are collected from the official website [15] of the Indian Meteorological Department and other online sources [16]. Format of the data available for the crop is shown in Table 2 and format for the historical data of physical factors of the crop lifecycle is shown in Table 3. It is as follows. The *rain* is average monthly rainfall, *max* is maximum temperature in the month, *min* is minimum temperature in a month, *hum* is average monthly humidity in percentage, *slp* is mean sea level pressure in hPa, *ws* is mean wind speed in km/h, *maxws* is maximum sustained wind speed in km/h and *days* is number of days of rain occurred in the month.

Table 2. Historical data of the yield Since 1973 to 1979 of pearl millet (bajra) in Jaipur, Rajasthan

Year	Production in tones	Area in Hectare	Yield in Kg/Ha
1973	166.00	315	527.00
1974	66.00	228	289.00
1975	76.00	185	411.00
1976	59.00	213	277.00
1977	32.00	174	184.00
1978	144.00	200	720.00
1979	72.00	202	356.00

Table 3. Historical climate data of July Since 1973 to 1979 in Jaipur, Rajasthan

Year	rain	max	min	Hum	Slp	ws	maxws	days
1973	126.4	33.7	26.1	71.8	997.4	9.6	20.5	11
1974	369.4	33.9	24.5	71.4	996.4	6.6	17.5	14
1975	377.4	33.5	24.5	71.8	998.9	7.5	17.6	4
1976	208.8	33.6	25.7	69.9	997.4	6.5	15.5	10
1977	385.1	31	24.6	85.1	996.6	4.6	12.2	17
1978	452.2	31.6	24.5	81.6	998.3	6.1	14.7	16
1979	128.3	128.3	25.4	66.6	998.8	7.2	19.3	11

4.2   Results and Discussion

As discussed above we consider 24 factors as the input variables and the crop yield as the output variable. As few input factors may be redundant, hence irrelevant, which affects accuracy of the results severely, we remove the redundancy using correlation analysis. The correlation shows whether and how strongly the pairs of variables are related. Its value, which is known as correlation coefficient r, ranges between +1 and -1. The closer the value of r to +1 or -1, the closer the two variables are. If r is close to 0 the variables are not related, if r is positive the variables are positively correlated and if r is negative the variables are negatively correlated. However, the correlation doesn't support the causality, i.e., any change in one variables never cause the effect to the other variable.

Table 4. 6 factors after correlation matrix reduction

Factors
July number of days of rain
August rainfall
August maximum temperature
August humidity
September humidity
September number of days of rain

After correlation analysis the 24 input variables are reduced to 6 only as shown in Table 4. Our objective is to minimize the average forecasting error rate (AFER) [6], which is shown as given in equation 9.

$$AFER = \sum_{i=1}^{n} \left(\frac{\left(\frac{abs(forecasted\ value\ i - actual\ value\ i)}{actual\ value\ i} \right)}{n} \right) * 100 \qquad (9)$$

Table 5. Comparison of the results for the data set

Case	No. of inputs	No. of hidden neurons	Structure	Training Data (%)	Testing data (%)	AFER (%)
1	6	10	06-10-01	60	40	15.89
2	6	12	06-12-01	60	40	13.79
3	6	12	06-12-01	70	30	03.82
4	6	12	06-12-01	80	20	05.20

Here, n is size of the dataset. We experiment with different structures of artificial neural network and with different ratio of training to testing data of the available dataset using MATLAB. The best results are obtained with 12 numbers of neurons in the hidden layer and training to testing data ratio of 8:2 (refer, case 3 in Table 5). Figure 6 shows the regression plot of case 3. We see that almost all the values are close to the actual value as the regression value R for test data is 0.90365 which is close to 1.

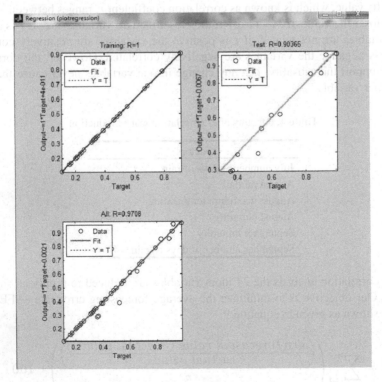

Fig. 6. Regression plot for case 3

Table 6. Final forecasted results for Jaipur region

Year	Yield in Kg/Ha	Forecasted yield in Kg/Ha	Year	Yield in Kg/Ha	Forecasted yield in Kg/Ha
1973	544.00	527.00	1993	578.00	578.00
1974	289.00	289.00	1994	952.00	935.00
1975	425.00	408.00	1995	459.00	442.00
1976	289.00	272.00	1996	697.00	658.44
1977	187.00	187.00	1997	867.00	850.00
1978	731.00	714.00	1998	1122.00	1053.29
1979	357.00	357.00	1999	663.00	663.00
1980	561.00	544.00	2000	612.00	493.00
1981	391.00	591.00	2001	1156.00	1139.00
1982	646.00	505.36	2002	408.00	391.00
1983	595.00	578.00	2003	1700.00	1644.45
1984	612.00	595.00	2004	1428.00	1450.77
1985	357.00	340.00	2005	799.00	782.00
1986	578.00	578.00	2006	1190.00	1173.00
1987	561.00	561.00	2007	1530.00	1457.26
1988	731.00	714.00	2008	1564.00	1547.00
1989	1037.00	1040.44	2009	816.00	816.00
1890	901.00	669.51	2010	1377.00	1343.00
1991	544.00	527.00	2011	1581.00	1635.03
1992	935.00	910.22	2012	816.00	1329.80

The final forecast results are shown in Table 6. The actual yield is also shown for a comparison. The same is presented in Figure 7 in graphical form. It is observed that

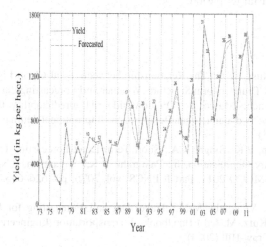

Fig. 7. Comparison between actual yield and forecasted yield

except for few erring years, e.g., 1982, 1990, 2000, 2012, the actual yield and the forecasted yield are very close to each other. We further compare our results with the results obtained by other models proposed using fuzzy logic for forecasting the crop yield [7, 9] and find that our results are much superior (refer, Table 7). It is probably because the fuzzy models completely ignore the important physical factors, e.g., temperature, humidity, rainfall, which heavily affects the crop yield and consider only previous year's yield for forecasting.

Table 7. Comparison of results

Model	AFER (%)
Kumar et al. (2010) [9]	11.40
Kumar and Kumar (2012) [7]	21.87
Our Proposed Method	03.82

5   Conclusion

In this work, we present a back propagation artificial neural network model for forecasting of crop yield. In absence of any method to select the values of artificial neural network parameters we use trail-and-error approach. The Artificial neural network is trained to minimize the value of AFER (average forecasting error rate). Unlike the fuzzy models available in the literature, our method uses the important physical factors also for yield forecast. The proposed model is tested on the data of the pearl millet (bajra) in the Jaipur region of Rajasthan, India. The proposed method obtains very good results as the AFER is only 03.82% in comparison to the competing fuzzy models where AFER is much higher. Though the results are good enough to forecast yield with high accuracy, the model may be improved further if more physical factors and other economic and technological factors are included along with crop yield data for larger period.

References

1. Metzger, E., Nuss, W.A.: The Relationship between Total Cloud Lightning Behavior and Radar-Derived Thunderstorm Structure. Weather and Forecasting 28(1), 237–253 (2013)
2. Rubia, A., Sanchis-Marco, L.: On downside risk predictability through liquidity and trading activity: A dynamic quantile approach. International Journal of Forecasting 29(1), 202–219 (2013)
3. Jain, A., Singh, P.K., Singh, K.A.: Short Term Load Forecasting Using Fuzzy Inference and Ant Colony Optimization. In: Panigrahi, B.K., Suganthan, P.N., Das, S., Satapathy, S.C. (eds.) SEMCCO 2011, Part I. LNCS, vol. 7076, pp. 626–636. Springer, Heidelberg (2011)
4. Chatterjee, A., Venigalla, M.M.: Travel Demand Forecasting for Urban Transportation Planning. In: Kutz, M. (ed.) Handbook of Transportation Engineering, vol. 34, ch. 7, pp. 7.1–7.34. McGraw-Hill (2004)

5. Davis, D.F., Mentzer, J.T.: Organizational factors in sales forecasting management. International Journal of Forecasting 23(3), 475–495 (2007)
6. Lee, W.W., Henschel, H., Madnick, S.E.: A Framework for Technology Forecasting and Visualization. MIT Sloan Research Paper No. 4757-09 (2009), http://ssrn.com/abstract=1478054 or http://dx.doi.org/10.2139/ssrn.1478054
7. Kumar, S., Kumar, N.: Fuzzy Time Series based Method for Wheat production Forecasting. International Journal of Computer Applications 44(12), 5–10 (2012)
8. http://www.preservearticles.com/2011101215204/what-are-the-factors-that-affects-agriculture-in-india.html
9. Kumar, N., Ahuja, S., Kumar, V., Kumar, A.: Fuzzy time series forecasting of wheat production. International Journal on Computer Science and Engineering 02(03), 635–640 (2010)
10. Crone, S.F., Dhawan, R.: Forecasting Seasonal Time Series with Neural Networks: A Sensitivity Analysis of Architecture Parameters. In: International Joint Conference on Neural Networks, pp. 2099–2104 (2007)
11. Sivanandam, S.N., Sumathi, S.: Introduction to Neural Networks Using MATLAB 6.0. Tata McGraw Hill (2005)
12. Kandil, N., Khorasani, K., Patel, R.V., Sood, V.K.: Optimum Learning Rate for Backpropagation Neural Networks. In: Canadian Conference on Electrical and Computer Engineering (CCECE/CCGEI 1993), pp. 465–468 (1993)
13. http://www.rajasthanstat.com/agriculture/2/stats.aspx
14. http://www.krishi.rajasthan.gov.in/
15. http://www.imd.gov.in/section/nhac/mean/110_new.htm
16. http://www.tutiempo.net/en/Climate/Jaipur_Sanganer/423480.htm

Non-linear Dynamic System Identification Using FLLWNN with Novel Learning Method

Mihir Narayan Mohanty[1], Badrinarayan Sahu[1],
Prasanta Kumar Nayak[2], and Laxmi Prasad Mishra[1]

[1] Siksha 'O' Anusandhan University
{mihirmohanty,badrinarayandsahu}@soauniversity.ac.in,
pnayak28@gmail.com
[2] Synergy Institute of Technology
laxmimishra@soauniversity.ac.in

Abstract. Nonlinear dynamic systems are characterized with uncertainties in terms of structure and parameters. These uncertainties cannot be described by deterministic models. The modelling and identification of nonlinear dynamic systems through the measured experimental data is a problem in engineering and technical processes. Therefore, field of system identification have become an important area of research. Fuzzy technology is an effective tool for dealing with complex nonlinear processes that are characterized with uncertain factors. In this paper, a novel approach based on Local Linear method learning in dynamical filter weights neurons for the identification of non-linear dynamic systems is presented. The fuzzy wavelet neural network combines wavelet theory with fuzzy logic and neural networks. Learning fuzzy rules and parameter update in fuzzy wavelet neural network is based on gradient decent method. The proposed approach is said to be Fuzzy Local Linear Wavelet Neural Network based model. It has been explained through examples. The structure is tested for the identification with both wavelet neural network and Fuzzy Local Linear Wavelet Neural Network that shows the comparative performance.

Keywords: System Identification, Non-linear System, Wavelet Neural Network, Fuzzy Wavelet Neural Network, Local Linear Wavelet Neural Network, Fuzzy Local Linear Wavelet Neural Network.

1 Introduction

System identification is an area of research and has evolved during the last two to three decades. It involves finding a relation between the input and output of the system. Identification is basically the process of developing or improving a mathematical representation of a physical system using experimental data. Recently authors are proposed to design fuzzy wavelet neural network (FWNN)[3] for function learning and identification by tuning fuzzy membership functions and wavelet neural networks. The structure of FWNN is based on the basis of fuzzy rules including wavelet functions in the consequent parts of rules. Some of them also designed for controllers based on fuzzy wavelet neural sliding mode controller (AFWN-SMC). FWNN models

B.K. Panigrahi et al. (Eds.): SEMCCO 2013, Part II, LNCS 8298, pp. 332–341, 2013.

have been used for identification and prediction also [1-3]. But one of the main problems for effective control of an uncertain system is the creation of the proper knowledge base for the control system. Hence in [4], authors developed that each fuzzy rule includes a wavelet function in the consequent part of the rule. The parameter update rules of the system are based on the gradient descent method (GDA). The structure was verified for the identification as well as the control of the dynamic plants. The performance of the FWNN structure is illustrated by applying to a nonlinear dynamic plant that has fast local variation as compared with Adaptive Neuro-Fuzzy Inference System (ANFIS) model [5]. Further, attention was in learning and some techniques have been applied. Accelerated hybrid learning algorithm is proposed for the training of FWNNs. The algorithm gives the initial parameters by the clustering algorithm and then updates them with a combination of back propagation and recursive least-squares methods [6]. The parameters are updated in the direction of steepest descent but with a local adaptive learning rate that is different for each epoch which has been taken care in this work.

FWNN have been widely used in many applications. For solving the majority of approximation problems, NNs require a large number of neurons. But the NNs may get stuck on a local minimum of the error surface, and the network convergence rate is generally very slow. A WNN has a nonlinear regression structure that uses localized basis functions in the hidden layer to achieve the desired input– output mapping. The integration of the localization properties of wavelets and the learning abilities of NN results in the advantages of WNN over NN for complex nonlinear system modelling, and some researchers have used such structures for solving approximation, classification, prediction and control problems. The FWNN is a combined structure based on fuzzy rules that includes wavelet functions in their consequent parts. In many research, the strength of FWNNs for function learning has been shown [7-10]. They have shown a fuzzy wavelet network that is based on multi-resolution analysis of wavelet transforms and fuzzy concepts to approximate random nonlinear functions. In [11], Fuzzy NNs are used for direct adaptive control of dynamic plants and for robust adaptive control or robot manipulators, and in [12], a recurrent fuzzy network is used for nonlinear modelling where as in [13], a Takagi-Sugeno-Kang(TSK)-type recurrent neuro-fuzzy NN(TRFN) is developed. The membership functions are chosen from a family of scaling functions, and the fuzzy system is developed by using wavelet techniques.

2   Proposed Method

2.1   Wavelet Neural Network

Wavelet networks uses wavelet functions as hidden neuron activation functions. It helps to determine the neural network parameters and number of hidden neurons during training. The output of wavelet neural network is given by

$$y(x) = \sum_{m=1}^{M} \omega_m \psi_m(x) = \sum_{m=1}^{M} \omega_m |a_m|^{-\frac{1}{2}} \psi_m\left(\frac{x - b_m}{a_m}\right) \tag{1}$$

Where ψ_m is the wavelet activation function of mth unit of the hidden layer and ω_m is the weight connecting the mth unit of the hidden layer to the output layer unit. The $\psi_m(x)$, is called as mother wavelet and the parameters a_m and b_m are the scale and translation parameters and x represents inputs to the WNN model. In consequent part of fuzzy rules, the Mexican hat wavelet function is used and the mother wavelet is represented by

$$\psi_m(x) = \frac{1}{\sqrt{|a|}}(1 - 2x^2)\exp(\frac{-x^2}{2}) \tag{2}$$

A shortcoming of WNN is being removed by LLWNN and is explained.

2.2   Local Linear Wavelet Neural Network

In Local Linear Wavelet Neural Network (LLWNN), the number of neurons in the hidden layer is equal to the number of inputs and the connection weights between the hidden layer units and output units are replaced by a local linear model. It has advantages as the learning efficiency and the structure transparency. The output of local linear wavelet neural network is given by

$$y = \sum_{m=1}^{M}(\omega_{m0} + \omega_{m1}x_1 + \omega_{m2}x_2 + \dots\dots + \omega_{nm}x_n)|a_m|^{-\frac{1}{2}}\psi_m\left(\frac{x - b_m}{a_m}\right) \tag{3}$$

where $x = \lfloor x_1, x_2, \dots\dots x_n \rfloor$ and the linear model is given by

$$L_m = (\omega_{m0} + \omega_{m1}x_1 + \omega_{m2}x_2 + \dots\dots + \omega_{nm}x_n) \tag{4}$$

The activities of linear models $L_m(m = 1, 2, \dots\dots, M)$ are determined by the associated locally active wavelet functions. The basic structure is shown in Fig. 1.

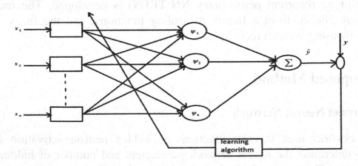

Fig. 1. Block diagram of LLWNN for System Identification

2.3 Fuzzy Local Linear Wavelet Neural Network

Figure 2 shows the block diagram for FLLWNN. The FLLWNN can be described by a set of fuzzy rules R^i : If x_1 is A_1^i, x_2 is A_2^i....... And x_q is A_q^i

$$\text{Then } y_i = w_i \sum_{j=1}^{q} \psi_{ij}(x_j)$$

The nonlinear parameters of the FLLWNN are updated by the following relation.

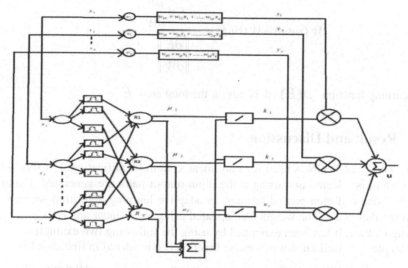

Fig. 2. Block diagram of FLLWNN for System Identification

$$a_{ij}(t+1) = a_{ij}(t) - \eta_{ij} \frac{\partial E_p}{\partial a_{ij}} + \lambda(a_{ij}(t) - a_{ij}(t-1)) \tag{5}$$

$$b_{ij}(t+1) = b_{ij}(t) - \eta_{ij} \frac{\partial E_p}{\partial b_{ij}} + \lambda(b_{ij}(t) - b_{ij}(t-1)) \tag{6}$$

$$c_{ij}(t+1) = c_{ij}(t) - \eta_{ij} \frac{\partial E_p}{\partial c_{ij}} + \lambda(c_{ij}(t) - c_{ij}(t-1)) \tag{7}$$

$$\sigma_{ij}(t+1) = \sigma_{ij}(t) - \eta_{ij} \frac{\partial E_p}{\partial \sigma_{ij}} + \lambda(\sigma_{ij}(t) - \sigma_{ij}(t-1)) \tag{8}$$

where $1 \leq i \leq c$ is the number of fuzzy rules; $1 \leq j \leq q$ is the input dimension; λ is the momentum that is used to speed up the learning process. η is the local learning rate that is updated for each parameter separately.

2.4   Adaptive Learning Method

In adaptive back propagation (ABP) learning algorithm, the network weight update rule is chosen such that the error function is forced to behave in a certain manner that accelerates convergence. As in back propagation network (BPN), the weight update is given by

$$\Delta W = W(new) - W(old) - \eta \frac{\partial E}{\partial W} \tag{9}$$

The weight update equation used in ABP algorithm is

$$W(new) - W(old) - \frac{\rho(E)(\frac{\partial E}{\partial W})}{\left\| \frac{\partial E}{\partial W} \right\|^2} \tag{10}$$

The learning function $\rho(E)$ depends on the total error E.

3   Result and Discussion

In this work, FLLWNN is used for non-linear system identification. For this, a reference system is selected and using it the input-output pairs are generated. Using this, error is found and then passed through an adaptive learning algorithm where weight updating takes place. The weights are updated using local linear and back propagation learning method. It has been explained by using the following two examples:

Example-1. A well known piecewise function is considered in first case [5].

$$f(x) = \begin{cases} -2.186x - 12.864 & -10 \leq x \leq -2 \\ 4.246 & -2 \leq x < 0 \\ 10e^{-0.05x-0.5} \sin[(.03x+.7)x] & 0 \leq x \leq 10 \end{cases} \tag{11}$$

In this example, we have sampled 200 points that are distributed uniformly over [-10, 10] as training data. Despite of low number of epochs, the convergence speed is much higher than previous works. For comparison, this function is approximated by first applying Local Linear Wavelet Neural Network (LLWNN) and then using Fuzzy Local Linear Wavelet Neural Network (FLLWNN) for whole of the parameters. For the purpose of comparison, the root mean square error (RMSE) is used as the performance criterion.

$$RMSE = \sqrt{\frac{\sum_{l=1}^{L}(y_l - y_l^d)^2}{\sum_{l=1}^{L}(y_l^d - \bar{y})^2}} , \text{ where } \bar{y} = \frac{1}{L}\sum_{l=1}^{L} y_l^d \text{ and } y_l^d \text{ is the desired output,}$$

y_l is the estimated output and L is the number of training data. For example 1, the results of identification and error show from Fig. 3 to Fig. 6 respectively.

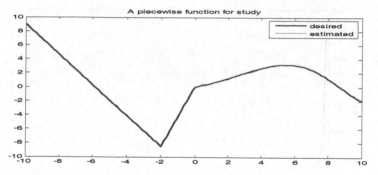

Fig. 3. Identification of a piecewise function using LLWNN

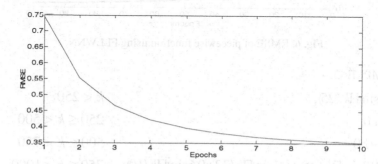

Fig. 4. RMSE of a piecewise function using LLWNN

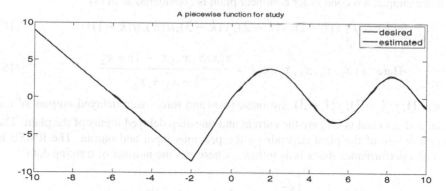

Fig. 5. Identification of piecewise function using FLLWNN

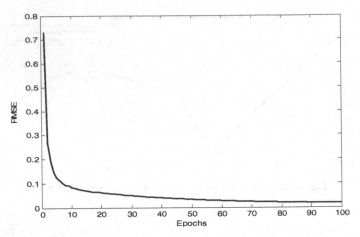

Fig. 6. RMSE of piecewise function using FLLWNN

EXAMPLE -2: -

$$u(k) = \begin{cases} \sin(\Pi k/25), & k < 250 \\ 1.0, & 250 \le k < 500 \\ -1.0 & 500 \le k < 750 \\ 0.3\sin(\Pi k/25) + 0.1\sin(\Pi k/32 + 0.6\sin(\Pi k/10), & 750 \le k < 1000 \end{cases} \quad (13)$$

In this example, a second order nonlinear plant is considered as in [4],

$$y(k) = f(y(k-1), y(k-2), y(k-3), u(k), u(k-1)) \quad (14)$$

Here $f(x_1, x_2, x_3, x_4, x_5) = \dfrac{x_1 x_2 x_3 x_5 (x_3 - 1) + x_4}{1 + x_3^2 + x_2^2} \quad (15)$

$y(k-1), y(k-2), y(k-3)$ are one-, two- and three- step delayed outputs of the plant, and u(k) and u(k-1) are the current and one-step delayed inputs of the plant. The current output of the plant depends on the previous input and output. The RMSE is used as a performance index is as follows, where k is the number of training data.

$$RMSE = \sqrt{\dfrac{\sum_{i=1}^{K}(y(k+1) - y_d(k+1))^2}{K}} \quad (16)$$

For example 2, the results of identification and error show from Fig. 7 to Fig. 10 respectively.

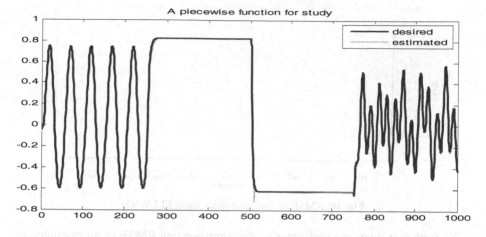

Fig. 7. Identification of nonlinear plant using LLWNN

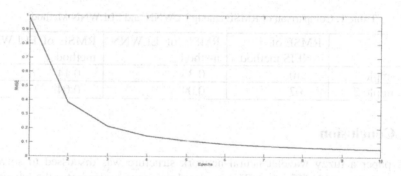

Fig. 8. RMSE of nonlinear plant using LLWNN

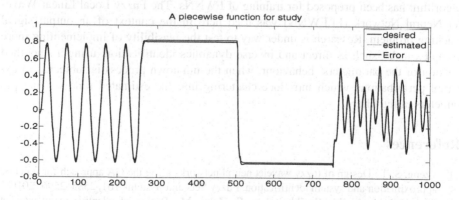

Fig. 9. Identification of nonlinear plant using FLLWNN

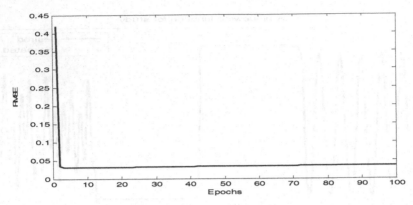

Fig. 10. RMSE of nonlinear plant using FLLWNN

To further evaluate the performance, the corresponding RMSE of all examples are summarized in Table 1.

Table 1. Comparison of RMSE among LLWNN and FLLWNN Method

	RMSE of ANFIS method	RMSE of LLWNN method	RMSE of FLLWNN method
Example-1	.40	0.35	0.14
Example-2	.07	0.09	0.04

4   Conclusion

In this paper a fuzzy wavelet neural network structure was discussed to solve the problem of system identification. The proposed structure incorporates the advantages of wavelet function, neural networks and fuzzy logic. An accelerated hybrid learning algorithm has been proposed for training of FWNNs. The Fuzzy Local Linear Wavelet Neural Network (FLLWNN) was used here in the context of an output signal tracking problem. Research is under way to test the feasibility of implementing more complex tasks, such as direct and inverse dynamics identification, using a smoothed version of the parameters' behaviour, when the unknown process is subjected to external perturbations which introduce chattering into the estimated time varying parameters of the filters.

References

1. Tzeng, S.-T.: Design of fuzzy wavelet neural networks using the GA approach for function approximation and system identification. Fuzzy Sets and Systems 161, 2585–2596 (2010)
2. Shahriarikahkeshi, M., Sheikholeslam, F., Zekri, M.: Design of adaptive fuzzy wavelet neural sliding mode controller for uncertain nonlinear systems. ISA Transactions 52, 342–350 (2013)

3. Yilmaz, S., Oysal, Y.: Fuzzy Wavelet Neural Network Models for Prediction and Identification of Dynamical Systems. IEEE Transactions on Neural Networks 21(10), 1599–1609 (2010)
4. Abiyev, R.H., Kaynak, O.: Fuzzy wavelet neural networks for identification and control of dynamic plants-A novel structure and a comparative study. IEEE Trans. Ind. Electron. 55(8), 3133–3140 (2008)
5. Abiyev, R.H., Kaynak, O.: Identification and control of dynamic plants using fuzzy wavelet neural networks. In: Proc. IEEE Int. Symp. Intell. Control, pp. 1295–1301 (2008)
6. Davanipoor, M., Zekri, M., Sheikholeslam, F.: Fuzzy Wavelet Neural Network With an Accelerated Hybrid Learning Algorithm. IEEE Transactions on Fuzzy Systems 20(3), 463–470 (2012)
7. Zhang, Q., Benviste, A.: Wavelet networks. IEEE Trans. Neural Netw. 3(6), 889–898 (1992)
8. Zhang, J., Walter, G.G., Miao, Y., Lee, W.N.W.: Wavelet neural networks for function learning. IEEE Trans. Signal Process. 43(6), 1485–1497 (1995)
9. Wai, R.J., Chang, J.M.: Implementation of robust wavelet-neural network control for induction motor drive using sliding-mode design technique. IEEE Trans. Ind. Electron. 50(4), 733–748 (2003)
10. Ho, D.W.C., Zhang, P.A., Xu, J.: Fuzzy wavelet neural network for function learning. IEEE Trans. Fuzzy Syst. 9(1), 200–211 (2001)
11. Da, F., Song, W.: Fuzzy neural networks for direct adaptive control. IEEE Trans. Ind. Electron. 50(3), 507–513 (2003)
12. Lee, C.H., Theng, C.C.: Identification and control of dynamic systems using recurrent fuzzy neural network. IEEE Trans. Fuzzy Syst. 8(4), 349–366 (2000)
13. Juang, C.F.: A TSK – type recurrent fuzzy network for dynamic systems processing by neural network and genetic algorithm. IEEE Trans. Fuzzy Syst. 10(2), 155–170 (2002)

Analysis of Transient Stability Based STATCOM for Neural Network Controller in Cascaded Multilevel Inverter

P.K. Dhal[1] and C. Christober Asir Ranjan[2]

[1] Department of EEE, Veltech DR.RR&DR.SR Technical University, Chennai
[2] Department of EEE, Pondicherry Engineering College, Pondicherry
pradyumna.dhal@rediffmail.com, asir_70@ hotmail.com

Abstract. This paper is proposed a neural controller for static time critical error and better damping oscillations after a short circuit fault is cleared. The neural network is approached for estimation of the control and operating parameters of STATCOM .It is used for improving voltage profile in power system. So STATCOM is an important voltage source converter device. It is used in voltage control mode or reactive power injection mode. To achieve this idea, a controller is designed based on energy function lyapunov. The neural controller is employed to the system for enhancement the transient stability. The performance is analyzed using MATLAB/SIMULINK.

Keywords: Neural Controller, Multilevel Inverter, STATCOM, Transient Stability.

1   Introduction

The static synchronous compensator (STATCOM) using voltage source inverters has been accepted as a competitive alternative to the conventional static VAr compensator (SVC) using thyristor-controlled reactors STATCOM functions as a synchronous voltage source. It can provide reactive power compensation without the dependence on the ac system voltage. By controlling the reactive power, a STATCOM can stabilize the power system, increase the maximum active power flow and regulate the line voltages. Faster response makes STATCOM suitable for continuous power flow control and power system stability improvement. The interaction between the AC system voltage and the inverter-composed voltage provides the control of the STATCOM var output. When these two voltages are synchronized and have the same amplitude. So the active and reactive power outputs are zero. However, if the amplitude of the STATCOM voltage is smaller than that of the system voltage, it produces a current lagging the voltage by 90° and the compensator behaves as a variable capacitive load. The reactive power depends on the voltage amplitude. This amplitude control is done through the leading the STATCOM voltage, it is possible to charge or discharge the dc capacitor; as a consequence change the value of the dc voltage and the STATCOM's operational characteristics and the compensator behaves as an inductive load, which reactive value depends on the voltage amplitude. Making

B.K. Panigrahi et al. (Eds.): SEMCCO 2013, Part II, LNCS 8298, pp. 342–353, 2013.

the STATCOM voltage higher than the AC system voltage the current will lead the voltage by 90°. To overcome the limitations of semiconductor device, many new techniques are developed. They are multiple switching elements in one leg of an inverter, series connected inverter and parallel connected inverters. Among these various multilevel topologies, the cascaded multilevel inverter can implement a high number of levels [13].

In conventional cascaded multilevel inverter use fundamental switching frequency to generate step waveform at low harmonic distortion and keep the switching loss as low as possible. But the inverter unit's duty cycles are different from each other. Due to unequal duty cycle the inverter units cannot equally share the exchanged power with the utility grid. In STATCOM is to balance the dc-link voltages and additional auxiliary inverters is used to exchange the energy among various capacitors [7]. The disadvantage is high cost and complexity in hardware design. To eliminate unequal duty cycles, it is required dc capacitance of each inverter unit is calculated according to the corresponding duty cycle. But in practical application modular design is very difficult. By using proposed method inverter unit's fundamental output voltage are equalized. Consequently, all the inverter units can equally share the exchanged power with the utility grid and the dc-link voltage balancing control can be simplified [12]. A special gating pattern is used for maintain the dc capacitor charge balance and equalize the current stress of the switching device. In this paper, design rules for creating neural controller is very effective. This article on a STATCOM Control for transient stability improvement has proposed.

2   Cascaded Multilevel Inverter

Fig. 1 shows the basic structure of cascaded multilevel inverter with separate dc source. For a three phase system, the output voltage of the three cascaded inverters can be connected either star or delta.

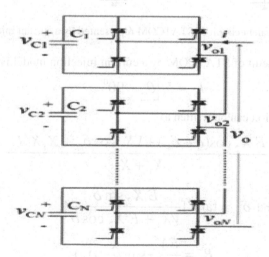

Fig. 1. Shows the basic structure of cascaded Multilevel Inverter

3   STATCOM

The STATCOM with DC link and a link type GTO converter. Its simplest form includes only one capacitor displaying a single-phase power system and single infinite bus. A major element modeling is that the system can be given it like a current source model, STATCOM performance. It can usually drive for more reactive to consider or before the current phase of the STATCOM are for power system to inject. Because this model at this stage it with the ability that each waveform is STATCOM Sinusoidal current favorite for a very short time and accurately can be produced. The STATCOM is comprised a voltage source shunt converter connected through a transformer and filter across a load bus where the voltage is to be regulated [10] [11]. The shunt converter is a modeled as a controllable voltage source generated by the inverting action of the converter with a DC voltage applied through a charged capacitor. The static synchronous compensator is based on the principle that a voltage source inverter generates a controllable AC voltage source behind a transformer leakage reactance. So that the voltage difference across the reactance produces active and reactive power exchange between the STATCOM and the transmission network [2]. The converter controls the current injected to the power system and the energy exchanges by the STATCOM which is limited by the capacitor stored energy. Only reactive power can be exchanged in steady state. The terminal voltage almost independent of their form a reactive current source STATCOM Parallel is shown in Fig. 2.

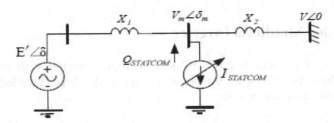

Fig. 2. Equivalent circuit of STATCOM represented by a current injection model

The equivalent circuit of STATCOM by a current injection model is given by

$$I_S = I_S \lfloor \theta_m - 90^0 \tag{1}$$

The voltage equation can be written as

$$V_m = \frac{E' X_2 \cos(\delta - \delta_m) + VX_1 \cos \delta_m + X_1 X_2 I_s}{X_1 + X_2} \tag{2}$$

$$\text{And } \delta_m = \tan^{-1}[\frac{E' X_2 \sin \delta}{VX_1 + E' X_2 \cos \delta}] \tag{3}$$

$$P_O = \frac{E' V_m}{X_1} \sin(\delta - \delta_m) \tag{4}$$

The output electrical power P_o of generator is connected with STATCOM. So it can be written as $P_e = Po$ (without STATCOM) $+ K I_S \sin (\delta - \delta_m)$ (5)

The energy function (V) of a power system with STATCOM is written by

$$V(\delta,\omega) = V_K(\omega) + V_P(\delta) + V(\delta) + V_C(\delta) \tag{6}$$

Here V_K is kinetic energy, V_k is the potential energy of the system without STATCOM , V_p is the additional component of potential energy of STATCOM and V_C is the constant energy at the post fault equilibrium and speed ($\omega_s = 0$).The first integral of the motion[8][9]. It constitutes an energy function is given by

$$V(\delta,\omega) = [\int_0^\omega M \,\omega d\,\omega] - [\int_{\delta s}^\delta Mfo(x)dx] - [\int_{\delta s}^\delta MIsf_1(x)dx \tag{7}$$

The equation (8) can be written as again

$$V(\delta,\omega) = [\int_0^\omega M \,\omega d\omega] + [\int_{\delta s}^\delta (-P_m + P_0)d\delta + [\int_{\delta s}^\delta KIs \sin(\delta - \delta_m)d\delta \tag{8}$$

The STATCOM is placed at the location where it provides the maximum output electrical power. So $E' = V$ and $X_1 = X_2$, the output electrical power has the maximum value. The value of δ_m is given by $\delta_m = 2\delta$. The energy function V of a power system with STATCOM is given by

$$V(\delta,\omega) = [\tfrac{1}{2}M\omega] + [-P_m\delta + P_0^{max}\cos\delta] + [KIs\cos\tfrac{\delta}{2}] + V_c \tag{9}$$

The above equation (10) that $KIs\cos\tfrac{\delta}{2} =$ the potential energy function. Similarly the continuous nonlinear control of the STATCOM is given by $Is = K\omega\sin\delta$.

Now the single line diagram is representing grid network with STATCOM as shown in figure 3.

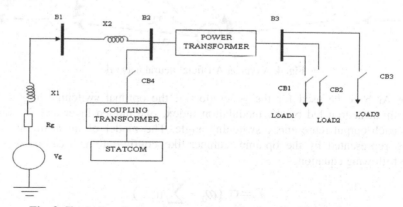

Fig. 3. Single line diagram representing grid network with STATCOM

At the time of starting the source voltage is such that the STATCOM is inactive. It neither absorbs nor provides reactive power to the network. The following load sequence is tested and results are taken. At t=0.06 sec STATCOM is connected to the system by switching circuit breaker CB4. At t=0.1 load 1 is connected by switching CB1. At t= 0.3 load 2 is connected by switching CB2. At t= 0.5 load 2 is connected by switching CB3. STATCOM system is given in the Appendix.

4   Neural Network Approach

A typical multilayer ANN is shown in Fig. 4. It consists of one input layer, a middle layer and an output layer, where each layer has a specific function.   The input accepts an input data and distributes it to all neurons in the middle layer. The input layer is usually passive and does not alter the input data. The neurons in the middle layer act as feature detectors. They encode in their weights a representation of the features present in the input patterns. The output layer accepts a stimulus pattern from the middle layer and passes a result to a transfer function block which usually applies a nonlinear function and constructs the output response pattern of the network. The number of hidden layers and the number of neurons in each hidden layer depend on the network design consideration and there is no general rule for an optimum number of hidden layers or nodes [3] [4].

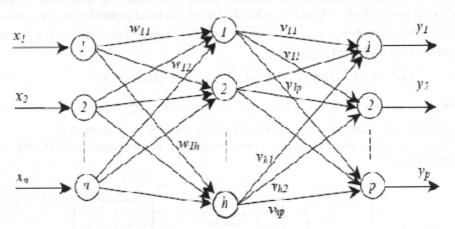

Fig. 4. A typical Artificial neural network

The ANN to be used for the generation of the optimal switching angles has a single input neuron fed by the modulation index, one hidden layer and Y outputs where each output represents a switching angle. The model of an artificial neuron can be represented by the op-amp summer-like configuration. It can be described by the following equation:

$$Y = \sigma \ (\omega_0 + \sum_{i=1}^{k} w_i x_i)$$ (10)

Where,

Y = the output of the neuron, x_i = the ith input to the neuron, w_i = the ith connection weight, ω_0 = the bias weight, σ = the transfer function of the neuron, k - the number of connections with the neurons in the preceding layer. So the sigmoid transfer function used in output layer has the form given by: $\sigma_1(x) = \dfrac{1}{1+e^{-\alpha x}}$.

Where α is the co-efficient or gain which adjusts the slope of the function that change between two asymptotic values (0 and +1). The sigmoid function is nonlinear, monotonic and differentiable. It has the largest incremental gain at zero signals. In the hidden layer, the Gaussian transfer function has been used [5] [6].

5   Indirect Supervised Training of Neural Network

Back propagation training algorithm is a supervised learning algorithm for multilayer feed forward neural network. It is a supervised learning algorithm in both input and target output. It provides for training network. The error data at the output layer is calculated using network output and target output. Then the error is back propagated to intermediate layers, allowing incoming weights to these layers to be updated. This algorithm is based on the error-correction learning rule. Basically the error back-propagation process consists of two passes through the different layers of the network: a forward pass and a backward pass. In the forward pass, input vector is applied to the network, and its effect propagates through the network, layer by layer. Finally, a set of outputs is produced as the actual response of the network. During the forward pass the synaptic weights of network are all fixed. During the backward pass, on the other hand, the synaptic weights are all adjusted in accordance with the error-correction rule [1]. The actual response of the network is subtracted from a desired target response to produce an error signal. This error signal is then propagated backward through the network against direction of synaptic connections. Hence the name is called as "error back-propagation". The synaptic weights are adjusted so as to make the actual response of the network move closer the desired response. The ANN is trained by the back-propagation algorithm of the error between the desired solutions of the nonlinear system equations to enhance the transient stability and the output of this equation using the switching angle given by the ANN [7] [8] as shown in figure 5. The training algorithm (BPA) is summarized as follows:

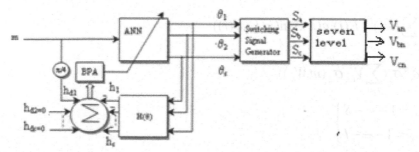

Fig. 5. Indirect Training of Artificial Neural Network (ANN) for harmonic elimination

The ANN is trained by the back-propagation algorithm of the between the desired solutions of the nonlinear system equations to enhance the transient stability and the output of this equation using the switching angle is given by ANN. The training algorithm is summarized as follows:

Step 1: Define the nodes 'W' of the Gaussian functions and Random initialization of the weights 'V'.

Step 2: Present at the input of a network the value of a network the value of the modulation index m.

Step 3: Calculate the output of the neurons of the hidden layer and the output layer i.e Hidden layer: σ_2 (m, W) with $W = [w_1, w_2 \text{ --------- } w_l]^T$, l. It is the number of the neurons in the hidden layer. The output layer:

$$\theta = \sigma_1(V, \sigma_2(m, W)), size V = (S, l).$$

Step 4: Standardize the outputs of the network of neuron between 0 and $\dfrac{\pi}{2}$.

Step 5: Apply the ANN outputs to the nonlinear system equation $H(\theta)$

Step6: Calculate the total error $E = H_d(\theta) - H(\theta)$ and

$$E^2 = (H_d(\theta) - H(\theta)^T)(H_d(\theta) - H(\theta))$$

Step 7: Back Propagate error on the network using gradient descent algorithm

$$V^{new} = V^{old} - \eta_v \frac{1}{2} \frac{\partial E^2}{\partial V}$$

$$V^{new} = V^{old} + \eta_v E \frac{\partial H}{\partial \theta} \frac{\partial \theta}{\partial V}$$

$$\frac{\partial H}{\partial \theta} = \begin{pmatrix} \sin(\theta_1) & -\sin(\theta_2) & (-)^{s+1}\sin(\theta_s) \\ \sin(5\theta_1) & -\sin(5\theta_2) & (-)^{s+1}\sin(5\theta_s) \\ \sin(n\theta_1) & -\sin(n\theta_2) & (-1)^{s+1}\sin(n\theta_s) \end{pmatrix}$$

Step8: Adapt the weights recursively by

$$V_{i,j}^{new} = V_{i,j}^{old} + \eta_v \delta_i^1 \sigma_2(m, W_j)$$

With

$$\delta_i^0 = \sum_{k=1}^{s} (-1)^{i+1} E(i).n(k).\sin(n(k).\theta(i))$$

$$\delta_i^1 = \delta_i^0 \sigma_1(\sum_{k=1}^{l} V_{i,k} \sigma_2(m.W_k))$$

and $\begin{cases} i = 1 - - - S \\ j = 1 - - - l \end{cases}$

$V = $ Random initialization of weight

Step9: Repeat steps 3 to end until obtaining the desired precision.

After the termination of the training phase, the obtained ANN can be used to generate the control sequence of the inverter as shown in Fig.6.

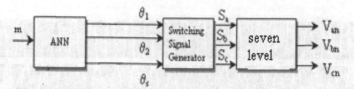

Fig. 6. Generating switching angles by using an ANN

6   Simulation Result

Fig. 11 shows the output voltage at various load conditions without controller and Fig. 12 shows the real and reactive power of the system at bus 3 without controller. Fig. 13 shows the voltage at bus 3 by using neural controller. Fig 14 shows the real and reactive power of the system at bus 3 by using neural controller. From the graph it is inferred that transient period is reduced and also voltage is regulated. Reactive power and active power are analyzed. By comparing without compensator, the time critical error is reduced in Neural Controller.

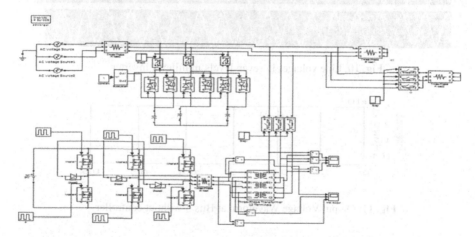

Fig. 7. Simulation of Cascaded Multilevel inverter

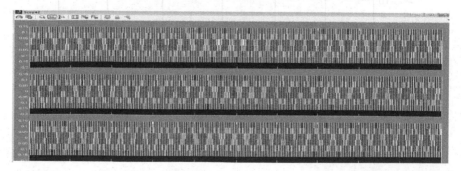

Fig. 8. Phase currents in seven levels multilevel inverter

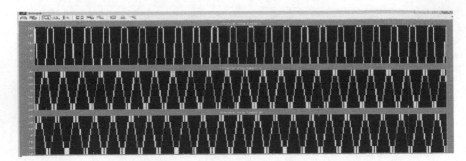

Fig. 9. Line currents in seven levels multilevel inverter

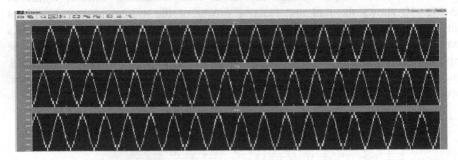

Fig. 10. Line voltages in seven levels multilevel inverter

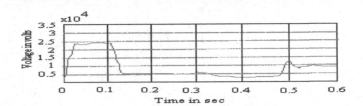

Fig. 11. Output Voltage Waveform at Bus 3 without controller

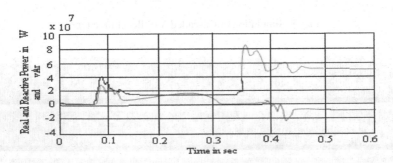

Fig. 12. Real and Reactive at Bus 3 without controller

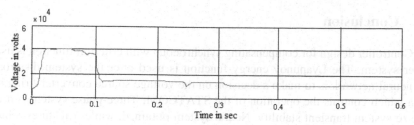

Fig. 13. Output Voltage waveform at Bus 3 with neural control

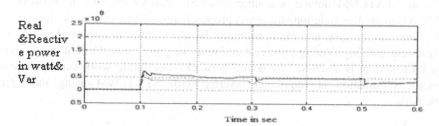

Fig. 14. Real and Reactive Power at Bus 3 with neural control

Comparison of time critical

Table 1.

Controller	Without Controller	Neural controller
Time Critical (Seconds)	0.0054	0.00505

Table 2.

Without Controller				With Neural Controller			
Time in sec	Voltage in KV	Real Power in Watts	Reactive Power in Var	Time in sec	Voltage in KV	Real Power in Watts	Reactive Power in Var
0	0	0	0	0	0	0	0
0.02	2.5	0	0	0.02	2.0	0	0
0.06	3.4	0	0	0.06	4.0	0	0
0.1	3.4	0	0	0.1	3.5	0	0
0.12	0.62	4.0	2.2	0.12	1.62	0.5	0.65
0.2	0.6	2.0	0.8	0.2	1.62	0.46	0.51
0.28	0.6	2.0	0.8	0.28	1.60	0.46	0.5
0.30	0.6	1.8	1.0	0.3	1.60	0.4	0.52
0.40	0.4	1.0	0.40	0.40	0.8	0.38	0.5
0.44	0.4	1.0	0.40	0.44	0.8	0.38	0.5
0.50	0.4	-1.8	0.40	0.50	1.0	0.38	0.5
0.52	1.0	-0.9	8.40	0.52	1.0	0.36	0.32
0.54	1.5	0.0	4.4	0.54	1.0	0.4	0.4
0.60	1.4	-0.9	6.0	0.60	1.0	0.45	0.45

7   Conclusion

The Controller design for compensating synchronous with criterion function is used in power system. The Lyapunov energy function is used after the system disturbance. The neural network is to make a decision on the voltage source converter firing angle alpha which controls the operation of the STATCOM. Three-phase system is used to analyze system transient stability. Neural system obtained, while it features robust in dealing with uncertain system. So the stability criteria Lyapunov will also meet. A 100Mvar STATCOM device is connected to the 230-kV (L-L) grid network. A multilevel optimal modulation strategy is proposed for STATCOM is incorporated in system line. So the system is easily balanced. Neural Control is employed to enhance the transient stability. Voltage and real and reactive power waveform at bus 3 under open loop system is discussed by neural network. The future work can be done in harmonic elimination at multilevel inverter with STATCOM using intelligent controllers.

APPENDIX

For STATCOM
Rated Power = 100 MVAr
Rated voltage= 138 kV
Interface inductor (L) = 2.86 mH
Resistance (Rs) = 0.0898 Ω
For Power Transformer (Y/Y)
Rated Voltage 220 kV/33 kV
Rated Power: 300 MVA
Three Phase Load

For grid
Rated Voltage: 230 kV
Short Circuit Capacity: 10000 MVA

For Coupling Transformer (Y/Y)
Rated Voltage 138 kV/230 kV
Rated Power: 100 MVA

Load 1:
P= 100 MW
Q= 80 MVAr

Load 2:
P= 70 MW
Q= 50 MVAr

Load 3:
P= 60 MW
Q= 40 MVAr

References

[1] Mohaghegi, S., Valle, Y.D., Venayagamoorthy, G.K., Harley, R.G.: A comparison of PSO and backpropagation for training RBF neural networks for identification of a power system with STATCOM. In: Proceedings of the IEEE Swarm Intelligence Symposium, June 8-10, pp. 381–384. IEEE Xplore Press (2005)
[2] Chu, C.C., Tsai, H.C.: Application of Lyapunov-Based Adaptive Neural Network Controllers for Transient Stability Enhancement. Power and Energy Society General Meeting, pp. 1–6 (2008)
[3] Mohaddes, M., Gole, A.M., McLaren, P.G.: A Neural Network controlled Optimal pulse-width modulated STATCOM. IEEE Transactions on Power Delivery 14(2), 481–488 (1999)

[4] Namikawa, Tani: Building Recurrent Neural Networks to Implement Multiple Attractor Dynamics Using the Gradient Descent Method. Advances in Artificial Neural Systems 2009, 1–11

[5] Mishra, S.: Neural-Network-Based Adaptive UPFC for Improving Transient Stability Performance of Power System. IEEE Trans. Neural Networks 17(2), 461–470 (2006)

[6] Esfahani, N., Abazari, S., Arab: A New Fuzzy-Neural STATCOM Controller for Transient Stability Improvement. Majlesi Journal of Electrical Engineering 3(2) (2009)

[7] Shishebori, A., Taki, F., Abazari, S., Arab, G.: Comparison of ANFIS based SSSC, STATCOM and UPFC Controllers for Transient Stability Improvement. Majlesi Journal of Electrical Engineering 4(3) (2010)

[8] Murillo-Perez, J.L.: Steady-State Voltage Stability with STATCOM. IEEE Transactions on Power Systems 21(3) (2006)

[9] Haque, M.H.: Improvement of First Swing Stability Limit by Utilizing Full Benefit of Shunt FACTS Devices. Transactions on Power Systems 19(4), 1894–1902 (2004)

[10] Chandrakar, V.K., Kothari, A.G.: Comparison of RBFN Based STATCOM, SSSC and UPFC Controllers for Transient Stability Improvement. In: Power Systems Conference and Exposition, pp. 784–791 (2006)

[11] Xavier, S.A.E., Venkatesh, P., Saravanan, M.: Design of Intelligent Controllers for STATCOM. In: IEEE POWERCON 2008, New Delhi, pp. 1–7 (2008)

[12] Mohagheghi, S., Park, J.W., Venayagamoorthy, G.K., Harley, R.G., Crow, L.: An Adaptive Neural Network Identifier for Effective Control of a Static Compensator Connected to a Power System. In: Proceedings of the International Joint Conference on Neural Networks, vol. 4, pp. 2964–2969 (2003)

[13] Murillo-Perez, J.L.: Steady-State Voltage Stability with STATCOM. IEEE Transactions on Power Systems 21(3) (2006)

Emotion Recognition System by Gesture Analysis Using Fuzzy Sets

Reshma Kar[1], Aruna Chakraborty[2], Amit Konar[1], and Ramadoss Janarthanan[3]

[1] Department of Electronics and Tele-Communication Engineering,
Jadavpur University, Kolkata
[2] Department of Computer Science & Engineering,
St. Thomas' College of Engineering & Technology, Kolkata, India
[3] Department of Computer Science & Engineering, TJS Engineering College, Chennai, India
rkar317@gmail.com, stcet@rediffmail.com,
konaramit@yahoo.co.in, srmjana_73@yahoo.com

Abstract. Gestures have been called the leaky source of emotional information. Also gestures are easy to retrieve from a distance by ordinary cameras. Thus as many would agree gestures become an important clue to the emotional state of a person. In this paper we have worked on recognizing emotions of a person by analyzing only gestural information. Subjects are initially trained to perform emotionally expressive gestures by a professional actor. The same actor trained the system to recognize the emotional context of gestures. Finally the gestural performances of the subjects are evaluated by the system to identify the class of emotion indicated. Our system yields an accuracy of 94.4% with a training set of only one gesture per emotion. Apart from this our system is also computationally efficient. Our work analyses emotions from only gestures, which is a significant step towards reducing the cost efficiency of emotion recognition. It may be noted here that this system may also be used for the purpose of general gesture recognition. We have proposed new features and a new classifying approach using fuzzy sets. We have achieved state of art accuracy with minimal complexity as each motion trajectory along each axis generates only 4 displacement features. Each axis generates a trajectory and only 6 joint trajectories among all joint trajectories are compared. The 6 motion trajectories are selected based on maximum motion, as maximum moving regions give more information on gestures. The experiments have been performed on data obtained from Microsoft Kinect sensors. Training and Testing were subject gender independent.

Keywords: Type-1 Fuzzy Sets, Gesture Recognition, One-shot Learning, Emotion Recognition.

1 Introduction

Health experts have long been discussing on the bad effects of sitting for prolonged periods in front of the computer, the side effects including, eye problems, back pain and obesity. In such a scenario, developing a gestural interface which works on

B.K. Panigrahi et al. (Eds.): SEMCCO 2013, Part II, LNCS 8298, pp. 354–363, 2013.

human gestures can be a solution to avoid diseases which originate from sedentary working style. Some thinkers also believe, that sedentary habits such as sitting in front of the computer for prolonged periods; is against healthy evolution Fig 1. We have developed a gesture recognition system by recognizing human emotional gestures, as recognizing human emotions is the fundamental step to develop a more natural Human-Computer Interface. The only modality considered is body gesture, which can be extracted even if the camera is located far away from the subject. It is a one-shot learning system performing in real time and it yet achieves state of art accuracy. None of its one-shot learning counterparts have been able to perform similarly [19]. Also it may be noted that our experimental data was gender independent.

Fig. 1. Change in posture pattern because of non-gestural computing interface

Fuzzy logic has been extensively studied and applied for gesture recognition; the main reason being its accommodation for uncertainty that is associated with human gestures. Uncertainty associated with devices collecting images/videos [2], [5], [14] has been modeled in a fuzzy manner and also uncertainty associated with body structure and action sequence. Most commonly, features have been identified by taking into account the similarity between the observed training features and input features [1] Fang et al. [9] reported a system using two data gloves and three position trackers as input devices and a fuzzy decision tree as a classifier to recognize Chinese Sign Language (CSL) gestures. The average classification rate of 91.6% was achieved over a very impressive 5113-sign vocabulary in CSL. Schwier et al. combined hidden markov models with fuzzy logic [3]. Lin et al. [4] combined the superior classification power of a support vector machine and the efficient humanlike reasoning of a fuzzy neural network for pattern classification. Fuzzy neural networks have also interested many researchers [4], [14], [17]. Although less training data were required for these algorithms, heavy computation could not be avoided. Some of these techniques were combined with validation techniques [1], [4], [11]. Fuzzy clustering techniques were also popular. Fuzzy control techniques [15], [16] were also popular in robotic control. Sotelo et al. used fuzzy logic to manage uncertainty occurring due to image occlusion and 3D displacement [5]. The fuzzy K-means clustering and linear discriminant classifier (LDC) are proposed for the training and classification of the hand orientation classifier [7]. The work presented by Sarkar et al. [9] proposes fuzzy logic (as Jiang and Wang [10]) to elucidate up to what extent a user is under stress. Furthermore, it introduces an approach oriented to improve HCI. Sugeno and Mamdani type inference systems [13], [17], [18], in general rule based inference systems in general have generated a lot of interest.

Our approach works with only displacement and expansion properties, yet achieves a very good accuracy with minimal complexity. This is because:

- We have proposed expansion and displacement features which are independent of the subject's height, weight or position in general.
- Our algorithm is also time efficient; this is because of two factors; the first reason being that we do not match entire motion trajectories but only 4 parameters extracted from each of the selected 6 motion trajectories. Secondly our algorithm considers only six trajectories with maximum quantity of motion, as these trajectories yield most information of the gesture.
- In our approach we have considered the 3 axes of movement separately, which ensured that negative movement along one axis does not neutralize positive movement along another axis. Each axes of each body part yields four features namely averages of two most repeated cycles and maximum positive and negative displacements.
- We have modeled intra-personal variance, by analyzing intra-gesture dynamics. The entire process is illustrated with a block diagram given in Fig 2. Each of these modules are then explained. Complexity is minimized as only the six trajectories with maximum quantity of motion are matched against their respective training set Gaussian curve.

We have trained the algorithm using gestures of a person expressing the 5 emotions, Happy, Anger, Fear, Disgust and Surprise separately. These gestural clues are obtained mainly from our extensive literature review and were validated by a professional actor. Data training was done by the actor and testing was performed on gestures of the other 10 subjects. Thus we have a testing set of 50 cases (10 subjects * 5 emotions). The accuracy obtained for all emotions was 94.4% which is better than most of its counterparts [19].

2   System Overview

The algorithm employs dimension reduction based on Quantity of Motion (QoM). Each body joint has 3 motion trajectories along the 3 axes. Thus, for 20 body joints there will be 20x3(60) motion trajectories. We evaluate expansion parameters of the right hand and displacement parameters of the 6 motion trajectories with maximum QoM. The parameters are listed in table 1. The memberships of gesture in each emotion are found by evaluating closeness of the test parameters to training parameters. The entire methodology is illustrated with a block diagram.

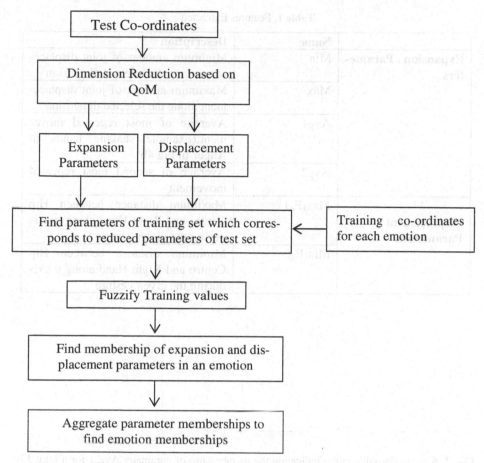

Fig. 2. Overview of the Fuzzy Gesture Recognition approach

Dimension Reduction: Quantity of Motion (QoM) or amount of detected motion has been used in many cases as a low level feature of gesture expression [20], [21]. In our experiments, we consider another aspect of QoM; we use it for dimension reduction. As it is natural for humans to consider most moving parts of body more informative, we also, induce our system to filter the most moving body joints as more relevant.

Feature Extraction: Form each of the joint trajectories with maximum quantity of motion (QoM) we select the displacement features. Expansion parameters are distance between hip center and right hand, as right hand is mostly active and dominant hand in humans. Here α may indicate X, Y or Z axis.

Table 1. Features Extracted

	Name	Description
Expansion Parameters	Min	Minimum amount of joint displacement along the selected dimension
	Max	Maximum amount of joint displacement along the selected dimension
	Avg1	Average of most repeated movement.(example shaking hands in Anger in Fig 4b)
	Avg2	Average of second most repeated movement
Displacement Parameters	$Max(E_\alpha)$	Maximum distance between Hip Centre and Right Hand along α axis during the given gesture
	$Min(E_\alpha)$	Minimum distance between Hip Centre and Right Hand along α axis during the given gesture

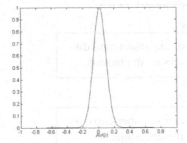

Fig. 3. Sample Gaussian curve indicating the membership of parameter Avg 1 for a joint J in emotion "Angry". X axis indicates feature value Y axis indicates membership.

Fuzzification of values: Since emotions are fuzzy parameters of a human mind set, we have fuzzified the displacement and expansion parameters to find displacement and expansion memberships in emotions. To fuzzify the variables we have, constructed Gaussian curves with peaks at extracted displacement and expansion parameters. Also we have determined intrapersonal variance by calculating the variance of movement of a particular joint for a selected gesture. Let M be the set of displacements of any joint j along any axis. Let there be a set of n displacements. Then,

$$\text{Intra-personal variance for parameters of joint } j = \frac{\sum_{i=1}^{n}(|Mi| - M')}{n}$$

$$\text{where, } M' = \frac{\sum_{i=1}^{n}(|Mi|)}{n}$$

Where, Mi indicates the ith displacement of joint j along a fixed axis. The peak of the Gaussian curve for a joint i representing an emotion of class c is taken as the observed parameter training value. Fig 3 shows a generated sample membership curve.

2.1 Matching Test Gesture with Trained Gestures to Find Out Emotion Indicated by Test Gesture

1. For a given test gesture we extract joint co-ordinate vectors and select 6 with maximum QoM.
2. From each selected 6 joint co-ordinate vectors we extract 4 displacement features. Apart from this we also extract 6 expansion parameters. Thus we have extracted 6x4 displacement parameters + 6 expansion parameters.
3. Gaussian curves are constructed with peaks at corresponding training parameter values.
4. Variance of each of the curve indicating a parameter extracted from a joint is variance of intra-personal displacement for that joint.
5. The 6 displacement parameter vectors extracted, each containing Avg1, Avg2, Max and Min are plotted on their corresponding Gaussian curves.
6. Thus we get 6 membership vectors for displacement features, each containing 4 memberships of AVG1, AVG2, MAX and MIN in the trained emotion. For all 6 parameter vectors:

$$\mu_E(\text{Avg1}) = \frac{\sum_{i=1}^{6} \mu_E(Avg1_i)}{6}$$

$$\mu_E(\text{Avg2}) = \frac{\sum_{i=1}^{6} \mu_E(Avg2_i)}{6}$$

$$\mu_E(\text{Max}) = \frac{\sum_{i=1}^{6} \mu_E(Max_i)}{6}$$

$$\mu_E(\text{Min}) = \frac{\sum_{i=1}^{6} \mu_E(Min_i)}{6}$$

where i denotes the vector to which a parameter belongs to

7. The net memberships of displacement parameters in emotion E are calculated as follows:

$\mu_E^{net}(\text{displacement}) = 0.3 \times \mu_E(\text{Avg1}) + 0.2 \times \mu_E(\text{Avg2}) + 0.25 \times \mu_E(\text{Max}) + 0.25 \times \mu_E(\text{Min})$

8. The weights given to membership values are based on the following philosophy; as Max and Min are based on displacement they share 50% priority and Avg1 and Avg2 share the remaining 50% priority as they are based on movement repetition Avg1 being repeated more often repeated gets more weight (30%) than Avg2 (20%). As maximum and minimum displacements are both equally important in determining motion, both get equal priority (25% each).
9. We also get 6 memberships of expansion parameters in each emotion from their corresponding training expansion parameter membership curves.
10. The net expansion parameter membership in emotion E is calculated as

$\mu_E^{net}(\text{expansion}) = \min(\mu_E(\text{expansion parameters})) joints \, \omega, \forall \, axes \, \gamma$

11. The membership of gesture G in emotion E is calculated as

$$\mu_E(G) = \mu_E^{net}(displacement) \times \mu_E^{net}(expansion)$$

12. Winning emotion is the emotion with maximum $\mu_E(G)$ value.

3   Experimental Details

3.1   Experiment Design

As an input set skeletal co-ordinates of emotionally indicative nature are taken. Since all subjects may not be similarly vivid in expressing their emotions through gestures, a professional actor is chosen to train the subjects how a vividly emotional gestural expression may be portrayed. The same actor also performs in front of the Kinect and the system analyses the X, Y and Z co-ordinates of the body joints obtained from Kinect. When the subjects perform any test gesture in front of the Kinect, it processes the X, Y and Z co-ordinates and matches the obtained features with the features it has processed by analyzing the actor's performance. The performance is assigned a class to which acted performances lie closest to. Some of the skeleton overviews are given in Fig 4. For evaluating displacement; we consider 3 axes separately as aforementioned. These views of skeleton have been stimulated my Matlab software by plotting the body joint co-ordinates from Kinect machine. Some gesture stills have been shown. Five emotions: Anger, Disgust, Fear, Happy and Surprise have been studied.

3.2   Experiment Modality and Result Analysis

The sole modality of the experiment was gesture. The gestures were analyzed by evaluating direction of and magnitude of repetitive movements (Avg1, Avg2), direction and magnitude of movements of joint co-ordinates (Max, Min), and expansion (maximum and minimum distance of right wrist from hip center along each axis for a gesture).The confusion matrix of the system is given in Table 2.From Table 2 we can see that "Surprise" class is sometimes confused with "Happy" or "Fear" class because the gestures are almost similar. In Table 3 some emotion recognition methods and are compared with our proposed approach.

Table 2. Confusion Matrix for Emotion Recognition

	Anger	Disgust	Fear	Happy	Surprise
Anger	100%				
Disgust		98%	2%		
Fear			96%	2%	2%
Happy				92%	8%
Surprise			6%	8%	86%

Table 3. Performance in comparison to other methods

Approach	Accuracy
SVM classification, facial expression and gesture features, CCA feature fusion[21]	89.57%
SVM classification, facial expression and gesture features, Direct feature fusion[21]	74.57%
HNB classifier, correlation based feature selection of gesture[20]	61%
Proposed Approach	94.4%

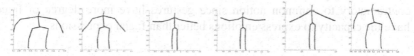

Fig. 4a. Expanding arms upwards to indicate happiness

Fig. 4b. Shaking Wrist and stamping feet to indicate anger

Fig. 4c. Turning body away in disgust. It may be noted here that our algorithm performs well even with bent knees coming due to loose clothes around knees.

Fig. 4d. Hands moving towards head and outwards in surprise

Fig. 4e. Body moving backwards and hands protecting body in fear

4   Conclusion

An efficient and novel system has been developed which evaluates and recognizes emotional gestures with single training only. It is a real time system and can be experimented on for more purposes like person recognition and emotion detection from dances. It tackles time complexity well and has incorporated fuzzy system to allow for the uncertainty involved in emotions. It achieves an accuracy of 94.4% based on only gestural clues. The best accuracy obtained for a one shot learning system for gesture recognition is around 90% [19]. The major drawback of this system is that the subjects need to be trained in order to vividly express their emotions as all subjects may not be equally expressive in projecting their emotions through gestures. However there are a lot of applications of this gesture recognition system as it is a real time system. Also we have used only cameras for data extraction which means minimum user hindrance. Also gestures are a better source of emotional information from a distance; wherein face bay not be visible, as gestures can be extracted by low end cameras also. The system can also be used for threat detection. It may be noted here that contradictory to common notion since gestures have more degree of freedom, they have the capacity to express emotions better than facial expressions.

References

1. Ju, Z., Liu, H.: A unified fuzzy framework for human-hand motion recognition. IEEE Transactions on Fuzzy Systems 19(5), 901–913 (2011)
2. Liao, J., Bi, Y., Nugent, C.: Using the Dempster–Shafer theory of evidence with a revised lattice structure for activity recognition. IEEE Transactions on Information Technology in Biomedicine 15(1), 74–82 (2011)
3. Schwier, J.M., Brooks, R.R., Griffin, C.: Methods to window data to differentiate between Markov models. IEEE Transactions on Systems, Man, and Cybernetics, Part B: Cybernetics 41(3), 650–663 (2011)
4. Lin, C.T., Yeh, C.M., Liang, S.F., Chung, J.F., Kumar, N.: Support-vector-based fuzzy neural network for pattern classification. IEEE Transactions on Fuzzy Systems 14(1), 31–41 (2006)
5. Sotelo, M.P., Desseree, E., Moreau, J.M., Shariat, B., Beuve, M.: 3-D Model-Based Multiple-Object Video Tracking for Treatment Room Supervision. IEEE Transactions on Biomedical Engineering 59(2), 562–570 (2012)
6. Fang, G., Gao, W., Zhao, D.: Large vocabulary sign language recognition based on fuzzy decision trees. IEEE Transactions on Systems, Man and Cybernetics, Part A: Systems and Humans 34(3), 305–314 (2004)
7. Zhang, X., Chen, X., Li, Y., Lantz, V., Wang, K., Yang, J.: A framework for hand gesture recognition based on accelerometer and EMG sensors. IEEE Transactions on Systems, Man and Cybernetics, Part A: Systems and Humans 41(6), 1064–1076 (2011)
8. Zadeh, L.A.: Fuzzy logic = computing with words. IEEE Transactions on Fuzzy Systems 4(2), 103–111 (1996)
9. Sarkar, N., Smith, C.A.: A novel interface system for seamlessly integrating human-robot cooperative activities in space. Technical Report, NASA Institute for Advanced Concepts (2002)
10. Jiang, M., Wang, Z.: A method for stress detection based on FCM algorithm. In: 2nd International Congress on Image and Signal Processing, CISP 2009, pp. 1–5. IEEE (2009)
11. Guney, K., Sarikaya, N.: Comparison of Mamdani and Sugeno fuzzy inference system models for resonant frequency calculation of rectangular microstrip antennas. Progress In Electromagnetics Research B 12, 81–104 (2009)

12. Bailador, G., Guadarrama, S.: Robust gesture recognition using a prediction-error-classification approach. In: IEEE International Fuzzy Systems Conference, 2007 (FUZZ-IEEE 2007), pp. 1–7. IEEE (2007)
13. de Santos Sierra, A., Sánchez Ávila, C., Casanova, J.G., del Pozo, G.B.: A stress-detection system based on physiological signals and fuzzy logic. IEEE Transactions on Industrial Electronics, 58(10), 4857-4865 (2011)
14. Várkonyi-Kóczy, A.R., Tusor, B.: Human–computer interaction for smart environment applications using fuzzy hand posture and gesture models. IEEE Transactions on Instrumentation and Measurement 60(5), 1505–1514 (2011)
15. Álvarez, M., Galán, R., Matía, F., Rodríguez-Losada, D., Jiménez, A.: An emotional model for a guide robot. IEEE Transactions on Systems, Man and Cybernetics, Part A: Systems and Humans 40(5), 982–992 (2010)
16. Liu, H.Y., Wang, W.J., Wang, R.J., Tung, C.W., Wang, P.J., Chang, I.P.: Image Recognition and Force Measurement Application in the Humanoid Robot Imitation. IEEE Transactions on Instrumentation and Measurement 61(1), 149–161 (2012)
17. Yang, F., Li, Y.: Set-membership fuzzy filtering for nonlinear discrete-time systems. IEEE Transactions on Systems, Man, and Cybernetics, Part B: Cybernetics 40(1), 116–124 (2010)
18. Kadkhodaie-Ilkhchi, A., Monteiro, S.T., Ramos, F., Hatherly, P.: Rock recognition from mwd data: A comparative study of boosting, neural networks, and fuzzy logic. IEEE Geoscience and Remote Sensing Letters 7(4), 680–684 (2010)
19. Castellano, G., Villalba, S.D., Camurri, A.: Recognising human emotions from body movement and gesture dynamics. In: Paiva, A.C.R., Prada, R., Picard, R.W. (eds.) ACII 2007. LNCS, vol. 4738, pp. 71–82. Springer, Heidelberg (2007)
20. Castellano, G., Mortillaro, M., Camurri, A., Volpe, G., Scherer, K.: Automated analysis of body movement in emotionally expressive piano performances. Music Perception: An Interdisciplinary Journal 26(2), 103–119 (2008)
21. Gunes, H., Shan, C., Chen, S., Tian, Y.: Bodily Expression for Automatic Affect Recognition. Advances in Emotion Recognition. Wiley-Blackwell

Automatic Eye Detection in Face Images for Unconstrained Biometrics Using Genetic Programming

Chandrashekhar Padole[1,2] and Joanne Athaide[1,3]

[1] Technical Consultant, IRDC India, Mumbai (Thane), India
chandupadole@yahoo.com
www.irdcindia.com
[2] Research Scholar at Dept. of Informatics, University of Beira Interior, Covilha, Portugal
[3] Design Engineer, CoMira Solutions Inc, Pittsburgh, Pennsylvania, USA

Abstract. Automatic extraction of eyes is a very important step in face detection and recognition system since eyes are one of the most stable features of the human face. In this paper, we present a novel technique using genetic programming for determining the classifier function to be used in the automatic detection of eyes in facial images. The feature terminals fed to the system are Gabor wavelet filtered image, mean, standard deviation and vertical position. Gabor wavelet transform has the optimal basis to extract local features. To find the Gabor wavelet to filter the image, we make use of Levenberg-Marquardt optimization. For the fitness function, we have used the concept of localization fitness, which is incorporated in the calculation of the precision and recall values to be included in fitness. We tested our system on the face images from the ORL databases and have presented our results. The result shows the effectiveness and flexibility provided by genetic programming in deciding the classifier for the detection of eyes in face images.

1   Introduction

Identification of people using Face Recognition is a trivial task for humans. The latest available cameras can capture images with equal and far greater resolution as that of the human eye. But the system to process these images for recognition of human faces is still nowhere near that of the human brain. This problem has attracted significant attention [15] across the research community. Face recognition systems are most widely used for time attendance systems, access control systems including gates and entrances at corporate or residential enclosures, visitor management systems etc. and vital part of biometrics systems in the case of unconstrained set-up. For face recognition, several features such as eyes, nose, lips etc are used. Among these, eyes are the most salient features to be detected by human eyes and hence, image processing algorithms. Another important point in face recognition algorithms is the alignment of facial images which has a large impact on recognition accuracy [16]. The best way to perform alignment is by locating the eye positions. More recently, the facial area around the vicinity of eyes are used for periocualr recognition for the person identification, where iris recognition becomes implausible due to large camera-subject distance [24, 25, 26]. This inspired us to find the effective and flexible solution for the localization of eyes in the facial images.

B.K. Panigrahi et al. (Eds.): SEMCCO 2013, Part II, LNCS 8298, pp. 364–375, 2013.

The classification method we will be using is Genetic Programming (GP). GP is a relatively new approach which was introduced by Koza in 1992 [10] in his work Genetic programming: on the programming of computers by means of natural selection. GP is a part of evolutionary computation which is inspired by the principles of natural evolution as introduced by Charles Darwin in On the Origin of Species: By Means of Natural Selection or the Preservation of favored Races in the Struggle for Life [17] in 1859.

Several eye detection methods have been developed for different purposes such as drowsiness detection [18], driver fatigue detection and as a preliminary step to face detection. Red-eye detection has been developed as well in many works. For detecting eyes, entropy of different regions of a face image is found in [1]. It is assumed that the eye region will have the highest entropy and this is used to find eye regions. In another system [2], Haar wavelets are used along with AdaBoost system for eye detection. SVM has been used as well for this purpose in [3], [8]. A terrain map and Gaussian mixture model has been used [5].

Our work takes a cue from the work done in [14] in which Genetic Programming was used for object detection. A sweeping window is used to collect the features which were pixel statistics. But instead of using pixel statistics, we have use Gabor wavelets to filter the image. The dimensions of the Gabor wavelet are calculated by using Levenberg-Marquandt algorithm. This wavelet filtered image along with vertical position information is used as features fed to the GP system. So far to our knowledge, there have not been any attempt to use the genetic programming, effective and flexible way, to detect the eye locations. Though, there are several attempts of using the genetic algorithm for eye detection. In section 2 we explain the basics of a GP system. Then in section 3 we explain the architecture of our system. In section 4 we explain our results and then the conclusions and scope for future work.

2   Genetic Programming

GP can be summarized as a supervised learning method in which a number of 'computer programs' are initialized randomly. Selected features are extracted from the data set which are called as 'terminals'. These are given as inputs to the system to the initialized programs and a 'fitness function' is used to evaluate the programs. This fitness function is a very important part of the GP system. It must be carefully formulated to as to find the 'program' which will give the optimum solution. It assigns a fitness value to each possible fixed-length character string in the population. The best programs are 'reproduced' or inserted into the next population. 'Crossover' operations are performed on some of the good programs in which two 'parent' programs are combined to form child programs which are also evaluated and then inserted into the new population. 'Mutation' operations are performed as well on the good programs and are inserted into the population. The basic flow of a GP system is shown in figure 1. GP is used widely to solve two problems i.e. classification and regression. In this work we use it for classification.

3   Eye Detection System

The GP system described above is used. In this section we will describe the collection of features which will be used in the eye detection system.

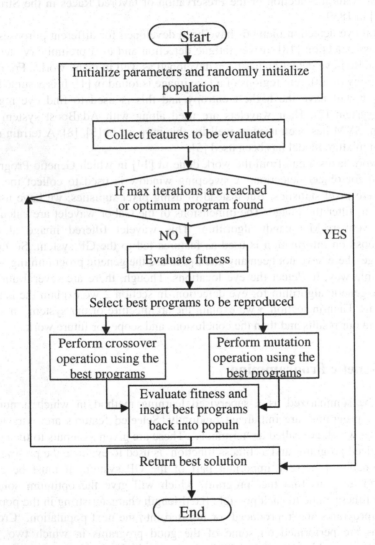

Fig. 1. Flowchart of GP system

3.1   Features Collection

The major feature used for eye detection is the Gabor filtered wavelet. The wavelet transform can perform multi-resolution time-frequency analysis. Gabor wavelet transform are the optimal basis to extract local features for several reasons [20]: The biological motivation is, the simple cells of the visual cortex of mammalian brains are best modeled as a family of self-similar 2D Gabor wavelets while the mathematical and empirical motivation is that Gabor wavelet transform has both the multi-resolution and multi-orientation properties and are optimal for measuring local spatial frequencies. The Gabor function can be defined as:

$$g(x, y) = K \exp(-\pi(a^2(x-x_0)_r^2 + b^2(y-y_0)_r^2))$$
$$\exp(j(2\pi(u_0 x + v_0 y) + P)) \tag{1}$$

where, K: scales the magnitude of the Gaussian envelope.
(a, b) : Scale the two axis of the Gaussian envelope.
θ : Rotation angle of the Gaussian envelope.
(x_0, y_0) : Location of the peak of the Gaussian envelope.
(u_0, v_0) : Spatial frequencies of the sinusoid carrier in Cartesian coordinates.
P: Phase of the sinusoid carrier

Below in figure 2, we have shown some Gabor wavelets of varying scales, frequencies and orientations.

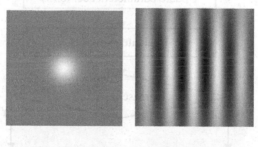

(a) (50,50), 0 degrees, 0 Hz (b) (50,50), 0 degrees, 5 Hz

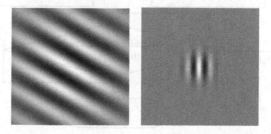

(c) (50,50), 30 degrees, 5 Hz (d) (10,10), 90 degrees, 10 Hz

Fig. 2. Gabor wavelets with varying scales, phase angles and frequencies

The pixel values of the Gabor wavelets shown above vary between 0 and 1. As it can be seen a variety of configurations for filters can be used. The challenging task is to find out which wavelet will give us the best output for the eye detection system. In other words, the filtered image should be such that the eyes stand out. In order to converge upon the optimal wavelet, we use Levenberg-Marquardt optimization.

The Levenberg-Marquardt (LM) algorithm is an iterative technique that locates the minimum of a multivariate function that is expressed as the sum of squares of non-linear real-valued functions [21, 22]. It can be thought of as a combination of steepest descent and the Gauss-Newton method. When the current solution is far from the correct one, the algorithm behaves like a steepest descent method: slow, but guaranteed to converge. When the current solution is close to the correct solution, it becomes a Gauss-Newton method. The block diagram of L-M algorithm is shown in figure 3.

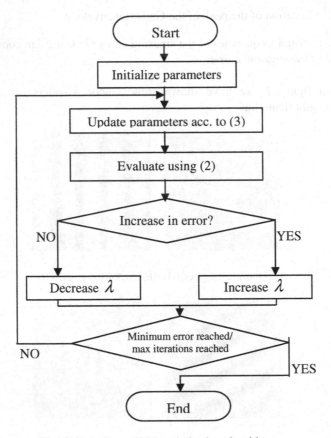

Fig. 3. Flowchart of LM optimization algorithm

In brief, the working of LM can be shown as follows. The function to be minimized can be given as

$$f(x) = \frac{1}{2}\sum_{j=1}^{m} r_j^2(x) \tag{2}$$

In our case the function is minimum when the when the wavelet correctly filters out the eyes. We used the ORL database with the manual annotation of eye positions. Using the LM algorithm, the updating of the parameters can be found as

$$x_{i+1} = x_i - (H + \lambda diag \mid H \mid)^{-1} \nabla f(x_i) \tag{3}$$

where H is the hessian of $f(x)$. The algorithm is as follows

Thus the LM algorithm will converge as it approaches the optimal wavelet. Using this wavelet, the image is filtered.

Fig. 4. (a) Face image, (b) Optimal Gabor wavelet (c) Filtered image

The above figure 4(b) shows the optimal Gabor wavelet obtained after running the mentioned LM optimization or the face image, fig 4(a). The fig 4(c) shows the gabor output of optimal filter parameters. It can be seen that it highlights the eyes albeit with other regions as well. They can be eliminated by using some more features which are described further.

Second and third features used are mean and standard deviation. They can be obtained using the formulas below.

$$\bar{X} = \frac{\sum_{i=1}^{n} X_i}{N} \tag{4}$$

$$\sigma = \sqrt{\frac{\sum_{i=1}^{n}(X_i - \bar{X})^2}{N}} \tag{5}$$

where N = the total number of pixels in the window which are being considered,

X_i = the ith pixel and

$\overline{X}$ = the mean of pixels for i=1 to N

σ = the standard deviation of the pixels under the window.

The fourth feature used is the vertical position of the eyes. Since we are only working with face images, it can be assumed that the eyes will be somewhere in the lower parts of the upper half of the image. Hence we take the vertical height of the pixels as well as a feature. The features fed to a GP system are called as its terminals. For collection of features, the concept of sweeping window with fixed step size to reduce computations is used as used in our earlier work [9].

3.2   Function Set

The function set contain the four standard arithmetic and conditional operation: FuncSet = {+, −, *, /, if}. The +, −, and * operators are usual addition, subtraction and multiplication, while / represents "protected" division. The *if* function returns its second argument if the first argument is positive or returns its third argument otherwise.

3.3   Fitness Function

Using the above function sets and terminals, programs are randomly generated. These programs need to be evaluated so that they can be 'evolved'. These programs are generated as shown in [14]. This evaluation is done using the Fitness Function. At the heart of the genetic programming problem lies the fitness function formulation. This function must give a measure of how well evolved the program is. We used precision and recall values to calculate fitness value. The fitness function we are using was used for object localization using GP by Zhang and Malcolm Lett [23]. We use it for eye detection. They introduced the "Relative Localization Weighted F-measure" (RLWF), which attempts to acknowledge the worth of individual localizations made by the genetic program. Precision refers to the number of objects correctly detected by a GP system as a percentage of the total number of object detected by the system. Recall refers to the number of objects correctly detected by a system as a percentage of total number of target objects in a data set. In this fitness function, we don't just say 1=correct localization and 0=incorrect localization, but we use the scale [0,1] to signify how 'worthy' each localization is. We call this value as *localization fitness* LF. It is calculated based on the Euclidean distance between the current position and the correct position (closest object center). LF=1 indicates that the localization made by the function is the correct localization and LF=0 indicates it is not close to a correct localization position. LF can be calculated as follows:

$$LF(x, y) = \begin{cases} 1 - \dfrac{\sqrt{x^2 + y^2}}{r}, & if \sqrt{x^2 + y^2} \le r \\ 0, otherwise \end{cases} \tag{6}$$

where $\sqrt{x^2 + y^2}$ is the distance of the classification position (x,y) from target object centre, and r is called the "localization fitness radius", defined by the user. In this system, r is set to a half of the square size of the input window, which is also the radius of the largest object.

The precision and recall are calculated by taking the localization fitness for all the localizations of each object and dividing this by the total number of localizations or total number of target objects respectively.

$$Precision = \frac{Sum(LF \text{ for all localization positions})}{\text{Total no. of localization positions}} \tag{7}$$

$$Re\,call = \frac{\text{Number of objects localized}}{\text{Total number of objects to be localized}} \tag{8}$$

$$Fitness = \frac{2X \Pr ecisionX \operatorname{Re} call}{\Pr ecision + \operatorname{Re} call} \tag{9}$$

Hence while calculating precision, for every localization position, a value between 1 and 0 will be used depending on how "precise" each localization is. This is divided by the total number of objects. Hence for a perfect case where each position represents the object at the exact center, precision value will be 1. Hence it is the measure of false alarms and trying to reduce those. However, this leaves a loophole. In the case where all object are not localized, one can still achieve precision 1. Hence recall value is used which checks for localization of all objects. Hence recall = 1 indicates that all objects are classified regardless of how good the precision is. Hence this measures detection ratio. Hence both these measures completely describe the fitness function which is given in eqn. (9).

3.4   Parameters and Termination Criteria

The parameter values used in this approach are shown in table 1. In this approach, the learning/evolutionary process is terminated when one of the following conditions is met:

1) The detection problem has been solved on the training set, that is, all objects in each class of interest in the training set have been correctly detected with no false alarms. In this case, the fitness of the best individual program is zero.

2) The number of generations reaches the pre-defined number, max-generations.

Table 1. Parameters for GP Training

	Parameters	Values
Search Parameters	Population size Max. no. of generations	100 30
Genetic parameters	Reproduction rate Cross-rate Mutation-rate	10% 80% 10%
Fitness parameters	Classification fitness radius	5

4   Experimental Results

We use the images in the ORL database, a well-known free database of faces, to do our experiments. In this database, there are completely photographs of 40 persons, of which each one has 10 various views. The 10 views of the same person include faces looking to the right, to the left, downward and upward. All faces in this database are presented by images in gray-level with the size of 92×112.

Fig. 5. Results after testing on various subjects

Fig. 5. (*Continued.*)

Our system works well for images of persons without glasses. The first stage of the training process is to obtain the optimum Gabor wavelet (GW). We use 10 frontal face images to get it. One of the obtained GW is shown in Fig. 4(b). After that the actual system training takes place which is finding the program which will give the best solution combining the extracted features. For training of the system, we used images of faces without glasses. From the subject without glasses which are 25, we trained the system for 17 of these subjects and tested on the remaining 8. Some of the results obtained are shown below.

The sub-figures shown in the figure 5 presents the effectiveness and flexibility of the system. The flexibility in general is very useful parameter as it provides the way to adapt the systems to changing situations by updating the classifier using GP. A few false positives and negatives do exist. But they are at a minimum due to the robustness of the fitness function.

5   Conclusion

We have presented a novel system of eye detection using genetic programming. This is an approach that has not been used before. It has used a very powerful tool which has recently emerged to solve difficult classification problems: Genetic Programming. Since Gabor wavelets is a very good feature extractor, it was used for extracting one of the features or terminals for the GP system. These tools combined with the LM algorithm made for a very robust system. Genetic Programming has continued to prove itself as a very promising and intelligent system for solving classification problems and it could also be used to make system more adaptable for changing situations. Thus, GP based method can be used in unconstrained biometrics.

References

1. Hassaballah, M., Ido, S.: Eye detection using and Appearance Information, MVA2009 IAPR Conference on Machine Vision Applications, May 20-22, Yokohama, JAPAN (2009)
2. Wang, P., Green, M.B., Ji, Q., Wayman, J.: Automatic Eye Detection and Its Validation. In: Conference on Computer Vision and Pattern Recognition - Workshops, CVPR Workshops, p. 164. IEEE Computer Publication Society (2005)
3. Kim, H.-J., Kim, W.-Y.: Eye detection in facial images using Zernike moments with SVM. ETRI Journal 30(2), 335–337 (2008)
4. Zhou, Z.H., Geng, X.: Projection functions for eye detection. Pattern Recognition 37(5), 1049–1056 (2004)
5. Wang, J., Yin, L.: Eye Detection under Unconstrained Background by the Terrain Feature. In: IEEE International Conference on Multimedia and Expo, ICME 2005, pp. 1528–1531 (2005)
6. Zhu, Z., Ji, Q.: Robust real-time eye detection and tracking under variable lighting conditions and various face orientations. Journal on Computer Vision and Image Understanding - Special issue on Eye Detection and Tracking 98(1) (2005)
7. Wang, J., Yin, L.: Eye Detection Under Unconstrained Background by the Terrain Feature. In: IEEE International Conference on Multimedia and Expo, pp. 1528–1531 (2005)
8. Wang, Q., Yang, J.: Eye Location and Eye State Detection in Facial Images with Unconstrained Background. Journal of Information and Computing Science 1(5), 284–289 (2006)
9. Padole, C., Athaide, J.: Object Detection and Classification using Evolutionary Computations. International Journal on Science and Technology (2011)
10. Koza, J.R.: Genetic programming: on the programming of computers by means of natural selection. MIT Press, London (1992)
11. Daubechies, I.: The Wavelet Transform, Time-Frequency Localization and Signal Analysis. IEEE Trans. Information Theory 36(5), 961–1004 (1990)
12. Daugman, J.G.: Two-Dimensional Spectral Analysis of Cortical Receptive Field Profile. Vision Research 20, 847–856 (1980)
13. Daugman, J.G.: Uncertainty Relation for Resolution in Space, Spatial Frequency, and Orientation Optimized by Two-Dimensional Visual Cortical Filters. J. Optical Soc. Amer. 2(7), 1 (1985)
14. Zhang, M., Andreae, P., Pritchard, M.: Pixel statistics and false alarm area in genetic programming for object detection. In: Raidl, G.R., Cagnoni, S., Cardalda, J.J.R., Corne, D.W., Gottlieb, J., Guillot, A., Hart, E., Johnson, C.G., Marchiori, E., Meyer, J.-A., Middendorf, M. (eds.) EvoIASP 2003, EvoWorkshops 2003, EvoSTIM 2003, EvoROB/EvoRobot 2003, EvoCOP 2003, EvoBIO 2003, and EvoMUSART 2003. LNCS, vol. 2611, pp. 455–466. Springer, Heidelberg (2003)
15. Goldstein, A.J., Harmon, L.D., Lesk, A.B.: Identification of Human Faces. Proc. IEEE 59(5), 748–760 (1971)
16. Phillips, P.J., Moon, H., Rizvi, S.A., Rauss, P.J.: The feret evaluation methodology for face-recognition algorithms. IEEE Transactions on Pattern Analysis and Machine Intelligence 22(10), 1090–1104 (2000)
17. Darwin, C.: On the origin of species: By Means of Natural Selection or the Preservation of Favoured Races in the Struggle for Life. Murray, London (1859)

18. Tabrizi, P.R., Zoroofi, R.A.: Open/Closed Eye Analysis for Drowsiness Detection. In: First Workshops on Image Processing Theory, Tools and Applications, IPTA 2008, pp. 1–7 (2008)
19. Bala, J., DeJong, K., Huang, J., Vafaie, H., Wechsler, H.: Visual routine for eye detection using hybrid genetic architectures. In: Proceedings of the 13th International Conference on Pattern Recognition, vol. 3, pp. 606–610 (1996)
20. Shen, L., Bai, L.: A review of Gabor wavelets for face recognition. Patt. Anal. Appl. 9, 273–292 (2006)
21. Levenberg, K.: "A method for the solution of certain problems in least squares. Quart. Appl. Math. 2, 164–168 (1944)
22. Marquardt, D.: An algorithm for least-squares estimation of nonlinear parameters. SIAM J. Appl. Math. 11, 431–441 (1963)
23. Zhang, M.: Malcolm Lett. Genetic Programming for Object Detection: Improving Fitness Functions and Optimising Training Data 7(1), 12–21 (2006)
24. Santos, G., Proença, H.: Periocular Biometrics: An Emerging technology for Unconstrained Scenarios. In: Proceedings of the IEEE Symposium on Computational Intelligence in Biometrics and Identity Management – CIBIM 2013, Singapore, April 16-19, pp. 14–21 (2013)
25. Padole, C.N., Proenca, H.: Periocular recognition: Analysis of performance degradation factors. In: 2012 5th IAPR International Conference on Biometrics (ICB), March 29-April 1, pp. 439–445 (2012)
26. Park, U., Jillela, R.R., Ross, A., Jain, A.K.: Periocular Biometrics in the Visible Spectrum. IEEE Transactions on Information Forensics and Security 6(1), 96–106 (2011)

Neural Network Based Gesture Recognition
for Elderly Health Care Using Kinect Sensor

Sriparna Saha[1], Monalisa Pal[1], Amit Konar[1], and Ramadoss Janarthanan[2]

[1] Electronics & Telecommunication Engineering Department, Jadavpur University, India
[2] Computer Science and Engineering Department, TJS Engineering College, India
{sahasriparna,monalisap90}@gmail.com,
akonar@etce.jdvu.ac.in, srmjana_73@yahoo.com

Abstract. A simple method to detect gestures revealing muscle and joint pain is described in this paper. Kinect Sensor is used for data acquisition. This sensor only processes twenty joint coordinates in three dimensional space for feature extraction. The recognition part is achieved using a neural network optimized by Levenberg-Marquardt learning rule. A high recognition rate of 91.9% is achieved using the proposed method. This is also better than several algorithms previously used for elder person gesture recognition works.

Keywords: Elder, gesture, Kinect sensor, neural network.

1   Introduction

The identification of various body gestures and human behaviors falls within the sphere of gesture recognition. The main efficacy of gesture recognition is the analyzing of information that is entrenched in the gesture and is not communicated by speech or text [1], [2]. It is well thought-out as a way computer understands body language and thus, renders a better interface between human and computer than other various interfaces, e.g. text and graphical [3]. In our proposed work, we have dealt with 3D mode of gesture recognition for elderly health care. Gestures arising out of diseases related to muscle and joint pains, such as Lumbar spondylosis, Plantar fascitis, Tennis elbow, etc., are taken as the inputs in the system and Kinect sensor is employed to obtain the 3D representation of the body gestures using twenty body joint co-ordinates. Advantages of using this method accounts to faster processing as only the data for these twenty joints needs to be processed and also implementation of the system in real-time is achieved using Kinect sensor.

The medical diseases considered for this proposed work are the symptoms shown by elderly persons due to muscle and joint pains. These diseases occur due to injury, fatigue or aging and are further intensified due to the lifestyle of the disabled individuals. Thus the proposed algorithm can be utilized for home monitoring systems for aged persons. These diseases if not recognized in early stages produce adverse effects on their health and intensify to chronic stages.

B.K. Panigrahi et al. (Eds.): SEMCCO 2013, Part II, LNCS 8298, pp. 376–386, 2013.

A few research works have been done in this following area. The authors in [4] have proposed an algorithm, where silhouettes are extracted from elder persons using video sensor. The work suffers from a drawback of variation in the background. As the background of the monitored scenario can vary widely, this may lead to erroneous silhouettes and which further generates wrong results. Another scheme is proposed by authors in [5], employing the time-of flight camera. This algorithm is very much similar to our proposed work, as in [5] also the human body is modeled using body joints. The algorithm in [5] only addresses the fall detection of elder persons, while our work does not have this sort of limitation.

In our proposed work, we have employed Microsoft Kinect Sensor [6], [7], [8], [9], [10] for gathering the information regarding the various muscle and joint pains in elder persons. In [9], researchers have used Kinect sensor for recognizing four postures viz., standing, bending, lying and sitting using Support Vector Machine as classifier. We have created a large database comprising of 7 body gestures related to diverse muscle and joint pains for elderly health care. Thus, along with describing a method for gesture recognition, this work addresses the issues related to independent living and elderly healthcare.

In this work, we intend to make a real-time system which tracks the subject concerned and recognize whether the subject has any of the muscle and joint pains using Kinect sensor. Kinect sensor detects skeleton of the individual, using 20 body joint co-ordinates [11]. This tracking is possible if the subject situated in front of the Kinect sensor within a finite amount of distance using a set of visible and IR cameras. The elder persons generally perform their whole day activity while sitting on a chair. Thus we considered 7 different body gestures related to muscle and joint pains when the person is sitting on a chair. After collection of the body gestures, those are processed to produce 10 features from the skeleton structure. The recognition is accomplished using neural networks [12], [13] with Levenberg-Marquardt (LM) Optimization [14], [15]. In a real-time recognition scenario, when an elder performs his/her whole day activity, the Kinect sensor tracks the skeleton and matches each frame of the recording with the database and generate the best matched body gesture using neural network. In case the person possesses pain at any body part, the system recommends the subject to perform some exercises. If the pain persists the subject is advised to consult doctors. We have achieved a high recognition rate of 91.9% using the above mentioned method.

In section 2, method of study for the proposed work is illustrated by providing the description of Kinect sensor, concerned diseases related to muscle and joint pain and the explanation of neural network. Section 3 elaborately shows feature extraction procedure for 10 features. The experimental results are discussed in section 4 and section 5 concludes the paper providing future directions.

2   Method of Study

This section includes the description of Kinect sensor, concerned muscle and joint pains and neural network.

2.1   Kinect Sensor

The Kinect is an upcoming technology which basically looks like a webcam [7]. It has the appearance of a long horizontal bar with a motorized base. It tracks the skeleton of the person present in front of the sensor roughly within 1.2 to 3.5m or 3.9 to 11ft from the sensor. It has a set of visible IR and RGB cameras [11] as picturized in Fig. 1. The IR cameras are responsible for sensing the skeleton in three-dimensional space [16] and hence the body gestures irrespective of the color of the person's dress or distance from the camera are produced.

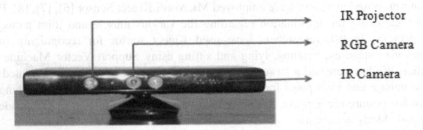

IR Projector

RGB Camera

IR Camera

Fig. 1. Kinect Sensor

2.2   Overview of Concerned Muscle and Joint Pains

Although there is no demarcation that marks the onset of old-age, it has been seen that pain at different muscle and joints starts on an average age of 40 years. Ten subjects, 7 female and 3 male in the age group of 40 years and above, have been asked to participate for the data acquisition. For each of the diseases, 50 sample gestures are obtained. The following 7 pains are frequently observed in the studied persons and a database is created after processing the data for these diseases. While making the database, it is kept in mind to include equal number of samples for pain at both right and left sides, where applicable.

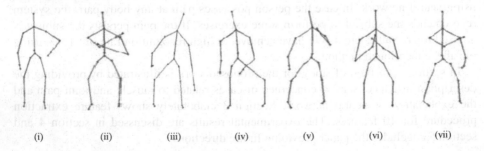

(i)   (ii)   (iii)   (iv)   (v)   (vi)   (vii)

Fig. 2. Data output from Kinect Sensor for the seven diseases considered. (i) Lumbar spondylosis, (ii) Tennis elbow, (iii) Plantar fasciitis, (iv) Osteoarthritis knee, (v) Cerviacal spondolysis, (vi) Osteoarthritis hand, (vii) Frozen shoulder.

Lumbar spondylosis is a joint problem caused due to degenerative changes in the lumbar spine. Pain is felt in lower back position. Fig. 2(i) shows the skeleton when the lower back is massaged by left hand due to this pain. Tennis elbow is a problem of tendon. The subject experiences pain over the lateral aspect of the elbow due to strain of the tendinous origin. The pain at right elbow is depicted by the skeleton in Fig. 2(ii). Plantar fascitis is also a disease related to tendon. Pain is faced at the heel due to strain of the plantar fascia. Fig. 2(iii) shows the skeleton of a person having pain at the left ankle. Osteoarthritis knee occurs due to degenerative changes of the knee leading to pain and stiffness of the joint. The skeleton of a person holding his right knee due to the pain is shown in Fig. 2(iv). The origin of Cerviacal spondolysis disease is the degenerative changes occurring in the cervical spine. The patient holds and tilts their neck to get some relief. The corresponding skeleton is given in Fig. 2(v) where the person has hold her neck with her left arm. The palm and fingers have several joints. The degenerative change of the joints of the hand which gradually leads to pain and stiffness is the cause of Osteoarthritis hand disease. The patient generally massages the painful hand with the other arm. The skeleton in Fig. 2(vi) shows the person facing pain in the right hand. Pain and stiffness occurs at the shoulder due to degenerative changes in the shoulder. The skeleton of a subject rubbing the left shoulder due to Frozen shoulder pain is given in Fig. 2(vii).

2.3   Neural Network with Levenberg-Marquardt Optimization

A feed forward neural network [12], [13], [17], [18], [19] is a type of a network which has a series of layers and a weighted sum of input flows in forward direction only. Each of the layers has connection only from its immediately previous layer. The layers between the input and output layers are called hidden layers. Although there can be many hidden layers, one hidden layer with several neurons fits any input-output mapping. If satisfactory results are not obtained, the number of neurons in the hidden layer is varied. For our work, we have obtained best performance with one hidden layer having 10 neurons. In order to obtain a mapping between two domains (input-output) a random set of weights has to be adapted so that error between desired and generated output is minimized. Back-propagation algorithm is one such model where weight adaption proceeds from the last to first layer. There are several weight adaptation techniques for implementing back propagation algorithm. Out of them, Levenberg-Marquardt optimization [15] has been used as it surpasses gradient descent search and conjugate gradient (or quadratic approximation) methods for medium-sized problems. The block diagram of the proposed work using neural network is depicted in Fig. 3.

The gradient descent learning (1) used by back-propagation algorithm converges very slowly as it takes very small step size which is some constant times the negative gradient instead of a step of fixed size in the direction of negative gradient of the error function.

$$w_{i+1} = w_i - \eta \nabla E(w) \ . \tag{1}$$

This results in quick movement in steep regions (large gradient) and slow movement in valley regions (small gradient) of the error surface. However, if the curvature information is taken into account, we can speed up the optimization technique. The second order information provides both the curvature and gradient but it is computationally expensive to calculate. Hence, most of the techniques approximate the curvature by function evaluation and the gradient using first order derivative.

The error surface is given by average squared error function (2) where $f(x;w)$ represents the output of the neural net as a function of input and weights, y is the desired output, $E(w)$ is the error which is a function of weights during the training phase and the averaging is done over the input and output pairs.

$$E(w) = \left\langle \left(f(x;w) - y \right)^2 \right\rangle . \tag{2}$$

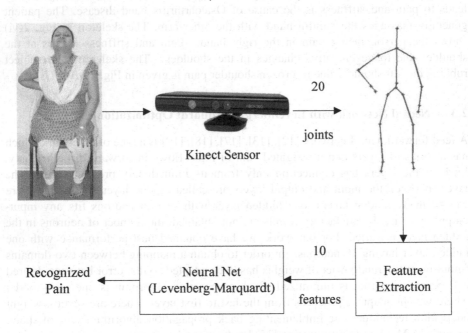

Fig. 3. Block Diagram of the Proposed Work

If E is quadratic in nature, we have a linear model with which we directly find the minimum without undergoing the steepest descent search. By approximating f as linear, the weight adaptation rule is slightly changed (3) where d is derivative and H is an approximation of Hessian matrix resulting from averaging the first order derivative.

$$w_{i+1} = w_i - H^{-1}d . \tag{3}$$

However, E may not always be a quadratic function but it can be treated so near the minimum. So, Levenberg blended these two approaches where at first the minimum is roughly estimated by the gradient descent learning and the quadratic approximation is then used to improve upon the previous result. Here, weights and all parameters are randomly initialized to generate the output and corresponding error. Then the Levenberg proposed optimization rule (4) is used. An increase in the error means quadratic approximation is failing and so λ is increased to use gradient descent and if error decreases, λ is decreased as minimum is nearby. The weights adaptation continues until error is within a prescribed threshold.

$$w_{i+1} = w_i - (H + \lambda I)^{-1} d . \tag{4}$$

Marquardt noticed that when λ is large, only gradient descent search occurs. He incorporated the insight of moving further in the direction in which gradient decreases to prevent getting trapped in a local minima. For this, in the original Levenberg equation, the identity matrix is replaced by diagonal of the Hessian matrix, which yielded the final Levenberg-Marquardt rule (5).

$$w_{i+1} = w_i - (H + \lambda diag[H])^{-1} d . \tag{5}$$

3   Feature Extraction

The data obtained using Microsoft Kinect consists of the Cartesian coordinates of the 20 different joints of the person facing the device. From this information, we extract features or valuable information that is used to differentiate a normal gesture from a gesture showing a muscle or joint pain. To form a feature vector, the following features are considered: distance between hand left (HaL) and hand right (HaR); elbow left (EL) and elbow right (ER); and knee left (KL) and knee right (KR). Not only distances between different joints but also angles formed at various joints are used as features. The following angles are considered: angle at elbow left, elbow right, knee left, knee right and spine (S). As angle calculation depends on vector algebra, we need coordinates of three vertices. So, angle such as that between shoulder left (SL), hip left (HiL) and knee left (KL) are measured as a feature. The same angle with the respective joints at the right side is also considered. Hence, we calculate a 1 by 10 feature vector for a frame as shown in Fig. 4.

$D\,(HaL,$ $HaR)$	$D\,(EL,$ $ER)$	$D\,(KL,$ $KR)$	θ (EL)	θ (ER)	θ (KL)	θ (KR)	θ (S)	$\theta\,(SL,$ $HiL,$ $KL)$	$\theta\,(SR,$ $HiR,$ $KR)$

Fig. 4. Feature Vector

Let there be two points V_1 (a_1,b_1,c_1) and V_2 (a_2,b_2,c_2). The distance between these two points is calculated as given by (6). We have taken Euclidean distance, as other distance metrics, like City Block, Chebyshev etc. are less precise.

$$\text{distance} = \sqrt{(a_1 - a_2)^2 + (b_1 - b_2)^2 + (c_1 - c_2)^2} \; . \tag{6}$$

Let there be 3 vertices V_1 (a_1,b_1,c_1), V_2 (a_2,b_2,c_2) and V_3 (a_3,b_3,c_3). Then, we have two vectors $\vec{v_1}$ (from V_2 to V_1) and $\vec{v_2}$ (from V_2 to V_3) as given by (7) and (8) respectively. The angle formed between these two vectors is given by (9).

$$\vec{v_1} = (a_1 - a_2)\vec{i} + (b_1 - b_2)\vec{j} + (c_1 - c_2)\vec{k} \; . \tag{7}$$

$$\vec{v_2} = (a_3 - a_2)\vec{i} + (b_3 - b_2)\vec{j} + (c_3 - c_2)\vec{k} \; . \tag{8}$$

$$\theta = \left[\frac{\tan^{-1}\left(\frac{\left| \vec{v_1} \times \vec{v_2} \right|}{\vec{v_1} \bullet \vec{v_2}} \right)}{\pi} \right] \times 180^o \; . \tag{9}$$

4   Experimental Results

After the above-mentioned ten features are calculated from the data of each sample a very large feature space is obtained. As the data is acquired from many subjects the distances used as feature have to be normalized. This is done with respect to the maximum value of the distance from any of the three distance feature of all the samples. This creates a subject-invariant data-set. Each of the columns of table 1 shows the features of a sample of a particular disease.

After the feature extraction step, 70% of the total feature space is taken as input and the neural network is trained by Levenberg-Marquardt learning rule [15]. The remaining data-set is divided equally for testing and validation. After the testing is over, classification accuracy is noted as the performance parameter. The overall accuracy is found to be 91.9%. The same data-set, used for training the neural network, is then used to train a Support Vector Machine (SVM) [20], [21], [22], [23] and a k-Nearest Neighbors (kNN) classifier [24], [25], [26], [27]. Then, the trained classifiers are tested with the remaining data-set. It is observed that the classification accuracy decreases.

Table 1. Feature vector of samples from each of the 7 gestures

Features	Gesture 1	Gesture 2	Gesture 3	Gesture 4	Gesture 5	Gesture 6	Gesture 7
D (HaL, HaR)	0.3929	0.2925	0.4327	0.2353	0.5370	0.0500	0.3463
D (EL, ER)	0.5295	0.3200	0.4810	0.3226	0.3840	0.4017	0.3086
D (KL, KR)	0.2479	0.2368	0.3010	0.3247	0.2791	0.2719	0.2728
θ (EL)	133.9250	143.8060	87.0081	144.3490	135.0660	80.4115	91.1978
θ (ER)	65.5103	57.6142	139.5170	118.8670	27.6181	81.5946	119.5570
θ (KL)	127.9930	127.7030	124.7170	108.1600	129.0380	117.9680	126.9930
θ (KR)	127.8040	126.1600	104.2230	121.6670	126.6810	118.5920	123.6570
θ (S)	141.2740	136.5250	164.3590	162.1730	129.1990	129.4690	134.4660
θ (SL, HiL, KL)	133.4650	136.4620	104.1750	107.2280	123.0930	142.4880	127.4220
θ (SR, HiR, KR)	143.6880	134.1040	109.4600	104.8500	126.4800	132.7030	129.3360

For successful recognition of body gestures, exercises corresponding to the recognized body gesture are shown in a video player for the real-time system. If the disease persists then the patient is recommended to seek advice from a doctor. For the preparation of the videos for the exercises, doctors are consulted.

Table 2. Recognition rate obtained with one-versus-one classification

Gesture	Accuracy with Neural Net (%)	Accuracy with SVM (%)	Accuracy with kNN (%)
1	90.37	85.71	84.12
2	92.54	71.43	74.50
3	98.11	85.71	83.47
4	85.37	100	98.54
5	95.28	71.43	84.91
6	87.94	100	94.86
7	93.72	85.71	98.20
Average	91.90	85.71	88.37

The proposed work not only produces better result with Neural Net than with SVM and k-NN classifiers, but it also outperforms the similar works performed in [5] and [9]. When our work is compared with the algorithms proposed in [5] and [9], we note that the proposed method yield higher accuracy covering a large spectrum of disorders while keeping the procedure simple. The comparison of the accuracy rates are collectively explained in Fig. 5.

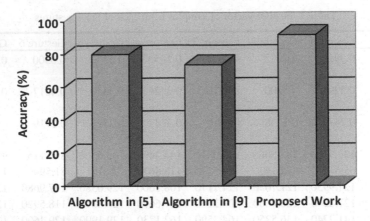

Fig. 5. Comparison of accuracies with respect to [5] and [9]

5   Conclusion

We have examined the seven different diseases causing pains at different body parts on people above 40 years of age. The proposed algorithm is validated using ten subjects. The performance of neural net with an accuracy of 91.9%, surpasses that of the SVM and kNN classifiers.

The drawback of the silhouette based algorithm [4] has been overcome with this work. Even if the background of the examined person varies, there is no effect on the proposed work. This is due to the reason that only the skeleton is tracked using the Kinect Sensor. On the other hand, our work has considered simple and large number of diseases commonly occurring in elderly persons as compared to [5] and [9].

In the future, we are going to concentrate on complex muscle and joint pains with a larger dataset.

Acknowledgments. We would like to thank University Grant Commission, India, University of Potential Excellence Programme (Phase II) in Cognitive Science, Jadavpur University. We are also thankful to the doctors of Calcutta Medical College and Hospital, specially Dr. Subhasish Saha, Head and Professor of Orthopedics Department, for his kind and generous support for preparation of the datasets.

References

1. Halder, A., Rakshit, P., Chakraborty, A., Konar, A., Janarthanan, R.: Emotion recognition from the lip-contour of a subject using artificial bee colony optimization algorithm. In: Panigrahi, B.K., Suganthan, P.N., Das, S., Satapathy, S.C. (eds.) SEMCCO 2011, Part I. LNCS, vol. 7076, pp. 610–617. Springer, Heidelberg (2011)
2. Chakraborty, A., Konar, A.: Emotional Intelligence: A Cybernetic Approach, vol. 1234. Springer (2009)

3. Saha, S., Ghosh, S., Konar, A., Nagar, A.K.: Gesture Recognition from Indian Classical Dance Using Kinect Sensor. In: 2013 Fifth International Conference on Computational Intelligence, Communication Systems and Networks (CICSyN), pp. 3–8 (2013)
4. Zhou, Z., Dai, W., Eggert, J., Giger, J.T., Keller, J., Rantz, M., He, Z.: A real-time system for in-home activity monitoring of elders. In: Annual International Conference of the IEEE Engineering in Medicine and Biology Society, EMBC, pp. 6115–6118 (2009)
5. Diraco, G., Leone, A., Siciliano, P.: An active vision system for fall detection and posture recognition in elderly healthcare. In: Design, Automation & Test in Europe Conference & Exhibition (DATE), pp. 1536–1541 (2010)
6. Liu, Y., Zhang, Z., Li, A., Wang, M.: View independent human posture identification using Kinect. In: 2012 5th International Conference on Biomedical Engineering and Informatics (BMEI), pp. 1590–1593 (2012)
7. Leyvand, T., Meekhof, C., Wei, Y.-C., Sun, J., Guo, B.: Kinect identity: Technology and experience. Computer 44(4), 94–96 (2011)
8. Tanabe, R., Cao, M., Murao, T., Hashimoto, H.: Vision based object recognition of mobile robot with Kinect 3D sensor in indoor environment. In: 2012 Proceedings of SICE Annual Conference (SICE), pp. 2203–2206 (2012)
9. Le, T.-L., Nguyen, M.-Q., Nguyen, T.-T.-M.: Human posture recognition using human skeleton provided by Kinect. In: 2013 International Conference on Computing, Management and Telecommunications (ComManTel), pp. 340–345 (2013)
10. Zhang, Z.: Microsoft kinect sensor and its effect. IEEE Multimedia 19(2), 4–10 (2012)
11. Dutta, T.: Evaluation of the Kinect^{TM} sensor for 3-D kinematic measurement in the workplace. Applied Ergonomics 43(4), 645–649 (2012)
12. Konar, A.: Artificial intelligence and soft computing: behavioral and cognitive modeling of the human brain, vol. 1. CRC Press (1999)
13. Konar, A.: Computational intelligence: principles, techniques and applications. Springer (2005)
14. Kermani, B.G., Schiffman, S.S., Nagle, H.T.: Performance of the Levenberg–Marquardt neural network training method in electronic nose applications. Sensors and Actuators B: Chemical 110(1), 13–22 (2005)
15. Lera, G., Pinzolas, M.: Neighborhood based Levenberg-Marquardt algorithm for neural network training. IEEE Transactions on Neural Networks 13(5), 1200–1203 (2002)
16. Solaro, J.: The Kinect Digital Out-of-Box Experience Computer, pp. 97–99 (2011)
17. Zhuang, H., Zhao, B., Ahmad, Z., Chen, S., Low, K.S.: 3D depth camera based human posture detection and recognition Using PCNN circuits and learning-based hierarchical classifier. In: The 2012 International Joint Conference on Neural Networks (IJCNN), pp. 1–5 (2012)
18. Li, S., Kwok, J.T., Wang, Y.: Multifocus image fusion using artificial neural networks. Pattern Recognition Letters 23(8), 985–997 (2002)
19. Brown, D.E., Corruble, V., Pittard, C.L.: A comparison of decision tree classifiers with backpropagation neural networks for multimodal classification problems. Pattern Recognition 26(6), 953–961 (1993)
20. Sevakula, R.K., Verma, N.K.: Support vector machine for large databases as classifier. In: Panigrahi, B.K., Das, S., Suganthan, P.N., Nanda, P.K. (eds.) SEMCCO 2012. LNCS, vol. 7677, pp. 303–313. Springer, Heidelberg (2012)
21. Das, S., Halder, A., Bhowmik, P., Chakraborty, A., Konar, A., Nagar, A.K.: Voice and facial expression based classification of emotion using linear support vector machine. In: 2009 Second International Conference on Developments in eSystems Engineering (DESE), pp. 377–384 (2009)

22. Cortes, C., Vapnik, V.: Support vector machine. Machine Learning 20(3), 273–297 (1995)
23. Zhan, Y., Shen, D.: Design efficient support vector machine for fast classification. Pattern Recognition 38(1), 157–161 (2005)
24. Wu, Y., Ianakiev, K., Govindaraju, V.: Improved<i> k</i>-nearest neighbor classification. Pattern Recognition 35(10), 2311–2318 (2002)
25. Cover, T., Hart, P.: Nearest neighbor pattern classification. IEEE Transactions on Information Theory 13(1), 21–27 (1967)
26. Wang, J., Neskovic, P., Cooper, L.N.: Improving nearest neighbor rule with a simple adaptive distance measure. Pattern Recognition Letters 28(2), 207–213 (2007)
27. Vidal Ruiz, E.: An algorithm for finding nearest neighbours in (approximately) constant average time. Pattern Recognition Letters 4(3), 145–157 (1986)

City Block Distance for Identification of Co-expressed MicroRNAs

Sushmita Paul and Pradipta Maji

Biomedical Imaging and Bioinformatics Lab
Machine Intelligence Unit, Indian Statistical Institute, Kolkata, India
{sushmita_t,pmaji}@isical.ac.in

Abstract. The microRNAs or miRNAs are short, endogenous RNAs having ability to regulate gene expression at the post-transcriptional level. Various studies have revealed that a large proportion of miRNAs are co-expressed. Expression profiling of miRNAs generates a huge volume of data. Complicated networks of miRNA-mRNA interaction increase the challenges of comprehending and interpreting the resulting mass of data. In this regard, this paper presents the application of city block distance in order to extract meaningful information from miRNA expression data. The proposed method judiciously integrates the merits of robust rough-fuzzy c-means algorithm and normalized range-normalized city block distance to discover co-expressed miRNA clusters. The city block distance is used to calculate the membership functions of fuzzy sets, and thereby helps to handle minute differences between two miRNA expression profiles. The effectiveness of the proposed approach, along with a comparison with other related methods, is demonstrated on several miRNA expression data sets using different cluster validity indices and gene ontology.

Keywords: MicroRNA, co expressed miRNAs, overlapping clustering, rough sets.

1 Introduction

MicroRNAs/miRNAs are a class of short approximately 22-nucleotide non-coding RNAs found in many plants and animals. They often act post-transcriptionally to inhibit mRNA expression. Hence, miRNAs are related to diverse cellular processes and regarded as important components of the mRNA regulatory network. Recent genome wide surveys on non-coding RNAs have revealed that a substantial fraction of miRNAs is likely to form clusters. The genes of miRNAs are often organized in clusters in the genome. It has been reported that at a very conservative maximum inter-miRNA distance of 1kb, over 30% of all miRNAs are organized into clusters [1]. Expression analyses showed strong positive correlations among the closely located miRNAs, indicating that they may be controlled by common regulatory element(s). In fact, experimental evidence demonstrated that clustered miRNA loci form an operon-like gene structure and that they are transcribed from common promoter. Existence of co-expressed miRNAs is also demonstrated using expression profiling analysis in [3]. Several miRNA clusters have been experimentally shown by RT-PCR or Northern blotting [6]. These findings suggest that members of

B.K. Panigrahi et al. (Eds.): SEMCCO 2013, Part II, LNCS 8298, pp. 387–396, 2013.
© Springer International Publishing Switzerland 2013

a miRNA cluster, which are at a close proximity on a chromosome, are highly likely to be processed as co-transcribed units. Expression data of miRNAs can be used to detect clusters of miRNAs as it is suggested that co-expressed miRNAs are co-transcribed, so they should have similar expression pattern. The complex networks of miRNA-mRNA interaction greatly increase the challenges of comprehending and interpreting the resulting mass of data [15]. A first step towards addressing this challenge is the use of clustering techniques, which is essential in the pattern recognition process to reveal natural structures and identify interesting patterns in the underlying data [21].

In this background, authors have used hierarchical clustering algorithms [15] and self organizing maps [2] to group miRNAs having similar function. Other clustering techniques such as k-means algorithm [12], graph theoretical approaches [4,11,24,26], model based clustering [9,10,19,27], density based approach [13], and nearest hyperplane distance neighbor based method [20], which have been widely applied to find co-expressed gene clusters, can also be used to group co-expressed miRNAs from microarray data.

However, one of the main problems in expression data analysis is uncertainty. Some of the sources of this uncertainty include imprecision in computations and vagueness in class definition. In this background, the possibility concept introduced by fuzzy sets [28] and rough sets [22] provides a mathematical framework to capture uncertainties associated with human cognition process. Therefore, fuzzy c-means [5] and different rough-fuzzy clustering algorithms such as rough-fuzzy c-means [16] and robust rough-fuzzy c-means [17] can be used to effectively handle these situations and to find co-expressed miRNA clusters.

In general, the quality of generated clusters is always relative to a certain distance measure. Different distance measures may lead to different clustering results. However, every distance measure tries to compute the dissimilarity among miRNAs present in different clusters. Several similarity or dissimilarity measures such as Euclidean distance, jaccard index, correlation coefficient, and city block distance (CBD) are used in various clustering algorithms. The performance of a clustering algorithm is highly dependant on the distance measure used. One of the important properties of the CBD, not shared by Euclidean distance, is dimensional additivity, that is, the total distance is a sum of the distances per dimension. Moreover, the time required to calculate the CBD is less than the time required to calculate the Euclidean distance.

In this regard, the paper presents a rough-fuzzy clustering algorithm, integrating the concepts of robust rough-fuzzy c-means algorithm [17] and normalized range-normalized city-block distance (NRNCBD), to discover co-expressed miRNAs from huge miRNA expression data. The use of the NRNCBD helps to handle minute differences between two miRNA expression profiles. Each cluster is represented by a set of three parameters, namely, a cluster prototype or centroid, a possibilistic lower approximation, and a probabilistic boundary. The cluster prototype depends on the weighting average of the possibilistic lower approximation and probabilistic boundary. The NRNCBD is used to calculate both possibilistic and probabilistic membership functions. The effectiveness of the NRNCBD over Euclidean distance is presented in this paper. The performance of the proposed miRNA clustering algorithm, along with a comparison with other related methods, is demonstrated on three miRNA expression data sets using standard cluster validity indices and gene ontology based analysis.

2 Proposed Clustering Method

This section describes the proposed miRNA clustering algorithm. It is developed by integrating judiciously robust rough-fuzzy c-means algorithm and the CBD.

The CBD, also known as the Manhattan distance or taxi distance, is closely related to the Euclidean distance. Whereas the Euclidean distance corresponds to the length of the shortest path between two points, the CBD is the sum of distances along each dimension. The distance between two objects x_i and x_j is defined as follows:

$$CBD(x_i, x_j) = \sum_{k=1}^{m} |x_{ik} - x_{jk}| \tag{1}$$

where m is the number of features of the objects x_i and x_j. As for the Euclidean distance, the expression data are subtracted directly from each other, and therefore should be made sure that they are properly normalized. There are many variants of the CBD. The normalized range-normalized CBD (NRNCBD) is defined as follows:

$$\mathcal{N}(x_i, x_j) = \frac{1}{m} \times \sum_{k=1}^{m} \left[\frac{|x_{ik} - x_{jk}|}{|k_{max} - k_{min}|} \right], \tag{2}$$

where k_{max} and k_{min} denote the maximum and minimum values along the kth feature, respectively. The following properties can be derived for the NRNCBD:

1. $0 \leq \mathcal{N}(x_i, x_j) \leq 1$.
2. $\mathcal{N}(x_i, x_j) = \mathcal{N}(x_j, x_i)$.
3. $\mathcal{N}(x_i, x_i) = 0$.
4. $\mathcal{N}(x_i, x_j) \leq \mathcal{N}(x_i, x_k) + \mathcal{N}(x_k, x_j)$.

The proposed rough-fuzzy clustering algorithm adds the concepts of fuzzy memberships, both probabilistic and possibilistic, of fuzzy sets, lower and upper approximations of rough sets, and the NRNCBD into c-means algorithm. While the integration of both probabilistic and possibilistic memberships of fuzzy sets enables efficient handling of overlapping clusters in noisy environment, the rough sets deal with uncertainty, vagueness, and incompleteness in cluster definition.

Let $X = \{x_1, \cdots, x_j, \cdots, x_n\}$ be the set of n objects and $V = \{v_1, \cdots, v_i, \cdots, v_c\}$ be the set of c centroids, where $x_j \in \Re^m$ and $v_i \in \Re^m$. Each of the clusters β_i is represented by a cluster center v_i, a lower approximation $\underline{A}(\beta_i)$ and a boundary region $B(\beta_i) = \{\overline{A}(\beta_i) \setminus \underline{A}(\beta_i)\}$, where $\overline{A}(\beta_i)$ denotes the upper approximation of cluster β_i.

In the proposed rough-fuzzy clustering algorithm, each cluster is represented by a centroid, a possibilistic lower approximation, and a probabilistic boundary. The lower approximation influences the fuzziness of final partition. According to the definitions of lower approximation and boundary of rough sets [22], if an object $x_j \in \underline{A}(\beta_i)$, then $x_j \notin \underline{A}(\beta_k), \forall k \neq i$, and $x_j \notin B(\beta_i), \forall i$. That is, the object x_j is contained in β_i definitely.

Hence, the memberships of the objects in lower approximation of a cluster should be independent of other centroids and clusters. Also, the objects in lower approximation should have different influence on the corresponding centroid and cluster. From the standpoint of "compatibility with the cluster prototype", the membership of an object in the lower approximation of a cluster should be determined solely by how far it is from the prototype of the cluster, and should not be coupled with its location with respect to other clusters. As the possibilistic membership v_{ij} depends only on the distance of object x_j from cluster β_i, it allows optimal membership solutions to lie in the entire unit hypercube rather than restricting them to the hyperplane. Whereas, if $x_j \in B(\beta_i)$, then the object x_j possibly belongs to cluster β_i and potentially belongs to another cluster. Hence, the objects in boundary regions should have different influence on the centroids and clusters, and their memberships should depend on the positions of all cluster centroids. So, in the proposed clustering algorithm, the membership values of objects in lower approximation are identical to possibilistic c-means as follows:

$$v_{ij} = \left[1 + \left\{\frac{\mathcal{N}(v_i, x_j)}{\eta_i}\right\}^{\frac{1}{(\acute{m}_2 - 1)}}\right]^{-1} ; \text{ where } \eta_i = \frac{\sum_{j=1}^{n} (v_{ij})^{\acute{m}_2} \mathcal{N}(v_i, x_j)}{\sum_{j=1}^{n} (v_{ij})^{\acute{m}_2}}; \quad (3)$$

subject to $0 < \sum_{j=1}^{n} v_{ij} \leq n, \forall i$; $\max_i \{v_{ij}\} > 0, \forall j$. The η_i represents the zone of influence or size of the cluster β_i. On the other hand, those in boundary region are the same as fuzzy c-means as follows:

$$\mu_{ij} = \left[\sum_{k=1}^{c} \left(\frac{\mathcal{N}(v_i, x_j)}{\mathcal{N}(v_k, x_j)}\right)^{\frac{1}{\acute{m}_1 - 1}}\right]^{-1}; \quad (4)$$

subject to $\sum_{i=1}^{c} \mu_{ij} = 1, \forall j$, and $0 < \sum_{j=1}^{n} \mu_{ij} < n, \forall i$. The parameters $\acute{m}_1 \in [1, \infty)$ and $\acute{m}_2 \in [1, \infty)$ are the probabilistic and possibilistic fuzzifiers, respectively. Note that $\mu_{ij} \in [0, 1]$ is the probabilistic membership function as that in fuzzy c-means [5] and $v_{ij} \in [0, 1]$ represents the possibilistic membership function that has the same interpretation of typicality as in possibilistic c-means [14].

The centroid is calculated based on the weighting average of the possibilistic lower approximation and probabilistic boundary. The centroid calculation for the proposed clustering algorithm is as follows:

$$v_i = \begin{cases} w\mathscr{C}_1 + (1-w)\mathscr{D}_1 & \text{if } \underline{A}(\beta_i) \neq \emptyset, B(\beta_i) \neq \emptyset \\ \mathscr{C}_1 & \text{if } \underline{A}(\beta_i) \neq \emptyset, B(\beta_i) = \emptyset \\ \mathscr{D}_1 & \text{if } \underline{A}(\beta_i) = \emptyset, B(\beta_i) \neq \emptyset \end{cases} \quad (5)$$

$$\text{where } \mathscr{C}_1 = \frac{\sum_{x_j \in \underline{A}(\beta_i)} (v_{ij})^{\acute{m}_2} x_j}{\sum_{x_j \in \underline{A}(\beta_i)} (v_{ij})^{\acute{m}_2}}; \text{ and } \mathscr{D}_1 = \frac{\sum_{x_j \in B(\beta_i)} (\mu_{ij})^{\acute{m}_1} x_j}{\sum_{x_j \in B(\beta_i)} (\mu_{ij})^{\acute{m}_1}}. \quad (6)$$

The parameters w and $(1-w)$ correspond to the relative importance of lower and boundary regions, respectively. Hence, the cluster prototypes or centroids depend on the parameters w and $(1-w)$, and fuzzifiers $\acute{m}_1$ and $\acute{m}_2$ rule their relative influence. The main steps of the proposed clustering algorithm proceed as follows:

1. Select c initial cluster prototypes using the NRNCBD based initialization method mentioned in [17].
2. Choose values for fuzzifiers $\acute{m}_1$ and $\acute{m}_2$, and calculate thresholds δ_1 and δ_2. Set iteration counter $t = 1$.
3. Compute v_{ij} by (3) for c clusters and n objects.
4. If v_{ij} and v_{kj} be the highest and second highest possibilistic memberships of object x_j and $(v_{ij} - v_{kj}) > \delta_1$ then $x_j \in \underline{A}(\beta_i)$.
5. Otherwise, $x_j \in B(\beta_i)$ and $x_j \in B(\beta_k)$ if $v_{ij} > \delta_2$. Furthermore, x_j is not part of any lower bound.
6. Compute μ_{ij} for the objects lying in boundary regions for c clusters using (4).
7. Compute new centroid as per (5).
8. Repeat steps 3 to 7, by incrementing t, until no more new assignments can be made.
9. Stop.

The performance of the proposed clustering algorithm depends on the values of two thresholds δ_1 and δ_2, which determine the cluster labels of all the miRNAs. In other word, the proposed clustering algorithm partitions the data set into two classes, namely, lower approximation and boundary, based on the values of δ_1 and δ_2. The thresholds δ_1 and δ_2 control the size of granules of the proposed clustering algorithm. In practice, the following definitions work well:

$$\delta_1 = \frac{1}{n}\sum_{j=1}^{n}(v_{ij} - v_{kj}); \quad \delta_2 = \frac{1}{\acute{n}}\sum_{j=1}^{\acute{n}} v_{ij} \tag{7}$$

where n is the total number of miRNAs, v_{ij} and v_{kj} are the highest and second highest memberships of object x_j. That is, the value of δ_1 represents the average difference of two highest possibilistic memberships of all the miRNAs in the data set. A good clustering procedure should make the value of δ_1 as high as possible. On the other hand, the miRNAs with $(v_{ij} - v_{kj}) \leq \delta_1$ are used to calculate the threshold δ_2, where $\acute{n}$ is the number of miRNAs those do not belong to lower approximations of any cluster and v_{ij} is the highest membership of miRNA x_j. That is, the value of δ_2 represents the average of highest memberships of $\acute{n}$ miRNAs in the data set.

3   Results and Discussions

In this section, the performance of the proposed method is compared with that of hard c-means (HCM) [12], fuzzy c-means (FCM) [8], rough-fuzzy c-means (RFCM) [16], robust rough-fuzzy c-means (rRFCM) [17], cluster identification via connectivity kernels (CLICK) [24], and self organizing map (SOM) [25]. The performance of the NRNCBD over Euclidean distance is also presented. In this work, publicly available three miRNA expression data sets with accession number GSE16473, GSE17155, and GSE29495 are used to compare the performance of different clustering methods. The data sets are downloaded from Gene Expression Omnibus (www.ncbi.nlm.nih.gov/geo/). For each data set, the number of clusters c is decided by using the CLICK [24] algorithm. The weight parameter w for rough-fuzzy clustering algorithms is set to 0.99, while the values of fuzzifiers $\acute{m}_1 = 2.0$ and $\acute{m}_2 = 2.0$. All the results are presented using Silhouette index [23], and Davies-Bouldin index [7]. The biological analysis of the obtained miRNA clusters is also studied using the gene ontology.

3.1 Performance of Different Distance Measures

Table 1 provides the comparative performance analysis of different c-means algorithms with Euclidean distance and the NRNCBD for three miRNA microarray data sets. The results of each c-means algorithm are reported for the optimal λ value. The optimal λ value has been used in initialization method, described in [17]. In most of the cases, the NRNCBD is found to improve the performance in terms of Silhouette and DB indices, irrespective of the c-means algorithms. Out of total 24 comparisons, the NRNCBD is found to provide significantly better results in 15 cases compare to the Euclidean distance. Also, the proposed NRNCBD based rough-fuzzy clustering algorithm achieves better performance in all 42 comparisons, irrespective of the c-means algorithms, cluster validity indices, distance measures, and miRNA data sets used. In this regard, it should be mentioned that the proposed algorithm with Euclidean distance is the rRFCM introduced in [17].

Table 1. Comparative Performance of Different C-Means Algorithms and Distance Measures

Methods / Algorithms	Microarray Data Sets	Silhouette Index		DB Index	
		Euclidean	NRNCBD	Euclidean	NRNCBD
HCM	GSE16473	**0.749**	0.564	**0.889**	3.037
	GSE17155	-1.000	**0.215**	8.000	**6.401**
	GSE29495	0.253	**0.759**	**3.982**	8.624
FCM	GSE16473	0.073	**0.169**	**2.977**	1115.042
	GSE17155	**0.132**	0.110	416.098	**128.1**
	GSE29495	**0.437**	0.271	**25.935**	1564.585
RFCM	GSE16473	0.262	**0.543**	**1.603**	2.924
	GSE17155	0.233	**0.369**	65.459	**4.896**
	GSE29495	**0.780**	0.759	58.539	**8.277**
Proposed	GSE16473	0.969	**0.971**	0.009	**0.007**
	GSE17155	0.415	**0.471**	0.674	**0.658**
	GSE29495	0.899	**0.928**	0.115	**0.092**

3.2 Performance of Different Clustering Algorithms

Table 2 presents the performance of different clustering algorithms. The results and subsequent discussions are presented with respect to the Silhouette and DB indices. From Table 2, it can be observed that the proposed method outperforms other clustering algorithms, irrespective of the quantitative indices and miRNA data sets used. The

Table 2. Performance of Different Clustering Algorithms

Validity Index	Methods/ Algorithms	Data Sets		
		GSE16473	GSE17155	GSE29495
Silhouette	CLICK	0.005	-0.101	-0.634
	SOM	0.059	-0.112	-0.540
	Proposed	0.971	0.471	0.928
DB	CLICK	2.277	13.016	450.689
	SOM	10.128	39.558	455.345
	Proposed	0.007	0.658	0.092

best performance of the proposed clustering algorithm is achieved due to the following reasons: (1) the city block distance used to calculate possibilistic and probabilistic membership functions, provides effective values for degree of belongingness of the miRNAs; (2) probabilistic membership function of the proposed clustering algorithm handles efficiently overlapping partitions, while the possibilistic membership function of lower approximation of a cluster helps to discover arbitrary shaped cluster; and (3) the concept of possibilistic lower approximation and fuzzy boundary of the proposed algorithm deals with uncertainty, vagueness, and incompleteness in class definition.

3.3 Biologically Significant Gene Clusters

DIANA microT v3.0 [18], a miRNA target prediction algorithm, is used to predict miRNA target genes for all miRNA clusters generated by different clustering algorithms. The genes that are targeted by 95% or more miRNAs in a particular miRNA cluster are used to calculate number of significant gene clusters. Fig. 1 presents the results for the molecular functions (MF), biological process (BP), and cellular components (CC) ontologies on three data sets. The gene ontology (GO) Term Finder is used to determine the statistically significant gene clusters produced by different algorithms for all the GO terms from the MF, BP, and CC ontologies. If any cluster of genes generates a p-value smaller than 0.05, then that cluster is considered as a significant cluster.

The upper portion of Fig. 1 presents the comparative results of the RFCM and proposed algorithm for the MF, BP, and CC ontologies, respectively. From the results, it is seen that the proposed algorithm generates more or comparable number of significant gene clusters in all cases. The middle portion of Fig. 1 reports the number of significant gene clusters generated by the HCM, FCM, and proposed algorithm for the MF, BP, and CC ontologies for all microarray data sets, respectively. All the results reported in this portion establish the fact that the proposed algorithm generates more or comparable number of significant gene clusters than that of other c-means algorithms in most of the cases. However, the proposed method generates more or comparable number of significant gene clusters in three cases, while the HCM with Euclidean distance generates more or comparable number of significant gene clusters in only one case CC ontology.

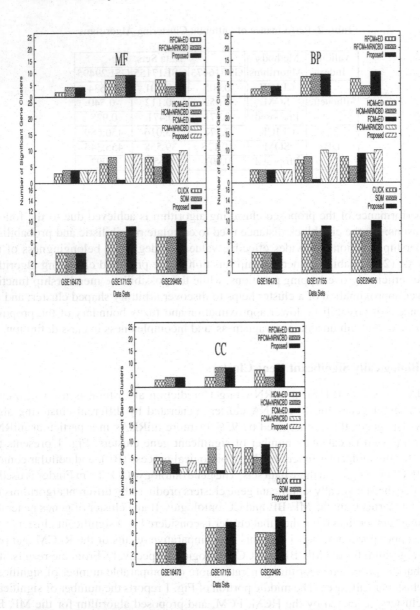

Fig. 1. Biologically significant gene clusters generated by different algorithms

Finally, the performance of CLICK, SOM, and proposed algorithm is compared in lower portion of Fig. 1 with respect to the number of significant gene clusters generated for MF, BP, and CC ontologies, respectively. From the results reported in this portion, it is seen that the proposed algorithm generates more or comparable number of significant gene clusters compare to both CLICK and SOM algorithms in all the cases.

4 Conclusion

In this paper, a new miRNA clustering algorithm has been presented. Integration of the merits of robust rough-fuzzy c-means algorithm and normalized range-normalized city block distance generates better results as compared to other c-means algorithms. The dimension additivity property of city block distance leads to better clustering solutions as compare to the Euclidean distance. The effectiveness of the proposed clustering algorithm, along with a comparison with other clustering algorithms, has been demonstrated on three miRNA microarray data sets.

Acknowledgements. This work is partially supported by the Indian National Science Academy, New Delhi (grant no. SP/YSP/68/2012). The work was done when one of the authors, S. Paul, was a Senior Research Fellow of Council of Scientific and Industrial Research, Government of India.

References

1. Altuvia, Y., Landgraf, P., Lithwick, G., Elefant, N., Pfeffer, S., Aravin, A., Brownstein, M.J., Tuschl, T., Margalit, H.: Clustering and Conservation Patterns of Human microRNAs. Nucleic Acids Research 33, 2697–2706 (2005)
2. Bargaje, R., Hariharan, M., Scaria, V., Pillai, B.: Consensus miRNA Expression Profiles Derived from Interplatform Normalization of Microarray Data. RNA 16, 16–25 (2010)
3. Baskerville, S., Bartel, D.P.: Microarray Profiling of microRNAs Reveals Frequent Coexpression with Neighboring miRNAs and Host Genes. RNA 11, 241–247 (2005)
4. Ben-Dor, A., Shamir, R., Yakhini, Z.: Clustering Gene Expression Patterns. Journal of Computational Biology 6(3-4), 281–297 (1999)
5. Bezdek, J.C.: Pattern Recognition with Fuzzy Objective Function Algorithms. Plenum, New York (1981)
6. Cai, X., Hagedorn, C.H., Cullen, B.R.: Human microRNAs are Processed from Capped, Polyadenylated Transcripts that can also Function as mRNAs. RNA 10, 1957–1966 (2004)
7. Davies, D.L., Bouldin, D.W.: A Cluster Separation Measure. IEEE Transactions on Pattern Analysis and Machine Intelligence 1, 224–227 (1979)
8. Dembele, D., Kastner, P.: Fuzzy C-Means Method for Clustering Microarray Data. Bioinformatics 19(8), 973–980 (2003)
9. Fraley, C., Raftery, A.E.: How Many Clusters? Which Clustering Method? Answers Via Model-Based Cluster Analysis. The Computer Journal 41(8), 578–588 (1998)
10. Ghosh, D., Chinnaiyan, A.M.: Mixture Modelling of Gene Expression Data from Microarray Experiments. Bioinformatics 18, 275–286 (2002)
11. Hartuv, E., Shamir, R.: A Clustering Algorithm Based on Graph Connectivity. Information Processing Letters 76(4-6), 175–181 (2000)
12. Heyer, L.J., Kruglyak, S., Yooseph, S.: Exploring Expression Data: Identification and Analysis of Coexpressed Genes. Genome Research 9(11), 1106–1115 (1999)
13. Jiang, D., Pei, J., Zhang, A.: DHC: A Density-Based Hierarchical Clustering Method for Time-Series Gene Expression Data. In: Proceedings of the 3rd IEEE International Symposium on Bioinformatics and Bioengineering, pp. 393–400 (2003)
14. Krishnapuram, R., Keller, J.M.: A Possibilistic Approach to Clustering. IEEE Transactions on Fuzzy Systems 1(2), 98–110 (1993)

15. Lu, J., Getz, G., Miska, E.A., Saavedra, E.A., Lamb, J., Peck, D., Cordero, A.S., Ebert, B.L., Mak, R.H., Ferrando, A.A., Downing, J.R., Jacks, T., Horvitz, H.R., Golub, T.R.: MicroRNA Expression Profiles Classify Human Cancers. Nature Letters 435(9), 834–838 (2005)
16. Maji, P., Pal, S.K.: RFCM: A Hybrid Clustering Algorithm Using Rough and Fuzzy Sets. Fundamenta Informaticae 80(4), 475–496 (2007)
17. Maji, P., Paul, S.: Rough-Fuzzy Clustering for Grouping Functionally Similar Genes from Microarray Data. IEEE/ACM Transactions on Computational Biology and Bioinformatics, 1–14 (2013)
18. Maragkakis, M., Alexiou, P., Papadopoulos, G.L., Reczko, M., Dalamagas, T., Giannopoulos, G., Goumas, G., Koukis, E., Kourtis, K., Simossis, V.A., Sethupathy, P., Vergoulis, T., Koziris, N., Sellis, T., Tsanakas, P., Hatzigeorgiou, A.G.: Accurate microRNA Target Prediction Correlates with Protein Repression Levels. BMC Bioinformatics 10(295) (2009)
19. McLachlan, G.J., Bean, R.W., Peel, D.: A Mixture Model-Based Approach to the Clustering of Microarray Expression Data. Bioinformatics 18, 413–422 (2002)
20. Pasluosta, C.F., Dua, P., Lukiw, W.J.: Nearest hyperplane distance neighbor clustering algorithm applied to gene co-expression analysis in alzheimer's disease. In: 2011 Annual International Conference of the IEEE Engineering in Medicine and Biology Society, EMBC, pp. 5559–5562 (2011)
21. Paul, S., Maji, P.: Robust RFCM Algorithm for Identification of Co-Expressed miRNAs. In: Proceedings of IEEE International Conference on Bioinformatics and Biomedicine, Philadelphia, USA, pp. 520–523 (2012)
22. Pawlak, Z.: Rough Sets: Theoretical Aspects of Resoning About Data. Kluwer, Dordrecht (1991)
23. Rousseeuw, J.P.: Silhouettes: A Graphical Aid to the Interpration and Validation of Cluster Analysis. Journal of Computational and Applied Mathematics 20, 53–65 (1987)
24. Shamir, R., Sharan, R.: CLICK: A Clustering Algorithm for Gene Expression Analysis. In: Proceedings of the 8th International Conference on Intelligent Systems for Molecular Biology, pp. 307–316 (2000)
25. Tamayo, P., Slonim, D., Mesirov, J., Zhu, Q., Kitareewan, S., Dmitrovsky, E., Lander, E.S., Golub, T.R.: Interpreting Patterns of Gene Expression with Self-Organizing Maps: Methods and Application to Hematopoietic Differentiation. Proceedings of the National Academy of Sciences, USA 96(6), 2907–2912 (1999)
26. Xing, E.P., Karp, R.M.: CLIFF: Clustering of High-Dimensional Microarray Data via Iterative Feature Filtering Using Normalized Cuts. Bioinformatics 17(1), 306–315 (2001)
27. Yeung, K.Y., Fraley, C., Murua, A., Raftery, A.E., Ruzz, W.L.: Model-Based Clustering and Data Transformations for Gene Expression Data. Bioinformatics 17, 977–987 (2001)
28. Zadeh, L.A.: Fuzzy Sets. Information and Control 8, 338–353 (1965)

Extreme Learning Machine Approach
for On-Line Voltage Stability Assessment

P. Duraipandy[1] and D. Devaraj[2]

[1] Department of Electrical and Electronics Engineering, Velammal College of Engineering
and Technology, Madurai District, Tamilnadu, India
[2] Department of Computer Science Engineering, Kalasalingam University,
Virudhunagar District, Tamilnadu, India
vai_2k4@yahoo.co.in, deva230@yahoo.com

Abstract. In recent years, voltage instability has become a major threat for the operation of many power systems. This paper proposes a scheme for on-line assessment of voltage stability of a power system for multiple contingencies using an Extreme Learning Machine (ELM) technique. Extreme learning machines are single-hidden layer feed- forward neural networks, where the training is restricted to the output weights in order to achieve fast learning with good performance. ELMs are competing with Neural Networks as tools for solving pattern recognition and regression problem. A single ELM model is developed for credible contingencies for accurate and fast estimation of the voltage stability level at different loading conditions. Loading margin is taken as the indicator of voltage instability. Precontingency voltage magnitudes and phase angles at the load buses are taken as the input variables. The training data are obtained by running Continuation Power Flow (CPF) routine. The effectiveness of the method has been demonstrated through voltage stability assessment in IEEE 30-bus system. To verify the effectiveness of the proposed ELM method, its performance is compared with the Multi Layer Perceptron Neural Network (MLPNN). Simulation results show that the ELM gives faster and more accurate results for on-line voltage stability assessment compared with the MLPNN.

Keywords: Extreme learning machine, loading margin, voltage stability assessment.

1 Introduction

Voltage stability is one of the challenging problems faced by the power utilities. Due to economic reasons arising out of deregulation and open market of electricity, modern day power systems are being operated closer to their stability limits. If a contingency occurs in an already stressed system, stability may be lost, leading to the most critical outcome of voltage instability process: the so-called voltage collapse. Voltage collapse which occurs due to the inability of the system to meet the reactive power requirements of the system is observed by a sudden decline in system-wide

B.K. Panigrahi et al. (Eds.): SEMCCO 2013, Part II, LNCS 8298, pp. 397–405, 2013.
© Springer International Publishing Switzerland 2013

voltages. This change in voltage is so rapid that voltage control devices may not be able to take corrective action rapidly enough to prevent cascading blackouts.

Online voltage stability monitoring is becoming an integral part of the modern day Energy Management Systems (EMS) so that corrective measures can be taken to avoid system black-out. Several approaches have been proposed for analyzing the voltage stability problem. They can be broadly classified into static and dynamic approaches. The static approach [1–9] is based on the steady-state load flow model. In the dynamic approach [10-11] the power system is represented by a dynamic model and time domain simulations are carried out using a comprehensive set of initial and transient conditions to compute the voltage stability level. These analytical methods require significantly large computational time. For online applications, there is a need for quick detection of the potentially dangerous situations of voltage instability so that necessary actions may be taken to avoid the occurrence of voltage collapse in a power system.

Alternatively, Artificial Neural Network (ANN) model can be developed for on-line assessment of voltage stability. Several voltage stability prediction studies have been carried out by using ANN model. In [13], an Artificial Neural Network (ANN)–based approach has been proposed for contingency ranking. A set of feed forward neural networks were developed to estimate the voltage stability level at different load conditions for the selected contingencies. S. Chakrabarti [14] proposed a methodology for online voltage stability monitoring using artificial neural network (ANN) and a regression based method of selecting features for training the ANN. Separate ANNs were used for different contingencies. In [15], a Radial Basis Function (RBF) networks was proposed for fast contingency ranking. An adaptive RBF network has been proposed in [16] for multicontingency voltage stability monitoring in which sequential learning strategy is used along with regularization technique to design RBFNN and weights in output layer are determined using linear optimization. A network pruning strategy is used to limit the growth of network size due to adaptive training. Jayashankar etal. [17] proposed feedforward back propagation network to estimate voltage stability index for various load conditions and the optimal location for placement of TCSC is identified for improving the voltage stability in power system. In [18], an artificial neural network (ANN)-based approach was proposed for on-line voltage security assessment. The proposed approach uses radial basis function (RBF) networks to estimate the voltage stability level of the system under contingency state. In [19], an ANN based algorithm was proposed to estimate the voltage magnitude of each critical bus in a power system under normal and/or contingent states. The learning speed of feedforward neural network is in general slower and it has been a major bottleneck in their applications. Two key reasons behind may be: (1) the slow gradient-based learning algorithms are extensively used to train neural networks, and (2) all the parameters of the networks are tuned iteratively by using such learning algorithms.

In this paper, an Extreme Learning Machine model [22] is developed for on-line voltage stability assessment. ELM is a single hidden layer feedforward network where the input weights are chosen randomly and the output weights are calculated analytically. The learning speed of ELM is extremely fast. Unlike traditional gradient-based learning algorithms which only work for differentiable activation functions, ELM works for all bounded non constant Piecewise continuous activation functions. Unlike traditional gradient-based learning algorithms facing several issues like local minima, improper learning rate and over fitting, etc, ELM tends to reach the solutions straightforward without such trivial issues. The training data required to develop the ELM model is generated by conducting off-line contingency analysis by varying the load at the load buses. The effectiveness of the proposed method is demonstrated through stability assessment in IEEE 30-bus test system.

2   Voltage Stability Assessment

Voltage stability is concerned with the ability of the power system to maintain acceptable voltages at all the system buses under normal conditions as well as after being subjected to a disturbance. Thus the analysis of voltage stability deals with finding the voltage levels at all buses in the system under different loading conditions to ascertain the stability limit and margin. Voltage stability is commonly analyzed by employing two techniques, namely time-domain (dynamic) simulation and steady-state analysis. Depending on the stability phenomenon or phenomena under investigation, one or both of these techniques may be applied. Studies have been performed to predict voltage collapse with both static and dynamic approaches.

System dynamics influencing voltage stability are usually slow. Therefore many aspects of the problem can be effectively analyzed by using static methods, which allow examinations of a wide range of system conditions and if appropriately used, can provide much insight into the nature of the problem and identify the key contributing factors. For static voltage stability studies of a power system, the loading of the system is increased incrementally and slowly (in certain direction) to the point of voltage collapse. The MW-distance to this point called loading margin is a good measure of system voltage stability limit (Fig. 1).

At the loadability limit, or tip of the nose curve, the system Jacobian of the power flow equations will become singular as the slope of the nose curve become infinite. Thus, the traditional Newton-Raphson method of obtaining the load flow solution will break down. In this case, a modification of the Newton-Raphson method known as the continuation method is employed. The continuation method introduces an additional equation and unknown into the basic power flow equations. The additional equation is chosen specifically to ensure that the augmented Jacobian is no longer singular at the loadability limit. The additional unknown is often called the continuation parameter. The formulation of continuation power flow method is given in Appendix A.

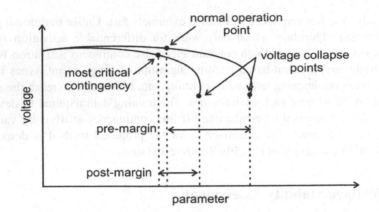

Fig. 1. Loading Margin

3   Proposed Approach for Voltage Stability Assessment

This paper proposes a scheme for on-line assessment of voltage stability of a power system for multiple contingencies using an Extreme Learning Machine (ELM). A single ELM model is developed for credible contingencies to accurately estimate the voltage stability level at different loading conditions. Loading margin is taken as the indicator of voltage instability. Precontingency voltage magnitudes and phase angles at the load buses are taken as the input variables. The training data are obtained by running Continuation Power Flow (CPF) routine. The training data for the development of ELM is generated as per the following procedure:

1.   First, a range of situations is generated by randomly perturbing the load at all buses from the base case value and by adjusting the generator output in proportion to the output in the base case condition. For each load-generation pattern, load flow study is conducted to obtain the pre-contingency quantities.
2.   Next, for each load-generation pattern, the single line-outages specified in the contingency list are simulated sequentially and the maximum loading parameters are evaluated by running CPF.

After training, the generalization performance of the network is evaluated with the 250 test data. The proposed method can be used for on-line voltage stability assessment in large scale power systems.

4   Extreme Learning Machine

ELM [21, 22] provides a unified learning platform with a widespread type of feature mappings and can be applied in regression and multiclass classification applications directly. ELM is a single hidden layer feedforward network where the input weights are chosen randomly and the output weights are calculated analytically. For hidden neurons, many activation functions such as sigmoidal, sine, Gaussian and hard-limiting function can be used and the output neurons have a linear activation function. ELM uses non-differentiable or even discontinuous functions as an activation function. In ELM, the input weights and hidden biases are randomly chosen. The output weights obtained using the Moore-Penrose (MP) generalized inverse. After the input weights and the hidden layer biases are chosen randomly, SLFNs can be simply considered as a linear system and the output weights (linking the hidden layer to the output layer) of SLFNs can be analytically determined through simple generalized inverse operation of the hidden layer output matrices. Based on this concept, this paper proposes a simple learning algorithm for SLFNs called extreme learning machine (ELM) whose learning speed can be thousands of times faster than traditional feedforward network learning algorithms like back-propagation (BP) algorithm while obtaining better generalization performance. Different from traditional learning algorithms the proposed learning algorithm not only tends to reach the smallest training error but also the smallest norm of weights. Therefore, the proposed learning algorithm tends to have good generalization performance for feedforward neural networks.

5   Simulation Results

This section presents the details of the simulation study carried out on IEEE 30- bus system for on-line estimation of voltage stability level using the proposed method. IEEE 30 –bus system consists of 6 generator buses, 24 load buses and 41 transmission lines. For this test system, based on the contingency analysis conducted at different loading conditions, seven single line outages 1-2, 28-27, 27-30, 27-29, 2-5, 9-10, 4-12 were identified as severe cases. ELM model is developed for the selected contingencies to estimate the voltage stability level at different loading conditions. Precontingency voltage magnitudes and phase angles at the load buses are taken as the input variables. Loading margins for seven credible contingencies are the outputs of ELM.

The input features after normalization along with the output are used to train the network as mentioned above. The networks are trained until the network reaches the mean square error of 0.0001.

After training, the generalization performance of the network is evaluated with the 250 test data. The performance of the developed ELM model is given in Table 1. From these results it is evident that the ELM takes less time for training and exhibits better generalization performance than the MLPNN network.

Table 1. Performance Comparison of ELM with MLPNN and SVM

Parameters	ELM	MLPNN	SVM
Number of input variables	48	48	48
Number of output variables	7	7	7
Training data	750	750	750
Testing data	250	250	250
Testing error	0.000565	0.0112	0.001924
Training time (s)	0.046875	84.952	2.9219

Comparison between the actual values of loading margin calculated from CPF and ELM for one loading scenario is presented in Table 2 and for random 10 loading conditions is shown in Fig. 2.

Table 2. Comparison of ELM output with CPF result

Line outaged		ELM output		CPF result	
		λ_{max}	Rank	λ_{max}	Rank
1	2	0.2612	1	0.2612	1
2	5	2.0411	5	2.0410	5
4	12	2.7010	7	2.7010	7
9	10	2.4207	6	2.4207	6
28	27	1.4144	2	1.4144	2
27	29	2.0143	4	2.0143	4
27	30	1.8089	3	1.8089	3

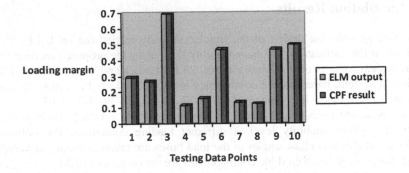

Fig. 2. Comparison of ELM output and CPF result for line outage 1-2

The result shows the agreement between the actual ranking and the ranking based on the output of the ELM. After training, the developed network is able to estimate the voltage stability index accurately within a short duration i.e., 1.4844 seconds when compared to time taken to compute loading margin of 7 line outages using conventional power flow method i.e., 12.575 seconds. This shows that the proposed method can be used for on-line voltage stability assessment in large scale power systems.

6   Conclusion

In this paper, an Extreme Learning Machine technique is presented for on-line voltage stability assessment. The ELM model was developed to estimate the voltage stability level for severe contingencies. Precontingency voltage magnitudes and phase angles at the load buses are chosen as the input features to the ELM and the corresponding loading margins for the credible contingencies are taken as the outputs of the network.

For large power systems, training separate ELMs for all contingencies is a demanding task. The proposed method allows the use of a single ELM for different contingencies. The contingencies considered are the outage of transmission lines, one at a time. The effectiveness of the method has been demonstrated through voltage stability assessment in IEEE 30-bus system. Test results show that the ELM gives faster and more accurate results for on-line voltage stability assessment considering multiple contingencies compared with the MLPNN.

References

1. IEEE Special Publication, 90TH0358-2-PWR: Voltage stability of power systems: concepts, analytical tools and industry experience (1990)
2. Tiranuchit, Thomas, R.J.: A Posturing Strategy against Voltage Instabilities in Electric Power Systems. IEEE Transactions on Power Systems 3(1), 87–93 (1998)
3. Löf, P.A., Smed, T., Anderson, G., Hill, D.J.: Fast calculation of a voltage stability index. IEEE Transactions on Power Systems 7, 54–64 (1992)
4. Kessel, P., Glavitsch, H.: Estimating the voltage stability of power systems. IEEE Transactions on Power Systems 1(3), 346–354 (1986)
5. Gao, B., Morison, G.K., Kundur, P.: Voltage stability evaluation using modal analysis. IEEE Transactions on Power Systems 7(4), 1529–1542 (1992)
6. Lof, P.A., Anderson, G., Jill, D.J.: Voltage stability indices for stressed power system. IEEE Transactions on Power Systems 8(1), 326–335 (1993)
7. Canizares, C.A., de Souza, A.Z., Quintana, V.H.: Comparison of performance indices for detection of proximity to voltage collapse. IEEE Transactions on Power Systems 11(3), 1441–1450 (1996)
8. Canizares, C.A., Alvarado, F.L., DeMarco, C.L., Dobson, I., Long, W.F.: Point of collapse methods applied to ac/dc power systems. IEEE Transactions on Power Systems 7(2), 673–683 (1992)
9. Ajjarapu, V., Christy, C.: The continuation power flow: A tool for steady state voltage stability analysis. IEEE Transactions on Power Systems 7(1), 416–423 (1992)
10. Morison, G.K., Gao, B., Kundur, P.: Voltage stability analysis using static and dynamic approaches. IEEE Transactions on Power Systems 8, 1159–1165 (1993)
11. Pal, M.K.: Voltage stability conditions considering load characteristics. IEEE Transactions on Power Systems 7, 243–249 (1992)
12. Karlsson, Hill, D.J.: Modeling and identification of nonlinear dynamic loads in power systems. IEEE Transactions on Power Systems 9, 157–163 (1994)
13. Devaraj, D., Preetha Roselyn, J., Uma Rani, R.: Artificial neural network model for voltage security based contingency ranking. Applied Soft Computing 7, 722–727 (2007)
14. Chakrabarti, S.: Voltage stability monitoring by artificial neural network using a regression-based feature selection method. Expert Systems with Applications 35, 1802–1808 (2008)
15. Devaraj, D., Yegnanarayana, B., Ramar, K.: Radial basis function networks for fast Contingency Ranking. Electric Power and Energy Systems Journal 24, 387–395 (2002)
16. Chakrabarthi, S., Jeyasurya, B.: Multi-contingency voltage stability monitoring of a power system using an adaptive radial basis function network. Electric Power and Energy Systems Journal 30, 1–7 (2008)
17. Jayashankar, V., Kamaraj, N., Vanaja, N.: Estimation of voltage stability index for power system employing artificial neural network technique and TCSC placement. Neurocomputing 73, 3005–3011 (2010)

18. Devaraj, D., Preetha Roselyn, J.: On-line voltage stability assessment using radial basis function network model with reduced input features. Electrical Power and Energy Systems Journal 33, 1550–1555 (2011)
19. Aravindhababu, P., Balamurugan, G.: ANN based online voltage estimation. Applied Soft Computing 12, 313–319 (2012)
20. Nizam, M., Mohamed, A., Al-Dabbagh, M., Hussain, A.: Using Support Vector Machine for Prediction of Dynamic Voltage Collapse in an Actual Power System. Proceedings of World academy of Science, Engineering and Technology 31, 711–716 (2008)
21. Huang, G.-B., Zhu, Q.-Y., Siew, C.-K.: Extreme learning machine: theory and applications. Neurocomputing 70, 489–501 (2006)
22. Huang, G.-B., Zhou, H., Ding, X., Zhang, R.: Extreme Learning Machine for Regression and Multiclass Classification. IEEE Transactions on Systems, Man, and Cybernetics 42(2), 513–529 (2012)

Appendix: A

A.1   Formulation of Continuation Power Flow

The continuation power flow analysis [9] uses iterative predictor and corrective steps (Fig.A.1). The predictor step will start from point A, from which the estimate solution is obtained from tangent of ABC triangle. Then corrector step determines the solution by using conventional power flow. The further increase in load voltage is then predicted on a new tangent predictor.

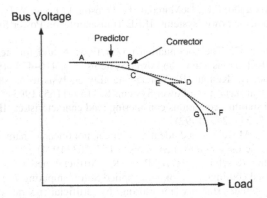

Fig. A.1. The Predictor – corrector scheme used in the Continuation Power Flow

The load flow equation consisting of load factor can be written as:

$$F(\delta, V, \lambda) = 0 \qquad (A.1)$$

Where λ = the loading parameter
         δ = the vector of bus voltage angle
         V   = the vector of bus voltage magnitude

From the Newton-Raphson load flow calculation is expressed as:

$$P_i - \sum_{j=1}^{N} Y_{ij} V_i V_j \cos(\delta_i - \delta_j - \theta_{ij}) = 0 \tag{A.2}$$

$$Q_i - \sum_{j=1}^{N} Y_{ij} V_i V_j \sin(\delta_i - \delta_j - \theta_{ij}) = 0 \tag{A.3}$$

The system has N node and N_q number of source including slack bus. The total number of equation equal $2N-N_q-1$.

The new load flow equations consists of load factor (λ) are expressed as:

$$P_{Li} = P_{L0} + \lambda(K_{Li} S_{\Delta base} \cos \phi_i) \tag{A.4}$$

$$Q_{Li} = Q_{L0} + \lambda(K_{Li} S_{\Delta base} \sin \phi_i) \tag{A.5}$$

where

P_{Li}, Q_{Li} = the active and reactive power respectively,

K_{Li} = the constant for load changing at bus I, and

$S_{\Delta base}$ = the apparent power which is chosen to   provide appropriate scaling of λ.

Then the active power generation term can be modified to

$$P_{Gi} = P_{G0}(1 + \lambda K_{Gi}) \tag{A.6}$$

Where

P_{G0} = the initial value of active power generation,

P_{Gi} = the active power generation at bus I, and

K_{Gi} = the constant of changing rate in generation.

A.   Predictor step

In the predictor step, a linear approximation is used to estimate the next solution in order to adjust the state variables. Taking the derivative of both side of (A.1), it can be expressed as:

$$F_\delta d\delta + F_V dV + F_\lambda d\lambda = 0 \tag{A.7}$$

$$\begin{bmatrix} F_\delta & F_V & F_\lambda \end{bmatrix} \begin{bmatrix} d\delta \\ dV \\ d\lambda \end{bmatrix} = 0 \tag{A.8}$$

B.   Corrector step

The load flow equations are selected by

$$\begin{bmatrix} F(\delta, V, \lambda) \\ X_k - \eta \end{bmatrix} = [0] \tag{A.9}$$

Where

X_k= the state variable selected as continuation parameter at k iterative and

η = the predicted value of X_k.

Quadratic Fuzzy Bilevel Chance Constrained Programming with Parameters Following Weibull Distribution

Animesh Biswas[1,*] and Arnab Kumar De[2]

[1] Department of Mathematics, University of Kalyani
Kalyani – 741235, India
abiswaskln@rediffmail.com
[2] Department of Mathematics, Academy of Technology
G.T. Road, Adisaptagram, P.O.-Aedconagar
Dist – Hooghly, Pin – 712121, India
arnab7339@yahoo.co.in

Abstract. This paper presents a fuzzy goal programming approach for solving quadratic fuzzy bilevel programming problems with probabilistic constraints containing Weibull distributed fuzzy random variables. In the proposed methodology the problem is first converted into an equivalent quadratic fuzzy bilevel programming model by applying chance constrained programming technique developed with the use of α −cuts in a fuzzily defined stochastic decision making situation. Then the developed model is transferred into an equivalent deterministic one by using the method of defuzzification based on probability density function of the corresponding membership functions. The individual optimal value of the objective of each decision makers is found in isolation to construct the quadratic fuzzy membership goals of each of the decision makers. The quadratic membership goals are then converted into linear goals by applying approximation techniques. A weighted minsum goal programming method is then applied to achieve the highest membership degree of each of the membership goals of decision makers in the decision making context. Finally a comparison is made on the applied approximation techniques with the help of using distance function. An illustrative numerical example is provided to demonstrate the applicability of the proposed methodology.

Keywords: Bilevel programming, Weibull distribution, Fuzzy nonlinear programming, Fuzzy Chance Constrained programming, Fuzzy goal programming.

1 Introduction

In the real life decision making problems the decision makers (DMs) often faces various types of vagueness in which randomness and fuzziness are the most crucial ones. To deal with such type of uncertainties, there exist two typical approaches, viz.,

---

* Corresponding author.

B.K. Panigrahi et al. (Eds.): SEMCCO 2013, Part II, LNCS 8298, pp. 406–418, 2013.

probability theoretic approach and fuzzy set theoretic approach. One well defined methodology for treating problems involving probabilistic data is known as chance constrained programming (CCP) [1]. Solving fuzzy CCP (FCCP) has attracted more attention in recent years to the researchers. In FCCP probabilistic and fuzzy aspects are combined to provide an efficient technique to describe real-life problems where uncertainty and imprecision of information co-occur. However, this kind of combination with fuzzy and stochastic uncertainties creates great challenges to the researcher [2,3] to find an efficient solution in the decision making contexts.

In mathematical optimization, bilevel programming problem (BLPP) establishes its greater applicability in different real life hierarchical decision making problems. Candler and Townsley [4] first introduced the concept of BLPP. It is a powerful and robust technique for solving hierarchical decision making problem with a structure of two levels in a highly conflicting decision making situation. The upper level decision maker is known as leader and the lower level decision maker is termed as follower. In most of the decision making situation it is found that the parameters involved with BLPP are based on prediction of future conditions which inevitably contains some degree of uncertainty. Under this context the classical approaches fails to give satisfactory solution which would be acceptable to both the DMs. To deal with such types of problems Zimmermann [5] first applied fuzzy set theory in decision making problems with several conflicting objectives. In 1996 Lai [6] introduced the concept of fuzzy sets in a hierarchical decision making context. The main difficulty of fuzzy programming (FP) approach is that the objectives of the DMs are conflicting. So there is possibility of rejecting the solution again and again by the DMs and the solution process is continued by redefining the membership functions repeatedly until a satisfactory solution is obtained. This make solution process very lengthy and tedious one.

To overcome such difficulty fuzzy goal programming (FGP) procedure, introduced by Mohamed [7], is applied indecision making problems. In the recent past FGP approaches to solve BLPPs have been discussed by Moitra and Pal [8], Biswas and Bose [9], and others.

The class of BLPPs which are associated with fuzzy random variables (FRVs) in the objective of the DMs and the constraints are termed as fuzzy bilevel chance constrained programming (FBLCCP). In the recent times there is an increase emphasizing on different solution aspects and methodologies of this kind of decision making problems. Very recently Biswas and Modak [10] develop a new solution technique for FBLCCP in which the constraints of the problem are involved with normally distributed FRVs. Among the various types of probability distributions, Weibull distribution [11] plays an important role for its wide applications in survival analysis, reliability engineering and failure analysis, weather forecasting and many other real life decision making areas. Solution techniques for FBLCCP problems with FRVs following Weibull distribution is yet to appear in the literature.

Further it may found in a FBLCCP that objectives of the DMs are nonlinear in nature. To solve nonlinear objectives, different classical approaches have been developed in the literature. Two methods of approximation of nonlinear objectives, viz., Taylor series approximation [12] and piecewise linear approximation method [13], are frequently used in a nonlinear decision making environment.

In this paper a FBLCCP is considered in which the objectives of the DMs are quadratic in nature and the parameters are fuzzily defined. Again the system constraints are involved with some FRVs following Weibull distribution. At first the quadratic FBLCCP (QFBLCCP) model is converted into its equivalent quadratic fuzzy BLPP (QFBLPP) using CCP technique developed for FRVs following Weibull distribution by α-cut of fuzzy numbers. Then the QFBLPP is transformed into quadratic BLPP (QBLPP) using the method of defuzzification [14]. FGP approach is considered to solve the QBLPP by developing nonlinear membership goals of the objective of the DMs. A weighted minsum goal programming model is developed after linearizing the nonlinear goals by using approximation techniques for finding most compromise solution in the decision making arena.

2   Preliminaries

The basic ideas which are necessary in the treatise of formulating the proposed model are described in this section.

Trapezoidal fuzzy number: A trapezoidal fuzzy number, $\tilde{A}$, is a quadruplet (a^1, a^2, a^3, a^4) whose membership function, $\mu_{\tilde{A}}(x)$, is defined by

$$\mu_{\tilde{A}}(x) = \begin{cases} \frac{x-a^1}{a^2-a^1} & if \quad a^1 \leq x \leq a^2 \\ 1 & if \quad a^2 \leq x \leq a^3 \\ \frac{a^4-x}{a^4-a^3} & if \quad a^3 \leq x \leq a^4 \\ 0 & otherwise \end{cases} \tag{1}$$

It is to be noted here that if in a trapezoidal fuzzy number, $a^2 = a^3 = a$ then that number is converted into a triangular fuzzy number (a^1, a, a, a^4) with the corresponding changes in its membership function. For simplicity, in the subsequent texts of this article, a triangular fuzzy number would be denoted by the triple (a^1, a, a^4).

α-cut of a fuzzy number: α-cut of a fuzzy number $\tilde{A}$ is a crisp set which is denoted by $\tilde{A}[\alpha]$ and defined by $\tilde{A}[\alpha] = \{x \in \mathbb{R} : A(x) \geq \alpha, 0 < \alpha \leq 1\}$, where $\mathbb{R}$ represents the set of real numbers considered as the universe of discourse on which the fuzzy number $\tilde{A}$ is defined.

First decomposition theorem: Every fuzzy set $\tilde{A}$ defined on Y, some universal set of discourse, can be represented in the form $\tilde{A} = \bigcup_{\alpha \in (0,1]} \alpha \cdot \tilde{A}[\alpha](x)$, where $\bigcup$ is considered as the standard union on fuzzy sets.

Fuzzy random variable: Let X be a continuous random variable with probability density function $f(x,v)$, where v is a parameter describing the density function. If v is considered as fuzzy number $\tilde{v}$, then X becomes a fuzzily described random variable with density $f(x,\tilde{v})$. A fuzzy random variable on a probability space (Ω, Φ, P) is a fuzzy valued function $X : \Omega \to \Phi_0(\mathbb{R})$, $\omega \to X_\omega$ such that for every Borel set B of $\mathbb{R}$ and for every $\alpha \in (0, 1], (X[\alpha])^{-1}(B) \in \Phi$, where $\Phi_0(\mathbb{R})$ and $X[\alpha]$ are the set of fuzzy numbers and the set valued function, respectively. The set valued function, $X[\alpha]$, has the form $X[\alpha] : \Omega \rightarrow 2^{\mathbb{R}}$, $\omega \rightarrow X_{\omega}[\alpha] = \{x \in \mathbb{R} : X_{\omega}(x) \geq \alpha\}$. Fuzzy random variables are found by using decomposition theorem on fuzzy numbers as $X = \cup_{\alpha \in (0,1]} \alpha . X[\alpha]$

Proportional probability distribution: Consider a probability density function $f_{\tilde{A}}(x) = c\mu_{\tilde{A}}(x)$ associated with $\tilde{A}$, where c is a constant obtained by using the property of probability density function $\int_{-\infty}^{\infty} f_{\tilde{A}}(x)\, dx = 1$, i.e. $\int_{-\infty}^{\infty} c\mu_{\tilde{A}}(x)\, dx = 1$.

Mellin Transform: The Mellin transform $M_X(t)$ of a probability density function $f(x)$ is written as $M_X(t) = \int_0^{\infty} x^{t-1} f(x) dx$

Here it is to be pointed out that the expected value of the function x^{t-1} is given by $E(X^{t-1}) = \int_{-\infty}^{\infty} x^{t-1} f(x) dx$. As x is non-negative,

$$E(X^{t-1}) = \int_0^{\infty} x^{t-1} f(x) dx = M_X(t). \text{ Thus } E(X) = M_X(2).$$

2.1 Defuzzification with Probability Density Function from Membership Function [14]

Let $\tilde{A} = (a^1, a^2, a^3, a^4)$ be a trapezoidal fuzzy number. Then the crisp value is obtained by finding the expected value using the probability density function corresponding to the membership function of the trapezoidal fuzzy number.

Now probability density function of a random variable involved with trapezoidal fuzzy number $\tilde{A}$ is consider as $f_{\tilde{A}}(x) = c\mu_{\tilde{A}}(x)$, where $\mu_{\tilde{A}}(x)$ is defined in (1). The value of c is then calculated as $\quad c = \dfrac{2}{(a^4 + a^3 - a^1 - a^2)}$

Thus the proportional density function of the random variable corresponding to a trapezoidal fuzzy number $\tilde{A}$ is given by

$$f_{X_{\tilde{A}}}(x) = \begin{cases} \dfrac{2(x-a^1)}{(a^2-a^1)(a^4+a^3-a^1-a^2)} & if \quad a^1 \leq x \leq a^2 \\ \dfrac{2(a_4-x)}{(a^4-a^3)(a^4+a^3-a^1-a^2)} & if \quad a^3 \leq x \leq a^4 \\ \dfrac{2}{(a^4+a^3-a^1-a^2)} & if \quad a^2 \leq x \leq a^3 \\ 0 & otherwise \end{cases} \qquad (2)$$

Again by Mellin transform, the expression of $M_{X_{\tilde{A}}}(t)$ is found as

$$M_{X_{\tilde{A}}}(t) = \frac{2}{(a^4+a^3-a^1-a^2)t(t+1)} \left[\frac{\{(a^4)^{t+1}-(a^3)^{t+1}\}}{(a^4-a^3)} - \frac{\{(a^2)^{t+1}-(a^1)^{t+1}\}}{(a^2-a^1)} \right]$$

Thus the mean of the random variable $X_{\tilde{A}}$ is obtained as

$$E(X_{\tilde{A}}) = M_{X_{\tilde{A}}}(2) = \frac{1}{3}(a^4 + a^3 + a^1 + a^2 + \frac{(a^1 a^2 - a^3 a^4)}{(a^4+a^3-a^1-a^2)}) \qquad (3)$$

Similarly, the mean of a random variable corresponding to a triangular fuzzy number $\tilde{A} = (a^1, a, a^4)$ is given by

$$E(X_{\tilde{A}}) = M_{X_{\tilde{A}}}(2) = \frac{1}{3}(a^4 + a + a^1). \qquad (4)$$

With the consideration of the above ideas the QFBLCCP model is derived in the following section.

3   Formulation of QFBLCCP Model

In BLPP both the DMs are motivated to cooperate with each other and each DM tries to optimize his/her own benefit, paying serious attention to the interest of the other. The generic form of QFBLCCP problem is represented as

Find $X(x_1, x_2, \ldots, x_n)$ so as to

$$\text{Max}_{X_1}\ Z_1(X) = \sum_{j=1}^{n} \tilde{c}_{1j} x_j + \frac{1}{2}\sum_{j=1}^{n}\sum_{k=1}^{n} \tilde{d}_{1jk}\, x_j x_k$$

where for given X_1 ; X_2 solves

$$\text{Max}_{X_2}\ Z_2(X) = \sum_{j=1}^{n} \tilde{c}_{2j} x_j + \frac{1}{2}\sum_{j=1}^{n}\sum_{k=1}^{n} \tilde{d}_{2jk}\, x_j x_k$$

$$\text{subject to}\ \text{Pr}\left(\sum_{j=1}^{n} \tilde{a}_{ij} x_j \le \tilde{b}_i\right) \ge 1 - \gamma_i \qquad ; i = 1, 2, \ldots, m$$

$$x_j \ge 0 \qquad ; j = 1, 2, \ldots, n. \tag{5}$$

Here $\tilde{b}_i (i = 1, 2, \ldots, m)$ represents Weibull distributed FRVs; $\tilde{c}_{1j}, \tilde{d}_{1jk}, \tilde{c}_{2j}, \tilde{d}_{2jk} (j, k = 1, 2, \ldots, n)$ and $\tilde{a}_{ij}$ are considered as fuzzy numbers and $\gamma_i \in [0,1]$. The decision vector $X_1 = (x_{11}, x_{12}, \ldots, x_{1n_1})$ is controlled by the leader and the decision vector $X_2 = (x_{21}, x_{22}, \ldots, x_{2n_2})$ is controlled by follower; $X_1 \cup X_2 = X = (x_1, x_2, \ldots, x_n) \in \mathbb{R}^n$ with $n_1 + n_2 = n$.
As $\tilde{b}_i$ is Weibull distributed FRV, its probability density function is written as

$$f\left(b_i\ ; \tilde{\beta}_i, \tilde{\lambda}_i\right) = \left(\frac{p_i}{s_i}\right)\left(\frac{b_i}{s_i}\right)^{p_i-1} e^{-\left(\frac{b_i}{s_i}\right)^{p_i}}, p_i \in \tilde{\lambda}_i[\alpha], s_i \in \tilde{\beta}_i[\alpha]$$

where the support of $\tilde{b}_i$ is the set of non-negative real numbers. Here $\tilde{\lambda}_i[\alpha], \tilde{\beta}_i[\alpha]$ are the α–cut of fuzzy numbers $\tilde{\lambda}_i, \tilde{\beta}_i$ whose support are the set of positive real numbers.

3.1   QFBLPP Construction

In this subsection a technique for converting the QFBLCCP problem into its equivalent QFBLPP form is discussed. The chance constraints in model (5) are given by $\text{Pr}\left(\sum_{j=1}^{n} \tilde{a}_{ij} x_j \le \tilde{b}_i\right) \ge 1 - \gamma_i; i = 1, 2, \ldots, m.$

Now considering $\tilde{A}_i = \sum_{j=1}^{n} \tilde{a}_{ij} x_j$ the above constraints reduces to the following form as $\text{Pr}\left(\tilde{A}_i \le \tilde{b}_i\right) \ge 1 - \gamma_i.$

Now considering α –cuts of each fuzzy numbers associated with the constraints, and applying CCP technique the following calculations are derived as

$$\int_{u_i}^{\infty} \left(\frac{p_i}{s_i}\right)\left(\frac{b_i}{s_i}\right)^{p_i-1} e^{-\left(\frac{b_i}{s_i}\right)^{p_i}} db_i \ge 1 - \gamma_i \text{ , where } (s_i \in \tilde{\beta}_i[\alpha], p_i \in \tilde{\lambda}_i[\alpha], u_i \in \tilde{A}_i[\alpha])$$

$$i.e. u_i \le s_i \left[\ln \left(\frac{1}{1-\gamma_i} \right) \right]^{\frac{1}{p_i}} \quad ; i = 1, 2, \dots, m$$

Since this inequality is true for all $\alpha \in (0, 1]$, the expression can be written in terms of α-cut as

$$\tilde{A}_i[\alpha] \le \tilde{B}_i[\alpha](\ln \frac{1}{1-\gamma_i})^{\frac{1}{\tilde{\lambda}_i[\alpha]}} i.e. \sum_{j=1}^{n} \tilde{a}_{ij}[\alpha]x_j \le \tilde{B}_i[\alpha](\ln (\frac{1}{1-\gamma_i}))^{\frac{1}{\tilde{\lambda}_i[\alpha]}}; i = 1, 2, \dots, m$$

Now using first decomposition theorem, the above equation is reduced to the following form as

$$\sum_{j=1}^{n} \tilde{a}_{ij}x_j \le \tilde{B}_i(\ln (\frac{1}{1-\gamma_i}))^{\frac{1}{\tilde{\lambda}_i}} \quad ; i = 1, 2, \dots, m$$

Hence the QFBLCCP model (5), is converted into the equivalent FP problem by using the derived methodology as

Find $X(x_1, x_2, \dots, x_n)$ so as to

$$\text{Max}_{X_1} Z_1(X) = \sum_{j=1}^{n} \tilde{c}_{1j}x_j + \frac{1}{2}\sum_{j=1}^{n}\sum_{k=1}^{n} \tilde{d}_{1jk} x_j x_k$$

where for given X_1 ; X_2 solves

$$\text{Max}_{X_2} Z_2(X) = \sum_{j=1}^{n} \tilde{c}_{2j}x_j + \frac{1}{2}\sum_{j=1}^{n}\sum_{k=1}^{n} \tilde{d}_{2jk} x_j x_k$$

subject to $\sum_{j=1}^{n} \tilde{a}_{ij}x_j \le \tilde{B}_i(\ln (\frac{1}{1-\gamma_i}))^{\frac{1}{\tilde{\lambda}_i}} \quad ; i = 1, 2, \dots, m$

$$x_j \ge 0 \qquad ; j = 1, 2, \dots, n \qquad\qquad (6)$$

Here $\tilde{c}_{1j}, \tilde{d}_{1jk}, \tilde{c}_{2j}, \tilde{d}_{2jk} (j = 1, 2, \dots, n ; k = 1, 2, \dots, n)$ are considered as triangular fuzzy numbers with the forms $\tilde{c}_{1j} = (c_{1j}^1, c_{1j}, c_{1j}^4)$, $\tilde{d}_{1jk} = (d_{1jk}^1, d_{1jk}, d_{1jk}^4)$, $\tilde{c}_{2j} = (c_{2j}^1, c_{2j}, c_{2j}^4), \tilde{d}_{2jk} = (d_{2jk}^1, d_{2jk}, d_{2jk}^4)$, $\tilde{a}_{ij}$ are considered as trapezoidal fuzzy numbers with the form $\tilde{a}_{ij} = (a_{ij}^1, a_{ij}^2, a_{ij}^3, a_{ij}^4); (i = 1, 2, \dots, m ; j = 1, 2, \dots, n)$. Also the parameters $\tilde{\lambda}_i, \tilde{B}_i$ of the fuzzy random variable are taken as triangular fuzzy numbers with the form $\tilde{\lambda}_i = (\lambda_i^1, \lambda_i, \lambda_i^4)$ and $\tilde{B}_i = (\beta_i^1, \beta_i, \beta_i^4)$. ; $(i = 1, 2, \dots, m)$.

3.2   Derivation of QBLPP Using Method of Defuzzification

The fuzzy numbers are defuzzified in this subsection to find a QBLPP model of the given problem. Defuzzification of fuzzy numbers is a process that maps a fuzzy number to a crisp number. The crisp values associated with the fuzzy numbers of model (6) are obtained by the method of defuzzification [14] with probability density function of the corresponding membership functions are given as

$$\hat{c}_j^{(1)} = \frac{c_{1j}^1 + c_{1j} + c_{1j}^4}{3} \quad ; \hat{d}_{jk}^{(1)} = \frac{d_{1jk}^1 + d_{1jk} + d_{1jk}^4}{3} ; \hat{c}_j^{(2)} = \frac{c_{2j}^1 + c_{2j} + c_{2j}^4}{3};$$

$$\hat{d}_{jk}^{(2)} = \frac{d_{2jk}^1 + d_{2jk} + d_{2jk}^4}{3} ; \hat{\lambda}_i = \frac{\lambda_i^1 + \lambda_i + \lambda_i^4}{3} ; \hat{\beta}_i = \frac{\beta_i^1 + \beta_i + \beta_i^4}{3}; k = 1, 2, \dots, n$$

$$\hat{a}_{ij} = \frac{1}{3}(a_{ij}^1 + a_{ij}^2 + a_{ij}^3 + a_{ij}^4 + \frac{a_{ij}^1 a_{ij}^2 - a_{ij}^3 a_{ij}^4}{a_{ij}^3 + a_{ij}^4 - a_{ij}^1 - a_{ij}^2}); i = 1,2,\dots,m \; ; j = 1,2,\dots,n.$$

Thus the equivalent deterministic model of the QFBLPP (6) is stated as

Find $X(x_1, x_2, \dots, x_n)$ so as to

$$\text{Max}_{X_1} \, Z_1(X) = \sum_{j=1}^n \hat{c}_j^{(1)} x_j + \frac{1}{2}\sum_{j=1}^n \sum_{k=1}^n \hat{d}_{jk}^{(1)} x_j x_k$$

Where for given $X_1 \; ; X_2$ solves

$$\text{Max}_{X_2} \, Z_2(X) = \sum_{j=1}^n \hat{c}_j^{(2)} x_j + \frac{1}{2}\sum_{j=1}^n \sum_{k=1}^n \hat{d}_{jk}^{(2)} x_j x_k$$

Subject to $\sum_{j=1}^n \hat{a}_{ij} x_j \leq \hat{\beta}_i (\ln(\frac{1}{1-\gamma_i}))^{\frac{1}{\lambda_i}} \; ; i = 1,2,\dots,m$

$$x_j \geq 0 \qquad\qquad ; j = 1,2,\dots,n \qquad\qquad (7)$$

4   Development of QFGP Model

In a bilevel system, it can reasonably be assumed that both the DMs are motivated to cooperate with each other and each one tries to optimize his/her own benefit paying serious attention to the benefit of the others.

Now both the leader and follower optimize their objective independently under the same set of system constraints defined in (7).

Let $[x_k^b \; ; Z_k^b] = [x_{k1}^b, x_{k2}^b, \dots, x_{kn}^b \; ; Z_k^b]$ and $[x_k^w \; ; Z_k^w] = [x_{k1}^w, x_{k2}^w, \dots, x_{kn}^w \; ; Z_k^w](k = 1,2)$ be the best and worst independent solutions of the objectives of the respective DMs. Hence the fuzzy objective goal for each of the corresponding DMs is expressed as: $Z_k \gtrsim Z_k^b$ for $k = 1,2$.

In a bilevel decision making context, it is to be realized that the full achievement of the respective goal values of the DMs are not always possible due to conflicting nature of the objectives of the DMs and also due to the scarcity of limited resources in the decision making context. Again values lower than the worst values of the objectives of the DMs are completely unacceptable to the DMs. Hence the membership functions of the defined fuzzy goals are formulated as

$$\mu_{Z_k(x)} = \begin{cases} 0 & if \quad Z_k \leq Z_k^w \\ \frac{Z_k - Z_k^w}{Z_k^b - Z_k^w} & if \quad Z_k^w \leq Z_k \leq Z_k^b (k = 1, 2) \\ 1 & if \quad Z_k \geq Z_k^b \end{cases} \qquad (8)$$

The membership function defined above are now converted into the membership goals by introducing under- and over- deviational variables and assigning the highest membership value (unity) as the aspiration level to each of them. Then the QFGP model of the corresponding QBLPP (7) is presented as:

Find $X(x_1, x_2, \ldots, x_n)$
so as to Min D $= \sum_{k=1}^{2} w_k d_k^-$
and satisfy

$$\frac{z_1 - z_1^w}{z_1^b - z_1^w} + d_1^- - d_1^+ = 1 \ , \ \frac{z_2 - z_2^w}{z_2^b - z_2^w} + d_2^- - d_2^+ = 1 \ ,$$

subject to

$$\sum_{j=1}^{n} \hat{a}_{ij} x_j \leq \hat{\beta}_i (\ln \left(\frac{1}{1-\gamma_i}\right))^{\frac{1}{\lambda_i}} \ ; i = 1, 2, \ldots, m$$

$$x_1, \ x_2, \ d_1^-, d_1^+, d_2^-, d_2^+ \geq 0 \text{ with } d_1^-.d_1^+ = d_2^-.d_2^+ = 0 \tag{9}$$

where $w_k = \frac{1}{z_k^b - z_k^w}$ (k= 1, 2) represents fuzzy weight corresponding to the membership goals of the DMs.

5   Linearization of QFGP Model

Since the membership goals are quadratic in form, first order Taylor's series approximation technique [12] and piecewise linear approximation technique [13] are used to convert the defined membership goals to linear forms and thereby obtaining most suitable solution in the decision making arena.

5.1   Taylor's Series Approximation

To linearize the membership goals by using Taylor series linear approximation technique, the initial point is considered as the best solution point arrived by the leader and follower in the process of solving individual objective. Thus applying linearizing technique the defined membership functions are approximated as

$$\mu_{Z_k(x)} \cong$$
$$\mu_{Z_k(x)}\Big|_{x_k^b} + \left(x_1 - x_{k1}^b\right)\left(\frac{\partial}{\partial x_1}\mu_{Z_k(x)}\right)\Big|_{x_k^b} + \cdots + \left(x_n - x_{kn}^b\right)\left(\frac{\partial}{\partial x_n}\mu_{Z_k(x)}\right)\Big|_{x_k^b}$$

$$= \tau_{Z_k(x)}, \text{ say, for } k = 1, 2. \tag{10}$$

Thus the linearized model of (9) is stated as

Find $X(x_1, x_2, \ldots, x_n)$
so as to Min D $= \sum_{k=1}^{2} w_k d_k^-$
and satisfy $\tau_{Z_1(x)} + d_1^- - d_1^+ = 1$;
$\tau_{Z_2(x)} + d_2^- - d_2^+ = 1$

$$\sum_{j=1}^{n} \hat{a}_{ij} x_j \leq \hat{\beta}_i (\ln \left(\frac{1}{1-\gamma_i}\right))^{\frac{1}{\lambda_i}} \ ; i = 1, 2, \ldots, m$$

$$x_j \geq 0 \qquad ; j = 1, 2, \ldots, n \tag{11}$$

5.2   Piecewise Linear Approximation

In this technique each objective of the DMs are expressed in the form

$$Z_k(x) = \sum_{j=1}^n f_{kj}(x_j) \text{for} k = 1,2$$

Thus the membership goals in (9) are expressed as

$$\frac{\sum_{j=1}^n f_{kj}(x_j) - z_k^w}{z_k^b - z_k^w} + d_k^- - d_k^+ = 1 \ , \ k = 1,2.$$

To linearize the quadratic form of $f_{kj}(x_j)$, the grid points for the variable $x_j (j = 1,2,..,n)$ are chosen as $a_{jp} (p = 0,1,..,p_j)$. Now, introducing new variables $y_{jp} (p = 0,1,..,p_j)$, x_j is expressed as

$$x_j = \sum_{p=0}^{p_j} a_{jp} y_{jp},$$

where $\sum_{p=0}^{p_j} y_{jp} = 1 (y_{jp} \geq 0)$ with $a_{j0} = l_j$ and $a_{jp_j} = u_j$.

Then the piecewise approximated linear form of the $f_{kj}(x_j)$ is expressed as

$$F_{kj} = \sum_{p=0}^{p_j} y_{jp} f_{kj}(a_{jp}) \qquad k = 1,2 \qquad (12)$$

where l_j and u_j are the respective lower and upper bounds of x_j. Using the relation in (12) the executable linear FGP model is presented as

Minimize D $= \sum_{k=1}^2 w_k d_k^-$
So as to satisfy

$$\frac{\sum_{j=1}^n F_{1j} - z_1^w}{z_1^b - z_1^w} + d_1^- - d_1^+ = 1 \ ,$$

$$\frac{\sum_{j=1}^n F_{2j} - z_2^w}{z_2^b - z_2^w} + d_2^- - d_2^+ = 1$$

subject to $\sum_{j=1}^n \hat{a}_{ij} (\sum_{p=0}^{p_j} y_{jp} a_{jp}) \leq \hat{\beta}_i (\ln (\frac{1}{1-\gamma_i}))^{\frac{1}{\lambda_i}} \ ; i = 1,2,....,m$

$$y_{jp} \geq 0 \ (j = 1,2,..,n ; p = 0,1,..,p_j) \qquad (13)$$

At most two y_{jp} may be positive and if two are positive, they must be consecutive.

To ensure the above conditions binary variable Z_{jp} $(j = 1,2,..,n ; p = 0,1,..,p_j - 1)$ are to be introduced. The required restriction are then appeared as

$$y_{j0} \leq Z_{j0}; y_{jp} \leq Z_{jp-1} + Z_{jp}, p = 0,1,..,p_j - 1; y_{jp_j} \leq Z_{jp_j-1}; \sum_{j=0}^{p_j-1} Z_{jp} = 1 \quad (14)$$

The derived two models (11) and (13) including constraints in (14) are then solved independently using minsum goal programming to achieve most compromise solution in a linearized decision making context.

6   Comparison of Decisions Using Distance Function

In BLPP, distance function is used to make appropriate measure regarding achievement of the goals of the leader and follower in the decision making context.

The concept of ideal point dependent solution and the use of distance function for group decision analysis were studied by Yu [15]. In the present study, since the aspired level of each of the membership goals is unity, the point consisting of the highest membership value of each of the goals would represent the ideal point. The Euclidean distance function is expressed as

$$d = \{\textstyle\sum_{k=1}^{2}(1 - \mu_k)^2\}^{\frac{1}{2}}$$ (15)

where μ_k represents the achieved membership value of the objective goal of the k-th level decision maker under the different linearization technique.

Now it can be easily be realized that the linearization technique under which the value of d is found to be minimum would be considered as appropriate solution technique of the proposed model in the current decision making situation.

To illustrate the proposed approach, a numerical example is solved in the next section.

7   A Numerical Example

The following QFBLCCPP is considered to explore the application potentiality of the proposed approach

Find $X(x_1, x_2, \ldots, x_n)$
so as to
$$\text{Max}_{x_1} \ Z_1 = \tilde{6}x_1 + \tilde{3}x_2 + \widetilde{-1}x_1^2 + \widetilde{-1}x_2^2$$
$$\text{Max}_{x_2} \ Z_2 = \tilde{1}x_1 + \tilde{5}x_2 + \widetilde{-1}x_2^2$$
subject to $\Pr(\tilde{1}x_1 + \tilde{1}x_2 \le \tilde{b}_1) \ge 0.85, \ \Pr(\tilde{3}x_1 + \tilde{2}x_2 \le \tilde{b}_2) \ge 0.75,$

$$\Pr(\tilde{2}x_1 + \tilde{1}x_2 \le \tilde{b}_3) \ge 0.72, \ x_1, x_2 \ge 0$$ (16)

Here $\tilde{b}_1, \tilde{b}_2, \tilde{b}_3$ represents Weibull distributed independent fuzzy random variables. The parameters of the distribution are taken as triangular fuzzy numbers with the form
$$\tilde{\lambda}_1 = \widetilde{0.5} = (0.4, 0.5, 0.6), \tilde{\beta}_1 = \widetilde{186} = (184, 186, 188), \tilde{\beta}_2 = \widetilde{118} = (115, 118, 121),$$
$$\tilde{\lambda}_3 = \widetilde{0.25} = (0.20, 0.25, 0.30), \tilde{\beta}_3 = \widetilde{589} = (585, 589, 593).$$

Also the coefficients of the objectives are also taken as triangular fuzzy number with the values

$$\tilde{6} = (4, 6, 9), \tilde{3} = (2, 3, 5), \widetilde{-1} = (-1.5, -1, -0.5), \widetilde{-1} = (-1.1, -1, -.15),$$
$$\tilde{1} = (0.95, 1, 1.05), \tilde{5} = (4.5, 5, 5.8), \widetilde{-1} = (-1.04, -1, -0.03).$$

The coefficients of the probabilistic constraints are taken as trapezoidal fuzzy numbers as

$$\tilde{1} = (0.2, 0.8, 1, 1.2), \tilde{1} = (0.4, 1, 1.6, 2), \tilde{3} = (1, 2, 3, 4), \tilde{2} = (0.5, 1.5, 2.5, 3),$$
$$\tilde{2} = (1, 1.8, 2.2, 3), \tilde{1} = (0.5, 1, 1.5, 2).$$

On the basis of the method of defuzzification with probability density function and CCP technique the above model (16) can be expressed as

Find $X(x_1, x_2, \ldots . x_n)$ so as to

$\text{Max}_{x_1} Z_1 = 6.33x_1 + 3.33x_2 - x_1^2 - 0.75x_2^2$

$\text{Max}_{x_2} Z_2 = x_1 + 5.1x_2 - 0.69x_2^2$

subject to $0.78x_1 + 1.24x_2 \leq 4.92$

$2.67x_1 + 1.86x_2 \leq 9.78$

$2x_1 + 1.25x_2 \leq 6.86$

$\quad x_1, x_2 \geq 0$ (17)

Now each DM considers their objective independently and then solve with respect to the system of constraints in (17) to find the best and worst values of the objectives. The results are obtained as

$x_1 = 2.427, x_2 = 1.605$ with $Z_1^b = 12.885$;

and $x_1 = 1.566, x_2 = 2.983$ with $Z_2^b = 10.639$.

Then the worst values of the objective of the respective DMS are

$Z_1^w = 10.720 \quad and \quad Z_2^w = 8.835$

Then the fuzzy goals of the objectives are found as: $Z_1^b \gtrsim 12.885$ and $Z_2^b \gtrsim 10.639$. Therefore the membership goal of the leader and follower are expressed as

$\mu_{Z_1}(x) = \frac{6.33x_1 + 3.33x_2 - x_1^2 - 0.75x_2^2 - 10.720}{2.165} + d_1^- - d_1^+ = 1$

$\mu_{Z_2}(x) = \frac{x_1 + 5.1x_2 - 0.69x_2^2 - 8.835}{1.804} + d_2^- - d_2^+ = 1$

These nonlinear membership goals are first linearized by Taylor series approximation method as discussed in subsection 4.1 and then solving the developed model subject to the system constraints defined in (17), the solutions are achieved as

$x_1 = 1.8, x_2 = 2.608$ with objective values $Z_1 = 11.737$ and $Z_2 = 10.408$.

Similarly, linearizing the membership goals of DMs using piecewise approximation technique, as described in subsection 4.2, and then solving the achieved subject to the system constraints defined in (17) the solutions are found as

$x_1 = 1.992, x_2 = 2.3$ with objective values $Z_1 = 12.333$ and $Z_2 = 10.072$.

The solutions achieved by two approximation techniques are summarized in the following table:

Table 1. Result comparisons of two approximation techniques

Linearization technique	Solution point	Objective values	Membership values	Euclidean distance
Taylor series approximation technique	$x_1 = 1.8$ $x_2 = 2.608$	$Z_1 = 11.737$ $Z_2 = 10.408$	$\mu_1 = 0.58$ $\mu_2 = 0.87$	$d = 0.44$
Piecewise linear approximation method	$x_1 = 1.992$ $x_2 = 2.3$	$Z_1 = 12.333$ $Z_2 = 10.072$	$\mu_1 = 0.74$ $\mu_2 = 0.68$	$d = 0.41$

The comparison shows that better solution is obtained in the process of piecewise linear approximation method than Taylor series approximation method.

It is to be mentioned here that Taylor series approximation provides estimation based on the selection of initial solution points. Also some round-off errors may occur in practical decision situations. On the other hand, since piecewise linear approximation approach approximate the nonlinear functions in a piecewise manner, the error estimation becomes less in comparison to the Taylor series approximation method.

8   Conclusions

In this paper, methodological development of solving a QFBLCCP model is discussed systematically using a combination of probabilistic and fuzzy concepts in a hierarchical decision making environment for finding most satisfactory solution to the DMs for overall benefit of the organization. In the solution process, two well-known linear approximation techniques are employed for solving QFBLPP and the achieved solutions are compared using distance function to measure the suitability of two different solution techniques. The proposed procedure can be extended to solve any nonlinear fuzzy hierarchical decision making problems involving fuzzy parameters and fuzzy random variables following different types of probability distributions. The proposed methodology can also be applied to different real life planning problems for obtaining satisfactory solution in a hierarchical decision making environment. However, it is hoped that the proposed procedure may act as a pioneer into the way of making decision from some nonlinear imprecisely defined probabilistic hierarchical decision making environment.

Acknowledgements. The authors are thankful to the anonymous reviewers for their comments and suggestions to improve the clarity and quality of the paper. This work is partially supported by DST-PURSE Program, University of Kalyani, Kalyani, India.

References

1. Charnes, A., Cooper, W.W.: Chance-constrained programming. Management Science 6, 73–79 (1962)
2. Liu, B.: Fuzzy random chance-constrained programming. IEEE Transactions on Fuzzy Systems 9, 713–720 (2001)
3. Biswas, A., Modak, N.: On solving chance constrained programming problems involving uniform distribution with fuzzy parameters. Intelligent Decision Technologies 7, 151–159 (2013)
4. Candler, W., Townsley, R.: A linear two-level programming problem. Computers and Operations Research 9, 59–76 (1982)
5. Zimmermann, H.J.: Fuzzy programming and linear programming with several objective functions. Fuzzy Sets and Systems 1, 45–55 (1978)

6. Lai, Y.J., Hwang, C.L.: Fuzzy Mathematical Programming Methods and Applications. Springer (1996)
7. Mohamed, R.H.: The relationship between goal programming and fuzzy programming. Fuzzy Sets and System 89, 215–222 (1997)
8. Moitra, B.N., Pal, B.B.: A fuzzy goal programming approach for solving bilevel programming problems. In: Pal, N.R., Sugeno, M. (eds.) AFSS 2002. LNCS (LNAI), vol. 2275, pp. 91–98. Springer, Heidelberg (2002)
9. Biswas, A., Bose, K.: A fuzzy programming approach for solving quadratic bilevel programming problems with fuzzy resource constraints. International Journal of Operational Research 12, 142–156 (2011)
10. Modak, N., Biswas, A.: A fuzzy programming approach for bilevel stochastic programming. AISC (in Press)
11. Johnson, N.L., Kotz, S., Balakrishnan, N.: Continuous Univariate Distributions-I, 2nd edn. John Wiley and Sons, New York (1994)
12. Ignigio, J.P.: Goal Programming and Extensions. Massachusetts, Lexington (1976)
13. Bazaraa, M.M., Sherali, H.D., Shetty, C.M.: Nonlinear Programming Theory and Algorithms. John Wiley & Sons, New York (1993)
14. Barik, S.K., Barik, M.P.: Probabilistic Quadratic Programming Problems with Some Fuzzy Parameters. Advances in Operations Research 13 (2012)
15. Yu, P.L.: A class of solutions for group decision problems. Management Science 19, 936–946 (1973)

Message Passing Methods
for Estimation of Distribution Algorithms
Based on Markov Networks

Roberto Santana, Alexander Mendiburu, and Jose A. Lozano

Intelligent Systems Group
Department of Computer Science and Artificial Intelligence
University of the Basque Country (UPV/EHU)
Paseo Manuel de Lardizabal 1, 20080, San Sebastian, Guipuzcoa, Spain
{roberto.santana,alexander.mendiburu,ja.lozano}@ehu.es

Abstract. Sampling methods are a fundamental component of estimation of distribution algorithms (EDAs). In this paper we propose new methods for generating solutions in EDAs based on Markov networks. These methods are based on the combination of message passing algorithms with decimation techniques for computing the maximum a posteriori solution of a probabilistic graphical model. The performance of the EDAs on a family of non-binary deceptive functions shows that the introduced approach improves results achieved with the sampling methods traditionally used by EDAs based on Markov networks.

Keywords: estimation of distribution algorithms, message passing, Markov networks, probabilistic modeling, belief propagation, abductive inference.

1 Introduction

Genetic Algorithms that apply simple genetic operators are usually unable to identify the problem variables that interact and therefore they are not very efficient at the time of generating solutions. Extensive research has been devoted to design heuristic recombination operators based on a priori information about the problem domain and adaptive genetic operators that attempt to identify and preserve the linkage between the variables. However, these are not general and robust solutions to these problems.

Estimation of distribution algorithms (EDAs) [4,11] are evolutionary algorithms (EAs) that deal in a different way with the "building-block identification" and "building-block mixing or exchange" questions [16]. EDAs use machine learning techniques to learn a probabilistic model from the selected solutions and to sample new solutions from this model. There is overwhelming evidence that probabilistic modeling of selected solutions is a very competitive approach to the "linkage problem" as known in EAs [3,5,20].

The choice of the probabilistic model in EDAs influences the type of problems that can be successfully addressed and the machine learning algorithms used to

B.K. Panigrahi et al. (Eds.): SEMCCO 2013, Part II, LNCS 8298, pp. 419–430, 2013.
© Springer International Publishing Switzerland 2013

learn the models and to sample from them. One class of EDAs able to represent higher order interactions between the variables are EDAs that use Markov networks [13,18,20]. Sampling methods commonly applied by this type of EDAs can transfer the information contained in the Markov models to the generated solutions but are computationally costly [21]. In this paper we propose the combination of message passing algorithms [12] with decimation strategies [1] for generating solutions in EDAs based on Markov networks.

The paper is organized as follows. In the next section, we review two typical examples of EDAs based on Markov networks. Section 3 presents factor graphs, message passing algorithms, and decimation methods for computing the (MAP) of a factor graph. Section 4 introduces three variants of algorithms for generating solutions in EDAs. The experimental results on the validation of our proposal are given in Section 5. The conclusions of our paper are presented in Section 6.

2   Markov Network Factorized Distribution Algorithm and the Markovianity Based Optimization Algorithm

Let $\mathbf{X} = (X_1, \ldots, X_n)$ denote a vector of discrete random variables. We will use $\mathbf{x} = (x_1, \ldots, x_n)$ to denote an assignment to the variables. S will denote a set of indices in $\{1, \ldots, n\}$, and X_S (respectively x_S) a subset of the variables of $\mathbf{X}$ (respectively $\mathbf{x}$) determined by the indices in S. We will work with positive distributions denoted by p. $p(x_S)$ will denote the marginal probability for $\mathbf{X}_S = \mathbf{x}_S$. We use $p(x_i \mid x_j)$ to denote the conditional probability distribution of $X_i = x_i$ given $X_j = x_j$.

The Markov network factorized distribution algorithm (MN-FDA) [13] and the Markovianity based optimization algorithm (MOA) [19,21] are two different approaches to the use of undirected graphical models to represent probabilistic dependencies in EDAs. MN-FDA can capture some of the dependencies that acyclic models like trees are not able to represent, however the number of these dependencies that it is able to represent is rather limited. The reason for this limitation is that MN-FDA represents dependencies using a junction graph of bounded complexity [15]. A good characteristic of MN-FDA is that it samples new solutions using probabilistic logic sampling (PLS), which is a very efficient sampling procedure. MOA is a more powerful algorithm in terms of the number of probabilistic dependencies that it is able to capture. Nevertheless, it requires to use the Gibbs sampling (GS) algorithm to sample this model. GS is a computationally costly algorithm.

2.1   MN-FDA

MN-FDA defines a factorization in which the factors correspond to a set of maximal cliques organized as a labeled junction graph (JG). The cliques in the factorization can be ordered in such a way that at least one of the variables in every clique is not contained in the previous nodes in the ordering. MN-FDA allows the existence of cycles between the factors, therefore expanding the class of distributions represented by junction trees [13].

Algorithm 1. MN-FDA

---

1 Set $t \Leftarrow 0$. Generate $N \gg 0$ points randomly.

2 **do** {

3   Evaluate the points using the fitness function.

4   Select a set D_t^S of $k \leq N$ points according to a selection method.

5   Learn an undirected graphical model from D_t^S.

6   Generate the new population sampling from the model.

7 $t \Leftarrow t + 1$

8 } **until** Termination criteria are met

The general steps of MN-FDA are shown in Algorithm 1. The steps that describe the way the probabilistic model is learned are shown in Algorithm 2. In this paper, we use the G-test of independence [6] to detect dependencies. G-tests are a subclass of likelihood ratio tests, a general category of tests that have many uses for testing the fit of data to mathematical models. To compute the test, we use the relationship between the G-test and the mutual information:

$$G(X_i, X_j) = 2NMI(X_i, X_j) \tag{1}$$

where MI is the mutual information and N is the number of samples.

Since the use of the G-statistics implies a different way to determine the relationships between variables and different characteristics of the learning algorithm, we call the MN-FDA that uses this test as MN-FDA^G.

Algorithm 2. Model learning in MN-FDA

---

1 Learn an independence graph $\mathcal{G}$ using the G-test.

2 If necessary, refine the graph.

3 Find the set L of all the maximal cliques of $\mathcal{G}$.

4 Construct a labeled JG from L.

5 Find the marginal probabilities for the cliques in the JG.

Details on the algorithms used for refining the graph, finding the maximal cliques, and constructing the labeled JG are given in [14]

2.2 MOA

MOA [19,21] exploits the Markovianity or local Markov property of Markov networks. Its workflow is described in Algorithm 3.

Algorithm 3. Markovianity based optimization algorithm

---

1   Set $t \Leftarrow 0$. Generate M points randomly
2   **do** {
3   Evaluate the points using the fitness function.
4   Select a set D_t^S of $N \leq M$ points according to a selection method.
5   Estimate the structure of a Markov network from D_t^S.
6   Estimate the local Markov conditional probabilities, $p(x_i|N_i)$, for each
         variable X_i as defined by the undirected structure.
7   Generate M new points sampling from the Markov network.
8       $t \Leftarrow t + 1$
9   } **until** Termination criteria are met

To learn the Markov network structure, first the mutual information for each pair of variables in computed. Then, an edge between two variables is created if the mutual information between them is higher than a given threshold. Here we compute the threshold, TR, as $TR = avg(MI) * sig$, where $avg(MI)$ is the average of the elements of the mutual information matrix and sig is the significance parameter. Following [21], we set $sig = 1.5$. If the number of neighbors of a variable is higher than an allowed maximum number, N_{neigh}, then only the N_{neigh} neighbors that have the highest mutual information are kept.

MOA uses a Gibbs sampler with r steps, where $r = n \times ln(n) \times IT$, and IT, the *iteration coefficient*, is set to 4. In the particular case of binary representation, the probability of $x_i = 1$ given the value of its neighbors N_i is $p(x_i = 1|N_i) = \frac{e^{p(x_i=1,N_i)/T}}{e^{p(x_i=1,N_i)/T}+e^{p(x_i=0,N_i)/T}}$, where T is the *temperature coefficient* that controls the convergence of the Gibbs probability distribution. More details on the learning and sampling procedures used by MOA can be obtained from [21].

3   Message Passing and Decimation Methods Methods on Factor Graphs

A *factor graph* [2] is a bipartite graph that can serve to represent the factorized structure of a distribution. It has two types of nodes: variable nodes, and factor nodes. Variable nodes are indexed with letters starting with i, and factor nodes with letters starting with a. The existence of an edge connecting variable node i to factor node a means that x_i is an argument of function f_a in the referred factorization.

Belief propagation (BP) [12] is an inference method used to calculate the marginal probabilities of a probabilistic model. It is usually applied after some evidence about the observed states of the variables has been incorporated to the model. A key characteristic of the BP algorithm is that the inference is done using message-passing between nodes. Each node sends and receives messages until a stable situation is reached. Messages, locally calculated by each node, comprise statistical information concerning neighbor nodes.

When the algorithm converges (i.e. messages do not change), marginal functions (sum-product) or max-marginals (max-product) are obtained as the normalized product of all messages received by X_i. For the the max-product approach, each variable in the optimal solution is assigned the value given by the configuration with the highest probability at each max-marginal.

Decimation strategies [1] are used to solve constraint satisfaction problems. They work by repeatedly fixing variable values and simplifying the constraints without reconsidering earlier decisions. They can be seen as a divide and conquer approach in which the problem is split and simplified at each step.

In the context of EDAs, we will apply a decimation strategy to find an approximate solution to the maximum a posteriori probability (MAP) configuration of a factor graph representing a probability distribution. At each step of the simple BP-decimation algorithm the idea is to identify the variable X_i that is almost certainty to have a given value in the problem's most probable configuration. First, max-BP is run. Then, the variable X_i with the largest likelihood on one of its configurations is identified and fixed to its most probable value. In the next step, the variable node X_i is removed from the factor graph, and all factors that contain X_i are reduced by eliminating the tuples which force X_i to take a value different from the one fixed. The cycle is repeated until all variables are fixed. The BP-decimation scheme used in this paper is based on the *decmap* program included in the libDAI implementation [9].

4   New Methods for Generating Solutions in EDAs Based on Markov Networks

We propose two different ways for using the information contained in the Markov networks for generating new solutions: 1) Adding the most probable configuration and 2) Using the most probable configuration as a template for crossover.

In Algorithm 4, the MAP is generated using BP-decimation and it is passed to the new generation together with the elitist solutions E, and the $N - |E| - 1$ solutions generated from the probabilistic model using GS or PLS. This is essentially the same idea used in previous EDA work on the use of the most probable configurations [7,8]. However, there are also some relevant differences:

- The factor graph is constructed from a Markov network that will represent two different types of structural information. Reduced set of cliques, for MN-FDA^G, and neighborhood based cliques, for MOA.
- Three different methods are used to compute the most probable configuration: junction-tree-based method for computing exact MAP, loopy belief propagation (LBP) for computing approximate MAP, and decimation-based LBP for computing approximate MAP [9].
- An archive is used as a memory of the EDA to avoid adding MAPs already found in previous generations. The archive stores at most one new MAP in each generation.

Algorithm 4. Insert-MAP

1	Learn the Markov network model MN.
2	Generate the set S of $N - |E| - 1$ solutions according to generation method.
3	Compute the factor graph FG.
4	Generate a MAP solution from FG.
5	Form the new population with S, E, and the MAP solution.

The effect of the Insert-MAP strategy will depend on the choice of the inference algorithm. Very often for MOA the application of an exact inference procedure is infeasible due to the dimension of the junction tree. In these situations no MAP solution is added to the population.

In Algorithm 5, the MAP is used as a template for recombining the information of the solutions in the current population with the global information contained in the Markov model. Recombination guarantees that partial configurations that coincide with the MAP will remain in the next population. In Algorithm 5, inference is applied only once in each generation and PLS or Gibbs sampling are not applied. It has been acknowledged [22] that operators that generate offspring through combination of global statistical information and the local information of solutions found so far (e.g., guided mutation) can improve search efficiency.

Algorithm 5. Template-MAP

1	Learn the Markov network model MN.
2	Compute the factor graph FG.
3	Obtain MAP solution from FG.
4	**for** $i = 1$ **to** $N - |E|$
5	Apply uniform crossover between solution x^i and MAP solution.

5   Experiments

To evaluate the algorithms introduced in this paper we use separable additively decomposable functions (ADFs) defined on discrete non-binary variables.

$$f^c_{deceptivek}(\mathbf{x}) = \sum_{i=1}^{\frac{n}{k}} F_{dec}(x_{k\cdot(i-1)+1} + x_{k\cdot(i-1)+2} + \cdots + x_{k\cdot i}, k, c) \qquad (2)$$

$$F_{dec}(x_1, \ldots, x_k, k, c) = \begin{cases} k \cdot (c-1), & for \ \sum_{i=1}^{k} x_i = k \cdot (c-1) \\ k \cdot (c-1) - \sum_{i=1}^{k} x_i - 1 \ otherwise \end{cases} \qquad (3)$$

The general deceptive function $f^c_{deceptivek}(\mathbf{x})$ of order k [17] is formed as an additive function composed by the function $F_{dec}(x_1, \ldots, x_k, k, c)$ evaluated on substrings of size k and cardinality c, i.e. $x_i \in \{0, \ldots, c-1\}$. This family of functions is a generalization of the binary $f_{deceptivek}(\mathbf{x})$ to variables with non-binary values. Its difficulty increases with the cardinality of the variables (c) and the size of the definition sets (k).

We compare the algorithms in terms of their critical population size to reach the optimum and the average number of evaluations needed. The critical population size is computed as the minimum population size needed to reach the optimum in $l = 30$ successive experiments and the average number of evaluations is computed from a maximum of $r = 30$ independent computations of the critical population size (less than r if it was not possible to find a critical population size in all the runs). The population size is started at $N = 32$ and doubled if the algorithm does not converge in the l experiments until a maximum $N = 131072$. The maximum number of generations was $g = 40$. Truncation selection, $T = 0.5$, is applied together with best elitism in which the complete selected population is passed to the next generation.

There are two factors that define the different variants we compare:

1. EDAs (MN-FDA^G and MOA)
2. Strategy for generating new solutions: S1) Insert-MAP. S2) Template-MAP. S3) Insert-MAP + Template-MAP

We also evaluate the influence that using different inference methods has in the behavior of the EDA. Four inference methods are compared:

1. NoMAP: No MAP is computed. Instead a solution generated using PLS, GS, or template crossover is added to the population.
2. Exact: Exact inference based on a junction tree
3. BP: Belief propagation
4. Dec-BP: Decimation BP

The choice of MN-FDA^G or MOA influences the type of undirected model that is learned from data but also the strategy used for generating new solutions. When Insert-MAP is combined with NoMAP it means that no MAP is computed and therefore the original method used by MN-FDA^G or MOA to generate new solutions is applied. In total, we compare $2 \times 3 \times 4 - 2 = 22$ variants of the algorithms.

We investigate the performance of MN-FDA^G and MOA using function $f^c_{deceptivek}(\mathbf{x})$, $k \in \{3, 4, 5\}$, $c \in \{2, 3, 4, 5\}$. We are interested in evaluating the behavior of the EDAs when the size of the definition sets and the number of values of each variable are increased.

Table 1 shows the number of successful runs of different EDAs variants when the definition sets of the functions are increased from $k = 3$ to $k = 5$. Each cell of the table groups the number of successful runs for 4 different cardinality values $c \in \{2, 3, 4, 5\}$. Therefore the maximum number of successful runs is 120.

A number of observations can be made from the analysis of Table 1:

Table 1. Results of the EDAs variants for $f^c_{deceptivek}(\mathbf{x})$, $k \in \{3,4,5\}$, $c \in \{2,3,4,5\}$. Number of runs that achieved the optimum.

Problems	Gen. Method	MN-FDA^G				MOA			
		NoMAP	Exact	BP	Dec-BP	NoMAP	Exact	BP	Dec-BP
$n = 30, k = 3$	$s1$	90	120	120	120	120	120	120	120
	$s2$	90	0	0	0	120	0	0	0
	$s3$	90	120	119	119	120	117	113	118
$n = 32, k = 4$	$s1$	60	90	90	90	56	57	57	58
	$s2$	60	0	0	0	56	0	0	0
	$s3$	60	85	88	88	54	30	30	30
$n = 30, k = 5$	$s1$	30	60	60	60	30	30	30	30
	$s2$	30	0	0	0	30	0	0	0
	$s3$	30	60	60	60	30	30	30	30

- As the size of the definition sets is increased the results of all algorithms deteriorate.
- Insert-MAP is a marginally better strategy than Insert-MAP+MAP-Template for MN-FDA^G, and a better strategy for MOA, as it can be observed for $n = 32, k = 4$.
- For Insert-MAP, there are not important differences between exact and approximate inference algorithms.
- MAP-Template is the worst generation strategy for all the problems.

We also investigate the number of function evaluations required by the algorithms to find the optimum for each combination of k and c. Figures 1, 2, and 3 show this information as boxplots. On each box, the central mark is the median number of evaluations from those runs (out of 30) in which the optimum was found. The edges of the box are the 25-th and 75-th percentiles. The whiskers extend to the most extreme datapoints the plotting algorithm considers to be not outliers, and the outliers are plotted individually as crosses.

A first finding from the analysis of the figures is that, for a fixed k, as the cardinality of the variables is increased, all algorithms dramatically decrease their performance. This can be seen in the fact that some of the algorithms are not able to find the optimum even once, and in the dramatic increase in the number of evaluations. For a fixed c (e.g., $c = 2$), the number of evaluations also increases with k. The combination of a high cardinality and a high definition set is particularly harmful to all the algorithms. For $c = 5$, only functions with $k = 3$ are solved.

Figures 1, 2, and 3 reveal that Insert-MAP is a more efficient algorithm than No-MAP and Insert-MAP+MAP-Template. The advantage of using Insert-MAP over No-MAP can be clearly observed for $c = 5$ for which MN-FDA^G with No-MAP never finds the optimum. The figures help to realize that Insert-MAP outperforms Insert-MAP+MAP-Template significantly. For all combinations of c and k the average number of evaluations needed by Insert-MAP is smaller than that needed by Insert-MAP+MAP-Template. Another interesting observation can be made from the analysis of the outliers in Figure 2, ($k = 4, c = 2$). Although the average behavior of MOA is worse than MN-FDA^G for $s1$, there are runs were the number of evaluations needed by MOA to find the optimum is smaller than the number of evaluations required by the best run of MN-FDA^G. This fact indicates that MN-FDA^G is more stable but MOA can eventually require a smaller number of evaluations in some runs.

Once possible explanation of the poor performance achieved by Template-MAP is that it produces a lack of diversity in the population that leads to search stagnation. Insert-MAP+MAP-Template attempts to counteract this effect but the result does not outperform Insert-MAP. Another issue that should be taken into account in the analysis of the experiments is that the critical population size has been computed by requiring to reach the optimum in $l = 30$ successive experiments. This is a very strong condition and may explain that for some functions the success rate is close but not equal to 30.

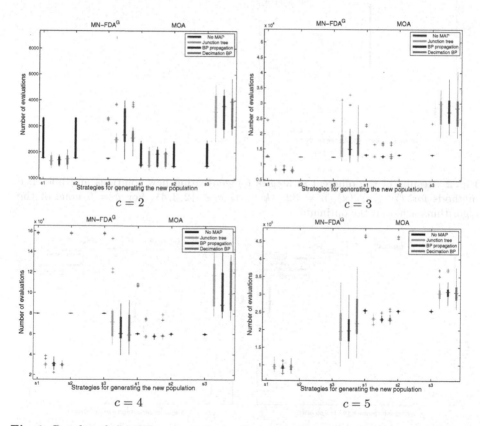

Fig. 1. Results of the different strategies for generating new solutions and inference methods for $f_{deceptivek}^c(\mathbf{x})$, $n = 30$, $k = 3$, $c \in \{2, 3, 4, 5\}$

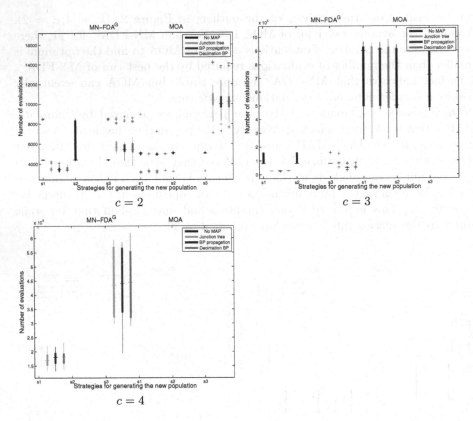

Fig. 2. Results of the different strategies for generating new solutions and inference methods for $f_{deceptivek}^c(\mathbf{x})$, $n = 32$, $k = 4$, $c \in \{2, 3, 4\}$. For $c = 5$ none of the algorithms achieved the optimum.

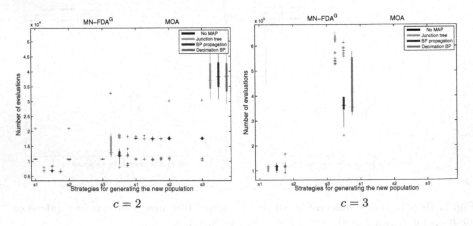

Fig. 3. Results of the different strategies for generating new solutions and inference methods for $f_{deceptivek}^c(\mathbf{x})$, $n = 30$, $k = 5$, $c \in \{2, 3\}$. For $c \in \{4, 5\}$ none of the algorithms achieved the optimum.

6 Conclusions

In this paper we have introduced new strategies for generating solutions in EDAs based on Markov networks and presented ways in which they can be combined. We have compared exact and approximate inference strategies in the context of EDAs based on Markov networks and we have shown that the choice of the inference procedure can help to dramatically reduce the number of evaluations.

It has been acknowledged [10] that "While the computation of the conditional probabilities and even learning of the Markov network structure can be efficiently done, efficient sampling of Markov networks is still an unsolved problem." The same argument has been exposed or implicitly assumed by other authors from the field. Although we do not claim that the use of inference techniques contribute to a more accurate sampling of the Markov network probability distribution, our experiments show that focusing on the MAP of the Markov network can actually improve the optimization results. The lesson to be taken is that the sampling problem could be somewhat relaxed by aiming at directly generating the solutions with highest probabilities instead of sampling the full distribution using Gibbs sampling. This is what strategies for generating new solutions based on approximate inference methods for MAP are able to do.

Acknowledgements. This work has been partially supported by Saiotek and Research Groups 2007-2012 (IT-242-07) programs (Basque Government), TIN2010-14931, and COMBIOMED network in computational biomedicine (Carlos III Health Institute).

References

1. Kroc, L., Sabharwal, A., Selman, B.: Message-passing and local heuristics as decimation strategies for satisfiability. In: Proceedings of the 2009 ACM Symposium on Applied Computing, pp. 1408–1414. ACM (2009)
2. Kschischang, F.R., Frey, B.J., Loeliger, H.A.: Factor graphs and the sum-product algorithm. IEEE Transactions on Information Theory 47(2), 498–519 (2001)
3. Larrañaga, P., Karshenas, H., Bielza, C., Santana, R.: A review on probabilistic graphical models in evolutionary computation. Journal of Heuristics 18(5), 795–819 (2012)
4. Larrañaga, P., Lozano, J.A. (eds.): Estimation of Distribution Algorithms. A New Tool for Evolutionary Computation. Kluwer Academic Publishers, Boston (2002)
5. Lozano, J.A., Larrañaga, P., Inza, I., Bengoetxea, E. (eds.): Towards a New Evolutionary Computation: Advances on Estimation of Distribution Algorithms. Springer (2006)
6. McDonald, J.: Handbook of biological statistics, vol. 2. Sparky House Publishing, Baltimore (2009)
7. Mendiburu, A., Santana, R., Lozano, J.A.: Introducing belief propagation in estimation of distribution algorithms: A parallel framework. Technical Report EHU-KAT-IK-11/07, Department of Computer Science and Artificial Intelligence, University of the Basque Country (October 2007)

8. Mendiburu, A., Santana, R., Lozano, J.A.: Fast fitness improvements in estimation of distribution algorithms using belief propagation. In: Santana, R., Shakya, S. (eds.) Markov Networks in Evolutionary Computation, pp. 141–155. Springer (2012)

9. Mooij, J.: libDAI: A free and open source C++ library for discrete approximate inference in graphical models. The Journal of Machine Learning Research 11, 2169–2173 (2010)

10. Mühlenbein, H.: Convergence theorems of estimation of distribution algorithms. In: Shakya, S., Santana, R. (eds.) Markov Networks in Evolutionary Computation, pp. 91–108. Springer (2012)

11. Mühlenbein, H., Paaß, G.: From recombination of genes to the estimation of distributions I. Binary parameters. In: Voigt, H.-M., Ebeling, W., Rechenberg, I., Schwefel, H.-P. (eds.) PPSN 1996. LNCS, vol. 1141, pp. 178–187. Springer, Heidelberg (1996)

12. Pearl, J.: Causality: Models, Reasoning and Inference. Cambridge University Press (2000)

13. Santana, R.: A markov network based factorized distribution algorithm for optimization. In: Lavrač, N., Gamberger, D., Todorovski, L., Blockeel, H. (eds.) ECML 2003. LNCS (LNAI), vol. 2837, pp. 337–348. Springer, Heidelberg (2003)

14. Santana, R.: Estimation of distribution algorithms with Kikuchi approximations. Evolutionary Computation 13(1), 67–97 (2005)

15. Santana, R.: MN-EDA and the use of clique-based factorisations in EDAs. In: Shakya, S., Santana, R. (eds.) Markov Networks in Evolutionary Computation, pp. 73–87. Springer (2012)

16. Santana, R., Larrañaga, P., Lozano, J.A.: Research topics on discrete estimation of distribution algorithms. Memetic Computing 1(1), 35–54 (2009)

17. Santana, R., Ochoa, A., Soto, M.R.: Solving problems with integer representation using a tree based factorized distribution algorithm. In: Electronic Proceedings of the First International NAISO Congress on Neuro Fuzzy Technologies. NAISO Academic Press (2002)

18. Shakya, S., McCall, J.: Optimization by estimation of distribution with DEUM framework based on Markov random fields. International Journal of Automation and Computing 4(3), 262–272 (2007)

19. Shakya, S., Santana, R.: An EDA based on local Markov property and Gibbs sampling. In: Keijzer, M. (ed.) Proceedings of the 2008 Genetic and Evolutionary Computation Conference (GECCO), pp. 475–476. ACM, New York (2008)

20. Shakya, S., Santana, R. (eds.): Markov Networks in Evolutionary Computation. Springer (2012)

21. Shakya, S., Santana, R., Lozano, J.A.: A Markovianity based optimisation algorithm. Genetic Programming and Evolvable Machines 13(2), 159–195 (2012)

22. Zhang, Q., Sun, J., Tsang, E.P.K.: Evolutionary algorithm with guided mutation for the maximum clique problem. IEEE Transactions on Evolutionary Computation 9(2), 192–200 (2005)

Application of Neural Networks to Automatic Load Frequency Control

Soumyadeep Nag and Namitha Philip

Dept. of Electrical and Electronics Engineering, SRM University, Chennai, India
{Soumyadeepnag,namithaphilip2703}@gmail.com

Abstract. This paper is intended to present the benefits of the application of artificial neural network to automatic load frequency control. The power system model has been simulated and the conventional PI controller has been replaced by the artificial neural network controller wherein, we have trained the neural controller to behave as a PI controller. The strategy has been successfully tested for both a single area as well as multi area systems using MATLAB/SIMULINK. With the help of a neural controller we have been able to achieve a smaller transient dip as well as faster stabilization of frequency.

1   Introduction

In a power system there has to be perfect balance between the power generated and the power consumed. Any change in load is immediately sufficed by the change in frequency and conversion of energy stored as momentum of the system into electrical energy, until the time taken by the speed sensors, governors, amplifiers and actuators to respond to the change in load. The steam valves are opened and the system frequency is then restored to its normal value. It is imperative to mention that the control measures are most effective once the control elements are automatic devices. Power system loads and losses are sensitive to frequency.

Once a generating unit is tripped or a block of load is added to the system, the power mismatch is initially compensated by an extraction of kinetic energy from system inertial storage which causes a declining system frequency. As frequency decreases, the power taken by load also decreases. Equilibrium for large systems is often obtained when the frequency sensitive reduction of loads balances the output power of the tripped unit or that delivered to the added block of load at the resulting (new) frequency. If this effect halts the frequency decline it usually does so in less than 2 seconds. If the mismatch is large enough to cause the frequency to deviate beyond the governor dead band of generating units, their output will be increased by governor action. For such mismatches, equilibrium is obtained when the reduction in the power taken by loads plus the increased generation due to governor action compensates for the mismatch. Such equilibrium is normally obtained within a dozen seconds after the tripping of a unit or connection of the additional load.

B.K. Panigrahi et al. (Eds.): SEMCCO 2013, Part II, LNCS 8298, pp. 431–441, 2013.
© Springer International Publishing Switzerland 2013

The frequency of a generating system is affected by the change in the real power and the voltage of the system by the change in the reactive power. Although active and reactive powers have combined effects over the frequency and voltage the control problem of voltage and frequency can be decoupled. Hereafter we have decoupled the problem of frequency variations to be affected by the change in real power and the change voltage as a result of variation in reactive power. These two parameters (voltage and frequency) determine the quality of the system and hence impose a constraint on the system such that the system needs to maintain the deviations in these parameters within certain limits. Oscillation around the steady state values may result in system instability and may destroy the balance in real and reactive power. Thus a control is necessary to control the changes in the frequency and hence prevent the system from entering into an unstable state.

Any mismatch between generation and demand causes the system frequency to deviate from scheduled value. Thus high frequency deviation may lead to system collapse. This necessitates an accurate and fast acting controller to maintain constant nominal frequency. The limitations of the conventional controls viz., Integral, PI, and PID are slow and lack of efficiency in handling system non linearities.

Many works have been conducted in the field of neural control. In [1] an accurate simulation of a heating coil is considered for the comparison of the performance of a PI controller and a neural network, which is trained to predict the steady-state output of the PI controller, and a combination of PI and neural network. It is observed that the neural network when trained as a PI controller after a training of approximately 500 epochs, considerably reduced the average error between the set point and actual temperature to a level below that observed with the PI controller alone. Neural networks can be employed to develop a model reference adaptive control, as in [2] where an MRAC has been employed to supervise the control of a chemical plant with significant process delay. In [3] Neural network based PI controllers and PID controllers are designed and simulated so as to increase the accuracy of position in a pneumatic servomotor. Neural Network based PI and PID controllers have a simple structure which makes them easier to be implemented and enhances performance with a better efficiency than its individual working has been shown. In [4] Khepera mobile robot is considered in the case of obstacle avoidance behavior and conclusions that fuzzy is efficient for realization of simple tasks whereas neural networks have a better learning ability.

Most of the industrial processes today implement PI or PID controllers in order to achieve steady state or dynamic control over the process, but the these controllers have a high rise time, high settling time and also a high peak even when the settings are optimum and the gain is adjusted to its critical value. The main aim of the paper is to display the superior efficiency of neural controllers over conventional PI controllers through an application in the field of power system frequency control. The paper boasts of the simplicity and efficiency of the technique.

Here we observe the effectiveness of the ANN applied techniques. The results of ANN being applied to the ALFC have been really appreciable in the sense that,

- The transient dip has been reduced to a great extent (almost halved) in both cases, two area as well as a single area system.
- The time required for the system to achieve system frequency has also decreased

The paper is organized as follows, section 2 discusses the conventional approach to the problem, section 3 discusses a neural approach to the problem and Section 4 discusses the results of the simulation.

2   Automatic Load Frequency Control

2.1   The Single Area Model

The ALFC loop shown in fig.1 (a) is called the primary ALFC loop. It achieves the primary goal of real power balance by adjusting the turbine output ΔPm to match the change in load demand ΔPO.

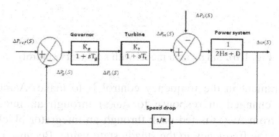

Fig. 1(a). Single area model

The transfer function of the system is given as [5]: -

$$KG(s)H(s) = \frac{1}{R} \frac{1}{(2Hs + D)(1 + \tau_g s)(1 + \tau_T s)}$$

$$\frac{\Delta\omega(s)}{-\Delta P_L(s)} = \frac{(1 + \tau_g s)(1 + \tau_T s)}{(2Hs + D)(1 + \tau_g s)(1 + \tau_T s) + \frac{1}{R}}$$

$$\Delta\omega(s) = -\Delta P_0(s)T(s)$$
$$\Delta\omega_{ss} = (-\Delta P_0)R$$

The above equation gives the steady state value of the frequency drift following a load disturbance and it can be inferred that the system's new operating frequency will be less than the nominal value due to the load disturbance. However from the stability point of view, the frequency drift should be brought down to zero or to a level acceptable for stable operation and this is done with the help of a secondary loop shown below.

2.2   The Single Area Model with Secondary Control

The ALFC loop shown in Fig. 1(a) achieves the primary goal of real power balance by adjusting the turbine output ΔPm to match the change in load demand ΔPo. But a change in load results in a steady state frequency deviation. The restoration of the frequency to the nominal value requires an additional control loop called the supplementary loop. This objective is met by using an integral controller which makes the frequency deviation zero. The ALFC with the supplementary loop is generally called the AGC. The block diagram of an AGC is shown figure 1(b).

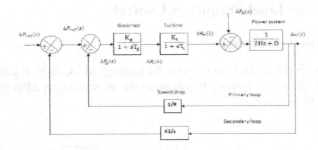

Fig. 1(b). Single area model with secondary control

The main requirement in the frequency control is to make- Δω=0. So the speed changer setting is changed in response to Δω(s) through an integrator. For this purpose the signal from Δω(s) is fed back through an integrator block (1/s) to adjust ΔPref so as to bring the frequency to the steady state value. Because of the secondary loop the steady state value of Δω(s)=0. Thus the integral action results in automatic adjustment of ΔPref so as to make Δω=0. This action is rightly called Automatic Generation Control.

The transfer function with the integral group is given below [5],

$$\omega = \frac{1}{D + \frac{1}{R}}[\Delta P_{Ref} - \Delta P_O]$$

2.3   Two Area Model

he model is similar to the Single Area System but with the additional input of ΔP_{12}. Suppose there is a change in load (ΔPo) in area1, the frequencies of the two area systems settle to a steady state value.

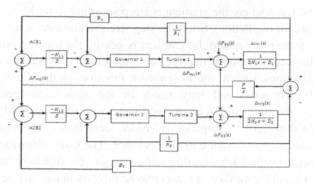

Fig. 1(c). Two area system with secondary control

3 Neural Control

3.1 Neural Networks

A neural network is a mathematical model of the brain that is inspired from the working of a biological neural network and consists of a cluster of neural neurons. Neural networks are applied in the field of robotics, data mining, recognition and control and to many other problems that involve high dimensionality, high degree of non-linearity and a complex relation between the input and output.

Here we train the neural network to behave as a PI controller. The neural network takes the load change as the input and produces an output control signal that is required to stabilize the frequency oscillations. The number of neurons in the hidden layer is determined by observing the MSE.

3.2 Levenberg Marquardt Algorithm

The Levenberg–Marquardt algorithm [6,7], which was independently developed by Kenneth Levenberg and Donald Marquardt, provides a numerical solution to the problem of minimizing a nonlinear function. It is fast and has stable convergence. In the artificial neural-networks field, this algorithm is suitable for training small- and medium-sized problems.

Many other methods have already been developed for neural-networks training. The steepest descent algorithm, also known as the error backpropagation (EBP) algorithm [8,9], dispersed the dark clouds on the field of artificial neural networks and could be regarded as one of the most significant breakthroughs for training neural networks. Many improvements have been made to EBP [10,11,12,13], but these improvements are relatively minor [14,15,16,17,18]. The EBP algorithm is still widely used today; however, it is also known as an inefficient algorithm because of its slow convergence. There are two main reasons for the slow convergence: the first reason is that its step sizes should be adequate to the gradients. Logically, small step sizes should be taken where the gradient is steep so as not to rattle out of the required minima (because of oscillation). So, if the step size is a constant, it needs to be chosen small. Then, in the place where the gradient is gentle, the training process would be very slow. The second reason is that the curvature of the error surface may not be the same in all directions, such as the Rosenbrock function, so the classic "error valley" problem [19] may exist and may result in the slow convergence. The slow convergence of the steepest descent method can be greatly improved by the Gauss–Newton algorithm [20]. Using second-order derivatives of error function to "naturally" evaluate the curvature of error surface, The Gauss–Newton algorithm can find proper step sizes for each direction and converge very fast; especially, if the error function has a quadratic surface, it can converge directly in the first iteration. But this improvement only happens when the quadratic approximation of error function is reasonable. Otherwise, the Gauss–Newton algorithm would be mostly divergent.

The Levenberg–Marquardt algorithm blends the steepest descent method and the Gauss–Newton algorithm. Fortunately, it inherits the speed advantage of the Gauss–Newton algorithm and the stability of the steepest descent method. It's more robust than the Gauss–Newton algorithm, because in many cases it can converge well even if the error surface is much more complex than the quadratic situation. Although the Levenberg–Marquardt algorithm tends to be a bit slower than Gauss–Newton algorithm (in convergent situation), it converges much faster than the steepest descent method. The basic idea of the Levenberg–Marquardt algorithm is that it performs a combined training process: around the area with complex curvature, the Levenberg–Marquardt algorithm switches to the steepest descent algorithm, until the local curvature is proper to make a quadratic approximation; then it approximately becomes the Gauss–Newton algorithm, which can speed up the convergence significantly.

Table 1. Update rules for various algorithms

Algorithms	Update Rules	Convergence	Computation Complexity
EBP algorithm	$w_{k+1}=w_k-\alpha g_k$	Stable, slow	Gradient
Newton algorithm	$w_{k+1}=w_k-H_k^{-1}g_k$	Unstable, fast	Gradient & Hessian
Gauss-Newton algorithm	$w_{k+1}=w_k-(J_k^T J_k)^{-1}J_k e_k$	Unstable, fast	Jacobian
Levenberg-Marquardt algorithm	$w_{k+1}=w_k-(J_k^T J_k+\mu I)^{-1}J_k e_k$	Stable, fast	Jacobian
NBN algorithm	$w_{k+1}=w_k-Q_k^{-1}g_k$	Stable, fast	Quasi Hessian

Table 2. Comparison of training algorithms

Algorithms	Convergence Rate (%)	Average Iteration	Average Time
EBP algorithm(α=0)	100	1646.52	320.6
Newton algorithm(α=100)	79	171.48	36.5
Gauss-Newton algorithm	3	4.33	1.2
Levenberg-Marquardt algorithm	100	6.18	1.6

The comparison of various algorithms is presented in Table 1and 2. One may notice that: (1) for the EBP algorithm, the larger the training constant α is, the faster and less stable the training process will be; (2) Levenberg–Marquardt is much faster than the EBP algorithm and more stable than the Gauss–Newton algorithm.

For more complex parity-N problems, the Gauss–Newton method cannot converge at all, and the EBP algorithm also becomes more inefficient to find the solution, while the Levenberg–Marquardt algorithm may lead to successful solutions.

4   Results and Simulation

The following figures demonstrate the models and their simulation results. A reduction in the transient dip and a reduction in peak time can be observed in case of a single area as well as a 2 area system. Fig 2(a) displays a model for comparing the frequency response of a neural control and that of a PI control in a single area system and Fig 2(b) displays the simulation results of the model of a single area system. Fig 4 (c) represents a 2 area system where Fig 2 (d) displays neural control in a 2 area system and Fig 2 (e) displays the simulation results of the 2 area system.

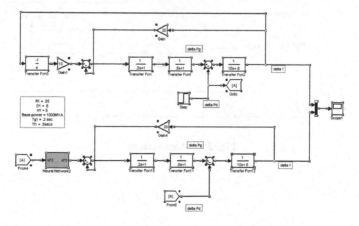

Fig. 2(a). Neural control in a single area system

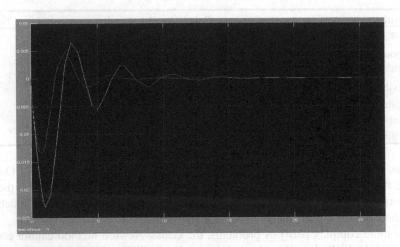

Fig. 2(b). Frequency response of a single area system

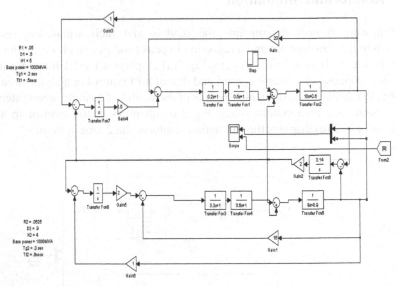

Fig. 2(c). Area system

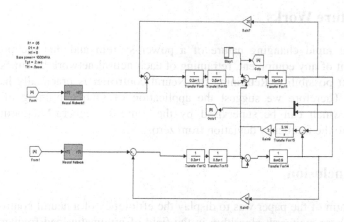

Fig. 2(d). :Neural Control in a 2 area system

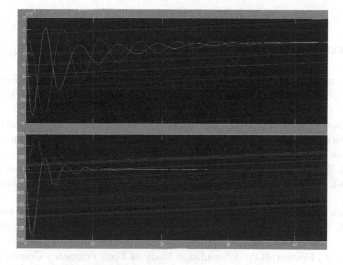

Fig. 2(e). Frequency response of a 2 area

Table 3 summarizes the decrease in Peak time and settling time and also a reduction in transient dip of frequency. Through neural control we have been able to achieve 40% reduction in settling time and 10-30% reduction in peak time.

Table 3. Comparison between a PI and Neural controller

	Peak Time	Settling time	Peak	Load
PI control	1 sec	16.5 sec	-0.024	.33
Neural control	.85 sec	10 sec	-0.0134	.33
PI controller	1 sec	16 sec	-0.0375	.54
Neural controller	.7 sec	9.5 sec	-0.0222	.54

5   Future Works

Due to the rapid changing nature of a power system and due the possibility of replacement of any equipment, retraining of each neural network becomes a practical and evident possibility. Retraining the Neural controller is practically harassing for the users. Therefore we suggest the application of Online training of the neural controller which can be supervised by the same Levenberg-Maquardt algorithm according to the frequency deviation from zero.

6   Conclusion

The main aim of the paper was to display the efficiency of a neural controller trained with levenberg-maquardt algorithm in the field of automatic load frequency control. The results achieved are truly appreciable and inspire further work in this particular sector.

References

1. Anderson, C.W., Hittle, D.C., Katz, A.D., Matt Kretchmar, R.: Reinforcement Learning. Neural Networks and PI Control Applied to a Heating Coil, Colorado State University (2000)
2. Douratsos, I., Barry Gomm, J.: Neural Network based model reference Adaptive Control for processes with time delay. International Journal of Information and Systems Sciences 3(1), 161–179 (2007)
3. Hassan, M.Y., Kothapalli, G.: Comparison Between Neural Network Based PI and PID Controllers. In: 2010 7th International Multi-Conference on Systems, Signals and Devices (2010)
4. Godjevac, J.: Comparitive study of fuuzy control, neural network control and neuro-fuzzy control, Swiss Federal Institute of Technology, Technical Report no. 103/95 (February 1995)
5. Usman, A., Divakar, B.P.: A Simulation Study of Load Frequency Control of Single and Two Area Systems, Department of Electrical and Electronics Engineering, vol. 3, pp. 161–179. Reva Institute of Technology and Management (2007)
6. Levenberg, K.: A method for the solution of certain problems in least squares. Quarterly of Applied Mathematics 5, 164–168 (1944)
7. Marquardt, D.: An algorithm for least-squares estimation of nonlinear parameters. SIAM Journal on Applied Mathematics 11(2), 431–441 (1963)
8. Rumelhart, D.E., Hinton, G.E., Williams, R.J.: Learning representations by back-propagating errors. Nature 323, 533–536 (1986)
9. Wilamowski, B.M., Torvik, L.: Modification of gradient computation in the back-propagation algorithm. In: Artificial Neural Networks in Engineering (ANNIE 1993), November 14-17, St. Louis, MO (1993)
10. Andersen, T.J., Wilamowski, B.M.: A modified regression algorithm for fast one layer neural network training. In: World Congress of Neural Networks, Washington, DC, July 17-21, vol. 1, pp. 687–690 (1995)

11. Wilamowski, B.M.: Neural networks and fuzzy systems. In: Chaps. 124.1 to 124.8 in The ElectronicHandbook, pp. 1893–1914. CRC Press, Boca Raton (1996)
12. Wilamowski, B.M., Chen, Y., Malinowski, A.: Efficient algorithm for training neural networks with one hidden layer. In: 1999 International Joint Conference on Neural Networks (IJCNN 1999), Washington, DC, July 10-16, pp. 1725–1728 (1999); #295 Session: 5.1
13. Wilamowski, B.M.: Neural networks and fuzzy systems. In: Bishop, R.R. (ed.) Mechatronics Handbook, ch. 32, pp. 33-1–32-26. CRC Press, Boca Raton (2002)
14. Wilamowski, B., Hunter, D., Malinowski, A.: Solving parity-n problems with feedforward neural network. In: Proceedings of the IJCNN 2003 International Joint Conference on Neural Networks, Portland, OR, July 20-23, pp. 2546–2551 (2003)
15. Yu, H., Wilamowski, B.M.: C++ implementation of neural networks trainer. In: 13th International Conference on Intelligent Engineering Systems (INES 2009), Barbados, April 16-18 (2009)
16. Wilamowski, B.M.: Neural network architectures and learning algorithms. IEEE Industrial Electronics Magazine 3(4), 56–63 (2009)
17. Yu, H., Wilamowski, B.M.: C++ implementation of neural networks trainer. In: 13th International Conference on Intelligent Engineering Systems (INES 2009), Barbados, April 16-18 (2009)
18. Osborne, M.R.: Fisher's method of scoring. International Statistical Review 86, 271–286 (1992)
19. Werbos, P.J.: Back-propagation: Past and future. In: Proceedings of International Conference on NeuralNetworks, San Diego, CA, vol. 1, pp. 343–354 (1988)

RNN Based Solar Radiation Forecasting Using Adaptive Learning Rate

Ajay Pratap Yadav, Avanish Kumar, and Laxmidhar Behera

Department of Electrical Engineering
Indian Institute of Technology, Kanpur, India
{ajaypratapyadav,avanishkumar007}@gmail.com, lbehera@iitk.ac.in

Abstract. The estimation of solar irradiation data is very important for renewable energy and solar energy systems applications. The forecasts can be used to predict the output power of photovoltaic systems installed in power systems and control the output of other generators to meet the electricity demand. In this paper, a Recurrent Neural Network(RNN) model is used to forecast the Daily, Mean Monthly and Hourly Solar Irradiations using the recorded meteorological data. Here, an adaptive learning rate is proposed for the RNN. The results of the RNN is compared with that of a Multi Layer perceptron(MLP). It is found that the RNN with the adaptive learning rate gives a better performance than the conventional feed forward network.

Keywords: Adaptive Learning Rate, Recurrent Neural network(RNN), Solar Radiation forecasting, Time Series Prediction.

1 Introduction

The amount of energy that the sun delivers to earth is many times more than all the world's power needs. It doesn't give off carbon dioxide emissions and its free. This has encouraged a lot of research in the field of solar energy. The cumulative installed capacity of solar photovoltaic reached roughly 65 gigawatts at the end of 2011 from 1.5 gigawatts in 2000[1]. Therefore, solar radiation forecasting has become of prime importance as it helps in predicting the output of photovoltaic systems and plays a huge role in their long term and short term planning.

There has been a lot of research work where Artificial Neural Networks is used to forecast solar irradiation values from meteorological data [4–6]. If we compare the conventional algorithms based on local linear models, ANN is a better option as it provides nonlinear parametric models. Authors in [5] used a Multi layer perceptron and an ad hoc time series pre-processing to develop a methodology for the daily prediction of global solar radiation on a horizontal surface tracking the sun. Its performance is better as compared to other predictors like ARIMA, Bayesian inference, Markov chains and k-Nearest-Neighbors predictors. Authors in [7] used Radial Basis Function (RBF) networks for daily global solar radiation data prediction from sunshine duration and air temperature.

B.K. Panigrahi et al. (Eds.): SEMCCO 2013, Part II, LNCS 8298, pp. 442–452, 2013.

1.1   Solar Irradiation

Solar irradiation is the measure incident of total amount of solar radiation transmitted to the surface of the Earth's atmosphere in a given unit of time. It is expressed in watt*hours/m². The solar irradiation can be represented in three ways.

(a) Direct Normal Irradiation(DNI)
(b) Diffuse Horizontal Irradiation(DHI)
(c) Global Horizontal Irradiation(GHI)

Direct Normal Irradiance is the amount of solar radiation received per unit area by a surface that is always held perpendicular to the rays that come in a straight line from the direction of the sun. While in Diffuse Horizontal Irradiance, the radiation scattered by molecules and particles is considered and that need not arrive on a direct path from the sun, it comes equally from all directions. Global Horizontal Irradiance is the total amount of radiation received per unit area by a surface horizontal to the ground. It is composed of both Direct Normal Irradiance and Diffuse Horizontal Irradiance, can be expressed as

$$GHI = DNI * cos(\theta) + DHI \qquad (1)$$

where θ is the angle between the incoming sun rays to the normal to the surface.

1.2   Why Solar Irradiation Forecasting Is Needed?

The forecasted values of solar irradiation can be used for variety of applications. Short term forecasting can be used to predict the output of the photovoltaic systems. This can further be used for controlling the output of other generators in the grid or planning the installation of new systems. Forecasted monthly mean data of solar radiation is needed for calculating the long term performance of solar energy systems. The forecasted results can also be used to increase the integration limit of the renewable energy systems into the electric grid. Figure 1

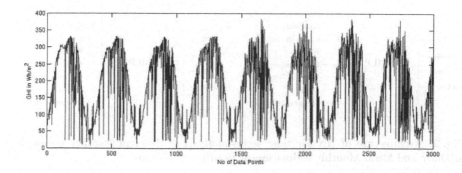

Fig. 1. Variation of GHI with time(days)

shows the variation of GHI at a certain time against time(days). It can be observed here that the variation of GHI follows a pattern. Therefore, the irradiation values is not entirely unpredictable.

2   Problem Formulation

The meteorological studies suggest that solar irradiation reaching earth depends on other weather parameters like temperature, humidity, rainfall etc [4]. So, we can use neural networks and train it to give solar irradiation values as output while feeding these weather parameters as inputs. As a result, we will have a model which gives us solar irradiation values if these weather data is given to it. In this paper, we will use the old recorded data of solar irradiations and different weather parameters and develop such a neural network model. Once we have such a model, we can even forecast the future solar irradiation values provided we have the future values of different weather parameters. Therefore, for solar irradiation forecasting we need to first use the recorded data of these weather parameters and perform a time series analysis to get their future values and then give it to the neural network model to predict the solar radiation values.

2.1   Data

The meteorological data which has been used here were recorded in Rajasthan, India. The site is located at 26.487475 latitude, 73.12122 longitude and having an elevation of 237 meter from the sea level. We have a total 13 years of data i.e. from Jan 1999 to Feb 2013 recorded on a half an hour basis. The meteorological parameters used are day, month, year, time (UTC +5.5), temperature (°C), relative humidity (%), wind speed (m/s), wind direction (deg), dew point temperature (°C), rainfall in kg/m^2 and atmospheric pressure (hPa) that were finally used to estimate DNI,GHI and DIF in Wh/m^2.

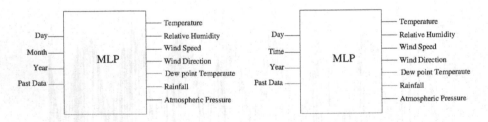

Fig. 2. Architecture of NN for time series analysis of different weather parameters (a)Daily and Mean Monthly estimation(b) Hourly estimations

2.2   Model Development

The meteorological parameters mentioned before are used as inputs to the neural networks to predict the DNI,GHI and DIF. We use the old values of these parameters to form a training data set for the neural networks. Once the training is over, we can perform the forecasting. But for forecasting, these inputs must also be predicted. So, a separate time series prediction is done for these input parameters using feed forward neural networks(MLP). For this time series prediction, we have used a set of MLP networks for each parameter with the architecture shown in fig 2. For our calculations, we have used a MLP network with the structure of [8-10-10-1] i.e. 8 inputs, 2 hidden layers with 10 neurons and 1 output. As shown in figure 2, we give day, month, year and the parameter's past 5 values as inputs to the MLP to get the future values of the parameter we want to know. Therefore, in this way we calculate the future values of different parameters and use it for the solar irradiation forecasting. In our problem, we will feed these forecasted weather parameters to a recurrent neural network with an adaptive learning rate to get the solar irradiation values. We will also use a separate MLP network in place of the RNN for comparison.

In this paper, we have made three kinds of forecasting. First, the daily solar irradiation values corresponding to 11-12am for the entire year of 2012. Second, the hourly solar irradiation values for the first three month of 2012. Finally, the monthly mean values of solar irradiation for each month of 2012 is also calculated. The number of hidden layers and number of neuron were chosen on the basis of hit and trial. The monthly mean solar irradiation is calculated by taking the monthly average of daily solar irradiation. Since the desired values are known, the performance of the models can be analyzed and compared.

2.3   Performance Evaluation

The performance of the models were evaluated by three statistical indices, i.e. the coefficient of determination (R^2), root mean square error $(RMSE)$, and the mean absolute error (MAE). The R^2 is a measure of how successful the model evaluation is in explaining the variation of the data. The value of RMSE gives information on the short term performance of the correlations. The MAE gives the absolute value of the bias errors. The lower value of RMSE and MABE shows better estimation.

Let us assume N is the number of test data. If $e_1, e_2....e_N$ is the error in the test data sets then,

$$RMSE = \sqrt{\frac{e_1^2 + e_2^2 + ...e_N^2}{N}} \tag{2}$$

$$MAE = \frac{|e_1| + |e_2| + ...|e_N|}{N} \tag{3}$$

$$R^2 = \frac{\sum_{i=1}^{N}(y_i - \overline{y}_d)^2}{\sum_{i=1}^{N}(y_i - \overline{y}_d)^2 + \sum_{i=1}^{N}(y_i - y_{d_i})^2} \tag{4}$$

where $\overline{y}_d$ is the mean of desired data set.

3   Recurrent Neural Networks

Recurrent Neural Network (RNN) is a class of neural network with feedbacks. In such a network, the next state is a function of the current input together with the present state of the network. Thus, these networks have some memory. This feature of RNN can be utilized in solar forecasting calculations. Figure 3 shows us the feedbacks in a RNN. This means that the current output depends upon previous values of output.

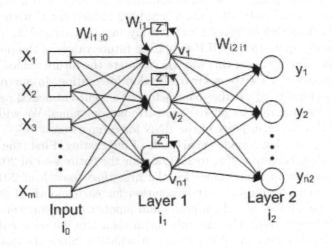

Fig. 3. The structure of RNN used

3.1   Recurrent Neural Network Learning Algorithm

In figure 3, a three-layered recurrent neural network is shown which comprises an input layer (i_0), a hidden layer(i_1) and an output layer (i_2). The objective of the algorithm is to adjusts the weights $W_{i_2 i_1}$ and $W_{i_1 i_0}$ such that the cost function $E(t)$ is minimized. The instantaneous cost function in error can be expressed as

$$E(t) = \sum_{i_2=1}^{n_2} E_{i_2}(t) = \frac{1}{2} \sum_{i_2=1}^{n_2} (y_{i_2}^d(t) - y_{i_2}(t))^2 \tag{5}$$

The input to the i_1^{th} neuron of hidden layer is given by

$$h_{i_1}(t) = \sum_{i_o=1}^{m} W_{i_1 i_o}(t) x_{i_0}(t) + W_{i_1} v_{i_1}(t-1) \tag{6}$$

where v_{i_1} is the output of i_1^{th} neuron of hidden layer given by

$$v_{i_1}(t) = \psi(h_{i_1}(t)) = \frac{1}{1 + e^{-h_{i_1}(t)}} \tag{7}$$

Here $\psi(.)$ is the sigmoidal activation function. Now, input to the i_2^{th} neuron of output layer is

$$h_{i_2}(t) = \sum_{i_1=1}^{n_1} W_{i_2 i_1}(t) v_{i_1}(t) \tag{8}$$

The final output of the i_2^{th} neuron of output layer is given by

$$y_{i_2}(t) = v_{i_2}(t) = \frac{1}{1 + e^{-h_{i_2}(t)}} \tag{9}$$

Update of the Weights Connecting the Output Layer and Hidden Layer. The gradient descent algorithm can be used to update the weights as [9]

$$W_{i_2 i_1}(t+1) = W_{i_2 i_1}(t) + \eta \delta_{i_2}(t) v_{i_1}(t) \tag{10}$$

where,

$$\delta_{i_2}(t) = \left[y_{i_2}^d(t) - y_{i_2}(t) \right] \times y_{i_2}(t) \times (1 - y_{i_2}(t)) \tag{11}$$

ans η is the learning rate.

Recurrent Weights Update. Similarly, applying the gradient descent algorithm will give

$$W_{i_1}(t+1) = W_{i_1}(t) + \eta v_{i_1}(t)(1 - v_{i_1}(t)) v_i(t-1) \sum_{i_2=1}^{n_2} (\delta_{i_2} W_{i_2 i_1}(t)) \tag{12}$$

Update of the Weights Connecting the Input Layer and Hidden Layer

$$W_{i_1 i_0}(t+1) = W_{i_1 i_0}(t) + \eta P(t) \sum_{i_2=1}^{n_2} (\delta_{i_2}(t) W_{i_2 i_1}(t)) \tag{13}$$

where $P(t) = \frac{\delta v_{i_1}(t)}{\delta W_{i_1 i_0}(t)}$ and it can be shown that

$$
\begin{aligned}
P(t) &= \frac{\delta v_{i_1}(t)}{\delta W_{i_1 i_0}(t)} = \frac{\delta v_{i_1}(t)}{\delta h_{i_1}(t)} \times \frac{\delta h_{i_1}(t)}{\delta W_{i_1 i_0}(t)} \\
&= v_{i_1}(t)(1 - v_{i_1}(t)) \times \left[x_{i_o}(t) + W_{i_1}(t) \frac{\delta v_{i_1}(t-1)}{\delta W_{i_1 i_0}(t)} \right] \\
&= v_{i_1}(t)(1 - v_{i_1}(t)) \times [x_{i_o}(t) + W_{i_1}(t) P(t-1)] \tag{14}
\end{aligned}
$$

Eqn 14 is the recursive relation in $P(t)$ and $P(t-1)$. It can be implemented in real time. The learning rate η is considered to be fixed in this derivation. Next, an adaptive learning rate will be derived which will replace the constant value here in this derivation.

3.2 Recurrent Neural Network with an Adaptive Learning Rate

In [8], authors have proposed an adaptive learning rate for a feed forward network. Here, it is observed that a similar adaptive learning rate can also be derived for the recurrent neural network.Therefore, using the results in [8]

$$
\begin{aligned}
\mathbf{W}_{i_2 i_1}(t+1) &= \mathbf{W}_{i_2 i_1}(t) + \mu \dot{\mathbf{W}}_{i_2 i_1}(t) \\
&= \mathbf{W}_{i_2 i_1}(t) + \left(\mu \frac{||\mathbf{e}||^2}{||\mathbf{J}^T \mathbf{e}||^2} \right) \mathbf{J}^T \mathbf{e}
\end{aligned}
\tag{15}
$$

So, the adaptive learning rate for the RNN will be

$$
\eta_a = \mu \frac{||\mathbf{e}||^2}{||\mathbf{J}^T \mathbf{e}||^2}
\tag{16}
$$

where $\mathbf{e} = [y_d^1 - y^1, y_d^2 - y^2, ...]^T$ and

$$
\mathbf{J} = \frac{\delta \mathbf{y}}{\delta \mathbf{W}_{i_2 i_1}}
$$

here, μ is selected heuristically and in order to avoid numerical instability.

4 Estimation of Solar Irradiations

4.1 Daily and Mean Monthly Solar Irradiations

For the daily solar irradiation prediction, we have chosen the interval 11-12am for which we will make the forecasting. As the meteorological data is from Jan 1999 to Feb 2013, a subset of data from 11-12am is taken for daily irradiation calculation. Therefore, the data corresponding to 11:48am from Jan 1999 to December 2011 is taken to build the input-output data set for training and the forecasting is made for the year 2012. Therefore, we have 4748 number of input-output data for training while 366 number of test points for forecasting. The Monthly Mean solar irradiation is calculated by taking the monthly average of Daily solar irradiation. Since the desired values are known, the performance of the models can be analysed and compared.

Simulation Results. In this paper, the RNN which gives the final solar irradiation values has the structure of [7-15-3] i.e. 7 inputs, 15 neurons in the hidden layer and 3 outputs. For comparison we have also used a MLP with the structure of [7-10-10-3] in place of the RNN. Figure 4 and 5 show the GHI forecasting for an entire year for an interval of 11-12 am by RNN and MLP networks respectively. Figure 6 compares the monthly mean solar irradiation calculation. In both the cases we can observe that the performance of RNN with an adaptive learning rate is better than that of MLP. Table 1 compares the performance on the basis of various indices.

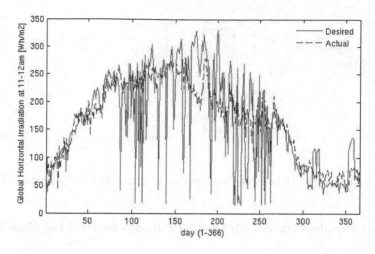

Fig. 4. Daily Global Horizontal Irradiation(GHI) at 11-12am $[Wh/m^2]$ using RNN

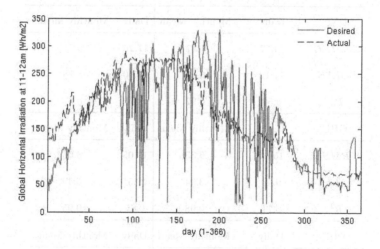

Fig. 5. Daily Global Horizontal Irradiation(GHI) at 11-12am $[Wh/m^2]$ using MLP

4.2 Estimation of Hourly Solar Irradiation

For the hourly forecasting, first the data is converted from half hourly basis to hourly basis by down sampling by a factor of 2. We have calculated the hourly irradiation of each month separately. For example, if we consider the month of january, the input to the RNN is the subset of the whole data which contain the irradiation values of january month only from 1999 to 2011. The total number of training data for the month with 31 days were 9672 and the number of testing data were 744.

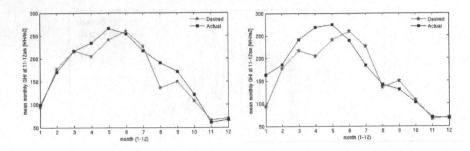

Fig. 6. Mean Monthly global solar radiation at 11-12am $[Wh/m^2]$ using (a) RNN (b) MLP

Table 1. Comparison between RNN and MLP Results for Daily and Mean Monthly Irradiations

	RNN [7-15-3]		MLP [7-10-10-3]	
DNI	Daily	Monthly Mean	Daily	Monthly Mean
%RMSE	14.57	6.37	17.26	9.71
%MAE	11.12	6.09	13.60	8.28
R^2	0.58	0.92	0.52	0.87
GHI	Daily	Monthly Mean	Daily	Monthly Mean
%RMSE	15.54	5.35	17.05	8.66
%MAE	9.42	3.94	12.51	6.49
R^2	0.71	0.98	0.65	0.95
DIF	Daily	Monthly Mean	Daily	Monthly Mean
%RMSE	14.94	4.47	16.45	9.4
%MAE	10.04	3.36	12.03	7.59
R^2	0.67	0.98	0.66	0.95

Simulation Results. The RNN which gives the final solar irradiation values has the structure of [7-15-3]. For comparison we have also used a different MLP with the structure of [7-10-10-3] in place of the RNN. Figure 7 shows the hourly solar irradiation forecasting for all the 31 days of January 2012. Figure 8 shows the forecasting for a random day of January. Note that the peaks in the figure 7 represent one day of the month while figure 8 is a zoomed version of one such

Table 2. Results of Hourly Solar Irradiations using RNN [7-15-3]

	DNI			GHI			DIF		
	%RMSE	%MAE	R^2	%RMSE	%MAE	R^2	%RMSE	%MAE	R^2
Jan	14.15	7.18	0.71	9.30	5.05	0.90	10.38	7.12	0.86
Feb	9.45	4.43	0.91	8.49	4.03	0.92	6.67	4.2	0.90
Mar	11.38	5.50	0.81	13.32	7.73	0.82	8.41	4.72	0.88

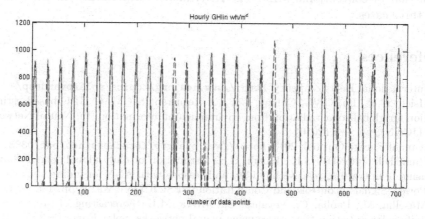

Fig. 7. Hourly Solar irradiation forecasting for 31 days of January $[Wh/m^2]$

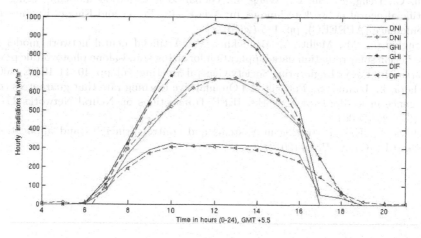

Fig. 8. Hourly Solar irradiation $[Wh/m^2]$ forecasting for a random day of January against time

peak. Table 2 shows the performance of RNN for the first three months on the basis of various indices.

5   Conclusion

In this paper, a single layer Recurrent Neural Network(RNN) is used to estimate the different solar irradiations i.e. Direct Normal Irradiance (DNI), Global Horizontal Irradiance (GHI) and Diffuse Horizontal Irradiance (DHI). Daily, Mean monthly and hourly values of the irradiance are predicted using the meteorological data of different weather parameters. The results of [9] regarding the adaptive learning rate has been extended to the recurrent neural network. The performance of the proposed RNN with the adaptive learning rate is compared with that of conventional MLP. The RNN model outperforms the MLP in all the three cases.

References

1. International Energy Agency, http://www.iea.org/topics/solarpvandcsp/
2. Hsieh, C.Y., Lu, C.W., Chiang, C.T.: A Recurrent S CMAC GBF based estimation for global solar radiation from environmental information. In: Neural Networks (IJCNN), pp. 1–5 (2010)
3. Annual Energy Outlook 2013, http://www.eia.gov/forecasts/aeo/pdf/0383.pdf
4. Rani, B.I., Rao, D.V.S.K., Ilango, G.S.: Estimation of daily global solar radiation using temperature, relative humidity and seasons with ANN for indian stations. In: Power, Signals, Controls and Computation (EPSCICON), vol. 1, pp. 1–6 (2012)
5. Musellia, M., Paolia, C., Voyanta, C., Niveta, M.L.: Forecasting of prepro-cessed daily solar radiation time series using neural networks. Solar Energy 84(12), 2146–2160 (2010)
6. Liu, C., Deng, F., Su, G., Wang, Z.: Global solar radiation modeling using the artificial neural network technique. In: Asia-Pacific Power and Energy Engineering Conference (APPEEC), pp. 1–5 (2010)
7. Menghanem, M., Mellit, A., Bendekhis, M.: Artificial neural network model for prediction solar radiation data: application for sizing stand-alone photovoltaic power system. In: Power Engineering Society General Meeting, vol, pp. 40–44. IEEE (2005)
8. Behera, L., Kumar, S., Patnaik, A.: On adaptive learning rate that guarantees convergence in feedforward networks. IEEE Transactions on Neural Networks 17(5), 1116–1125 (2006)
9. Behera, L., Kar, I.: Intelligent Systems and control principles and applications. Oxford University Press (2010)

Energy Efficient Aggregation in Wireless Sensor Networks for Multiple Base Stations

Nagarjuna Reddy Busireddy and Siba K. Udgata

School of Computer and Information Sciences
University of Hyderabad, India, 500046
nagarjuna.busireddy@gmail.com, udgatacs@uohyd.ernet.in

Abstract. Data aggregation is essential for wireless sensor networks (WSN) where energy resources are limited. Due to scarce energy resources, construction of data aggregation tree in WSN from group of source nodes to sink nodes with less energy consumption is challenging. In this work, we propose a method to determine the aggregation tree with less energy consumption using Artificial Bee Colony (ABC) algorithm, which is a swarm intelligence technique. We compute the fitness (energy consumption of whole network) by considering multiple algorithms in the same network and then evolving the solution until fitness value is minimum. Our preliminary results suggest that, under investigated scenarios, the usage of ABC algorithm for aggregation in WSN with multiple base stations can achieve energy savings over Shortest path tree data aggregation and Ant colony data aggregation with multiple base stations.

Keywords: WSN, Aggregation, Energy Efficient, ABC Algorithm.

1 Introduction

Wireless Sensor Network (WSN) consists of large number of sensor nodes, where each node is connected to one or more sensor nodes. Each node contains a radio transceiver, a micro controller, an electronic circuit for interfacing with the sensors and an energy source. WSNs have a wide range of potential applications to industry, science, transportation, civil infrastructure and security. Power supplies of WSNs are limited and the positions of the sensor nodes are usually not predetermined and deployed randomly in inaccessible geographic areas and disaster locations [5]. The applications like forest monitoring, wild life monitoring and battlefield surveillance etc. can not replace the batteries by reaching the sensor node. This implies that the sensor nodes are expected to perform sensing and communication for long time with no maintenance or reorganization. The lifetime of a sensor network can increase by using energy efficiently. The energy consumption of each and every sensor node in the sensor network can be balanced with the use of multiple base stations.

The sensor nodes monitor a geographical area and collect sensory information. Sensory information is communicated to the base station through wireless hop by hop transmissions. To conserve energy this information is aggregated at

B.K. Panigrahi et al. (Eds.): SEMCCO 2013, Part II, LNCS 8298, pp. 453–464, 2013.
© Springer International Publishing Switzerland 2013

intermediate sensor nodes by applying a suitable aggregation function on the received data. Aggregation reduces the amount of network traffic which helps to reduce energy consumption on sensor nodes [4]. Optimal aggregation tree problem is NP-Hard [7] which is equivalent to Steiner tree and weighted set cover [1] problems. Approximation algorithms for finding optimal aggregation are Greedy Incremental Tree (GIT), Shortest Paths Tree (SPT) and Center at Nearest Source (CNS) [4]. The Shortest Path Tree problem is to find the set of edges connecting all nodes such that the sum of the edge lengths from the root to each node is minimized.

Sensor nodes around the base station become bottlenecks and deplete their battery energy much faster than other nodes. A natural solution to such a problem is to have multiple base stations, so that the load is distributed evenly among all nodes [6]. If one of the base station malfunctions due to some reason, the nodes that are connected to the malfunctioned base station will switch to the nearest base station that is working properly.

In this paper, an Artificial Bee Colony(ABC) algorithm is proposed to find data aggregation tree in a WSN for reducing the energy consumption. The intermediate nodes that have more than one children are known as aggregation nodes. The aggregation node will combine data coming from a group of source nodes and transmits it to the nearest base station. With multiple base stations, the energy consumption of sensor nodes in the region is balanced by switching from the current base station to another active base station.

Rest of the paper is organized as follows. sections 2 presents a brief review of the literature. section 3 describes the algorithm and working principle of artificial bee colony algorithm. Experimental setup and results obtained are discussed in section 4 followed by conclusions and future work in section 5.

2   Related Work

Data aggregation is essential for WSN, lot of researchers have made effort on this area. To save energy, the data coming from different sources are aggregated by eliminating redundancy and minimizing the number of transmissions. Minimizing the number of non source nodes in the aggregation tree also minimizes energy consumption in the whole network.

Design of an efficient data aggregation technique with efficient use of the resources can reduce communications among nodes. Most of data aggregation techniques are not designed for large scale WSNs. The application like static time driven monitoring system provides redundant information to the user. For example, temperature information in the field is almost same, it is redundant data. For sending the redundant data to the base station lots of sensors deplete their energy for transmission purpose. A dynamic data aggregation method was proposed for large scale WSN with degree of aggregation based on dynamic decision making [16].

Number of routing protocols for wireless sensor networks have been developed using the principles of swarm intelligence. The natural systems of inspiration from the foraging behaviors of ant and bee colonies, show the desirable interest in context of network routing, and in particular of routing in wireless sensor networks. An extensive survey of these protocols, the general principles of swarm intelligence and its application to the routing is described in [19].

An ant based algorithm is proposed to find an aggregation tree [9]. In this paper, every source is assigned to an ant. Each ant tries to get the path between source and sink. If any ant finds an already existing path, it adds more pheromone to the path and chooses that path for onward transmission. Like this if all ants use the existing path, the energy consumption is less [12] [3]. The results are compared with the Greedy Incremental Tree Algorithm [4], ant-0, ant-1 and ant-2. The ant-0 algorithm works by using extended hop count 0. ant-1 and ant-2 algorithms(ALG) work by using extended hop count 1 and 2 respectively.

One of the main problems to be solved in WSNs operation is the routing problem. The main goal of WSN routing is to prolong the lifetime of the network and prevent connectivity errors by employing aggressive energy management techniques. A routing approach is proposed based on Artificial Bee Colony (ABC) [13] [15] algorithm of which preliminary performance results presented is tested by round based network lifetime. With this test, complexity analysis of the model is also studied. ABC algorithm is utilized to develop the routing strategy for time-based WSN applications by transferring data periodically [20].

3   Artificial Bee Colony Algorithm

Artificial bee colony algorithm is a population based meta-heuristic optimization algorithm, which is inspired by the intelligent foraging behavior of natural honey bee swarm. This algorithm was proposed by Dervis Karaboga [13], later developed by Karaboga and Basturk [10] [11][8]. ABC algorithm is used in WSN like deployment [17] [14], coverage [21], routing [20] etc. ABC algorithm is also used for other engineering applications [18]. Naturally there are three types of bees Employed bees, Onlooker bees and scout bees. In the similar way, ABC also consist 3 types of bees.

3.1   ABC Algorithm Overview

In artificial bee colony, the assumption is that one bee is associated with one food source. Food sources are assumed as solutions. As the food source is having nectar amount as a measurement, solutions are also associated with fitness. Depending on the problem in consideration, the solution with least fitness or maximum fitness is considered as best solution. The sudo code of the ABC is described in Algorithm.1.

Initialization Phase: In the first step, each bee is randomly initialized with a solution. The fitness of each solution is evaluated. The best solution is identified based on the fitness value.

Employed Bee Phase: For each solution have to find the neighboring solution. That means, searching for better solution with in the region of current solution.

Algorithm 1: Pseudo code of ABC

---

generate n_e random solutions $S_1, S_2, ..., S_{n_e}$ [Getting path from each source to the nearest base station];

best_sol := best solution among $S_1, S_2, ..., S_{n_e}$ [Less energy consumption solution among all solutions] ;

while *max cycle number* **do**

    foreach *Employed bee* **do**
        N_e := Generate_Neighboring_Solution(S_e);
        [If neighboring solution not get path to all sources];
        if *(N_e == $\emptyset$)* **then**
            replace S_e with random solution;
        else if *(N_e is better than S_e)* **then**
            S_e := N_e;
            $count_e$:= 0 ;
        end
        $count_e$:= $count_e$ + 1;
    end

    foreach *Onlooker bee* **do**
        o := Roulette_Wheel_Selection($S_1, S_2, ..., S_{n_e}$);
        N_o := Generate_Neighboring_Solution(S_o);
        if *(N_o == $\emptyset$)* **then**
            replace S_o with random solution;
        else if *(N_o is better than S_o)* **then**
            S_o := N_o;
            $count_e$:= 0;
        else
            $count_e$:= $count_e$ + 1;
        end
    end

    foreach *Employed bee* **do**
        if *(S_e is better than best_sol)* **then**
            best_sol := S_e;
        end
    end

    if *($count_e$ $\geq$ maxcount)* **then**
        replace S_e with random solution;
    end
end
return best_sol;

The reason behind finding the neighboring solution is motivated from the nature itself, because in the nature if there is a good food source, there is high probability of another good food source availability. If that neighbor solution is better than the current solution, current solution replaced with the neighbor solution. In case if neighboring solution is unable to generate, replace the solution with random solution.

Onlooker Bee Phase: Instead of finding neighboring solution to every solution, select some solutions randomly. For this purpose, generally either roulette wheel selection, or binary tournament selection was used. For those randomly selected solutions, generate the neighboring solution and store it, instead of replacing as soon as we find better solution. At the end of the iteration, compare the generated neighbor solutions with existing solution. If they are better, replace the old ones with new solutions.

Scout Bee Phase: If a solution is neither worst than neighbor solution nor replaced by random solution, and if this continues after some number of iterations the employed bee associated with that solution becomes scout bee. The scout bee replaces the existing solution with new random generated solution.

3.2 ABC for Data Aggregation in WSN with Multiple Base Stations

Initialization Phase

1. The path between each and every source to the nearest base station by making the overlapping nodes as aggregation nodes is a solution.
2. The path between source and nearest base station was found using Breadth First Search (BFS) technique.
3. The BFS begins at a source node and inspects all the neighboring nodes. Then for each of those neighbor nodes in turn, it inspects their neighbor nodes which were unvisited, and so on. Once it reaches the nearest base station, it will retrieve the path from source to the nearest base station.

Employed Bee Phase

1. Generate the neighboring solution to every solution.
   (a) For each node, check for existed path in one hop neighbors.
   (b) If exists switch to that path.
   (c) Otherwise traverse in previous path.
   (d) This process continues until each source finds its path to the nearest base station.
2. Check whether neighboring solution is better than existing solution.
3. If yes replace the existing solution with neighboring solution.

Onlooker Bee Phase

1. Instead of finding neighboring solution to every solution, select some solutions randomly.
2. To select a solution randomly **roulette wheel selection** has been used.

3. If f_i is the fitness of individual i in the population, its probability of being selected is

$$p_i = \frac{f_i}{\sum_{j=1}^{N} f_j}$$

where N is the number of individuals in the population.

Scout Bee Phase

1. Find out which solution has the highest *count* value in total solutions.
2. Check whether that highest trial value is greater than *maxcount*.
3. If yes replace respective solution with random solution.

4   Experimental Setup and Results

The simulation are carried out on a Windows 32-bit system with Intel Core2 Duo, 3.00GHz processor. Matlab version 7.8 is used to perform all experiments. The sensor nodes are distributed randomly in $100m \times 100m$ grid. All sensor nodes are assumed to have the same transmission range. The neighbors of each sensor node are identified by using euclidean distance. If the euclidean distance between two sensor nodes is less than the communication range, these sensor nodes are said to be neighbors. In the Euclidean plane, if $p = (p1, p2)$ and $q = (q1, q2)$ then the distance is given by

$$d(\mathbf{p}, \mathbf{q}) = \sqrt{(p_1 - q_1)^2 + (p_2 - q_2)^2}.$$

An energy consumption model described in [2] is used to estimate the power consumption. The energy consumption for sending a packet is determined by a cost function

$$E_{send} = E_{trans} * s + E_{amp} * d^2$$

where E_{send} is the energy cost of sending a bit, s is the packet size, E_{amp} is the energy consumed in the amplifier, E_{trans} is the energy consumed for sending a bit and d is the distance of message transmission. The simulation parameters used for the experimental setup is shown in Table 1.

Table 1. Simulation Parameters

Symbol	Definition	Setting
E_{rec}	Receiver electronics	$50_{nJ/bit}$
E_{trans}	Transmitter electronics	$50_{nJ/bit}$
E_{amp}	Transmit Amplifier	$0.1_{nJ/bit/m^2}$
DP_{size}	Size of data packet	$64bytes$
S_{energy}	Initial energy of sensor	$0.25J$

The energy consumption for receiving a message is determined by a cost function

$$E_{receive} = E_{rec} * r$$

where E_{rec} is the energy cost of receiving a bit, and r is the packet size.

Fig.1. shows an initial setup that contains 500 sensor nodes and 3 base stations. In those 500 sensor nodes, 250 nodes are used as source nodes. The transmission range is $12m$. Nodes that are represented by $*$ (red) are source nodes and nodes represented by $+$ (green) are intermediate nodes. The nodes $501-503$ are base stations and these are represented with $*$ (blue). Fig.2. to Fig.4. shows the final networks obtained after performing the SPT, ANT and ABC algorithm for multiple base stations respectively, for the same network.

Fig. 1. Initial setup

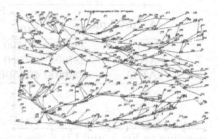

Fig. 2. SPT ALG for aggregation in WSN with multiple base stations

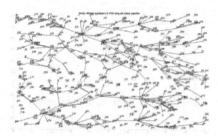

Fig. 3. ACO ALG for aggregation in WSN with multiple base stations

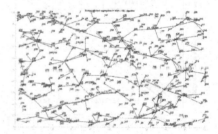

Fig. 4. ABC ALG for aggregation in WSN with multiple base stations

Table 2. to Table 5. shows the total energy consumption of the network in nano joulels for SPT, ANT and ABC algorithms. For each set of sources, the reported results are the average of four different sets of sources(instances). The minimum energy consumption is shown in bold phases in the table i.e. ABC.

Fig. 5. to Fig. 8. plots the energy consumption of whole network for a set of sources on x(axis) and energy in nano joules in y(axis). Here we have taken four networks, in each network the number of set of sources is varied (100, 200, 300 etc.), for each set of sources, the average of four different instances is considered.

Fig.5. shows the energy comparison of 500 sensors with variable number of sources. The network is configured in 100*100 grid, each sensor transmission range is fixed at 12 and only one base station is considered. Fig.6. represents same as Fig.5. but with three base stations. It shows the total energy consumption in the network with the three base station is less compare to total energy

Table 2. Energy consumption (nano joules) for 500 sensors and 1 base station

Algorithms	Number of Sources					
	70	140	210	280	350	420
SPT	348300	531400	688300	832600	963900	1082500
ANT	303200	470500	625200	768000	912200	1054400
ABC	248000	413700	566800	726900	879300	1034300

Table 3. Energy consumption (nano joules) for 500 sensors and 3 base stations

Algorithms	Number of Sources					
	70	140	210	280	350	420
SPT	336500	543700	694300	833100	960500	1091200
ANT	287900	460300	613700	769500	905500	1053200
ABC	233600	403500	559300	722300	873700	1034200

consumption in the network with one base station. The numerical data corresponding to Fig.5. and Fig.6. are tabulated in Table 2. and Table 3. respectively.

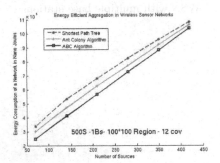

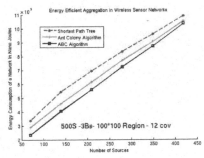

Fig. 5. Energy comparison of ALGs for 500 sensors and 1 base station

Fig. 6. Energy comparison of ALGs for 500 sensors and 3 base stations

Table 4. Energy consumption (nano joules) for 1500 sensors and 1 base station

Algorithms	Number of Sources					
	220	440	660	880	1100	1320
SPT	1105400	1685200	2137700	2543900	2929200	3269700
ANT	905900	1406800	1865000	2319000	2754700	3185400
ABC	744000	1232100	1707300	2183700	2658000	3130700

Fig.7. shows the energy comparison of 1500 sensors with variable number of sources. The network is configured in 200*200 grid, each sensor transmission range is fixed at 15 and only one base station is considered. Fig.8. represents same as Fig.7. but with ten base stations. It shows the total energy consumption in the

Table 5. Energy consumption (nano joules) for 1500 sensors and 10 base stations

Algorithms	Number of Sources					
	220	440	660	880	1100	1320
SPT	917700	1532200	2020000	2460800	2862100	3254100
ANT	785000	1308000	1793000	2260700	2714800	3163700
ABC	**671500**	**1177200**	**1671000**	**2151700**	**2637400**	**3118500**

network with the ten base stations is less compare to total energy consumption in the network with one base station. The numerical data corresponding to Fig.7. and Fig.8. are tabulated in Table 4. and Table 5. respectively.

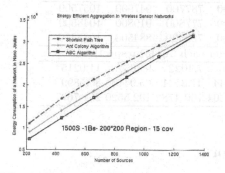

Fig. 7. Energy comparison of ALGs for 1500 sensors and 1 base station

Fig. 8. Energy comparison of ALGs for 1500 sensors and 3 base stations

It is observed that with increase in number of base stations, energy consumption of the whole network is decreces. ABC algorithm is performing better, if the number of source nodes is approximately half the number of total sensor nodes. If all the sensors in the network act as sources, energy consumption of every aggregation algorithm is the same.

Table 6. Energy consumption for 500 sensors and 1 base station with respect to less cpu time

ALG/sources	80	160	240	320	400	480
SPT	313300	514400	642100	787700	947900	1057500
ANT	319200	490100	628600	777800	919800	1048500
ABC	261300	422600	571800	736600	888200	1037300
Number of seconds usage of cpu time for each alg for respective sources						
SPT	1.9110	3.6348	5.6316	7.5426	9.4069	10.9357
ANT	8.3461	18.1819	32.5340	47.9079	64.5142	82.4621
ABC	7.6986	15.10870	23.8058	31.55120	38.18120	45.7863

SPT algorithm takes little CPU time compared to ANT and ABC but the energy efficiency is very less and there is no way to improve the energy efficiency even if we run the SPT algorithm for more time. ABC algorithm is more energy efficient compared to ANT if both these algorithms are allowd to run for almost same time [Table 6]. But if ABC algorithm is executed for more time, the energy efficiency still increases. Thus it can be concluded that ABC algorithm performs better in terms of energy efficiency in comparison to SPT and ANT if all the algorithms are executed for a fixed time. ABC still gives better performance if executed for more time period[Table 7].

Table 7. Energy consumption for 500 sensors and 1 base station with respect to more cpu time

ALG/sources	80	160	240	320	400	480
SPT	313300	514400	642100	787700	947900	1057500
ANT	319200	490100	628600	777800	919800	1048500
ABC	251700	421300	565700	729300	884500	1037300
Number of seconds usage of cpu time for each alg for respective sources						
SPT	1.8174	3.6192	5.5146	7.4022	9.1651	11.0215
ANT	8.2915	19.0555	34.6244	47.3541	65.9416	85.5899
ABC	42.7755	85.5665	123.6464	160.4782	192.5520	261.7697

5   Conclusions and Future Work

In this work, we have modeled the data aggregation tree problem in WSN with less energy consumption. The importance of energy efficiency and aggregation in WSN are explained. We used Ant colony and Artificial Bee Colony Algorithms to solve the problem and to find a set of optimal data aggregation trees across the total network. We have extended data aggregation problem for multiple base stations also. The performance of ABC is compared with ANT and SPT algorithm for aggregation in WSN with multiple base stations for variable number of sources and base stations. Simulation results and analysis show that ABC algorithm is more energy efficient than ANT and SPT algorithms for data aggregation in WSN with multiple base stations. It is also observed that with same aggregation efficiency, ABC is energy efficient compared to SPT and ANT algorithms.

In future we proposed to extend this work to find out dynamic aggregation trees in WSN for mobile base stations.

References

1. Back, T., Schutz, M., Khuri, S.: A comparative study of a penalty function, a repair heuristic, and stochastic operators with the set-covering problem. In: Alliot, J.-M., Ronald, E., Lutton, E., Schoenauer, M., Snyers, D. (eds.) AE 1995. LNCS, vol. 1063, pp. 320–332. Springer, Heidelberg (1996)

2. Heinzelman, W.R., Chandrakasan, A., Balakrishnan, H.: Energy-efficient communication protocol for wireless microsensor networks. In: Proceedings of the 33rd Annual Hawaii International Conference on System Sciences, pp. 1–6 (January 2000)
3. Intanagonwiwat, C., Estrin, D., Govindan, R., Heidemann, J.: Impact of Network Density on Data Aggregation in Wireless Sensor Networks. Technical Report 01-750, University of Southern California (November 2001)
4. Krishnamachari, B., Estrin, D., Wicker, S.: The Impact of Data Aggregation in Wireless Sensor Networks. In: International Workshop of Distributed Event Based Systems (DEBS), Vienna, Austria, pp. 575–578 (July 2002)
5. Akyildiz, I., Su, W., Sankarasubramaniam, Y., Cayirci, E.: Wireless Sensor Networks: A Survey. Computer Networks 38, 393–422 (2002)
6. Gandham, S.R., Dawande, M., Prakash, R., Venkatesan, S.: Energy Efficient Schemes for Wireless Sensor Networks with Multiple Mobile base stations. In: Global Telecommunications Conference, pp. 377–381 (December 2003)
7. Al-Karaki, J.N., Ul-Mustafa, R., Kamal, A.E.: Data Aggregation in Wireless Sensor Networks - Exact and Approximate Algorithms. In: The Proceedings the International Workshop on High-Performance Switching and Routing, Phoenix, pp. 241–245 (April 2004)
8. Karaboga, D.: An idea based on honey bee swarm for numerical optimization. Technical Report TR06, Computer Engineering Department, Erciyes University, Turkey (2005)
9. Misra, R., Mandal, C.: Ant-aggregation: Ant Colony Algorithm for optimal data aggregation in Wireless Sensor Networks. In: IFIP International Conference on Wireless and Optical Communications Networks, 5pages (2006)
10. Basturk, B., Karaboga, D.: An artificial bee colony (ABC) algorithm for numeric function optimization. In: Proceedings of the IEEE Swarm Intelligence Symposium, pp. 12–14 (May 2006)
11. Karaboga, D., Basturk, B.: A powerful and efficient algorithm for numerical function optimization: artificial bee colony (ABC) algorithm. Journal of Global Optimization, 459–471 (2007)
12. Liao, W.-H., Kao, Y., Fan, C.-M.: An Ant Colony Algorithm for Data Aggregation in Wireless Sensor Networks. In: International Conference on Sensor Technologies and Applications, pp. 101–106 (2007)
13. Karaboga, D., Basturk, B.: On the performance of artificial bee colony(ABC) algorithm. Applied Soft Computing, 687–697 (2008)
14. Udgata, S.K., Sabat, S.L., Mini, S.: Sensor deployment in irregular terrain using artificial bee colony algorithm. In: World Congress on Nature and Biologically Inspired Computing, pp. 1308–1313 (2009)
15. Sabat, S.L., Kumar, K.S., Udgata, S.K.: Differential evolution and swarm intelligence techniques for analog circuit synthesis. In: World Congress on Nature and Biologically Inspired Computing, pp. 468–473 (2009)
16. Karim, L., Nasser, N., Abdulsalam, H., Moukadem, I.: An Efficient Data Aggregation Approach for Large Scale Wireless Sensor Networks. In: IEEE Global Telecommunications Conference, pp. 1–6 (2010)
17. Mini, S., Udgata, S.K., Sabat, S.L.: Sensor deployment in 3-D terrain using artificial bee colony algorithm. In: Panigrahi, B.K., Das, S., Suganthan, P.N., Dash, S.S. (eds.) SEMCCO 2010. LNCS, vol. 6466, pp. 424–431. Springer, Heidelberg (2010)
18. Sabat, S.L., Udgata, S.K., Abraham, A.: Artificial bee colony algorithm for small signal model parameter extraction of MESFET. Eng Appl. Artif. Intell., 689–694 (2010)

19. Muhammad, S., Di Caro, G.A., Farooq, M.: Swarm intelligence based routing protocol for wireless sensor networks: Survey and future directions. In: Information Sciences, vol. 181, pp. 4597–4624. Elsevier (2011)
20. Okdem, S., Karaboga, D., Ozturk, C.: An Application of Wireless Sensor Network Routing based on Artificial Bee Colony Algorithm. In: IEEE Congress on Evolutionary Computation (CEC), pp. 326–330 (2011)
21. Mini, S., Udgata, S.K., Sabat, S.L.: Artificial bee colony based sensor deployment algorithm for target coverage problem in 3-D terrain. In: Natarajan, R., Ojo, A. (eds.) ICDCIT 2011. LNCS, vol. 6536, pp. 313–324. Springer, Heidelberg (2011)

An Intelligent Method for Handoff Decision in Next Generation Wireless Network

Laksha Pattnaik, Mihir Narayan Mohanty, and Bibhuprasad Mohanty

ITER, Sikshya O Anusandhan University, Bhubaneswar, Odisha, India
{laksha008,mihir.n.mohanty,bmohanty.iit07}@gmail.com

Abstract. The vision of Next-Generation networks is to be heterogeneous in nature with an increasing demand in wireless networks. Many wireless networks are deployed with widely varying characteristics. As various networks have widely different characteristics, it is difficult to maintain the quality of service after executing a handoff from one network to another network. Maintaining the quality of service, based on applications, during the handoff in heterogeneous networks needs an intelligent handoff decision mechanism. In order to utilize the full heterogeneous networks, the mobile terminal may handoff from one network to another by many reasons. Development of efficient handoff algorithm for cost-effective, and that can enhance the capacity as well as quality of service of cellular system. A fuzzy based handoff algorithm is proposed in this paper as a solution to this problem. Handoff on the basis of ratio of slopes of normal signal loss to the actual signal loss is presented. The fuzzy based solution is supported by analytical solution. Simulation results show that compared to other vertical handoff algorithms, the proposed algorithm gives better performance for different traffic classes.

Keywords: Next Generation Wireless Network, Handoff Decision, Intelligent Method, Fuzzy Logic.

1 Introduction

In Next-Generation (NG) hybrid wireless networks, it is assumed that Mobile-Controlled Handover can substitute the current handoff mechanism in homogeneous networks. The presence of heterogeneity in wireless technology has paved the way to provide global information access to users on the move. In case of number of mobile networks, the problem of handoff and managing the mobility is an important parameter which affects the performance dramatically. So we need different handoff schemes that consider the current situations [1, 2]. Quality of Service (QoS) is one of the key operations in cellular mobile communication systems that is accomplished by the system and is imperceptible for the user. The continuity of a call is maintained when mobile moves from one cell area to another. The handoff initiation in cellular systems depends on many environmental and system parameters. Various handoff initiation algorithms are available and most of them are based on relative signal strength (RSS) measurements [3, 4]. The parameters which affect the hand-off vary with respect to the type of geographical location of the mobile terminal (MT) and various atmospheric conditions. Therefore, for improving the handoff performance it is necessary to use an appropriate path loss model and proper parameter values [5, 6].

B.K. Panigrahi et al. (Eds.): SEMCCO 2013, Part II, LNCS 8298, pp. 465–475, 2013.

Currently, there are various wireless access networks deployed and these different types of access technologies give users great flexibility in choosing services, which can be different in QoS support, business models, and service providers. Realization of seamless handovers to the best network selection can be obtained by using intelligent handover decision strategies [7-8]. A proper scheme of handoff between neighboring cells in different type of network is needed. The design of handover decision strategy to support seamless handover scenarios and also used to obtain QoS and AAAC (Authentication, Authorization, Accounting and Charging) information from candidate networks with minimum signaling overhead [9].   Handoff decision must be adaptively set based on the type of network it presently resides and the one it is attempting handoff with through some predefined rules. These schemes were depended on the speed of the mobile terminal to make a decision of the handoff initiation RSS threshold value. The handoff types based on channel usage, microcellular and multilayered systems and network characteristics has been explained in [10-12].

In order to maintain reliable communication in a microcellular/ macrocellular/ hybrid system new and better handoff algorithms must be developed. We have proposed a fuzzy based handoff algorithm as a solution to this problem. Fuzzy set theory allows a linguistic representation of the control and operational laws of a system. The main strength of fuzzy set theory is that it excels in dealing with imprecision. Thus, fuzzy sets chosen in this work have smooth membership function that increases or decreases gradually.

This paper is organized as follows. Section 2 provides the knowledge and idea of handoff. Section 3 depicts the methods for hand-off decision. The result of performance is discussed in section 4 and finally in section 5, it concludes the work.

2   Hand-off

Handoff is defined as the process of changing the current radio channel to a new radio channel which mainly takes place because of the movement of mobile unit and unfavorable radio conditions (deterioration of received signal quality) inside an individual cell or between a numbers of adjacent cells. A handoff algorithm with fixed parameters cannot perform well in different system environments. QoS is achieved with a good mechanism to handle handoff between two dissimilar networks, called vertical handoff. Vertical handoff mechanisms involve three different phases of operations: system discovery, handoff decision process and handoff execution. Some research has been conducted to model the performance of heterogeneous networks. In [13-15], fuzzy logic-based vertical handover decision is applied by considering a combination of various parameters such as price, RSS variation, traffic, sojourn time, available network bandwidth, monetary cost, user preferences, dwell time, etc. In heterogeneous networks, Vertical handoffs can be initiated for convenience rather than connectivity reasons. A decision algorithm gives a better performance when several parameters are considered, more so when a combination of static and dynamic parameters are considered. The decision may depend on various groups of parameters such as,

- Network- Related Parameters - Bandwidth, Latency, RSS, SIR, Cost, Security etc.
- Terminal Related Parameters - Velocity, Battery power, Location Information, Distance etc.
- User-Related Parameters - user profile and preferences
- Service Related Parameters - service capacities, QoS etc.

2.1   Issue in Hand-off

While the mobile is moving, if it detects that the signal strength of current network is less than a predetermined threshold value, it scans the available foreign network set. The mobile client needs to obtain the information about the foreign networks.

Relative signal strength chooses the strongest received base station at all times. The decision is based on an averaged measurement of the received signal. *Relative signal strength with hysteresis and threshold* hands a user over to a new base only if the current signal level drops below a threshold and the target base station is stronger than the current one by a given hysteresis margin. The rapid decrease in received signal strength may cause the call drop and that cannot be supported by handoff algorithms. This nature of the decaying signal can be determined with the slope or tangent of angle subtended by the two corresponding points on signal line with respect to two axes. Slope ratio (S_r) can be defined as the ratio between normal to actual signals and depicted in Fig. 1 [16].

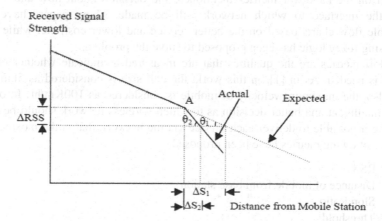

Fig. 1. Slope of actual signal and expected signal

From the geometry of Fig. 1, slope of normal signal can be represented as,

$$\tan \theta_1 = \frac{\Delta RSS}{\Delta S_1}$$

(1)

and slope of actual signal with rapid decrease can be represented as,

$$\tan \theta_2 = \frac{\Delta RSS}{\Delta S_2} \tag{2}$$

Hence, the slope ratio of normal to actual signal can be represented as

$$S_r = \frac{\tan \theta_1}{\tan \theta_2} \tag{3}$$

For different values of θ_1 and θ_2 various values of S_r are obtained. But for handoff to take place θ_2 must always be greater than θ_1.

Automation and adaptability is one of the solutions with fuzzy logic based in this work to decide hand-off and switch over automatically.

3   Methods for Hand-off Decision

The potential capacity benefits of mobile-initiated vertical handovers are substantial. However, it is important to choose the correct VHO criteria in order to achieve optimum load balancing and equilibrium states [17]. Pervasive systems are context aware and need to adapt to context changes, including network disconnections and changes in network Quality of Service (QoS). Vertical handover is one of many possible adaptation methods. It allows users to roam freely between heterogeneous networks while maintaining the continuity of their applications. In [18], S. Balasubramaniam, et. al., proposed a vertical handover mechanism suitable for multimedia applications in pervasive systems. They focused on the handover decision making process which uses context information regarding user devices, user location, network environment and requested QoS.

Based on the handover metrics mentioned, the decision about how and when to switch the interface to which network will be made. Many papers have given reasonable flow charts based on the better service and lower cost, etc. while in this work, using fuzzy logic has been proposed to solve the problem.

Handoff metrics are the qualities that are measured to indicate whether or not a handoff is needed. As in [1], in this work, the cell size is considered as 5km radius each. Also, the maximum velocity of mobile is considered as 100Km/hr. In order to take an intelligent and better decision as to which wireless network should be chosen and make it possible to deliver each service via the network that is the most suitable, for it the following metrics have been proposed.

- RSS
- Distance of mobile from base station
- Slop Ratio
- Threshold

The consideration of the above parameters in various ways, the block diagrams of the fuzzy inference systems are shown from Fig. 2 to Fig. 4.

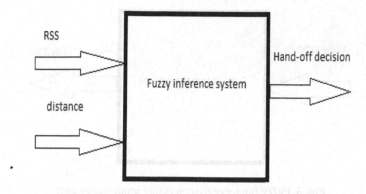

Fig. 2. Block Diagram of Fuzzy Inference System (using input RSS & distance)

This system consists of two membership functions for handoff initiation: Received Signal Strength (RSS), and distance as shown in Fig. 2. The elements in membership function have a varying degree of membership in a set. The membership values are obtained by mapping the values obtained for a particular parameter onto a membership function. The membership functions are listed in Table-1. Here triangular membership function is used whose formula is as follows:

$$trimf(x; a, b, c) = \max\left(\min\left(\frac{x-a}{b-a}, \frac{c-x}{c-b}\right), 0\right) \quad (2)$$

Table 1. Membership values of membership function

Linguistic variable	Fuzzy set
RSS	{weak, medium, strong}
Distance	{low, medium, high}
Handoff decision	{no change, handoff}

These membership functions ranges from -20 to 70.These fuzzified data will be passed to the inference engine, and is matched against a set of fuzzy rules using fuzzy techniques to produce output fuzzy sets. This is based on the fuzzy rule of IF-THEN. It decides whether handoff is necessary or not. By using the fuzzy sets of the inputs the IF-THEN rules are implemented. In the next step, the output fuzzy sets are passed to the defuzzifier for computation of output.

Mamdani based FIS has been considered for such process, where one of the membership functions is considered for handoff initiation is Slope ratio (SR) as shown in Fig. 3. The procedure for assigning the membership values to the membership function is as same as previous process described.

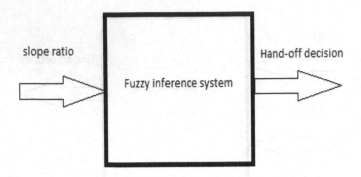

Fig. 3. Fuzzy Inference System (using input slope ratio)

Table 2. Membership values of membership function

Linguistic variable	Fuzzy set
Slope ratio	{low, medium, high}
Handoff decision	{no change, handoff}

The fuzzified data is passed to the inference engine to match against a set of fuzzy rules using fuzzy techniques to decide the output. The fuzzy rules for the system are implemented in IF-THEN format. The fuzzy rules provides knowledge base to the system and results in proper handoff. In the same manner, all the parameters (i.e., RSS, SR, threshold) are verified with the Mamdani based FIS and is shown in Fig. 4.

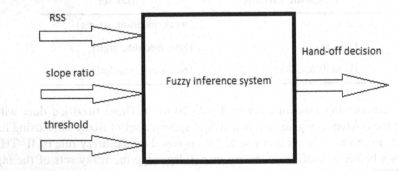

Fig. 4. Mamdani base fuzzy inference system (using input RSS, slope ratio & threshold)

This system has three membership functions for handoff initiation i.e. Received Signal Strength (RSS), Slope ratio (SR) and Threshold. The membership functions are mentioned in Table-3.

Table 3. Membership values of membership function

Linguistic variable	Fuzzy set
RSS	{weak, medium, strong}
Slope ratio	{low, medium, high}
Threshold	{low, medium, high}
Handoff decision	{no change, handoff}

The fuzzified data matched with fuzzy rules to produce output fuzzy sets. The rules for the system are implemented to obtain the decision of hand-off.

Defuzzification

In this work, centroid principle method is chosen for defuzzification to obtain the crisp set. It consists of finding the centroid of the area under the curve by the output MF and its abscissa is taken as the crisp value. The method is also commonly known as center of gravity or center of area defuzzification. It was developed by Sugeno in 1985. But this method is difficult computationally for complex membership functions. The centroid defuzzification technique can be expressed as

$$x_{COG} = \frac{\int_z \mu_A(x) x \, dx}{\int_z \mu_A(x) \, dx}$$

where z_{COG} is the crisp output, $\mu_A(z)$ is the aggregated membership function and z is the output variable.

This method determines the centre of the area of the combined membership functions [19].

4   Result and Discussion

Using fuzzy logic a softer handoff decision can be drawn. It has been observed better performance as compared to the work done in [14-15]. Here, the handoff decision using parameters like RSS, distance, slope ratio and threshold have been analyzed. When RSS increases, the handoff decision is taken as NO; that implies no handoff is required. Similarly when distance of MT from the base station increases, handoff is required. Hence for adaptive handoff decision, RSS value is set for particular distance so as to minimize the false handoff initiation and handoff failure.

Fig. 5 (a) and (b) shows the output after de-fuzzification of the mapped inputs with fuzzy rules.

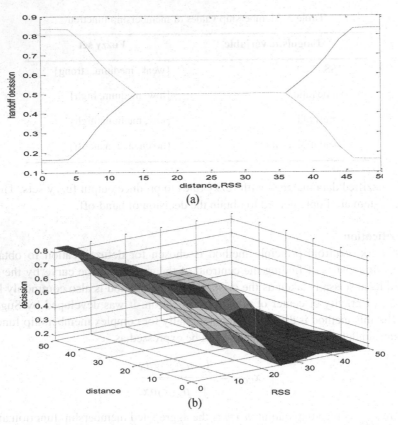

(a)

(b)

Fig. 5. (a) and (b) Variation of handoff decision with respect to distance and RSS

The slope ratio is inversely proportional to the hand off decision. Higher the value of slope ratio, lower the hand off value. Higher slope ratio means the actual signal strength approaches the normal or expected signal strength. By determining the slope ratio, the value of RSS can be monitored. Hence, we can take a decision on hand off. The relation between slope ratio and hand off decision is shown in Fig. 6.

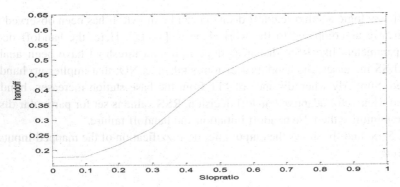

Fig. 6. Variation of handoff decision w.r.t. slope ratio

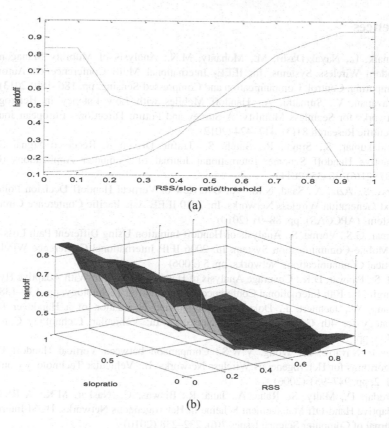

Fig. 7. (a) and (b) variation of handoff decision with respect to RSS, slope ratio, threshold

A relation between handoff decision with respect to RSS, slope ratio and threshold is shown Fig. 7 (a) and (b).

5   Conclusion

We presented a Fuzzy based intelligent approach for handover decision algorithm designed for NG and multi-technology environments. The simulation is carried out using MATLAB 7.5 platform and the results obtained. From the results obtained, it is concluded that the proposed FUZZY rule-based technique gives better performance for different types of applications. The fuzzy membership functions help in making a clear distinction among the parameters of the networks and the fuzzy rule base is used to compute the handoff decisions. Results obtained using the proposed technique show better performance for decision. In this paper a new fuzzy based handoff algorithm capable of responding to the fast changes that occur in a microcellular environment is presented. These results are to be expected because fuzzy algorithms are superior to conventional ones when working in areas of uncertainties.

References

1. Patnaik, L., Nayak(Dash), M., Mohanty, M.N.: Analysis of Mobility Management in Modern Wireless Systems. In: IEEE- International Multi Conference on Automation, Computing, Control, Communication and Compressed Sensing, pp. 186–189 (2013)
2. Saravanan, V., Sumathi, A.: Handoff Mobiles with Low Latency in Heterogeneous Networks for Seamless Mobility: A Survey and Future Directions. European Journal of Scientific Research 81(3), 417–424 (2012)
3. Nandakumar, S., Singh, R., Singh, S.: Traffic Driven & Received Signal Strength Adaptive Handoff Scheme. International Journal of Computer Applications (0975 – 8887) 21(6), 30–35 (2011)
4. Rizvi, S., Aziz, A., Saad, N.M.: An Overview of Vertical Handoff Decision Policies for Next Generation Wireless Networks. In: 2010 IEEE Asia Pacific Conference Circuits and Systems (APCCAS), pp. 88–91 (2010)
5. Tomar, G.S., Verma, S.: Analysis of Handoff Initiation Using Different Path Loss Models in Mobile Communication System. In: 2006 IFIP International Conference Wireless and Optical Communications Networks, pp. 5 (2006)
6. Lal, S., Panwar, D.K.: Coverage Analysis of Handoff Algorithm With Adaptive Hysteresis Margin. In: 10th International Conference on Information Technology, pp. 133–138 (2007)
7. Zhang, W., Jaehnert, J., Dolzer, K.: Design and Evaluation of a Handover Decision Strategy for 4th Generation Mobile Networks. In: Vehicular Technology Conference, vol. 3, pp. 1969–1973 (2003)
8. Stevens-Navarro, E., Wong, V.W.S.: Comparison between Vertical Handoff Decision Algorithms for Heterogeneous Wireless Networks. In: Vehicular Technology Conference, vol. 2, pp. 947–951 (2006)
9. Sarddar, D., Maity, S., Raha, A., Jana, R., Biswas, U., Naskar, M.K.: A RSS Based Adaptive Hand-Off Management Scheme In Heterogeneous Networks. IJCSI International Journal of Computer Science Issues 7(6), 232–238 (2010)
10. Smaoui, I., Zarai, F., Kamoun, L.: An Anticipated Handoff Management Mechanism for Next Generation Wireless Networks. In: Mosharaka International Conference on Communications, Propagation and Electronics, pp. 1–6 (2008)
11. Vakili, V.T., Moghaddam, S.S.: Optimum Selection of Handoff Initiation Algorithm & Related Parameters. In: International Conference on Communication Technology Proceedings, vol. 1, pp. 563–567 (2000)
12. Ekiz, N., Salih, T., Küçüköner, S., Fidanboylu, K.: An Overview of Handoff Techniques in Cellular Networks. International Journal of Information Technology 2(2), 132–136 (2006)
13. Ezzouhairi, A., Quintero, A., Pierre, S.: A fuzzy decision making strategy for vertical handoffs. In: Canadian Conference on Electrical and Computer Engineering, Ontario, Canada, pp. 000583–000588 (2008)
14. He, Q.: A fuzzy logic based vertical handoff decision algorithm between WWAN and WLAN, 2nd International Conference on Networking and Digital Society (ICNDS), vol 2. (Wenzhou, China, 2010), pp. 561–564. (2010)
15. Yang, T., Rong, P.: A fuzzy logic vertical handoff algorithm with motion trend decision. In: 6th International Forum on Strategic Technology (IFOST), Harbin, China, vol. 2, pp. 1280–1283 (2011)

16. Balasubramaniam, S., Indulska, J.: Vertical handover supporting pervasive computing in future wireless networks. Elsevier Science Publishers 27(8), 708–719 (2004)
17. Dimitriou, N., Mertikopoulos, P., Moustakas, A.L.: Vertical Handover between Wireless Standards. In: IEEE International Conference on Communications, pp. 3269–3273 (2008)
18. Rappaport, T.: Wireless Communication: principles and practice, 2nd edn. Pearson Education, India
19. Rao, D.H., Saraf, S.S.: Study of Defuzzification Methods of Fuzzy Logic Controller for Speed Control of a DC Motor. IEEE Transactions, 782–787 (1995)

Path Planning for the Autonomous Underwater Vehicle

Andrey Kirsanov, Sreenatha G. Anavatti, and Tapabrata Ray

School of Engineering and Information Technology, University of New South Wales,
Canberra, ACT, 2600, Australia
z3397566@student.adfa.edu.au

Abstract. This paper introduces a novel method to find the optimal path for Autonomous Underwater Vehicles (AUVs). AUVs have gained importance over the last few years as service and research tools in a variety of applications. Path planning is one of the challenging tasks when dynamic obstacles are encountered. The Dijkstra's algorithm is modified suitably to account for static as well as dynamic obstacles by adding an Additional Part (AP). In addition, the proposed algorithm takes into account the dynamics of the water flow and corrects the path suitably. Only two-dimensional routes are considered in the applications. The numerical results show that the proposed algorithm is effective in finding optimal paths.

Keywords: Autonomous Underwater Vehicle, path planning, collision avoidance, Dijkstra's algorithm, Graph theory.

1   Introduction

AUVs are increasingly employed while the technology is applied to survey and exploration to meet the deepwater challenges. One of the major challenges with AUVs is to design a suitable path planning algorithm to circumvent obstacles. In particular, when the dynamic obstacles are considered, brings in more complexity. The path optimization algorithm needs to navigate the AUV without human intervention [1,2].

A number of different algorithms are available to find the optimal path, such as: Dijkstra's algorithm, Bellman-Ford algorithm, Floyd-Warshall algorithm, Johnson algorithm [3]. All these algorithms are based upon the graph theory and could be applied to calculate the optimal path for the AUV. These algorithms need to be modified suitably, if they are employed for the underwater robots.

In the proposed algorithm, the first step is dividing the area of obstacles and area of all possible paths [4] using the input from standards of World Geodetic System (WGS) and Automation Identification System (AIS). The output data includes the coastline, waterways, shoals, obstacles and depth. All data types are composed of an array of nodes. All nodes of the map are processed and connected by edges to each other. The AP part of the algorithm complements the Dijkstra's algorithm. Thus the algorithm is made up of the two areas of path planning: obstacles and trajectories. The AP of the algorithm can handle dynamic obstacles as well. Along with this, the effect

B.K. Panigrahi et al. (Eds.): SEMCCO 2013, Part II, LNCS 8298, pp. 476–486, 2013.

of flow is considered and an optimal path is computed in the presence of flows. This is carried out as the addition of a correction matrix. The correction matrix has weights based on the graph theory. Thus, an optimal trajectory is created that can be employed for navigation and control of the AUV.

The methodology of the technique is discussed in Section 2. Section 3 deals with collision avoidance in the presence of dynamic obstacles. The effect of flow is discussed in Section 4. The paper is concluded in Section 5 with some remarks on the methodology.

2   Methodology

To find the optimal trajectory, the graph theory with Dijkstra's algorithm [5] is used. Dijkstra's algorithm is complemented by a special algorithm Graph [6]. Graph's algorithm generates a graph of all possible paths. There are two main functions in the proposed program. First function is *CrossTest*. Consider two edges t_1 and t_2 with the nodes at the ends (Figure 1, 2). Let the coordinates of nodes be; $x_{i1}, y_{i1}, x_{i2}, y_{i2}$ and $x_{j1}, y_{j1}, x_{j2}, y_{j2}$ (Figure 1);

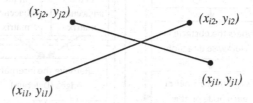

(x_{j2}, y_{j2}) (x_{i2}, y_{i2})

(x_{i1}, y_{i1}) (x_{j1}, y_{j1})

Fig. 1. Two edges intersecting each other

where:

$$0 < t_1 < 1, \, 0 < t_2 < 1 \qquad (1)$$

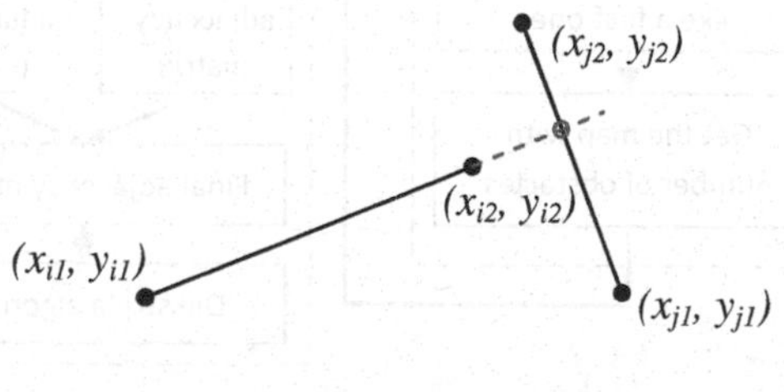

(x_{j2}, y_{j2})

(x_{i2}, y_{i2})

(x_{i1}, y_{i1})

(x_{j1}, y_{j1})

Fig. 2. Two non-intersecting edges

where:

$$t_1 > 1, \quad 0 < t_2 < 1 \qquad (2)$$

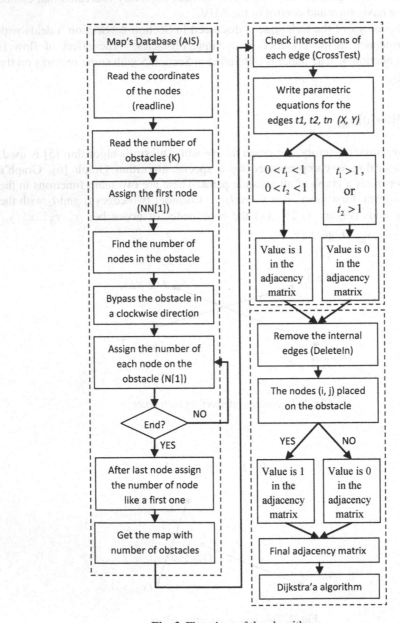

Fig. 3. Flowchart of the algorithm

The equations of the coordinates of nodes are described by;

$$x = x_{i1}t_1 + (1-t_1)x_{i2};$$
$$y = y_{i1}t_1 + (1-t_1)y_{i2};$$
$$x = x_{j1}t_2 + (1-t_2)x_{j2};$$
$$y = y_{j1}t_2 + (1-t_2)y_{j2}.$$

(3)

where:

$$0 < t_1 < 1, \, 0 < t_2 < 1.$$

(4)

If the system Eq. (3) has a solution for the condition Eq. (4), the edges are intersected. If it is not or the determinant is equal to zero, the edges do not intersect. The determinant of the system Eq. (3) has the form;

$$(x[j2] - x[j1]) \cdot (y[i1] - y[i2]) +$$
$$+ (x[i1] - x[i2]) \cdot (y[j1] - y[j2])$$

(5)

The determinant is obtained from the matrix:

$$\begin{bmatrix} 1 & 0 & -x_{i1} + x_{i2} & 0 \\ 0 & 1 & -y_{i1} + y_{i2} & 0 \\ 1 & 0 & 0 & -x_{j1} + x_{j2} \\ 0 & 1 & 0 & -x_{i1} + x_{j2} \end{bmatrix}$$

(6)

The edges are parallel and there are no restrictions with t_1 and t_2 if the determinant is zero. These edges do not intersect each other and will be included to the number of graph edges with Dijkstra'a algorithm. The program *CrossTest* goes through all the nodes in pairs and if the edge do not intersect with the other edges of the graph, it will be considered by Dijkstra's algorithm. The symmetry of the adjacency matrix of the graph is used to accelerate this process. The adjacency matrix has $a_{ij} = 0$ if there is no edge from the node i to node j, otherwise $a_{ij} = 1$. The matrix and numbers of the nodes are used by Dijkstra'a algorithm. The number of the nodes is taken to be increasing along the contour of the obstacles in the clockwise direction. The edges in obstacles are divided as; edges which come inside the contour from corner nodes and edges which come outside the contour of obstacles from corner nodes. For example, the edge in the sea is a possible trajectory for the AUV [7]. Function DeleteIn determines the edges which go into the contour.

Bypassing ends of the edges of the unit vector ([k,j]) and unit vector of the edge of two adjacent edges ([k,k-1], [k,k+1]) differ by the sign (Figure 3) depending on whether the direction is clockwise or anti-clockwise. The sign of bypass is determined by the sign of double area of the corresponding triangle and is calculated by Green's formula (the function is DeleteIn).

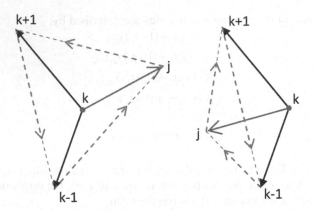

Fig. 4. Traversing nodes in a counter clockwise and clockwise directions

$$2S = \sum_{n=1}^{3}(x_{n+1}y_n - x_n y_{n+1}) \qquad (7)$$

$$x_4 = x_1, y_4 = y_1 \qquad (8)$$

The function returns "0" if the edge is inside, otherwise it returns "1". The auxiliary function F calculates the sum of;

$$x_{n+1}y_n - x_n y_{n+1} \qquad (9)$$

In this case, it is important to determine the direction of the contour nodes. Function DeleteIn deletes all edges which do not have any crossing with each other but are placed inside of the contour.

Adjacency matrix A is formed when the function DeleteIn is applied when there are unnecessary edges. In the loop of all the obstacles *(ii=1..k)*, two nested loops are written. The first loop is calculated from corners i of obstacle ii, and second loop is calculated from the end of edges inside the obstacle and goes from i+2 to the last node of the obstacle. It should be noticed that the second loop is smaller than the first loop because the edges located on the borderline of obstacle are not considered. Elements of the matrix a_{ij} are multiplied by the value of the function DeleteIn and then the result is assigned to the matrix a_{ij} again. In adjacency matrix, the edge is removed if the value of function DeleteIn is 0 indicating an inside edge, otherwise the edge remains.

Consider the example shown in Fig. 5. There are two obstacles with nine nodes. The function DeleteIn returns the values of $a_{5,1} = 0, a_{5,2} = 0, a_{5,3} = 1$. Similarly the nodes 7, 8 and 9 are considered. Fig.6 shows different obstacles along with all the edges possible for the nodes. The edges inside the obstacle are removed and the optimal path is obtained using the Dijkstra's algorithm.

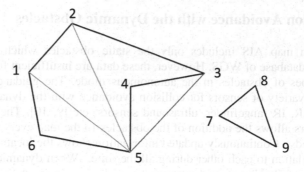

Fig. 5. Obstacles

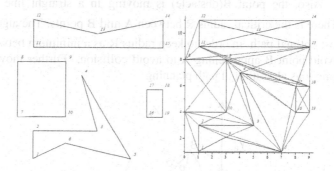

Fig. 6. Creating obstacles and displaying of all edges

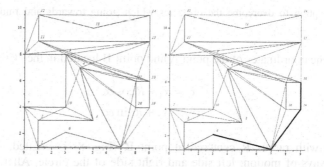

Fig. 7. Removing the edges from obstacles and finding the optimal path

3   Collision Avoidance with the Dynamic Obstacles

The navigation map AIS includes only the static obstacles which are displayed initially in the database of WGS. However, these data are insufficient for safe passing through all types of obstacles in the autonomous mode. The guidance and control system uses a variety of sensors for collision avoidance with the dynamic obstacles, such as: LIDAR, IR rangefinder, ultrasound sensors, etc [9, 10]. The data obtained from the sensors allows the addition of the obstacles to the map every sampling time (e.g., 0.5 seconds). Continuously updated information shows the location of obstacles and AUV in relation to each other during all the time. When dynamic obstacles are encountered, the following algorithm works.

Let point A be the object of control (AUV) (Fig. 8, 9). Point B is a moving obstacle. Point A in the XY coordinate system is moving in a straight line $x = x_A$ at a speed v_A. Also, the point B(obstacle) is moving in a straight line $y = y_B$ at a speed v_B. There is the critical radius R between A and B points. The algorithm has to find the most optimal path in order to keep radius R as a minimum between points A and B to avoid point B approaching A to avoid collision. Further movement of the point A is previous algorithm of path planning.

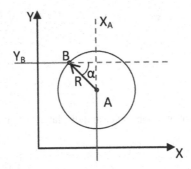

Fig. 8. The option to overcome the obstacles which going towards and finding the critical radius R

Linking the coordinates of the point A and point B located in the "Critical area";

$$x_B = x_A - R\cos\alpha;$$
$$y_B = y_A + R\sin\alpha. \tag{10}$$

A circle with radius R centered at point B (Fig. 8) is created. The point A has a two ways of motion: left side and right side of the circle. Alternatively, there is a possibility of moving straight back if the point B is within the critical radius R (Fig. 9).

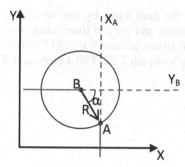

Fig. 9. Collision avoidance by going backward as an alternative way of the point A

The first option is overcoming the obstacles by point A going towards B. The vehicle (point A) moves along the trajectory:

$$x = R\cos(kt-\alpha)+x_B +v_B t;$$
$$y = R\sin(kt-\alpha)+y_B.$$

(11)

where $k = v_A / R$ provided that the point A moves the circumference length $2\pi R$ at a speed v_A during the period $2\pi R / v_A$, and bypassing ends when the point A reaches the straight line $x = x_A$. As a result, one can find the bypassing period of the point A. The second option to avoid the obstacles is going backward. Now, the point A is moving along a trajectory

$$x = R\cos(-kt-\alpha)+x_B +v_B t;$$
$$y = R\sin(-kt-\alpha)+y_B.$$

(13)

This problem has a numerical solution. Assume $v_A =10, v_B =2, R=150, \alpha =\pi/3$. Fig. 10 shows the options to avoid the moving obstacle B.

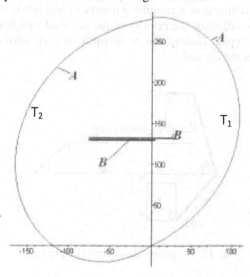

Fig. 10. Path followed by the vehicle

The blue lines indicate the path taken by the vehicle (point A) to overcome the obstacle B by going backwards and the red lines while moving towards the obstacle. The period to overcome the obstacles are; T1 = 39.71246547 and T2 = 52.04941998 accordingly. The total length of path T2 is 520.4 units and T1 is 397.1 units.

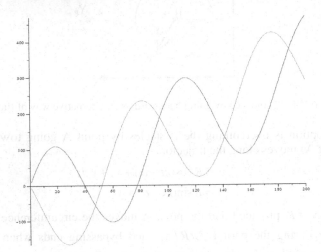

Fig. 11. The graphical solution of the finding the periods T1 and T2

4   Path Planning with Flow

Autonomy and speed of reaching a destination is an important criterion in the development of the AUV [11, 12]. If one can account for the effect of flows (water flow), then the path planning will significantly improve these parameters.

The first step in this direction is creating a matrix of weights to calculate the power of flow [13, 14]. This will show the priority of the selected path between the edges in a map. The second step is finding the most optimal path with minimum weight. Finally the trajectories are created.

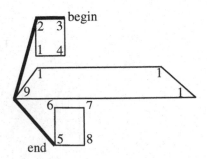

Fig. 12. The path without correction factors

As shown in Fig. 12, the starting point is 3 and the goal point is 5. The bold line is the trajectory of the AUV. After the addition of the correction matrix due to flow, one gets;

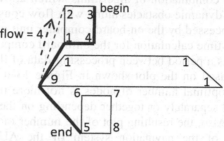

Fig. 13. The path with correction factors

Assuming a flow of strength of 4 units, the total length of the new path is 9.20823962 units as compared t0 9.19214935 units without the correction.

5   The Optimization of the Number of Points with Respect to Time

Generally, there will be restrictions on the processing of points (nodes) at a time. It is caused by the hardware capabilities of the guidance and control system [13, 14]. A large number of points increase the computational time, particularly with dynamic objects. At the same time, lesser number of points may not give a proper image of the map. Fig. 14 shows the plot of numbers of points vs computation time with and without flow taken into consideration.

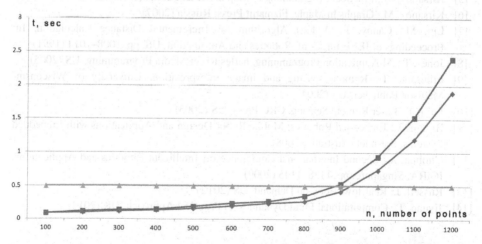

Fig. 14. A plot of the number of points on the time ⬥ path planning; ■ path planning with flows; ▲ optimal time calculation

6   Concluding Remarks

The paper presents a combination of algorithms which allows finding the optimal path with static and dynamic obstacles along with flow considerations. All results are collected and processed by the on-board computer unit of guidance and control system. The optimal time calculation for the on-board computer unit is 0.5 seconds per time. This time is a period between processing data of the map and getting the new information. Based on the plot shown in Figure 13 it is possible to make a conclusion that the optimal number of nodes is not more than 900. Each of these methods can be used separately or together depending on the needs of the guidance and control system. Also, the resulting plot of the number of points on the time will optimize the range of the navigation system of the AUV, depending on the performance of the on-board computer unit.

References

[1] Yuh, J.: Design and Control of Autonomous Underwater Robots: A Survey. Kluwer Academic Publisher, Netherlands (2000)

[2] Griffiths, G.: Technology and Applications of Autonomous Underwater Vehicles. Taylor & Francis Inc., UK (2003)

[3] Zilouchian, A.: Intelligent Control Systems Using Soft Computing Methodologies. CRC Press, USA (2000)

[4] Merrigan, M.: A Refinement to the World Geodetic System 1984 Reference Frame, pp. 2–4. Institute of Navigation (2002)

[5] Kirsanov, M.: Practical Programming in Maple. MPEI Publisher, Russia (2011)

[6] Kirsanov, M.: Graphs in Maple. Fizmatlit Press, Russia (2007)

[7] Lin, M., Canny, J.: A Fast Algorithm for Incremental Distance Calculation. In: Proceedings of IEEE Int. Conf. Robotics and Automation, US, pp. 1008–1014 (1991)

[8] Jones, T.: AI Application Programming. harles River Media Programming, US (2005)

[9] Lillesand, T.: Remote sensing and image interpretation. University of Wisconsin-Madison Publisher, US (2004)

[10] Fujii, T.: Laser Remote Sensing. CRC Press, US (2005)

[11] Braunl, T.: Embedded Robotics: Mobile Robot Design and Applications with Embedded Systems. Springer, Australia (2008)

[12] Guohua, X.: Second International Conference on Intelligent Robotics and Applications, ICIRA, Singapore, pp. 1138–1145 (2009)

[13] Russell, J.: Realflow, Book on Demand, US (2012)

[14] Jiyuan, T.: Computational Fluid Dynamics: A Practical Approach, UK (2012)

A Game Theoretic Approach for Reliable Power Supply in Islanded DG Grids

Rohan Mukherjee[1], Rupam Kundu[1], Sanjoy Das[2],
Bijaya Ketan Panigrahi[3], and Swagatam Das[4]

[1] Electronics and Telecommunication Engineering Department, Jadavpur University
[2] Department of Electrical and Computer Engineering, Kansas State University, USA
[3] Electrical Engineering Department, Indian Institute of Technology Delhi
[4] Electronics and Communication Sciences Unit, Indian Statistical Institute, Kolkata
{rohan.mukherjii,rupam2422}@gmail.com,
sdas@ksu.edu, bkpanigrahi@ee.iitd.ac.in, swagatam.das@isical.ac.in

Abstract. Game theory applies mathematical models in deciding interactions among people and their outcome. Mixed strategy Nash equilibrium in general exists in every game with a finite set of actions. Correlated equilibrium is a new solution concept in game theory that is more general than Nash Equilibrium and can be formulated with more accuracy on solutions. In this paper a Correlated Equilibrium based control has been extended to an Islanded Microgrid structure which depicts that scenario in smart-grids when it is isolated from the main power supply during power scarcity. The game theory based control has been shown to perform exceedingly well for the islanded scenario considering multi-agent structure. The individual agents are segregated by a superagent as potential buyers and sellers.A novel problem formulation is proposed and a Constrained variant of a newly proposed Differential Evolution Algorithm, ADE-LbX has been used for solving the non linear optimization problem. The final outcome has shown that the overall utility or satisfaction of agents is maximized extensively after energy trading besides maintaining trade advantage for each agent.

Notation

1. **Loads**
   L_i: Load of agent i.
   α_i: Fraction of L_i consumed by agent i; $0 \leq \alpha_i < 1$.

2. **Sources**
   G_{PVi}: Photovoltaic power generated by agent i.
   G_{Bi}: Non-critical load of agent i.

3. **Marginal Utility**
   $U(\alpha_i L_i)$: Utility of agent i consuming fraction α_i of L_i.
   $= (1 - (\exp(-4 * \alpha_i)))$

B.K. Panigrahi et al. (Eds.): SEMCCO 2013, Part II, LNCS 8298, pp. 487–498, 2013.

Utility function is formulated as an exponentially saturating curve following the law of diminishing returns: which states that there is more utility or benefit from utilizing initial percentage of something utilizable, than utilizing the later part and the overall curve stagnates finally[3]. $[\alpha_i \in [0, 1]$

4. **Trading**
   $\triangle P_i$: Power surplus/deficit of agent i.

5. $\triangle P_i = G_{PVi} + G_{Bi} - \alpha_i L_i$.

6. **S**: Set of selling agents.
   S$=i \mid \triangle P_i > 0$.

7. **B**: Set of buying agents.
   B$=i \mid \triangle P_i < 0$.

8. $S(\triangle P_i)$: Selling price of $\triangle P_i$ units to agent $i \in$ **S**.

9. $B(\triangle P_i)$: Buying price of $\triangle P_i$ units to agent $i \in$ **B**.

1   Introduction

Definition 1. *Game theory is a study of how agents interact with each other for making decisions. Formally it is a study of mathematical models of conflict and cooperation between intelligent rational decision-makers for strategic decision making [1,2,7]. Game theory has lots of applications in economics, political science, and psychology, as well as logic and biology.*

Definition 2. *In multiplayer non-cooperative games, Nash equilibrium is a solution concept in which each and every player has no advantage in deviating from its own strategy unilaterally when other players are fixed in their choice. The corresponding pay-offs constitute the Nash Equilibrium.[2,4]*

The modern game-theoretic concept of Nash Equilibrium is instead defined in terms of mixed strategies, where players choose a probability distribution over possible actions. In every game a pure strategy Nash Equilibrium might not exist. *John Forbes Nash* in his 1951 article *"Non-Cooperative Games"* proved that at least one mixed strategy Nash Equilibrium must exist in any game with a finite set of actions.

Correlated equilibrium introduced by *Robert Aumann* is a much recent proposition which is a solution concept more general than Nash Equilibrium.

Definition 3. *In Correlated Equilibrium the control resides on a super agent who assigns public signal based on which each player chooses its action.If every agent would not want to deviate from their assigned strategies for maximizing their utility, the distribution is said to be a correlated equilibrium.*

A strategic game of N players is characterized by an action set A_i and each player has an assigned u_i denoting its utility for choosing strategy a_i. The (N, A_i, u_i) game is thus comprised of strategies a_i, $a_i \in A_i$ and remaining players choose strategy profiles described by $N - 1$ tuple $a - 1$. The utility of i-th player is thus $u_i(a_i, a - i)$.

$\phi : A_i \longrightarrow A_i$ is a strategy modification for player i i.e. ϕ tells a player to play with action $\phi(a_i)$ when instructed to play a_i.

Let (Ω, π) be a countable probability space. For each player i, let P_i be his information partition, q_i be i's posterior and let $S_i : \Omega \longrightarrow A_i$, assigning the same value to states in the same cell of i's information partition. Then $((\Omega, \pi), P_i)$ is a correlated equilibrium of the strategic game (N, A_i, u_i) if for every player i and for every strategy modification ϕ:

$$\sum_{\omega \in \Omega} q_i(\omega) u_i(s_i, s_{-i}) \geq \sum_{\omega \in \Omega} q_i(\omega) u_i(\phi(s_i), s_{-i})$$

That is, $((\omega, \pi), P_i)$ can be said to be a correlated equilibrium if there exists no such player who can possibly improvise on its expected utility by any possible strategy modification.

Example 1. In game theory, battle of the sexes (BoS), [2] is a two-player coordination game shown in Table 1 where Husband and Wife play the game with individual probabilities $p, 1 - p, q$ and $1 - q$ respectively. The payoff of wife is

Table 1. Battle of Sexes

		Husband	
		Opera	*Game*
		p	$1 - p$
Wife	*Opera* q	$(2, 4)$	$(0, 0)$
	Game $1 - q$	$(0, 0)$	$(2, 4)$

given in the first value in each set whereas the payoff of the husband is given in the second ordinate. Clearly there exists two pure strategy Nash Equilibrium at $(Opera, Opera)$ and $(Game, Game)$ and also a mixed strategy Nash equilibrium if both husband and wife go to their preferred event $\frac{2}{3}$ times. The expected payoff for each individual will be $\frac{4}{3}$ respectively. The utility calculation for wife $U(W)$ is shown as below:

$$U(W) = 2pq + 4(1 - p)(1 - q).$$

So, for maximizing $U(W)$, we equate: $\frac{\partial}{\partial p} U(W) = 0$, which results in $q = \frac{2}{3}$. Therefore the $U(W) \mid_{max}$ equals $\frac{4}{3}$. Similar calculations hold for husband with $p = \frac{1}{3}$ and $U(H) \mid_{max} = \frac{4}{3}$.

Now if we consider a correlated strategy pair as given in Table 2 the total utility for wife will be: $U(W) = 2 * p_{OO} + 0 * p_{OG} + 0 * p_{GO} + 4 * p_{GG}$. If wife is instructed to go to *Opera* by a super agent her expected payoff will be $2 * p_{OO} + 0 * p_{OG}$ and if she disobeys her payoff will be $0 * p_{OO} + 4 * p_{OG}$. Again if she is instructed to go to *Game* her expected payoffs for the above two cases will be $0 * p_{GO} + 4 * p_{GG}$ and $2 * p_{GO} + 0 * p_{GG}$. Hence wife will benefit by obeying the super agent only if: $2 * p_{OO} + 0 * p_{OG} > 0 * p_{OO} + 4 * p_{OG}$ and $0 * p_{GO} + 4 * p_{GG} > 2 * p_{GO} + 0 * p_{GG}$ respectively. Similar explanation holds for husband, which yields $4 * p_{OO} + 0 * p_{GO} > 0 * p_{OO} + 2 * p_{GO}$ and $0 * p_{OG} + 2 * p_{GG} > 4 * p_{OG} + 0 * p_{GG}$. Maximizing the total utility of each agent $U(W)$ and $U(H)$ with the above constraints along with $p_{OO} + p_{OG} + p_{GO} + p_{GG} = 1$ we get an expected reward of 3 for each player which happens to be much higher than Mixed Strategy Nash Equilibrium.

Table 2. Battle of Sexes

		Husband	
		Opera(O)	Game(G)
Wife	Opera(O)	p_{OO}	p_{OG}
	Game(G)	p_{GO}	p_{GG}

That is if both the players could agree to toss a coin and if the result is heads, then both play *Opera*. or, both play *Game* then both players would benefit more.

2   Islanding- A Brief Overview

Definition 4. *Islanding [5] refers to the condition of a smart grid problem [3,6] in which a distributed (DG) generator continues to power a location even though electrical grid power from the electric utility is no longer present.*

The common example of islanding is a grid supply line that has solar panels attached to it. In the case of a blackout, the solar panels will continue to deliver power as long as brightness is sufficient. In this case, the supply line becomes an "island" with power surrounded by a "sea" of unpowered lines.

In intentional islanding, the generator disconnects from the grid, and forces the distributed generator to power the local circuit. Intentional islanding is the purposeful sectionalization of the utility system during widespread disturbances to create power "islands". These islands can be designed to maintain a continuous supply of power during disturbances of the main distribution system. The distributed energy resources can then supply the load power demand of the islands created until reconnection with the main utility system occurs.

3 Problem Formulation

3.1 Objectives and Constraints

1. Power Balance Constraint
$\sum_i (G_{PVi} + G_{Bi} - \alpha_i L_i) = 0.$

2. Utility Objective
Maximize: $\Lambda = \sum_i U(\alpha_i L_i).$

3. Agent Objective
Maximize: $\prod_i = S(\triangle P_i) - B(\triangle P_i) + U(\alpha_i L_i)$

3.2 Correlated Equilibrium Approach

The idea behind the following formulation is to distribute the excess powers of some agents to the agents having deficits, provided that the agents sacrificing excess powers are getting incentives in return or their utility gets maximized. Thus during islanding the outage can be handled effectively by efficient allocation of excess powers among agents.

– Scenario: The utility for all agents is to be maximized such that no agent loses in trading. The power trade is to beneficial for all and the total utility of load consumption by the society is to maximized. The power balance constraints must also be satisfied such that there is no loss in power being traded.

– Some Sellers can sell surplus power which are identified by the superagent. The microgrid verifies whether the α metric of the agent is above the mean value for the entire islanded agents. If it is so then it is classified as a potential seller. So sellers can adopt two strategies as instructed by the superagent: **Strategies:** Sell/NoSell

– Remaining units (B) can buy power. It readily follows that if the α metric of some agents falls below the mean value of α for all agents it gets classified as a potential buyer. So buyers can adopt two strategies as instructed by the superagent: **Strategies:** Buy/NoBuy

The Superagent will thus send signals to sellers (S) & buyers (B) as per the algorithm.

– Seller Payoffs: $\alpha_{(i,\bar{S})} > \alpha_{(i,S)}.$
a. Sell: $U(S) = S(G_{PVi} + G_{Bi} - \alpha_{(i}, S)L_i) + U(\alpha_{(i,S)} L_i).$
b. No Sell: $U(\bar{S}) = U(\alpha_{(i,\bar{S})} L_i).$

– Buyer Payoffs:$\alpha_{(i,\bar{B})} < \alpha_{(i,B)}$.
   a. Buy:$U(B) = B(G_{PVi} + G_{Bi} - \alpha_{(i,S)}L_i) + U(\alpha_{(i,B)}L_i)$.
   b. No Buy:$U(\bar{B}) = U(\alpha_{(i,\bar{B})}L_i)$.

Correlated Equilibrium Formulation for Constraints Determination. Here we consider the cases where the microgrid as a superagent instructs the potential buyers and sellers with their corresponding strategies to play. The equilibrium is ensured only when each agent does not lose by obeying the superagent while the overall utility of the total number of agents is maximized. This ensures that the overall benefit of the society is maximized by trading while nobody loses in its value of trade. The different cases by which the superagent instructs the agents are illustrated.

• **Case-1:** Buyer $i \in \mathbf{B}$ is receiving signal B

a. Expected payoff $U(B \mid B)$ if it is buying:
Determine users $\alpha_{(i,B|B)}$ if buying $(\alpha_{(i,\bar{B}|B)} < \alpha_{(i,B|B)})$.
Determine expected payoff,$U(B \mid B) = -B(\alpha_{(i,B)}L_i - G_{PVi} + G_{Bi}) + U(\alpha_{(i,B)}L_i)$.

b. Expected payoff $U(\bar{B} \mid B)$ if it is not buying:
Determine users $\alpha_{(i,(\bar{B}|B))}$ if not buying $(\alpha_{(i,B|B)} < \alpha_{(i,B|B)})$.
Determine expected payoff, $U(\bar{B} \mid B) = U(\alpha_{(i,\bar{B})}L_i)$.

– Criterion for utility gain of buyers by obeying the super agent:
$U(B \mid B) > U(\bar{B} \mid B)$
$-B(\alpha_{(i,B)}L_i - G_{PVi} + G_{Bi}) + U(\alpha_{(i,B)}L_i) > U(\alpha_{(i,\bar{B})}L_i)$.

• **Case-2:** Buyer $i \in \mathbf{B}$ is receiving signal $\bar{B}$

a. Expected payoff $U(\bar{B} \mid \bar{B})$ if it is not buying:
Determine users $\alpha_{(i,\bar{B}|\bar{B})}$ if not buying $(\alpha_{(i,\bar{B}|\bar{B})} > \alpha_{(i,B|\bar{B})})$.
Determine expected payoff, $U(\bar{B} \mid \bar{B}) = U(\alpha_{(i,\bar{B})}L_i)$.

b. Expected payoff $U(B \mid \bar{B})$ if it is buying:
Determine users $\alpha_{(i,(B|\bar{B}))}$ if not buying $(\alpha_{(i,\bar{B}|\bar{B})} > \alpha_{(i,B|\bar{B})})$.
Determine expected payoff,$U(B \mid \bar{B})=B(G_{PVi}+G_{Bi}-\alpha_{(i,B)}L_i)+U(\alpha_{(i,B)}L_i)$.

– Criterion for utility gain of buyers by obeying the super agent::
$U(\bar{B} \mid \bar{B}) > U(B \mid \bar{B})$
$U(\alpha_{(i,\bar{B})}L_i) > B(G_{PVi} + G_{Bi} - \alpha_{(i,B)}L_i) + U(\alpha_{(i,B)}L_i)$.

• **Case-3:** Seller $i \in \mathbf{S}$ is receiving signal S

a. Expected payoff $U(S \mid S)$ if it is selling:
Determine users $\alpha_{(i,S|S)}$ if selling $(\alpha_{(i,\bar{S}|S)} < \alpha_{(i,S|S)})$.
Determine expected payoff, $U(S \mid S) = S(\alpha_{(i,S)}L_i - G_{PVi} + G_{Bi}) + U(\alpha_{(i,S)}L_i)$.

b. Expected payoff $U(\bar{S} \mid S)$ if it is not selling:
Determine users $_{(i,}(\bar{S} \mid S))$ if not selling $(\alpha_{(i,\bar{S}|S)} < \alpha_{(i,S|S)})$.
Determine expected payoff, $U(\bar{S} \mid S) = U(\alpha_{(i,\bar{S})}L_i)$.

– Criterion for utility gain of sellers by obeying the super agent::
$U(S \mid S) > U(\bar{S} \mid S)$
$S(\alpha_{(i,S)}L_i - G_{PVi} + G_{Bi}) + U(\alpha_{(i,S)}L_i) > U(\alpha_{(i,\bar{S})}L_i)$.

• **Case-4:** Seller $i \in \mathbf{S}$ is receiving signal $\bar{S}$

a. Expected payoff $U(\bar{S} \mid \bar{S})$ if not selling:
Determine users $\alpha_{(i,\bar{S}|\bar{S})}$ if not selling $(\alpha_{(i,\bar{S}|\bar{S})} > \alpha_{(i,S|\bar{S})})$.
Determine expected payoff, $U(\bar{S} \mid \bar{S}) = U(\alpha_{(i,\bar{S})}L_i)$.

b. Expected payoff $U(S \mid \bar{S})$ if selling:
Determine users $\alpha_{(i,(S|\bar{S}))}$ if not selling $(\alpha_{(i,\bar{S}|\bar{S})} > \alpha_{(i,S|\bar{S})})$.
Determine expected payoff, $U(S \mid \bar{S}) = S(G_{PVi} + G_{Bi} - \alpha_{(i,S)}L_i) + U(\alpha_{(i,S)}L_i)$.

– Criterion for utility gain of sellers by obeying the super agent::
$U(\bar{S} \mid \bar{S}) > U(S \mid \bar{S})$
$U(\alpha_{(i,\bar{S})}L_i) > S(G_{PVi} + G_{Bi} - \alpha_{(i,S)}L_i) + U(\alpha_{(i,S)}L_i)$.

• Therefore the problem is:

Maximize: $\Lambda = \sum_i U(\alpha_i L_i)$.
subject to the Correlated Equilibrium constraints:

1. $-B(\alpha_{(i,B)}L_i - G_{PVi} + G_{Bi}) + U(\alpha_{(i,B)}L_i) > U(\alpha_{(i,\bar{B})}L_i)$.

2. $U(\alpha_{(i,\bar{B})}L_i) > B(G_{PVi} + G_{Bi} - \alpha_{(i,B)}L_i) + U(\alpha_{(i,B)}L_i)$.

3. $S(\alpha_{(i,S)}L_i - G_{PVi} + G_{Bi}) + U(\alpha_{(i,S)}L_i) > U(\alpha_{(i,\bar{S})}L_i)$.

4. $U(\alpha_{(i,\bar{S})}L_i) > S(G_{PVi} + G_{Bi} - \alpha_{(i,S)}L_i) + U(\alpha_{(i,S)}L_i)$.

4 Algorithm

The initial settings of each agent are computed. The production:consumption ratio is classified as α for each agent. The agents will recompute their α based on trading. The average value of α helps in distinguishing between $\mathbf{S}$ and $\mathbf{B}$. Based on their classification the constraints are formulated as shown previously.

The functional value $\sum_i U(\alpha_i L_i)$ is also set up. The agents along with their functional value and constraints are optimized as a Constrained Differential Evolution algorithm [8].

Differential evolution (DE) is a popular heuristic that is widely applied as an optimizer to real world problems of varied complexity and dimensionality. It is mostly used an an optimizer to static unimodal fields with sufficient advantage in complexity of the algorithm and runtime. It has shown to provide excellent solutions to a varied range of problems which includes its variants to be extended to multimodal, dynamic, as well constrained field of optimization. Here the constraints are formulated as a measure of penalty which is subtracted from the original functional value for optimization.

Very recently a strong modification on Differential Evolution, ADE-LbX [9] has been proposed which aims at having an explorative coverage of the entire search space rather than selective search biased to Cartesian Co-ordinates as in classical Differential Evolution. The algorithm is composed of strong components like a local best mutation schemes and L-best crossover merged with adaptive parameters F and Cr. The strength of the algorithm lies in its searching ability that can search an entire portion of the Gaussian Hyper-sphere marked by its two parents responsible for the mutation. The explorative search is suitable and more promising than other heuristics especially when search space is complicated, convoluted and high-dimensional in nature. The ADE-LbX has been implemented here to cater to these conditions and the constraints that make the search challenging.

Pseudo Code

Step 1. Set data for each home agent, G_{PVi} and L_i.

Step 2. Compute α_i for each agent: $\alpha_i = (G_{PVi} + G_{Bi})/L_i$

Step 3. Compute $\bar{\alpha} = mean(\alpha)$

Step 4. **For** each agent

       If $\alpha_i > \bar{\alpha}$

           Classify it as seller

       Else Classify it as buyer.

       End if

     End for

Step 5. Compute constraints for each agent.

Step 6. Optimize α for all agents by Differential Evolution using benchmark as $\sum_i U(\alpha_i L_i)$ and using all the constraints.

---

5   Experimental Settings

In the following section we discuss in details the set of parameters used to validate the problem formulation described above. The Number of Agents is kept fixed at $N = 40$. All agents are assumed to have G_{PVi} and G_{Bi} generation. The range of L_i and G_{PVi} are defined within $[5, 4]$ and $[3, 4]$(in KWH). The value of G_{Bi} is kept fixed as 1KWH for all agents. The Selling Price and Buying price are assumed to be fixed at 10 cents/KW. All the runs have been taken on a machine with Windows 7 64-bit configuration, 4GB RAM, 500GB hard disk and

2.26 GHz Intel Core i3-350M Processor. The parametric settings assumed here are approximately similar to real scenarios but they can be adjusted according to the problem considered. However, the performance of the correlated equilibrium approach to optimize the total utility of agents in islanded microgrids is independent of any parametric settings considered.

6 Results and Discussions

The α values of all the agents are shown in Fig 1. The algorithm is tested on a sample microgrid scenario representing outage for 40 agents. The G_{PVi} generation of each home along with its battery capacity G_{Bi} and demands L_i are as per Experimental Settings. The α metrics are segregated for sellers and buyers separately for better analysis of the results.

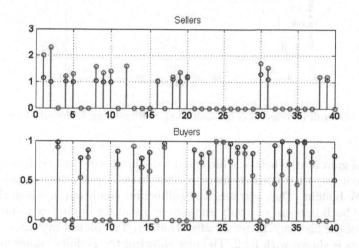

Fig. 1. Final α for both Buyers and Sellers

The initial α values are marked in red and the final values after optimization is shown in blue. For the sellers it can be observed that their α happens to be higher than average α for all the agents. More over many of them has α that happens to be greater than 1 that is their production is more than their consumption. Hence they try to sell this off during outage for more profit. Even if the α metric is not more than one the sellers are identified by their α metrics being greater the average value for all. Hence the sellers are those agents who have already satisfied much of its load demand. As the utility of each agent with increasing load decreases they can trade off their power for more profit by selling. The final α values are observed in Fig 1 which shows that that the sellers has traded off much of their power resulting in lower α. However their α is seldom less than one because after that they have to compromise their utility more for profit. The buyers who are in demand for energy gain by buying the powers as sold by the

Table 3. Performance Comparison of ADE-Lbx as compared to various other algorithms

Algorithms	ADE-Lbx	JADE	DE	PSO	GA
Final Value of $\sum U(\alpha_i)$	39.8979	37.2387	34.5730	27.5507	32.4973

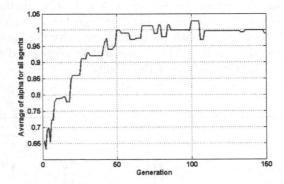

Fig. 2. Overall increase of α by optimizing utility using Differential Evolution

sellers and gain in α. Their α is increased with increasing utility. However all of them do not buy their entire demand as they have to pay a buying price for the power they bought. They settle in an equilibrium condition in which they have advantage both in terms of utility and money spent for buying extra power. The overall α of the agents is increased after trading. The plot of average α with DE generations is shown with fig 2. The plot showing the penalty values decreasing with iterations is shown in figure 3.

The performance of the algorithm has also been compared to several state-of the-arts. The final sum of utilities for all the agents has been taken as a metric of comparison. The average of 50 runs has been taken for a fair comparison. All the algorithms have been run on similar operating conditions. The results have been compared with JADE[10][11], the most recent adaptive variant of DE, original DE, PSO and GA and reported in Table 3. The results signify that ADE-LbX is the best of the state-of-the-arts in terms of the final value reached and signify its use in the islanded microgrid problem. The algorithm is run only for 150 generations and best DE individual is reported as the final α metric for all the agents.

Runtime for the algorithm as a function of the number of agents has been enumerated in Table 4. The runtime signifies that the controlling substation will not have a problem in evaluating the correct condition for the Microgrid before sending out the appropriate signals to the agents with respect to time. An outage is expected to last nearly 2-3 hours on average and an evaluation time in minutes

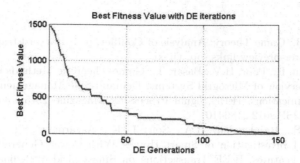

Fig. 3. Decrease of the Penalty Values with iterations

Table 4. Runtime for ADE-LBX Algorithm

No of agents	Runtime
20	28.56 secs
40	49.74 secs
60	1.23 mins
80	1.87 mins
100	2.76 mins

is not expected to hamper the situation because a Microgrid itself takes couple of minutes before islanding a part of the agent as it needs to retrieve the network condition of those agents before islanding.

7   Conclusion and Future Works

Game theory is successfully applied to a multi agent islanded DG scenario in smart grids. Correlated Equilibrium is used as a possible means of control algorithm formulation. A variant of Differential Evolution, ADE-LbX is used an optimizing tool in the problem with superior results. The algorithm has been applied over a sample islanded scenario of 40 agents of varying generation and load characteristics. Results show that the final utility of the entire society is maximized which implies that most of the agents could use a healthy amount of their load even when the entire neighbourhood is cut-off from main power grid. The results have also been compared with state-of-the arts and shown to outrun them by good margin. The low value of final penalty of the solution implies that the power balance constraints is minimal and the trading value of each agent is positive i.e. no agent loses by trading in terms of trade utility. Future work includes extending the problem to include critical loads i.e. the loads in which the power is to be ensured in any situation like the hospital or industrial loads etc. Moreover trading values can be made adaptive to the power availability of the sellers or power demand of the buyers.

References

1. Myerson, R.B.: Game Theory: Analysis of Conflict, p. 1. Harvard University Press (1991); Chapter-preview links, pp. vii–xi
2. Saad, W., Zhu, H., Poor, H.V., Basar, T.: Game-Theoretic Methods for the Smart Grid: An Overview of Microgrid Systems, Demand-Side Management, and Smart Grid Communications. IEEE Signal Processing Magazine 29(5), 86–105 (2012), doi:10.1109/MSP.2012.2186410
3. Kahrobaee, S., Rajabzadeh, R.A., Soh, L.-K., Asgarpoor, S.: A Multiagent Modeling and Investigation of Smart Homes With Power Generation, Storage, and Trading Features. IEEE Transactions on Smart Grid 4(2), 659–668 (2013), doi:10.1109/TSG.2012.2215349
4. Zhou, Q., Tesfatsion, L., Liu, C.-C., Chu, R.F., Sun, W.: A Nash approach to planning merchant transmission for renewable resource integration. IEEE Transactions on Power Systems (99), 1, doi:10.1109/TPWRS.2012.2228239
5. Dou, C.-X., Liu, B.: Multi-Agent Based Hierarchical Hybrid Control for Smart Microgrid. IEEE Transactions on Smart Grid 4(2), 771–778 (2013), doi:10.1109/TSG.2012.2230197
6. Maity, I., Rao, S.: Simulation and Pricing Mechanism Analysis of a Solar-Powered Electrical Microgrid. IEEE Systems Journal 4(3), 275–284 (2010), doi:10.1109/JSYST.2010.2059110
7. Couchman, P., Kouvaritakis, B., Cannon, M., Prashad, F.: Gaming Strategy for Electric Power With Random Demand. IEEE Transactions on Power Systems 20(3), 1283–1292 (2005), doi:10.1109/TPWRS.2005.851954
8. Das, S., Suganthan, P.N.: Differential evolution a survey of the state-of-the-art. IEEE Transactions on Evolutionary Computation 15(1), 4–31 (2011)
9. Mukherjee, R., Debchoudhury, S., Kundu, R., Das, S., Suganthan, P.N.: Adaptive Differential Evolution with Locality based Crossover for Dynamic Optimization. In: 2013 IEEE Congress on Evolutionary Computation (CEC), June 20-23, pp. 63–70 (2013)
10. Zhang, J., Sanderson, A.C.: JADE: Self Adaptive Differential Evolution with Fast and Reliable Convergence Performance. In: IEEE Congress on Evolutionary Computation(CEC) (2007)
11. Minhazul Islam, S.K., Das, S., Ghosh, S., Roy, S., Suganthan, P.N.: An Adaptive Differential Evolution Algorithm with Novel Mutation and Crossover Strategies for Global Numerical Optimization. IEEE Trans. on Systems, Man, and Cybernetics, Part B: Cybernetics 42(2), 482–500 (2012)

Classification of Day-Ahead Deregulated Electricity Market Prices Using DCT-CFNN

S. Anbazhagan and Narayanan Kumarappan

Department of Electrical Engineering, Annamalai University, Annamalai Nagar,
Chidambaram, Cuddalore District, Tamil Nadu, India, 608002
s.anbazhagan@gmx.com, kumarappan_n@hotmail.com

Abstract. Artificial neural networks (ANNs) are promising methods for the pattern recognition and classification. In this paper applies ANN to day-ahead deregulated energy market prices. The optimal profit is determined by applying a perfect price forecast. A price forecast with a less prediction errors, yields maximum profits for market players. The numerical electricity price forecasting is high in forecasting errors of various approaches. In this paper, discrete cosine transforms (DCT) based cascade-forward neural network (CFNN) approach (DCT-CFNN) is used to classify the electricity markets of mainland Spain and New York is presented. These electricity price classifications are important because all market participants do not to know the exact value of future prices in their decision-making process. In this paper, classifications of electricity market prices with respect to pre-specified electricity price threshold are used. In this proposed approach, all time series (historical price series) are transformed from time domain to frequency domain using DCT. These discriminative spectral coefficient forms the set of input features and are classified using CFNN. It has been observed that features selected from spectral domain improve the classification accuracy. The proposed model is more effective compared to some of the most recent price classification models.

Keywords: Price forecasting, Discrete cosine transforms, Cascade-forward neural network, Electricity price classification, Electricity market.

1   Introduction

The industries like oil and gas, airlines, banking, auto-manufacturing etc. had already showed very good performance in deregulation. Although electricity is a different type of commodity which cannot be stored in bulk quantity and also related to the interconnected grid management, beyond above features electric supply industries will also show the good results as deregulated industries. In most countries, oil and gas industry was deregulated before the electric supply industries. After looking at the performance of other sectors, the electric supply industries were deregulated [1].

In a deregulated electricity market, producers submit selling bids to the market operator consisting in energy blocks and their corresponding minimum selling prices, and consumers submit buying bids to the market operator consisting in energy blocks

B.K. Panigrahi et al. (Eds.): SEMCCO 2013, Part II, LNCS 8298, pp. 499–510, 2013.
© Springer International Publishing Switzerland 2013

and their corresponding maximum buying prices. In turn, the market operator clear the market using an appropriate market clearing procedure then that results in hourly energy prices and accepted selling and buying bids. Both producers and consumers use day-ahead price forecasts to derive their respective bidding strategies to the electricity market. Therefore, accurate price estimates are crucial for producers to maximize their profits and for consumers to maximize their utilities. Forecasting electricity prices is difficult because unlike demand series, price series present such characteristics as nonconstant mean and variance and significant outliers [2].

The electricity price forecasting errors generally range from approximately 5% to 36% and vary based on the technique used and the market analyzed. This range of error, however, is relatively high when compared to that of short-term electric load forecasting where errors usually range from 1% to 3% [3].

It is perceived from the existing literature [6-12] that traditional price forecasting approaches are generally developed for numerical prediction or point-forecasting. That is, existing approaches try to predict the exact value of prices at future hours by approximating the true underlying price formation process. However, not all market participants know the exact value of future prices in their decision-making process. Many demand-response products are designed having certain thresholds for electricity prices in mind, such as the hour-ahead dispatchable load program in the Ontario market. Another example of threshold-based decision making can be found in electricity consumers with on-site generation facilities. These facilities only purchase electricity from the grid if the electricity market prices are below the marginal cost of operating the on-site electricity generation equipment. In these types of applications where the exact value of prices is not primarily required, the point-price forecasting problem can be reduced to price classification sub problems in which the class of future prices is of interest [3].

The key uncertainties associated with those electricity prices are fuel prices, future addition of generation and transmission capacity, regulatory structure and rules, future demand growth, plant operations and climate changes [15]. For instance, electricity price depends on its previous values (historical values) and load values [16].

Prediction under soft-computing models, such as artificial neural networks (ANN), intelligent algorithms and hybrid intelligent approaches were used. Some of the soft-computing models include feed forward neural networks (FFNNs) technique [13], CFNN technique [13] and DCT based NN approach (DCT-NN) technique [14] are used. In particular, neural networks have been used to solve problems such as load/price predictions and classification, component and system fault diagnosis, security assessment, unit commitment etc. Electricity price classification has become an important research area in electrical engineering in recent years. Among the different approaches of classification systems, application of cascade-forward neural network (CFNN) input featured by discrete cosine transform (DCT) has been adopted in this paper because of its ability to learn complex and non-linear relationships that are difficult to model with conventional approaches.

An ANN input-output mapping is learned from historical examples, thus there is no need to model the system. Hence in this paper proposes a DCT input featured CFNN (DCT-CFNN) approach to classify next-week prices in the electricity markets of mainland Spain and New York. The day-ahead price classification method is as an alternative to numerical price forecasting. In price classification, predictions are made with respect to whether the price is above or below pre-specified price thresholds defined by users based on their operation and planning objectives. Price classification is specifically useful when the exact value of future prices is not critically important [3]. The main contribution of this paper is proposing a day-ahead price classification that could be realized using DCT input featured CFNN, trained by the levenberg-marquardt (LM) algorithm.

The price evaluation is different in different markets and therefore large variations exist in price-classification accuracy achieved by different models across different electricity markets [10]. Therefore, the Spanish market is taken as a real-world case study with sufficient non linear behavior and time variant functional relationship [2], [6]. The proposed approach is compared with FFNN, CFNN, and DCT-NN approaches, to show its good classification accuracy and less computation time.

The rest of the paper is organized as follows. The section 2 presents data source and proposed approach to classify electricity prices using their dataset. Section 3 presents the numerical results of proposed approach from a real-world case study based on the electricity markets of mainland Spain and New York. Finally, the conclusions are presented in section 4.

2   Methodology

This section describes the data source and proposed DCT-CFNN classification model to day-ahead price classification in mainland Spain and New York electricity markets.

2.1   Data Source

In order to perform the research reported in this paper, the electricity prices data taken from mainland Spain's daily trading reports, presented on a monthly basis and New York Independent System Operator (NYISO), CAPITL zone customized on yearly reports were used. The Spain and NYISO data set consists of market clearing price (MCP) [17] and locational-based marginal price (LBMP) [18]. Different sets of lagged prices (are transformed from time domain to frequency domain using DCT) have been proposed as input features for the price classification. The lags of P_{h-1}, P_{h-2}, P_{h-3}, P_{h-24}, P_{h-25}, P_{h-48}, P_{h-49}, P_{h-72}, P_{h-73}, P_{h-96}, P_{h-97}, P_{h-120}, P_{h-121}, P_{h-144}, P_{h-145}, and P_{h-168} are transformed from time domain to frequency domain using DCT considered in which as the input features for the proposed approach.

Four classification thresholds are considered for the mainland Spain market for the year 2002: $T_1 = 0$, $T_2 = 37$, $T_3 = 74$ and $T_4 = 158$ with all in euro per megawatt hour and New York market for the year 2010: $T_1 = 17$, $T_2 = 49$, $T_3 = 98$ and $T_4 = 189$ with all in dollar per megawatt hour. T_1, T_4, T_2 and T_3 are the price floors, price cap, annual average and twice the annual average of the prices in mainland Spain and New York.

Normally, the price thresholds based on their own operating criteria were defined by the users. For the above price thresholds, the class distribution is

- Class 1: (Prices between T_1 and T_2)
- Class 2: (Prices between T_2 and T_3)
- Class 3: (Prices between T_3 and T_4)

For electricity price classification, target prices belongs to particular class are applied with target as "1" to the corresponding class and target as "0" to the rest of the classes. All patterns have sixteen features. These features are DCT transformed lagged prices.

2.2   Classification of Electricity Prices Using DCT-CFNN Approach

The proposed DCT-CFNN approach to classify electricity prices is based on a coordination of DCT and CFNN. In this approach, all time series (historical price series) are first transformed from time domain into a frequency domain using DCT. This step is crucial because it helps reducing the correlation between the features in time domain and in revealing the hidden information about the series. Then, these discriminative spectral co-efficient forms the set of input features and are classified using CFNN. Finally, CFNN classify the future behavior of the prices that classify the actual prices.

Discrete Cosine Transform. In most real world time series, consecutive values of a time series are usually not independent, but highly correlated. This makes it difficult to develop effective feature selection techniques that work directly on the time series data. To alleviate the problem, time series can be transformed from time domain into another domain in order to de-correlate the time features and reveal the hidden structure of the series. This paper, describes the DCT time series transformation technique.

The DCT attempts to de-correlate the time series. After de-correlation each transformed co-efficient can be encoded independently without losing efficiency. DCT is a Fourier related transform is similar to discrete fourier transform, but uses only cosine functions instead of using both cosines and sines. It transforms the input signal from time domain to frequency domain, which highlights the periodicity of the signal.

The DCT definition of a 1-D (one dimension) sequence of $f(x)$, length N is

$$C(u) = \alpha(u) \sum_{x=0}^{N-1} f(x) \cos\left[\frac{(2x+1)u\pi}{2N}\right] \tag{1}$$

for $x = 0,1,2,\ldots,N-1$. In equation (1), $\cos\left[\dfrac{(2x+1)u\pi}{2N}\right]$ is called forward DCT transformation kernel. In $C(u)$ for $u = 0,1,2,\ldots,N-1$ in equation (1) are called DCT transform coefficients of $f(x)$.

In this approach, the inverse transformation is not used. In equation (1), $\alpha(u)$ is defined as

$$\alpha(u) = \begin{cases} \sqrt{\dfrac{1}{N}} & for \quad u = 0 \\[3mm] \sqrt{\dfrac{2}{N}} & for \quad u \neq 0 \end{cases} \tag{2}$$

It is clear from the equation (1) that $u = 0$, $C(u = 0) = \sqrt{\dfrac{1}{N}} \sum_{x=0}^{N-1} f(x)$. thus, the first

transform co-efficient is the average value of the time series. In literature, this value is referred to as the DC co-efficient. All other transform co-efficient are called the AC co-efficient.

In this paper, the DCT is used. It is chosen because it offers the following desirable properties:

1)   DCT co-efficient are always real numbers;
2)   DCT can handle effectively, the time series with trends;
3)   When successive values are highly correlated, DCT achieves better energy concentration.

Cascade-Forward Neural Network. The ANN models are trained in such a way that a particular input leads to a specific target output. There are generally four steps in the training and testing process (1) assembling the training data, (2) creating the network, (3) training the network, and (4) computing the network response to new inputs.

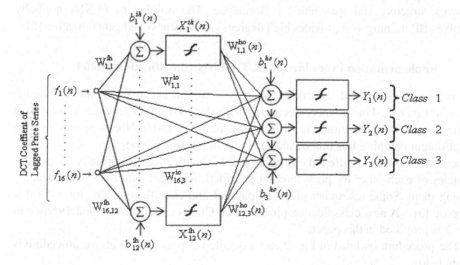

Fig. 1. Implementation of DCT-CFNN approach for electricity price classification

In this paper, a CFNN was used for electricity price classification. In this CFNN model (with one input layer, one hidden layer and one output layer), the first layer has connecting weights with the input layer and each subsequent layer has weights coming from the input as well as from all previous layers is shown in Fig. 1. The hidden layer neurons (12 neurons) and the output layer neurons (three neurons) use nonlinear hyperbolic-tangent-sigmoid and pure linear activation functions respectively. In this system, sixteen inputs are featured, and electricity price classification outputs are used to classify electricity prices. Equations used in the CFNN classification model with only one hidden layer are shown in (3) and (4).

Outputs of the hidden layer neurons are:

$$\vec{X}^{ih}(n) = 2/(1 + \exp(-2 * (W^{ih}(n) * \vec{f}(n) + \vec{b}^{ih}(n)))) - 1 \tag{3}$$

Output of the network is:

$$\vec{Y}(n) = W^{io}(n) * \vec{f}(n) + W^{ho}(n) * \vec{X}^{ih}(n) + b^{ho}(n) \tag{4}$$

Where $W^{ih}(n)$ are the weights from the input to the hidden layer and $\vec{b}^{ih}(n)$ are the biases of the hidden layer, $W^{io}(n)$ are the weights from the input to the output layer, $W^{ho}(n)$ are the weights from the hidden layer to the output layer and $b^{ho}(n)$ are the biases of the output layer, $\vec{f}(n)$ values are the input features. $\vec{Y}(n)$ values are the outputs for the electricity price class, and n is training pattern index.

Like FFNNs, CFNN uses BP algorithm for updating of weights but the main symptoms of the network is that each neuron is related to all previous layer neurons. In [4], several neural network topologies were evaluated and it was found that CFNN with BP training provides the best performance in terms of convergence time, optimum network structure and recognition performance. The training of FFNNs normally involves BP training as it provides high degrees of robustness and generalization [5].

2.3   Implementation Procedure of DCT-CFNN Classification Model

As previously described, electricity price is a nonlinear, time variant and multi-variable function. For instance, electricity price depends on its previous values, load values, available generation, etc. It is very hard for a single NN to capture correct input/output mapping function of such a signal in all time periods [16]. However, our experience shows that different electricity price classifications can usually cover deficiencies of each other for price forecast provided; a correct data flow is constructed among them. Some researcher proposed parallel and classification structures for this purpose [3].   A new classification procedure of CFNN classification model shown in Fig. 2 is proposed in this paper.

The procedure outlined in Fig. 2 and a detailed explanation of above procedure is given below.

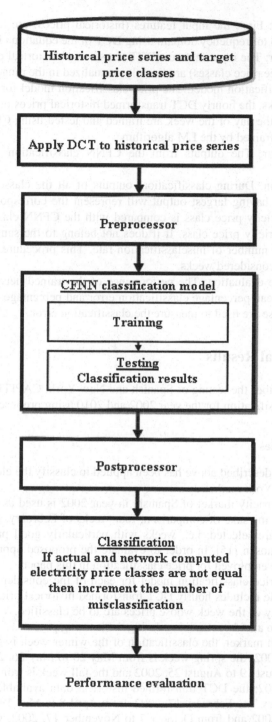

Fig. 2. The classification procedure of DCT-CFNN approach

1) Apply DCT: First, the input features (historical prices) are transformed from time domain to frequency domain using DCT of the equation (1).
2) Preprocessor: The input features (DCT transformed historical prices) and target outputs (three price classes) are linearly normalized in the range of {-1, 1}.
3) CFNN classification model: The price classification model for each of the considered weeks, the hourly DCT transformed historical prices of the past 42 days previous to the day of the week are trained and tested using CFNN of equation (3) and (4), trained by the LM algorithm.
4) Postprocessor: The outputs from the CFNN classification model were denormalized.
5) Classification: During classification, outputs of all the classes are compared. The classes having largest output will represent the corresponding class. The actual electricity price class is compared with the CFNN classification model output electricity price class. If it does not belong to the same class, then increment the number of misclassification rate. This procedure is repeated until each of the considered weeks.
6) Performance evaluation: The performance of the trained network is then evaluated by mean percentage classification error and percentage classification accuracy. These are used to measure the classification error.

3   Numerical Results

This section describes the testing of Spanish and New York, CAPITL zone electricity markets price classification for the year 2002 and 2010 using proposed approach.

3.1   Case Studies

The methodology described above has been applied to classify the electricity prices of Spanish and New York markets.

Day-ahead electricity market of Spanish, in year 2002 is used as test case in price classification. For the sake of comparison, four weeks of February, May, August and November 2002 are selected, i.e., weeks with particularly good price behavior are deliberately not chosen [15]. In order to evaluate the proposed approaches, the most volatile prices, are employed for price classification in this paper.

To build the price classification model for each of the considered weeks, the information available includes hourly DCT transformed historical prices of the 42 days previous to the day of the week whose prices are to be classified. Very large training sets are not used to avoid overtraining during the learning process.

For the Spanish market, the classification of the winter week is from February 18 to February 24, 2002, the spring week is from May 20 to May 26, 2002, the summer week is from August 19 to August 25, 2002 and the fall week is from November 18 to November 24, 2002; the DCT transformed historical data available includes hourly prices from January 7 to February 17, 2002, from April 8 to May 19, 2002, from July 8 to August 18, 2002 and from October 7 to November 17, 2002, which are used to classify the respective week.

Real data of the New York electricity market in year 2010 are also considered for examination. For the sake of fair comparison, the four weeks of February, May, August, and November (months 2, 5, 8, and 11) are selected. The winter week is February 15 to February 21, 2010; historical data available includes hourly prices from January 4 to February 14, 2010. The spring week is May 15 to May 21, 2010; historical data includes prices from April 3 to May 14, 2010. The summer week is August 15 to August 21, 2010; historical data includes prices from July 4 to August 14, 2010. The fall week is November 15 to November 21, 2010; historical data includes prices from October 4 to November 14, 2010.

In this paper, the input features (DCT transformed historical prices) and target output (three price classes) are linearly normalized in the range of {-1, 1}. The outputs from the CFNN classification model were de-normalized before being presented in performance evaluation.

The performance of the trained network is then evaluated by comparison of the network output with its actual value via statistical evaluation indices. The mean percentage classification error (MPCE) and percentage classification accuracy (PCA) are used as the overall measures of classification error in this paper.

The MPCE can be defined as

$$MPCE = 100 \times \left(\frac{N_{mc}}{N_{tot}} \right) \qquad (5)$$

The PCA is given by

$$PCA = \left(\frac{N_{tot} - N_{mc}}{N_{tot}} \right) \times 100 \qquad (6)$$

Where N_{mc} and N_{tot} are the number of misclassified and total number of classified hours, respectively.

3.2   Classification of Electricity Prices with DCT-CFNN Approach

In DCT-CFNN classification model, the architecture and training are determined using stochastic approach. Several attempts were made until the proper number of hidden layers and numbers of neurons in hidden layer were reached. The network architecture selected after many attempts produced minimal error in both training and testing.

The CFNN classification model have input layer composed of sixteen neurons, hidden layer composed of twelve neurons and output layer with three neurons. The multi-layer neural network is selected as the network type with LM training. The DCT-CFNN classification model is implemented using the MATLAB neural network toolbox. The size of the input pattern is 16 (DCT transformed historical price series) $\times$ 1008 (42 days training period $\times$ 24 hours), and the size of the target pattern is 3 (three price classes) $\times$ 1008 in DCT-CFNN classification model.

Table 1. Statistical analysis for four weeks obtained with the DCT-CFNN approach on Spanish and New York market for the year 2002 and 2010

Classification Week	Spanish Market		New York Market	
	MPCE	PCA	MPCE	PCA
Winter	3.0	97.02	3.6	96.43
Spring	1.8	98.21	3.0	97.02
Summer	4.2	95.83	3.0	97.02
Fall	3.6	96.43	6.6	93.45
Average	3.2	96.87	4.1	95.98

The MPCE and PCA obtained by proposed DCT-CFNN classification model to electricity price classification were presented in Table 1 for both the markets. The first column indicates the classification week, the second and third column indicates MPCE and PCA for Spanish market, the fourth and fifth column indicates MPCE and PCA for New York market. It is observed that the MPCE and PCA obtained using proposed approach for the Spanish and New York electricity market has an average value of 3.2% and 96.87%; 4.1% and 95.98% respectively. The MPCE and PCA results confirm that the proposed DCT-CFNN classification model is capable of classifying the electricity market prices efficiently.

3.3 Comparison with Other Approaches

Different approaches are tested for Spanish market and results of these analyses are compared. Table 1 gives statistical analysis for four weeks obtained with the DCT-NN approach on Spanish and New York market for the year 2002 and 2010. Table 2, shows the comparison between the proposed DCT-CFNN approach and three other approaches (FFNN, CFNN, and DCT-NN) on Spanish market for the year 2002. From the same Table 2, it is observed the minimum MPCE and maximum PCA is 3.2% and 96.87% respectively occurred on an average in DCT-CFNN approach for price classification when compared with three other approaches for all the four weeks of Spanish market in year 2002.

Table 2. Comparative MPCE and PCA results between the various methods on Spanish market for the year 2002

Method	Classification Week				Average	
	Winter	Spring	Summer	Fall	MPCE	PCA
FFNN [21]	3.6	3.0	4.8	5.4	4.2	95.83
CFNN [21]	3.0	3.0	4.8	4.8	3.9	96.13
DCT-NN [22]	3.0	1.8	4.8	4.2	3.5	96.58
DCT-CFNN	3.0	1.8	4.2	3.6	3.2	96.87

Improvement in the average MPCE of the proposed approach with respect to the NN, CFNN and DCT-NN approaches are 1.0%, 0.7%, and 0.3% and improved percentage average error of MPCE are 23.8%, 18.0%, and 8.6% on Spanish market. So, we can easily say that DCT-CFNN approach possesses better classifying abilities than three other approaches and its performance was least affected by the price volatility. Finally, the proposed DCT-CFNN approach provides a very powerful tool of easy implementation for electricity price classification.

The simulations were carried out in AMD processor with 2GHz and 1GB RAM. Moreover, the proposed approach presents lower modeling complexity: the average computation time is less than 25ms. In a deregulated electricity market, the fast classification of prices would help the power trading market and independent players with better bidding strategies for efficient operation and increase in savings and social benefit.

4   Conclusion

This paper presented a comprehensive model for day-ahead electricity price classification using a DCT-CFNN approach in the mainland Spain and New York deregulated markets. The electricity price depends on its previous values (historical values) and load values. In price classification, predictions are made with respect to whether the price is above or below the pre-specified price thresholds used. To verify the price classification ability of the proposed approach, yielding an average weekly MPCE and PCA for the Spanish and New York electricity were close to 3.2% and 96.87%; 4.1% and 95.98% which shows a better capability to improve the problem of classifying price spikes. The test results showed that the proposed price classification model, especially the MPCE and PCA results of the proposed DCT-CFNN classification model is a good tool for price classification in terms of efficiency as well as heuristic compared to three other classification models on Spanish market. The research work is underway in order to develop better feature selection algorithm for different power markets and classification models.

References

1. Singh, S.N.: Electric Power Generation, Transmission and Distribution. Prentice-Hall, India (2008)
2. Conejo, A.J., Plazas, M.A., Espinola, R., Molina, A.B.: Day-ahead electricity price forecasting using the wavelet transform and ARIMA models. IEEE T. Power Syst. 20, 1035–1042 (2005)
3. Zareipour, H., Janjani, A., Leung, H., Motamedi, A., Schellenberg, A.: Classification of Future Electricity Market Prices. IEEE T. Power Syst. 26, 165–173 (2011)
4. Qahwaji, R., Colak, T.: Neural Network-based Prediction of Solar Activities. In: Proceedings of 3rd International Conference on Cybernetics and Information Technologies, Orlando, Florida, USA (2006)
5. Kim, J., Mowat, A., Poole, P., Kasabov, N.: Linear and non-linear pattern recognition models for classification of fruit from visiblenext term–near infrared spectra. Chemometr. Intell. Lab. 51, 201–216 (2000)
6. Amjady, N., Hemmati, H.: Day-ahead price forecasting of electricity markets by a hybrid intelligent system. Eur. Trans. Elect. Power 19, 89–102 (2009)

7. Aggarwal, S.K., Saini, L.M., Kumar, A.: Day-ahead price forecasting in Ontario electricity market using variable-segmented support vector machine-based model. Elect. Power Compon. Syst. 37, 495–516 (2009)
8. Saini, L.M., Aggarwal, S.K., Kumar, A.: Parameter optimisation using genetic algorithm for support vector machine-based price-forecasting model in national electricity market. IET Gen. Transm. Distrib. 4, 36–49 (2010)
9. Zhang, L., Luh, P.B.: Neural network-based market clearing price prediction and confidence interval estimation with an improved extended Kalman filter method. IEEE T. Power Syst. 20, 59–66 (2005)
10. Aggarwal, S.K., Saini, L.M., Kumar, A.: Electricity price forecasting in deregulated markets: A review and evaluation. Int. J. Elec. Power 3, 13–22 (2009)
11. Unsihuay-Vila, C., Zambroni de Souza, A.C., Marangon-Lima, J.W., Balestrassi, P.P.: Electricity demand and spot price forecasting using evolutionary computation combined with chaotic nonlinear dynamic model. Int. J. Elect. Power 32, 108–116 (2010)
12. Shafie-khah, M., Moghaddam, M.P., Sheikh-El-Eslami, M.K.: Price forecasting of day-ahead electricity markets using a hybrid forecast method. Energ. Convers. Manage. 52, 2165–2169 (2011)
13. Anbazhagan, S., Kumarappan, N.: A neural network approach to day-ahead deregulated electricity market prices classification. Electr. Pow. Syst. Res. 86, 140–150 (2012)
14. Anbazhagan, S., Kumarappan, N.: Day-ahead deregulated electricity market price classification using neural network input featured by DCT. Int. J. Elec. Power 37, 103–109 (2012)
15. Catalão, J.P.S., Mariano, S.J.P.S., Mendes, V.M.F.: Short-term electricity prices forecasting in a competitive market: A neural network approach. Electr. Pow. Syst. Res. 77, 1297–1304 (2007)
16. Amjady, N., Keynia, F.: Application of a new hybrid neuro-evolutionary system for day-ahead price forecasting of electricity markets. Appl. Soft Comput. 10, 784–792 (2010)
17. Spanish Electricity Market Website, http://www.omel.com
18. New York Electricity Market Website, http://www.nyiso.com

Multi-Objective Approach
for Protein Structure Prediction

S. Sudha[1,*], S. Baskar[1], and S. Krishnaswamy[2]

[1] Thiagarajar College of Engineering, Madurai, India
{ssj,sbeee}@tce.edu
[2] Centre of Excellence in Bioinformatics, Madurai Kamaraj University, Madurai, India
krishna@mrna.tn.nic.in

Abstract . This work proposes to optimize Protein Structure Prediction (PSP) using multi-objective ab initio approach. This paper addresses an application of modified NSGA-II (MNSGA-II) by incorporating controlled elitism and Dynamic Crowding Distance (DCD) strategies in NSGA-II for PSP by minimizing free Potential Energy (PE) and minimizing Solvent Accessible Surface area (SAS). In this model, a trigonometric representation is used to compute backbone and side-chain torsion angles of protein atoms. Free energy is calculated using Chemistry at HARvard Macromolecular Mechanics (CHARMm -22). SAS is calculated using dssp program. Both objectives together evaluate the structures of protein conformations. The evolution of protein conformations is directed by optimization of protein energy and surface area contributions using MNSGA-II. To validate the Pareto-front obtained using MNSGA-II, reference Pareto-front is generated using multiple runs of single objective optimization (RGA) with weighted sum of objectives. TOPSIS technique is applied on obtained non-dominated solutions to determine Best Compromise Solution (BCS). Result of MNSGA-II is compared with NSGA-II. The proposed model is validated with Met-enkephalin, a benchmark protein, obtaining very promising results.

Keywords: Protein Structure Prediction, Free Potential Energy, Solvent Accessible Surface Area, modified NSGA-II, Pareto-front, Best Compromise Solution.

1 Introduction

One of the most important open problems in molecular biology is the prediction of the spatial conformation of a protein from its primary structure, i.e. from its sequence of amino acids. The classical methods for structure analysis of proteins are X-ray crystallography and nuclear magnetic resonance (NMR). Unfortunately, these techniques are expensive and can take a long time. On the other hand, the sequencing of proteins is relatively fast, simple, and inexpensive. As a result, there is a large gap between the number of known protein sequences and the number of known three-dimensional protein structures. This gap has grown over the past decade and is

---

* Corresponding author.

B.K. Panigrahi et al. (Eds.): SEMCCO 2013, Part II, LNCS 8298, pp. 511–522, 2013.
© Springer International Publishing Switzerland 2013

expected to keep growing, as a result of the various genome projects worldwide. Therefore, computational methods are needed as they could provide a faster and economic way to tackle the PSP problem.

There are three major approaches to predict the native state of this problem: 'comparative modelling', 'threading', and 'ab initio prediction'. Comparative modelling exploits the fact that evolutionarily related proteins with similar sequences, as measured by the percentage of identical residues at each position based on an optimal structural superposition, often have similar structures. Threading methods compare a target sequence against a library of structural templates, producing a list of scores. The scores are then ranked and the fold with the best score is assumed to be the one adopted by the sequence. Finally, the ab initio prediction methods consist in modeling all the energies involved in the process of folding, and then in finding the structure with lowest free energy. This approach is based on the 'thermodynamic hypothesis', which states that the native structure of a protein is the one for which the free energy achieves the global minimum. While ab initio prediction is clearly the most difficult, it is arguably the most useful approach [1].

2   Literature Review

Proteins usually fold into the conformation with the lowest free energy, so protein structure prediction is essentially a search amongst all possible conformations of an amino acid sequence for the conformation with the lowest free energy. As PSP using ab initio approach can be considered as a search problem, the search space is determined by all possible rules involved in the folding process of a protein. Such a space is huge and very complex.   Evolutionary Algorithms are more suitable, because EAs are characterized by very good search capabilities and have the ability to escape from local optima. Authors of [2-4] used torsion angle model, HP model and Lattice model respectively to solve PSP using EAs. All these methods consider PSP as single-objective optimization problem to minimize potential energy. This potential energy function is used to find the three-dimensional native conformation with minimum energy from a protein sequence of amino acids.

The single objective approach works well when one objective to optimize or all the objectives are not in conflict with each other. When a problem requires optimizing several objectives at a time and they can be difficult to combine into in a single function, single objective approach will not work well. Because, in this, the search space is highly complex and it is often impossible to find a single optimal solution.

In this scenario, one is usually interested in finding a set of solutions that presents a good compromise among all the objectives. Such solutions are generally denoted as the Pareto set, because based on the notion of Pareto dominance. Rather than combining the multiple objectives into a single fitness function, a better approach to find this optimal set is to optimize the objectives separately, i.e., treat the problem as a multi-objective problem. EAs are particularly suited for tackling multi-objective optimization problems, mainly due to the population-based nature of EAs. This allows the generation of several elements of the Pareto set in a single run. Some of the best known multi-objective EAs (MOEAs) are NSGA, SPEA, NSGA-II, SPEA-II and PAES-II [5].

Several prediction methods have considered PSP problem as a multi-objective optimization problem (MOP). In [6], authors developed MI-PAES as a modified version of PAES using a torsion angles model. A parallel multi-objective optimization was performed by using Chemistry at HARvard Macromolecular Mechanics (CHARMM) energy function in [7]. Authors of [8] proposed a multi-objective Feature Analysis and Selection Algorithm (MOFASA) in order to solve the Protein Fold Recognition (PFR) problem. In [9], an I-PAES algorithm is used as search procedure for exploring the space of the PSP problem. The concept of bond and non-bond energies is included in the fitness function of this approach. MOEA is proposed in [10] for the protein contact map prediction problem and the scheme is based on the Strength Pareto Evolutionary Algorithm (SPEA) for the PSP problem. The novelty in prediction is based on a set of amino acid properties [10].

So for, authors of multi-objective optimization in PSP have used bonded and non-bonded energies as their conflicting objectives. But, in this work, for the first time, potential energy and accessible surface area are considered as two conflicting objectives and Modified NSGAII is used to solve the problem.

The flow of the paper is as follows: Section 3 describes the formulation of two objectives; Section 4 explains the Modified NSGAII algorithm; Section 5 discusses about the results and Pareto fronts.

3   Objective Functions Formulation

Protein Structure Prediction Problem has been formulated as Multi-objective problem by minimizing the potential energy as well as minimizing the accessible surface area of a protein to improve the structure of protein. Fig 1. shows the plotting of two objectives for the random 100 solutions. As the plotting is not linear, it is shown that the considered two objectives are conflicting.

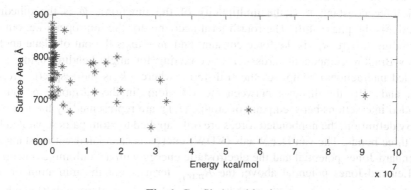

Fig. 1. Conflicting objectives

3.1   Potential Energy

The force field refers to the form and parameters of mathematical functions used to describe the potential energy of a protein.   The force field encapsulates both bonded terms relating to atoms that are linked by covalent bonds, and nonbonded (also called "non-covalent") terms describing the long-range electrostatic and van der Waals forces. The total energy in an additive force field can be written as $E_{total} = E_{bonded} + E_{nonbonded}$ where the components of the covalent and non-covalent contributions are given by

$$E_{bonded} = E_{bonds} + E_{angles} + E_{dihedrals} + E_{impropers} + E_{Urey-Bradley}$$
$$E_{nonbonded} = E_{vanderWaals} + E_{electrostatic}$$

CHARMM (Chemistry at HARvard Macromolecular Mechanics) is widely used set of force fields for molecular dynamics. There are several versions of the CHARMM force field available like CHARMM19, CHARMM22, or CHARMM27. CHARMM22 (released in 1991) and CHARMM27 (released in 1999) are the most recent versions of the force field. For purely protein systems, the two are equivalent [11]. The potential energy function for CHARMM22 is given below in eqn (1).

$$V = \sum_{bonds} k_b (b - b_0)^2 + \sum_{angles} k_\theta (\theta - \theta_0)^2 + \sum_{dihedrals} k_\phi [1 + cos(n\phi - \delta)] +$$
$$\sum_{impropers} k_\omega (\omega - \omega_0)^2 + \sum_{Urey-Bradley} k_u (u - u_0)^2 + \sum_{nonbonded} \epsilon \left[\left(\frac{R_{min_{ij}}}{r_{ij}} \right)^{12} - \left(\frac{R_{min_{ij}}}{r_{ij}} \right)^6 \right] + \frac{q_i q_j}{\epsilon r_{ij}} \tag{1}$$

The first term in the energy function accounts for the bond stretches. k_b, is the bond force constant and $b - b_0$ is the distance from equilibrium that the atom has moved. The second term in the equation accounts for the bond angles, where, k_θ is the angle force constant and $\theta - \theta_0$ is the angle from equilibrium between 3 bonded atoms. The third term is for the dihedrals (a.k.a. torsion angles) where k_ϕ is the dihedral force constant, n is the multiplicity of the function, ϕ is the dihedral angle and δ is the phase shift. The fourth term accounts for the impropers, i.e. out of plane bending, where k_ω is the force constant and $\omega - \omega_0$ is the out of plane angle. The Urey-Bradley component (cross-term accounting for angle bending using 1, 3 nonbonded interactions) comprises the fifth term, where k_U is the respective force constant and U is the distance between the 1,3 atoms in the harmonic potential. Nonbonded interactions between pairs of atoms (i, j) are represented by the last two terms. By definition, the nonbonded forces are only applied to atom pairs separated by at least three bonds. The van Der Waals (VDW) energy is calculated with a standard 12-6 Lennard-Jones potential and the electrostatic energy with a Coulombic potential. In the Lennard-Jones potential above, the $R_{min_{ij}}$ term is not the minimum of the potential, but rather where the Lennard-Jones potential crosses the x-axis (i.e. where the Lennard-Jones potential is zero).

3.2   Accessible Surface Area

The Solvent Accessible Surface Area (SAS) describes the area over which contact between protein and solvent can occur. The solvent accessible surface is defined as the locus of the centre of a probe sphere (representing the solvent molecule) as it rolls over the van der Waals surface of the protein. The original motivation for the calculation of the accessible surface was the study of the protein-folding problem and hydrophobicity. The size of the solvent accessible surface area buried in an interaction between protein units can be used to discriminate between crystal packing and a functional protein-protein interaction.

An effect of using different van der Waals' radii is that Hydrogen atoms are not considered individually in the calculations. The van der Waals' radii used for non-hydrogen atoms are modified to account for the implicit presence of hydrogen. The choice of van der Waals' radii used in the calculations would also be expected to have an effect on the estimates of ASA[12].

While defining the accessible surface area, draw spheres of radii $r + r_w$ around each atom of the protein structure; r is the van der Waals radius of the atom and r_w is the radius of a sphere simulating a water molecule, typically 1.4 A. The spheres intersect, and the accessible surface area of the atom is: $A = S - B$, in which S is the total surface area of the sphere S attached to that atom, $S = 4\pi(r + r_w)^2$ and B (buried surface area) is the area cut out of the surface of S by all intersecting spheres. SAS is calculated using DSSP software [13].

4   Modified NSGA-II (MNSGA-II)

NSGA-II algorithm [14] incorporates advanced concepts like elitism, fast non-dominated sorting and diversity maintenance along the Pareto-optimal front, but, still it cascades a bit to maintain lateral diversity and uniform distribution of non-dominated solutions. Emphasis on lateral diversity is essential to elude too much exploitation than exploration and hence need to have better convergence of search algorithm. Uniform distribution of non-dominated solutions is necessary to cover the entire Pareto-front. The proposed, enhanced concept called controlled elitism, which maintains the diversity of non-dominated front laterally, overcomes shortcomings of NSGA-II.   Also, Luo et al.'s[15] DCD improves distribution of non-dominated solutions in NSGA-II.

4.1   Controlled Elitism

A new concept called 'controlled elitism' incorporated [16] in NSGA-II restricts the number of individuals in the current best non-dominated front adaptively and maintains a predefined distribution of individuals in each front. First, the combined parent and offspring population $R_t = Pop_t \cup Off_t$ is sorted for non-domination. Let K be the number of non-dominated fronts in the combined population (of size $2N$). According to the geometric distribution, the maximum number of individual allowed in the jth front $(j = 1,2,...,K)$ in the new population of size N_j is given in eqn. (2).

$$N_j = N \frac{1-r}{1-r^k} r^{j-1}$$ (2)

r is the reduction rate. Since $r < 1$, the maximum allowable number of individuals in the first front is the highest. Thereafter, each front is allowed to have an exponentially reducing number of solutions.

4.2   Dynamic Crowding Distance (DCD)

In MOEAs, the horizontal diversity of Pareto-front is very important. The horizontal diversity is often realized by removing excess individuals in the non-dominated set (NDS) when the number of non-dominated solutions exceeds population size. NSGA-II uses crowding distance (CD) measure as given in eqn. (3) to remove excess individuals. The individuals having lower value of CD are preferred over individuals with higher value of CD in removal process.

$$CD_i = \frac{1}{N_{obj}} \sum_{g=1}^{N_{obj}} |f_{i+1}^g - f_{i-1}^g|$$ (3)

where N_{obj} is the number of objectives, f_{i+1}^g is the gth objective of the $i + 1^{th}$ individual and f_{i-1}^g is the gth objective of the $i - 1^{th}$ individual after sorting the population according to CD value. The major drawback of crowding distance is lack of uniform diversity in obtained non-dominated solutions as illustrated in Fig. 2.

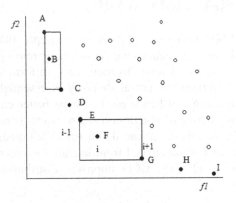

Fig. 2. Crowding Distance of individuals

In Fig.2, if normal crowding distance method is adopted then the individuals C–E are deleted from NDS, since they have small CD values. Because of that, some parts of Pareto-front are too crowded and some parts are with sparseness. Also, CD of B is small, because one side of the rectangle is short, while another side is long. However, the CD of F is large because the length of one side almost equal to another side. If one individual must be removed between the individuals B and F, because of small CD value, individual B will be removed and F will be retained in NDS. But, in order to get good horizontal diversity the individual B should be maintained, because the individual B helps to maintain uniform spread. To overcome this problem, DCD method is recently suggested in [15]. In this approach, one individual with lowest DCD value every time is removed and recalculates DCD for the remaining individuals. The individuals in DCD [16] are calculated as follows:

$$DCD_i = \frac{CD_i}{log\left(\frac{1}{Var_i}\right)} \tag{4}$$

where CD_i is calculated by Eqn. (3), Var_i is based on

$$Var_i = \frac{1}{N_{obj}} \Sigma_{g=1}^{N_{obj}} (|f_{i+1}^g - f_{i-1}^g| - CD_i)^2 \tag{5}$$

Var_i is the variance of CDs of individuals which are neighbors of the ith individual. Var_i can give information about the difference variations of CD in different objectives. In Fig. 1, the individual B has larger value of Var_i than the individual F and DCD of B is larger than F. Therefore, the individuals similar to B in the NDS will have more chance to retain.

4.3   DCD Algorithm

Suppose the population size is N, the non-dominated set at t^{th} generation is R_t and its size is M.

If M > N, DCD based strategy is used to remove M-N individuals from non-dominated set. The summary of DCD algorithm is given below:

    if $|R_t| \le N$ then
                Stop the population maintenance.
    else
                Calculate individuals DCD in the $|R_t|$ based on Eqn. (4).
                Sort the non-dominated set, $|R_t|$ based on DCD.
                Remove the individual which has the lowest DCD value in the $|R_t|$.
                end

4.4   Algorithmic Steps of Proposed Approach

Input   Initial random Pop_0

Output   non-dominated Pop_t to form Pareto optimal front

Initialize $dim, xl, xu, pop_{size} N, pc, pm, \eta_c, \eta_m, r, max_{gen}$

Algorithm

                Set Gen_count $t = 0$;
                Generate $Pop_t [N]$ within xl and xu limits;
                Calculate fitness (Pop_t)
                            $CHARMMFit (Pop_t)$;
                            $DSSPFit(Pop_t)$;
                loop until ($t \le max_{gen}$)
                            Generate Off_t from crowded_tour_sel(Pop_t),SBX(Pop_t)

and poly_mut(Pop_t);
Generate Combined_pop $R_t = Off_t \cup Pop_t$;
Perform non_dom_sort(R_t) to find various $PF_i = 1, 2, \ldots etc$;
Apply N_Dom_Improved_dcd_controlled_elitism(R_t);
$M = $ size(non_dom_set);
if $M > N$

      remove $M - N$ individuals from M using DCD;
      $Pop_{t+1} = $ crowded_tour_sel($R_t(M - N)$);

else

      $Pop_{t+1} = $ crowded_tour_sel($R_t(M)$);
Calculate fitness (Pop_{t+1});

End

5   Results and Discussion

In this paper, Protein Structure Prediction is solved as multi-objective problem. The proposed model is validated with Met-enkephalin, a benchmark protein. For multi-objective procedure, Modified NSGAII is used by incorporating controlled elitism and Dynamic Crowding Distance (DCD) strategies in NSGA-II for PSP by minimizing free potential energy (PE) and minimizing solvent accessible surface area (SAS). NSGA-II is also applied to compare the performance of MNSGA-II. For single objective optimization RGA is used. The algorithms are developed in MATLAB and are executed for 10 runs. Table1 lists the optimal parameters selection for the three algorithms.

Table 1. Optimal Parameters selection

Parameters	RGA	NSGA-II	MNSGA-II
Pop Size N_p	300	300	300
Max. no. of generations	300	300	300
Dimensions	22	22	22
probability of crossover P_c	0.8	0.8	0.8
probability of mutation P_m	1/(0.2*dim)	1/(0.2*dim)	1/(0.2*dim)
Crossover Index η_c	---	1	1
Mutation Index η_m	---	50	50

Table 2 shows the optimized results of potential energy (PE) and solvent accessible surface area (SAS) minimum for Met-enkephalin obtained using MNSGA-II and NSGA-II from 5 best runs. Since MNSGA-II adopts lateral diversity, more exploration than exploitation made better convergence of this search algorithm.

Table 2. Optimized minimum of potential energy and accessible surface area from 5 runs

Runs	MNSGA-II		NSGA-II	
	Min. PE kcal/mol	Min. Surface area Å	Min. PE kcal/mol	Min. Surface area Å
Run1	-28.604	452.745	-22.4186	483.920
Run2	-28.6222	452.653	-22.9262	514.865
Run3	-28.6307	452.634	-22.9247	476.871
Run4	-28.2879	459.165	-23.0285	495.296
Run5	-28.6605	476.317	-22.7156	509.286

Table 3 shows the optimized results of potential energy (PE) and solvent accessible surface area (SAS) minimum for Met-enkephalin obtained using RGA, MNSGA-II and NSGA-II.

Table 3. optimized results of energy (PE) and surface area (SAS)

Objectives	RGA	MNSGA-II	NSGA-II
Potential Energy kcal/mol	-29.12	-28.66	-23.0285
Surface Area Å	449.14	452.634	476.87

The Reference Front is generated using multiple runs of single objective optimization by minimizing weighted sum of objectives. The Best Compromise Solution (BCS) is obtained using TOPSIS [18] method. Table 4 and Figure 3 show the BCS performance comparison of MNSGA-II and NSGA-II with RGA.

Table 4. Comparison of the results Modified NSGA-II and NSGA-II

	RGA	BCS of MNSGA-II	Deviation	BCS of NSGA-II	Deviation
Potential Energy	-29.12	-6.4146	77.9%	18.3613	163%
Surface area	447.14	624.038	39.6%	639.588	43%

The BCS score of MNSGA-II is not only closer to true ideal solution, but far away from the false ideal solution. Controlled elitism used in MNSGA-II maintains the diversity of non-dominated front laterally, which overcomes shortcomings of NSGA-II. Also Table 4 shows that deviation of BCS of NSGA-II is more than MNSGA-II from the minimum solution of Single objective optimization.

The Root Mean Square Deviation of the minimum solutions and the Best Compromise Solution of MNSGA-II with 1PLW[19] and Scheraga[20] structures are calculated using Pymol [21] and the results are shown in Table 5. 1PLW is NMR structure and Scheraga structure is experimentally proven bench mark structure for Met-Enkephalin.

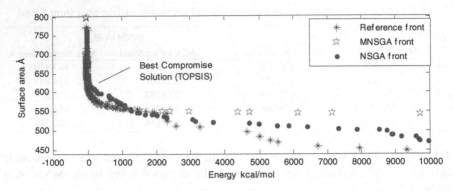

Fig. 3. Reference Pareto front vs MNSGA and NSGA fronts

Table 5. RMSD with 1PLW and Scheraga structures

	RMSD with 1PLW		RMSD with Scheraga	
	All Atoms	C atoms	All Atoms	C atoms
Minimum Potential Energy Solution	3.27	1.78	1.59	**0.33**
Best Compromise Solution	**2.86**	**1.68**	**1.52**	0.65
Minimum Accessible Area Solution	3.09	1.85	3.97	2.13

RMSD values of Best Compromise Solution with 1PLW and RMSD of all atoms with Scheraga structure are smaller than other best solutions, while RMSD of C atoms with Scheraga structure is slightly more than RMSD value of Minimum Potential Energy Solution.

Figure 4a shows the structural superimpose of minimum solutions and best compromise solution with 1PLW for all atoms, whereas Figure 4b shows the structural superposition with Scheraga structure.

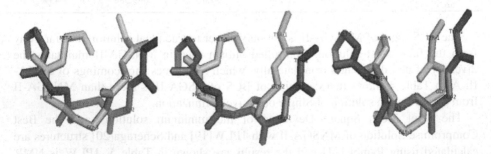

Fig. 4a. Superimpose of solutions with 1PLW   (Dark Gray – 1PLW, light Gray- predicted solutions)

From Table 5 values and Figures 4a & 4b, it is well known that Best Compromise Solution is performing better than the minimum solutions of Potential Energy and Accessible Surface Area.

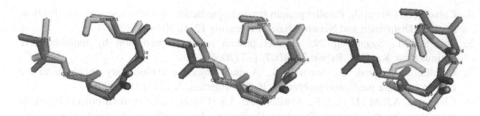

Fig. 4b. Superimpose of solutions with Scheraga (Dark Gray – 1PLW, light Gray- predicted solutions)

Since this solution compromises both the objectives, the deviation of this structure with original structures is marginal. Also, this solution is not only closer to true ideal solution, but far away from the false ideal solution.

6   Conclusions

In this work, Protein structure Prediction is treated as multi-objective problem by minimizing the Potential energy and minimizing solvent accessible surface area of a protein. Modified NSGAII has been implemented. Met-enkephalin, a benchmark protein, is used as test data. The force field CHARMM-22 and DSSP software are used to calculate potential energy and Accessible Surface area respectively. The performance of MNSGA-II and NSGA-II approaches are compared. An appreciable improvement on lateral diversity and uniformity measure without affecting convergence metric is observed in Pareto-front obtained using MNSGA-II when compared to NSGA-II. The RMSD results show that the Best Compromise Solution is compromising the ideal solutions and is better than the minimum solutions of Potential energy and surface area of MNSGA-II.

References

1. ERCIM News, http://www.ercim.eu/publication/Ercim_News/enw43/bernasconi.html
2. Cui, Y., Chen, R.S., Hung, W.: Protein folding simulation with genetic algorithm and super secondary structure constraints. Proteins: Structure, Function and Genetics 31, 247–257 (1998)
3. Unger, R., Moult, J.: Genetic algorithms for protein folding simulations. Biochim. Biophys. 231, 75–81 (1993)
4. Hoque, T., Chetty, M., Sattar, A.: Extended hp model for protein structure prediction. J. Comput. Biol. 16(1), 85–103 (2009)
5. Coello, C.A., Van Veldhuizen, D.A., Lamont, G.B.: Evolutionary Algorithms for Solving Multi-Objective Problems. Kluwer Academic Publishers (2002)
6. Judya, M., Ravichandrana, K., Murugesan, K.: A multi-objective evolutionary algorithm for protein structure prediction with immune operators. Comp. Methods in Biomechanics and Biomedical Engineering 12(4), 407–413 (2009)

7. Calvo, J.C., Ortega, J.: Parallel protein structure prediction by multiobjective optimization. Parallel, Distributed and Network-based Processing 12(4), 407–413 (2009)
8. Shi, S.Y.M., Suganthan, N.: Parallel protein structure prediction by multiobjective optimization. KanGAL Report 2004007, 1–7 (2004)
9. Cutello, V., Narzisi, G., Nicosia, G.: A multi-objective evolutionary approach to the protein structure prediction problem: J. R. Soc. Interface 3, 139–151 (2006)
10. Chamorro, A.E.M., Divina, F., Aguilar-Ruiz, J.S., Cortés, G.A.: A multi-objective genetic algorithm for the Protein Structure Prediction. In: Intelligent Systems Design and Applications ISDA 2011, pp. 1086–1090 (2011)
11. NIH Center for Macromolecular Modeling, & Bioinformatics, http://www.ks.uiuc.edu/
12. Wodak, S.J., Janin, J.: Analytical approximation to the accessible surface area of proteins. Proc. Nati. Acad. Sci. USA 77(4), 1736–1740 (1980)
13. Centre for Molecular and Biomolecular Informatics, http://swift.cmbi.ru.nl/gv/dssp
14. Deb, K., Pratap, A., Agarwal, S., Meyarivan, T.: A fast elitist multiobjective genetic algorithm: NSGA-II. IEEE Trans. Evol. Comput. 6(2), 182–197 (2002)
15. Luo, B., Zheng, J., Xie, J., Wu, J.: Dynamic crowding distance – a new diversity maintenance strategy for MOEAs. In: Proceedings of the IEEE International Conference on Natural Computation, pp. 580–585 (2008)
16. Jeyadevi, S., Baskar, S., Babulal, C.K., Willjuice Iruthayarajan, M.: Solving multiobjective optimal reactive power dispatch using modified NSGA-II. Int. J of Electrical Power and Energy Systems 33(2), 219–228 (2011)
17. Kannan, S., Baskar, S., Mccalley, J.D., Murugan, P.: Application of NSGA-II algorithm to generation expansion planning. IEEE Trans. Power System 24(1), 454–461 (2009)
18. Deb, K., Tewari, R., Dixit, M., Dutta, J.: Finding trade-off solutions close to KKT points using evolutionary multi-objective optimization. IIT Kanpur, KanGAL Report Number 2007006 (2007)
19. Biological Macromolecular Resource, Protein Data Bank, http://www.pdb.org/
20. Li, Z., Scheraga, H.A.: Structure and free energy of complex thermodynamic systems. Journal of Molecular Structures 179, 333 (1988)
21. An open-source molecular visualization system, http://www.pymol.org/

Clustering Based Analysis of Spirometric Data Using Principal Component Analysis and Self Organizing Map

Mythili Asaithambi[1], Sujatha C. Manoharan[2,] and Srinivasan Subramanian[1]

[1] Department of Instrumentation Engg., MIT Campus, AnnaUniversity, Chennai, India
[2] Department of Electronics and Communication Engineering, CEG Campus,
Anna University, Chennai, India
mythiliasaithambi@gmail.com

Abstract. Spirometry is a valuable tool used for respiratory diagnoses and assessment of disease progression. It measures air flow to help make a definitive diagnosis of pulmonary disorder and confirms presence of airway obstruction. In this work, clustering based classification of spirometric pulmonary function data has been attempted using Principal Component Analysis (PCA) and Self Organising Map (SOM). Pulmonary function data (N=100) are obtained from normal and obstructive subjects using gold standard Spirolab II spirometer. These data are subjected to PCA to extract significant parameters relevant to the cluster structure. The clustering analysis of the significant spirometric parameters is further enhanced using self organizing map and classification of spirometric data is achieved. It is observed from results that FEV_1, PEF and $FEF_{25-75}\%$ are found to be significant in differentiating normal and obstructive subjects. SOM based classification is able to achieve accuracy of 95%. This cluster based method of feature reduction and classification could be useful in assessing the pulmonary function disorders for spirometric pulmonary function test with large dataset.

Keywords: Spirometry, principal component analysis, self organizing map, clustering.

1   Introduction

Pulmonary Function Test (PFT) measures how well the lungs take in and release air and how well they move from the atmosphere into the body's circulation. This test performs complete evaluation of the respiratory system. Spirometry is a most commonly used PFT for assessing lung function by measuring the total volume of air expelled from the lungs after a maximal inhalation. It monitors disease progression in chronic obstructive pulmonary disease, assess one aspect of response to therapy, and perform pre-operative assessment [1]. Spirometry is a reliable method of identifying obstructive illness and is used to grade the disease severity [2].

The dynamic interrelationships of flow and volume parameters obtained during various time intervals from spirometer are displayed as graphical loop called spirogram. Respiratory diseases and their severity are interpreted based on these

B.K. Panigrahi et al. (Eds.): SEMCCO 2013, Part II, LNCS 8298, pp. 523–533, 2013.

graphical patterns and the parameters obtained from them [3]. Some of the important parameters obtained from the maneuver are Forced Expiratory Volume of air in one second (FEV_1), Forced Vital Capacity (FVC), Peak Expiratory Flow (PEF), Forced Expiratory Flow at 25% of FVC ($FEF_{25}\%$), Forced Expiratory Flow at 25-75% of FVC ($FEF_{25-75}\%$), Forced Expiratory Flow at 50% of FVC ($FEF_{50}\%$), Forced Expiratory Flow at 75% of FVC ($FEF_{75}\%$), Forced Inspiratory volume at first second (FIV_1), percentage of Forced Inspiratory Volume at first second ($FIV_1\%$) and Forced Inspiratory Vital Capacity (FIVC).

Automated diagnosis methods that evaluate respiratory flow volume patterns for appropriate clinical interpretation are very much essential [3,4]. Data clustering is a common technique employed for multi-label classification. It has been used in many fields, including machine learning, data mining, pattern recognition, image analysis and bioinformatics [5,6]. Clustering performs classification of data by finding natural groups using unsupervised learning [7]. Cluster analysis divides data into clusters such that similar data objects belong to the same cluster and dissimilar data objects to different clusters. As large number of parameters could be extracted from spirometer, there may be chance of misclassification of pulmonary disease [8]. Hence there is a need for data reduction of significant parameters for appropriate interpretation.

Principal Component Analysis (PCA) is a mathematical procedure that uses an orthogonal transformation to convert a set of observations of possibly correlated variables into a set of values of uncorrelated variables called principal components [9]. The mathematical approach used in PCA is called eigen analysis. The eigenvector associated with the largest eigenvalue has the same direction as the first principal component. The first principal component accounts for as much of the variability in the data as possible, and each succeeding component accounts for as much of the remaining variability as possible. The main objectives of the PCA are to reduce the dimensionality of the data set and to identify new meaningful underlying variables. Segmentation of retinal images is investigated extensively using PCA has been reported [10]. Feature extraction of biometric identifier, Finger-Knuckle-Print (FKP), is done using Principal Component Analysis (PCA) technique [11]. PCA is also performed to identify the transnational terrorism [12]. PCA is powerful used for processing and visualizing the data [13, 14]. PCA approach could be used to reduce the dimension of input parameters of clustering routine [15]. Interdependency of the measured and predicted parameters of flow volume spirometric data has been analyzed using PCA [16, 17].

The SOM is an unsupervised neural network that characterizes a relatively massive amount of data and performs clustering based classification [18]. It projects a high dimensional input space on a two-dimensional output space. Unique feature of SOM is that it can use neighbourhood kernels to preserve and also control the topological structure of high-dimensional input data [19]. The projection is topological preserving, that is, where patterns that are similar in terms of the input space are mapped to geographically close locations in the output space. The SOM is composed of a set of nodes arranged in a geometric pattern, typically a two dimensional lattice. Each node is associated with a weight vector W with the same dimension as the input space. Learning in SOM is based on competitive learning where these output nodes of the network compete among themselves to be activated or fired. Only one output node, or one node per group, is ON at any one time. The output nodes that win the competition are called winner-take-all nodes [20, 21]. SOM algorithm can serve as an abstraction of data set, scalable to large datasets and it is robust to the missing data and rare outliers [22]. In this work, spirometric parameters are obtained from normal and obstructive subjects and are subjected to PCA. The clustering based classification using SOM is performed with significant parameters as inputs.

2   Methodology

The spirometer recordings are carried out on adult volunteers (N = 100) for the present study. The age, gender and race of the subject are recorded and height, weight are being measured before recording. The portable Spirolab II spirometer with a gold standard volumetric transducer is used for the acquisition of the data.

In this work, acquired data is pre-processed using PCA before feeding it to the clustering algorithm. The most significant parameters of the spirometric pulmonary data are derived using PCA. Principal component analysis is a statistical method to estimate the most influenced common stochastic series by analyzing cross-sectional correlation. It is utilized for extracting high dimensionality by constructing a linear projection of the spirometric data set in the two dimensional space. Principal component analysis is performed on the symmetric Covariance matrix or on the symmetric Correlation matrix. These matrices can be calculated from the data matrix.

The spirometric data for 100 subjects is arranged in the form of matrix. PCA transforms the data by extracting statistically independent components and arranging them in the order of relative significance. The original feature space consists of 14 spirometric parameters of normal and obstructive subjects. PCA is employed in transforming this feature space into a new space and the components that account for most of the variability are retained whereas the remaining components are ignored. In PCA method, spirometric data arranged in the form of matrix of size 100 X 14 is reduced into a covariance matrix A of size 14 X 14, where the columns corresponds to number of principal components and rows are associated with the spirometric variables. The covariance matrix A is given by

$$\Phi_{jk} = \frac{1}{n}\sum_{i=1}^{n}(x_{ji} - \overline{x}_j)(x_{ik} - \overline{x}_k), \ j \neq k \tag{1}$$

where $\overline{x}$ is mean of m variables in the matrix. The Principal Components (PCs) are determined as the Eigenvectors of the covariance matrix A. Eigen values $(\lambda_1, \lambda_2, ..., \lambda_m)$ can be found by solving the determinant equation $|(\Phi - \lambda I)| = 0$. Then PCs of the covariance matrix Φ can be generated using a process of singular value decomposition, which is given by

$$\Phi = E \wedge E^T \tag{2}$$

The set of PCs is then represented as a linear combination of the original variables. PCA uncovers combinations of the original variables which describe the dominant patterns and the main trends in the data. This is done through an Eigen vector decomposition of the covariance matrix of the original variables [16]. The extracted latent variables are orthogonal and they are sorted according to their Eigen v alues [21]. The percentage of variance (PV) for the principal components can be calculated by

$$PV = \frac{\lambda_k}{\lambda_1 + \lambda_2 + ... + \lambda_m} \times 100\%$$

(3)

The PCA from the perspective of statistical pattern recognition is an effective technique for dimension reduction [22]. The principal components that explain the maximum percentage variance are chosen and the corresponding component magnitudes are analyzed. The spirometric variables corresponding to these components are considered as the most significant features. The three parameters having highest magnitudes in the loadings of the principal components are chosen for further cluster based classification using SOM.

SOM consists of two layers; the input layer and the output layer. The output layer is composed of a set of nodes arranged in a two dimensional lattice. Each neuron from the output layer has a double representation, one is its position in the grid and another is its weight vector. The dimension of the weight vector equals the dimension of the input data vectors. In the training process, the weights are gradually changed in order to span the weight vectors across the input data set. The training is based on competitive and cooperative learning [23].

In the SOM network, the input pattern x represented by vector of length 3 corresponding to significant features is presented to a two dimensional map of 25 X 25 nodes. During each training cycle t_k, every input pattern corresponding to 100 subjects is considered in turn and the best matching weight vector W, also called winner node is determined such that

$$\|x - w_i\| = \min \|x - w_i\|, \quad (i = 0, 1, ..., N)$$

(4)

The weights of the neuron, which resembles the most to that input data, are updated. The weight vectors are updated using the following adaptation function.

$$w_i(t_k + 1) = \begin{cases} w_i(t_k) + [a(t_k)(w_i(t_k) - x)] \, for \, i \, \varepsilon \, N_i(t_k) \\ w_i(t_k), otherwise \end{cases}$$

(5)

where $a(t_k)$ is the learning coefficient that decreases over time and $N_I(t_k)$ is the set of nodes considered to be in the topological neighbourhood of node i, the winner node. Node i represent the neuron that maximally responds to the input signal, i.e., its weight vector matches most closely, among all the Kohonen layer nodes, to that of the input vector. N_I contains all nodes that are within a certain radius from node i. The weight vectors of all the nodes within the set N_I are updated at the same rate [21].

When the SOM has been trained, the centroids of the input patterns that create winning neuron are identified as cluster centers. The SOM network is used for classification of normal and obstructive subjects. The performance of classification is evaluated by accuracy, sensitivity and specificity. The performance of a clustering and classification system can be measured by the clustering accuracy and the classification accuracy [24]. The clustering accuracy is defined as

$$\text{Clustering Accuracy} = \text{Number of correct clustering combinations/}$$
$$\text{Number of total combinations} \qquad (6)$$

Correct clustering indicates the number of clusters determined by the algorithm that are matched to the number of classes present in the spirometric data.

3   Results and Discussion

The spirometric pulmonary function test is assessed using gold standard Spirolab II flow-volume spirometer. Spirometric parameters are obtained and they are subjected to PCA.

The statistical analysis consisting mean and standard deviation of the principal components for the normal and obstructive subjects are presented in Table 1. The mean values of these principal components in normal subjects are distinctly higher than those of the obstructive subjects. The standard deviations for all the principal components for both normal and obstructive subjects are found to be high.

The percentage variance obtained by various principal component for normal and obstructive data are shown in Figure 2. It is illustrated that the first two PCs account for 90% of variance. The higher percentage variance indicated that these PCs are sufficient to explain the similarity pattern of each data and capture most of the discrimination capability. These principal components alone are enough to guide clustering and removing features with low variance provides a more robust clustering.

Table 1. Mean and standard deviation of the 11 principal components

Principal components	Mean ± Standard deviation	
	Normal	Obstruction
PC1	0.1941±0.2737	-0.0135±0.3329
PC2	0.0775±0.3255	-0.0340±0.3142
PC3	0.1264±0.2871	0.0529±0.3226
PC4	0.0142±0.3158	0.0804±0.2860
PC5	0.1451±0.2534	0.0694±0.3168
PC6	0.0044±0.2891	0.0442±0.3128
PC7	0.0587±0.3102	0.0466±0.2910
PC8	0.0113±0.3160	0.1518±0.2692
PC9	0.0652±0.3087	0.2024±0.2343
PC10	0.0285±0.3148	0.0053±0.3162
PC11	0.0283±0.3148	0.0853±0.3032

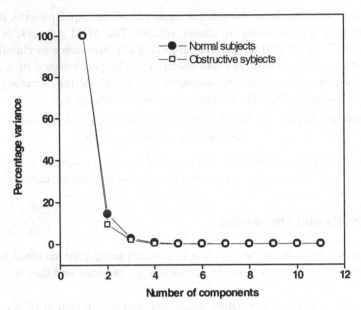

Fig. 1. Percentage variance obtained by various principal components

PC1 and PC2 obtained for normal subjects represented as weighted linear combination of original parameters are given in equations 7 and 8.

$$PC1 = -0.26(FVC)+0.49(FEV_1)+0.45(PEF)+0.24(FEV_1\%) -0.32(FEF_{25-75}\%)-0.25(FEF_{25}\%)-0.18(FEF_{75}\%)$$
$$-0.34(FEF_{50}\%)-0.28(FIVC)-0.28(FIV_1)-0.14(FIV_1\%) \tag{7}$$

$$PC2 = -0.16(FVC)+0.52(FEV_1)+0.45(PEF)+0.08(FEV_1\%) -0.33(FEF_{25-75}\%)-0.19(FEF_{25}\%)-0.36(FEF_{75}\%)$$
$$-0.3(FEF_{50}\%)-0.22(FIVC)-0.21(FIV_1)-0.4(FIV_1\%) \tag{8}$$

PC1 and PC2 obtained for obstructive subjects represented as weighted linear combination of original parameters are given in equations 9 and 10.

$$PC1 = 0.43(FVC)+0.49(FEV_1)-0.41(PEF)+0.06(FEV_1\%) -0.32(FEF_{25-75}\%)-0.21(FEF_{25}\%)-0.14(FEF_{75}\%)$$
$$-0.20(FEF_{50}\%)-0.36(FIVC)-0.20(FIV_1)-0.13(FIV_1\%) \tag{9}$$

$$PC2 = 0.43(FVC)+0.60(FEV_1)-0.31(PEF) -0.14(FEF_{25-75}\%)-0.26(FEF_{25}\%)-0.15(FEF_{75}\%) -0.24(FIVC)$$
$$-0.29(FIV_1)-0.11(FIV_1\%) \tag{10}$$

It is found that the coefficients of PC1 and PC2 of normal subjects corresponding to spirometric parameters FEV_1 and PEF have the largest magnitude. Similarly, spirometric parameters FVC and FEV_1 contribute the largest magnitude in obstructive subjects. It illustrates that these parameters are the significant components extracted from overall spirometric data set using correlation matrix. The corresponding component loading plots for normal and obstructive subjects are shown in Figures 2 and 3 respectively. It is found that the parameters FEV_1 and PEF of normal subjects have similar magnitude and grouped to form cluster 1. Similarly, all the other spirometric parameters FVC, $FEF_{25-75}\%$, $FEF_{25}\%$, $FEF_{75}\%$, $FEF_{50}\%$, FIVC, FIV_1, $FIV_1\%$ have negative magnitudes and form cluster 2. The parameters FEV_1, FEV_1 %, FVC and $FEF_{50}\%$ of obstructive subjects form cluster 1 and all the other spirometric parameters $FEF_{25-75}\%$, $FEF_{25}\%$, $FEF_{75}\%$, FIVC, FIV_1, $FIV_1\%$ and PEF have negative magnitudes and form cluster 2.

The significant parameters obtained from the PCA are given as the inputs to the self organizing map. Each pattern is presented and the best matching weight vector W for the present input is determined. The visualization map of SOM for classification of normal and obstructive subjects is shown in Figure 4. It is found that nodes corresponding to each class are clustered together and are mapped to geographically close locations in the output space. The classification accuracy for various number of SOM units for normal and obstructive subjects are presented in Table 2. It is observed that error is minimum for dimension of 5 X 5 for normal and obstructive subjects. The performance of the network in classifying normal and obstructive values is then calculated using true positive rate and false positive rate.

It is observed that high values of classification accuracy, specificity and sensitivity are obtained for model with 25 neurons. It is also observed that high values of clustering accuracy are obtained for the same number of neurons.

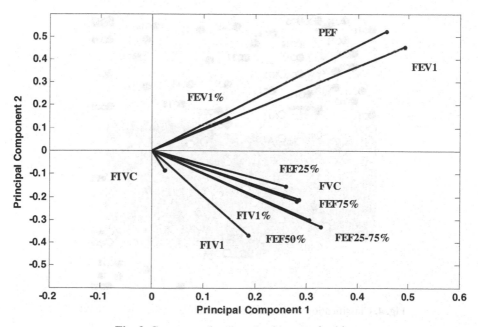

Fig. 2. Component loading plot for normal subjects

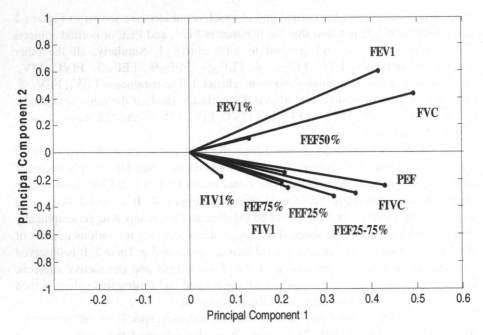

Fig. 3. Component loading plot for obstruction subjects

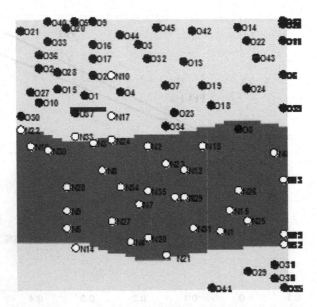

Fig. 4. Classification of normal and obstructive subjects using SOM

Table 2. Classification performance for various dimensions of SOM classifier

Number of neurons	Classification accuracy (%)	Clustering accuracy (%)
25	95	95
30	87.65	88.75
40	93.9	96.25
50	89.02	91.25
60	93.75	93.75

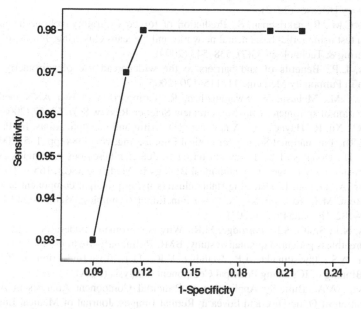

Fig. 5. ROC analyses for SOM classifier with 25 neurons

The ROC curves for SOM model with varied number of neurons (25, 30, 40, 50, and 60) is shown in Fig 5. Results demonstrate that SOM model with 25 neurons achieved better classification accuracy.

4   Conclusions

Spirometry is the most frequently performed pulmonary function test and is an essential tool for the diagnosis of respiratory diseases. The clinical utility of spirometer depends on the accuracy, performance of the subject and on the measured and predicted values [16]. It is also reported that a large database is to be analyzed by the physician to investigate the pulmonary function abnormalities [8]. Hence there is a need to provide automated diagnostic support to the physician using cluster based classification schemes. In this work, clustering based classification of normal and obstruction subjects are analyzed using PCA and SOM. Results show that PCA could extract significant parameters that are required for classification. These components provide a good stable clustering solution without any significant compromise on quality of clusters. The clustering based SOM classification could achieve accuracy of 95 % with dimension of 5 X 5 neurons. It is observed that the proposed model can be used to enhance the diagnostic relevance of pulmonary function test.

References

1. Gordon, D.: Spirometry: Thinking Beyond the COPD Gold Standard: The Journal of Respiratory Diseases (2012)
2. Sujatha, C.M., Ramakrishnan, S.: Prediction of forced expiratory volume in pulmonary function test using radial basis neural networks and k-means clustering. Journal of Medical Engineering & Technology 33(7), 538–543 (2009)
3. Thomas, L.P.: Benefits of and barriers to the widespread use of spirometry. Current Opinion in Pulmonary Medicine 11, 115–120 (2005)
4. Sujatha, C.M., Mahesh, V., Swaminathan, R.: Comparison of two ANN methods for classification of spirometer data. Measurement Science Review 8(3), 53–57 (2008)
5. Kwan, C., Xu, R., Hayness, L.: A new data clustering and its applications. In: Proceeding of SPIE The International Society for Optical Engineering, vol. 4384, pp. 1–5 (2001)
6. Warren, H., Douglas, T.S.: Fuzzy clustering to detect tuberculous meningitis-associated hyperdensity in CT images. Computational Biology in Medicine 38(2), 165–170 (2007)
7. Ben Hur, A., Guyon, I.: Detecting stable clusters using principal component analysis. In: Brownstein, M.J., Kohodursky, A. (eds.) Functional Genomics: Methods and Protocols, pp. 159–182. Humana Press (2003)
8. Roberts, N.J., Smith, S.F., Partridge, M.R.: Why is spirometry underused in the diagnosis of the breathless patient: a qualitative study. BMC Pulmonary Medicine 11, 37 (2011)
9. Banthia, A.S., Jayasumana, A.P., Malaiya, Y.K.: Data Size Reduction for Clustering-Based Binning of ICs Using Principal Component Analysis (PCA)
10. Mudassar., A.A., Butt, S.: Application of Principal Component Analysis in Automatic Localization of Optic Disc and Fovea in Retinal Images. Journal of Medical Engineering 2013 (2013), doi: http://dx.doi.org/10.1155/2013/989712
11. Neware, S., Mehta, K., Zadgaonkar, A.S.: Finger Knuckle Identification using Principal Component Analysis and Nearest Mean Classifier. International Journal of Computer Applications (0975 – 8887) 70(9) (May 2013)
12. Gaibulloev, K., Sandler, T., Sul, D.: Common drivers of transnational terrorism: principal component analysis. Create Research Archive - Published Articles & Papers: Paper 144 (2013)
13. Tipping, M.E., Bishop, C.M.: Mixtures of probabilistic principal component analysers. Neural Computation 11, 443–482 (1999)
14. Koua, E.L.: Using self-organizing maps for information visualization and knowledge discovery in complex geospatial datasets. In: Proceedings of the 21st International Cartographic Conference (ICC), Durban, South Africa, pp. 1694–1702 (2003)
15. Kiang, M.Y., Kumar, A.A.: Comparative analysis of an extended SOM network and K-means analysis. Journal International Journal of Knowledge-Based and Intelligent Engineering Systems, 9–15 (2004)
16. Kavitha, A., Sujatha, M., Ramakrishnan, S.: Evaluation of flow–volume spirometric test using neural network based prediction and principal component analysis. Journal of Medical System 35, 127–133 (2011)

17. Kavitha, A., Sujatha, M., Ramakrishnan, S.: Evaluation of Forced expiratory volume prediction in spirometric Test Using Principal Component Analysis. Int. J. Biomedical Engineering and Technology 5(2/3) (2011)
18. Zhang, J., Fang, H.: Using Self-Organizing Maps to Visualize, Filter and Cluster Multidimensional Bio-Omics Data, http://dx.doi.org/10.5772/51702
19. Marc, T.: A unified continuous optimization framework for centre – based clustering methods. Journal of Machine Learning Research 8, 65–102 (2007)
20. David, G., Antonio, S., Daniel, R., Alberto, M.C.: Embedded system for diagnosing dysfunctions in the lower urinary tract. In: Proceedings of the ACM Symposium on Applied Computing, Seoul, Korea, pp. 1695–1699 (2007)
21. Aguado, D., Montoy, T., Borras, L., Seco, A., Ferrer, J.: Using SOM and PCA for analyzing and interpreting data from a P-removal SBR. Eng. Appl. Artif. Intel. 21(6), 919–930 (2008)
22. Haykin, S.: Neural Networks a Comprehensive Foundation, 2nd edn. Pearson Education, India (2008)
23. Kohonen, T.: Self-organizing maps, 3rd edn. Springer (2000)
24. Chattopadhyay, M., Dan, P.K., Mazumdar, S.: Principal component analysis and Self-organizing map for visual clustering Of machine-part cell formation in Cellular manufacturing system. Systems Research Forum 5(1), 25–51 (2011)

Feature Selection of Motor Imagery EEG Signals Using Firefly Temporal Difference Q-Learning and Support Vector Machine

Saugat Bhattacharyya[1,4], Pratyusha Rakshit[1],
Amit Konar[1], D.N. Tibarewala[2,4], and Ramadoss Janarthanan[3,5]

[1] Dept. of Electronics and Telecommunication Engg.,
[2] School of Bioscience and Engg.,
[3] Computer Science Dept.
[4] Jadavpur University, Kolkata
[5] TJS Engineering College, Chennai, India
{saugatbhattacharyya@live.com, pratyushar1@gmail.com,
konaramit@yahoo.co.in, biomed.ju@gmail.com, srmjana_73@yahoo.com}

Abstract. Electroencephalograph (EEG) based Brain-computer Interface (BCI) research provides a non-muscular communication to drive assistive devices using movement related signals, generated from the motor activation areas of the brain. The dimensions of the feature vector play an important role in BCI research, which not only increases the computational time but also reduces the accuracy of the classifiers. In this paper, we aim to reduce the redundant features of a feature vector obtained from motor imagery EEG signals to improve their corresponding classification. In this paper we have proposed a feature selection method based on Firefly Algorithm and Temporal Difference Q-Learning. Here, we have applied our proposed method to the wavelet transform features of a standard BCI competition dataset. Support Vector Machines have been employed to determine the fitness function of the proposed method and obtain the resultant classification accuracy. We have shown that the accuracy of the reduced feature are considerably higher than the original features. This paper also demonstrates the superiority of the new method to its competitor algorithms.

Keywords: Brain-Computer Interfacing, Electroencephalography, Firefly Algorithm, Temporal Difference Q-Learning, Support Vector Machines, Wavelet Transforms.

1 Introduction

Brain-Computer Interfacing (BCI) has been one of the most widely studied field in rehabilitation engineering in the last few decades. BCI provides a direct pathway between the brain and an external prosthetic device without involving the use of any muscles [1], [2]. Initially, BCI aimed at providing a neuro-muscular rehabilitation to patient suffering from Amytropic Lateral Sceloris (ALS), Paralysis,

B.K. Panigrahi et al. (Eds.): SEMCCO 2013, Part II, LNCS 8298, pp. 534–545, 2013.

Amputees and like [3]-[4], but in recent times it has found use in other general applications like communication and control, robotics and gaming [5]-[6].

Elecroencephalography (EEG) is the most widely used brain measure in BCI research because it is non-invasive, portable, easy to use, easy availability and the best temporal resolution. Now, EEG-based BCI consists of the following modules: a) Pre-processing, where the frequency band and the electrodes are selected, b) Feature Extraction, where the relevant features are extracted and c) Classification, where the different mental states are recognized. Sometimes, the dimension of the feature vectors after feature extraction is very large. The high dimension of the feature vectors increases the possibility of an increase in the redundant features, which increases the computational load and may decrease the overall performance of the classifiers [10]-[12]. In recent times, researchers have employed algorithms like Principal Component Analysis (PCA) [13], Independent Component Analysis (ICA) [14], Sequential Forward Floating Search (SFFS)[15], Genetic Algorithm [16] to decrease the dimensions of the feature vector without removing the relevant discriminating features.

In this study, we have aimed to reduce the dimensions of a feature vector using a novel technique based on a synergistic operation between an evolutionary algorithm (EA) and a supervised learning classifier. In the proposed evolutionary learning framework, a number of trial solutions come up with different pre-defined number of features for the same dataset. Then a pseudo data set is formed from the original dataset such that each data point only consists of the selected features (represented by solution EA). Precision of each possible combination of selected features is quantitatively evaluated with the classification accuracy obtained by testing the learning classifier. Then, through a mechanism of mutation and natural selection, eventually, the best solutions start dominating the population, whereas the bad ones are eliminated. Ultimately, the evolution of solutions comes to a halt (i.e., converges) when the fittest solution represents a near-optimal partitioning of the data set with respect to the employed validity index. In this way, the optimal pre-defined number of features can be located in one run of the evolutionary optimization algorithm.

In this paper, we have used a standard BCI Competition dataset [17] which classified between left and right hand motor imagery. Energy distribution [21], [22] of wavelet coefficients [20] obtained from our standard dataset are used as feature vectors in this study. This feature vector is fed to our proposed feature selection algorithm based on EA to obtain a reduced feature set which is fed to the SVM classifier. Hence the proposed methodology requires an EA for global search of optimal features and a supervised learning classifier for judgment of correctness of selecting the features (in terms of classification accuracy). The evolutionary component has been realized here by Firefly Algorithm with Temporal Difference Q-Learning (FA-TDQL) algorithm for its proven merits in global optimization [23]. It includes a Firefly Algorithm (FA) [24] for global exploration and a Temporal Difference Q-Learning (TDQL) [25] for adaptive selection of memes. These two modules work in a synergistic manner to improve the quality of solutions for a given optimization problem. The results obtained in this study have shown a considerable increase in the performance of the classifier, both in terms of accuracy and computational costs.

The rest of this paper is organized as follows. In Section 2, we have described our proposed framework for feature selection. Section 3 describes the dataset and the data analysis techniques employed in this study, followed by a discussion of the results in Section 4. The concluding remarks are provided in Section 5.

2   The Proposed Framework

2.1   Problem Definition

Let $\mathbf{data}_{N \times D} = \{\overrightarrow{data_1}, \overrightarrow{data_2}, \ldots, \overrightarrow{data_N}\}$ be a set of N patterns or data points, each having D features and an assigned class label $l \epsilon [1, K]$ for K classes. Given such $\mathbf{X}_{N \times D}$ matrix, a feature selection algorithm tries to find out an optimal set of d features ($d < D$). Since d number of features can be selected in a number of ways, an objective function (some measure of the adequacy of the optimal feature selection) must be defined. The problem then turns out to be one of finding a set of $d(< D)$ features of optimal or near-optimal adequacy, as compared to all other feasible solutions. For this task we have employed the use Firefly Algorithm with Temporal Difference Q-Learning (FA-TDQL) algorithm.

2.2   Firefly Algorithm with Temporal Difference Q-Learning (FA-TDQL)

In the proposed method, the process of adaptive selection of step size α in (6) using (3) from the meme pool, followed by one step of FA and reward/penalty updating in the Q-table is continued until the condition for convergence of the AMA is satisfied. The row indices of the Q-table represent states $S_1, S_2, \ldots, S_{NP}$ of the population of fireflies obtained from the last iteration of the FA-TDQL algorithm. The column indices of the Q-table correspond to uniformly quantized values of the step sizes to be used in the evolutionary algorithm. Let the parameter under consideration be α with possible quantized values $\alpha_1, \alpha_2, \ldots, \alpha_{10}$. Then $Q(S_i(t), 10\alpha_j)$ represents the total reward given to a member at state S_i for selecting $\alpha = \alpha_j$. Principles used in designing the FA-TDQL are introduced below.

Initialization. FA-TDQL starts with a population of NP fireflies with D-dimensi-onal position vectors within the prescribed minimum and maximum bounds: $\overrightarrow{Z_{min}} = \{z_{min-1}, z_{min-2}, \ldots, z_{min-D}\}$ and $\overrightarrow{Z_{max}} = \{z_{max-1}, z_{max-2}, \ldots, z_{max-D}\}$.

Hence, we may initialize the jth component of the ith vector at generation $t = 0$ as

$$z_{i,j}(t) = z_{j-min} + rand_{i,j}(0, 1) \times (z_{j-max} - z_{j-min}) \qquad (1)$$

The entries for the Q-table are initialized as small values. If the maximum Q-value attainable is 100, then we initialize the Q-values of all cells in the Q-table as 1.

Adaptive Selection of Parameters in FA. The probability of selection of $\alpha = \alpha_j$ from the meme pool $\alpha_1, \alpha_2, \ldots, \alpha_{10}$ is given by

$$P(\alpha_j) = Q(S_i(t), 10\alpha_j) / \sum_{l=1}^{10} Q(S_i(t), 10\alpha_l) \tag{2}$$

The random selection of α is realized by generating a random number r between $(0, 1)$ such that

$$\sum_{m=1}^{j-1} P(\alpha = \alpha_m) < r \leq \sum_{m=1}^{j} P(\alpha = \alpha_m)$$
$$\Rightarrow \frac{\sum_{m=1}^{j-1} Q(S_i(t), 10\alpha_m)}{\sum_{m=1}^{10} Q(S_i(t), 10\alpha_l)} < r \leq \frac{\sum_{m=1}^{j} Q(S_i(t), 10\alpha_m)}{\sum_{m=1}^{10} Q(S_i(t), 10\alpha_l)} \tag{3}$$

Firefly Algorithm. In the Firefly Algorithm (FA), each firefly changes its position iteratively by moving towards brighter and more attractive locations of other fireflies in order to obtain optimal solutions. The attractiveness of a firefly $\overrightarrow{Z_i}(t)$ to other more attractive one $\overrightarrow{Z_j}(t)$. The attractiveness β of each firefly is described by a monotonically decreasing function of the distance $dist_{ij}$ between any two fireflies [24] as given in (4).

$$\beta(dist_{ij}) = \beta_0 exp(-\gamma \times dist_{ij}^m), m \geq 1 \tag{4}$$

where β_0 denotes the maximum attractiveness (at $r = 0$) and γ is the light absorption coefficient, which controls the decrease of the light intensity and

$$dist_{i,j} = \| \overrightarrow{Z_i}(t) - \overrightarrow{Z_j}(t) \| = \sqrt{\sum_{k=1}^{D} (z_{i,k}(t) z_{j,k}(t))^2} \tag{5}$$

The movement of ith firefly $\overrightarrow{Z_i}(t)$ to another more attractive (brighter) j^{th} $\overrightarrow{Z_j}(t)$ firefly at the tth generation is determined by the following form [24].

$$z_{i,k}(t+1) = z_{i,k}(t) + \beta(dist_{i,j}) \times (z_{j,k}(t) - z_{i,k}(t)) + \alpha \times (rand - 0.5) \tag{6}$$

Here $rand$ is a random number generator uniformly distributed in the range $(0, 1)$ and $k\epsilon[1, D]$. For most cases step size $\alpha\epsilon(0, 1)$, $\beta_0 = 1$. In practice the light absorption coefficient γ[24] varies from 0.1 to 10.

Ranking of the Members and State Assignment. Let fit_i be the fitness of the ith firefly in the last iteration. A ranking policy is designed to compute normalized cost function $fit_i / \sum_{j=1}^{NP} fit_j, \forall i$, and then sort them in descending order.

Reward/Penalty-Based Q-Table Updating. If the fitness of the firefly increases due to transition from S_i to S_k on selection of α_j, then $Q(S_i(t), \alpha_j)$ will be updated following (7) with a positive reward function: $reward(S_i, 10_j) =$ increase in fitness function of the firefly,

$$Q(S_i(t+1), 10\alpha_j) = (1-\rho)Q(S_i(t+1), 10\alpha_j)$$
$$+\rho(reward(S_i(t+1), 10\alpha_j) + \delta max_{\alpha'}Q(S_k(t+1), 10\alpha')) \qquad (7)$$

else $Q(S_i(t), 10\alpha_j)$ will be evaluated by (7) with a negative $reward = -K$, of constant value, however, small. Here ρ and λ represent the learning rate and the discount factor, respectively [25].

Convergence. After each evolution, we repeat from step-2 until the termination condition is satisfied.

2.3   Solution Representation and Cost Function Evaluation

In the proposed method, for N data points, each D dimensional, and user-specified maximum number of features $d\epsilon[1, D]$, a solution is a vector of real numbers of dimension $Dim = d$ for K number of classes. The d entries of a solution of FA-TDQL, $\overrightarrow{X_i}$ are positive integers numbers in $[1, D]$. The value of $x_{ij} = p(p\epsilon[1, D])$ indicates that the pth feature is activated i.e., to be really used for classifying the data. As an example, consider the solution encoding scheme in Fig. 1. Let, there are $D = 8$ features, among which, the second, third, fourth, fifth and seventh ones have been activated for $d = 5$.

In order to judge the quality of the feature selection yielded by such a solution a pseudo data set **data$'_{N \times d}$** is constructed from the original one **data$_{N \times D}$**. **Data$'_{N \times d}$** consists of all the N−data points. However, each data $\overrightarrow{data'_j}, j = [1, N]$ is formed by extracting only the d features (encoded by the solution $\overrightarrow{Z_i}$) from the original data point $\overrightarrow{data_j}, j = [1, N]$. In other words,

$$\overrightarrow{data'_{j,k}} = \overrightarrow{data_{j, \overrightarrow{X_{i,k}}}} for j = [1, N], k = [1, d] \qquad (8)$$

The mechanism is elucidated in Fig. 1. Now the reduced data set **data$'_{N \times d}$** is decomposed into **training − dataset** and **testing − dataset**. The **training− dataset** with the class level l, l ϵ [1, K] of each data point is then fed to the SVM classifier. After training, the **testing − dataset** is fed to the SVM classifier. Since the **testing − dataset** have their nominal classes known to the user, we also compute the mean number of correctly classified data points i.e., the classification accuracy for different number of features. This is the average number of objects that were assigned to classes according to the nominal classification. The classification accuracy obtained by the SVM classifier is an indication of the quality of the solution $\overrightarrow{Z_i}(t)$. In the proposed feature selection method using FA-TDQL-SVM, classification accuracy is used for fitness function evaluation.

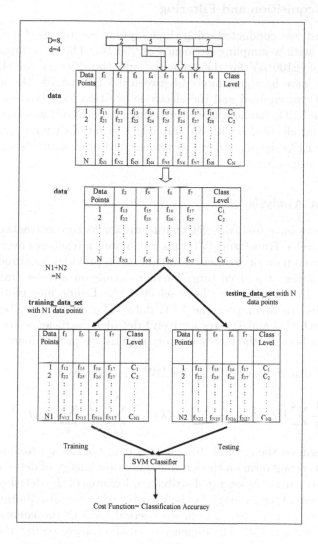

Fig. 1. Proposed methodology for feature selection

3   Data Analysis

3.1   The Dataset

The dataset used in this study was obtained from the BCI Competition 2008-Graz dataset B. This data set consists of EEG data from 9 subjects of a study published in [17]. Because of space constraint, the details of the dataset are not explained in this paper and can be found in [17].

3.2   Data Acquisition and Filtering

The experiment was conducted using three bipolar recordings (C3, Cz and C4) were recorded with a sampling frequency of 250 Hz. The recordings had a dynamic range of ±100 μV for the screening and the ±50 μV for the feedback sessions. They were bandpass-filtered between 0.5 Hz and 100 Hz, and a notch filter at 50 Hz was enabled and the electrode position Fz served as ground. In addition to the EEG channels, the electrooculogram (EOG) was recorded using three monopolar electrodes with an amplifier setting of dynamic range ±1 μV [17]. From the EEG signals, the eye movement and blink artifacts were removed using the EOG signals.

3.3   Wavelet Analysis

In this study, we have used wavelet transforms for feature extraction the given EEG data. Wavelet Transform (WT) has its obvious advantages over techniques based on time-domain or frequency-domain as it provides localized frequency related information at a given time. Further details on wavelet transforms are found in [20]. In our study, we have selected the Daubechies mother wavelet of order 4 (db4) to decompose the EEG data. The energy distribution of the third and fourth (D3 and D4, respectively) detailed coefficients are selected as feature vectors because the motor imagery signals are predominant at 8 -12 Hz and 16-24 Hz.

The energy distribution [21], [22] for DWT is given as

$$\frac{1}{N}\sum_t |f(t)|^2 = \frac{1}{N_J}\sum_k |a_J(k)|^2 + \sum_{J=1}^{N}(\frac{1}{N_J}\sum_k |d_J(k)|^2) \tag{9}$$

The first term on the right of (9) denotes energy of the approximation coefficients and the second term on the left of (9) denotes energy of detail coefficients. The second term gives the energy distribution features of the detail coefficient of the distorted signal which extracts the features of power distribution [21], [22]. The feature vector is prepared from the second term of the equation for each electrode (C3, Cz and C4). The dimensions of the feature vector, thus obtained is 822.

3.4   Support Vector Machine

The Support Vector Machine (SVM) has two purposes in this study: a) First, it is used to provide the fitness function to our proposed algorithm, b) Secondly, to determine the performance of our approach. Support Vector Machines (SVM) are a set of supervised learning methods based on Statistical Learning Theory. SVM finds the global minimum and its performance depends upon a selected kernel, where the user only selects the error penalty parameter [27], [28]. A SVM constructs an N-dimensional hyperplane that optimally separates the data in two categories, which is specified by the support vectors. SVM can deal with large feature spaces as the complexity does not depend upon the dimension of the features. Further details of the SVM classifier is given in [27], [28].

4   Results and Discussions

In this study, we have reduced the feature set from its original dimension of 822 to various smaller dimensions. The average classification accuracy for a given dimension d is given in Table 1. It is observed that on reduction of the dimensions of the feature vectors, our proposed algorithm have shown an improvement in the classification accuracy as compared to the original feature vector. It is noted that there is an improvement of accuracy in the range d = 200 to 500, but the accuracy decreases below d=200. Also, from Table 1, we have observed that the computational time (C.T.) of the algorithm keeps improving for every reduction of the dimensions of the feature vector. Thus, based on these two observations, we are able to maintain a trade-off between the accuracy and computational time by selecting an appropriate dimension d.

Here, we have also compared the performance of FA-TDQL to Principal Component Analysis (PCA)[13], Sequential Forward Search (SFS)[15], Genetic Programming (GP)[29], Genetic Algorithm (GA)[30], Differential Evolution (DE)[31], Particle Swarm Optimization (PSO)[32] and Artificial Bee Colony (ABC)[33]. The input parameters for each competitor algorithm is given in Table 2 and the comparisons based on the average classification accuracy and computational time for the reduced feature dimensions d =50, 300 and 600, are discussed in Table 3. It is observed that the FA-TDQL performs better than the competitor algorithms in

Table 1. Average Classification Accuracy for the given dataset using FA-TDQL-SVM

Subject ID	Average Classification Accuracy for given dimension d (k=10) in %									
d=	50	100	200	300	400	500	600	700	800	822
B0101T	83.33	83.33	88.89	91.67	91.67	91.67	91.67	88.89	88.89	88.89
B0102T	80.56	80.56	83.33	91.67	86.11	86.11	86.11	86.11	86.11	86.11
B0201T	83.33	83.33	88.89	88.89	91.67	88.89	88.89	86.11	86.11	86.11
B0202T	83.33	83.33	80.56	83.33	83.33	77.78	80.56	75.00	75.00	75.00
B0301T	86.11	86.11	83.33	86.11	83.33	80.56	77.78	77.78	77.78	77.78
B0302T	80.56	80.56	83.33	77.78	77.78	77.78	77.78	77.78	77.78	75.00
B0401T	83.33	83.33	83.33	86.11	86.11	86.11	86.11	86.11	83.33	83.33
B0402T	85.71	85.71	90.47	90.47	92.85	92.85	88.09	85.71	85.71	85.71
B0501T	86.11	86.11	88.89	88.89	86.11	86.11	86.11	86.11	83.33	83.33
B0502T	78.57	78.57	83.33	85.71	85.71	83.33	83.33	83.33	80.95	80.95
B0601T	80.56	86.11	83.33	88.89	88.89	88.89	86.11	86.11	86.11	83.33
B0602T	88.89	91.67	94.44	94.44	94.44	91.67	91.67	88.89	86.11	86.11
B0701T	77.78	75.00	77.78	80.56	75.00	77.78	77.78	77.78	75.00	75.00
B0702T	80.56	80.56	83.33	83.33	83.33	83.33	83.33	77.78	80.56	80.56
B0801T	81.25	81.25	87.50	85.41	83.33	83.33	83.33	81.25	81.25	81.25
B0802T	80.56	80.56	86.11	83.33	83.33	83.33	83.33	83.33	83.33	83.33
B0901T	77.78	77.78	80.56	80.56	77.78	77.78	77.78	77.78	77.78	77.78
B0902T	80.56	80.56	86.11	83.33	80.56	80.56	83.33	80.56	80.56	80.56
C. T. (sec)	98.59	98.02	101.85	105.56	107.09	120.60	136.25	182.96	279.24	295.49

Table 2. Parameters used in the competitor algorithms

	Algorithms					
Parameters	GP	GA	DE	PSO	ABC	FA-TDQL
Population Size	50	50	50	50	50	500
Mutation Probability	0.1	0.25	×	×	×	×
Crossover Probability	0.85	0.75	0.90	×	×	×
Scale Factor	×	×	(0,2]	×	×	×
Inertia Factor ω	×	×	×	0.7	×	×
C_1, C_2	×	×	×	2	×	×
Limit Cycle	×	×	×	×	50	×
β_0	×	×	×	×	×	1
Light Absorption Coefficient γ	×	×	×	×	×	2
Learning Rate ρ	×	×	×	×	×	0.25
Discount Factor δ	×	×	×	×	×	0.8

Table 3. Comparison of Performances of FA-TDQL with other competitive algorithms (d=50, 300, 600)

Reduced Dimension d	Algorithms	Average Classification Accuracy	Computational Time (in seconds)
	PCA	42.51	**65**
	SFS	57.43	87
	GP	61.46	117
50	GA	69.19	121
	PSO	70.57	107
	DE	72.62	97
	ABC	74.31	115
	FA-TDQL	**77.85**	92
	PCA	74.45	**94**
	SFS	75.13	100
	GP	77.26	147
300	GA	80.75	160
	PSO	82.45	145
	DE	83.20	134
	ABC	84.75	140
	FA-TDQL	**89.14**	105
	PCA	60.65	**117**
	SFS	68.62	131
	GP	70.05	176
600	GA	71.32	182
	PSO	74.37	153
	DE	74.94	150
	ABC	77.13	167
	FA-TDQL	**80.21**	119

terms of accuracy. The proposed algorithm takes longer only as compared to the statistical features selector (PCA and SFS) but takes a significantly lesser time in comparison to the evolutionary features selector (GP, GA, DE, PSO and ABC).

5   Conclusion

This paper proposes a novel technique for feature selection based on a Firefly Algorithm with Temporal Difference Q-Learning and Support Vector Machine classifier. Our proposed approach is validated on a standard datasets using Wavelet Transforms for feature vector preparation. The results shows that an improvement of accuracy is observed when the feature set is approximately half of its original size, containing mostly the relevant features. Simultaneously the computational complexity has also reduced. Further study in this direction will aim to optimize the feature selection, extraction and classification techniques to implement in real-time application towards an artificial limb control.

Acknowledgments. I would like to thank University Grants Commission, India, University of Potential Excellence Programme (Phase II) in Cognitive Science, Jadavpur University and Council of Scientific and Industrial Research, India.

References

1. Tavella, M., Leeb, R., Rupp, R., Millan, J.R.: Towards Natural Non-invasive Hand Neuroprostheses for Daily Living. In: 32nd Annual Int. Conf. IEEE EMBS, pp. 126–129 (2010)
2. Muller-PutzGernot, R., Reinhold, S., Pfurtscheller, G., Neuper, C.: Temporal coding of brain patterns for direct limb control in humans. J. Fron. Neurosci. 4, 1–11 (2010)
3. Conradi, J., Blankertz, B., Tangermann, M., Kunzmann, V., Curio, G.: Brain-computer interfacing in tetraplegic patients with high spinal cord injury. Int. J. Bioelectromagnetism 11(2), 65–68 (2009)
4. Prasad, G., Herman, P., Coyle, D., McDonough, S., Crosbie, J.: Applying a brain-computer interface to support motor imagery practice in people with stroke for upper limb recovery: a feasibility study. J. Neuroeng. and Rehab. 7(1), 60–76 (2010)
5. Vaughan, T.M., Heetderks, W.J., Trejo, L.J., Rymer, W.Z., Weinrich, M., Moore, M.M., Kubler, A., Dobkin, B.H., Birbaumer, N., Donchin, E., Wolpaw, E.W., Wolpaw, J.R.: Brain computer interface technology: A review of the second international meeting. IEEE Trans. Neural Syst. Rehab. Eng. 11(2), 94–109 (2003)
6. Wolpaw, J.R., Birbaumer, N., Heetderks, W.J., McFarland, D.J., Peckham, P.H., Schalk, G., Donchin, E., Quatrano, L.A., Robinson, C.J., Vaughan, T.M.: Brain computer interface: a review of the first international meeting. IEEE Trans. Rehabilitation Eng. 8(2), 164–173 (2000)
7. Anderson, R.A., Musallam, S., Pesaran, B.: Selecting the signals for a brain-machine interface. Curr. Opin. Neurobiol. 14(6), 720–726 (2004)
8. Dornhege, G., Millan, J.R., Hinterberger, T., McFarland, D.J., Muller, K.R.: Toward Brain-Computer Interfacing. MIT Press, Massachusetts (2007)

9. Sanei, S., Chambers, J.A.: EEG Signal Processing. John Wiley & Sons, West Sussex (2007)
10. Theodoridis, S., Koutroumbas, K.: Pattern Recognition. Academic Press (2006)
11. Rakotomamonjy, A., Guigue, V., Mallet, G., Alvarado, V.: Ensemble of svms for improving brain computer interface. In: Int. Conf. on Artificial Neural Networks (2005)
12. Lotte, F., Congedo, M., Lecuyer, A., Lamarche, F., Arnaldi, B.: A review of classification algorithms for eeg-based brain-computer interfaces. J. Neural Eng. 4 (2007)
13. Abdi, H., Williams, L.J.: Principal component analysis. Wiley Interdisciplinary Reviews: Computational Statistics 2, 433–459 (2010)
14. Comon, P.: Independent component analysis: a new concept. Signal Processing 36(3), 287–314 (1994)
15. Pudil, P., Novovicova, J., Kittler, J.: Floating search methods in feature selection. Pattern Recognition Letters 15, 1119–1125 (1994)
16. Hao, H., Liu, C.-L., Sako, H.: Comparison of Genetic Algortihm and Sequential Search Methods for Classifier Subset Selection. In: 7th Int. Conf Document Analysis & Recognition (ICDAR) (2003)
17. Leeb, R., Lee, F., Keinrath, C., Scherer, R., Bischof, H., Pfurtscheller, G.: Brain-computer communication: motivation, aim and impact of exploring a virtual apartment. IEEE Trans. Neural Sys. & Rehab. Engg. 15, 473–482 (2007)
18. Tamraz, J.C., Comair, Y.G.: Atlas of regional anatomy of the brain using MRI with functional correlates. Springer (2006)
19. Pfurtscheller, G., Lopes da Silva, F.H.: Event-related EEG/MEG synchronization and desynchronization: basic principles. J. Clin. Neurophysiology 110, 1842–1857 (1999)
20. Darvishi, S., Al-Ani, A.: Brain-computer interface analysis using continuous wavelet transform and adaptive neuro-fuzzy classifier. In: 29th Int. Annu. Conf. IEEE Eng. Med. Biol. Soc., pp. 3220–3223 (2007)
21. Gaing, Z.L., Huang, H.S.: Wavelet Based Neural Network For Power Disturbance Classification. IEEE Trans. Power Delivery 19(4), 1560–1568 (2004)
22. Kocaman, C., Ozdemir, M.: Comparison of Statistical Methods and Wavelet Energy Coefficients for Determining Two Common PQ Disturbances: Sag and Swell. In: Int. Conf. Electrical & Electronics Engg., ELECO 2009, pp. I-80–I-84 (2009)
23. Bhowmik, P., Rakshit, P., Konar, A., Nagar, A.K., Kim, E.: FA-TDQL: an adaptive memetic algorithm. In: Congress on Evolutionary Computation, pp. 1–8 (2012)
24. Yang, X.S.: Firefly algorithms for multimodal optimization. In: Watanabe, O., Zeugmann, T. (eds.) SAGA 2009. LNCS, vol. 5792, pp. 169–178. Springer, Heidelberg (2009)
25. Mitchell, T.: Machine Learning. McGraw Hill (1997)
26. Das, S., Abraham, A., Konar, A.: Automatic clustering using an improved differential evolution algorithm. IEEE Transactions on Systems, Man, and Cybernetics Part A: Systems and Humans 38(1) (2008)
27. Vapnik, V.: The Nature of Statistical Learning Theory. Springer, New York (1995)
28. Alpaydin, E.: Introduction to Machine Learning. MIT Press, Massachusetts (2009)
29. Neshatian, K., Zhang, M., Johnston, M.: Feature Construction and Dimension Reduction Using Genetic Programming. In: Orgun, M.A., Thornton, J. (eds.) AI 2007. LNCS (LNAI), vol. 4830, pp. 160–170. Springer, Heidelberg (2007)

30. Yang, S.X., Hu, Y., Meng, M.Q.H.: A Knowledge Based GA for Path Planning of Multiple Mobile Robots in Dynamic Environments. In: IEEE Conf. Robotics, Automation & Mechatronics, pp. 1–6 (2006)
31. Storn, R., Price, K.V.: Differential Evolutiona simple and efficient heuristic for global optimization over continuous spaces. J. Global Optimization 11(4), 341–359 (1997)
32. Chakraborty, J., Konar, A.: A Distributed Multi Robot Path Planning Using Particle Swarm Optimization. In: 2nd Nat. Conf. Recent Trends in Information Systems, pp. 216–221 (2008)
33. Bhattacharjee, P., Rakshit, P., Goswami, I., Konar, A., Nagar, A.K.: Multi-robot path-planning using artificial bee colony optimization algorithm. In: Third World Congress on Nature & Biologically Inspired Computing, pp. 219–224 (2011)

Optimal Build-or-Buy Decision for Component Selection of Application Package Software

P.C. Jha[1], Ramandeep Kaur[2], Shivani Bali[3], and Sushila Madan[1]

[1] University of Delhi, Delhi, India
[2] Institute of Information Technology & Management
[3] Lal Bahadur Shastri Institute of Management, Delhi
{Jhapc,sushila_lsr}@yahoo.com, {rrdk_07,lbsshivani}@gmail.com

Abstract. Application Package Software (APS) is a collection of software programs developed for the purpose of being licensed to third-party organizations. Examples of APS include accounting systems, human resources software, and enterprise resource planning (ERP) software. With the advancement in Information technology, Component Based Software Engineering (CBSE) has emerged for rapid assembly of flexible modular software systems. It promotes software re-use for large software systems by purchasing components in the form of commercial-off the shelf components from the vendor. If the required component is not available in the market, then it has to be developed in-house. This decision of whether to buy the component or build from the scratch is known as build-or-buy decision. Through this paper, we shall discuss a framework that will help the developer to decide whether to buy or to build software components while designing a fault-tolerant modular software system. This paper proposes optimization models for optimal component selection for a fault-tolerant modular software system under the Recovery Block Scheme (RBS).

Keywords: Application Package Software (APS), Commercial-off-the Shelf (COTS), Build-or-Buy, Recovery Block Scheme (RBS).

1 Introduction

Opportunities in technology and variation in global markets, force organizations to be more market oriented, futuristic and knowledge driven with a flexible infrastructure. This kind of an advancement help organizations' business practices and procedures to sustain in a competitive environment [1]. APS has emerged over the past decade and were introduced into organizations to solve their problems and to provide an integrated and holistic view of the business from a single information and IT structure. Most of the large organizations have already adopted these software and more of small- and medium-sized enterprises (SMEs) too are finding it cost effective and a competitive necessity for sustainability. These APS are developed using Component Based software Engineering (CBSE) approach. This approach has a great potential for reducing development time and cost. CBSE process starts with identification of users as well as developers requirements. After the analysis of the

B.K. Panigrahi et al. (Eds.): SEMCCO 2013, Part II, LNCS 8298, pp. 546–558, 2013.

requirements, a design of the software system is developed. CBSE approach follows a modular design and is composed of various modules and each module is more manageable and developed by integrating components. The cost and quality of a modular software system are majorly affected by selection of suitable components. The developers have different options for the development of these small independent components such as choosing from available Commercial-off-the shelf (COTS) components developed by different developers, in-house development from the scratch, or modifying the functioning of some existing in house components [2].COTS components are used without any code modification and inspection. The information on cost, reliability, execution time and delivery time of COTS components are generally given by the respective vendor. The components, which are not available in the market or cannot be purchased economically, can be developed within the organization. The strategy of developing software by assembling a mix of COTS and in-house build components is known as *build-or-buy*. This strategy tends to provide higher quality software, within a specified budget and delivery time.

In this paper we shall focus on a framework that helps the developers to decide whether, buying or building, the components of software architecture is beneficial, on the basis of various factors, *viz.*, cost, reliability, execution time and delivery time. Very few researchers have taken into account the execution time behavior of software functions. Through this paper we aim at proposing a model of component selection for a fault tolerant modular software system that more indulgently incorporates execution time. The execution time taken by the software to perform a function is important for a developer as well as user. Long execution time for performing a function may cause dissatisfaction and lead to low productivity of the system. The reliability of software can be improved during the software development life cycle through the application of reliability improvement technique, such as fault tolerance. Two of the best-known fault tolerant software design methods are N-version programming and Recovery block scheme. The basic mechanism of both the schemes is to provide redundant software to tolerate software failures. This paper discusses bi-objective optimization model which maximizes reliability and minimizes cost of the software system with the threshold on reliability, execution time and delivery time.

The rest of the paper is organized as follows. Section 2 presents a review of the previous work done in the field of fault tolerant software systems. In section 3, a decision framework is given by formulating optimization model for selection of components in design of fault tolerant modular software system. The fuzzy solution methodology is also explained in this section. In section 5, a case study on development of APS for Academic Institution is given. Finally, some conclusions are furnished in section 5.

2   Literature Review

Two of the most widely discussed fault tolerant techniques in the literature are N-version programming and recovery block scheme. From past few decades tremendous efforts have been spent to study fault tolerant architecture in software systems. Scott et al., (1983, 1984 &1987) introduced data domain reliability models of several fault-tolerant software schemes, including N-version programming (NVP), Recovery Block

(RB), and Consensus Recovery Block (CRB)). Laprie et al, (1990) presented a simple cost model for the N-version programming and recovery block fault-tolerant software systems. On contrary, limited contributions have been brought to support the selection of components on the basis of their non – functional characteristics (such as performance and reliability). As a consequence, software developers have no automated tools to support the analysis "aimed at characterizing the performance and reliability behavior of software applications based on the behavior of the "components" and the "architecture" of the application" [4, 5]. Tang et.al, (2011) proposed an optimization model to solve component selection problem by considering the concept of reusability and compatibility matrix. The model can be used to assist software developers in selecting software components when multi-applications are undertaken concurrently. Jadhav & Sonar, (2011) proposed hybrid knowledge based system approach which can be used by decision makers as a tool for software selection as it supports various software evaluation activities such as: choosing criteria for software evaluation; specifying and changing user requirements of the software package; determining the fit between software package and user needs of that package; and for reusing knowledge/experience.

3   Decision framework for Component Selection Using Build-or-Buy Strategy

Software system are usually developed using modular techniques and are required to perform one or more functions as specified by the user. Each function is performed by executing a module wherein each module is build up by integrating alternatives. These alternatives can be a mix of COTS and in-house developed components. Each module may be called by more than one function assuming that functionally equivalent and independently developed alternatives of modules are available, each with an estimated reliability, cost, execution time and delivery time. The schematic representation of the software system is given in Figure 1.

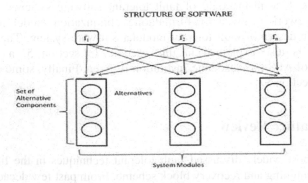

Fig. 1. Software System

The alternatives of modules within a software system can be differentiated on the grounds of cost and non-functional attributes. Purchase of high quality COTS products can be justified by the frequent use of the module. Also effective test cases and testing effort is required so as to improve the reliability of the in-house build component. This leads to an increase in cost. So this paper aims at minimizing the cost by simultaneously maximizing the system reliability. The estimation of cost and reliability of an in-house component can be done on the basis of fundamental attributes of development process. For instance, the cost of any component may be directly dependent upon the developer skills while the component reliability may be associated with the amount of testing. Hence, our model solution provides an optimal combination of COTS/in-house components for a fault tolerant modular software system under recovery block scheme. The model presents a trade-off between cost and reliability, under the limitations of reliability, execution time and delivery time.

3.1 Notations

Table 1. Model Notations

R	System reliability measure
C	Overall system cost
f_l	Frequency of use, of function l
s_l	Set of modules required for function l
R_i	Reliability of module
L	Number of functions the software is required to perform
N	Number of modules in the software
m_i	Number of alternatives available for module i
N_{ij}^{tot}	Total number of test cases performed on j^{th} in-house built component of ith module
N_{ij}^{suc}	Total number of successful test cases performed on j^{th} in-house built component of ith module
t_1	Probability that next alternative is not invoked upon failure of the current Alternative
t_2	Probability that a correct result is judged wrong
t_3	Probability that an incorrect result is accepted as correct
X_{ij}	Event that output of jth component of ith module is rejected
Y_{ij}	Event that correct result of jth component of ith module is accepted
r_{ij}	Reliability of jth component of ith module
C_{ij}	Cost of jth COTS alternative of ith module
s_{ij}	Reliability of jth COTS alternative of ith module
d_{ij}	Delivery time of jth COTS alternative of ith module
c_{ij}	Unitary development cost of jth in-house component of ith module
t_{ij}	Estimated development time of jth in-house component of ith module
τ_{ij}	Average time required to perform a test case for j^{th} in-house component of ith module

Table 1. (*Continued.*)

π_{ij}	Probability that a single execution of software fails on a test case chosen from a certain input distribution of jth in-house build component of ith module
ρ_{ij}	the probability that the jth in-house developed alternative of ith module is failure free during a single run given that N_{ij}^{suc} test cases have been successfully performed
R_o	Thresh hold on module reliability
D_T	Thresh hold on delivery time
E_l	Execution time of the lth function
T_{ij}	Execution time of jth COTS component of ith module
Te_{ij}	Execution time of jth in-house build component of ith module
y_{ij}	$\begin{cases} 1 & \text{if } jth \text{ component of } ith \text{ module is in-house built} \\ 0 & \text{otherwise} \end{cases}$
x_{ij}	$\begin{cases} 1, & \text{if the } jth \text{ COTS alternative of the } ith \text{ module is chosen} \\ 0, & \text{otherwise} \end{cases}$

3.2   Model Assumptions

The optimization model is based on the following assumptions:

1. Software is developed using modular approach where the number of modules considered are finite.
2. Each module is a logical collection of several independent developed components. The components available are also finite in number.
3. A software system is required to perform a known number of functions. The program written for a function can call a series of modules. A failure occurs if a module fails to carry out an intended operation.
4. Codes written for integration of modules don't contain any bug.
5. Several alternatives are available for each module.
6. Fault tolerant architecture is desired in the modules (it has to be within the specified budget). Independently developed alternatives (COTS or in-house build components) are attached in the modules and work similar to the recovery block scheme discussed in [4,6].
7. Redundancy is allowed in the modules. For each module more than one component can be selected.
8. The cost of an alternative is the development cost, if developed in house; otherwise it is the buying price for the COTS product. Reliability for all the COTS components are known and no separate testing is done.
9. Cost and reliability of an in-house component can be specified by using basic parameters of the development process, e.g. a component cost may depend on a measure of developer skills, or the component reliability depends on the amount of testing.
10. Different COTS alternatives with respect to cost, reliability and delivery time of a module are available.
11. Different In-house alternatives with respect to unitary development cost, estimated development time, average time and testability of a module are available.

3.3   Model Formulation

In the optimization model, it is assumed that the alternatives of module are in RB. The model is formulated for the structure given in Figure 1. RB requires n alternatives of a program and a testing segment called acceptance test (AT). Whenever an alternative fails, the testing segment activates the succeeding alternative. The function of the testing segment is to ensure that the operation performed by an alternative is correct. If the output of the alternative is incorrect, then the testing segment recovers the initial state and activates the next alternative.

3.3.1   Optimization Model

Let S be a software architecture made of n modules, with a maximum number of m_i alternatives (i.e. COTS or in-house) available for each module. Therefore, optimization model for component selection can be written as follows:

$$Maximize \quad R = \sum_{l=1}^{L} f_l \prod_{i \in S_l} R_i \tag{1}$$

$$Minimize \quad C = \sum_{i=1}^{n} \sum_{j=1}^{m_i} \left[c_{ij} \left(t_{ij} + \tau_{ij} N_{ij}^{tot} \right) y_{ij} + C_{ij} x_{ij} \right] \tag{2}$$

$$Subject \ to \quad X \in S = \{ \ x_{ij}, y_{ij}, z_{ij} \ are \ decision \ variables \ |$$

$$\sum_{i \in S_l} \sum_{j=1}^{m_i} Te_{ij} y_{ij} + T_{ij} x_{ij} \le E_l; l = 1, 2, ..., L \tag{3}$$

$$(t_{ij} + \tau_{ij} N_{ij}^{tot}) y_{ij} + d_{ij} x_{ij} = D_{ij}; i = 1, 2, ..., n; j = 1, 2, .., m_i \tag{4}$$

$$\max(D_{ij}) \le DT$$

$$R_i = \sum_{j=1}^{m_i} z_{ij} \left[\prod_{p=1}^{j-1} P(X_{ip})^{z_{ip}} \right] P(Y_{ij})^{z_{ij}} \ge R_0; i = 1, 2, ..., n \tag{5}$$

$$P(X_{ij}) = (1 - t_1) \left[(1 - r_{ij})(1 - t_3) + r_{ij} t_2 \right] \tag{6}$$

$$P(Y_{ij}) = r_{ij} (1 - t_2) \tag{7}$$

$$N_{ij}^{suc} = (1 - \pi_{ij}) N_{ij}^{tot}; i = 1, 2, ..., n; j = 1, 2, ..., m_i \tag{8}$$

$$\rho_{ij} = \frac{(1 - \pi_{ij})}{(1 - \pi_{ij}) + \pi_{ij} (1 - \pi_{ij})^{N_{ij}^{suc}}}; i = 1, 2, ..., n; j = 1, 2, ..., m_i \tag{9}$$

$$r_{ij} = \rho_{ij} y_{ij} + s_{ij} x_{ij}; i = 1, 2, ..., n; j = 1, 2, ..., m_i \tag{10}$$

$$y_{ij} + x_{ij} = z_{ij}; i = 1, 2, .., n; j = 1, 2, ..., m_i \tag{11}$$

$$\sum_{j=1}^{m_i} z_{ij} \ge 1; i = 1, 2, ..., n \tag{12}$$

$$x_{ij} = \{0, 1\}; i = 1, 2, ..., n; j = 1, 2, .., m_i \tag{13}$$

$$y_{ij} = \{0, 1\}; i = 1, 2, ..., n; j = 1, 2, .., m_i \tag{14}$$

$$z_{ij} = \{0, 1\}; i = 1, 2, ..., n; j = 1, 2, .., m_i \} \tag{15}$$

The above formulation pertaining to the problem (P1) can be expressed based on the objective functions, constraints applicable and the formula derivation. Here, the objective function (1) maximizes the system reliability through a weighted function of modular reliability. Higher weights may be allocated to the modules that are invoked more frequently. These weights may depend on decision maker's preference. The objective function (2) minimizes the overall cost of the system. Constraint (3) is the execution time constraint that provides maximum threshold on execution time of all functions. Constraint (4) is the threshold on the delivery time while constraints (5), (6) and (7) estimate reliability of each module under recovery block scheme. As it has been assumed that the exception raising and control transfer programs work perfectly, a module fails if all attached alternatives fail.

Constraint (8) is the testability condition representing number of successful test cases performed on in-house developed components whereas constraint (9) calculates the probability of failure free in house developed test cases and constraint (10) is the reliability of both in-house and COTS products. Constraint (11) ensures that the alternative is either COTS or in-house build component whereas constraint (12) specifies that redundancy is allowed at modular level. Constraint (13), (14) and (15) shows rejection or selection of a particular component.

3.3.4   Fuzzy Approach for finding Solution

Crisp optimization models are based on the assumption that in the software development process all the parameters and goals are precisely known. But in real practical problems there are incompleteness and unreliability of input information. Fuzzy optimization is a flexible approach that permits more adequate solutions of real problems in the presence of vague information, providing the well-defined mechanisms to quantify the uncertainties directly. The representative linear membership functions for the two objectives are defined as follows:
The membership function of the goal of reliability is given as:

$$
\mu_{R(x)} = \begin{cases} 1, & \text{if } R(x) \geq R_u \\ \dfrac{R(x) - R_l}{R_u - R_l}, & \text{if } R_l < R(x) < R_u \\ 0, & \text{if } R(x) \leq R_u \end{cases} \tag{16}
$$

where R_l is the worst lower bound and R_u is the best upper bound of reliability objective.

The membership function of the goal of cost is given as:

$$
\mu_{C(x)} = \begin{cases} 1, & \text{if } C(x) \leq C_l \\ \dfrac{C_u - C(x)}{C_u - C_l}, & \text{if } C_l < C(x) < C_u \\ 0, & \text{if } C(x) \geq C_u \end{cases} \tag{17}
$$

where C_u is the worst upper bound and C_l is the best lower bound of the execution time. Following Bellman-Zadeh's maximization principle [13] and using the above defined fuzzy membership functions; the fuzzy multi-objective optimization model for the problem (P1) is formulated as (P2) as follows.

$$Maximize \quad \lambda$$
$$Subject\ to \quad \lambda \leq \mu_{R(x)}$$
$$\lambda \leq \mu_{C(x)}$$
$$0 \leq \lambda \leq 1$$
$$X \in S$$

The optimal value of λ represents the best compromise solution between two objective functions. The solution to the above problem gives the optimal mix of components (COTS or In-house) selected that maximizes reliability and minimizes overall cost of the system developed.

4   Case Study

Many software companies are in the business of developing APS system for various organizations and institution. Software companies have to face a challenge of developing software which is cost effective, timely delivered and also reliable. The organizations which are in the process of acquiring software system also want to have a system which takes minimum execution time. Hence, a case study of 'Academic Institution' software system is presented to illustrate the given methodology.

The methodology is applied to select right mix of components for development of fault-tolerant modular software system. The optimal solution of the optimization model will give a set of components, either in-house built or COTS, so as to have a system which is highly reliable and within a budget. A real world case problem is selected to illustrate the application of the given approach. The selected organization is a management institute which is in the business of providing post graduate management courses to graduate students. The institute was facing a problem of integration and functional performance of various departments. In order to resolve this issue, a team of professors, would like to make a decision to have a customized software system to increase communication between departments, to implement new technologies, to lower administrative task and cost, improve faculty's workload, to manage students database, to ease out admission, examination and placement process, maintain inventory, to enhance organizational flexibility, etc. The team of professors had then selected a software company who will develop a software system for their institute. Brainstorming sessions were organized in the institute with members of different department and their functional requirements were identified and given to the software development company.

Software Development Company adopts CBSE approach for development of software system for this academic institution. Also, CBSE approach of software development follows a modular approach. Therefore, software development team of the company has identified seven software modules which can perform almost all the functions given by the institute and is given in Table 2.

Table 2. Functional requirement of Academic Institution Software

Modules	Functional Requirements
Admission	✓ Defining admission types and preferences ✓ Category, Mandatory original documents required ✓ Payment modes ✓ Rules of seat distribution & cancellation of admission ✓ Admission listing with gender and branch wise ✓ Confirmed admissions with admission type details ✓ Cancelled admissions with amount return details ✓ Provision for allotment of enrollment number to students ✓ Issuing I-cards ✓ Original documents submitted and pending for submission
Academics	✓ Defining branch wise subjects ✓ Defining criteria for internal evaluation and marks scored ✓ Defining criteria for external evaluation and marks scored ✓ Provision to capture marks scored (internal + external) ✓ Provision to display results using graphical charts ✓ Analyzing results using class and section wise ✓ Records of summer training and end-term projects
Payroll/HR	✓ Salary summary (Pay Slip) ✓ Leaves management ✓ Attendance monitoring ✓ Income tax computation ✓ Provident Fund statutory report ✓ Recruitment ✓ Management performance tracking ✓ Skill set management ✓ Employee training ✓ Employee performance evaluation ✓ Administration ✓ Facility management
Events	✓ Details of cultural events ✓ Details academic events ✓ Sponsorships details ✓ Organizing Faculty Development Programs (FDP) ✓ Organizing Management Development Programs (MDP) ✓ Provision for registration for participating in above events ✓ Maintaining photographs of events
Alumini/ Placement	✓ Registration of Ex-students in the Alumni association ✓ Maintaining Ex-students records with their batch and contact details ✓ Provision to define council members of the alumni association ✓ Provision to define terms and conditions for registration ✓ Re-union planning ✓ Provision to update contact information and current profile ✓ Provision to maintain placement records of past few years ✓ Provision to give details of placements batch-wise ✓ List of companies who visit for placement ✓ Provision for making placement schedule ✓ Maintaining students profile for placement and summer internships. ✓ Graphical reports of placements, batch wise and area wise

Table 2. (*Continued.*)

Accounts/ Finance	✓ Periodic and as on date balance sheet ✓ Periodic profit & loss ✓ Bank receipts and payment vouchers ✓ Cash receipts and payment vouchers ✓ Tracking of sales tax forms to be issued and received ✓ Ratio Analysis ✓ Cash flow ✓ Fund flow ✓ Budget analysis ✓ Fixed asset management ✓ Asset purchase sale ✓ Asset scraps
Store	✓ Classifications of Items upto 5 levels ✓ Godown wise classification wise stock ✓ Auto Indent facility for Items going below Re-Order Level ✓ Goods Receipt Register ✓ Requisition Status Register ✓ Items list below Re-order level ✓ Items list below Minimum level

Table 3. Data Set of COTS components

Module	Alternatives	Cost	Reliability	Delivery Time	Execution Time
Admission	x_{11}	13	0.99	2	0.29
	x_{12}	10	0.93	3	0.43
	x_{13}	12	0.96	3	0.36
Academics	x_{21}	16	0.89	2	0.71
	x_{22}	14	0.85	3	0.92
Payroll/ HR	x_{31}	6	0.87	2	0.92
	x_{32}	4	0.84	3	0.99
	x_{33}	8	0.92	1	0.78
	x_{34}	7.5	0.94	3	0.8
Events	x_{41}	4.5	0.66	3	0.99
	x_{42}	5.5	0.7	5	0.95
Alumni/ Placement	Not available	-	-	-	-
Accounts/ Finance	x_{61}	6.8	0.89	1	0.88
	x_{62}	5.7	0.86	1	0.9
	x_{63}	5.5	0.85	2	0.91
Store	x_{71}	5.8	0.72	1	0.96
	x_{72}	6.2	0.76	2	0.92

As discussed earlier, each module is built-up by integrating components. These components can be either readymade components, known as COTS or in-house build components that can be developed within the organization. COTS vendor provides information on cost, reliability, delivery time and execution time of each component. The software development team estimates values of cost, reliability, development time, execution time of in-house build components. The objective of the software development team is to take a decision on selection of right mix of components which will help in developing software which is highly reliable, within a budget, delivered on time and also takes less execution time. After collecting all possible information about all the modules, the software development team identified some vendors from where the desired COTS components are available. The software development team had collected information on various parameters of COTS components and is given in the Table 3.

These components can be purchased as COTS and also we assume that the software development company has the capability to build these components in-house. The software development team compares in-house build components with that of COTS, with respect to cost, reliability, delivery time and execution time. The components (either one of the available COTS components or an in-house developed one) which satisfy these criterions will get selected for the final development of software. Sometimes, there may be a situation that for particular module a COTS component is not available in the market, and then in-house development of that component becomes a mandatory decision. We can see from table 2 that for module 5 no COTS component is available, therefore, development of this component becomes a must decision irrespective of the cost involved. Data set for in-house built component is given in Table 4.

The initial parameters, given in Table 3, help in estimating cost, reliabilities and development time of in-house built component. In total twenty three components are available to the software development team, out of these seven are in-house build components and fifteen COTS components. The decision maker has to evaluate each component on the basis of different parameters *viz.*, cost, reliability, delivery time and execution time. Therefore, a scientific method of mathematical optimization has been adopted to deal with such a situation that involves too many decision variables. For this an optimization model was formulated and is given in section 3.3.1. The solution of the model is given below:

Table 4. Data Set for In-house components

Module	Components	Cost	Development Time	Execution Time
Admission	y_1	10	5	0.36
Academics	y_2	11	6	0.50
Payroll/ HR	y_3	10	3	0.84
Events	y_4	6	4	0.85
Alumni/ Placement	y_5	11	3	0.78
Accounts/ Finance	y_6	6	2	0.92
Store	y_7	8	1	0.94

Once the optimization model is formulated for the above case study the next step is to determine the solution of each single objective problem so as to find the upper and lower bounds as follows:

Objective	X^1 (upper bound)	X^2 (lower bound)
Reliability	0.96	0.54
Cost	87	82

The various thresholds on different constraints were assumed as:

E_l	DT	R_o
15	6 weeks	0.60

Then fuzzy problem is developed and solved using a software package LINGO [3,14]. The solution thus obtained is:

Module	Components selected	Reliability	Cost	λ
1	x_{13}	0.60	86.24	0.15
2	x_{22}			
3	x_{32}			
4	$x_{41}, x_{42},$			
5	y_{51}			
6	x_{63}			
7	x_{72}			

5   Conclusions

In this paper, we have presented a bi-objective optimization model for optimal selection of components using build-or-buy approach under Recovery Block Scheme. The objective of the problem consists of the maximization of reliability and minimization of cost, under the limitations of reliability, execution time and delivery time. The proposed methodology involves subjective judgment from software development team. Fuzzy approach is used in this context to deal with the imprecision caused due to subjective judgment. The usefulness of the model is illustrated using a case study of Academic Institution. The solution to the case study gives the optimal mix of components selected (both in-house and COTS) based on the criteria of maximizing reliability and minimizing cost.

References

1. Onut, S., Efendigil, T.: A theoretical model design for ERP software selection process under the constraints of cost and quality: A fuzzy approach. Journal of Intelligence & Fuzzy Systems 21, 365–378 (2010)
2. Cortellessa, V., Marinelli, F., Potena, P.: An optimization framework for "build-or-buy" decisions in software architecture. Computers and Operations Research, Elsevier Science, 35-10, 3090–3106 (2008)
3. http://www.lindo.com
4. Jung, H.W., Choi, B.: Optimization models for quality and cost of modular software system. European Journal of Operations Research 112, 613–619 (1998)

5. Jung, H.W.: Optimizing value and cost in requirement analysis. IEEE Software, 74–78 (1998)
6. Jadhav, A.S., Sonar, R.M.: Framework for evaluation and selection of the software packages: A hybrid knowledge based system approach. The Journal of Systems and Software 84, 1394–1407 (2011)
7. Laprie, J.-C., Arlat, J., Beounes, C., Kanoun, K.: Definition and analysis of hardware- and software-fault-tolerant architectures. Computer, 39-51 (1990)
8. Scott, R.K., Gault, J.W., McAllister, D.F., Wiggs, J.: Experimental validation of six fault-tolerant software reliability models. IEEE Fault Tolerant Comput. Syst. 14, 102–107 (1984)
9. Scott, R.K., Gault, J.W., McAllister, D.F.: The consensus recovery block. In: Proc. Total Systems Reliability Symp., pp. 74–85 (1983)
10. Scott, R.K., Gault, J.W., McAllister, D.F.: Modeling fault tolerant software reliability. In: Proc. Third Symp. Reliability in Distributed Software and Database Systems, pp. 15–27 (1983)
11. Scott, R.K., Gault, J.W., McAllister, D.F.: Faulttolerant software reliability modeling. IEEE Trans. Soft. Eng. 13(5), 582–592 (1987)
12. Tang, J.F., Mu, L.F., Kwong, C.K., Luo, X.G.: An optimization model for software component selection under multiple applications development. European Journal of Operational Research 212, 301–311 (2011)
13. Bellman, R.E., Zadeh, L.A.: Decision making in a fuzzy environment. Manag. Sci. 17, 141–164 (1970)
14. Schrage, L.: Optimization Modeling with LINDO. Duxbury Press, CA (1997)

Text and Data Mining to Detect Phishing Websites and Spam Emails

Mayank Pandey, Vadlamani Ravi*

Institute for development and research in banking technology Castle Hills,
Road No.1, Masab Tank, Hyderabad-57, India
mayank08p@gmail.com, rav_padma@yahoo.com

Abstract. In this paper, we performed phishing and spam detection using text and data mining. For phishing websites detection, we extracted 17 features from the source code and URL of the websites and for spam-email detection we applied text and data mining in tandem. In both studies, we achieved high sensitivity compared to previous studies and also provided decision rules.

Keywords: Phishing, spam, text mining, data mining, feature selection.

1 Introduction

Daily millions of user across the world access internet for communication and business purpose. Phishing attack is the most serious threat for financial as well as non financial institution. It is defined as a criminal mechanism employing both social engineering and technical proficiency to steal consumer's personal identity data and financial account credentials [33]. The existing email filtering techniques have been found ineffective to control the phishing attack [14]. Therefore, we propose a method using text and data mining techniques to predict phishing attacks correctly.

Our method predicts whether a websites is phishing or not based on the source code and URL of that website. Also, the URL is used for checking the results of search engine, blacklist and SSL certificate of a website. The combination of these two approaches proved potent in detecting phishing websites accurately.

Spam emails are unsolicited commercial or bulk email, which may contains link of phishing websites or malware hosting websites and it is sent to a group of people who do not request for it. The spam emails consume a lot of time of the user for de-tecting it and also they contain unwanted message which can harm or provide losses to users [6, 24, 25, 26]. A study estimated that from our daily emails 70% of them are spam emails.The cost affected by spam emails to companies around the world is approximately $20 billion in a year and it is growing at the rate of 100% a year [8, 22]. So, the spam emails need to be identified accurately by the system.

Several mechanisms have been proposed to overcome the spam identification problem. Most of the researchers have used textual part of data from Spamassassin database, but here we used data from Enron-spam corpus which contains a variety of

---

* Corresponding author.

B.K. Panigrahi et al. (Eds.): SEMCCO 2013, Part II, LNCS 8298, pp. 559–573, 2013.
© Springer International Publishing Switzerland 2013

spam emails. We developed spam emails prediction model based on the textual part of emails. For detecting the phishing websites we used the same method as followed by the Lakshmi and Vijaya [15] and He et al. [12]. Our major contributions in this research are as follows: (i) Detection of two cyber frauds viz., phishing and spamming by a GP classifier. It is like genetic algorithms (GA) but here each individual is a computer program (ii) We provide decision rules (iii) further, we constructed hybrid classifiers to get decision rules with best classifier. The rest of the paper is organized as follows: Literature review is presented in Section 2. Proposed methodology is pre-sented in section 3, followed by dataset description in section 4; results and discussion in section 5 and finally conclusion in section 6.

2   Literature Review

A lot of research is reported to detect phishing websites and phishing emails using different approaches. He et al. [12] constructed a framework by combining two approaches CANTINA, a content based approach to detect phishing websites [27], Anomaly based phishing webpage detection [19] and PILFER, a method to detect phishing emails. They obtained better results with 97.33% True Positive on first dataset and 97% True Positive on second using SVM classifier. Lakshmi and Vijaya [15] used 17 features extracted from source code of phishing webpages, URLs and from web, including 100 phishing and 100 legitimate sites, taken from Phishtank [28]. They obtained highest accuracy of 98.5% using J48. Islam [14] combined Support Vector Machine (SVM), Naïve Bayes (NB), Decision Tree (DT), Random Forest (RF), Instance-Based Learner (IB1) and adaboost classifiers. They reported an average accuracy of 97%. ALmomani et al. [4] proposed fuzzy neural network model for detecting phishing emails. The dataset is collected from PhishingCorpus [29] for phishing e-mails and SpamAssassin [30] for legitimate e-mails. , They obtained RMSE value 0.12 and NDEI value 0.21 in phishing emails prediction. Afroz [3] proposed a new mechanism, called PhishZoo, for detecting web phishing using profiling and Fuzzy matching. In their research, they described the problems of blacklist and whitelist approach [7, 13]. They obtained 97.14% sensitivity using PhishZoo, which is higher compared to other tools like Netcraft [31] and Firefox version 3. Fergus [10] used classifier ensembles for phishing detection and obtained very good results. Abu-Nimeh et al. [2] reported that RF yielded highest accuracy of 92.28% in detecting phishing emails. Basnet [5] selected 16 features from the URL and some keywords of phishing webpage and obtained highest accuracy of 97.99% with BSVM and NN. Maher et al. [16] proposed fuzzy Techniques and reported the highest website phish-ing rate 86.2% representing very phishy website.. Also, Maher et al. [17] proposed fuzzy data mining for detecting e-banking phishing websites and reported 83.7% phishing website rate representing very phishy website..

For spam detection Abi-Haidar [1] proposed Adaptive Spam Detection Inspired by the Immune System and cross regulation model, of Carneiro et al. [32]. They ob-tained improved results with the help of bio-inspired model. Another spam filtering with Naïve Bayes is conducted by Metsis [18]. They obtained 97.53% spam recall using MV Bool. Version of Naïve Bayes. Diesner [9] proposed Exploration of the Enron Email Corpus using network analytic techniques. They investigated the Enron-email dataset. In their report they suggested that in October, 2001 the network had been denser, more centralized and more connected than in October, 2000. Using the text categorization, Fumera [11] developed spam filtering model and reported false positive below 2% and false negative below 20%. Our motivation behind this research was to generate the efficient phishing website detection model by enhancing the result of previous research and provide decision rules, which will help in decision making.

3   Proposed Methodology

3.1   System Architecture

In identifying a phishing website, we consider the source code and URL part of a web-site, we can extract a lot of information which discriminates phishing and legitimate sites. Following Lakshmi and Vijaya [15], we extracted the source code of the web-sites and analyzed it along with URL of the websites to get information, which is used to predict the phishing websites. Fig. 1 depicts the schematic of the architecture pro-posed in our study. We extracted source code of each of the web pages and parsed it using HTML parser to obtain useful and required contents. Here, PHP is used for extracting the source code of webpage. After getting the parsed data the next step is identity extraction and feature extraction.

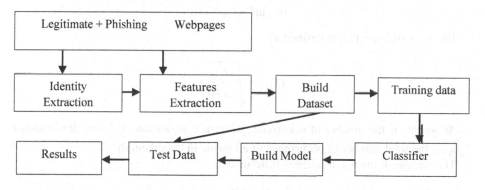

Fig. 1. Used framework in this research for predicting phishing websites and spam emails

Text mining is used in the identity extraction phase. We extracted the features from source code and URL of the websites. For spam detection, we followed the same approach used for client based phishing detection [20]. We analyzed textual part of spam and legitimate emails. We calculated frequency of the each term presented in the textual data and selected those terms, which had higher frequencies. These select-ed terms are used as input features and document-term-matrix is built from selected features. Here, we constructed 6 datasets using the textual part of emails.

3.2   Identity Extraction in Phishing Detection

In this research, identity extraction is a very important phase which confirms the iden-tity of a webpage using certain keywords. These keywords describe the functionality of the website and these identities of a website cannot be altered or replicated by the phishing websites. However, if they do changes in these identities, then it affects the ownership of website. The identity keywords extracted from the META Title Tags, META Description Tag, META Keyword Tags and HREF <a> Tags of webpage's source code.

The META tag used to provide structured metadata about a Web page.. The META description tag is a HTML attribute that provides explanation of the content of web pages. The META Keyword Tag is a brief and concise keyword list of most important terms of a webpage. The importance of this tag is it may define the identity of a web page based on its content. The HREF attribute specifies the URL of the page which the link goes to (www.w3schools.com). When a user clicks on hyperlink, it has to redirect to the concerned web page. Phishers can't change the destination site of a webpage hyperlink. So it will redirect to the legitimate websites. The HREF tags have the high chance to be identity of a webpage because it contains the URL which points to the domain name of a webpage.

After extracting the relevant features related to identity from the webpage source code, the unstructured source code needs to be converted into structured one. To do this, we remove stop words such as http, www, at, com, etc and perform other text mining tasks like filtering and stemming. Further, tf-idf weight is calculated for each of the keywords relevant to identity. We selected first five keywords as identity sets which obtained high tf-idf value. The following formula is used to calculate the tf-idf:

$$\text{tf} - \text{idf} = \text{tf}_{ij} * \text{idf}_i$$

The term frequenct tf_{ij} is defined as

$$tf_{ij} = \sqrt{\frac{n_{ij}}{\sum_k n_{kj}}}$$

Where n_{ij} is the number of occurrence of term t_i in document d_j and denominator $\sum_k n_{kj}$ is the total number of occurrence of all terms in document dj.

The document inverse frequency is defined as

$$\ln\left(\frac{|D|}{|\{d_j : t_i \in d_j\}| + 1}\right)$$

Where |D| is the total number of documents in a dataset, and is doc-ument frequency i.e. the total number of documents, where term t_i appears. The term which will have high tf-idf value has the high probability to present in all documents. So, the above formula is used to choose five identities from each websites source code which is termed as identity set. This process is performed to extract the keywords, which are used to generate the vectors of two features.

3.3   Feature Extraction

Feature extraction plays a crucial role for accurate and efficient prediction of phishing websites and spam emails. For phishing website detection, we constructed dataset by extracting the features from source code of web pages, URLs and from the web. In these 3 sources, we can find various factors which will distinguish between phishing and legitimate websites. We followed the same approach as [15] for extracting the features.

For spam email detection, we extracted features from textual data of spam and legitimate emails. Here, each feature is selected based on their occurrence in the documents. We kept the threshold as 300 (randomly) and we used those features, which had more number of occurrences than threshold. In this research, we worked on 6 datasets after converting the unstructured data into structured datasets using the textual part of emails. In the dataset-I we used 42 features, 40 in the dataset-II, 30 in the dataset-III, 23 in the dataset-IV, 27 in the dataset-V and 32 features in the dataset-VI. The features extracted from spam emails are considered based on their relevance and frequency in the emails.

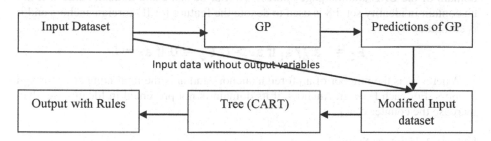

Fig. 2. Proposed methodology to construct hybrid classifier

Feature1: Foreign Anchor
An anchor tag contains href attribute whose value is a URL to which the page is linked with. If the domain name in a URL is not similar to that in page URL then it is called foreign anchor. Too many foreign anchors in a website is a sign of phishing website. So, all the <a> tags in a webpage are collected and checked for foreign anchor. If the number of foreign domain exceeds 5, then the feature F1 is assigned -1 else 1.

Feature2: Nil Anchor
Nil anchor denotes that the page is linked with none. The value of the href attribute of <a> tag will be null. The values that denote nil anchor are about: blank, JavaScript:; JavaScript: void(0),#. If these values exist then the feature F2 is assigned 1, else 0.

Feature3: IP Address
The main aim of phishers is to earn money without investment. So, they do not buy domain names for their fake website. Most phishing websites contain IP address as their domain name. If the domain name is an IP Address then the F3 is 1 else 0.

Feature 4 and 5: Dots in Page Address and Dots in URL
The page address and URL in the source code should not contain more number of dots. If they contain more number of dots then it is the sign of phishing website. If the page address contains more than five dots then the value of the feature F4 is 1 or else

0. All the URL's in the source code are checked for more number of dots if they contain F5 is 1 or else F5 is 0.

Feature 6 and 7: Slash in page address and URL:
The page address and URL should not contain more number of slashes. If they contain more than five slashes then the URL is considered to be a phishing URL and the value of F6 is assigned as 1. If the page address contains less than 5 slashes, the value of F6 is 0. Similarly for all the URL's in the source code, number of slashes is checked and if they contain more number of slashes F7 is 1 else F7 is 0.

Feature 8: Foreign Anchor in Identity Set
If the website is legitimate, then both the URL and the page address will be similar and it will be present in the identity set. But while considering phishing website, the domain of the URL and the page address will not be same and domain name will not be contain in identity set. F8 is used to denote the feature for ID foreign anchors and it is computed by

$$F_8 = a_{id}/a_f \text{ if } a_f > 0, F_8 = 0 \text{ if } a_f = 0$$

Where, a_{id} is the number of a_{id} foreign anchors and a_f is the total number of foreign anchors. For each Foreign Anchors, if its domain is not presented in Identity Set than increase the counter of a_{id}.

Feature 9: Using @ Symbol
Presence of @ symbol in page address indicates that, all text before @ is comment. So the page URL should not contain @ symbol. If the page URL contains @ symbol, the value of F9 is 1 else F9 is 0.

Feature 10: Server Form Handler (SFH)
Forms are used to pass data to a server. Action is one of the attributes of form tag, which specifies the URL to which the data should be transferred. In the case of phishing website, it specifies the domain name, which embezzles the credential data of the user. Even though some legitimate websites use third party service and hence contain foreign domain, it is not the case for all the websites. The value of the feature F10 is 1, if the following conditions hold. 1) The value of the action attribute of form tag comprise foreign domain, 2) value is empty, 3) value is # and 4) Value is void. If the value of the action attribute is its own domain then, F10= 0.

Feature 11: Foreign Request
Websites request images, scripts, CSS files from other websites. Phishing websites to imitate the legitimate website request these objects from the same page as legitimate one. The domain name used for requesting will not be similar to page URL. Request URLs are collected from the src attribute of the tags <img> and <script>, background attribute of body tag, href attribute of link tag and code base attribute of object and applet tag. If the domain in these URLs is foreign domain then the value of F11 is 1 else F11 is 0.

Feature 12: Foreign request URLs in Identity set:
If the website is legitimate, the page URL and URL used for requesting the objects such as images, scripts etc., will be same and the domain name will be present in the identity set. Request URLs are checked for their existence in identity set. F12 is used to denote the feature for ID foreign requests and it is computed by

$$F_{12} = a_{id}/a_f \text{ if } a_f > 0, F_{12} = 0 \text{ if } a_f = 0$$

Where, a_{id} is the number of a_{id} foreign request and a_f is the total number of foreign requests. For each Foreign request, if its domain is not presented in Identity Set than increase the counter of a_{id}.

Feature 13: Cookie
Web cookie used to store the web information. The domain attribute of cookie holds the server domain, which set the cookies. It will be a foreign domain for phishing website. If the value of the domain attribute of cookie is a foreign domain then F12 is 1, otherwise F13 is 0. Some websites do not use cookies. If no cookies found then F13 is 0.5.

Feature 14: SSL Certificate
All legitimate websites will have SSL certificate. But phishing websites do not have SSL certificate. The SSL certificate of a website is extracted by providing the page address. If SSL certificate exists then the value of the feature F14 is 0. If there is no SSL certificate then the value of F14 is 1.

Feature 15: Search Engine
If the website is legitimate and if the page URL is given to any search engine, the first 5 results produced will be about the concerned website. If the page URL is fake, the results will not be related to the concerned website. If the first 5 results from the search engine are similar to the page URL then F15 is 0 or else F15 is 1.

Feature 16: "Whois" Lookup
"Whois" is a request response protocol used to fetch the registered customer details from the database. The database contains the information about the registered users such as registration date, duration, expiry date etc. The legitimate site owners are the registered users of "whois" database. The details of phishing website will not be available in "Whois" database. "Whois" database is checked for the existence of the data pertaining to a particular website. If exists then the value of F16 is 0 or else the value is 1.

Feature 17: Blacklist
Blacklist contains list of suspected websites. It is a third party service. The page URL is checked against the blacklist. If the page URL is present in the blacklist, it is considered to be a phishing website and the value of F17 is assigned as 1 or else the value is 0. Thus, a set of 17 features are extracted from the HTML source code and URL of a website by developing PHP code and the feature vectors are generated for all the websites.

In the feature number 8 & 12, we used different technique from previous research for generating the feature's vector. Here, we made this features categorical to numerical, which increase the importance of these features for classifying the phishing and legitimate records.

3.4   Feature Selection

In this study, we performed t-statistic based feature selection on phishing website dataset. In the phishing website data, for all 17 features we calculated t-value. Further, we selected top 9 features out of 17 features and fed them to the classifiers. Table 1 presents t-value for all 17 features and the bold faced ones are the selected features.

3.5   Hybridization of Classifiers

In order to find maximum output from classifiers, we developed hybrid classifier. In order to extract rules from the best stand-alone classifier, we fed the output of the best stand-alone classifier to another one that generates if-then rules. Here, GP yielded the best result in both the datasets. But GP is a black box, as it doesn't provide decision rules. Therefore, to get decision rules out of the trained GP, we hybridized GP with CART. Fig. 2 depicts the methodology used to construct the hybrid classifier.

Table 1. Keywords Extracted from Phishing website dataset and their t-Statistic Value

Keyword	t-statistic value	Keyword	t-statistic value
Search Engine	14.52	Foreign Request	2.38
Foreign Requesturl in ID	10.88	Using @ Symbol	2.28
Foreign Anchor in ID Set	8.96	Dots in Page Add	1.81
SSL Certificate	6.17	Whois Lookup	1.42
Blacklist	4.92	Nil Anchor	1.13
Foreign Anchor	4.84	Server form Handler	1.07
Cookie	4.25	Dots in URL	1.02
Slash in Page Add	4.04	IP Address	1.007
Slash in URL	2.74		

4   Data Description

For phishing website detection, we analyzed 200 URLs collected from PhishTank (www.phishtank.com), in which 50% are phishing website's URLs and rest are legitimate website's URLs. The dataset is built by extracting the features from webpage's source code, URL and from the web. For spam detection we collected emails from

Enron-spam corpus (http://csmining.org/index.php/enron-spam-datasets.html). This corpus contains large number of spam as well as legitimate emails. We analyzed 6 datasets for spam email detection and in each dataset the ratio of spam & legitimate emails were 50-50%. For extracting the features we used textual part of the email.

5   Results and Discussion

5.1   Experiment - I

In the first experiment, we performed phishing websites detection using text and data mining techniques. The results obtained by applying the trained classification model on test data are presented in this section. We used Genetic Programming (GP), Logistic Regression (LR), Probabilistic Neural Network (PNN), Multi Layer Perceptron (MLP), Classification and Regression Tree (CART) and hybridized GP+CART classifier to train the classifiers. Sensitivity is used to evaluate the performance of the classifier. Table 2 presents the average results of 10-fold cross validation experiments obtained by the above techniques as well as the number of rules yielded by the hybrid classifiers. Here, GP yields the best results with 99% sensitivity, followed by CART, GP+CART, GP+DT, LR and MLP.

Compared to results of Lakshmi & Viajaya [15], where they obtained 98.5% accuracy using J48 technique, we obtained better results using GP as 99.5% accuracy and 99% sensitivity. While, GP yielded the best result, it remains a black box, as it does not provide rules. Thus, to obtain the decision rules, we hybridized GP with CART and again performed our experiment. Further, we needed to select one model as best, which provides decision rules also. In Table 2, we can see that there is not much difference between the classifier's sensitivity. Further, since GP yielded numerically best results, we performed t-test between GP and other classifiers to see whether there is any statistically significant difference or not.

Table 4 presents the decision rules obtained by GP+CART. We performed 10-fold cross validation. However, on average we obtained 5.5 no of rules. Here, we presented decision rules obtained in the fold that yielded best results. Using t-statistic based feature selection we selected 9 features out of 17 and fed them to the classifiers. The results are presented in Table 2. Here also, the GP yielded the best accuracy and sensitivity of 98%, 99% respectively. The average number of rules yielded by CART and GP+CART is 4.5 and 5.6 respectively.

While comparing the results of with and without feature selection, it turned out that the classifiers yielded approximately the same results. Hence, we conducted t-test to see if the difference between sensitivities in both cases is statistically significant. The t-statistic values computed for GP, LR, PNN, MLP, CART and GP+CART are 0.6, 0.26, 0, 0.22, 0.77 and 0.77 respectively. The t-value is less than 2.83 for all the classifiers. It means in all classifiers, using only 9 features, we are able to get statistically the same sensitivity and also, the average number of rules is decreased with feature selection, which is a significant result of the study.

Table 2. Average 10-Fold Results of Phishing website data

Classifier	Without Feature Selection				With Feature Selection				t-statistic value (Sensitivity)
	Sen	Spec	Acc	No of Rules	Sen	Spes	Acc	No of Rules	
GP	**99**	**100**	**99.5**	NA	**98**	**100**	**99**	NA	0.6
LR	91	88	89.5	NA	90	90	90	NA	0.26
PNN	89	90	89.5	NA	89	86	87.5	NA	0
MLP	89	80	84.5	NA	88	86	87	NA	0.22
CART	94	90	92	6.6	92	88	90	**4.5**	0.77
GP+ CART	94	87	90.5	**5.5**	92	90	91	5.6	0.77

Table 3. t-test based model comparison

Classifiers	t-statistic value (Sensitivity)	
	Without FS	With FS
GP vs. CART+GP	2.61	2.49
GP vs. CART	2.61	2.49
GP+CART vs. CART	0	0

Table 4. Decision rules yielded by GP+CART in predicting phishing websites

SN	If-then rules	Class
1	SEARCH_ENGINE <= 0.5.	Legitimate
2	SEARCH_ENGINE > 0.5 && FOREIGN_REQUEST_ IN_ID <= 0.02 && SSL_CERTIFICATE <= 0.5.	Legitimate
3	SEARCH_ENGINE > 0.5 && FOREIGN_REQUEST_IN_ID <= 0.02 && SSL_ CERTIFICATE > 0.5 && FOREIGN_REQUEST <= 0.5.	Legitimate
4	SEARCH_ENGINE > 0.5 && FOREIGN_REQUEST_IN_ID <= 0.02 && SSL_ CERTIFICATE > 0.5 && FOREIGN_REQUEST > 0.5.	Phishing
5	SEARCH_ENGINE > 0.5 && FOREIGN_REQUESTURL_IN_ID > 0.02	Phishing

Table 3 presents t-test results among the classifiers based on sensitivity. Here, we found that the GP is not statistically significantly different from the hybrid classifier GP+CART and CART because t-value is less than 2.83 in both the cases with or without feature selection. Therefore, we can prefer GP+CART or CART, which provided decision rules for phishing website detection. Afterwards, we performed t-test between GP+CART and CART and obtained t-value 0 in both the cases. Thus, there is no statistically significant difference between these two classifiers. However, from Table 2, we found that with 17 features, on average GP+CART provided 5.5 rules, whereas CART provided 6.6 rules. So, in this dataset GP+CART is preferable. In the dataset with 9 features, on average CART provided 4.5 rules, whereas GP+CART provided 5.6 rules on average. Thus, CART is the preferable classifier in this dataset. In conclusion we can say that, in both the datasets, there is no statistically significant difference between the classifiers GP+CART, and CART but we can go with such classifier which provides less number of rules.

5.2   Experiment-II

Here, we performed spam email detection. We analyzed 6 datasets containing large scale of spam emails. We employed LR, CART, GP, MLP and PNN for classification purpose and followed 10-fold cross validation testing. Table 5 presents the average 10-fold results of all the datasets. In the datasets 1 & 4, LR performed the best, while in the dataset 2 & 3, MLP yielded the best results. In the dataset 5 & 6, PNN significantly outperformed other techniques. Further, in each dataset, we performed t-test between the best performing technique versus others to check the statistical significant difference, based on sensitivity (see Table 6). In the dataset 1, we performed

Table 5. Average 10-fold results of all the 6 Spam datasets

Technique		Datasets						
		1	2	3	4	5	6	Avg
LR	Sen	93.3	95	92.7	97.3	86.5	81.1	90.9
	Spe	81.3	86.6	85.6	82.7	90.6	75.7	83.7
	Acc	87.3	90.8	89.1	90.1	88.5	74.3	86.7
CART	Sen	93.3	92.9	91.3	96.2	90.8	83	91.2
	Spe	82.1	90.3	89.4	89.1	88.5	80.3	86.6
	Acc	87.7	91.6	90.4	92.6	89.6	81.7	88.9
	Rules	27.8	27.3	25.6	24.1	27.4	29.6	26.9
GP	Sen	92.4	93.8	92.6	96.7	91.8	81.6	91.5
	Spe	86.2	90.4	90.6	89.8	90.8	82.4	88.3
	Acc	89.3	92.1	91.6	93.2	91.3	82	89.9
MLP	Sen	93.1	96.3	94.3	95.9	91.1	84.9	92.6
	Spe	87	93.5	93.7	91.1	92.4	86	90.6
	Acc	90.1	94.9	94	93.5	91.7	85.5	91.6
PNN	Sen	38.3	45.9	64.9	24.3	96.9	97.7	61.3
	Spe	96.5	99.5	98	98.3	61.6	34.6	81.4
	Acc	67.4	72.7	81.4	61.3	79.2	66.2	71.3

Table 6. t-test comparison results between the techniques in all 6 datasets

Dataset	Technique Comparison		t-value
1	LR Vs	CART	0.001
		GP	0.68
		MLP	0.11
		PNN	**23.69**
2	MLP Vs	LR	**3.01**
		CART	**6.87**
		GP	**5.76**
		PNN	**50.23**
3	MLP Vs	LR	1.98
		CART	**3.82**
		GP	2.35
		PNN	**29.22**
4	LR Vs	CART	1.69
		GP	0.84
		MLP	2.3
		PNN	**12.07**
5	PNN Vs	LR	**11.94**
		CART	**9.58**
		GP	**9.19**
		MLP	**8.16**
6	PNN Vs	LR	**22.29**
		CART	**15.69**
		GP	**11.86**
		MLP	**18.36**

t-test between LR and other techniques. Here, we preferred CART as best technique because there is no statistical significant difference between CART and LR and CART provides decision rules. Similarly, in the dataset-2, MLP is best technique because other techniques are statistical significant different to MLP. In the dataset-3, MLP, LR and GP have no statistical difference, so we can choose any one of them. In the same way, CART is the best in dataset-4, because CART and LR are statistically indifferent. While in the dataset-5 & 6, PNN is best technique. Here, CART is the only technique which provides decision rules. In the past, Abi-Haider and Rocha [1] have also analyzed the 6 datasets. They also performed 10-fold cross validation and reported only accuracy and not sensitivity. Hence, we compare the accuracies obtained by them with that of the present work. On dataset-1, we achieved higher accuracy of 90.1% using MLP and they obtained 90% accuracy using Variable Trigonometric Threshold (VTT) technique developed by them. On dataset-2, we achieved 94.9% accuracy with MLP and they obtained 93% accuracy with Naïve Bayes. In dataset-3I we obtained 94% accuracy with MLP, whereas they obtained 92% accuracy with Naïve Bayes. In the case of dataset-4, we achieved 93.5% accuracy, while they obtained 95% with VTT technique. On dataset-5, we achieved 91.7% accuracy with MLP, whereas they obtained better accuracy of 95% with Naïve Bayes. In the dataset-6, we got 85.5% accuracy with MLP, while they obtained 90% with Naïve Bayes. On average of all the 6 datasets, we obtained 91.6% accuracy with MLP, whereas they obtained 91% with Naïve Bayes. Thus, in summary, the comparison yielded mixed results in terms of accuracy.

6   Conclusion

This research presents a detailed study to predict two common forms of cyber attacks viz., the phishing and spamming. For phishing detection we extracted features from source code of the webpage, URL and web. Further, in spam detection we constructed and analyzed 6 datasets, for which textual data is taken from enron-spam corpus. Here we used text mining and data mining in tandem. Here, LR, CART, GP, MLP and PNN for classification purpose and followed 10-fold cross validation testing. Even though GP yielded best results, in order to extract 'if-then' rules, it is hybridized with CART. Further, we performed t-test to check the statistical significant difference between the techniques. We obtained improved results compared to a previous study and also provided decision rules which hitherto no one has provided. In the spam detection case, we analyzed 6 datasets. In the dataset 1 & 4, CART is the preferred technique, while in the datasets 2 & 3 MLP yielded superior results. In the datasets 5 & 6, PNN significantly outperform other techniques.

References

1. Abi-Haidar, A., Rocha, L.M.: Adaptive Spam Detection Inspired by the Immune System. In: Bullock, S., Noble, J., Watson, R.A., Bedau, M.A. (eds.) Artificial Life XI: Eleventh International Conference on the Simulation and Synthesis of Living Systems, pp. 1–8. MIT Press (2008)
2. Abu-Nimeh, S., Nappa, D., Wang, X., Nair, S.: A comparison of machine learning techniques for phishingdetection. In: Proceedings of the APWG Ecrime Researchers Summit, Pittsburgh, USA (2007)
3. Afroz, S., Greenstadt, R.: PhishZoo: An automated web phishing detection approach based on profiling and fuzzy matching, Technical Report DU-CS-09-03, Department of Computer Science, Drexel University, Pennsylvania, USA (2009)
4. ALmomani, A., Wan, T.-C., Altaher, A., Manasrah, A., Eman, A., Anbar, M., Esraa, A., Ramadass, S.: Evolving fuzzy neural network for phishing emails detection. Journal of Computer Science 8(7), 1099–1107 (2012)
5. Basnet, R., Mukkamala, S., Sung, A.H.: Detection of phishing attacks: A machine learning approach. In: Prasad, B. (ed.) Soft Computing Applications in Industry. STUDFUZZ, vol. 226, pp. 373–383. Springer, Heidelberg (2008)
6. Boykin, P.O., Roychowdhury, V.P.: Leveraging Social Networks to Fight Spam. IEEE Computer 38(4), 61–68 (2005)
7. Chou, N., Ledesma, R., Teraguchi, Y., Boneh, D., Mitchell, J.C.: Client side defense against Web based Identity Theft. In: Proceedings of 11th Annual Network and Distributed System Security Symposium, San Diego, CA (2004)

8. Delany, S.J., Cunningham, P., Tsymbal, A., Coyle, L.: A case-based technique for tracking concept drift in spam filtering. Knowledge-Based Systems 18(4-5), 187–195 (2005)
9. Diesner, J., Carley, K.M.: Exploration of Communication Networks from the Enron Email Corpus. In: Proc. of Workshop on Link Analysis, Counterterrorism and Security, SIAM International Conference on Data Mining, Newport Beach, California, USA (2005)
10. Fergus, T., Joe, C.: Phishing detection using Classifier Ensembles, e-Crime Researchers Summit, Tacoma, WA, 1-9 (2009)
11. Fumera, G., Pillai, I., Roli, F.: Spam Filtering Based on the Analysis of Text Information Embedded into Images. The Journal of Machine Learning Researc 7, 2699–2720 (2006)
12. He, M., Horng, S.-J., Fan, P., Khan, M.K., Run, R.-S., Lai, J.-L., Chen, R.-J., Sutanto, A.: An efficient phishing webpage detector. Expert Systems with Applications: An International Journal 38(10) (2011)
13. Herzberg, A., Gbara, A.: TrustBar: Protecting web users from spoofing and phishing attacks, Cryptology ePrint Archive: Report 2004/155 (2004)
14. Islam, R., Abawajy, J.: A multi-tier phishing detection and filtering approach. J. Network and Computer Applications 36(1), 324–335 (2013)
15. Lakshmi, V.S., Vijaya, M.S.: Efficient prediction of phishing websites using supervised learning algorithms. In: International Conference on Communication Technology and System Design, vol. 30, pp. 798–805 (2011)
16. Maher, A., Hossain, M.A., Fadi, T., Dahal, K.: Intelligent phishing website detection using fuzzy Techniques. In: 3rd International Conference Information and communication technologies: From theory to applications, ICTTA, Damascus, Syria, pp. 1–6 (2008)
17. Maher, A., Hossain, M.A., Fadi, T., Dahal, K.: Intelligent phishing Detection System for e-Banking using fuzzy data mining. Expert Systems with Applications 37(12), 7913–7921 (2010)
18. Metsis, V., Androutsopoulos, I., Paliouras, G.: Spam Filtering with Naive Bayes – Which Naive Bayes? In: Third Conference on Email and Anti-Spam, Mountain View, California, USA (2006)
19. Pan, Y., Ding, X.: Anomaly based web phishing page detection. In: Twenty Second Annual Computer Security Applications Conference, pp. 381–392. IEEE Computer Society, Washington, DC (2006)
20. Pandey, M., Ravi, V.: Detecting Phishing emails using Text and Data mining. In: Proceedings of Internation Conference on Computational Intelligence and Computing Research (ICCIC 2012), Coimbatore, India, pp. 249–254 (2012)
21. Ravi, V., Lal, R., Rajkiran, N.: Foreign exchange rate prediction using Computational Intelligence Methods. International Journal of Computer Science and Industrial Management Applications 4, 659–670 (2012) ISSN 2150-7988
22. Spira, J.: Spam E-Mail and its Impact on IT Spending and Productivity, Basex Report (2003), http://www.basex.com/poty2003.nsfl
23. The Anti Phishing Working Group, http://www.antiphishing.org
24. Wei, C.-P., Chen, H.-C., Cheng, T.-H.: Effective spam filtering: A single-class learning and ensemble approach. Decision Support System 45(3), 491–503 (2008)
25. Whitworth, B., Whitworth, E.: Spam and the social-technical gap. IEEE Computer 37(10), 38–45 (2004)
26. Zhang, V., Zhu, J., Yao, T.: An evaluation of statistical spam filtering techniques. ACM Transactions on Asian Language Information Processing 3(4), 243–269 (2004)
27. Zhang, Y., Hong, J., Cranor, L.: CANTINA: A content-based approach to detecting phishing web sites. In: Proceedings of the international World Wide Web Conference, Banff, Alberta, Canada, May 8-12 (2007)

28. Phishtank, `http://www.phishtank.com`
29. PhishingCorpus,
    `http://monkey.org/~jose/wiki/doku.php?id=PhishingCorpus`
30. SpamAssassin, `http://www.spamassassin.apache.org`
31. Netcraft, `http://toolbar.netcraft.com/`
32. Carneiro, J., Leon, K., Caramalho, Í., van den Dool, C., Gardner, R., Oliveira, V., Bergman, M., Sepúlveda, N., Paixão, T., Faro, J.: When three is not a crowd: a Cross regulation Model of the dynamics and repertoire selection of regulatory CD4 T cells. Immuno-logical Reviews 216(1), 48–68 (2007)
33. Anti Phishing Working Group, `http://www.apwg.com`

Intelligent Fault Tracking by an Adaptive Fuzzy Predictor and a Fractional Controller of Electromechanical System – A Hybrid Approach

Tribeni Prasad Banerjee[1] and Swagatam Das[2]

[1] B.C Roy Engineering College, Durgapur
[2] Electronics and Communication Sciences Unit, Indian Statistical Institute, Kolkata
tribeniprasad.banerjee@bcrec.ac.in, swagatam.das@ieee.org

Abstract. In this paper we proposed a Fuzzy Fractional order Proportional-integral-derivative (FOPID) controller for electromechanical actuated worm gear operated fuel shut off valve. An adaptive fuzzy fractional control system (FFCS) is used to reduce the fault of a critical mechanical element in the air-craft component. In Aircraft operator and the maintenance people starving to reduce the cost of aircraft maintenance. So the condition based monitoring and control for electromechanical system is very popular recently.

Keywords: Fuzzy controller, Mechatronics System Maintenance, Proportional Integral and Derivative control, Fractional Control.

1   Introduction

Aircraft system researchers are continually striving to control of a mechatronics system. Whilst at the same time ensuring that the aircraft safety, reliability and integrity are not compromised. The mechanical systems produce motions or transfer forces or torques. Most of the electromechanical systems gears and rolling elements are the major component to driving the system. Now in sophisticated micromechanical (such as aircraft control valve) component it is almost everywhere observed that the mechanical systems, the actuators, the sensors, and the microelectronics are increasingly integrated forming the total compact unit. Thus, a real time health prediction is required to forecast the future condition of the component health so that timely controller can take necessary action automatically or maintenance can be done by the observer manually.

Even In recent years, several diagnostic and prognostic models based on statistical, artificial intelligence (AI) and soft computing (SC) techniques has been proposed [1-4] and getting the satisfactory results. In [5] presented combining with Particle swam optimization (PSO) [6] other hybrid computational intelligence (CI) techniques like [7] for automated selection of features and detection of motor fault.

Fault occurrence in any electromechanical system is very much uncertain. Such that, to overcome any uncertainty some time as we used our brain and experience to predict the next situation and act accordingly the intelligent system also try to mimic

B.K. Panigrahi et al. (Eds.): SEMCCO 2013, Part II, LNCS 8298, pp. 574–582, 2013.
© Springer International Publishing Switzerland 2013

the same logic to overcome the uncertain failure. In system condition prediction can be divided into major two categories: model based (or physics based) and data driven [1]. Among the most capable data-driven methods, neural networks and fuzzy systems are widely used to forecast and predict the electromechanical system conditions. Recently, various neural networks based techniques successfully applied in the prediction of rotating mechanical system conditions [8, 9].In some of the recent works researcher hybridized the two methods like neuro-fuzzy [10] and support vector machine (SVM) combine with sensor data fusion[7] has also been used for fault classification.

However, after many investigation and experiments shows that the hybrid approaches gives the better performance so in this paper we proposed a fuzzy predictor based fractional order PID control system. The uncertainty of the system failure can be minimized by predicting and controlling the system response has been shown in the results. As we know that fuzzy systems can make use of human domain expertise via a series of IF-THEN rules, then it can be integrated with control logic to carry out uncertainty management and fault condition prediction. There are various problem of designing a robust fault-detection system for uncertain T-S fuzzy models [11]. In [12], the author investigates and proposed a method of robust fault detection for a class of nonlinear time-delay systems. The discrete-time networked systems with unknown input and multiple state delays has also been investigated [13]. In [14], the problem of adaptively compensating actuator uncertainties was addressed in a feedback based framework. It is valuable to point out that most results concerning actuator faults reported in the literature only considered bias faults. Controlling with compensating faults and applied to an implementation in to a lower cost technology for future aircraft did not attract enough attention, which motivates this paper. It can advance transportation and also prompt global strike capabilities. Such complex technological system attracts considerable interests from the control research community and aeronautical engineering in the past couple of decades and significant results were reported [15,16].

The rest of this paper is organized as follows. In Section 2, the T-2 fuzzy model, and FOPID controller is first briefly recalled. In Section 3, problem description and how uncertain faults are integrated in such model and the FTC objective is discussed. The main technical results of this paper are given, which include fault detection, isolation, estimation and fault-tolerant control scheme is presented in Section 4. The dynamics and simulation results of proposed system are presented to demonstrate the effectiveness of the proposed technique. Finally, Section 5 draws the conclusion.

2   Basic Definition and Preliminaries of Type-2 Fuzzy Logic System and Fractional Order Control

Type-2 fuzzy sets are used to handle uncertainties. Zadeh [17] first introduced the concept of type-2 fuzzy sets as an extension of the concept of a commonly used type-1 fuzzy set. As we know type-2 fuzzy logic system (FLS) includes a fuzzifier, a rule base, a fuzzy inference engine, and an output processor. Different from a type-1 FLS, the output processor includes a type reducer and a defuzzifier: the type reducer generates a type-1 fuzzy set output and the defuzzifier produces a crisp number. Like a type-1 FLS, a type-2 FLS is also characterized by IF-THEN rules, but its antecedent or consequent sets are type 2. As we understand that the basic distinction between type-1and type-2 is associated with the nature of the membership functions, which is not important while forming rules. The structure of the rules remains same in the type-2 case, the only differences being that now some or all of the set involved are of type -2.

Consider a type-2 FLS having p inputs, $x_1 \in X_1, x_2 \in X_2, \ldots x_p \in X_p$, and one output $y \in Y$. Let us suppose that it has M rules where the lth rule has the form

$$R^l : \textbf{IF } x_1 \text{ is } \tilde{F}^l_1 \text{ and } x_2 \text{ is } \tilde{F}^l_2 \text{ and} \ldots \text{ and } x_p \text{ is } \tilde{F}^l_p,$$

Then

$$y \text{ is } \tilde{G}^l. \tag{1}$$

This rule represents a type-2 fuzzy relation between the input space $X_1 \times X_2 \times \ldots \times X_p$ and the output space Y of the FLS. We denote the membership function of this type-2 relation as $\mu_{\tilde{F}^l_1 \times \ldots \times \tilde{F}^l_p \to \tilde{G}^l(x,y)}$, where, $\tilde{F}^l_1 \times \ldots \times \tilde{F}^l_p$ denotes the Cartesian product of $\tilde{F}^l_1, \tilde{F}^l_2, \ldots, \tilde{F}^l_p$, and $X = \{x_1, x_2, \ldots, x_p\}$.

Fractional order dynamic systems and controllers, is based on fractional order calculus [18]. Fractional calculus is a branch of mathematical analysis that studies the possibility of taking real number power of the differential operator and integration operator. In [19] it was advocated that fractional order calculus would play a major role in an intelligent mechatronic system. In conventional gears has more friction but worm gears is pure sliding and these attractive features desirable in aerospace application. Worm gears are frequently used in electro-mechanical systems. The friction plays a dominant role in the performance of the worm gear system [20, 21]. In FOPID controller I and D operations are usually of fractional order, therefore besides setting the proportional, derivative and integral constants K_p, T_d, T_i we have two more parameters: the order of fractional integration λ and that of fractional derivative μ. Finding an optimal set of values for K_p, T_i, T_d, λ, and μ to meet the user specifications for a given plant (worm gear teeth friction minimization control) parameter in multi-dimensional hyperspace.

3   Problem Description and Mathematical Model of the System

The electromechanical motor fault prediction and precisely tracking is a great challenge. In this paper a new fuzzy adaptive predictor is proposed to monitoring the system performance and fractional control is coupled with it to improve tracking response with the uncertainty. A new intelligent Fault Tolerant Control (FTC) law has been proposed in this paper which can reduce the observer error and improve the predicted and tracking performance.

From the previous type 2 fuzzy definition in section II, we can easily write the overall fuzzy system is inferred as follows:

$$\begin{cases} \dot{x}(t) = \sum_{i=1}^{r} h_i\left(z(t)\right)\left(A_i x(t) + B_i u(t)\right) \\[2mm] y(t) = \sum_{i=1}^{r} h_i\left(z(t)\right) C_i x(t) \end{cases} \tag{2}$$

where $h_i\left(z(t)\right)$ is defined as

$$h_i\left(z(t)\right) = \frac{\prod\limits_{j=1}^{n} M_{ij}\left[z(t)\right]}{\sum\limits_{i=1}^{r} \prod\limits_{j=1}^{n} M_{ij}\left[z(t)\right]}, i = 1,2.....r \tag{3}$$

where $M_{ij}\left[z(t)\right]$ is the grade of membership of $z_j(t)$ in M_{ij} Now, the control objective is re-defined as follows. An adaptive fault tolerant control approach is proposed to make system (2) stable in normal and uncertain faulty conditions. Under normal condition (no fault), a state feedback fractional control input $u(t)$ is designed, such that the system (2) is stable. Meanwhile, the FDI algorithm is working. As soon as an observer predicts a fault it is identified and captured, by the fault estimation algorithm. The predicted estimation is used to compensate and reduces a proper control input $u(t)$ and the feedback error, such that the system (2) is compensate the error and still maintained the high tracking and stable responses under faulty case.

A fuzzy state space observer is used in order to detect the fault. This can be written in more general as follows:

$$u_i^f(t) = \left(1 - \rho(t)\right)u_i(t) + \sum_{j=1}^{p_i} g_{i,j} f_{i,j}(t) \tag{4}$$

where $f_{i,j}(t), i=1,...., m, j=1,....p_i$ denotes a bounded signal, p_i is a known positive constant, $g_{i,j}$ denotes an unknown constant.

Remark 1: A new adaptive compensation control is added which can reduce the effect of drift faults, and a satisfactory tracking performance can still be maintained.

Remark 2: Using MATLAB Fuzzy toolbox is used to simulate and simulink is used to validate the system.

In order to display the superiority of the proposed T-2FFOPID (Type-2 Fuzzy Fractional order PID) system clearly, the measure criterion of mean square error (MSE) is introduced as follows:

$$MSE(e_i) = \frac{1}{T} \int_0^T |e_i(t)|^2 \, dt$$

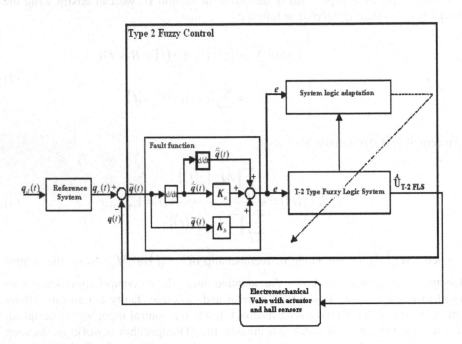

Fig. 1. Type-2 fuzzy control scheme to predict the uncertain fault

4   Experimental Results and Discussions

The Fractional order system with fuzzy predictive controller for the first time to control worm gear friction is applied in this paper. These innovative predictive maintenance solutions, utilizing condition-monitoring systems are currently under testing in order to support the introduction of new electrically actuated aircraft fuel control valve systems to provide reliability assurances. An embedded intelligent CBM and control method has been introduced in this paper. This would allow pre flight warning that can help to reducing fault. Controlling the friction by fractional order PID (FOPID) controllers based on the Fuzzy prediction is presented in this paper. Fractional calculus can provide novel and higher performance extension for FOPID controllers. The obtained results give experimental evidence of the capability of the algorithm and the proposed model. The experimental results are a significant contribution of this work and have been obtained through the development of a suitable software solution that allows interfacing the fuzzy algorithm with the sensors and the actuator. The all experiment and the test of the system have been done in laboratory and the control parameter settings done by experimental testing.

The data acquisition and the simulation we use standard PC with XP, Core 2 Duo Processor, 1Gb RAM, and the LabVIEW software of National Instrument and there data acquisition system. We use T-2FFOPID control, for this complex advanced control with multiple inputs and single outputs. Following the same fundamental principles, we use our computer and data acquisition hardware to take sensor measurements, compare the measured values with the desired set points in software, and update output signals accordingly. There are a number of advantages to using a Industrial PC for control applications that lead to flexibility, high performance, and customization. The simulation has carried out in MATLAB simulink platform coupling with LabVIEW software.

Figure 2 shows that, when an fault occurs in the system, an residual is generated since the residual signal (green color signal) deviates significantly from actual response (pink color signal). From figure 3, we can see that, when an actuator fault occurs, with only FOPID fault compensation, the observation errors do not converge zero. However, T2-FFOPID compensating for the fault, the error system becomes stable, as shown in Figure 4. From Figures 2 and 5, we can clearly draw the conclusion that both faults prediction and compensating the observer response can be estimated accurately and promptly.

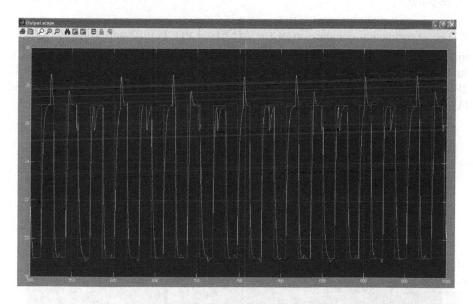

Fig. 2. Uncertain faults with uncontrolled prediction response

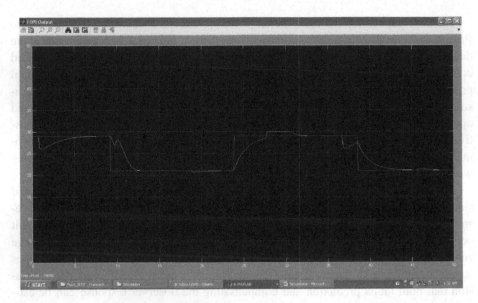

Fig. 3. Uncertain faults is captured and compassioned with predicted output and FOPID tracking response

The experimental comparison of for $MSE(e_i)$,PD, FOPID and T-2FFOPID control schemes due to periodic squire input commands at five different conditions is summarized in Table 1. According to the tabulated measurements, the proposed T-2FFOPID system indeed yields the superior control performance than the PD, and FOPID control system.

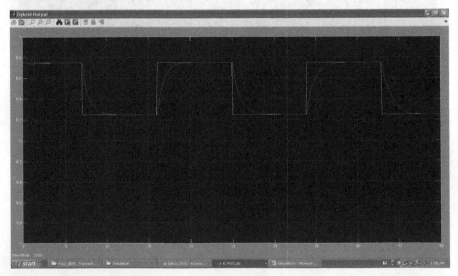

Fig. 4. Uncertain faults is captured and compassioned with predicted output and T2FFOPID position tracking response

Table 1. Experimental Comparison of PD, FOPID, T-2 FFOPID

	PD	FOPID	T-2FFOPID
E_1	1.429	1.129	0.416
E_2	2.432	1.332	0.480
E_3	4.370	3.370	2.330
E_4	3.493	2.450	1.890
E_5	4.550	3.150	3.164

5   Conclusion and Future work

In this paper presents a new fuzzy uncertainty prediction and tracking methods. A new hybrid control methods applied to ensure precise control into electromechanical on-off valve motion. The advantage of the proposed system is show finally, by the results of evidence that the use of a detailed and validated model of the system can produce a complete process of good performance.

References

1. Jardine, A.K.S., Lin, D., Banjevic, D.: A review on machinery diagnostics and prognostics implementing condition-based maintenance. Mechanical System Signal Processing 20, 1483–1510 (2006)
2. Hardman, W.: Mechanical and propulsion systems prognostics (2004); US navy strategy and demonstration. JOM 56(3), 21–7
3. Hardman, W., Hess, A., Sheaffer, J.: SH-60 helicopter integrated diagnostic system (HIDS) program—diagnostic and prognostic development experience. In: Proceedings of the IEEE Aerospace Conference, Aspen, CO, USA, March 6-13, p. 473
4. Samanta, B.: Gear fault detection using artificial neural networks and support vector machines with genetic algorithms. Mechanical System Signal Process 18, 625–644 (2004)
5. Samanta, B., Nataraj, C.: Prognostics of machine condition using soft computing. Robotics and Computer-Integrated Manufacturing 24(6) (2008); 17th International Conference on Flexible Automation and Intelligent Manufacturing, pp. 816–823 (December 2008)
6. Kennedy, J., Eberhart, R.C.: Particle swarm optimization. In: Proceedings of the IEEE International Conference on Neural Networks, IV, pp. 1942–1948. IEEE Service Center, Piscataway (1995)
7. Banerjee, T.P., Das, S.: A Support Vector Machine based Multi-Sensor Data Fusion for Motor Fault Detection. Information Sciences 217, 25, 96–107 (2012)
8. Tse, P., Atherton, D.: Prediction of machine deterioration using vibration based fault trends and recurrent neural networks. Journal of Vibration and Acoustics 121, 355–362 (1999)
9. Gebraeel, N., Lawley, M., Liu, R., Parmeshwaran, V.: Residual life predictions from vibration-based degradation signals: a neural network approach. IEEE Transactions on Industrial Electronics 51(3), 694–700 (2004)
10. Zhao, F., Chen, J., Guo, L., Lin, X.: Neuro-fuzzy based condition prediction of bearing health. Journal of Vibration and Control 15(7), 1079–1091 (2009)

11. Nguang, S.K., Shi, P., Ding, S.: Fault detection for uncertain fuzzy systems: An LMI approach. IEEE Trans. Fuzzy Syst. 15(6), 1251–1262 (2007)
12. Bai, L., Tian, Z., Shi, S.: Robust fault detection for a class of nonlinear time-delay systems. Journal of the Franklin Institute 344(6), 873–888 (2007)
13. He, X., Wang, Z.D., Zhou, D.H.: Robust fault detection for networked systems with communication delay and data missing. Automatica 45, 2634–2639 (2009)
14. Li, S., Tao, G.: Feedback based adaptive compensation of control system actuator uncertainties. Automatica 45, 393–404 (2009)
15. Cheng, Y., Jiang, B., Fu, Y., Gao, Z.: Robust observer based reliable control for satellite attitude control systems with sensor faults. Int. J. of Innovative Computing Information and Control 7(7B), 4149–4160 (2011)
16. van Soest, W.R., Chu, Q.P., Mulder, J.A.: Combined feedback linearization and constrained model predictive control for entry flight. AIAA Journal of Guidance, Control, and Dynamics 29(2), 427–434 (2006)
17. Zadeh, L.: The concept of a linguistic variable and its application to approximate reasoning—I. Information Sciences 8, 199–249 (1975)
18. Oldham, K.B., Spanier, J.: The Fractional Calculus. Academic Press, New York (1974)
19. Podlubny, I.: Fractional-order systems and $PI^{\lambda}D^{\mu}$ controllers. IEEE Trans. on Automatic Control 44(1), 208–213 (1999)
20. Biswas, A., Das, S., Abraham, A., Dasgupta, S.: Design of fractional order controllers with an improved differential evolution. Engineering Applications of Artificial Intelligence 22(2), 343–350 (2009)
21. Banerjee, T.P., Saha, S., Das, S., Abraham, A.: An Application of Fractional Intelligent Robust Controller for Electromechanical Valve. In: Proceedings of the World Congress on Information and Communication Technologies (WICT 2011), pp. 368–372 (2011)

Differential Evolution and Bacterial Foraging Optimization Based Dynamic Economic Dispatch with Non-smooth Fuel Cost Functions

Kanchapogu Vaisakh[1], Pillala Praveena[1], and Kothapalli Naga Sujatha[2]

[1] Department of Eelctrical Engineering, AU College of Engineering, Andhra University, Visakhapatnam-530003,AP,India
[2] Department of Eelctrical and Electronics Engineering, JNTUH College of Engineering, Jagityal-505501,AP,India
{vaisakh_k,knagasujatha}@yahoo.co.in, nambaripraveena@yahoo.com

Abstract. The Dynamic economic dispatch (DED) is an optimization problem with an objective to determine the optimal combination of power outputs for all generating units over a certain period of time in order to minimize the total fuel cost while satisfying dynamic operational constraints and load demand in each interval. Recently social foraging behavior of Escherichia coli bacteria has been explored to develop a novel algorithm for distributed optimization and control. The Bacterial Foraging Optimization Algorithm (BFOA) is currently gaining popularity in the community of researchers, for its effectiveness in solving certain difficult real-world optimization problems. This article comes up with a hybrid approach involving Differential Evolution (DE) and BFOA algorithm for solving the DED problem of generating units considering valve-point effects. The proposed hybrid algorithm has been extensively compared with the classical approach and those reported in the literature. The new method is shown to be statistically significantly better on two test systems consisting of five and ten generating units.

1   Introduction

Dynamic economic dispatch is an extension of the conventional economic dispatch problem used to determine the optimal generation schedule of on-line generators, so as to meet the predicted load demand over certain period of time at minimum operating cost under various system and operational constraints. Due to the ramp-rate constraints of a generator, the operational decision at hour t may affect the operational decision at a later hour. For a power system with binding ramp-rate limits, these limits must be properly modeled in production simulation. The DED is not only the most accurate formulation of the economic dispatch problem but also the most difficult dynamic optimization problem.

In the literature, DED problems have been addressed with convex cost functions [1]–[3]. However, in reality, large steam turbines have steam admission valves, which contribute non-convexity in the fuel cost function of the generating units [4]-[6].

B.K. Panigrahi et al. (Eds.): SEMCCO 2013, Part II, LNCS 8298, pp. 583–594, 2013.
© Springer International Publishing Switzerland 2013

Accurate modeling of DED problem will be improved when the valve point loadings in the generating units are taken into account. Furthermore, they may generate multiple local optimum points in the solution space. Previous efforts on solving DED problem have employed various mathematical programming methods and optimization techniques. Traditional methods like gradient projection method [1], Lagrangian relaxation [7], dynamic programming and so on, when used to solve DED problem, suffer from myopia for nonlinear, discontinuous search spaces, leading them to a less desirable performance and these methods often use approximations to limit complexity.

The stochastic search algorithms such as genetic algorithm (GA) [4],[8], evolutionary programming (EP) [5],[9],[10], simulated annealing (SA) [11], and particle swarm optimization (PSO) [6] may prove to be very effective in solving nonlinear ED problems without any restriction on the shape of the cost curves. They often provide a fast, reasonable nearly global optimal solution. The setting of control parameters of the SA algorithm is a difficult task and convergence speed is slow when applied to a real system. Though the GA methods have been employed successfully to solve complex optimization problems, recent research has identified some deficiencies in GA performance. This degradation in efficiency is apparent in applications with highly epistatic objective functions. Moreover, the premature convergence of GA degrades its performance and reduces its search capability that leads to a higher probability toward obtaining a local optimum [12]. EP seems to be a good method to solve optimization problems, when applied to problems consisting of more number of local optima the solutions obtained from EP method is just near global optimum one. Also GA and EP take long simulation time in order to obtain solution for such problems. All these methods use probabilistic rules to update their candidates positions in the solution space..

Recently, SA [13], hybrid EP-SQP [14], DGPSO [15] and hybrid PSO-SQP [16] methods are proposed to solve dynamic economic dispatch problem with nonsmooth fuel cost functions. These hybrid methods utilize local searching property of Sequential quadratic programming (SQP) along with stochastic optimization techniques to determine the optimal solution of DED problem. Differential Evolution is one of the excellent evolutionary algorithms [17]. DE is a robust statistical method for cost function minimization, which does not make use of a single parameter vector but instead uses a population of equally important vectors.

The BFOA is currently gaining popularity in the community of researchers, for its effectiveness in solving certain difficult real-world optimization problems. This article comes up with a hybrid approach involving Particle Swarm Optimization (PSO) and BFOA algorithm for solving the DED problem of generating units considering valve-point effects. The proposed hybrid algorithm has been extensively compared with the classical approach. The new method is shown to be statistically significantly better on two test systems consisting of five and ten generating units. The results obtained through the proposed method are compared with those reported in the literature.

2   Formulation of DED Problem

The classic DED problem minimizes the following incremental cost function associated to dispatchable units:

$$Min \quad F = \sum_{t=1}^{T}\sum_{i=1}^{N} F_{it}(P_{it}) \quad (\$) \tag{1}$$

where F is the total generating cost over the whole dispatch period, T is the number of intervals in the scheduled horizon, N is the number of generating units, and $F_{it}(P_{it})$ is the fuel cost in terms of its real power output Pit at time t. Taking into account of the valve-point effects, the fuel cost function of ith thermal generating unit is expressed as the sum of a quadratic and a sinusoidal function in the following form

$$F_{it}(P_{it}) = a_i P_{it}^2 + b_i P_{it} + c_i + \left| e_i \sin(f_i(P_{i\min} - P_{it})) \right| \quad (\$/h) \tag{2}$$

where a_i, b_i, and c_i are cost coefficients, e_i, f_i are constants from the valve point effect of the ith generating unit, and P_i is the power output of the ith unit in megawatts.

The minimization of the generation cost is subjected to the following equality and inequality constraints:

1) Real power balance constraint

$$\sum_{i=1}^{N} P_{it} - P_{Dt} - P_{Lt} = 0 \tag{3}$$

where t = 1, 2, ..., T. PD_t is the total power demand at time t and PL_t is the transmission power loss at time t in megawatts. PL_t is calculated using the B-Matrix loss coefficients and the general form of the loss formula using B-coefficients is

$$P_{Lt} = \sum_{i=1}^{N}\sum_{j=1}^{N} P_{it} B_{ij} P_{jt} \tag{4}$$

2) Real power generation limit

$$P_{i\min} \le P_{it} \le P_{i\max} \tag{5}$$

where P_{imin} is the minimum limit, and P_{imax} is the maximum limit of real power of the ith unit in megawatts.

3) Generating unit ramp rate limits

$$P_{it} - P_{i(t-1)} \le UR_i, \qquad i = 1, 2, 3, \dots\dots\dots, N$$

$$P_{i(t-1)} - P_{it} \le DR_i, \qquad i = 1, 2, 3, \dots\dots\dots, N \tag{6}$$

where UR_i and DR_i are the ramp-up and ramp-down limits of ith unit in megawatts. Thus the constraint of (6) due to the ramp rate constraints is modified as

$$\max(P_{i\min}, P_{i(t-1)} - DR_i) \le P_{it} \le \min(P_{i\max}, P_{i(t-1)} + UR_i) \qquad (7)$$

such that

$$P_{it,\min} = \max(P_{i\min}, P_{i(t-1)} - DR_i) \qquad \text{and}$$

$$P_{it\max} = \min(P_{i\max}, P_{i(t-1)} + UR_i) \qquad (8)$$

4) Constraint satisfaction technique

3   Brief Overview of BFOA and DE Based Hybrid Algorithm

In this section we briefly outline both the BFOA and the DE algorithms

The DE has reportedly outperformed powerful meta-heuristics like genetic algorithm (GA) and particle swarm optimization (PSO) [18]. Practical experiences suggest that the DE may occasionally stop proceeding towards the global optima, while the population has not converged to a local optima or any other point. Occasionally even new individuals may enter the population but the algorithm does not progress by finding any better solutions. This situation is usually referred to as *stagnation*. The DE also suffers from the problem of premature convergence [19] where the population converges to some local optima of a multimodal objective function loosing its diversity.

On the other hand, experiments with several benchmark functions reveal that the BFOA possesses a poor convergence behavior over multimodal and rough fitness landscapes as compared to other bio-inspired optimization techniques like GA, PSO etc. [20]. Its performance is heavily affected with the growth of search space dimensionality. Previously to improve the performance of the DE, some attempts have been made to hybridize it with a few local search techniques, and meta-heuristics like PSO [19-21]. Recently in 2007 Kim et al. developed a hybrid approach involving the GA and the BFOA for function optimization. Their algorithm outperformed both the GA and the BFOA over several numerical benchmarks and a practical PID tuner design problem. In the present work following the same train of thought, we have incorporated an adaptive chemotactic step borrowed from the realm of the BFOA into the DE.

The computational chemotaxis in the BFOA serves as a stochastic gradient descent based local search. It was seen to greatly improvise the convergence characteristics of the classical DE. The resulting hybrid algorithm is referred here as the CDE (Chemotactic Differential Evolution).

In the CDE, each trial solution vector first undergoes an adaptive computational chemotaxis. The trial solution is visualized as an E.coli bacterium. During the process of chemotaxis, bacterium in proximity of venomous substance takes larger chemotactic step to move towards the nutrient substances. Before each movement, it is ensured that bacterium moves in the direction of increasing nutrient substance concentration, i.e., region with smaller objective function value.

After this, it is subjected to the DE mutation. For the trial solution vector in population three vectors, other than the previous one, are selected. One of the three vectors is added with scaled difference of the remaining two. The vector thus produced probabilistically interchanges its components with the original vector (just like genes of two chromosomes). Offspring vector replaces the original one if the objective function value is smaller for it. The process is repeated several times over the entire population in order to obtain the optimal solution. The brief pseudo-code of the algorithm has been provided below:

The CDE (Chemotactic DE) Algorithm

Initialize parameters $S, N_C,, N_S,, C(i)(i = 1,2...N), F, CR$.

Where,

S: The number of bacteria in the population,

D: dimension,

Nc: no. of chemotactic steps,

C(i) : the size of the step taken in the random direction specified by the tumble.

F: scale factor for DE type mutation

CR: crossover Rate.

Set $j = 0; t = 0$;

Chemotaxis loop: $j = j + 1$;

Differential evolution mutation loop: $t = t + 1$;

$\theta(i, j, t)$ denotes the position of the i-th bacterium in the j-th chemotactic and t-th differential evolution loop.

for $i = 1, 2, \ldots , S$, a chemotactic step is taken for i-th bacterium.

(a) Chemotaxis loop:

(i)   Value of the objective function $J(i, j, t)$ is computed where $J(i, j, t)$ symbolizes value of objective function at j-th chemotaxis cycle for i-th bacterium at t-th DE mutation step.

(ii) $Jlast = J(i, j, t)$ we store this value of objective function for comparison with values of an objective function yet to be obtained in future.

(iii)   Tumble: generate a random vector $\Delta(i) \in \Re^D$ with each element

   $\Delta_m(i) = 1, 2, ..., D$ is a random number on [-1, 1].

(iv)   Move: $\theta(i, j+1, t) = \omega.\theta(i, j, t) + C(i).(\Delta(i) / \sqrt{\Delta(i).\Delta^T(i)})$.

   Where ω = inertia factor which is generally equals to 1 but becomes 0.8 if the function has an optimal value close to 0.

   $C(i)$ =   step   size   for k-th bacterium   =

   $((J(i, j, t))^{1/3} - 20) / ((J(i, j, t))^{1/3} + 300)$ Step size is made an increasing function of objective function value to have a feedback arrangement.

(v) $J(i, j, t)$ is computed.

(vi)   Swim: We consider here only i-th bacterium is moving and others are not moving.

Now let $m = 0$;

while $m < Ns$ (no of steps less than max limit).

Let $m = m + 1$;

If $J(i, j, t) < J_{last}$ (if going better)

$$J_{last} = J(i, j, t).$$

And let, $\theta(i, j+1, t) = \omega.\theta(i, j, t) + C(i).(\Delta(i) / \sqrt{\Delta(i).\Delta^T(i)})$.

Else, $m = Ns$ (end of while loop);

for i = 1, 2, . . . , S, a differential evolution mutation step is taken for i-th bacterium.

(b) Differential Evolution Mutation Loop:

(i)   For each $\theta(i, j+1, t)$ trial solution vector we choose randomly three other distinct vectors from the current population namely $\theta(l) + F.(\theta(m) - \theta(n))$, such that $i \neq l \neq m \neq n$

(ii) $V(i, j+1, t) = \theta(l) + F.(\theta(m) - \theta(n))$,

where, $V(i, j + 1, t)$ is the donor vector corresponding to $\theta(i, j+1, t)$.

(iii)   Then the donor and the target vector interchange components probabilistically to yield a trial vector $U(i, j + 1, t)$ following:

$U_p(i, j+1, t) = V_p(i, j+1, t)$ If $(rand_p(0,1) \leq CR)$ or $(p = rn(i))$

$\theta_p(i, j+1, t)$ If $(rand_p(0,1) > CR)$ or $(p \neq rn(i))$ for p-th dimension.

Where $rand_p(0,1) \in [0,1]$ is the p-th evaluation of a uniform random number generator. $rn(i) \in \{1, 2, ..., D\}$ is a randomly chosen index which ensures that $U(i, j+1, t)$ gets at least one component from $V(i, j + 1, t)$.

(iv) $J(i, j + 1, t)$ is computed for trial vector.

(v)   If

$(U(i, j+1, t)) < J(\theta(i, j+1, t)), \theta(i, j+1, t+1) = U(i, j+1, t)$

Original vector is replaced by offspring if value of objective function for it is smaller.

If $j < Nc$, start another chemotaxis loop.

4   Simulation Results and Discussion

A DE and BFA algorithm for the DED problem described above has been applied to five-unit and ten-unit systems with non-smooth fuel cost function to demonstrate the performance of the proposed method. The simulations were carried out on a PC with Pentium IV 3.1-GHZ processor. The software is developed using the MATLAB 7.1. The number of trials have been conducted with changes in the size of population, number of generations, and number of trials per iteration in order to obtain the best values to achieve the overall minimum cost of generation. The best solution obtained through the proposed method is compared to those reported in the recent literature.

4.1   Classical Method

The classic DED problem minimizes the following incremental cost function associated to dispatchable units:

Example-1: 5–unit system: The cost coefficients, generation limits, load demand in each interval and ramp-rate limits of five-unit sample system with valve-point loading is taken from Ref. [13]. The scheduling time horizon is one day divided into 24 intervals. The transmission losses are calculated using B-coefficient loss formula. The optimal dispatch of real power for the given scheduling horizon using the proposed method has been obtained. The best total production cost obtained using classical method is $51119.9. The cost of generation and power loss during 24 time periods are shown in Figs.1 and 2 respectively. The sum of total generating power in each interval satisfies the load demand plus transmission losses.

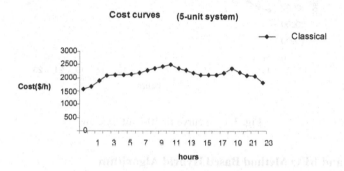

Fig. 1. Cost curve fir 5-Unit System

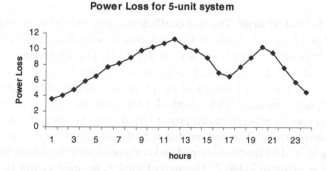

Fig. 2. Power Loss for 5-Unit System

Example-2: 10 – Unit System: In this example, the DED problem of the 10-unit system is solved by the proposed method by neglecting transmission losses in order to compare the results of the proposed method with hybrid methods such as Hybrid EP-SQP, Deterministically guided PSO and Hybrid PSO-SQP algorithms reported in literature [14], [15], and [16]. The load demand of the system was divided by 24 intervals. The system data for ten-unit sample system is taken from the Ref. [14]. Transmission losses have been ignored for the sake of comparison of results with those reported in literature. The cost of generation during 24 time periods is shown in Figs.3.

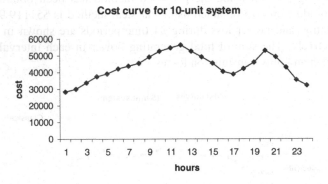

Fig. 3. Cost curve fir 10-Unit System

4.2   DE and BFO Method Based Hybrid Algorithm

The DED problem minimizes the following incremental cost function associated to dispatchable units:

Example-1: 5–Unit System: The cost coefficients, generation limits, load demand in each interval and ramp-rate limits of five-unit sample system with valve-point loading are given in Appendix, which is taken from Ref. [13]. The scheduling time horizon is one day divided into 24 intervals. The transmission losses are calculated using B-coefficient loss formula. The results of the proposed method are compared with that of the simulated annealing (SA) method [13] and are given in Table 1. The comparison of cost of generation and power loss during 24 time periods are shown in Figs.4 and 5 respectively, The optimal dispatch of real power for the given scheduling horizon using hybrid method is obtained and compared with the results reported in the literature and is given in Table 2. The sum of total generating power in each interval satisfies the load demand plus transmission losses.

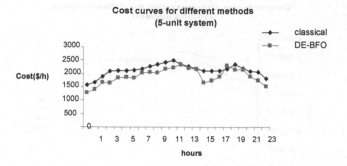

Fig. 4. Comparison of cost with classical and hybrid method for 5-Unit System

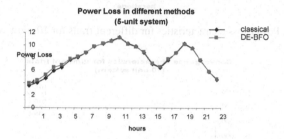

Fig. 5. Comparison of Power Loss with classical and hybrid method for 5-Unit System

Table 1. Best Cost of Generation for 5-unit system using hybrid and SA method

METHOD	TOTAL FUEL COST(DOLLARS/24H)
CLASSICAL	**51119.9**
DE-BFOA	46013.0
SA METHOD	47356.0

Example-2: 10 – Unit System: In this example, the DED problem of the 10-unit system is solved by the proposed method by neglecting transmission losses in order to compare the results of the improved DE method with hybrid methods such as Hybrid EP-SQP, Deterministically guided PSO and Hybrid PSO-SQP algorithms reported in literature [14], [15], & [16]. The load demand of the system was divided by 24 intervals. The system data for ten-unit sample system is taken from the Ref. [14]. Transmission losses have been ignored for the sake of comparison of results with those reported in literature. The convergence characteristics of maximum fitness and cost of generation for different trials for 10-unit system are shown in Figs.6 and 7 respectively. The comparison of cost of generation during 24 time periods is shown in Fig.8. The comparison of cost of optimum scheduling of generating units for 24 hours using proposed method and the methods reported in the literature is given in Table 2.

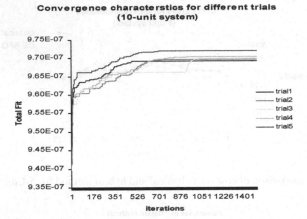

Fig. 6. Power loss characteristics for different trails for 10- unit system

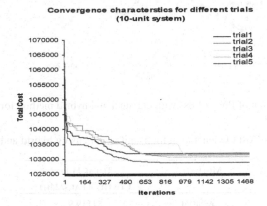

Fig. 7. Generation Cost characteristics for different trails for 10- unit system

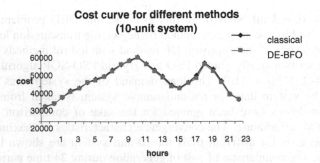

Fig. 8. Comparison of cost of generation with classical and hybrid method for 10 unit system

Table 2. Comparison of Best Cost of Generation for 10-unit system

METHOD	TOTAL FUEL COST($/24H)
DE-BFOA	1028800
HYBRID EP-SQP[14]	1031746
DGPSO[15]	1028835

5 Conclusions

In this paper an hybrid method based on DE and BFA algorithm by combining the DE based mutation operator with bacterial chemotaxis for determination of optimal solution for DED problem with the generator constraints has been presented. The presented scheme attempts to make a judicious use of exploration and exploitation abilities of the search space and therefore likely to avoid false and premature convergence. The feasibility of the proposed method was demonstrated with five and ten-unit sample systems. The test results reveals that the optimal dispatch solution obtained through the DE-BFA lead to less operating cost than that found by other methods, which shows the capability of the algorithm to determine the global or near global solution for DED problem. The proposed approach outperforms SA, hybrid EP-SQP, DGPSO and PSO-SQP methods for DED problems in terms of quality of solution with better performance

References

1. Passino, K.M.: Biomimicry of Bacterial Foraging for Distributed Optimization and Control. IEEE Control Systems Magazine, 52–67 (2002)
2. Mishra, S.: A hybrid least square-fuzzy bacterial foraging strategy for harmonic estimation. IEEE Trans. on Evolutionary Computation 9(1), 61–73 (2005)
3. Tripathy, M., Mishra, S., Lai, L.L., Zhang, Q.P.: Transmission Loss Reduction Based on FACTS and Bacteria Foraging Algorithm. In: PPSN, pp. 222-231 (2006)
4. Kim, D.H., Cho, C.H.: Bacterial Foraging Based Neural Network Fuzzy Learning. In: IICAI, pp. 2030-2036 (2005)
5. Holland, J.H.: Adaptation in Natural and Artificial Systems. University of Michigan Press, Ann Harbor (1975)
6. Kennedy, J., Eberhart, R.: Particle swarm optimization. In: Proceedings of IEEE International Conference on Neural Networks, pp. 1942–1948 (1995)
7. Storn, R., Price, K.: Differential evolution – A Simple and Efficient Heuristic for Global Optimization over Continuous Spaces. Journal of Global Optimization 11(4), 341–359 (1997)
8. Kim, D.H., Abraham, A., Cho, J.H.: A hybrid genetic algorithm and bacterial foraging approach for global optimization. Information Sciences 177(18), 3918–3937 (2007)

9. Mladenovic, P., Kovacevic-Vuijcic, C.: Solving spread-spectrum radar polyphase code design problem by tabu search and variable neighborhood search. European Journal of Operational Research 153, 389–399 (2003)
10. Stephens, D.W., Krebs, J.R.: Foraging Theory. Princeton University Press, Princeton (1986)
11. Yao, X., Liu, Y., Lin, G.: Evolutionary programming made faster. IEEE Transactions on Evolutionary Computation 3(2), 82–102 (1999)
12. Angeline, P.J.: Evolutionary optimization versus particle swarm optimization: Philosophy and the performance difference. In: Porto, V.W., Waagen, D. (eds.) EP 1998. LNCS, vol. 1447, pp. 84–89. Springer, Heidelberg (1998)
13. Ratnaweera, A., Halgamuge, K.S.: Self organizing hierarchical particle swarm optimizer with time-varying acceleration coefficients. IEEE Transactions on Evolutionary Computation 8(3), 240–254 (2004)
14. Attaviriyanupap, D., Kita, H., Tanaka, E., Hasegawa, J.: A hybrid EP and SQP for dynamic economic dispatch with nonsmooth incremental fuel cost function. IEEE Trans. Power Syst. 17(2), 411–416 (2002)
15. Granelli, G.P., Marannino, P., Montagna, M., Silvestri, A.: Fast and efficient gradient projection algorithm for dynamic generation dispatching. In: Proc. Inst. Elect. Eng., Gener. Transm. Distrib., vol. 136(5), pp. 295–302 (1989)
16. Li, F., Morgan, R., Williams, D.: Hybrid genetic approaches to ramping rate constrained dynamic economic dispatch. Elect. Power Syst. Res. 43(2), 97–103 (1997)
17. Han, X.S., Gooi, H.B., Kirschen, D.S.: Dynamic economic dispatch: feasible and optimal solutions. IEEE Trans. Power Syst. 16(1), 22–28 (2001)
18. Attaviriyanupap, D., Kita, H., Tanaka, E., Hasegawa, J.: A hybrid EP and SQP for dynamic economic dispatch with nonsmooth incremental fuel cost function. IEEE Trans. Power Syst. 17(2), 411–416 (2002)
19. Aruldoss Albert Victoire, T., Ebenezer Jeyakumar, A.: Deterministically guided PSO for dynamic dispatch considering valve-point effect. Elect. Power Syst. Res. 73(3), 313–322 (2005)
20. Aruldoss Albert Victoire, T., Ebenezer Jeyakumar, A.: Reserve constrained dynamic dispatch of units with valve-point effects. IEEE Trans. Power Syst. 20(3), 1273–1282 (2005)
21. Storn, R., Price, K.: Differential evolution – A simple and efficient heuristic for global optimization over continuous space. J. Global Optimization 11, 341–359 (1997)

Permutation Flowshop Scheduling Problem Using Classical NEH, ILS-ESP Operator

Vanita G. Tonge[1] and Pravin Kulkarni[2]

[1] Computer Technology,
Rajiv Gandhi college of Engg. Reasech and Technology, Chandrapur, India
vt238@rediffmail.com
[2] Information Technology
Rajiv Gandhi College of Engg. Reasech and Technology, chandrapur, India
kulkarnips1811@gmail.com

Abstract. This paper deals with the Permutation Flow Shop scheduling problem with the objective of minimizing the maximum completion time (makespan), which is associated with an efficient utilization of resources. A differential evolutionary algorithm with classical NEH, iterated local search and enhanced swap operator is proposed. The performance of proposed method is evaluated and results are compared with best metaheuristics GA, QIDE by taking examples from OR Library. Experimental results show the proposed method superiority for some earlier instances regarding solution quality.

1   Introduction

The permutation flowshop scheduling problem is normally classified as a complex combinatorial optimization problem, which consists of finding an optimal sequence for the jobs that optimizes some schedule performance measure. Usually, such measures are the maximum completion time (makespan), and the total flowtime. As it is well known, the first measure is associated with an efficient utilization of resources, and the second one with a faster response to job processing, therefore reducing in-process inventory. In this paper we try to implement classical NEH, ILS-ESP with DE with the objective of minimizing the makespan time. The problem class considered in this paper is as follows. N jobs 1, 2 ... n have to be processed on a set of m machines M1, M2 ...Mm. This problem must be completed with a series of assumptions: all jobs are independent and available at the time t = 0, all machines are permanently available, each job can be manufactured at a specific moment on a single machine, each machine can do a single operation at a specific time, the machine cannot be interrupted once it started an operation, the set-up and auxiliary times are included in the manufacturing times, if a machine is not available (being engaged in another operation) the following jobs are assigned to a waiting queue etc. A comprehensive list of these assumptions, grouped on categories, can be found in [1].

Flowshop Scheduling Problem (FSP) has an essential role in the field of combinatorial optimization problems. If the operations sequence or the technological

B.K. Panigrahi et al. (Eds.): SEMCCO 2013, Part II, LNCS 8298, pp. 595–605, 2013.
© Springer International Publishing Switzerland 2013

itinerary is the same for each job on the m given machines, then the problem is called Permutation Flowshop Scheduling Problem (PFSP). To solve the above problem we use Differential Evolutionary algorithm with classical NEH, Iterated local search and Enhanced swap operator. Techniques used in this paper are inspired from Mircea ANCĂU's proposed techniques [10].

DE is a population based algorithm. Population is generated randomly. Initially target population is evaluated and job sequence with minimum makespan value is considered as target vector then donor vector is generated by mutation. Crossover is occurred over target and donor vector to generate the trial vector. Finally selection is done between target vector and trial vector. Vector with minimum makespan value will be selected. Thus, this paper is organized as follows: In the next section we will briefly introduce the DE and notations (section 2). In section 3, the classical permutation flow shop problem statement is presented, and DE's computational complexity and previous results are looked at literature review in section 4. Section 5 describes the new approaches based on the NEH, ILS-ESP operator. A section 6 report on the proposed technique, section 7 is on computational experiment and comparison. We conclude, in section 8, with a summary discussion on further research

2   Differential Evolution Algorithm

Differential evolution (DE) is arguably one of the most powerful stochastic real-parameter optimization algorithms in current use. DE operates through similar computational steps as employed by a standard evolutionary algorithm (EA). The number of control parameters in DE is very few (F, Cr, and NP). The mutation scale factor F, the crossover constant Cr, and the population size NP. Each of these parameters has some influence on the performance of DE. A good volume of research work has been undertaken so far to improve the ultimate performance of DE by tuning its control parameters. Storn and Price in [8] have indicated that a reasonable value for NP could be chosen between 5-D and 10-D (D being the dimensionality of the problem), and a good initial choice of F was 0.5. The effective range of F is usually between 0.4 and 1. The parameter Cr controls how many parameters in expectation are changed in a population member. For low value of Cr, a small number of parameters are changed in each generation and the stepwise movement tends to be orthogonal to the current coordinate axes. On the other hand, high values of Cr (near 1) cause most of the directions of the mutant vector to be inherited prohibiting the generation of axis orthogonal steps. In project for first module we have used modified mutation operator to tune the mutation factor dynamically which improves the time complexity of DE algorithm.

The space complexity of DE is low as compared to some of the most competitive real parameter optimizers. This feature helps in extending DE for handling large scale and expensive optimization problems. Compared to most other EAs, DE is much more simple and straightforward to implement. Main body of the algorithm takes four to five lines to code in any programming language. [6], [7], [8].

The main steps of the DE algorithm are given below:

Initialization of parameters
Initialization of target population
Evaluation of target population
Find target vector
Generation=0
Repeat
Generation++
Mutation
Recombination
Evaluation
Selection
Find Trial vector
Update population
Until (termination criteria are met)

Fig. 1. Main steps of DE algorithm

2.1   Mutation

For each target vector $x_{i,\,G}$ a mutant vector is produced by

$$V_{i,\,G+1} = x_{i,\,G} + F * (x_{r1,\,G} - x_{r2,\,G}) \tag{1}$$

Where i, $r1$, $r2 \in \{1, 2, 3, NP\}$ are randomly chosen and must be different from each other. In eq. (1), F is the scaling factor which has an effect on the difference vector $(x_{r1,G} - x_{r2,G})$.

2.2   Crossover

The parent vector is mixed with the mutated vector to produce a trial vector $u_{ji,G+1}$

$$U_{j,i,G+1} = \begin{cases} V_{j,i,G+1} & if\ rand \le CR \\ X_{j,i,G} & if\ rand > CR \end{cases} \tag{2}$$

where $j = 1, 2, \ldots, D$; $rand$ [0, 1] is the random number; CR is crossover constant $\in$ [0; 1] i $\in$ (1,2,....,D) is the randomly chosen index.

2.3   Selection

All solutions in the population have the same chance of being selected as parents without dependence of their fittness value. The child produced after the mutation and crossover operations is evaluated. Then, the performance of the child vector and its parent is compared and the better one is selected. If the parent is still better, it is retained in the population.

3   Permutation Flowshop Scheduling Problem

By the concept of Group Technology (GT) the industrial parts are categorized according to different criteria, on part families (i.e. spindle family, gear family etc.). The most important feature of parts which belong to the same family is the technological itinerary, which is the same, no matter their size or specific geometry feature. The technological itinerary dictates the order in which the parts go by one machine to another, from rough material to final product. Optimal manufacturing means best quality and minimum price, while a minimum price involves always a minimum manufacturing time, essentially nowadays.

To generalize the above problem, we have to consider a set of n parts from the same family, which must be manufactured on m different machines. The main objective is to find the optimal order of parts manufacturing so that the total manufacturing time, denoted $Cmax$ (total completion time or makespan) is minimum. The values of the manufacturing time on each machine denoted P_{ij} ($i = 1, 2 \ldots n, j = 1, 2 \ldots m$), are   previously known, constant and positive. They include also all the necessary auxiliary times involved in the technological process. [2]

3.1   Notation

We will use the notation that follows:

J: set of n jobs J_i ($i=1\ldots n$)
M: set of m machines Mj ($j=1\ldots m$)
p_{ij}:   processing time of job J_i on machine M_j
C_i: completion time of job J_i
$Cmax$:   the maximum completion time of all jobs J_i. This is the schedule length, which is also called the makespan.

The optimal value of any criterion is denoted with an asterisk, *e.g.* C^*max denotes the optimal makespan value calculated as follows:

Let π be a sequence of all jobs and $C(j, k)$ denotes the completion time of Ojk.

$$C(\pi_1, 1) = P\pi 1, 1 \tag{3}$$

$$C(\pi_j, 1) = C(\pi_{j-1}, 1) + P_{\pi j}, 1 \; j=2,\ldots n \tag{4}$$

$$C(\pi_1, k) = C(\pi_1, k) + P_{\pi 1}, k \; k=2,\ldots m \tag{5}$$

$$C(\pi_j, k) = \max\{C(\pi_{j-1}, k), C(\pi_j, k-1) + P_{\pi j}, k\} \; j=2,\ldots n \; ; k=2,\ldots m \tag{6}$$

Then makespan can be defined as

$$Cmax(\pi) = C(\pi n, m).$$

So, the PFSP with the makespan criterion is to find a permutation $\pi *$ in the set of all permutations Π such that

$$Cmax(\pi*) \leq C(\pi n, m) \pi \Pi$$

4   Literature Review

Differential evolution (DE) is arguably one of the most powerful stochastic real-parameter optimization algorithms in current use. **Swagatam Das et al. (2011)** provide overall state-of-the-art research on and with DE. It includes brief introduction to DE, its control parameters and several promising variants of the conventional DE. The space complexity of DE is low as compared to some of the most competitive real parameter optimizers. Differential evolutionary algorithm is continuous nature algorithm which prohibits it to apply to combinatorial optimization problems. To compensate this drawback **M. Fatih Tasgetiren et al.** present a heuristic rule, called smallest parameter value first in the permutation. Iterated Local Search (ILS) is a powerful framework for developing efficient algorithms for the Permutation Flow Shop Problem (PFSP). These algorithms are relatively simple to implement and use very few parameters, which facilitates the associated fine-tuning process. Therefore, They constitute an attractive solution for real-life applications. **Angel A. Juan1 et al. (2008)** discuss some parallelization, parameterization, and randomization issues related to ILS-based algorithms for solving the PFSP. They analyzed: (a) is it possible to simplify even more the parameter setting in an ILS framework without affecting Performance? (b) How do parallelized versions of these algorithms behave as we simultaneously vary the number of different runs and the computation time? (c) For a parallelized version of these algorithms, is it worthwhile to randomize the initial solution so that different starting points are considered? And (d) are these algorithms affected by the use of a 'good-quality' pseudo-random number generator?

5   NEH

The NEH heuristic algorithm made by Nawaz *et al.* [3] is recognized by Taillard [4] as one of the efficient heuristic method in this field. NEH is based neither on Johnson's algorithm, nor on assigning weights techniques. First of all, the algorithm calculates the total completion time of each job taken by alone, on all machines. Then the jobs are sorted in descending order of these individual values. The total completion time for the first two jobs is calculated. There is taken the best one from two possible variant. It follows the third job from the ordered list. For this job there are three possible variants to place it in the manufacturing sequence. As in the precedent case, the variant with minimum completion time is selected, and so on, until all jobs are placed in the manufacturing sequence. In this way, the manufacturing sequence is generated, by placing each job Jk $(2 < k \leq n)$ in the most favorable position in the sequence $J1, J2\ldots Jk\text{-}1$ already formed. As a consequence, there are necessary $n \cdot (n - 1) / 2 - 1$ evaluation sequences to get the final result. Many other heuristic methods as Framinan *et al.* [5] are based on NEH and propose different starting sequences.

Let us consider following problem. Problem consist seven number of machine and seven numbers of jobs.

Table 1. Processing times p_{ij} for instance Car7

Machine/jobs	J1	J2	J3	J4	J5	J6	J7
M1	692	310	832	630	258	147	255
M2	581	582	14	214	147	753	806
M3	475	475	785	578	852	2	699
M4	23	196	696	214	586	356	877
M5	158	325	530	785	325	565	412
M6	796	874	214	236	896	898	302
M7	542	205	578	963	325	800	120

Step 1:   Columns 1 through 5: 3124   3097   3866   2948   3100

                     Columns 6 through 7: 4216   3533

Step 2:   6   3   7   1   5   2   4

                     Columns 1 through 5: 4216   3866   3533   3124   3100

                     Columns 6 through 7: 3097   2948

Step 3:   minmakespanTime = 5061

                     Seqe =   6   3

Step 4:   add third job to the sequence and find minimum makespan value and continue it until the last job.

                     Fitness = 6590. Job sequence = 5   4   2   6   7   3   1

5.1 Iterated Local Search and Enhanced Swap Operator

Local search algorithms (LSA) have a general behavior based on the following idea: take an initial solution and modify it until no further improvements are possible. These algorithms need to define a neighborhood function N which represents a map N: S->2^S, such that it defines for each solution s in the set of all feasible solutions S a subset N(s) ½ S of neighbors of s [1]. This function defines the structure over which the search must be done, and this structure is called search graph [4], fitness landscape [11], or state space. Iterated local search (ILS) is a very simple and powerful metaheuristic which consists in repeatedly applying a local search algorithm to solutions obtained by small modifications to one of the previously visited locally optimal solutions. The simplicity of ILS stems from the fact that typically only a few lines of code have to be added to an already existing local search algorithm. ILS is among the best performing approximation algorithms.

Procedure Iterated local Search ()
    Generate initial solution (so)
      s=local_Search (so)
      Repeat
      s1=Modify(s, history)
      s2=LocalSearch (s1)
      AcceptanceCriteria(s, s2, history)
      Until termination condition met
    End

Fig. 2. Iterated local Search

To apply an ILS algorithm to a given problem, four components have to be specified. These are mechanism to generate an initial solution, a procedure Modify that modifies the current solution s leading to intermediate solution s1 a procedure Local Search that takes s1 to a local minimum s2 and an Acceptance Criterion that decides to which solution the next time Modify is applied. An algorithmic scheme for ILS is given in Figure 2. ILS differs from other methods like simulated annealing and tabu search in the fact that it does not follow one trajectory in the search space but solution modifications which correspond to jumps in the search space are applied to allow leaving local minima.

During the perturbation process the so called 'enhanced-swap' operator is used. This is a very simple, fast, and efficient operator which basically do the following:(a) randomly selects (using a uniform distribution) two diffcrent jobs from the current solution; (b) interchanges both jobs, that is, interchange their positions in the permutation; and (c) applies a classical 'shift-to-left movement' -like the one proposed in the NEH heuristic- to each of those jobs following a left-to-right order. The idea here is that we first consider a subset of the sequence of jobs by looking at the left-most swapped job to all elements to its left. Then we shift the right-most job of this subset and tentatively insert it into all possible positions of the sequence of jobs in this subset. Next, we select the one that results in the minimum makespan. Afterwards, we take this subset and reinsert the other sequences that were taken out.

We then apply this idea again for the other swapped job. These 'shift-to-left' movements quickly determine which the best position for each job is when only the partial solution up to its position is considered. Figure 3 shows the pseudo-code associated with this perturbation operator. Notice that the proposed operator is really simple and it does not use any specific-value parameter that needs any complex fine-tuning process. [12].

Procedure ILS-ESP
Base Sol = ClassicalNEH
Base Sol = local Search (Base Sol)
Best Sol = Basc Sol
While stopping condition not met **do**
Current Sol= enhanced Swap (Base Sol)
Current Sol = local Search (current Sol)
Delta =cost (current Sol) – cost (Base Sol)
If delta < 0 **then**
Credit = - delta
Base Sol = current Sol
If cost (Base Sol) < cost (Base Sol) **then** Best Sol = Base Sol = Base Sol = **end if**
End if
If 0< delta <= credit **then**
Credit = 0
Base Sol = current Sol
End if
End while
Return Best Sol
      End

Fig. 3. ILS-ESP general procedure

6   Proposed Algorithm

Idea of the proposed algorithm is taken from "Combining Iterated Local Search and Biased Randomization for solving non-smooth flow-shop problems" presented by Albert Ferrer, Angel A. Juan, Helena R. Lourenço. Classical NEH algorithm and ILS-ESP is implemented with Differential Evolutionary algorithm. The proposed algorithm for the PFSP is coded in   MATLAB 10a. Population are constructed randomly. The perms () function is used. There is one limitation for perms () function in matlab10a that this function can not applicable for the length greater than 10. Due to this problem user defined perms () function has been generated which takes more time to execute a program. Although the proposed algorithm gives better result for some problem following figure shows algorithm of proposed plan.

>Initialize parameters and target population
>Evaluate target population
>NehR=classical NEH
>Search: =ILS (nehR, tareget_vector)
>**While** (not termination) do
>Obtain mutant population
>Obtain trial population
>Evaluate trial population
>Apply ESP
>Make selection
>Apply local search LS ()
>**Endwhile**
>**End**

Fig. 4. The Proposed algorithm

In step 1 we initialize population by considering 10*D, where D is the dimention. In next step target population is evaluated to find a vector with minimum makespan value known as target vector. In step 3, we have use classical NEH algorithm to get another permutation with minimum makespan value it is our second target vector. Both target vectors are passed to iterated local search to find vector with improved value. Then DE is applied to get Trial vector. Positioned based crossover operator is then applied over donor vector and trial vector. Positioned based crossover operator starts by selecting a random set of positions in the parent vector then filled the selected position by the corresponding positions of the second parent vector. Trial vector is passed to the enhanced swap operator. The process is continue till the maximum generation. The proposed algorithm is known as DENEH$_{ILS\_ESP}$.

7   Experimental Computations

In m-tech project we have implemented simple DE algorithm with modified mutation operator which tunes the mutation factor dynamically and position based crossover factor to improve the makespan value. In second module we use classical NEH and ILS-ESP operator. Both modules are implemented in matlab 10. For generating random permutations we have used matlab perms operator but due to limitation of perms operator we have to make some modification in that operator. The following table shows experimental results of DENEH$_{ILS\_ESP}$, which improves the value. It takes less CPUTIME for small problem whose job length is less than 10.

Table 2. Result for DENEHILS_ESP algorithm

Problem	Optimal value	DENEH$_{ILS\_ESP}$	Permutation						Cpu time in seconds
Car1 (11*3)	7038	7685	5 3 1 7 11 8 4 6 9 2 10						716.778232
Car2 (13*4)	7166	7952	7 3 4 1 9 8 11 2 13 12 5 10 6						1139.89
Car3 (12*5)	7312	6995	6 10 1 4 5 11 3 9 12 2 8 7						1132.883426
Car4 (14*4)	8003	8003	4 14 11 13 6 12 9 7 3 1 10 8 5 2						1140.282761
Car5 (10*6)	7720	7557	3 4 2 1 8 6 10 9 7 5						1136.895572
Car6 (8*9)	8505	8505	7 1 5 6 8 3 4 2						12.000066
Car7 (7*7)	6590	6590	5 4 2 6 7 3 1						12..361859
Car8 (8*8)	8366	8345	7 1 6 4 3 8 5 2						12.195967

Once all the trials were done, we transformed the data and used as the response variable of the experiment the following:

$$Relative\ Percentage\ Deviation(RPD) = \frac{Optimal\ Val - Obained\ val}{Obtained\ Val} \quad (7)$$

Where *Optimal Val is* the solution obtained by a given algorithm alternative on a given instance and *Obtained val* is the lowest makespan obtained in any experiment of the same instance. Following table shows the experimental results of DE algorithm for both modules. DEMP is the first module where we have implemented modified mutation operator and position based crossover operator and second module that is DENEH$_{ILS\_ESP}$. The examples are taken from OR library and results are compared with standard algorithm as follows. The results of car3, car5 and car8 problems are improved as compared to the optimal solution find in various algorithms. The RPD is shown in following table.

QIDE-Quantom inspired differential evolutionary algorithm [13].
GA-Genetic algorithm

Table 3. Comparative result of four different algorithms

Problem	GA	QIDE	DEMP	RPD	DENEH$_{ILS\_ESP}$	RPD
(11*3)	7038	7038	7038	0	7685	-8.419
(13*4)	7166	7166	7166	0	7952	-9.88431
(12*5)	7312	7312	7312	0	6995	4.531808
(14*4)	8003	8003	8003	0	8003	0
(10*6)	7720	7720	7720	0	7557	2.156941
(8*9)	8505	8505	8505	0	8505	0
(7*7)	6590	6590	6590	0	6590	0
(8*8)	8366	8366	8366	0	8345	0.251648

8   Conclusion

In this paper we proposed a differential evolutionary algorithm with classical NEH, iterated local search and enhanced swap operator. To check the proposed algorithm we have use carlier instances from OR library. The proposed algorithm DENEHILS_ESP gives improved result for some problem but due to perms() function's limitation implemented perms function take more time to execute and gives poor result. To overcome this disadvantage we proposed a recursive DE in next module which takes less time. In future we will also trying for improving perms function.

References

1. Gupta, J.N.D., Stafford Jr., E.: Flowshop scheduling research after five decades. European Journal of Operational Research 169, 699–711 (2006)
2. Ancău, M.: On Solving Flowshop Scheduling Problems. Proceedings of the Romanian Academy. Series A 13(1), 71–79 (2012)
3. Nawaz, M., Enscore Jr., E.E., Ham, I.: A heuristic algorithm for the m-machine, n-job flow-shop sequencing problem. OMEGA, The International Journal of Management Science 11(1), 91–95 (1983)
4. Taillard, E.: Some efficient heuristic methods for the flow-shop sequencing problem. European Journal of Operational Research 47, 67–74 (1990)
5. Framinan, J.M., Leisten, R., Rajendran, C.: Different initial sequences for the heuristic of Nawaz, Enscore and Ham to minimize makespan, idletime or flowtime in the static permutation flowshop sequencing problem. International Journal of Production Research 41(1), 121–148 (2003)
6. Das, S., Abraham, A., Chakraborty, U.K., Konar, A.: Differential evolution using a neighborhood based mutation operator. IEEE Trans. Evol. Comput. 13(3), 526–553 (2009)
[82] S

7. Rahnamayan, S., Tizhoosh, H., Salama, M.M.A.: Oppositionbased differential evolution. IEEE Trans. Evol. Comput. 12(1), 64–79 (2008)

8. Vesterstrøm, J., Thomson, R.A.: Comparative study of differential evolution, particle swarm optimization, and evolutionary algorithms on numerical benchmark problems. In: Proc. IEEE Congr. Evol. Comput., pp. 1980–1987 (2004)

9. Storn, R., Price, K.V.: Differential evolution: A simple and efficient adaptive scheme for global optimization over continuous spaces. ICSI, USA, Tech. Rep. TR-95-012 (1995), http://icsi.berkeley.edu/~storn/litera.html; Aarts E.H.L., Lenstra, J. K. (edis.): Local Search in Combinatorial Optimization. Wiley, Chichester (1997)

10. Dimitriou, T., Impagliazzo, R.: Towards a rigorous analysis of local optimization algorithms. In: 25th ACM Symposium on the Theory of Computing (1996)

11. Ancău, M.: On Solving Flowshop Scheduling Problem. Series A, vol. 13(1), pp. 71–79. Roceedings of the Romanian Academy (2012)

12. Weinberger, E.: Correlated and uncorrelated fitness landscapes and how to tell the difference. Biological Cybernetics 63, 325–336 (1990)

13. Juana, A.A., Lourencoþ, H.R., Mateoc, M., Castelláa, Q., Barriosa, B.B.: Ils-Esp: an Efficient, Simple, and Parameter-Free Algorithm for Solving the Permutation Flow-Shop Problem

14. Zheng, T., Yamashiro, M.: Quantom-Inspired Differential Evolutionary Algorithm for Permutative Scheduling Problem

15. Das, S., Suganthan, P.N.: Differential Evolution: A Survey of the State-of-the-art. IEEE Trans. on Evolutionary Computation 15(1), 4–31 (2011)

Analysis of Human Retinal Vasculature
for Content Based Image Retrieval Applications

Sivakamasundari J. and Natarajan V.

Department of Instrumentation Engineering, Madras Institute of Technology,
Anna University, Chennai, India
sivakamasundarij17@gmail.com

Abstract. In this work, an attempt has been made to analyse retinal images for Content Based Image Retrieval (CBIR) application. Canny edge based CBIR systems are developed with and without preprocessing techniques. Blood vessels of normal and abnormal retinal images are segmented using Canny edge method. The structural and texture based features are obtained from segmented images. Similarity comparison is carried out using Bhattacharyya distance measure. The retrieved images are ranked. Retrieval efficiency of the CBIR systems is compared based on their performance measures such as precision and recall. The results demonstrate that features derived using Canny with morphological preprocessing could differentiate normal and abnormal retinal images significantly. Precision and recall of the CBIR system using Canny with preprocessing is found to be better than without preprocessing. It appears that this CBIR system aids in diagnosis of retinal abnormalities.

Keywords: Retinal image, content based image retrieval, Canny edge detection, diabetic retinopathy, morphological operation.

1   Introduction

The human retina consist of different important anatomical structures such as blood vessels, optic disc and macula. Variations in these structures are related to pathological changes and provide information on severity of varios disease conditions [1]. The importance of retinal vessels in revealing the state of retinal disease such as glaucoma, age related macular degeneration, Diabetic Retinopathy (DR), hypertensive retinopathy and arteriosclerosis are assessed by observing the changes in blood vessel pattern [2].

The main cause of DR is uncontrolled blood glucose level elevation, which damages vessel endothelium and increases vessel permeability. The progression of DR leads to microaneurysms, neovascularization, hemorrhages, macular edema and retinal detachment [3]. Early recognition of changes in the blood vessel pattern can prevent major vision loss [4].

Fundus images are widely used by the medical community for large scale screening of patients. Manual delineation and detection of vessels become tedious when large numbers of images are acquired [5]. Hence there is a need for reliable automated method to extract and analyze vessels in retinal images.

B.K. Panigrahi et al. (Eds.): SEMCCO 2013, Part II, LNCS 8298, pp. 606–616, 2013.

The quality of an image is improved by suppressing the noise and emphasizing the objects that are used in segmentation. Preprocessing steps such as filtering, contrast stretching and equalizing uneven back ground illumination have been carried out to remove noise before segmentation [6]. Retinal images must be accurately segmented to extract sensitive objects present in the fundus image. Existing methods for vessel segmentation in retinal   images are based on various image processing algorithms such as edge detection, matched filters, adaptive   thresholding, intensity ridges, wavelets and vessel tracking methods [1-5].

Content Based Image Retrieval (CBIR) is a system for browsing, searching the query image and retrieving similar images from large databases. Similar images retrieved by the system with proven pathology can provide diagnostic support to physicians in their decision making process [7]. CBIR systems have been used in medical image retrieval fields such as CT, MRI, X-ray images and clinical processes applications [8, 9].

Retrieval based on statistical features of DR lesions using Fischer discriminant analysis has been carried out [10]. Automated disease separation methods to assist in CBIR for Stargardt's disease and age related macular degeneration have also been proposed [11]. A CBIR system for detection of maculopathy using symmetry based descriptor for retinal images has been attempted [4]. CBIR has been tested to diagnose diabetes related eye diseases [12]. SVM based Medical Image Annotation and   Retrieval System (MIARS) has been used for X-ray images such as skull, spine, arm and elbow [13].

In this work, an automated Canny edge based CBIR system for the identification of DR in retinal images is presented. The images are subjected to various preprocessing techniques such as green channel extraction and morphological operation and their results are analyzed. The segmentation of retinal blood vessels is carried out using Canny edge method. Structural and texture based features are extracted. Quantitative analyses are conducted using the derived features. Further, similarity matching is carried out using Bhattacharyya   distance measure. The performances of these CBIR systems are compared using precision and recall.

2   Methodology

The retinal images used for the analysis are taken from publicly available image database such as Digital Retinal Images for Vessel Extraction (DRIVE) and Diabetic Retinopathy database 1 (DIARETDB1). These are acquired using high sensitive color fundus camera with constant illumination, resolution, field of view, magnification and dilation procedures.

2.1   CBIR Framework

CBIR framework consists of two main subsystems namely, enrolment and query subsystem. The enrolment subsystem acquires information that will be stored in the database for later use. The query subsystem retrieves similar images from the retinal image database according to the user's query image [14].

2.2   Preprocessing

This system uses preprocessing techniques namely Green Channel (GC) extraction and morphological operation. The green channel extraction is applied on retinal images to improve the vessel-background contrast [15]. Morphological operators are used in the enhancement and segmentation of retinal images [5]. In this work, morphological operations such as top-hat and bottom-hat transformations are performed on the GC images. The top-hat operation enhances thin blood vessels and small lesions present in the retinal images. This enhancement is also used to compensate the non-uniform background illumination. The bottom-hat transform is applied to extract blood vessels and spots present in the retinal images [16, 17, 18].

2.3   Canny Edge Detection

Edges characterize the object boundaries and are useful for image segmentation, registration and identification of objects [19]. Canny edge detection algorithm runs in five separate steps. Smoothing is carried out on images to remove noise. Gradients are identified. Local maxima are marked as edges. Potential edges are determined by thresholding. Edges are tracked by suppressing all edges that are not connected to a strong edge.

2.4   Feature Extraction and Similarity Matching

In this work, shape feature is extracted using Canny edge detection [8, 9]. Texture features such as energy, contrast, entropy, homogeneity, maximum probability, mean and standard deviation are computed [20]. The structural feature, ratio of vessel to non vessel area is also calculated [14]. Bhattacharyya distance is used for the similarity matching of query and target images. The shorter distance corresponds to higher similarity in the matching process. For two normally distributed classes, the Bhattacharyya distance [21] D_B is   defined as follows:

$$D_B = \frac{1}{8}\left(\mu_q - \mu_t\right)^T \left[\frac{C_q + C_t}{2}\right]^{-1} \left(\mu_q - \mu_t\right) + \frac{1}{2}\ln\frac{\left|(C_q + C_t)/2\right|}{\left|C_q\right|^{1/2}\left|C_t\right|^{1/2}} \tag{1}$$

where μ_q, μ_t are the mean vectors and C_q, C_t are covariance matrices of the query image q and target image t respectively.

2.5   Performance Measures

Precision and recall are the performance measures to compute retrieval efficiency [7]. These measures are defined as:

$$\text{Precision} = \frac{\text{Number of relevant images retrieved}}{\text{Total number of images retrieved}} \tag{2}$$

$$\text{Recall} = \frac{\text{Number of relevant images retrieved}}{\text{Total number of relevant images in database}} \tag{3}$$

3   Results and Discussion

Retinal images of normal (25) and abnormal (25) are considered for analysis. The preprocessing stages of different normal and abnormal retinal images are shown in Fig. 1 and 2. Typical normal and abnormal gray scale images are shown in Fig. 1 (a) and 2 (a). The GC images are shown in Fig. 1 (b) and 2 (b). GC images are further enhanced using morphological operation as shown in Fig. 1 (c) and 2 (c). The Canny segmentation applied to gray scale images are depicted in Fig. 1 (d) and 2 (d). The Canny segmentation applied to GC images are shown in Fig. 1 (e) and 2 (e) and GC with morphological treated images are represented in Fig. 1 (f) and 2 (f).

It is observed from Fig. 1 (e) that the Canny method applied on GC image identified more blood vessels edges better than Canny method applied on gray scale image as shown in Fig. 1 (d). It is noticed from Fig. 1 (f) that the Canny method applied on GC with MO treated image is preserving the edges of thin blood vessels that are not visible in Canny method on gray and GC image as shown in Fig. 1 (e). Thin retinal blood vessel edges are also better visualized in Canny technique on GC with MO treated image as shown in Fig. 1 (f). This is because, morphological operator is able to improve the detection of blood vessels by eliminating uneven background illumination and linearly distributes the contrast value.

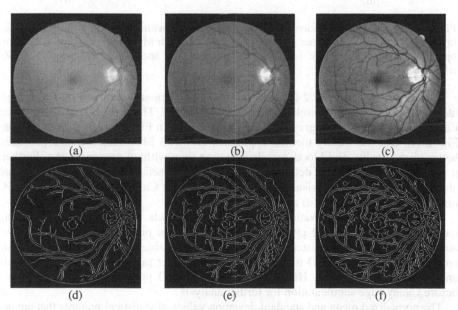

(a)   (b)   (c)

(d)   (e)   (f)

Fig. 1. Canny edge Segmentation of normal image using with and without preprocessing, (a) Gray scale image, (b) Green channel image, (c) GC with MO preprocessing, (d) Canny operation on gray scale image, (e) Canny operation on GC and (f) Canny operation on GC with MO treated image

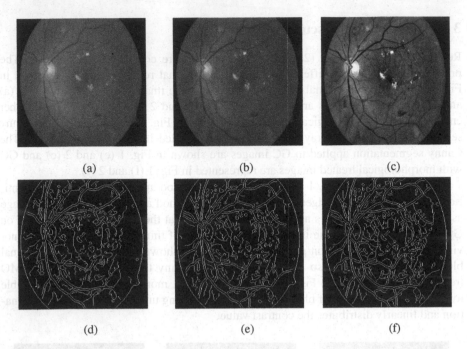

(a)   (b)   (c)

(d)   (e)   (f)

Fig. 2. Canny edge segmentation of abnormal image using with and without preprocessing, (a) Gray scale image, (b) Green channel image, (c) GC with MO preprocessing, (d) Canny operation on gray scale image, (e) Canny operation on GC and (f) Canny operation on GC with MO treated image

It is observed from Fig. 2 (e) that the Canny segmentation applied on GC image, identified retinal blood vessels and also abnormalities. These results are better than Canny method applied on gray scale image as shown in Fig. 2 (d). It is noticed from Fig. 2 (f), that the Canny method applied to GC with MO treated image provides, better visual quality and blood vessels detection than without preprocessing. Further, it is observed that the edge details of smaller blood vessels and disease conditions are also preserved and better visualized in Fig. 2 (f) than Canny on gray scale and GC images as shown in Fig. 2 (d) and 2 (e).

The Canny edge preservation on retinal blood vessels for different preprocessing methods are compared and given in Table 1. The edge pixel counts for normal and abnormal images are tabulated. It is observed from table that the Canny operation applied on the GC and MO treated images show better pixel counts than gray scale and GC enhanced images. Hence GC along with MO preprocessing is carried out before Canny edge segmentation for further analysis.

The normalized mean and standard deviation values of statistical features that are derived from Canny edge applied on GC and MO treated images are given in Table 2. The differences between normal and abnormal average values are also given. The separation between normal and abnormal images is considerably high for energy, contrast, entropy, mean than homogeneity, maximum probability and standard deviation. These features are statistically significant (p<0.0005). It is observed from Table 2 that the normalized average of energy, entropy and contrast of abnormal images show higher values due to high intensity variations of lesions and other non vessel structures.

Table 1. Comparison of edge preservation for with and without preprocessing

S.No	Preprocessing methods	Vessel pixel count	
		Normal image	Abnormal image
1	Gray scale and Canny	6065	6450
2	Green channel with Canny	6788	7397
3	Green channel and morphological operation with Canny	6928	7562

Table 2. Normalized average and standard deviation of statistical features

Features	Normal (Mean±SD)	Abnormal (Mean±SD)	Difference of normal and abnormal *
Energy	0.753±0.04	0.901±0.06	0.148
Contrast	0.779±0.03	0.913±0.05	0.134
Entropy	0.827±0.03	0.933±0.04	0.106
Homogeneity	0.987±0.00	0.972±0.06	0.015
Maximum probability	0.985±0.00	0.965±0.00	0.020
Mean	0.753±0.04	0.901±0.06	0.148
Standard deviation	0.882±0.02	0.955±0.02	0.073

$*p < 0.0005$ (highly statistically significant)

Contrast of abnormal images is high because, the intensity differences between neighboring pixels are large due to pathological regions present in the images. Energy is high for high contrast images. Homogeneity of normal images is high because the similarities between neighboring pixels are high. Whereas in abnormal images uniformity in neighboring pixels are less due to abnormalities.

The difference between normalized average ratio of vessel to non vessel area for different normal and abnormal images are given in Table 3. It is observed from Table 3 that the average ratio of vessel to non vessel area of normal and abnormal images for Canny with preprocessing is high. But this average ratio is less for Canny on gray scale images. This is because more number of vessel and pathological pixels are identified by Canny edge segmentation with preprocessing methods.

Table 3. Normalized average ratio of vessel to non vessel area for different normal and abnormal retinal images

Images	Ratio of vessel to vessel free area	
	Canny segmentation without preprocessing	Canny segmentation with Preprocessing *
Normal	0.704±0.09	0.782±0.04
Abnormal	0.850±0.06	0.989±0.06

*p < 0.0005(highly statistically significant)

It is also noticed that the average difference between the average ratio of vessel to non vessel area for normal and abnormal images are high (0.207) for Canny with preprocessing than Canny without preprocessing (0.146). This variation is considered as an important measure to differentiate normal and abnormal retinal images as this difference is higher than all other values given in Table 2. The p values obtained from t-test for this method is statistically significant (p<0.0005).

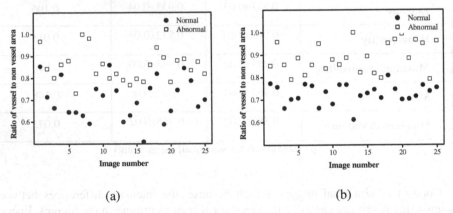

(a)   (b)

Fig. 3. Variation in the ratio of vessel to non vessel area for different normal and abnormal images, (a) Canny without preprocessing and (b) Canny with MO preprocessing

Fig. 3 (a) and (b) show the variation in the ratio of vessel to non vessel area for different normal and abnormal retinal images using Canny without preprocessing and with morphological preprocessing respectively. It is observed from Fig. 3 (b) that the parameter, ratio of vessel to non vessel area is able to differentiate the normal and abnormal images significantly using Canny with morphological preprocessing than without preprocessing. It is also observed that the values of ratio of vessel to non vessel area are more scattered for abnormal images. Due to pathological conditions and severity of disease, the vessel pattern varies highly in abnormal images, whereas normal images have similar vasculature pattern.

The retrieval is carried out for normal (40) and abnormal (40) retinal images. The retrieval performance such as precision and recall of the CBIR system using Canny method with and without preprocessing are given in Table 4. As precision and recall values are inversely proportional, these CBIR systems show high precision values than recall values. It is also observed from Table 4 that the   precision and recall for Canny with preprocessing are comparatively better than without preprocessing.

Table 4. Retrieval efficiency of CBIR systems based on Canny segmentation with and without preprocessing

Retrieval efficiency	Canny segmentation with preprocessing	Canny segmentation Without Preprocessing
Precision (%)	80	76
Recall (%)	38	34

Graphical User Interface (GUI) of input query with extracted feature vectors are shown in Fig. 4. Options are given to open, add and search images in the GUI. A normal retinal image is given as an input query. It accepts query image and display all its extracted feature values. Input images and features are added to different database. Fig. 5 shows the top eight ranked output images from the retrieved images. It is observed from Fig. 5 that all ranked images retrieved are normal images and have higher similarity with the input query.

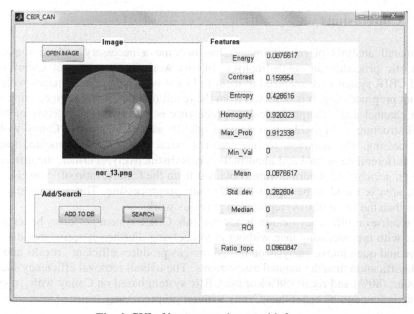

Fig. 4. GUI of input query image with features

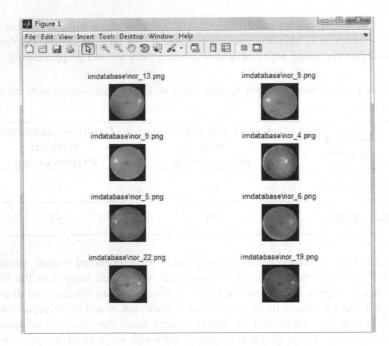

Fig. 5. GUI of output ranked images of CBIR system

4   Conclusions

Automated analysis of retinal images has become a necessary and an important diagnostic procedure in ophthalmology. In this work, performance of Canny edge based CBIR systems are analyzed to identify blood vessels in retinal images with and without preprocessing. It is observed from the result that the Canny segmentation with green channel and   morphological preprocessing is effective for detection of blood vessel structure and provides better visual quality when compared to Canny without preprocessing. The statistical texture features extracted from the segmented images could differentiate normal and abnormal images distinctively. Further, the difference between normal and abnormal value obtained from the feature, ratio of   vessel to non vessel area is found to be higher (0.207) with preprocessing. This is comparatively higher than the value (0.014) reported in previous work.

The retrieval efficiency demonstrates that this CBIR system performs better using Canny with preprocessing than without preprocessing. Further, it seems that the qualitative and quantitative analysis on retinal images produces efficient   results and less misclassification than the manual assessments. The overall retrieval efficiency such as precision (80%) and recall (38%) of the CBIR system based on Canny with   preprocessing is found to be better than Canny without preprocessing.

References

1. Niall, P., Tariq, M.A., Thomas, M., Deary, I.J., Baljean, D., Robert, H.E., Kanagasingam, Y., Constable, I.J.: Retinal image analysis: concepts, applications and potentiall. Progress in Retinal and Eye Research 25, 99–127 (2006)
2. Kavitha, G., Ramakrishnan, S.: Detection of blood vessels in human retinal images using Ant Colony Optimisation method. Int. J. Biol. Eng. Tech. 5, 360–370 (2011)
3. Marín, D., Aquino, A., Gegúndez-Arias, M.E., Bravo, J.M.: A new supervised method for blood vessel segmentation in retinal images by using gray-level and moment invariants-based features. IEEE Trans. Med. Imag. 30, 146–158 (2011)
4. Deepak, K.S., Gopal, D.J., Jayanthi, S.: Content-based retrieval of retinal Images for maculopathy. In: ACM Int. Health Informatics Symp., pp. 135–143 (2010)
5. Yong, Y., Shuying, H., Nini, R.: An automatic hybrid method for retinal blood vessel extraction. Int. J. Appl. Math. Comput. Sci. 18, 399–407 (2008)
6. Jamal, I., Akram, U., Tariq, A.: Retinal image preprocessing: background and noise segmentation. Telkomnika 10, 537–544 (2012)
7. Henning, M., Nicolas, M., David, B., Antoine, G.: A review of content-based image retrieval systems in medical applications-clinical benefits and future directions. Int. J. Med. Informatics 73, 1–23 (2004)
8. Ramamurthy, B., Chandran, K.R.: Content based image retrieval for medical images using Canny edge detection algorithm. Int. J. Comput. Appl. 17, 32–37 (2011)
9. Mohammadi, S.M., Helfroush, M.S., Kazemi, K.: Novel shape-texture feature extraction for medical X-ray image classification. Int. J. Innovative Computing Information and Control 8, 659–676 (2012)
10. Tobin, K.W., Abdelrahman, M., Chaum, E., Govindasamy, V.P., Karnowski, T.P.: A probabilistic framework for content-based diagnosis of retinal disease. In: Anal. Int. Conf. IEEE Eng. EMBS, pp. 6743–6746. Lyon, France (2007)
11. Acton, S.T., Soliz, P., Russell, S., Pattichis, M.S.: Content based image retrieval: The foundation for future case-based and evidence-based ophthalmology. In: IEE Int. Conf. on Multimedia and Expo ICME, Hannover, pp. 541–544 (2008)
12. Esnaashari., M., Amirhassan Monadjemi, S., Naderian, G.: A content-based retinal image retrieval method for diabetes-related eye diseases diagnosis. Int. J. Research and Reviews in Comput. Sci. 2, 1222–1227 (2011)
13. Mueen, A., Zainuddin, R., Sapiyan Baba, M.: MIARS: A medical image retrieval system. J. Med. Syst. 34, 859–864 (2010)
14. Sivakamasundari, J., Kavitha, G., Natarajan, V., Ramakrishnan, S.: Content based human retinal image retrieval using vascular feature extraction. In: Pan, J.-S., Chen, S.-M., Nguyen, N.T. (eds.) ACIIDS 2012, Part II. LNCS, vol. 7197, pp. 468–476. Springer, Heidelberg (2012)
15. Siddalingaswamy, P.C., Gopalakrishna Prabhu, K.: Automatic detection of multiple oriented blood vessels in retinal images. J. Biol. Sci. Eng. 3, 101–107 (2010)
16. Gonzalez, R.C., Woods, R.E., Eddins, S.L.: Digital image processing using Matlab. Pearson Education, Singapore (2005); Third Indian Reprint
17. Martin., D., Aquino., A., Gegundez-Arias., M.E., Bravo, J.M.: A supervised method for blood vessel segmentation in retinal images by using gray-level and moment in-variants-based features. IEEE Trans. Med. Imag. 30 (2011)

18. Ashok Kumar, T., Priya, S., Paul, V.: Automatic Detection of Vasculature from the Images of Human Retina Using CLAHE and Bitplane Decomposition. American Journal of Biomedical Imaging 1 (2013)
19. Canny, J.: A computational approach to edge detection. IEEE T. Pattern Analysis and Machine Intelligence 8, 679–698 (1986)
20. Manikandan, S., Rajamani, V.: A mathematical approach for feature selection and image retrieval of ultra sound kidney image databases. European J. Scientific Research 24, 163–171 (2008)
21. Choi, E., Lee, C.: Feature extraction based on the Bhattacharyya distance. Pattern Recog. 36, 1703–1709 (2003)

Activity Recognition Using Multiple Features, Subspaces and Classifiers

M.M. Sardeshmukh[1], M.T. Kolte[2], and D.S. Chaudahri[1]

[1] Electronics and Telecommunication Department, Government College of Engineering
Amravati India
manojsar@rediffmail.com
ddss@yahoo.com
[2] Maharashtra Institute of Technology College of Engineering Pune
Pune India
mtkolta@rediffmail.com

Abstract. The video analysis has become a centre of research in computer vision area. There are many application relies on the action recognition like surveillance, content based video retrieval etc. It's very crucial to devise the method that can discriminate one activity from all other activities in spite of presence of intra-class variability across the different subjects. In this paper, it is attempted to analyse the impact of each element present in action recognition method. Broadly, we considered here to observe the effect of various features, subspaces and classifiers. The experiments were performed with widely used, Weizmann dataset. The recognition results obtained with best method is up to 91%. The GEI, LDA, kNN method outperforms others. But, there is also a important capability lies with TGEI feature, which can distinguish the activities which are done only with movements of legs. The impact of each elements of the method is also observed

Keywords: Human activity recognition, GEI, REI, TGEI, LDA, PCA, kNN, ANN.

1 Introduction

Video events contain rich semantic information. Using computational approaches to analyze video events is very important for many applications due to the desire to interpret digital data in a way that is consistent with human knowledge. Cognitive video supervision and event analysis in video sequences is a critical task in many multimedia applications. Methods, tools and algorithms that aim to detect and recognize high level concepts and their respective spatio-temporal and causal relations in order to identify semantic video activities, actions and procedures have been in the focus of the research community over the last years. "Process of analyzing the behaviour representation of the object/s present in video is called as event recognition. The event may be coordinated with other objects or independent of other objects present in video". Examples of objects could be human, ball, trees, car etc.

B.K. Panigrahi et al. (Eds.): SEMCCO 2013, Part II, LNCS 8298, pp. 617–624, 2013.

In this work, "Event Recognition," "Behavior Recognition," and "Activity Recognition" can be used in identical context and interchangeably without losing consistency. critical public infrastructures), crisis management in public service areas (e.g., train stations, airports), security (detection of abnormal behaviours in surveillance videos) semantic characterization and annotation of video streams in various domains (e.g., broadcast or user-generated videos), etc. The traditional approaches for event detection in videos assume well structured environments and they fail to operate in largely unsupervised way under adverse and uncertain conditions from those on which they have been trained. Another drawback of current methods is the fact that they focus on narrow domains using specific concept detectors such as "human faces", "cars", "buildings". This work primarily aims to address the issue of detecting the abnormal behaviour of human beings or any moving entity.

The much of stress is given on feature representation methods in most of the literature as feature can be made invariance to view, temporal duration and rate. The proper selection or calculation of features can also make representation more inter-class discriminative. For performance measures of the activity recognition, in addition to the recognition accuracy for all events, the confusion matrix containing recognition accuracy for each of an event type can be one of the important measures to evaluate the performance of the algorithm. There could be also a comparison of recognition accuracy between single camera and multi-camera setups. The recognition accuracy for event classification can be compared versus following entities:

- each of the activity types,
- occlusion of different types and foreign objects like back-pack, loose clothes etc,
- variations in frame rate or temporal action rate,
- different viewing angles,
- different classifiers,
- number of dynamism (clusters),
  family of basis set.

This paper is organised as follows. The next section presents the brief review of relevant works done. Section 3 describes the various features, subspaces and classifiers. The experimental results are reported in section 4 and discussion over results obtained is elaborated in section 5 .The paper is concluded with in section 6 by highlighting the main contributions of this work.

2   Relevant Work

In one of the early papers in the area of activity recognition, Chomat et. al. [2] have presented the recognition of activities that was carried out using local appearance based features and classifying them with probabilistic classifier using Bay's rule. In order to extract local spatio-temporal appearance, gabor filters, in the form of spatio-temporal, were used to identify the each class of activity. The outputs of gabor filters were represented using multi-dimensional histogram. The recognition system was testes using the gesture sequences to be used in digital desk environment, where gesture interactions used as commands. In [1], One of the researcher constructed temporal pyramid of the entire video sequence by blurring and sub-sampling the sequence along the temporal direction only and captured temporal textures using filters (plenotic functions [3]) from each subsequence of pyramid. The temporal derivatives, which are above some threshold value, are considered further so that only space-time points, which contribute significantly to the motion of the activity, are included in its representation. The representation of training subsequences was clustered before the classification. The kinds of activity examples were used in the experiments were: walking, jogging, hand waving and walking in place.

In [4,5], Goerlick et. al. presented the approach that assigns a value for every internal point of the silhouette, reflecting the mean time required for a random walk beginning at the point to hit the boundaries. This function can be computed by solving Poisson's equation, with the silhouette contours providing boundary conditions. The application of this function is that it can be used to reliably extract various shape properties including part structure and rough skeleton, local orientation and aspect ratio of different parts, and convex and concave sections of the boundaries. These shape representation using Poisson's equation parameters are extended space-time shape (object) representation in the form of Hessian matrix parameters in [6,7]. The local features determined from the three eigen vectors and values, calculated from the Hessian matrix of Poisson equation at every point in the silhouette and placed in the set of local properties, namely plateness, stickness and ballness; determined from the eigen value's dominance. The video sequences obtained from 9 subjects with 9 activities were used to test the algorithm. The activities were: running, walking, jumping-jack, jumping-forward-on two legs, jumping in place on two legs, galloping sideways, waving two hands, bending. The similar work, but with difference image of consecutive frames instead of frame from video, was carried out by Hao et.al. in [8]. The neural network classifier was used in this work. Gkaleis et. al. decomposes a motion in activity as a combination of basic movement patterns, the so-called dynemes, calculated from fuzzy C-means (FCM) clustering method as described in [9]. The number of dynemes are decided from the leave-one-out cross-validation (LOOCV) procedure, which is an extension of the method described in [10]. Their algorithm combines fuzzy vector quantization (FVQ) of [11] using of posture vectors (column/row wise one-dimensional vector of binary silhouettes) and LDA to discover the most discriminative dynemes as well as represent and discriminate the different human movements in terms of these dynemes. This method was extended in [12, 13 and 14] for the multi-view videos. The training and testing videos were captures by multi-view cameras and dynemes were calculated from all the videos irrespective their view angles to make the motion representation and their classification view independent.

The work done in [15] by Bodor et. al. has proposed the scheme to make human motion classification view independent. In this method, training videos for each activity was captured using optimal view for particular activity. However, test video of any activity is acquired using fix numbers of camera with their fix positions. The 3D image reconstruction is used to have 3D data of activity and then 2D image from optimal view is rendered from 3D data. This optimal view image sequence is represented using the recursive filtering of two successive frames, each with different scaling factors.

3   Activity Recognition Techniques

The typical block diagram of action recognition is shown in figure 1. There are various techniques for activity recognition reported in the literature. We classify the on the basis of three criterions, namely, type of feature, subspace representation and classification methodology. The three features which are frequently applied so far are considered here and they are gait energy image (GEI) [16], Radon transform Energy image (REI) [17] and truncated GEI (TGEI) [18]. The GEI feature is calculated from silhouette of the subject obtained in each other frame of the activity video. The average of the silhouette images across the all frames involved in particular activity yields the GEI feature representation. The TGEI representation is obtained in the same way GEI is calculated but only with the 3rd of the height from the bottom so that only legs activity is included in the gait energy. In case radon transform, the each frame is transformed into radon coefficients and these coefficients are averaged across the all frames in video.

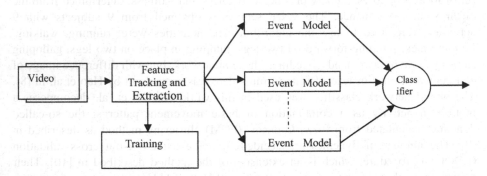

Fig. 1. Block diagram of Event modelling and Recognition

There is always possibility to have spurious information in the original feature space. The original feature space can be transformed into low dimensional feature subspace, which can precisely represent the every class of data. There are two popular subspaces, principal component analysis (PCA) and linear discriminate analysis (LDA). The PCA [20] is used to represent any class in more compact manner. However, it lacks in giving discriminate capability to class representation from classes. This shortcoming can be overcome in the LDA [19] subspace, where subspace is formed in order to maximize discriminancy between any two classes. The main advantage of the LDA is that it can automatically determine the low-dimensional feature subspace, where projected data from different classes would be separated according to their class labels.

The classifiers considered here are linear kNN classifier and nonlinear neural network classifier. Both have their advantages and disadvantages. The kNN classifiers need s k number of samples of each class in training data. This classifier gives the optimum performance for the optimal value of k [21]. However, when k-values approaches to the infinity then only the optimal behavior is assured. The non-linear classifier [22] in the form of feed-forward neural network using back-propagation algorithm used for optimizing the hidden layer weights can give optimum performance with less number of training samples.

4   Experimental Results

We have used widely used Weizmann dataset [5,6] for the analysis of various features, subspaces and classifiers. This dataset has sample videos for 9 activities. The classes of activities are bending (bend), walking (walk), jumping-forward (jump), jumping-in-place (pjump), running (run), gallop-side-ways (side), skipping (skip), wave one hand (wave1), wave two hands (wave2). Each of the activity type video was recorded from 7 different subjects.

The results depicting recognition accuracy for various features, subspaces and classifiers are shown in table 1 for two values of training samples, k= 3 & 4. The individual activity wise confusion matrix plots for four best methods are shown in figure 2. These best methods are i) kNN classifier in GEI feature space; ii) kNN classifier in REI feature space; iii) kNN classifier in GEI and LDA subspace and iv) kNN classifier in TGEI and LDA subspace

Table 1. Activity Recognition Performance with different methods

a)   Number of training samples, k=3

Subspace	GEI		REI		TGEI	
	kNN	NN	kNN	NN	kNN	NN
Feature (Original)	88.88	x	88.88	x	83.33	x
PCA	16.66	25.88	11.11	19.44	25	38.88
LDA	91.66	75	5.55	11.11	86.11	63.80

Table 2. Activity Recognition Performance with different methods

b)   Number of training samples, k=4

Subspace	GEI		REI		TGEI	
	kNN	NN	kNN	NN	kNN	NN
Feature (Original)	85.18	x	88.88	x	74.07	x
PCA	14.81	33.33	11.11	40.74	29.62	48.14
LDA	88.88	88.88	3.70	7.40	77.77	66.66

x-> Not calculated due to heavy computations and large feature input to the neural network (NN).

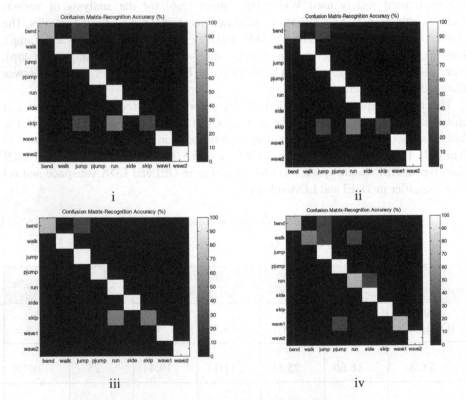

Fig. 2. The individual activity wise confusion matrix plots for four best methods, i) GEI and kNN; ii) REI and kNN ;iii) GEI, LDA and kNN and iv) TGEI, LDA and kNN

5   Discussion

The recognition accuracy reported in table 1 for no. of training samples, k= 3 & 4, clearly shows that PCA subspace miserably fails to represent the action precisely for all types features. The discriminant classifier LDA represents and classifies the action classes accurately in case of GEI and TGEI features. Due to variations in the intra-action variability across the subject because of the tendency that every person has their own style, neural network classifier suffers from over fitting and thus, gives worse performance. It is interesting to note that as number of training samples changes from 3 to 4, i.e. increases, there is no significant improvement observed in recognition accuracy.

The individual activity wise performance showing figure 2 shows the identical performance in case of GEI and REI original feature with kNN classifier. Both these methods gives fails in discriminating skip activity from jump and run activities. It can be seen in case of GEI, LDA and kNN that LDA subspace is successful in distinguishing skip action from jump but not from run activity. Interestingly, fourth method TGEI, LDA and kNN is able to completely separate skip action from both jump and run. The reason behind is that three activities skip, run and jump forward are different in only legs movement point of view. Thus TGEI feature and its discriminant subspace works well in classifying these activities accurately. This observation cal also be supported by observing the results obtained for activities of waving one and two hand, which are being misclassified in case of TGEI feature subspace, but not in other three cases. It is surprising to see that bend activity is sometimes being misclassified as jump action in all the methods.

6   Conclusion

The activity recognition is a critical element in various applications. We attempted to analyse the impact of various methods and their elements such as feature type, subspace and classifier. It has been observed that GEI and REI give identical result. The PCA subspace fails miserably, while LDA subspace outperform the result. There is an advantage in using TGEI is that it can very well distinguish the similar-looking activities but slightly different in leg movements. The results show that

References

1. Zelnik-Manor, L., Irani, M.: Event-based analysis of video. In: Proceedings of the 2001 IEEE Computer Society Conference on Computer Vision and Pattern Recognition, CVPR 2001, vol. 2, pp. II-123–II-130 (2001)
2. Chomat, O., Crowley, J.: Probabilistic recognition of activity using local appearance. In: IEEE Computer Society Conference on Computer Vision and Pattern Recognition, vol. 2, xxiii+637+663, p. 2 (1999)
3. Adelson, E.H., Bergen, J.R.: The plenoptic function and the elements of early vision. In: Computational Models of Visual Processing, pp. 3–20. MIT Press (1991)

4. Gorelick, L., Galun, M., Sharon, E., Basri, R., Brandt, A.: Shape representation and classification using the poisson equation. In: Proceedings of the 2004 IEEE Computer Society Conference on Computer Vision and Pattern Recognition, CVPR 2004, June-July 2 , vol. 2, pp. II-61–II-67 (2004)
5. Gorelick, L., Galun, M., Sharon, E., Basri, R., Brandt, A.: Shape representation and classification using the poisson equation. IEEE Transactions on Pattern Analysis and Machine Intelligence 28(12), 1991–2005 (2006)
6. Blank, M., Gorelick, L., Shechtman, E., Irani, M., Basri, R.: Actions as space-time shapes. In: Tenth IEEE International Conference on Computer Vision, ICCV 2005, vol. 2, pp. 1395–1402 (October 2005)
7. Gorelick, L., Blank, M., Shechtman, E., Irani, M., Basri, R.: Actions as space-time shapes. IEEE Transactions on Pattern Analysis and Machine Intelligence 29(12), 2247–2253 (2007)
8. Qu, H., Wang, L., Leckie, C.: Action recognition using space-time shape difference images. In: 2010 20th International Conference on Pattern Recognition (ICPR), pp. 3661–3664 (August 2010)
9. Gkalelis, N., Tefas, A., Pitas, I.: Combining fuzzy vector quantization with linear discriminant analysis for continuous human movement recognition. IEEE Transactions on Circuits and Systems for Video Technology 18(11), 1511–1521 (2008)
10. Zhu, M., Martinez, A.: Subclass discriminant analysis. IEEE Transactions on Pattern Analysis and Machine Intelligence 28(8), 1274–1286 (2006)
11. Karayiannis, N., Pai, P.-I.: Fuzzy vector quantization algorithms and their application in image compression. IEEE Transactions on Image Processing 4(9), 1193–1201 (1995)
12. Iosifidis, A., Nikolaidis, N., Pitas, I.: Movement recognition exploiting multi-view information. In: 2010 IEEE International Workshop on Multimedia Signal Processing (MMSP), pp. 427–431 (October 2010)
13. Iosifidis, A., Tefas, A., Pitas, I.: Person specific activity recognition using fuzzy learning and discriminant analysis. In: Euripean Signal Processing Conference (EUSIPCO) (2011)
14. Iosifidis, A., Tefas, A., Nikolaidis, N., Pitas, I.: Multi-view human movement recognition based on fuzzy distances and linear discriminant analysis. Computer Vision and Image Understanding 116(3), 347–360 (2012); Special issue on Semantic Understanding of Human Behaviors in Image Sequences
15. Bodor, R., Drenner, A., Fehr, D., Masoud, O., Papanikolopoulos, N.: View-independent human motion classification using image-based reconstruction. Image Vision Comput. 27(8), 1194–1206 (2009)
16. Han, J., Bhanu, B.: Individual recognition using gait energy image. IEEE Transactions on Pattern Analysis and Machine Intelligence 28(2), 316–322 (2006)
17. Boulgouris, N., Chi, Z.: Gait recognition using radon transform and linear discriminant analysis. IEEE Transactions on Image Processing 16(3), 731–740 (2007)
18. Bashir, K., Xiang, T., Gong, S.: Cross-view gait recognition using correlation strength. In: Proceedings of the British Machine Vision Conference, pp. 1109.1–109.11. BMVA Press (2010)
19. Swets, D.L., Weng, J.J.: Using Discriminant Eigenfeatures for Image Retrieval. IEEE Trans. Pattern Analysis and Machine Intelligence 18(8), 831–836 (1996)
20. Zhang, J., Yan, Y., Lades, M.: Face recognition: eigenface, elastic matching, and neural nets. Proceedings of the IEEE 85(9), 1423–1435 (1997)
21. Duda, R.O., Hart, P.E.: Pattern Classification and Scene Analysis. John Wiley & Sons, New York (1973)
22. Wan, E.W.: Neural network classification: A Bayesian interpretation. IEEE Trans. on Neural Networks 1(4), 303–305 (1990)

Advanced Optimization by Progressive Mapping Search Method of PSO and Neural Network

Dong Hwa Kim[1], Jin Ill Park[2], and X.Z. Gao[3]

[1] Department of Electronic and Control of Engineering
Hanbat National University, S. Korea
koreahucare@gmail.com
http://www.hucare.org
[2] Research Center
Vision System Com, S. Korea
[3] Department of Automation and Systems Technology
Aalto University School of Electrical Engineering, Finland
xiao-zhi.gao@aalto.fi

Abstract. This paper proposes a novel optimization approach by the fusion of the Progressive Mapping Search Method (PMSM) and the Neural Network (NN) aided Particle Swarm Optimization (PSO) that can obtain the global optimal solutions easily and speed up the overall search procedure. The PMSM merged with the NN and PSO has an important role as the navigation when the PSO is searching all the areas in order to acquire the optimum. It can help to improve the search capability of the original PSO method. That is, the PMSM together with the NN and PSO is trained to capture the PSO-searched solutions. To verify and demonstrate the effectiveness of our technique, we use a total of four test functions. The PMSM strategy employed in our paper is faster than the traditional PSO algorithm in all these four test functions. We also apply this new optimization scheme in the AVR (Automatic Voltage Regulator) system of the thermal power plant, which has resulted in faster and more stable responses.

Keywords: Progressive mapping search method, particle swarm optimization, neural network, hybrid systems, optimization, learning systems.

1 Introduction

During the past decades, artificial intelligence methods, such as fuzzy logic, neural networks, and genetic algorithm, have received significant attention as the intelligent and optimization tools [1, 2, 13, 14, 23]. There have also been considerable interests in exploring the fusion of the fuzzy logic and neural network systems, which combines the capability of the fuzzy reasoning to handle uncertain information and the capability of the artificial neural networks to learn from samples [24-26] so as to deal with nonlinearities and uncertainties in the real-world problems [8-10].

Recently, research interests have been focusing on the bio-based intelligence including IN (Immune network), PSO (Particle Swarm Optimization), GA (Genetic Algorithm), BF (Bacterial Foraging), etc. to acquire optimal solutions to a large

B.K. Panigrahi et al. (Eds.): SEMCCO 2013, Part II, LNCS 8298, pp. 625–638, 2013.

variety of engineering problems [3, 4, 12, 26, 27], because of their robustness and flexibility against dynamically changing systems and complex systems. The PSO has some similarities with the GA in the search process. That is, the PSO is an optimization algorithm for finding the optimal regions in the complex search spaces through the interaction of individuals in a population of particles. It usually uses two iterative procedures, one for the positions and the other one for the velocities of the particles. It also has certain degrees of flexibility in coping with various kinds of optimization problems. Unfortunately, selecting the best PSO parameters is always challenging in practice.

As a popular optimization algorithm, the PSO has been experimentally studied. There is still, however, no analytic way to choose a priori the best parameters. That is, the parameters of the velocity and position coefficients are usually randomly tuned or selected at each time step when we apply the PSO algorithm to handle engineering problems. There are different versions of the PSO algorithms, but we should answer the following two questions in the applications of the PSO: what kind of information each particle has access to, and how we can speed it up to get the optimal solutions. To address these two issues, we will study the hybrid PSO method in this paper. More precisely, when we use this PSO, we can have an advantage of a comparatively simple operation, and it is easier to understand its dynamics compared with the other computational techniques [8, 9]. Especially, our new PSO algorithm can yield a faster convergence speed in the search procedure, because it uses a smaller number of tunable parameters [6, 7, 9].

The Proportional-Integral-Derivative (PID) controller has been widely used because of its simplicity and robustness in power plants. Its tuning technology is an important research topic. However, using only the P, I, D parameters, it is often very difficult to control a power plant with complex dynamics. For example, power plants usually have a strong nonlinearity. To deal with these problems, as aforementioned, there has been a growing interest in the employment of the intelligent approaches, e.g., fuzzy inference systems, neural network, evolutionary algorithms, and their hybrid approaches [1, 18, 19].

In this paper, the NN is satisfactorily trained to enhance the performance of the regular PSO. The variables of the PSO can be suitably chosen depending on the applications, in which the algorithm is utilized. This paper is organized as follows. Section 2 describes and explains the underlying principles of the PSO algorithm and the role of the NN used in the paper. Section 3 proposes and studies the hybrid algorithm employing the NN trained PSO for optimization. Additionally, how it works with the PMSM system is suggested in this section. Section 4 shows the experimental study results based on using four test functions. Section 5 concludes our paper with some remarks and conclusions.

2   Characteristics of PSO and NN in a Hybrid System

2.1   Characteristics of PSO

As we know that the PSO conducts its search using a population of particles, which correspond to the individuals in the GA [4, 5]. A population of the particles is initially generated in a random way. Each particle represents a potential solution, and has a position represented by a position vector. A swarm of particles moves within the problem space, with the moving velocity of each particle represented by a velocity vector. At each time step, a function representing the quality measure is calculated. Each particle keeps track of its own best position, which is associated with the best fitness it has achieved so far in a vector. Furthermore, the best position among all the particles obtained in the present population is tracked as well. In addition to this global version, a local version of the PSO keeps track of the best position among all the topological neighbors of a particle. At each time step, by using the individually best position and the globally best position, a new velocity for the particles is updated by equation (1). In equation (1), the positive constants are set to be the uniformly distributed random numbers in [0, 1]. The term is always limited to a preset range. If the velocity violates this limit, it is reset within its proper limits. Obviously, changing the velocities of the particles in this way enables the particles to search around their individually best positions as well as globally best positions. The computation of the PSO method is simple and easy, and adds only a light computation load when it is incorporated into the GA. Furthermore, the flexibility of the PSO to control the balance between the local and global exploration of the problem space helps to overcome premature convergence problem in the GA by enhancing it search ability.

The characteristics of the hybrid system of the PSO and GA have been explored [1, 14-20]. Many researchers have been studying the hybridization of individual techniques to build up intelligent systems [1, 16-20]. A number of promising pproaches have been proposed to implement mixed control structures that combine a PID controller with the intelligent approaches [1, 20]. This paper focuses on a novel hybrid method using the NN and PSO. The position and speed vector of the PSO are:

$$v_{j,g}^{(t+1)} = w \cdot v_j^{(t)} + c_1^* rand()^* \left(pbest_{j,g} - k_{j,g}^{(t)} \right)$$
$$+ c_2^* Rand()^* \left(gbest_g - k_{j,g}^{(t)} \right)$$
$$j=1,2,...,n.$$
$$g=1,2,...,m.$$
$$k_{j,g}^{(t+1)} = k_{j,g}^{(t)} + v_{j,g}^{(t+1)}, \quad k_g^{min} \leq k_{j,g}^{(t+1)} \leq k_g^{max}$$

n : The number of the agents in each group.

m : The number of the members in each group.

t : The number of the reproduction steps.

$v_{j,g}^t$: The speed vector of agent j in the reproduction step of tth, and $v_g^{min} \leq v_{j,g}^t \leq v_g^{max}$.

$k_{j,g}^t$: The position vector of agent j in the reproduction step of tth.

w: Weighting factor.

c1, c2: Acceleration constant.

$rand$ ( ), $Rand$ ( ): Random values between 0 and 1.

$pbest(j,g)$: Optimal position vector of agent j.

$gbest$: Optimal position vector of group.

The values of the position vector and speed vector are determined by acceleration constant c1, c2. If these values are large, each agent moves to the target position with high speed and abrupt variation. If vice versa, the agents wander about the target place. As weighting factor w is for the searching balance of the agents, the value for the optimal search is given by

$$w = w_{max} - \frac{w_{max} - w_{min}}{iter_{max}} \times iter,$$ (2)

where v_{max}: Max mum value of w (0.9).

w_{min}: Minimum value of w (0.4).

$iter_{max}$: The number of the iterations.

$iter$: The number of the iterations at present.

The speed vector is limited by $v_g^{min} \le v_{j,g}^t \le v_g^{max}$. In this paper, the value of the speed vector for each agent is limited with 1/2 to avoid abrupt variation of the position vector. The details of each step in this hybrid optimization algorithm by the PSO and NN are shown in Fig. 3.

2.2   The Characteristics of NN as a Learning Tool

In this paper, the adaptive linear learning method (Adaline), suggested by Widrow and Hoff [1962], is used, and it has the structure of learning diagram as illustrated in Fig. 1.

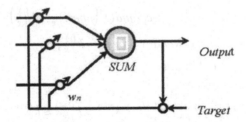

Fig. 1. Adaptive linear learning

This neural network is a supervised learning method, and the input patterns $x_i = [x_1, x_2, ..., x_n]^T$ are linearly independent. That is, the input-output relationship is linear in an Adaline. When the desired vector is $d_i = [d_1, d_2, ..., d_n]^T$, and the network output is y_i, the output is a weighted linear combination of the input vectors plus a constant bias value as in the following equation:

$$y_i(t) = \left(\sum_{j=1}^{n} w_i x_i(t) + b_o \right).$$ (3)

To find the optimal weights so as to get the desired output from (3), a cost function P(w) is defined to measure the system's performance error by

$$P(w) = \frac{1}{2}\left(\sum_{j=1}^{n}(d_i - y_i)^2\right) = \frac{1}{2}\left(\sum_{j=1}^{n}(d_i - w^T x_i)^2\right) \qquad (4)$$

The smaller $P(w)$ is, the better w will be, and $P(w)$ is normally positive. However, it approaches zero, when output y_i approaches the target vector d_i for i=1, 2,...,n. Usually, the mean squared error method is used to minimize $P(w)$. In summary, the running rule is

$$\Delta w_i = \alpha(d_i - w^T x_i) \qquad (5)$$

3   PMSM for the Optimal Solutions by NN Aided PSO

This paper suggests a novel optimization algorithm using the NN aided PSO learning algorithm. The NN has a role of function to increase the memory and training function in order to avoid repeatedly searching in those regions already searched in the past.

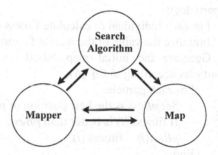

Fig. 2. Learning structure of Progressive Mapping Search Method (LSPM)

3.1   Navigation of a Mapping for Optimal Solutions

The architecture of a mapping is analogous to a navigation of cars in searching by maps. When the PSO searches the optimal solutions, it usually searches all the areas without using maps to decide where to go. However, in this paper, the PSO can search where and how to get to the optimal parameters or regions by using neural network as an efficient navigation tool. Therefore, it can obtain the optima in a faster and more effective way than the traditional approaches.

3.2   Apply the PMSM for PSO

To establish the algorithm in Eq. (6), we need to select the initial values of θ_0 and P_0. One way to avoid randomly determining these initial values is to collect the first n data points and solve θ_n and P_n directly from

$$\begin{cases} \mathbf{P}_n = (\mathbf{A}_n^T \mathbf{A}_n)^{-1} \\ \mathbf{\theta}_n = \mathbf{P}_n \mathbf{A}_n^T \mathbf{y}_n \end{cases} \tag{6}$$

where $[\mathbf{A}_n : \mathbf{Y}_n]$ is the data matrix composed of the first n data pairs. Therefore, we can start the iteration of this algorithm from the $(n + 1)$ th data sample.

Generally, the recursive least-squared estimator is used for acquiring the optimal solutions to the problem of $\mathbf{A}\mathbf{\theta} = \mathbf{Y}$. Note that the kth $(1 \le k \le m)$ row of $[\mathbf{A}_n : \mathbf{Y}_n]$, denoted by $[\mathbf{a}_k^T : \mathbf{y}_k]$, is sequentially obtained. It can be calculated as follows:

$$\begin{cases} \mathbf{P}_{n+1} = \mathbf{P}_n - \dfrac{\mathbf{P}_n \mathbf{a}_{n+1} \mathbf{a}_{n+1}^T \mathbf{P}_n}{1 + \mathbf{a}_{n+1}^T \mathbf{P}_n \mathbf{a}_{n+1}} \\ \mathbf{\theta}_{n+1} = \mathbf{\theta}_n + \mathbf{P}_{n+1} \mathbf{a}_{n+1} (y_{n+1} - \mathbf{a}_{n+1}^T \mathbf{\theta}_n) \end{cases} \tag{7}$$

```
Begin;
    Generate a random population of N solutions
(particles);
    For each individual i : calculate fitness (i);
    Initialize the value of the weight factor, w;
    Generate the initial map based on all the
particles according to Eq. (6);
    For each particle;
        Set pBest as the best position of particle i;
        If fitness (i) is better than pBest;
        pBest(i) = fitness (i);
    End;
    Set gBest as the best fitness of all particles;
    For each particle;
        For each candidate particle m;
            Calculate candidate particle velocity;
            Update candidate particle position;
        End;
        Choose the best candidate based on the
    map according to Eq. (8);
    End;
    Update the value of the weight factor, w;
    Update the map based on all the new
    particles according to Eq. (7);
    Check if termination = true;
End;
```

Fig. 3. Iteration process of fusion of PSO and PMSM algorithms

where k ranges from 0 to m-1, and the estimator uses all the m data pairs.

$$\begin{cases} \min|\hat{y}|, & \text{If global minimum} \\ \max|\hat{y}|, & \text{If global maximum} \end{cases} \quad (8)$$

Figure 3 shows the iteration procedure of our PMSM-based PSO search algorithm.

4 Experimental Verification Using Test Functions

4.1 Test Functions for Verification

We use a total of four test functions to examine and verify our optimization algorithm suggested by the PMSM of NN aided PSO, which are given in details as follows.

4.1.1 De Jong's Function 1

The simplest test function used is De Jong's function 1. It is also known as sphere model. It is continuous, convex, and unimodal:

$$f_1(x) = \sum_{i=1}^{n} x_i^2, \quad -5.12 \le x_i \le 5.12 \cdot \quad (9)$$

The global minimum is:

$$f_1(x) = 0, \quad x_i = 0, i = 1, 2, \ldots n.$$

4.1.2 Rosenbrock's valley (De Jong's function 2)

Rosenbrock's valley function is a classic optimization problem, also known as Banana function. The global optimum is inside a long, narrow, and parabolic shaped flat valley. To find the valley is trivial. However, the convergence to the global optimum is difficult, and thus this problem has been often used in assessing the performances of optimization algorithms.

$$f_2(x) = \sum_{i=1}^{n-1} 100 \cdot \left(x_{i+1} - x_i^2\right)^2 + \left(1 - x_i\right)^2, \quad -2.048 \le x_i \le 2.048 \cdot \quad (10)$$

The global minimum is:

$$f_{1b}(x) = 0, \quad x_i = 1, i = 1, 2, \ldots n.$$

4.1.3 Himmelblau Function

In mathematical optimization, the Himmelblau function is a multi-modal function often used to test the multi-modal optimization performances of optimization algorithms:

$$f_H(x) = (x_1^2 + x_2 - 11)^2 + (x_1 + x_2^2 - 7)^2, \qquad -5 \le x \le 5 \qquad (11)$$

The global minima are:

$f_H(3,2) = 0, f_H(-3.78, -3.28) = 0.0054,$

$f_H(-2.81, 3.13) = 0.0085, f_H(3.58, -1.85) = 0.0011$

4.1.4   Rastrigin's Function 6

Rastrigin's function is based on function 1 with the addition of cosine modulation to produce many local minima. Therefore, this test function is highly multimodal. However, the locations of the minima are regularly distributed.

$$f_6(x) = 10 \cdot n + \sum_{i=1}^{n} (x_i^2 - 10 \cdot \cos(2 \cdot \pi \cdot x_i)), \quad -5.12 \le x_i \le 5.12 \cdot \qquad (12)$$

The global minimum is

$f_{1b}(x) = 0, \quad x_i = 0, \ i = 1, 2, \ldots n.$

The optimization results of the above functions are demonstrated in Figs. 4 and 5.

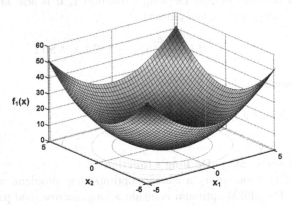

Fig. 4. (a). Experimental results after 100 iterations: De Jong's function 1

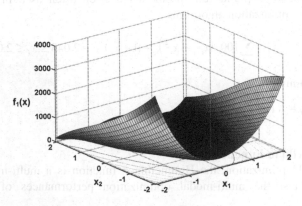

Fig. 4. (b). Experimental results after 100 iterations: Rosenbrock's valley function

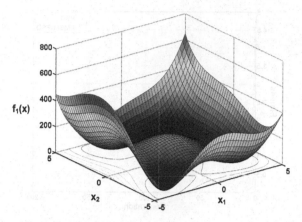

Fig. 4. (c). Experimental results after 100 iterations: Himmelblau's function

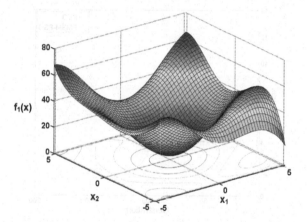

Fig. 4. (d). Experimental results after 100 iterations: Rastrigin's function 6

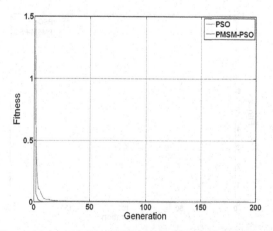

Fig. 5. (a). Convergence speeds of PSO and PMSM-PSO: De Jong's function 1

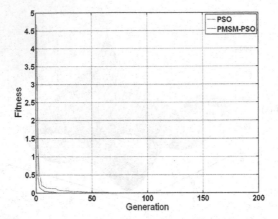

Fig. 5. (b). Convergence speeds of PSO and PMSM-PSO: Rosenbrock's valley

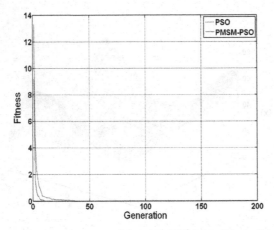

Fig. 5. (c). Convergence speeds of PSO and PMSM-PSO: Himmelblau's function

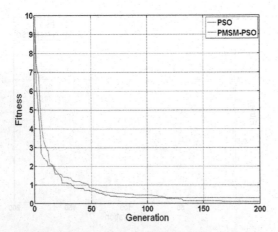

Fig. 5. (d). Convergence speeds of PSO and PMSM-PSO: Rastrigin's function 6

4.1.5   Application in AVR System

In this section, we apply our optimization approach to the AVR system of power plants, as shown in Fig. 8. The transfer function of the PID controller of the AVR system is given by [19-24]:

$$G(s) = k_p + \frac{k_i}{s} + k_d s ,$$ (12)

and the block diagram of the AVR system is illustrated in Fig. 6. The performance index of the control response is defined by

$$\min F(k_p, k_i, k_d) = \frac{e^{-\beta} \cdot t_s / \max(t)}{(1 - e^{-\beta}) \cdot |1 - t_r / \max(t)|} + e^{-\beta} \cdot Mo + ess$$

$$= \frac{e^{-\beta} \cdot (t_s + \alpha_2 \cdot |1 - t_r / \max(t) \cdot Mo|)}{(1 - e^{-\beta}) \cdot |1 - t_r / \max(t)|} + ess$$ (13)

$$= \frac{e^{-\beta} \cdot (t_s / \max(t) + \alpha \cdot Mo)}{\alpha} + ess$$

$$\alpha = (1 - e^{-\beta}) \cdot |1 - t_r / \max(t)| .$$

k_p, k_i, k_d : Parameter of PID controller.

β : Weighting factor.

Mo : Overshoot.

t_s : Settling time (2%).

ess : Steady-state error.

t : Desired settling time.

In (13), if the weighting factor, β, increases, the rising time of the response curve is short, and if β decreases, the rising time is long. The performance criteria used are defined as follows: $Mo = 50.61\%$, $ess = 0.0909, t_r = 0.2693(s), t_s = 6.9834(s)$.

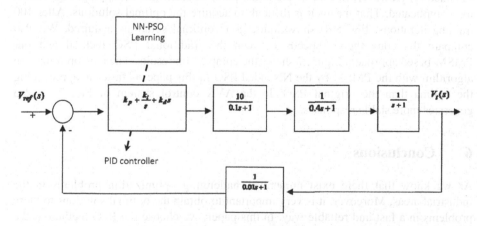

Fig. 6. AVR control system in power plant

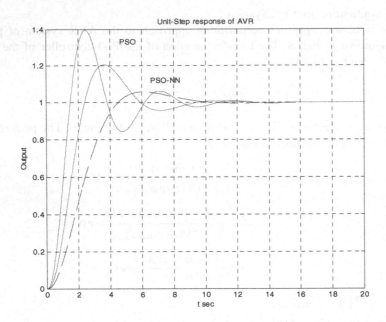

Fig. 7. Responses of PID controller with PSO and PSO-NN in AVR system

The simple crossover and dynamic mutation operators of the GA are used here. The numbers of the individuals are 50 and 200, and the initial values of the crossover and mutation are 0.6 and 0.5, respectively.

5   Experiment Results and Discussions

In the 3D mapping at the initial point of Fig. 4, some simulation results are fairly satisfactory. However, in case of the initial point of Rastrigin's mapping, Fig. 4(d) is too complicated. That means it is difficult to acquire the optimal solutions. After 100 training iterations, Fig. 5(d) shows quite good optimal solutions acquired. We also compare the convergence speeds between the traditional PSO method and our PMSM-based approach. Figure 7 shows the comparison results. The new optimization algorithm with the PMSM by the NN aided PSO in this paper is faster in approaching the optima than the original PSO. In the AVR control system of Fig. 7, it also generates more stable responses.

6   Conclusions

As we know that there exist numerous challenging optimization problems in the industrial areas. Moreover, it is very important to obtain the optimal solutions to these problems in a fast and reliable way. In this paper, we choose the PSO method as the principal optimization technique with embedded NN and PMSM. A novel hybrid search algorithm is proposed here, which can speed up the search process in obtaining the global optima in the PSO with employing the efficient training of an NN into the PSO. The NN trained PSO has certain milestones during the search for the optimal solutions just like a car has a navigation or map to search for the routes or ways so as to reach the final destinations. It is shown that the PMSM approach has been successfully trained in the proposed hybrid system. The NN can improve the performance of the original PSO, and our hybrid scheme of the NN and PSO is capable of yielding better optimal solutions. The new optimization method proposed in this paper can be further enhanced by making the entire PSO completely trained by others artificial intelligence techniques, such as different types of neural networks and fuzzy neural networks.

Acknowledgements. This work was supported by the Korea Research Foundation Grant funded by the Korean Government (MOEHRD, Basic Research Promotion Fund) (KRF-2009-013-D00046). X. Z. Gao's research was funded by the Academy of Finland under Grant 135225 and Finnish Funding Agency for Technology and Innovation (TEKES).

References

[1] Kim, D.H.: GA-PSO based vector control of indirect three phase induction motor. Applied Soft Computing 7(2) (March 2007)

[2] Du, J.-X., Huang, D.-S., Zhang, J., Wang, X.-F.: Shape matching using fuzzy discrete particle swarm optimization. IEEE (2005)

[3] Kennedy, J., Eberhart, R.C., Shi, Y.: Swam Intelligence. Morgan Kaufmann Publishers, San Francisco (2001)

[4] Kennedy, J., Eberhart, R.C.: Particle swarm optimization. In: Proc. IEEE International Conf. on Neural Networks, pp. 39–43. IEEE Service Center, Piscataway (1995)

[5] Elbeltagi, E., Hegazy, T., Grierson, D.: Comparison among five evolutionary-based optimization algorithms. In: Advanced Engineering Information, vol. 19, pp. 43–53 (2005)

[6] Secrest, B.R., Lamont, G.B.: Visualizing particle swarm optimization – Gaussian particle swarm optimization. In: Proc. of the 2003 IEEE Swarm Intelligence Symposium, SIS 2003, pp. 198–204 (April 2003)

[7] Panda, S., Padhy, N.P.: Comparison of particle swarm optimization and genetic algorithm for FACTS-based controller design. Applied Soft Computing (2007)

[8] Gaing, Z.-L.: A Particle Swarm Optimization Approach for Optimum Design of PID Controller in AVR System. IEEE Trans. on Energy Conversion 19(2) (June 2004)

[9] Shi, Y., Eberhart, R.: A modified particle swarm optimizer. In: Proc. IEEE World Congress on Computational Intelligence, pp. 69–73 (May 1998)

[10] Gaing, Z.-L.: A Particle Swarm Optimization Approach for Optimum Design of PID Controller in AVR System. IEEE Trans. Energy. Conv. 19(2), 384–391 (2004)

[11] Yoshida, H., Kawata, K., Fukuyama, Y.: A particle swarm optimization for reactive power and voltage control considering voltage security assessment. IEEE Trans. Power Syst. 15, 1232–1239 (2000)

[12] Angeline, P.J.: Using Selection to Improve Particle Swarm Optimization. IEEE Int. Conf., 84–89 (May 1998)

[13] Hwa, K.D., Hoon, C.J.: Robust PID controller tuning using multiobjective optimization based on clonal selection of immune algorithm. In: Negoita, M.G., Howlett, R.J., Jain, L.C. (eds.) KES 2004. LNCS (LNAI), vol. 3213, pp. 50–56. Springer, Heidelberg (2004)

[14] Kim, D.H.: Comparison of PID Controller Tuning of Power Plant Using Immune and Genetic Algorithm. Measurements and Applications. Ligano, Switzerland (July 2003)

[15] Juang, C.-F.: A Hybrid of Genetic Algorithm and Particle Swarm Optimization for Recurrent Network Design. IEEE Trans. Systems, Man and Cybernetics, Part B 34, 997–1006 (2004)

[16] Fogel, D.B.: Evolutionary Computation: Toward a New Philosophy of Machine Intelligence. IEEE Press, Piscataway (1995)

[17] Shi, Y., Eberhart, R.: A modified particle swarm optimizer. In: Proc. IEEE World Congress on Computational Intelligence, pp. 69–73 (May 1998)

[18] Whitley, D.: Genetic algorithms and neural networks. In: Winter, G., Periaux, J., Galan, M., Cuesta, P. (eds.) Genetic Algorithms Engineering and Computer Science, pp. 191–201. Wiley, New York (1995)

[19] Cordón, O., Herrera, F., Hoffmann, F., Magdalena, L.: Genetic Fuzzy Systems: Evolutionary Tuning and Learning of Fuzzy Knowledge Bases. World Scientific, Singapore (2001)

[20] Fong-Chwee, T.: Self-tuning PID controllers for dead time process. IEEE Trans. 35(1), 119–125 (1988)

[21] Wang, Y.-G.: PI tuning for processes with dead time. In: AACC 2000, Chicago, Illinois (June 2000)

[22] Kim, D.H.: Intelligent Tuning of the 2-DOF PID Controller On the DCS for Steam Temperature Control of Thermal Power Plant. In: IEEE Industrial Application Society. I&CPS 2002, Savannah, GA, USA (May 2002)

[23] : Auto-tuning of reference model based PID controller using immune algorithm. In: IEEE International Conference on Evolutionary Computation, Hawaii (May 2002)

[24] Lee, C.-H., Ten, C.-C.: Calculation of PID controller parameters by using a fuzzy neural network. ISA Transaction, 391–400 (2003)

[25] Lin, C.-L., Su, H.-W.: Intelligent control theory in guidance and control system design: an Overview. Proc. Natul. Sci., Counc. ROC(A) 24(1), 15–30 (2000)

[26] Fleming, P.J., Purshouse, R.C.: Evolutionary algorithms in control system engineering: A survey. Control Eng. Practice 10, 1223–1241 (2002)

[27] Ketata, R., De Geest, D., Titli, A.: Fuzzy controller: design, evaluation, parallel and hierarchical combination with a PID controller. Fuzzy Sets and Systems 71, 113–129 (1995)

[28] Montana, D.J., Davis, L.: Training feedforward networks using genetic algorithms. In: Proc. Int. Conf. Artificial Intelligence, Detroit, MI, pp. 762–767 (1989)

Optimal Placement of DG in Distribution System Using Genetic Algorithm

D. Sattianadan[1], M. Sudhakaran[2], S.S. Dash[1], K. Vijayakumar[1], and P. Ravindran[1]

[1] SRM University, Chennai, India
[2] Pondicherry Engg. College, Pondicherry, India
{sattia.nadan,ravindranpalanivel}@gmail.com,
{karan_mahalingam,munu_dash_2k}@yahoo.com,
kvijay_srm@rediffmail.com

Abstract. Power loss minimization is one of the important aspects in the distribution system..This paper deals with power loss minimization by the placement of distributed generators (DG) in the distribution system. The optimal location and sizing of DG for minimization of the power loss and cost of DG is found using GA. These two objectives power loss and cost are conflicting in nature. Moreover in such case only one compromised solution satisfying both objectives is obtained according to the choice of the decision maker. The Multi objective optimization algorithm (NSGA-II) is used to solve these two objectives to get a set of pareto optimal solutions. The simulation study is carried out on a 33 bus Distribution System for different load models.

Keywords: Distributed Generation, Voltage Stability Index, Genetic Algorithm, Load Factor, annual interest Rate, Operation and Maintenance cost.

1   Introduction

In current scenario, day by day the load demand increases rapidly due to Industrial and Domestic needs. On the other hand the conventional energy sources are decreasing rapidly, that makes finding an alternative source to meet the load demand, distributed generation is meant for that. It has huge potential benefits about which this paper is concerned. The distributed generation has been defined by many researchers [1,2], but in general a distributed generation is nothing but a small generator which is connected at the consumer terminal. Placement of DG plays an important role because the improper location may lead voltage instability and power loss [3]. Many research has been taken place to reduce the loss, in distribution system[4].

The analytical approaches for optimal placement of DG for loss reduction in distribution network have been found in [5]. Mallikarjuna used Simulated Annealing for determining the optimal location and size of DG units in a microgrid [6].Lalitha used fuzzy approach to find optimal DG localization [7].Tuba Gozel used loss sensitivity factor for the determination of the optimal size and location of DG to

B.K. Panigrahi et al. (Eds.): SEMCCO 2013, Part II, LNCS 8298, pp. 639–647, 2013.

minimize total power loss [8]. Hughifam used multi-objective function to minimize cost of energy losses, Investment cost of DG and Operation and maintenance cost [9]. Ochoa minimized real power loss and simple phase short circuit level [10]. Celli used multi objective approach, based on the non-dominated sorting Genetic Algorithm has been adopted to solve the optimal placement of different types of generation simultaneously [11]. Andrew used the Linear Programming Technique for placement of DG with multiple constraints [12]. Krueasuk used PSO to find optimal location and size of DG [13]. Vinoth Kumar addressed minimizing the multi objective index using genetic algorithm for the optimal Placement of DG[14].

Many researchers used various evolutionary methods for minimizing the power loss in the distribution system [15]. Multi objective optimization methods for optimizing two objectives are presented in [16][17].The inputs data for solving the 33 bus Distribution system [18]. Conventional optimization methods suffer from the local optimality problem and some of them usually require the function to have good characteristics, such as continuity, differentiability etc., this restricts the application of these traditional methods to a small range of real world problems. So in this paper real coded genetic algorithm is considered for solving the problem. The two objectives cost of DG and real power loss are minimized as a single objective function using GA by optimal sizing and location of DG in the Radial Distribution System.

Optimization methods available in specialized literature consider only one objective and provide only one solution which does not provide any choice to the operator. The Non-Dominated Sorting Genetic Algorithm (NSGA-II), one of the Pareto-based approach is used widely to solve the multi objective optimization problem. So in this paper the multi objective optimization method (NSGA II) [17] is used to solve these two objectives to get a set of pareto optimal solution.

2   Problem Formulation

In this paper, we have considered the balanced load in the system which can be represented either as constant power, constant current or constant impedance load. We have considered all the three types of load individually.

2.1   Multi Objective Optimization Problem formulation

The two objectives: Cost of DG and real power loss are conflicting in nature when one decreases the other increases and vice versa. So in this section both the objectives i.e. real power loss and cost of DG are minimized using a multi objective technique (NSGA-II).

Objective Function 1: Minimize the real power loss

$$\text{Min.}f1 = \sum_{b=1}^{Nb} (I_b^2).R_b \tag{1}$$

Where, b is the branch number, N_b is the total number of branches and I_b is the branch current

Objective Function 2: Minimize Cost of DG

Min. f2= C(PDG) = a + b * PDG

$$a = \frac{\text{Capital cost}\left(\frac{\$}{\text{Kw}}\right) * \text{Capacity (Kw)} * \text{Gr}}{\text{life time (year)} * 365 * 24 * \text{lf}}$$ (2)

$$b = \text{Fuel cost}(\$/\text{Kw}) + \text{O\&M Cost} (\$/\text{Kwh})$$

Where,
'Lf' is the Load Factor
'Gr' is the annual interest Rate
O&M is Operation and Maintenance cost.

The operational constraints of the system are the voltage at each bus of the distribution system.

$V_i(min) \leq V_i \leq V_i(max)$
Similarly the size of the DG is restricted between
$PDG_i(min) \leq PDG_i \leq PDG_i(max)$

3   Genetic Algorithm for Optimal Location of DG for Minimizing Power Loss and Cost of DG

Genetic algorithms are adaptive search algorithms premised on the evolutionary ideas of natural selection and genetics. The basic concepts of GAs are designed to simulate processes in natural system necessary for evolution, specifically those that follow the principles first laid down by Charles Darwin of survival of the fittest. Simple Genetic Algorithms (SGA) was first described by John Holland, who presented them as an abstraction of biological evolution and gave a theoretical mathematical framework for adaptation. GAs is based on models of genetic change in a population of individuals. These models consist of three basic elements, a 'fitness' measure which governs an individual's ability to influence. In GAs, selection and reproduction processes produce offspring for the next generation, and genetic operators that determine the genetic makeup of the off springs.

Algorithm

1.   Read system Data: line data, bus data
2.   Initialize GA parameters like population size, type of crossover, mutation, convergence criteria, crossover rate, mutation rate etc.

3.   Randomly generate the initial population i.e. (Control variables)

4.   Set iteration count k=1

5.   For the initial parents, run distribution power flow[18] and then evaluate the fitness function using equation (1). Check for voltage constraints if violated then select next parent.

6.   Select parent for crossover, based on minimum fitness function.

7.   Create a new particle using scattered cross over and constrained dependent mutation.

8.   Evaluate the fitness for the new particles (child). Combine the parents and child solution (n) and select best array (2n) solution based on the fitness value

9.   Check for the end condition

If the iteration counts greater than max, no of iteration then stop else go to step 4.

3.1   Multi-objective Optimization Algorithm for Optimal Placement of DG for Cost and Loss Minimization

The step by step procedure used for solving the proposed problem given in section 2 is stated as follows:

(1) Set up NSGA II parameters like population size, number of generations, distribution indices for the crossover (mu), and mutation (mum). Here mu and mum are taken 20 each.

(2) Read line data, bus data, incremental and decrement bidding costs for each generator. When applying evolutionary computation algorithm, the first step is to decide the control variables embedded in the individuals. In this work, the control variables are location and size of DG. Hence the control variables are generated randomly satisfying their operational constraints.

(3) For each chromosome of population, calculate objective function-1 using (6) and objective function-2 using (7).

(4) The equality and inequality constraints are handled in the Distribution Power Flow.

(5) Non-dominated sorting of the population is carried out. Then tournament selection is applied to select the best individuals based on crowding distance.

(6) Crossover and Mutation operators are carried out to generate offspring (Qt) and the new vectors obtained must satisfy the limits if not set it to the appropriate extreme.

(7) Calculate the value of each objective function of Qt and merge the parent and offspring population to preserve elites.

(8) Again perform non-dominated sorting of the combined population based on crowding distance measure and obtain the best new parent population (PT +1) of size N out of 2N population, so this would be the parents for the next generation and this process is carried out till a maximum number of generations are reached.

(9) Finally a Pareto front is achieved, that is, a set of solutions satisfying both objectives are obtained.

4   Results and Discussion

The optimal location of DG for various load models are obtained using VSI (Voltage Stability Index) given below

$$VSI(n_2) = V_{i4} - 4 * [R_i . R_i + Q_i . X_i]^2 - 4[R_i . X_i + Q_i . R_i]^2 * (V_{i4})^2 \qquad (3)$$

The DG size is varied in steps and the optimal location and size are obtained. The real power loss for various load models is shown in fig. 1. From the graph it is found that the location and size of DG are independent of load model. Since the power system loads are dynamic in nature and it is a combination of various load models, the optimal location and size obtained by this method is effective.

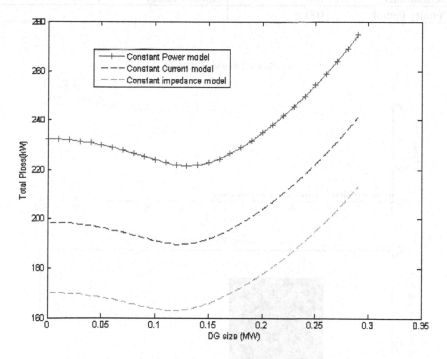

Fig. 1. Comparative Analysis of Load models using VSI- 33Bus System

4.1   Result: Phase-I

The optimal location and size obtained by this algorithm is compared with VSI for various load models are given in Table.1. The best solution and convergence characteristics and given in fig. 2. It is found that GA given better results when compared to VSI method. The losses obtained are less when compared to VSI, also the bus voltages are well within the limits. The effect on Bus Voltages for Constant Power model by the Placement of DG for the test system has been shown in fig.3. It is found that GA gave better voltage profile improvement compare to VSI used for GA given below.

Population Size : 20	Scaling Function : RANK
Selection Function : Stochastic Uniform	Mutation Function : Constraint Dependent
Crossover Function : Scattered	Crossover Fraction : 0.8
Generations : 100	Initial Penalty : 10
Penalty Factor : 100	

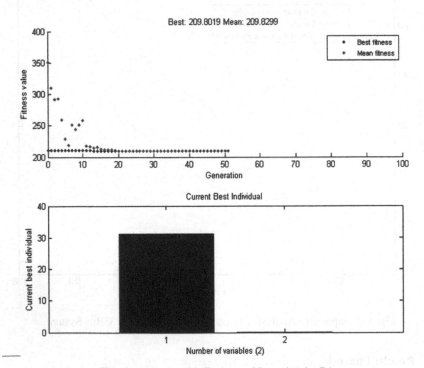

Fig. 2. Analysis of DG size and Location in GA

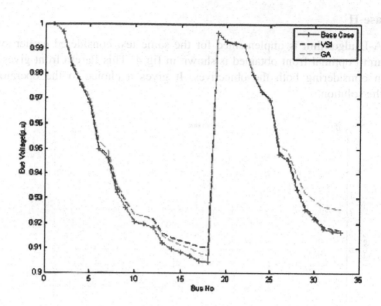

Fig. 3. Comparative Analysis of Bus Voltages for Constant Power model- 33Bus System

Table 1. Comparison of results obtained using GA and VSI

Test case	33 bus system					
Load Model	Constant Power model Base Case: Ploss = 232.28kW Qloss = 157.18kvar Min.Bus Voltage = 0.9043p.u		Constant Impedance model Base Case: Ploss =170.2kW Qloss = 114.5kvar Min.Bus Voltage = 0.9196p.u		Constant Current model Base Case: Ploss =198.54kW Qloss =133.95kvar Min.Bus Voltage = 0.9123p.u	
Approach	VSI	GA	VSI	GA	VSI	GA
Optimal location	18	32	18	32	18	32
Optimal Size of DG in MW	0.12	0.2	0.12	0.2	0.13	0.2
Ploss in kW	221.28	209.82	163.08	154.69	189.6	179.94
Qloss in kvar	149.14	141.80	109.26	103.91	127.44	121.16
Min.Bus Voltage(p.u)	0.9105	0.9077	0.9248	0.9222	0.9175	0.9153

4.2   Phase-II

The NSGA-II algorithm is implemented for the same test considered earlier system and the Pareto optimal front obtained is shown in fig 4. This Pareto front gives a set of solution considering both the objectives. It gives a choice to the operator for choosing the solution.

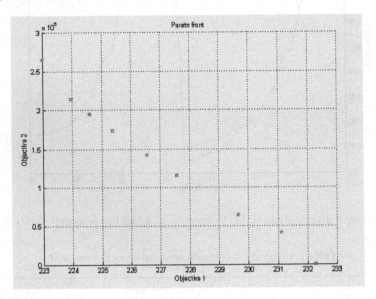

5   Conclusion

In this paper the optimal location and size of DG is obtained using VSI and compared with the results obtained using GA. GA is used simultaneously to find the location and size both to minimize the losses. Even though the size of DG obtained by GA is high, for this size the loss obtained by VSI method is greater than the loss obtained using GA. Using GA only one compromised solution satisfying both the objectives real power loss and cost of DG are obtained. Some times this may not be feasible for the operator to implement. So these two objectives are solved using (NSGA-II) to set of pareto optimal solution allowing the operator flexibility in implementation.

References

1. Ackermann, G.A., Sooder, L.S.: Distributed generation: A generation Electrical power systems research 57 (2001)
2. EI-Khattam, W., Salama, M.M.A.: Distributed generations technologies, definitions and benefits. Electrical Power Systems Research, 119–128 (2004)
3. Arya, L.D., Koshti, A., Choube, S.C.: Distributed generation planning using differential evolution accounting voltage stability consideration. Electrical Power and Energy Systems, 196–207 (2012)

4. Ghosh, S.: Optimal sizing and placement of distributed generation in a network system. Electrical Power and Energy Systems, 849–856 (2010)
5. Wang, C., Hashem Nehrir, M.: Analytical Approches for Optimal Placement of Distributed generation Sources in Power Systems. IEEE Transactions on Power Systems 19(4), 2068–2076 (2004)
6. Vallem, M.R., Mitra, J.: Siting and Sizing of Distributed Generation for Optimal Microgrid Architecture. In: IEEE Conference, pp. 611–616 (2005)
7. Lalitha, M.P., Reddy, V.C., Usha, V., Reddy, N.S.: Application of fuzzy and PSO for DG placement for minimum loss in radial distribution system. ARPN Journal of Engineering and Applied Sciences 5(4), 32–37 (2010)
8. Gozel, T., Hocaoglu, M.H.: An analytical method for the sizing and siting of distributed generators in radial systems. Electrical Power Systems Research, 912–918 (2009)
9. Haghifam, M.-R., Falaghi, H., Malik, O.P.: Risk-based distributed generation placement. IET Gener. Transm. Distrib. 2(2), 252–260 (2008)
10. Ochoa, L.F., Padilha, F.A., Harrison, G.P.: Evaluating distributed time-varying generation through a multi objective index. IEEE Trans. Power Delivery 23(2), 1132–1138 (2008)
11. Celli, G., Ghiani, E., Mocci, S., Pilo, F.: A multiobjective evolutionary algorithm for the sizing and sitting of distributed generation. IEEE Trans. 20(2), 750–757 (2005)
12. Keane, A., O'Malley, M.: Optimal Allocation of Embedded Generation on Distribution Networks. IEEE Transactions on Power Systems 20(3), 1640–1646 (2005)
13. Wichit, K., Weerakorn, O.: Optimal Placement of Distributed Generation Using Particle Swarm Optimization. M. Tech Thesis. AIT, Thailand (2005)
14. Vinothkumar, K., Selvan, M.P.: Impact of DG Model and Load Model on Placement of Multiple DGs in Distribution System. In: IEEE Conference, pp. 508–513 (2010)
15. Jaswanti, Thakur, T.: Minimum Loss Configuration of Power Distribution System. In: IEEE Conference (2009)
16. Abido, M.A.: Multiobjective Evolutionary Algorithms for Electric Power Dispatch Problem. IEEE Transactions on Evolutionary Computation 10(3), 315–329 (2006)
17. Abbass, H.A., Sarker, R.: The Pareto Differential Evolution Algorithm. International Journal on Artificial Intelligence Tools 11(4), 531–552 (2002)
18. Baran, M.E.W.E., Wu, F.F.: Network reconfiguration in distribution systems for loss reduction and load balancing. IEEE Transactions on Power Delivery 4(2) (April 1989)
19. Deb, K., Pratap, A., Agarwal, S., Meyarivan, T.: A Fast and Elitist Multiobjective Genetic Algorithm: NSGA-II. IEEE Trans. 6(2) (April 2002)

Intelligent Controllers in Path Tracking
of a Manipulator with Bounded Disturbance Torque

Neha Kapoor[1] and Jyoti Ohri[2]

[1] National Institute of Technology, Kurukshetra
[2] Associate Professor, National Institute of Technology, Kurukshetra
{ernehakapoor,ohrijyoti}@rediffmail.com

Abstract. Sliding mode controller (SMC) is an effective motion control strategy for robotic manipulator systems, which can ensure globally asymptotic stability. However, SMC suffer from chattering problem and a-priori knowledge of upper bound of the uncertainty is required for its effectiveness. In this paper, three main approaches naming Neural Network (NN), Fuzzy Logic (FL) and Adaptive Neuro Fuzzy Inference System (ANFIS) based adaptive intelligent SMC approach have been applied and analyzed for path tracking of a manipulator. These intelligent techniques are used to replace the signum function of sliding mode controller which results in increase of the robustness of the SMC with the elimination in the chattering. Also the maximum limit of the disturbance torque which these controllers can withstand without causing unstability has been observed. ANFIS controller has found to be the most capable to handle the maximum bounded disturbance torque; and also have the two main attractive features of minimum error and reduced chattering.

Keywords: Robotic Manipulator, Sliding Mode Controller (SMC), Neural Network (NN), Fuzzy Logic Controller (FLC), Adaptive Neuro Fuzzy Inference System (ANFIS).

1 Introduction

Robot manipulators are basically multi-degree-of-freedom positioning devices. The robot, as the "plant to be controlled", is a multi-input/multi-output, highly coupled, nonlinear mechatronic system. The main challenges in the robot control problem are the complexity of the dynamics and uncertainties. Main problems with the conventional control methodologies can be stated as: formulation of exact model of the manipulator to be controlled and controller is not able to cope with the disturbances and uncertainties or the sudden changes in the parameters of the manipulator. These create instability of the controller [1].

Although classical SMC is a powerful scheme for nonlinear systems with uncertainty, such as robotic manipulators, but this control scheme have important drawbacks such as chattering and large control authority, limiting its practical

B.K. Panigrahi et al. (Eds.): SEMCCO 2013, Part II, LNCS 8298, pp. 648–657, 2013.
© Springer International Publishing Switzerland 2013

applicability. Practically, it is impossible to find out the effect of all these uncertainties together. Hence, in order to guarantee the stability of the sliding mode control system, the boundary of the uncertainty has to be estimated.

Recently, much research work has been done to use soft computing methodologies such as artificial neural networks and fuzzy systems in order to improve the performance of SMCs [7-14].

Rest of the paper is organized as follows. Classical SMC for robotic manipulator is summarized in section II. The adaptive SMC using soft computing techniques for robot manipulator is presented in section III. The simulation results to demonstrate the effectiveness of the proposed control schemes are given in the section IV. Finally section V presents some concluding remarks.

2   Preliminaries

System Model and Dynamics
The dynamics of revolute joint type of robot can be described by following nonlinear differential equation [16],

$$M(q)\ddot{q} + V(q,\dot{q}) + G(q) + T_d = \tau \tag{1}$$

with $q \in R^n$ as the joint position variables, τ as vector of input torques, $M(q)$ is the inertia matrix which is symmetric and positive definite, $V(q,\dot{q})$ is the coriolis and centripetal matrix, $G(q)$ includes the gravitational forces and T_d is the upper limit of the bounded disturbance torque inserted in the robotic manipulator dynamics.

Sliding Mode Controller (SMC)
By defining the tracking error to be in the following form:

$$e = q - q^d \tag{2}$$

A conventional sliding surface corresponding to the error state can be represented as:

$$s(t) = \dot{e} + \Lambda_1 e \tag{3}$$

For this particular paper, a new integral term has been added to the classical sliding function; this integral term will improve the system performance

$$s(t) = \dot{e} + \Lambda_1 e + \Lambda_2 \int_0^t e \, dt \tag{4}$$

where Λ_1 and Λ_2 are constant positive definite diagonal matrices. The control input τ can be chosen as [15]

$$\tau = -M(\Lambda_1 \dot{e} + \Lambda_2 e - \ddot{q}^d) + V(\dot{q}^d - \Lambda_1 e - \Lambda_2 \int_0^t e \, dt) + G - As - K \tag{5}$$

where $A= diag[a_1, a_2 \ldots a_n]$, a_i is a positive constant, and K is chosen as

$$K = -ksgn(s) \tag{6}$$

where k= $[k_1, k_2, \ldots, k_n]$, k_i is also a positive constant.

3   Intelligent Techniques

a. Fuzzy Logic Controller (FLC)

Fuzzy Logic Controller provides an algorithm that connects linguistic control strategies with specific control strategies. Generally FLC has four main parts: fuzzification interface, knowledge base, inference engine and defuzzification interface.   Fuzzy systems rely on a set of rules. These rules allow the input to be fuzzy and more likely to be in natural way of human thinking. Main advantage of the FLC is that no precise model of the plant is required; hence able to cover almost all the uncertainties present in the manipulator. Discussing about some of the unavoidable drawbacks of the FLC is the memory requirements increases with the dimensions of the system. Also, FLC is discrete, hard to follow; rule base required is strong, hard to develop a model etc. Inference of rules and their tuning is not done in real world. The decision is made only after the output action has taken place; which can be avoided using neural network to tune parameter in real-time.

It is always difficult to tune the value of "K" in SMC. Two-input one-output fuzzy system is designed for this application, inputs taken are s and $\dot{s}$ while output is "K". Rule base used is given in Table 1. First input s has five membership functions and $\dot{s}$ has three membership functions. Output K has three membership functions.

Table 1. Rule base for tuning "K"

	NB	NS	Z	PS	PB
N	B	B	M	S	B
Z	B	M	S	M	B
P	B	S	M	B	B

Following abbreviations have been used for fuzzy control:
NB: Negative Big; NS: Negative Small; Z: Zero;
PS: Positive Small; PB: Positive Big; M: Medium.
Rule base followed is like,
If s is NS and $\dot{s}$ is P, then K is S.

b. Neural Network (NN)

Learning capability of the NN is used for learning non-linear functions for dynamics of a system. After learning, NN has a capability of generalization and then respond optimally to the unknown situations [18].Li sting some of the drawbacks of NN: there is no general way for deciding the network topologies, Numbers of neurons required are also has to be determined experimentally. Initially randomization of the weights results in poor control, failure and stability problems. Also, NN needs training before use, has high processing time, prone to generalization, have a problem of local minima.

Radial Bias Function Network (RBFN) is a type of neural network having great mapping ability. The structure of Radial Bias Function Network (RBFN) is shown in Fig. 1. This RBFN is used to find the gain of the SMC controller i.e. K. The input given to the network is the sliding function s and the output taken from the NN is K which is further given to the SMC torque equation.

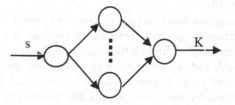

Fig. 1. General Structure of Neural Network

c. Adaptive Neuro Fuzzy Inference System (ANFIS)

Both the approaches, NN and FL discussed above have their own advantages and disadvantages. Fusion of both the schemes can enlarge the individual strengths and overcome their drawbacks. Neuro-fuzzy hybrid can produce a powerful intelligent system and has been proven in literature [17]. ANFIS is a feed forward adaptive NN that implies a fuzzy inference system through its structure and neurons. ANFIS architecture can be employed to model non-linear function, identify non-linear components on line in a control system. A Sugeno-type FIS structure with single output using a grid partition on the data is created here. Inputs given to the ANFIS are e and $\dot{e}$ with the output K.

4   Simulation and Results

Performances of the main controllers in this paper is testified by simulation of the controllers on a 2 DOF manipulator. Parameters of the manipulator model in (6) have been taken as:

$$M(q) = \begin{bmatrix} 8.77 + 1.02*\cos q2 & 0.76 + .51*\cos q2 \\ 0.76 + .51*\cos q2 & 0.62 \end{bmatrix}$$

$$V(q,\dot{q}) = \begin{bmatrix} -.51\sin (q2)\dot{q}2 & -.51\sin (q2)(\dot{q}1 + \dot{q}2) \\ -.51\sin (q2)\dot{q}1 & 0 \end{bmatrix}$$

$$G(q) = \begin{bmatrix} 74.48\sin (q1) + 6.174\sin(q1) + q2 \\ 6.174\sin(q1) + q2 \end{bmatrix}$$

Reference trajectory, ensuring the continuity in position, velocity and acceleration is given by (10) & (11) and represented in Figs. [2].

$$q^d{}_1 = [.3\sin(.7t-\Pi/2)+.3\sin(.1t-\Pi/2)+.7]; \tag{10}$$

$$q^d{}_2 = [.5\sin(.9*t-\Pi/2)+.5\sin(.1t-\Pi/2)+1.1]; \tag{11}$$

In this paper, simulation is done on MATLAB software. M file codes has been generated for various controllers; naming classical Sliding Mode Controller (SMC), Neural Network (NN), Fuzzy Logic Controller (FLC) and Adaptive Neuro Fuzzy Inference System (ANFIS).

It is a great misconception that exact dimensions and model of the disturbances are known. All the disturbances internal, external or random are unknown in nature. Hence, there is an urgent need of finding the upper bound values of these disturbances for various controllers. A wide scope of research is required in the field as literature is lacking in the particular area. Upper bound value of fixed bounded disturbance torque, T_d has been found by increasing it smoothly from zero to a value where the system becomes unstable. Value of the bounded disturbance torque is different for each and every controller.

a. Sliding Mode Controller (SMC)
Design parameters for SMC given in (4 & 5) are chosen by trial and error as:

$$\Lambda_1=\begin{bmatrix}1 & 0\\0 & 1\end{bmatrix}; \Lambda_2=\begin{bmatrix}20 & 0\\0 & 20\end{bmatrix}; A=\begin{bmatrix}1 & 0\\0 & 1\end{bmatrix}; k=\begin{bmatrix}20 & 0\\0 & 10\end{bmatrix};$$

It has been observed from the simulations that the maximum value of the fixed bounded torque which the basic SMC can withstand before showing instability is $T_d = [6.5; 0.85]$. With the increase in the value of the bounded disturbance torque beyond this value; system becomes unstable. Errors and torques for the joints 1 & 2 are given in Figs. [3 -5] respectively.

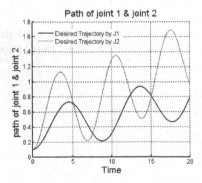

Fig. 2. Desired trajectory of joint angle 1 & 2

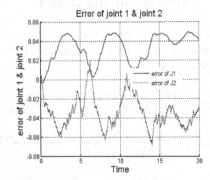

Fig. 3. Error of joint angle 1 & 2 in basic SMC

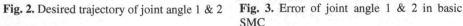

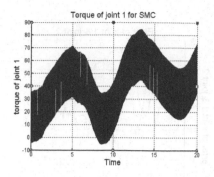

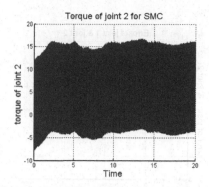

Fig. 4. Input Torque of joint 1 with basic SMC   **Fig. 5.** Input Torque of joint 2 with basic SMC

It can be observed from the Figs. 4 & 5 that input torque of the basic SMC is affected by a very huge chattering. Unstability in path tracking of the system for T_d having value greater than T_d= [6.5; 0.85] have been represented in Figs. [6 & 7]. Fig. 8 represents the error of the unstable basic SMC having input disturbance torque greater than the specified limit.

It can be observed from the Figs.[6-8] that the manipulator is unable to track the trajectory. Errors in joints 1 &2 are of the order 10^{20}. Input torques for joints 1 & 2 have also been found out of range. Similarly, all other controllers are unstable if the bounded torque given to the system is more than the specified maximum values.

From the chattering reduction point of view FLC has been found to give better results (ie smoothening of input torque) when compared the basic SMC.

b. Fuzzy Logic Controller (FLC)

The maximum value of the fixed bounded torque which can be given to FLC is T_d= [7.5; 1.5]. It can be seen that maximum value of the fixed bounded disturbance torque in FLC has increased when compared to basic SMC. Errors graphs for the joints 1 & 2 are given in Fig. 9.

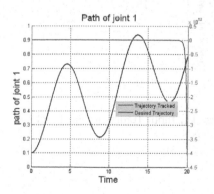

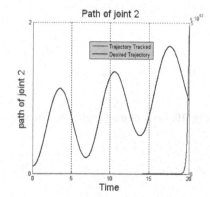

Fig. 6. Trajectory tracked by J1 with T_d greater than max. value in basic SMC

Fig. 7. Trajectory tracked by J2 with T_d greater than max. value in basic SMC

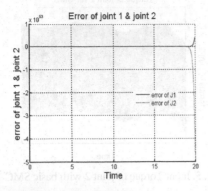

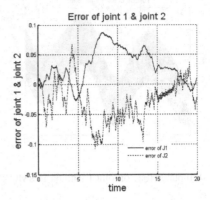

Fig. 8. Error of joint angle 1 & 2 in basic SMC in unstable condition

Fig. 9. Error of joint angle 1 & 2 in FLC

c.   Neural Network (NN)

The maximum value of the bounded torque which can be inserted in NN is $T_d=$ [7; 1.5]. Tracking errors and input torques for the joints 1 & 2 corresponding to this maximum value of torques are given in Figs. [10-11].

d.   Adaptive Neuro Fuzzy Inference System (ANFIS)

The maximum value of the bounded torque which can be given to ANFIS is $T_d=$ [14; 4.5]. It can be seen that ANFIS can withstand the maximum value of the bounded disturbance torque. Tracking errors for the joints 1 & 2 are given in Fig. 12.

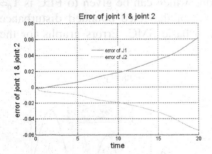

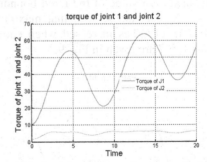

Fig. 10. Error of joint angle 1 & 2 in NN

Fig. 11. Input Torque in joint 1 and joint 2 with NN

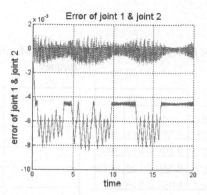

Fig. 12. Error of joint angle 1 & 2 in ANFIS

In the paper presented here, three mainly used intelligent techniques namely Fuzzy Logic (FL), Neural Network (NN) and Adaptive Neuro Fuzzy Inference System (ANFIS) has been reviewed and analyzed in terms of their general characteristics, advantages over classical controllers and disadvantages. Tracking performance for all the controllers discussed above has been represented in Figs. [13 & 14]. Performance indices used for the evaluation of the various controllers are maximum, minimum and mean square (mse) error, which have been recorded in table 2.

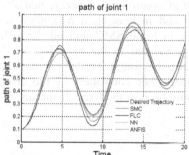

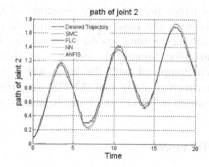

Fig. 13. Trajectory tracked by joint 1 with different controllers

Fig. 14. Trajectory tracked by joint 2 with different controllers

Table 2. Various Types of Errors for joint 1 & 2

Controller	error of joint1			error of joint2		
	max	min	mse	max	min	mse
SMC	0.909	4.7e-5	.0034	0.0903	1.6e-4	.0029
FLC	0.1058	4.2e-5	.0058	0.1326	1.6 e-4	.0055
NN	0.2396	2 e-5	.0106	0.2080	9.2 e-5	.0090
ANFIS	0.0106	1 e-4	8.6e-5	0.0027	1.6 e-4	2.7 e-6

Table 3. Maximum value of disturbance torques

Controller	Disturbance Torque	
	T_{d1}	T_{d2}
SMC	6.5	0.85
FLC	7.5	1.5
NN	7	1.5
ANFIS	14	4.5

From the Table 2 given further, it can be seen that maximum and mean square error (mse) of ANFIS is about 10 and 10^6 times lesser than the other controllers. From the observations of Table 3, it can be concluded that ANFIS controller is capable of handling the maximum disturbance torque.

5   Conclusion

This paper presents an investigation of the hybrid controllers of fuzzy, neural and anfis with the basic SMC. Starting from zero and increasing, a maximum fixed disturbance torque has been found and inserted in basic SMC and all the hybrid controllers. Simulation results have shown improvement in the hybrid controllers when compared with the basic SMC. It can also be found by the results of the experimental study that ANFIS outperforms than other controllers as the error is minimum in ANFIS and it can handle the maximum limit of the fixed disturbance.

References

1. Er, M.J., Yap, S.M., Yeaw, C.W., Luo, F.L.: A Review of Neural- Fuzzy Controllers for Robotic Manipulators. In: Proc. of IEEE Industry Applications Conference, IAS 1997, vol. 2, pp. 812–819 (1997)
2. Seraji, H.: Linear Multivariable Control of Robot Manipulators. In: Proc. of IEEE International Conference on Robotics and Automation, pp. 565–571 (April 1986)
3. Cervantes, I., Alvarrez, J.: On the PID tracking control of Robot Manipulators. Journal on Systems and Control Letters 42(1), 37–46 (2000)
4. Uebel, M., Minis, I., Cleary, K.: Improved Computed Torque Control for Industrial Robots. In: Proc. of Int. Conf. on Robotics and Automation, vol. 1, pp. 528–533 (May 1992)
5. Duy, N.T., Seegar, M., Peters, J.: Computed Torque Control with Nonparametric Regression Models. In: Proc. of IEEE Conf. in American Control, pp. 212–217 (August 2008)
6. Slotine, J.J.E., Li, W.: Adaptive Manipulator Control: A Case Study. Proc. of IEEE Trans. on Automatic Control 33(11), 995–1003 (1988)

7. Huang, S.J., Lee, J.S.: A Stable Self-Organizing Fuzzy Controller for Robotic Motion Control. Proc. of IEEE Trans. Ind. Electron. 47(2), 421–428 (2000)
8. Melin, P., Castillo, O.: Intelligent Control of Non-Linear Plants using type-2 fuzzy logic and neural networks. In: Proc. of IEEE Int. Joint Conf. on Neural Networks, vol. 2, pp. 1558–1562 (2003)
9. Vinh, T.Q., Giap, N.H., Kim, T.W., Jeong, M.G., Shin, J.H., Kim, W.H.: Adaptive robust fuzzy control and implementation for path tracking of a mobile robot. In: Proc. of IEEE Int. Symposium on Industrial Electronics, pp. 1943–1949 (July 2009)
10. Zhang, Y.Q., Kandel, A.: Compensatory neurofuzzy systems with fast learning algorithms. IEEE Trans. Neural Network 9(1), 83–105 (1998)
11. Yoo, B.K., Ham, W.C.: Adaptive Control of Robot Manipulator Using Fuzzy Compensator. Proc. of IEEE Trans. Fuzzy Syst. 8(2), 186–199 (2000)
12. Chang, Y.C.: Neural Network-based H-infinite Tracking Control for Robotic Systems. In: Proc. of Inst. Electr. Eng.-Control Theory Appl., vol. 147(3), pp. 303–311 (May 2000)
13. Li, W., Chang, X.G., Farrell, J., Wahl, F.M.: Design of an enhanced hybrid fuzzy P+ID controller for a mechanical manipulator. IEEE Transactions on Systems, Man, and Cybernetics—Part B: Cybernetics 31, 938–945 (2001)
14. Chang-Min, K., Seung-Kyu, P., Tae-Sung, Y., Doo-Hyeong, K., Gwang-Jo, C.: Comparative study of fuzzy PD control and PI control for heavy duty robot. In: Proc. of IEEE International Conference on Industrial Technology, ICIT 2009, pp. 1–5 (May 2009)
15. Kuo, T.C., Huang, Y.J.: Global Stabilization of Robot Control with Neural Network and Sliding Mode. Engineering Letters 16(1) EL_16_1_09
16. Spong, M.W., Vidyasagar, M.: Robot Dynamics and Control. Wiley-India Edition, New York
17. Li, W., Sun, Z.Q.: An Approach to Automatic Tuning of a Fuzzy Controller for Manipulators. In: Proc. of 1994 IEEE RSJ Int. Conf. on Intelligent Robots and Systems, vol. 1, pp. 634–640 (1994)

Multiscale and Multilevel Wavelet Analysis
of Mammogram Using Complex Neural Network

E. Malar, A. Kandaswamy, and M. Gauthaam

Department of Biomedical engineering, PSG College of Technology,Coimbatore
emalarpsg@gmail.com

Abstract . Mammography is an effective tool for early detection of breast cancer. The various abnormalities such as Microcalcification, Clusters, Masses, Spiculated lesions, Asymmetry and Architectural distortions are strong markers of breast cancer. Efficient diagnoses of these abnormalities from mammograms rely heavily on the kind of features extracted and the selection of classifier. In this paper, a novel methodology for microcalcification detection using multilevel wavelet analysis and Phase Encoded Complex Extreme Learning Machine is proposed. Generally, complex neural network operates only on complex features for classification. However, PECELM enables transforming the real-valued features to the complex domain to exploit the orthogonal decision boundaries of complex-valued classifiers for solving real-valued classification problems. This proposed methodology based on multiscale and multilevel Wavelet analysis on complex domain achieves an average efficiency of 95.41% and a maximum efficiency of 100%.

Keywords: Multiscale Wavelet Analysis, Mammogram Analysis, Breast cancer, Complex Neural Network, Phase encoded Complex Extreme Learning Machine.

1 Introduction

Breast Cancer is an important public health concern prevailing around the world. Breast cancer is the most frequently diagnosed cancer and the leading cause of cancer death among females, accounting for 23% of the total cancer cases and 14% of the cancer deaths [1]. Therefore, there is a need for the development of new approaches for the diagnosis of breast cancer at its early clinical course. The survival through breast cancer is found to be stage-dependent and the best survival is observed when diagnosed at early disease-stage [2-6].

Mammography is widely used for early detection, because, in many cases it can detect abnormalities such as masses, microcalcifications and other suspicious abnormalities up to two years before they are palpable. Evidence indicates that somewhere between 7-20% of mammograms with abnormalities currently detected also show signs in the previous mammogram when viewed in retrospect, which may be considered as false negative errors. On the other hand, about 65-80% of breast biopsies result in benign diagnosis, which may be considered as false positives

B.K. Panigrahi et al. (Eds.): SEMCCO 2013, Part II, LNCS 8298, pp. 658–668, 2013.

biopsies. Consequently, computer aided detection system aid radiologists in the process of detecting and localizing abnormalities and, as such, they can help avoid missed cancers and obviate benign biopsies.

Microcalcifications, tiny deposits of calcium present in breast tissue are potential indicators of breast cancer. Consequently, identification of microcalcifications from the dense breast tissue has been the subject of considerable study. Nikhil R.Pal et al [7] recommended a multistage detection system which engages online feature selection and mountain clustering system to locate the calcified region. The technique is tested on 17 mammograms comprising 10 abnormal and 7 normal images. Jiang et al [8] proposed a genetic algorithm design for optimized classification and detection of microclassification. It is reported that this experiment needs nearly 15 min to process 3000×5000 pixels image. Cristiane Bastos Rocha Ferreira and Dibio Leandro Borges [9] suggested fully automated mammogram analyses by constructing supervised classifier which is based on wavelet and special set of co-efficients. Hamid Soltanian-Zadeh et al [10] considered four different textures and shape feature extraction methods to classify mammograms as benign and malignant microcalcification. The multi-wavelet method surpassed the other methods and provides areas under ROC curve ranging 0.83 to 0.88 when using binary GA and 0.84 to 0.89 when using real- valued GA. Xinsheng Zhang [11] proposed a detection method based on ensemble learning method. Using a high-pass filter microcalcifications are enhanced and features are extracted and trained ensemble model is used as a classifier to detect microcalcifications.

The work presented here is an automated system for early identification of microcalcification from the last screening mammograms that employs advanced and novel image processing technique, the multi-resolution analysis. The proposed algorithm is implemented and tested on images obtained from mini-MIAS database. The mammographic images are pre-processed to remove label and background. Then Maximum Overlapping wavelet transform is employed to extract best wavelet features for classification. Existing microcalcification detection methods that employ neural networks for classification in the literature, mostly use real valued neural networks. Here, in this work a complex neural network called Phase Encoded Complex-valued Extreme Learning Machine proposed by R. Savitha *et. al.* [12] is used for classification. This complex neural network use complex activation function and it is are rated better than real valued neural networks due to its orthogonal decision boundaries. The proposed novel methodology proves to be effective in detecting microcalcifications than various tissue texture analyses as it provides 100% detection efficiency through Maximum Overlapping algorithm that constructs the best wavelet features and PECELM, a complex classifier.

The organisation of the paper is as follows: Section 1 provides introduction. The methodology used in the research is discussed in section 2. Section 3 presents the Performance study and Section 4 provides conclusion. The flow diagram of the proposed system is shown in Fig. 1.

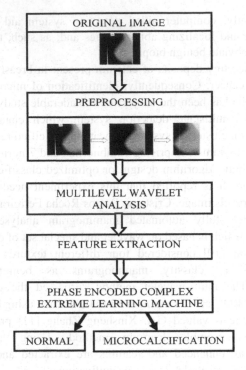

Fig. 1. Flow diagram of the proposed system

2 Methodology

2.1 Database

The mammographic images used in this work are collected from the Mammographic
Image Analysis Society (MIAS). Films have been digitized to 50 micron pixel edge
with a Joyce-Loebl scanning microdensitometer, a device linear in the optical density
range (0 - 3.2) and representing each pixel with an 8-bit word. It also includes
radiologist's truth-markings on the locations of any abnormalities that may be present.
The database has been reduced to a 200 micron pixel edge and padded/clipped so that
all the images are 1024 X 1024. The database contains images of 161 subjects with
both right and left breast images. This image database is being used by many
researchers and is considered to be a benchmark database [13].

2.2 Breast Region Extraction

The mammographic images from MIAS database contain labels, black background
and the breast region. It may also contain scribbling and other high intensity noises in
addition. The label and high intensity noises impede the performance of the system in
the identification of microcalcifications. After the input image is converted to binary,

the label is eliminated using connected component labelling algorithm and the breast region is extracted by thresholding with area being the criteria. In order to reduce the time consumed by the detection algorithm to work on the entire image, the black background is removed by slaughtering off the null rows and columns in the image. The entire process of pre-processing of mammogram image is depicted in Fig. 2.

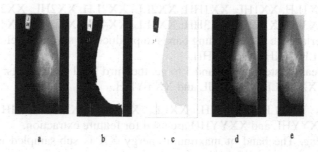

a   b   c   d   e

Fig. 2. Pre-processing (a) Raw image from the database (mdb211), (b) Image after binarization (c) Image showing connected components, (d) Image after label removal and (e) Image after black background removal

2.3   ROI Extraction

The pre-processed normal and microcalcification images are used for Region of interest (ROI) extraction. The ROI is manually cropped from these images to form sub-images of size 32x32. Since the number of microcalcification images in MIAS is just 25 while that of normal ones is 209, two sub-images were selected from each microcalcification images. And also each sub-image of microcalcification images is selected such that it contains microcalcification region within them. Thus a total of 70 normal sub-images and 50 microcalcification images are selected for the entire database.

2.4   Feature Extraction Using Multilevel Wavelet Analysis

Orthogonal wavelet transform allows an input image to be decomposed into a set of independent coefficients, corresponding to each orthogonal basis. Also, orthogonality implies that there is no redundancy in the information represented by the wavelet coefficients, which results in an efficient representation of desirable features [14 - 21].Haar wavelet is used for decomposition as it is best suited for extracting high frequency components (here microcalcifications) from an image. In the conventional wavelet technique, 4 sub-bands (LL, LH, HL and HH) are created at any level and the approximate band (LL_i) of each level is decomposed to extract the 4 bands of next level (LL_{i+1}, LH_{i+1}, HL_{i+1} and HH_{i+1}). As an alternative approach, at each level, the band of maximum energy is decomposed instead of the approximate band, as it contains enormous information. This band is further sub-sampled, filtered and interlaced to give the bands having the overlapping coefficients of all the sub-sampled bands. This technique is known as Maximum Overlapping Wavelet Transform algorithm [22].

Step 1. Decompose (UWT) the original image to produce sub-bands LL, LH, HL and HH (First level coefficients)

Step 2. Choose the band with the maximum energy (XX) for further decomposition.

Step 3. Subsample XX to produce XX1, XX2, XX3 and XX4.

Step 4: Decompose (UWT) the sub-sampled bands to 16 sub-bands:
XX1LL, XX1LH, XX1HL, XX1HH; XX2LL, XX2LH, XX2HL, XX2HH;
XX3LL, XX3LH, XX3HL, XX3HH; XX4LL, XX4LH, XX4HL, XX4HH

Step 5. Interlace the corresponding bands to produce the second level coefficients:
XXLL, XXLH, XXHL and XXHH.

Step 6. Repeat the steps 2, 3, 4 and 5 to get the third level coefficients:
XXYYLL, XXYYLH, XXYYHL and XXYYHH.

The bands LL, LH, HL, HH, XXLL, XXLH, XXHL, XXHH, XXYYLL, XXYYLH, XXYYHL and XXYYHH are used for feature extraction.

Sub-sampling. The band of maximum energy XX is sub-sampled in 4 different ways using masks S_a and S_b of size $\frac{N}{2}$ X N(for the image of dimension N X N) as follows,

$$XX1 = S_a XX S_a^T \tag{1}$$

$$XX2 = S_a XX S_b^T \tag{2}$$

$$XX3 = S_b XX S_a^T \tag{3}$$

$$XX4 = S_b XX S_b^T \tag{4}$$

Where, $S_a =$ zeros$\left(\frac{N}{2} \text{ X N}\right)$, with '0' replaced by '1' at positions $(i, 2*i-1)$,

$1 \leq i \leq \frac{N}{2}$

$S_b =$ zeros $\left(\frac{N}{2} \text{ X N}\right)$, with '0' replaced by '1' at positions $(i, 2*i)$, $1 \leq i \leq \frac{N}{2}$.

Interlacing. The coefficients are reconstructed back from their sub-sampled versions by interlacing as given below:

$$XXLL = S_a^T XX1LL S_a + S_b^T XX2LL S_a + S_a^T XX3LL S_b + S_b^T XX4LL S_b \tag{5}$$

$$XXLH = S_a^T XX1LH S_a + S_b^T XX2LH S_a + S_a^T XX3LH S_b + S_b^T XX4LH S_b \tag{6}$$

$$XXHL = S_a^T XX1HL S_a + S_b^T XX2HL S_a + S_a^T XX3HL S_b + S_b^T XX4HL S_b \tag{7}$$

$$XXHH = S_a^T XX1HH S_a + S_b^T XX2HH S_a + S_a^T XX3HH S_b + S_b^T XX4HH S_b \tag{8}$$

The features that are extracted for classifications are the energy, norm and infinity norm, given by equations 9 and 10.

$$\text{Energy} = \sum \sum \| M_{pq}(x, y) \|^2 \tag{9}$$

$$\text{Infinity norm} = \sum |x|^{p^{1/p}} \tag{10}$$

Where, P is the maximum row sum of x.

2.1 Classification Using Phase Encoded Complex Extreme Learning Machine

Neural networks have caught the eye of many researchers in the past two decades and find its application in diverse fields. The algorithms and techniques of neural network have evolved over the years with an aim of reducing the time consumption and improving the efficiency of the network. Most of the feed forward neural networks use gradient descent based learning methods which is susceptible to local minima and longer training epochs. However recently, Huang et al [23, 24 & 25] has put forth a technique called Extreme Learning Machine (ELM) which is not only more efficient but also takes lesser time for computation. Due to this reason ELM is extensively used for classification [26, 27,28 & 29].

Another factor that influences the efficiency of the network is the quality of feature presented to the network as inputs. In most of the applications where frequency domain features are used, not just magnitude information but phase information needs to be taken into account for efficient classification i.e., the input to the network needs to be presented in the form of complex. But due to the inability of real valued neural networks to process complex inputs, complex neural networks like Complex ELM are used. This complex ELM use complex activation function and such networks are called as fully complex valued Extreme Learning Machines which are rated better than real valued extreme learning machines due to their orthogonal decision boundaries [30]&[31].

Although complex valued extreme learning machines was primarily designed for complex inputs, real valued data can also be used as inputs to these networks. Aizenberg et. al. [32,33], was the first among many to suggest a complex-valued neuron network to solve real-valued classification problems. In this paper, we have used a network called `Phase Encoded Complex-valued Extreme Learning Machine (PE-CELM). In Phase Encoded Complex-valued Extreme Learning Machine (PE-CELM), at the input layer, to classify the real valued input using complex networks the real valued inputs are transformed into complex domain using the transformation function as given by equation (11).

$$Z_i = \exp(\pi X_i) \tag{11}$$

The PE-CELM network is designed with 36 input neurons, 2 output neurons and single hidden layer. The hidden neurons use fully complex valued activation function in the form of hyperbolic secant function represented by equation (12).

$$H_j = \text{sech}(u_j^T(z_t - v_j)) \tag{12}$$

where u_j is the complex-valued scaling factor, $j=1......h$ and v_j is the centre of the jth neuron, and $sech(x) = 2/(e^x + e^{-x})$. The output of the network can be found using the formula given in equation (13).

$$Y_i = \sum W_{ij} K_j \tag{13}$$

where W_{ij} are the complex-valued weight connecting the ith output neuron and the jth hidden neuron and K_j is jth hidden neuron. The output class can be found by using the equation (14).

$$C = \max(\text{real}(Y_i)) \tag{14}$$

3   Performance Study

The evaluation of the proposed method is presented in this section. A total of 120 images are used for the study, of which 90 samples are used for training the classifier while 30 is used for testing the classifier. The distribution of samples is given in Table 1. Training phase was carried out for different hidden neurons combination varied from 20 to 100. For each combination, the performance of the network was evaluated for 100 trials.

Table 1. Distribution of dataset used in the proposed system

	Normal	Microcalcification	Total
Training phase	53	37	90
Testing phase	17	13	30
Total	70	50	120

Fig. 3 is a 3-D graph that depicts the relationship between training efficiency, number of hidden neurons and number of trials. It is evident from the graph that training efficiency gradually increases as the number of hidden neurons increase.

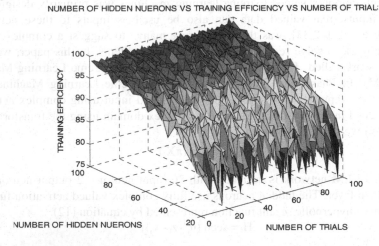

Fig. 3. Training Efficiency Vs Number of Hidden Neurons Vs Number of Trials

Fig. 4 is a 3-D graph that depicts the relationship between testing efficiency, number of hidden neurons and number of trials. It is evident from the graph that the testing efficiency gradually increases as the number of hidden neurons increase.

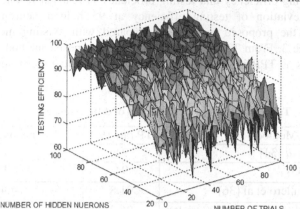

NUMBER OF HIDDEN NEURONS VS TESTING EFFICIENCY VS NUMBER OF TRIALS

Fig. 4. Testing Efficiency Vs Number of Hidden Neurons Vs Number of Trials

Table 2. Testing Efficiency for different hidden neurons

Hidden neuron	Testing efficiency			
	Average*	Std. Dev.	Max	Min
20	76.92	4.57	85.61	63.83
25	81.15	3.62	89.26	70.03
30	83.23	3.55	91.08	73.98
35	85.74	2.72	93.42	77.20
40	87.42	2.91	93.72	80.56
45	88.43	2.76	96.05	81.36
50	90.76	2.29	95.54	84.51
55	91.31	2.16	95.54	85.31
60	92.45	2.64	97.37	82.68
65	93.12	2.16	97.37	88.16
70	94.16	1.93	97.37	89.47
75	94.02	2.39	98.68	84.51
80	94.80	1.90	98.68	89.47
85	95.14	2.04	98.68	86.33
90	95.17	2.25	98.68	85.02
95	95.12	2.21	100	88.16
100	95.41	2.45	100	88.96

*Average for 100 trials

Table 2 gives details on testing efficiency for different number of hidden neurons. Maximum testing efficiency of 100% is realised at 95 hidden neurons while the minimum testing efficiency among different trials obtained is 63.23 at 20 hidden neurons. The average testing efficiency of 95.41% is obtained highest at 100 hidden neurons. Since the number of hidden neurons should be as less as possible in order to reduce the computational complexity, the optimum number of hidden neuron is 95 as both 100% training efficiency and testing efficiency is realised in one of the trials. The standard deviation of testing efficiency at 95 hidden neuron is 2.21.The performance of the proposed method is compared with existing methods and is depicted in Table 3. From Table 3 it is evident that proposed method is better than existing methods as TPR is sufficiently improved with reduction in number of false positives.

Table 3. Performance comparison of different methods

Methods	TP rate (%)	False positive per image
Songyang Yu et al [34]	94	1
Issam El-Naqa[35]	94	1
R. Gallardo-Caballero et al [36]	91.8	4.45
Proposed method (average for 100 trials)	96.2	0.03

3   Conclusion

In this study, results of a novel methodology to detect microcalcification are reported. The proposed system works on a 32x32 ROI. Maximum Overlapping algorithm is used to employ Wavelet Transform. Energy and Infinity Norm of various scales at various levels forms the feature. A complex network, PECELM is used for classification. The results indicate that proposed method is better than existing methods. A maximum efficiency of 100% and average efficiency of 95.41% is achieved in detecting microcalcifications from normal breast regions.

References

1. Jemal, A., Bray, F., Center, M.M., Ferlay, J., Ward, E., Forman, D.: Global cancer statistics. CA: A Cancer Journal for Clinicians 61, 69–90 (2011)
2. Doll, R., Payne, P., Waterhouse, J.: Cancer incidence in five continents, Vol. I. A Technical report, UICC, Geneva, Switzerland (1996)
3. Tabar, L., Fagerberg, G., Duffy, S.W., Day, N.E., Gad, A., Grontoft, O.: Update of the swedish two-country program of mammographic screening for breast cancer. Radiol. Clin. North. Am. 30, 187–210 (1992)
4. Kopans, D.: Breast Imaging. J.B. Lippincott Company, Philadelphia (1989)
5. Howard, J.: Using mammography for cancer control: An unrealized potential. CA-Cancer J. Clin. 37, 33–48 (1987)
6. Bird, R.E., Wallace, T.W., Yankaskas, B.C.: Analysis of cancers missed at screening mammography. Radiology 184, 613–617 (1992)
7. Pal, N.R., Bhowmick, B., Patel, S.K., Pal, S., Das, J.: A multi-stage neural network aided system for detection of microcalcifications in digitized mammograms. Neurocomputing 71, 2625–2634 (2008)
8. Jiang, J., Yao, B., Wason, A.M.: A genetic algorithm design for microcalcification detection and classification in digital mammograms. Computerized Medical Imaging and Graphics 31(1), 49–61 (2007)

9. Ferreira, C.B.R., Borges, D.L.: Analysis of mammogram classification using a wavelet transform decomposition. Pattern Recognition Letters 24(7), 973–982 (2003)
10. Soltanian-Zadeh, H., Rafiee-Rad, F., Pourabdollah-Nejad D, S.: Comparison of multiwavelet, wavelet, Haralick, and shape features for microcalcification classification in mammograms. Pattern Recognition 37(10), 1973–1986 (2004)
11. Zhang, X.: A New Ensemble Learning Approach for Microcalcification Clusters Detection. Journal of Software 4(9), 1014–1021 (2009)
12. Savitha, R., Suresh, S., Sundararajan, N., Kim, H.J.: Fast learning fully complex-valued classifiers for real-valued classification problems. In: Liu, D., Zhang, H., Polycarpou, M., Alippi, C., He, H. (eds.) ISNN 2011, Part I. LNCS, vol. 6675, pp. 602–609. Springer, Heidelberg (2011)
13. http://peipa.essex.ac.uk/info/mias.html
14. Bozek, J., Mustra, M., Delac, K., Grgic, M.: A Survey of Image Processing Algorithms in Digital Mammography. Rec. Advan. in Mult. Sig. Process. and Commun. 231, 631–657 (2009)
15. Yousef, W.A., Mustafa, W.A., Ali, A.A., Abdelrazek, N.A., Farrag, A.M.: On detecting abnormalities in digital mammography. In: IEEE 39th Applied Imagery Pattern Recognition Workshop (AIPR), pp. 1–7 (2010)
16. Strickland, R.N., Hahn, H.I.: Wavelet Transforms for Detecting Microcalcifications in Mammograms. IEEE Trans. Med. Imag. 15(2), 218–229 (1996)
17. Netsch, T., Peitgen, H.: Scale-Space Signatures for the Detection of Clustered Microcalcifications in Digital Mammograms. IEEE Trans. Med. Imag. 18(9), 774–786 (1999)
18. Clarke, L.P., Kallergi, M., Qian, W., Li, H.D., Clark, R.A., Silbiger, M.L.: Tree-Structured Nonlinear Filter and Wavelet Transform for Microcalcification Segmentation in Digital Mammography. Cancer Lett. 77, 173–181 (1994)
19. Qian, W., Clarke, L.P., Zheng, B., Kallergi, M., Clark, R.A.: Computer Assisted Diagnosis for Digital Mammography, IEEE Eng. Med. Biol. Mag. 14(5), 561–569 (1995)
20. Ramchandran, K., Vetterli, M., Herley, C.: Wavelets, Subband Coding, and Best Bases. Proc. IEEE 81(4), 541–560 (1996)
21. Mousa, R., Munib, Q., Moussa, A.: Breast cancer diagnosis system based on wavelet analysis and fuzzy-neural. Expert Systems with Applications 28, 713–723 (2005)
22. Petrou, M., García Sevilla, P.: Image Processing: Dealing with Texture. John Wiley & Sons, Ltd., Chichester (2006)
23. Huang, G.B., Zhu, Q.Y., Siew, C.-K.: Extreme Learning Machine: Theory and applications. Neurocomputing 70, 489–501 (2006)
24. Huang, G.-B., Zhu, Q.-Y., Siew, C.-K.: Extreme Learning Machine: A New Learning Scheme of Feedforward Neural Networks. In: Proc. Int. Joint Conf. Neural Networks, IJCNN, pp. 985–990 (2004)
25. Huang, G.-B., Siew, C.-K.: Extreme Learning Machine: RBF Network Case. In: Proc. ICARCV, pp. 1029–1036 (2004)
26. Huang, G.-B., Siew, C.-K.: Extreme Learning Machine with Randomly Assigned RBF Kernels. Int. J. Inf. Tech. 11(1), 16–24 (2005)
27. Zhang, R., Huang, G.-B., Sundararajan, N., Saratchandran, P.: Multicategory Classification Using an Extreme Learning Machine for Microarray Gene Expression Cancer Diagnosis. IEEE/ACM Trans. Comput. Biol. Bioinformatics 4(3), 485–495 (2007)
28. Wang, D., Huang, G.-B.: Protein Sequence Classification Using Extreme Learning Machine. In: Proc. Int. Joint Conf. on Neural Networks, vol. 3, pp. 406–1411 (2005)

29. Vani, G., Savitha, R., Sundararajan, N.: Classification of abnormalities in digitized mammograms using Extreme Learning Machine. In: Proc. Int. Conf. Control Automation Robotics & Vision (ICARCV), pp. 2114–2117 (2010)
30. Nitta, T.: On the inherent property of the decision boundary in complex valued neural networks. Neurocomputing 50, 291–303 (2003)
31. Nitta, T.: Orthogonality of decision boundaries of complex-valued neural networks. Neural Comput. 16(1), 73–97 (2004)
32. Aizenberg, I., Moraga, C.: Multilayer feedforward neural network based on multi-valued neurons (MLMVN) and a backpropagation learning algorithm. Soft Computing 11(2), 169–183 (2007)
33. Aizenberg, I., Paliy, D.V., Zurada, J.M., Astola, J.T.: Blur identification by multilayer neural network based on multivalued neurons. IEEE Trans. Neural Netw. 19(5), 883–898 (2008)
34. Yu, S., Guan, L.: CAD system for the automatic detection of clustered microcalcifications in digitized mammogram films. IEEE Transactions on Medical Imaging 19(2), 115–126 (2000)
35. El-Naqa, I., Yang, Y., Wernick, M.N., Galatsanos, N.P., Nishikawa, R.M.: A Support Vector Machine Approach for Detection of Microcalcifications. IEEE Trans. Med. Imaging 21(11), 1552–1563 (2002)
36. Gallardo-Caballero, R., García-Orellana, C.J., García-Manso, A., González-Velasco, H.M., Macías-Macías, M.: Independent Component Analysis to Detect Clustered Microcalcification Breast Cancers. The Scientific World Journal 2012, Article ID 540457, 6 pages (2012)

Author Index

Abdelaziz, Almoataz Y.   I-424, I-504
Abdelsalam, H.A.   I-504
Abdul Kadhar, K. Mohaideen   II-32
Abhyankar, A.R.   I-209
Agrawal, Sanjay   I-88
Ahmed, Sumaiya   I-68
Akella Venkata, Bharadwaj   I-366
Anavatti, Sreenatha G.   II-476
Anbazhagan, S.   II-499
Anumandla, Kiran Kumar   I-366
Aruna, M.   II-44
Arunachalam, Sundaram   I-354
Arya, K.V.   I-248
Asaithambi, Mythili   II-523
Athaide, Joanne   II-364

Babulal, C.K.   I-321, I-710
Bajer, Dražen   I-158
Bakkiyaraj, R. Ashok   I-580
Bali, Shivani   II-546
Banerjee, Abhik   II-119
Banerjee, Tribeni Prasad   II-574
Bansal, Jagdish Chand   I-248
Baskar, S.   II-32, II-511
Baskar, Subramanian   I-47, I-146, I-481
Basu, Debabrota   I-59, I-222, I-738
Bathrinath, Sankaranarayanan   I-377
Behera, Laxmidhar   II-442
Benala, Tirimula Rao   II-205
Bhattacharjee, Anup Kumar   I-436
Bhattacharya, Bidishna   I-78
Bhattacharyya, Dhruba Kumar   II-95
Bhattacharyya, Saugat   II-534
Bhuvaneswari, S.   II-44
Biswal, Bibhuti Bhusan   II-277
Biswas, Animesh   II-406
Biswas, Subhodip   I-222
Biswas (Raha), Syamasree   I-345
Burman, Ritambhar   I-274
Buyukdagli, Ozge   I-1, I-24

Cao, Cen   I-688
Cernea, Ana   I-642
Chakraborty, Aruna   II-354

Chakraborty, Niladri   I-78, I-133, I-189, I-345
Chatterjee, Sarthak   I-286
Chaturvedi, D.K.   II-132
Chaudahri, D.S.   II-617
Chaudhari, Devendra S.   II-156
Chaudhuri, Sheli Sinha   I-179, I-222
Chawla, Akshay   I-13
Chowdhury, Archana   II-55

Das, Asit Kumar   II-144
Das, Sanjoy   II-487
Das, Shantanu   I-457
Das, Swagatam   I-179, I-222, I-236,
    I-260, I-274, I-286, I-298, I-310, I-401,
    I-457, I-469, I-515, II-487, II-574
Dasgupta, Preetam   I-515
Dash, S.S.   II-639
De, Arunava   I-436
Deb, Kalyanmoy   I-13
Debchoudhury, Shantanab   I-59, I-738
Deep, Aakash   I-199
Deepamangai, P.   I-662
Deepika, T.J.   I-617
Dehuri, Satchidananda   II-205
Devaraj, D.   II-397
Devesh Raj, Mani   I-699
Devi, S.   I-673
Dewan, Hrishikesh   I-630, I-725
Dhal, P.K.   II-342
Dhingra, Atul   II-248
Dora, Lingraj   I-88
Du, Huimin   I-688
Dubey, Hari Mohan   I-568
Duraipandy, P.   II-397
Dutta, Malayananda   II-95

Elango, Murugappan   II-14
El-Fergany, Attia   I-424

Fernández-Martínez, Juan Luis   I-642

Ganguly, Srinjoy   I-401
Gao, Kai-Zhou   I-59, I-738

Gao, X.Z.   II-625
García-Gonzalo, Esperanza   I-642
Garg, Akhil   II-23
Gauthaam, M.   II-658
Geethanjali, M.   I-673
Ghosh, Arka   II-144
Ghoshal, Sakti Prasad   I-35, I-98, I-547,
    I-558
Ghoshal, S.P.   II-119
Goswami, Debdipta   I-286
Goswami, Rajib   II-95
Gunasundari, Selvaraj   II-214

Hanmandlu, Madasu   II-248
Hassanein, Osama   II-287
Hei, Xinhong   I-389

Indulkar, C.S.   II-237
Islam, R.   I-547

Jadon, Shimpi Singh   I-248
Jaipuria, Sanjita   II-69
Jana, Nanda Dulal   II-193
Janakiraman, S.   II-214
Janarthanan, Ramadoss   II-55, II-354,
    II-376, II-534
Jauhar, Sunil Kumar   I-199
Jegatheesan, R.   I-617
Jha, Panchanand C.   II-277, II-546
Jiang, Qiaoyong   I-389
Joe Amali, S. Miruna   I-146

Kabat, Manas Ranjan   I-68, I-590
Kanagaraj, Ganesan   II-14
Kandaswamy, A.   II-658
Kannan, B.K.V.   I-377
Kapoor, Neha   II-648
Kar, Rajib   I-35, I-98, I-547
Kar, Reshma   II-354
Karabulut, Korhan   I-1
Karthikeyan, P.   I-481
Kaur, Ramandeep   II-546
Kesavadas, C.   II-268
Kim, Dong Hwa   II-625
Kiran, Deep   I-209
Kirsanov, Andrey   II-476
Kiziay, Damla   I-1
Kolte, Mahesh T.   II-156, II-617
Konar, Amit   II-55, II-354, II-376, II-534
Kotteeswaran, Rangasamy   I-333, I-750
Krishnanand, K.R.   II-107

Krishnaswamy, S.   II-511
Kudikala, Shravan   I-366
Kulkarni, Pravin   II-595
Kumar, Amioy   II-248
Kumar, Avanish   II-442
Kumar De, Arnab   II-406
Kumarappan, N.   II-499
Kumarappan, Narayanan   I-580, II-499
Kumari, R. Sheela   II-268
Kundu, Rupam   I-310, II-487
Kundu, Souvik   I-222

Laha, Dipak   II-308
Lozano, Jose A.   II-1, II-419

Madan, Sushila   II-546
Mahapatra, S.S.   II-69
Majhi, Babita   II-298
Maji, Pradipta   II-387
Majumder, Bodhisattwa Prasad   I-260
Malar, E.   II-658
Malik, L.G.   I-492
Mall, Rajib   II-205
Mallipeddi, Rammohan   I-170
Manadal, Kamal Krishna   I-345
Mandal, Durbadal   I-35, I-98, I-547
Mandal, Kamal K.   I-78, I-189
Manic, K. Suresh   I-110
Manoharan, P.S.   I-662
Manoharan, Sujatha C.   II-523
Maroosi, Ali   II-257
Martinović, Goran   I-158
Mathuranath, P.S.   II-268
Meena, Mukesh   II-319
Mendiburu, Alexander   II-1, II-419
Mini, S.   I-446
Mishra, Ambika Prasad   II-298
Mishra, Laxmi Prasad   II-332
Mohanty, Bibhuprasad   II-465
Mohanty, Mihir Narayan   II-332, II-465
Mohanty, Prases Kumar   I-527
Moirangthem, Joymala   II-107
Mukherjee, Rohan   I-310, II-487
Mukherjee, Satrajit   I-260
Mukherjee, Sudipto   I-286
Mukherjee, V.   I-558, II-119
Muniyandi, Ravie Chandren   II-257
Murthy, V. Venkata Ramana   II-85
Mutyalarao, M.   I-762

Nag, Soumyadeep   II-431
Naik, Anima   II-180
Natarajan, V.   II-606
Nayak, Prasanta Kumar   II-332
Nayak, Raksha B.   I-630, I-725
Ni, Qingjian   I-688

Ohri, Jyoti   II-648
Osama, R.A.   I-504

Padole, Chandrashekhar   II-364
Pal, D.   I-189
Pal, Kunal   I-298
Pal, Monalisa   II-376
Pan, Quan-Ke   I-24
Panda, Bishnupriya   II-298
Panda, Rutuparna   I-88
Panda, Sanjib Kumar   II-107
Panda, Sidhartha   I-537
Pandey, Mayank   II-559
Pandiarajan, K.   I-321
Pandit, Manjaree   I-568
Panigrahi, Bijaya Ketan   I-209, I-424,
    I-504, I-515, I-568, I-642, II-107, II-248,
    II-487
Pant, Millie   I-199
Parhi, Dayal R.   I-527
Park, Jin Ill   II-625
Parvathi, K.   II-180
Patel, Manoj Kumar   I-68
Patel, Rahila   I-492
Pati, Soumen Kumar   II-144
Patil, Chandrashekhar G.   II-156
Patra, Gyana Ranjan   I-179
Pattnaik, Laksha   II-465
Paul, Sujoy   I-274
Paul, Sushmita   II-387
Philip, Namitha   II-431
Piplai, Aritran   I-260
Ponnambalam, S.G.   I-377, II-14
Pradhan, Rohini   I-590
Praveena, Pillala   II-583
Premdayal, Sinha Anand   II-132

Raghuwanshi, M.M.   I-492
Raj, M. Xavier James   I-762
Raja, Nadaradjane Sri Madhava   I-110
Rajasekhar, Anguluri   I-457, I-469
Rajinikanth, V.   I-110

Rakshit, Pratyusha   II-55, II-534
Ram, Gopi   I-35
Ramalakshmi, A.P.S.   I-662
Ramalingam, K.   II-237
Ranjan, C. Christober Asir   II-342
Ravi, Vadlamani   II-559
Ravindran, P.   II-639
Ray, Tapabrata   II-287, II-476
Reddy Busireddy, Nagarjuna   II-453
Reddy, M. Umamaheswara   I-617
Rout, Minakhi   II-298
Rout, Umesh Kumar   I-537
Roy, Subhrajit   I-236

Sabarinath, Amaranathan   I-762
Sabarinath, Pandurengan   I-601
Sabat, Samrat L.   I-366, I-446
Sabura Banu, U.   I-413
Saha, Chiranjib   I-298
Saha, Sriparna   II-376
Saha, Suman K.   I-98
Sahoo, Satya Prakash   I-68, I-590
Sahu, Badrinarayan   II-332
Sahu, Rabindra Kumar   I-537
Sangeetha, N.   I-354
Sankar, S. Saravana   I-377
Santana, Roberto   II-1, II-419
Saranya, R.   I-354
Saravanan, R.   I-601
Sardeshmukh, M.M.   II-617
Sarkar, Soham   I-179
Satapathy, Suresh Chandra   II-180
Sattianadan, D.   I-652, II-639
Sen, Aritra   I-236
Sharma, Harish   I-248
Shaw, Binod   I-558
Shukla, Anupam   II-168
Shunmugalatha, A.   I-122
Si, Tapas   I-436
Sil, Jaya   II-193
Singh, Alok   II-85
Singh, N. Albert   II-268
Singh, Pramod Kumar   II-319
Singh, Raj Mohan   II-226
Sivakamasundari, J.   II-606
Sivakumar, Lingappan   I-333, I-750
Som, Trina   I-133
Somasundaram, Periyasami   I-699
Sreenatha, G.   II-287
Srivastava, Divya   II-226

Srivastava, Soumil   I-13
Subramanian, Srinivasan   II-523
Suchitra, D.   I-617
Sudana Rao, N. Madhu   II-44
Sudha, S.   II-511
Sudhakaran, M.   II-639
Suganthan, Ponnuthurai Nagaratnam
    I-24, I-59, I-170, I-738
Suganyadevi, M.V.   I-710
Sujatha, Kothapalli Naga   II-583
Sur, Chiranjib   II-168
Suresh Babu, B.   I-122
Susheela Devi, V.   I-630, I-725

Tai, Kang   II-23
Tamilselvi, Selvaraj   I-47
Tasgetiren, M. Fatih   I-1, I-24
Thansekhar, M.R.   I-601

Tibarewala, D.N.   II-534
Tonge, Vanita G.   II-595

Udgata, Siba K.   I-446, II-453
Udgir, Mugdha   I-568

Vaisakh, Kanchapogu   II-583
Varghese, Tinu   II-268
Velasco, Julian   I-642
Vidyasagar, S.   I-652
Vijayakumar, K.   I-652, II-639

Wang, Lei   I-389

Yadav, Ajay Pratap   II-442
Yang, Dongdong   I-389

Zou, Feng   I-389